Governing
States
& Localities

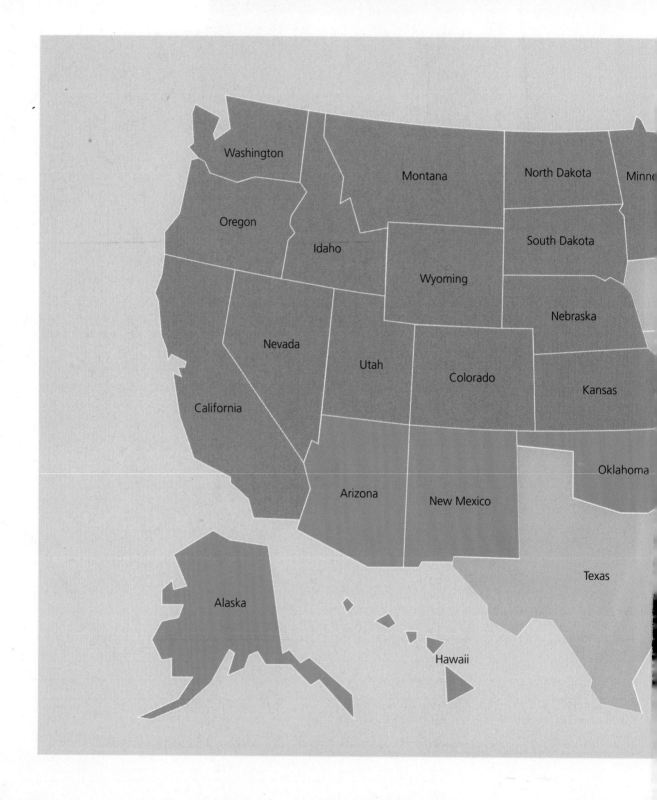

New Hampshire

Vermont

Maine

Massachusetts

New York

Rhode Island

Connecticut

Wisconsin

Michigan

Pennsylvania

New Jersey

Delaware

Maryland

owa

Ohio

Illinois

Indiana

West Virginia

Virginia

Missouri

Kentucky

North Carolina

Arkansas

Tennessee

South Carolina

Georgia

Alabama

Mississippi

Louisiana

Florida

Admission to the Union

- Original Ratifiers*
  December 1787–June 21, 1788
- June 25, 1788–1799
- 1800–1848
- 1849–1899
- Entered Union after 1900

Source: Bruce Wetterau, *Desk Reference on the States* (Washington, D.C.: CQ Press), 1999: 8–10.

* Until these first nine states ratified the Constitution, it technically was not in effect.

A CQ Press and **Governing** Magazine collaboration

Governing
States
Second Edition # & Localities

Kevin B. Smith, University of Nebraska–Lincoln

Alan Greenblatt, *Governing*

Michele Mariani, Pew Center on the States

CQ PRESS

A Division of Congressional Quarterly Inc.
Washington, D.C.

CQ Press
1255 22nd Street, NW, Suite 400
Washington, DC 20037

Phone, 202-729-1900; toll-free: 1-866-4CQ-PRESS (1-866-427-7737)

Web: www.cqpress.com

Cover and interior design and composition: Naylor Design Inc.

Editorial/Political Cartoons:
Copyright by Daryl Cagle 2007 and CagleCartoons.com. All rights reserved: 60
Created by Gene Packwood, reprint courtesy of Gene Packwood and the *Daily Commercial*: 65
Copyright 1962 by Bill Mauldin. Courtesy of the Mauldin Estate: 114
© Jeff Parker, *Florida Today,* and PoliticalCartoons.com: 246

Historic Alabama voter registration materials: 114–115
Courtesy of the Civil Rights Movement Veterans Web site (www.crmvet.org)

Photo credits:
Alamy: 367
Corbis: 550
Courtesy of Bill Chapin/Seattle Sea Hawks: 94
Courtesy of Hon. John A. Fritchey: 220
Courtesy of the Library of Congress: 72 (top), 148, 347, 516
Courtesy of national*atlas*.gov: 208
Image courtesy of The Meth Project: 533
Information as provided courtesy Ron Littlefield, Mayor of Chattanooga: 527
Photo courtesy of Mid-America Regional Council: 35
Photo courtesy of the Paul Pressau family: 496
Photo courtesy of South Dakota Department of Corrections: 72 (bottom)
Photo courtesy of Steve Barrett: 172
Photos courtesy of Massachusetts Turnpike Authority: 452
Photo used with permission, State Historical Society of Missouri, Columbia, and the *St. Louis-Post Dispatch*: 287
Reuters: 273, 433
AP Images: 3, 6, 11, 22, 27, 46, 90, 99, 108, 120, 132, 137, 179, 183, 188, 197, 207, 227, 233, 240, 267, 277, 327, 332, 352, 361, 382, 391 (top and bottom), 399, 409, 441, 465, 470, 491, 505, 508, 525, 529, 541, 545, 567

Printed and bound in the United States of America

12 11 10 09 08   1 2 3 4 5

Library of Congress Cataloging-in-Publication Data

Smith, Kevin B.
  Governing states and localities / Kevin B. Smith, Alan Greenblatt, Michele Mariani. — 2nd ed.
    p. cm.
  ISBN 978-0-87289-379-5 (alk. paper)
  1. State governments—United States—Textbooks. 2. Local government—United States—Textbooks. 3. Comparative government—Textbooks. I. Greenblatt, Alan. II. Mariani, Michele. III. Title.

  JK2408.S57 2007
  320.473—dc22

                                                                                              2007019221

To Brian and Pam Smith
Kevin B. Smith

For my son, Simon
Alan Greenblatt

To Brian
Michele Mariani

Brief Contents

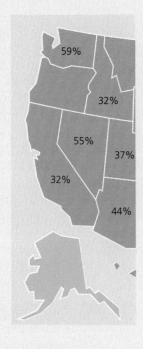

Brief Contents, *continued*

Contents

Chapter 3
Constitutions: Operating Instructions

4

5

Chapter 10   360
Local Government: Function Follows Form

Chapter 11   398
Metropolitics: The Hole Problem of Government

Tables, Figures, and Maps

Tables

Figures

Maps

Boxed Features

Local Focus

Policy in Practice

A Difference that Makes a Difference

About the Authors

Kevin B. Smith is professor of political science at the University of Nebraska—Lincoln. He is the author of *The Ideology of Education* and numerous scholarly articles on state politics and policy. He is also a former associate editor of *State Politics & Policy Quarterly.* Prior to becoming an academic he covered state and local politics as a newspaper reporter.

Alan Greenblatt has been writing about politics and government in Washington and the states for more than a decade. As a reporter at Congressional Quarterly, he won the National Press Club's Sandy Hume award for political journalism. Since joining the staff of *Governing* magazine, he has covered issues of concern to state and local governments, including budgets, taxes, and higher education. Along the way, he has written about politics and culture for numerous publications, including the *New York Times* and the *Washington Post.*

Michele Mariani is a senior associate with the Pew Center on the States, a unit of the Pew Charitable Trusts, where her responsibilities include oversight of the Government Performance Project, a regular assessment of state government management. Prior to joining Pew she wrote about government and business for newspapers and magazines, including *Governing,* where she was nominated for a National Magazine Award.

Preface

The primary goal of *Governing States and Localities* is to offer a comprehensive introduction to state and local government and to do it with a difference. This book is a unique collaboration between academic and professional writers that rests on a foundation of academic scholarship, more than a decade of experience teaching undergraduates about state and local government, and the insight and experience of writers and reporters from *Governing* magazine. As the preeminent publication covering state and local government, *Governing* offers unparalleled currency, data, inside knowledge, and know-how.

Like its predecessor, this second edition of *Governing States & Localities* aims to provide a fresh and contemporary perspective on state and local politics in terms of coverage and content as well as in the look and feel of the book. Taking full advantage of *Governing*'s award-winning reporting, the text deliberately follows the magazine's crisp newswriting style. The book's magazine-quality, full-color layout and design further enliven this vital subject. Our intent is to deliver a text that meets the highest academic and pedagogical standards while remaining engaging and easily accessible to undergraduates.

This second edition of the textbook contains a number of significant updates and revisions. An entirely new chapter on metropolitics (Chapter 11) has been added to more than double the coverage of politics at the substate level. Chapter 11 delves deeply into the structure of, and relations among, local governments in which economic, social, and thus political fates are tied to regional rather than to purely local trends. Growth patterns, governance challenges, and reform proposals are all considered from a local perspective in this chapter. All other chapters have been revised substantially, with content updated whenever possible to reflect the latest issues, trends, and political changes including:

- analysis of the results of the most recent legislative and gubernatorial elections;

- discussions of the most important state supreme court decisions and constitutional debates;

- the key changes in campaign and elections regulations;

- the ramifications of demographic changes like immigration and aging baby boomers on the political cultures of the different states;

- in-depth examination of recent events and issues that have impacted (and in some cases transformed) states and localities, such as Hurricane Katrina, gay marriage, and climate change.

New feature boxes, new examples, and new insights from the latest academic research also are included, along with one completely new feature: "How It Works." These figures break down some of the nuts-and-bolts functions of state and local governments—but by way of real examples—thus putting some flesh on what can seem to be abstract processes. In the chapter on legislatures, for instance, rather than the generic flowchart showing how a bill becomes a law, there's a feature that diagrams how a particular bill in Minnesota was actually introduced and made its way through that state's legislature, a process involving deformed frogs, some junior high school students, the bill's legislative sponsors, the media, and a host of other business and scientific organizations.

Although these represent significant revisions, the current edition retains the pedagogical philosophy of the comparative method. This approach compares similar units of analysis in order to explain *why* differences exist. As scholars know well, state and local governments make excellent units of analysis for comparison because they operate within a single political system. The similarities and differences that mark their institutional structures, laws and regulations, political cultures, histories, demographics, economies, and geographies mean that they make exciting laboratories for asking and answering important questions about politics and government. Put simply, their differences make a difference.

The appeal of exploring state and local government through comparison is not just that it makes for good political science. It is also a great way to engage students, as it gives undergraduates an accessible, practical, and systematic way to understand politics and policy in the real world. Students learn why even such seemingly personal concerns as why their tuition is so darned high are not just relevant to their particular situation and educational institution, but also are fundamental to the interaction of that institution with its state's political culture, economy, history, tax structure, and even the school's geographical and demographical position within the state and region. Using the comparative method, this book gives students the resources they need to ask and answer such questions themselves.

Key Features

This book includes a number of elements designed to showcase and promote the main themes of the text. A set of chapter-opening questions engages student interest and prompts them to look systematically for answers using the comparative method. The idea is not to simply spoon-feed the answers to students, but rather to demonstrate how the comparative method can be used to explore and explain questions about politics and policy.

Following the comparative questions, each chapter moves on to an opening vignette modeled after a lead in a news magazine article: a compelling story that segues naturally into the broader themes of the chapter. Many of these vignettes (as well as many of the feature boxes) represent original reporting by *Governing* writers.

The feature boxes in each chapter also emphasize and reinforce the comparative theme:

- "A Difference that Makes a Difference" boxes provide clear examples of how variation among states and localities can be used to explain a wide range of political and policy phenomena. These pieces detail the ways in which the institutions, regulations, political culture, demographics, and other factors of a particular state shape its constitution, the way its political parties function, how its citizens tend to vote, how it allocates its financial resources, and why its courts are structured the way they are, to name a few.

- The "Local Focus" boxes spotlight the ways localities function independently of the states and show how they are both constrained and empowered by intergovernmental ties. From battles to wrest control of their budgets from the state to constitutional restrictions on how they can tax and spend, these boxes showcase the rich variety that exists in these nearly eighty-seven thousand substate entities.

- "Policy in Practice" boxes demonstrate how different states and localities have interpreted and implemented legislation handed down from higher levels of government and the consequences of these decisions. Gubernatorial policy innovators in Wisconsin and Maryland, the surprising effects of new e-government tools, and the political and policy challenges involved in tuition hikes are just some of the issues addressed.

Another key feature that serves the comparative theme is the design and use of graphics and tables. More than twenty full-color fifty-state maps, including three unique cartograms, provide an intuitively easy way to grasp visual representation of the differences among states and localities, whether it is a measure of the size of state economies, the different party affiliation requirements for voting in direct primaries, methods of judicial selection, or state incarceration rates. Similarly, the nearly seventy tables and figures emphasize how states and localities differ and what these differences mean to politics and policy. State rankings of voter turnout rates, state-by-state data on per-pupil educational spending, recent regional murder rates, and many other features support comparisons made in the text.

To help students improve their fundamental grasp of the core functions of state and local government, as mentioned previously, we've created a new recurring feature called "How It Works" to give students an at-a-glance understanding of such things as how the constitutional amendment process operates, how governors exercise both their formal and informal powers to help pass legislation, and how a state budget gets created and approved. As well, a "state facts" feature is salted throughout the book's margins, designed to stimulate and maintain interest in the main themes being discussed in the text. Callout quotes in each chapter assist students in identifying key points along the way.

To help students assimilate content and review for tests, each chapter includes a set of highlighted key concepts. These terms are defined in the margins near the text where they are introduced and are compiled into a list at the end of each chapter with corresponding page numbers. We've also placed expanded and updated lists of Web links and lists of suggested readings, both with brief annotations, at the end of each chapter. A comprehensive glossary of key terms follows an appendix featuring state capitals and dates of entry into the Union and precedes the book's index.

Organization of the Book

The book is organized so that each chapter logically builds upon previous chapters. The first chapter, subtitled "They Tax Dogs in West Virginia, Don't They?," is essentially a persuasive essay that lays the conceptual groundwork for the book. Its aim is to convince students that state and local politics are important to their day-to-day lives and to their futures as professionals and as citizens. That is, it makes the case for why students should care about state and local politics. Along the way, it introduces the advantages of the comparative method as a systematic way to explore this subject. In introducing the book's approach, the chapter provides the basic context for studying state and local government, especially the differences in economics, culture, demographics, and geography that drive policy and politics at the regional level.

The next two chapters cover federalism and state constitutions. These chapters provide a basic understanding of what state and local governments are and what powers, responsibilities, and roles they have within the political system of the United States, as well as a sense of how they legally can make different political and policy choices. The next two chapters cover political attitudes and participation, and parties and interest groups. These chapters give students a coherent sense of the important mechanisms that link citizens to state and local governments.

Chapters 6–9 are separate treatments of the core institutions of government: legislatures, executives, courts, and the bureaucracy. There is special emphasis in each chapter on how variation in structure, powers, and responsibilities among these institutions has real-life implications for citizens of states and localities. Chapters 10 and 11 focus on local government. Chapter 10 concentrates on laying out the basic structure, authority, and responsibilities of local government. Chapter 11 examines the relations among local governments from a regional perspective. The final four chapters are devoted to specific policy areas: finance, education, crime and punishment, and health and welfare. These represent a selection of the most critical policy functions of state and local governments.

Ancillaries

We are pleased to offer an updated and significantly expanded suite of high-quality, classroom-ready instructor and student ancillaries to accompany the book. Written by Christopher Larimer of the University of Northern Iowa, the ancillaries are specifically tailored to the second edition of *Governing States & Localities*.

A set of downloadable instructor's resources is available free to adopters, including a comprehensive test bank of more than six hundred true/false, multiple-choice, fill-in-the-blank, and short-answer questions. Available in a number of formats, this test bank also can be used with *Respondus*—a flexible and easy-to-use test-generation software that allows professors to build, customize, and even integrate exams into course management platforms.

In addition, instructors will find more than two hundred PowerPoint lecture slides tailored to the text. These slides carefully detail the core concepts of each chapter, underscoring the book's comparative principles. New to this edition is a set of more than sixty interactive "clicker" slides for use in classrooms with personal response systems to help track participation, gauge comprehension, and instantly poll student opinion.

An Instructor's Manual with clear chapter summaries, downloadable lecture outlines, points for discussion, and sample syllabi for the course is included as well. Instructors have access to a full suite of .jpg and .ppt format files of all of the tables, figures, and maps in the book. These can be used to create additional PowerPoint slides or transparency masters when covering comparative data in the classroom or in discussion groups. In addition, these visuals can be imported into exams.

A host of new and improved student resources can be found on the book's Web site at http://college.cqpress.com/govstateandlocal, including chapter summaries with clear chapter objectives and a set of self-testing study questions, nearly three hundred self-grading comprehensive quiz questions, a set of flashcards for review of key concepts, crossword puzzles for each chapter, and a set of annotated links to important state and local Web sites.

Students and instructors alike will find *Governing* magazine's Web site especially useful for further research and in-class discussion. At www.governing.com, users of *Governing States & Localities* will find a menu of resources specially tailored to the book's content.

To help instructors bring the latest word from the states and localities into their classrooms, adopters will receive a free semester-long subscription to *Governing* magazine.

Acknowledgments

A lot of effort and dedication go into the making of a textbook like this, only a fraction of which is contributed by those whose names end up on the cover. Appreciation must be given, first and foremost, to Peter Harkness and Alan Ehrenhalt, publisher and executive editor, respectively, of *Governing*. Getting from the glimmer of an idea to an actual game plan for the project never would have happened without their vision, enthusiasm, and generous outlay of resources—meaning, graciously letting their reporters spend company time on such an endeavor.

Thanks are due to Christopher Larimer, who created the book's ancillaries, and to Jana Hudakova, who found herself unexpectedly developing an expertise in state politics when assigned as Kevin Smith's research assistant in 2006. She claimed to have enjoyed the experience, but has decided to finish her PhD in Germany, where people are less likely to pester her into looking up everything published in the last two years on, say, selection methods in state court systems.

To Elise Frasier, Charisse Kiino, and Lorna Notsch, the editorial team at CQ Press responsible for much of what happened from game plan to actualization, a single word: Thanks! The word is miserly compensation for their work, effort, and dedication, and in no way makes up for all the trouble we caused. Nonetheless, the thanks are most sincerely meant (again). Thanks also to CQ Press's Steve Pazdan, Margot Ziperman, and Paul Pressau, who each in their various ways helped usher this book through editing and production to bring it across the finish line. To our designer and compositor, Debra Naylor of Naylor Design Inc., we know you went above and beyond the call of duty, and we appreciate it very much.

We heartily thank our many reviewers, past and present, for their careful and detailed assistance with reading and commenting on the manuscript:

Sharon Alter, *William Rainey Harper Community College*
Jeff Ashley, *Eastern Illinois University*
Jenna Bednar, *University of Michigan*
Neil Berch, *West Virginia University*

John Bohte, *University of Wisconsin–Milwaukee*
Shannon Bow O'Brien, *University of Texas–Austin*
William Cassie, *Appalachian State University*
Douglas Clouatre, *Mid Plains Community College*
Gary Crawley, *Ball State University*
Warren Dixon, *Texas A&M University*
Jaime Dominguez, *DePaul University*
David H. Folz, *University of Tennessee*
Michael E. Greenberg, *Shippensburg University*
Dana Michael Harsell, *University of North Dakota*
Madhavi McCall, *San Diego State University*
Scott Moore, *Colorado State University*
Lawrence Overlan, *Bentley College*
Zachary Smith, *Northern Arizona University*
Kendra Stewart, *Eastern Kentucky University*
Charles Turner, *California State University–Chico*

We hope and expect that each of them will be able to find traces of their numerous helpful suggestions throughout this final product.

In addition, we would like to express our appreciation to a group of political scientists who pay attention not only to Washington, D.C., but also to what is happening throughout the rest of the country: the dean of governor-watchers, Thad Beyle, formerly of the University of North Carolina; Bruce Cain, University of California, Berkeley; Burdett Loomis, University of Kansas; Christopher Mooney, University of Illinois at Springfield; Alan Rosenthal, Rutgers University; and Larry Sabato, University of Virginia. All generously contributed their expertise when contacted by Alan Greenblatt. A special thanks also goes to Melissa Feinberg, an experienced government attorney and legal editor who wrote and has updated the deeply informative chapter on state courts.

Also owed thanks are the research staff at Georgetown University's Lauinger Library. Not only does this library buck current security-conscious trends by keeping its doors open to the public, but also it provides a safe haven for actual print copies of periodicals. Kudos.

Governing
**States
& Localities**

CHAPTER 1

Introduction
to State and Local Government
They Tax Dogs in West Virginia, Don't They?

Is government going to the dogs? State and local governments raise revenues in many different ways, including varying levels of income, sales, and property tax. They can tax virtually anything, including dogs. In some places a man's best friend is not only a family pet, but also a source of money for government.

1

What are the advantages and disadvantages of federalism?

What is the comparative method, and why is it a useful way to talk about state and local governments?

What role do state and local politics play in determining how much certain services— like a college education—cost?

It's generally reckoned that young people have little interest in politics. Don't tell that to eighteen-year-old Michael Sessions. He didn't just rock the vote in 2005. Oh, no. He won it.

Specifically, Sessions became the mayor of Hillsdale, Michigan, beating incumbent mayor Doug Ingles (age fifty-one) to become the youngest elected municipal executive in the United States. Mayor Sessions began his official duties while finishing his senior year in high school. Sessions is the antithesis of the stereotypical teenage political slacker. He registered to vote the day after his eighteenth birthday, researched issues carefully, and ran an aggressive campaign made all the more impressive by the fact that he was a write-in candidate (he was too young to actually qualify for the ballot). Sessions says he has "always been interested in politics." [1]

Winning office at so young an age makes Sessions an unusual politician, but it is his deep interest and involvement in politics that makes him an unusual young man. Fact is, what is generally reckoned is mostly true: young people have little interest in politics.

Consider the evidence. One recent survey of the "Dot.net" generation—those ages fifteen to twenty-six—concluded that people in this demographic "do not understand the ideals of citizenship, they are disengaged from the political process, they lack the knowledge necessary for effective self-government, and their appreciation and support of American democracy is limited." [2] The Higher Education Research Institute's annual survey of college students shows that only about one third of college freshmen believe that keeping up with political news is important. Only a quarter frequently discuss politics. And that is the *good* news—both of those numbers reflect four years of steady increases. [3] In the 2004 presidential election less than 42 percent of eighteen- to twenty-four-year-olds voted, whereas at least 50 percent of all other age groups cast ballots. Again, this is the good news—only 36 percent of this age group voted in the 2000 presidential election. [4]

Good news like that can certainly be read as bad news for a book like this. The typical college student is a white female between the ages of eighteen and twenty-four. She is a business or education major, leans slightly to the left politically, doesn't trust elected officials, has never participated in a political campaign, and does not believe politics is particularly relevant to her day-to-day life. [5] In other words, no Michael Sessions. A textbook on government and politics, if the polls and voting records are to be believed, is not likely to strike the typical college student as a must-read. And this is a textbook on state and local government no less, which tends not to enjoy the same high profile as national-level politics.

Of course, not too much should be read into this typical student, who, after all, is just a statistical composite, an average of the characteristics and attitudes of the U.S. college population at the beginning of the twenty-first century. College students are not all eighteen- to twenty-four-years old, they certainly are not all female, and their political attitudes fall across the entire ideological spectrum. This variation, though, does little to conceal the basic fact that for most young people, and for most college students, politics and government are not a number one interest. Or number two. State and local politics probably do not even make the top five. Or ten.

The variation in college students' backgrounds and beliefs, coupled with their general lack of interest in politics, obviously presents a challenge for a textbook like this. Readers with different characteristics, expectations, and attitudes are likely to come to a course in state and local politics with different, or perhaps indifferent, expectations. The one question most readers are likely to have is: Why should I care? Fair enough. Why should you care about politics and government? More specifically, why should you care about politics and government at the state and local level? The first goal of this textbook is to make the case that *everyone*—not just college students—has a vested interest in knowing more about state and local government.

The Impact of State and Local Politics on Daily Life

Why should you be interested in state and local politics? Government at this level plays a large, if largely invisible, role in your life. Regardless of what you are interested in—graduating, a career, relationships—state and local government shapes how, whether, and to what extent you are able to pursue these interests. As an example, consider your college education. The vast majority of college students in the United States—more than three quarters—attend public institutions of higher education.[6] Public colleges and universities are created and supported by state governments. For many readers of this textbook, the opportunity to get a college education is possible only because each state government created a system of higher education. These state governments require that taxpayers subsidize the studies of college students like you. The size of that subsidy determines the size of the tuition bill paid by most undergraduates. On average, about 36 percent of a public college's revenue comes from money the state appropriates, or sets aside. Less than 20 percent comes from tuition and fees paid by students. This means the relationship between state politics and your bank account is fairly direct: the greater the size of the state appropriation, the lower your tuition bill.[7]

If you attend a private college, you're not off the hook. State government still may play a significant role in covering the costs of your education. A quarter of the students at private, nonprofit schools receive grants or other

Eighty-six percent of California's 2,474,000 college students attend that state's public colleges; 56 percent of these students are female.

There really is no such thing as a typical college student. Jennifer Richardson (left) is a nineteen-year-old student at Mount Holyoke College in South Hadley, Massachusetts. Emma Ferguson (right), a fifty-year-old grandmother, is also a college freshman, who is going back to school to earn a bachelor's degree. One of the few things college students do have in common, however, is a general lack of interest in state and local government.

forms of financial aid directly funded by state governments.[8] In fact, undergraduates at private colleges receive on average more than $2,000 in state grants or other financial aid from state or local government. Not including tuition that amount of financial aid is several hundred dollars more than the average undergraduate at a public college receives from the state.[9]

State governments do not just determine what opportunities are available for higher education and how much those opportunities cost. Some states have curriculum mandates. You may be taking a course on state and local politics—and reading this book—because your state government decided that it was a worthy investment of your time and money. In Texas, for example, a state politics course is not just a good idea—it's the law. According to Section 51.301 of the Texas Education Code, in order to receive a bachelor's degree from any publicly funded college in the state, you must successfully complete a course on state politics.

Think that's a lot of regulation? The government's role in shaping your college education is actually pretty small. Compared to the heavy involvement of state and local governments in shaping K–12 education, colleges have free rein. In 2005, about 90 percent of students in grades 9–12 attended public high schools.[10] Local units of government operate most of these schools.[11] Private grade schools also are subject to a wide variety of state and local government regulations that range from teacher certification and minimum curriculum requirements to basic health and safety standards. Whether you attended public or private school—or were home schooled—at the end of the day you had no choice in the decision to get a basic grade

Governing States and Localities

school education. Although the minimum requirements vary, every state in the union requires at least a grade school education.

State and local governments do not exist simply to regulate large areas of your life, even if it sometimes seems that way. Their primary purpose is to provide services to their respective populations. By providing these services, state and local governments shape the social and economic lives of their citizens. Education is a good example of a public service that extends deep into the daily lives of Americans, but it is far from the only one. The roads you use to get to school are there because state and local authorities built them and maintain them. The electricity that runs your computer comes from a utility grid regulated by state government, local government, or both. State and local governments are responsible for the sewer and water systems that make the bathroom down the hall possible. They make sure that the water you drink is safe and that the burger, sushi, or salad you bought in your student union does not make you sick.[12] State governments determine the violations and punishments that constitute the criminal law. Local governments are responsible primarily for law enforcement and fire protection. The services state and local government supply are such a part of our lives that in many cases we only notice their absence—when the water does not run, when the school is closed—rather than their presence.

The Comparative Method in Practice: Yes, They Really Do Tax Dogs in West Virginia

Recognizing the impact of state and local government may be a reasonable way to spark an interest in the topic, but interest alone does not convey knowledge. A systematic approach to learning about state and local government is necessary to gain a coherent understanding of the many activities, responsibilities, and levels involved. In this textbook, that systematic approach is the **comparative method**, which uses similarities and differences as the basis for systematic explanation. Any two states or localities you can think of will differ in a number of ways. For example, they really do tax dogs in West Virginia. The state authorizes each county government to assess a fee for every dog within that county's jurisdiction. This is not the case in, say, New Jersey, where dogs live tax free.[13] Texas has executed hundreds of criminals since the moratorium, or ban, on the death penalty was lifted in the 1970s. Other states have executed none. In recent elections, Georgians sent a mixture of Republicans and Democrats to the House of Representatives (seven Republicans and six Democrats in 2006). The people of Massachusetts just sent Democrats (all ten seats in 2006). Differences between states and localities do not just involve such oddities as the tax status of the family pet or such big political questions as the balance of power in the House of Representatives. Those of you who do something as ordinary as buying a soda after class may pay more than your peers in other states or cities.

COMPARATIVE METHOD

A learning approach based on studying the differences and similarities among similar units of analysis (such as states).

Some readers of this textbook are certainly paying more in tuition and fees than those in other colleges. Why?

The comparative method answers such questions by systematically looking for **variance**, or differences, between comparable units of analysis. For our purposes, states are one comparable unit of analysis. Local governments—governments below the state level, such as county boards of commissioners and city councils—are another. This means they have basic similarities that make meaningful comparisons possible. One way to think of this is that the comparative method is based on the idea that you can learn more about apples by comparing them to other apples rather than to oranges or bananas.

Similarly, the argument is that you can learn about states by comparing them to other states. All fifty states are independent democratic governments free to make their own decisions as long as they stay within the broad confines of the single set of rules that is the U.S. Constitution. Their governmental structures are roughly the same. All have a basic division of powers among the executive, legislative, and judicial branches of government. There are different kinds and different levels of local government, but they share many of the same responsibilities. The similarities among states and among local governments make meaningful comparison possible. Their differences provide the opportunity to answer questions about politics and government.

The states may share similar political structures and follow the same set of rules, but they make very different choices. These differences have consequences. Take, for example, college tuition and fees. As noted earlier, there is a direct relationship between the size of a state government's contribution to higher education and a student's average tuition bill. Underlying this relationship is a set of differences that explains why your tuition bill is high (or low) compared to tuition charged by colleges in other states. Simply put, your tuition bill is comparatively higher (or lower) depending on the size of a state government's subsidy to higher education. A similar difference explains why some of you will pay more for a soda after class than others. The sales tax on a can of soda ranges from 0 to 9 percent depending on the city and state, hence different prices in different locales.[14] These examples demonstrate the essence of the comparative method: From your tuition bills to the price of soda, differences make a difference.

Such differences can lend themselves to very sophisticated statistical analyses. A professional policy analyst can use data on state higher education funding and tuition rates at state universities and colleges to provide a precise estimate of the relationship between the contributions from state government and your tuition bill: On average, for every $1,000 per student

The similarities among states and among local governments make meaningful comparison possible. Their differences provide the opportunity to answer questions about politics and government.

appropriation by state government, tuition and fees at public, four-year universities fall by a little more than $200.[15]

What's more, these differences can be used to answer "why" questions. For example, we know that how much a state gives to higher education helps determine how much you pay in tuition. So, you might want to know why some states provide more support to higher education than others. This is a question about one difference that can be answered by looking at other differences. What might these differences be? Well, they could range from partisan politics in a state's legislature to a state's traditions and history to its relative wealth. As a starting point for using the comparative approach to analyze such questions, consider the following basic differences among states and among localities:

Sociodemographics

The populations of states and localities vary enormously in size, age, and ethnicity. The particular mix of these characteristics, or **sociodemographics**, in a specific state or community has a profound impact on its politics. California is the most populous state in the nation, with about thirty-six million residents. Of those thirty-six million, more than 40 percent are minorities—many of which are first-generation or second-generation immigrants—and 14 percent live in poverty. Compare this with New Hampshire, which has about 1.3 million residents, 96 percent of whom are white, and only about 7 percent of whom live below the poverty line.[16] These population characteristics present different challenges to the governments in these two states. Differences in populations are likely to promote different attitudes and policies on welfare, affirmative action, bilingual education programs, even the role and responsibilities of government in general.

And it gets better. All of these population characteristics are dynamic. That is, they change. Between 2000 and 2005, the population of Flagler County, Florida, grew by more than 50 percent.[17] During roughly the same time period, the population of Arthur County, Nebraska, shrank by more than 10 percent. These population expansions and contractions create very different problems and policy priorities for local governments—the struggle to accommodate new growth in a fast developing area (Flagler County had 76,000 residents in 2005), versus the challenge of maintaining even basic services in a rural county in which there are ever fewer taxpayers to tax (Arthur County had only 378 residents in 2005).[18]

How are sociodemographics related to your tuition bill? Consider the age distribution from young to old of a state's population. There is less demand for college education among those older than sixty-five than there is among those in the traditional undergraduate demographic of eighteen to twenty-four. Given this, states with a higher percentage of their populations in older age groups face a different set of education policy pressures than those with higher concentrations of younger groups. States with large aging

Nevada continues to be the country's fastest growing state, with a nearly 3.5 percent increase in its population in 2005. Eleven percent of the state's population is currently sixty-five years of age or older, a 72 percent increase since 1990.

populations are likely to face less demand for higher education spending and more demand for public programs, such as healthcare, that address the needs of the elderly. Why do some states provide more support to higher education than others? At least a partial answer to this question is that different sociodemographics create different demands for higher education.

Study Map 1-1 for a moment. Believe it or not, you are actually looking at the United States. The reason the states look so strange is that this is a special kind of map called a cartogram. Instead of using actual geographical space to determine the size of a particular area represented in the map—the number of square miles in each state, for instance—cartograms use other variables to determine how size is represented. In this case, this cartogram measures the size of each state's population. This is another useful way to compare states. Notice how some states that are actually pretty big, like New Mexico at 122,000 square miles, are very small on this map because they have small populations. Other states that are actually really small, like Connecticut (only five thousand square miles), look much bigger

MAP 1-1 Population by State

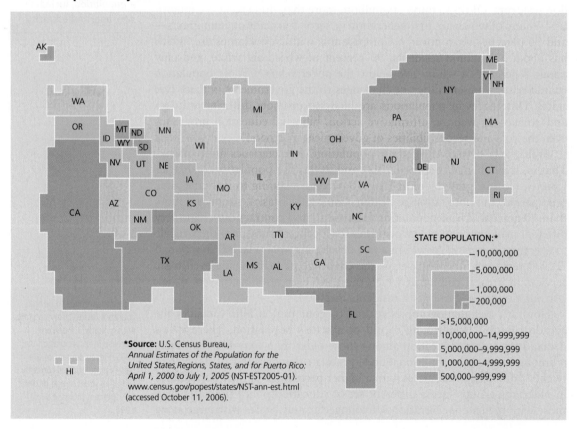

STATE POPULATION:*

- 10,000,000
- 5,000,000
- 1,000,000
- 200,000

>15,000,000
10,000,000–14,999,999
5,000,000–9,999,999
1,000,000–4,999,999
500,000–999,999

*Source: U.S. Census Bureau, *Annual Estimates of the Population for the United States, Regions, States, and for Puerto Rico: April 1, 2000 to July 1, 2005* (NST-EST2005-01). www.census.gov/popest/states/NST-ann-est.html (accessed October 11, 2006).

Governing States and Localities

on this map because they have large populations. Some states, like Virginia, don't look that different in size at all.

Culture and History

States and localities have distinct "personalities" that are apparent in everything from the "bloody bucket" shoulder patch worn by the Pennsylvania National Guard to the drawl that distinguishes the speech of West Texas natives. Some states have been part of the Union for more than two hundred years and still project an Old World connection to Europe. Others, notably Hawaii and Alaska, became states within living memory and are more associated with the Old West and the exoticism of the Pacific. New York City prides itself on being a cosmopolitan center of Western civilization. The visitor's bureau of Lincoln, Nebraska, touts its small-town ambience and Middle American values. These differences are more than interesting variations in accent and local points of pride. They are visible symbols that represent distinct values and attitudes. Political scientists generally accept that these differences extend to government and that each state has a distinct **political culture**, identifiable general attitudes and beliefs about the role and responsibility of government.

Daniel Elazar's *American Federalism: A View from the States* is the classic study of political culture. In this book, first published more than forty years ago, Elazar not only described different state cultures and created a classification of state cultures still in use today, he also explained why states have distinctly different political cultures. Elazar argued that political culture is a product of how the United States was settled. He said that

POLITICAL CULTURE
The attitudes and beliefs broadly shared in a polity about the role and responsibility of government.

Demographics and culture give each state and locality a unique "personality." In this picture, San Francisco's Chinatown prepares for the Chinese New Year, an important event in the city's calendar. Yet while many San Francisco businesses closed in order to prepare for an official celebration, in other cities the special day passed virtually unnoticed.

people's religious and ethnic backgrounds played the dominant role in establishing political cultures. On this basis there were three distinct types of settlers who fanned out across the United States in more or less straight lines from the East Coast to the West Coast. These distinct migration patterns created three different types of state political cultures: moralistic, individualistic, and traditionalistic.[19]

States with **moralistic** cultures are those in which politics is the means to try to achieve a good and just society. Such states tend to be clustered in the country's northern tier (New England, the upper Midwest, and the Pacific Northwest). Elazar argued that the Puritans who originally settled the Northeast came to the New World seeking religious freedom. Their political culture reflects a desire to use politics to construct the best possible society. Such a notion that government and politics represent the means to the greater good creates a society that values involvement in politics and views government as a positive force for addressing social problems. This general orientation toward government and politics spread along the northern and middle part of the country with successive waves of migration. Wisconsin, for example, is a classic moralistic state. First settled by Yankees, and later by Scandinavians, Germans, and Eastern Europeans, the state has long had a reputation for high levels of participation in politics (for example, high levels of voter turnout), policy innovation, and scandal-free government.

States with **individualistic** cultures have a different view of government and politics. In individualistic cultures, people view government as rather like an extension of the marketplace, something in which people participate for individual reasons and to achieve individual goals. Government should provide the services that people want, but it is not viewed as a vehicle to create a "good society" or to intervene in private activities. Politics in individualistic states is viewed like any other business. Officeholders expect to be paid like professionals, and political parties are, in essence, corporations that compete to provide goods and services to people. Unlike those in moralistic states, as long as the roads are paved and the trains run on time, folks in individualistic states tend to tolerate more corruption in government.

Why? In individualistic states, "Both politicians and citizens look upon political activity as a specialized one," Elazar writes, "and no place for amateurs to play an active role."[20] The roots of this view of government, according to Elazar, comes from the English, Scottish, Irish, and Germans who initially settled in states like Maryland, New Jersey, and Pennsylvania. They came to the United States in search of individual opportunity, not to construct some idealized vision of the good society. This "every man for himself" attitude was reflected in politics, and the individualistic culture was carried by subsequent waves of migration into places like Illinois and Missouri.

New Jersey is a good example of an individualistic state. The state, as political scientist Maureen Moakley puts it, "Has always been more of a polyglot than a melting pot."[21] Originally settled by waves of poor and uneducated immigrants in pursuit of the American Dream, in more recent times

A Difference that Makes a Difference:
Is It Better to Be a Woman in Vermont or a Gal in Mississippi?

According to the Institute for Women's Policy Research (IWPR), it is better to be a woman in Vermont than a gal in Mississippi.

Why? Well, in its 2004 analysis of the status of women in the states, the IWPR had several reasons for ranking Vermont as the best state for women and Mississippi as the worst. For example, in Vermont women had greater economic autonomy and enjoyed greater reproductive rights than women in Mississippi. This is only a partial answer to the question, however. To learn the rest of it, one must ask: *Why* do women have greater economic autonomy and more reproductive rights in Vermont than in Mississippi?

The comparative approach to answering this question involves looking for other differences between Vermont and Mississippi. Differences that might explain the variance in the status of women. Some candidates for those explanatory differences are presented in Table 1-1. This table shows the top five and the bottom five states in the IWPR rankings, the dominant political culture in these states, and the percent of state legislators who are women. Notice any patterns?

You may have caught that each of the top five states has either a moralistic or an individualistic culture. All of the bottom five states have traditionalistic cultures. Therefore, political culture might explain some of the difference in women's status. States in which the dominant political values stress the importance of everyone getting involved might offer more opportunities for women. So might states in which such values emphasize hard work as the predominant basis for getting ahead in life. States in which the dominant political values stress leaving the important decisions to established elites might offer fewer opportunities, since traditionally, elites have been male.

Also, take a look at the proportion of females in the state legislatures. On average, about 30 percent of state legislators in the top five states are women. In the bottom five states, that average is more than halved—only about 13 percent of state legislators are women. This is a difference that can have considerable impact. A number of studies show that women legislators tend to support more progressive policies, are more likely to pay attention to

TABLE 1-1

Politics and the Status of Women in the States: Some Variables

Five Best States for Women	Dominant Political Culture	Percentage of State Legislators Who Are Women
1. Vermont	Moralistic	30.4%
2. Connecticut	Individualistic	28.9
3. Minnesota	Moralistic	31.3
4. Washington	Moralistic	33.3
5. Oregon	Moralistic	27.8
Five Worst States for Women	**Dominant Political Culture**	**Percentage of State Legislators Who Are Women**
46. Oklahoma	Traditionalistic	14.8%
47. Arkansas	Traditionalistic	17
48. Kentucky	Traditionalistic	11.6
49. South Carolina	Traditionalistic	8.2
50. Mississippi	Traditionalistic	13.8

Sources: Center for American Women and Politics, "Fact Sheet: Women in State Legislatures 2006," www.cawp.rutgers.edu/Facts4. html (accessed April 4, 2006); Institute for Women's Policy Research, *The Status of Women in the States,* 2004, www.iwpr.org/States2004/ SWS2004/index.htm (accessed April 4, 2006); and Daniel Elazar, *American Federalism: A View from the States* (New York: Crowell, 1966).

women's issues, and are more likely to push these issues into law.*

Thus, states that have more women in their legislatures are more likely to respond to issues such as reproductive rights, violence against women, child support policies, and family leave benefits. All of these contribute to IWPR's calculations. Why is Vermont a better state for women than Mississippi? A comparative answer to that question is that Vermont has a political culture that is more likely to encourage and support political participation by women, and it also has a greater female presence in its state legislature.

*Michele Swers, "Understanding the Policy Impact of Electing Women: Evidence from Research on Congress and State Legislatures," *PS: Political Science and Politics* 34, no. 2 (2001): 217–220.

it has become home to more than a million foreign-born residents and large racial and ethnic minority populations. The result is a fragmented political culture in which many residents feel more connected to local communities than to the state. One poll conducted in 2003 found that only one in twenty-five residents could correctly identify which party controlled the state's government.[22] Not surprisingly given all of this, New Jersey has strong laws that give the state's more than five hundred local governments more power than localities in other states.

In **traditionalistic** cultures, politics is the province of elites, something that average citizens should not concern themselves with. Traditionalistic states are, as their name suggests, fundamentally conservative, in the sense of preserving a well-established society. Like moralistic states, traditionalistic states believe that government serves a positive role. But there is one big difference: traditionalistic states believe the larger purpose of government is to maintain existing social orders. Those at the top of the social structure are expected to play a dominant role in politics, and power is concentrated in the hands of these elites. Traditionalistic states tend to be rural states (at least historically) in which agriculture, rather than a broader mix of competing commercial activities, is the main economic driver.

Traditionalistic cultures tend to be concentrated in the Deep South, in states such as Georgia, Mississippi, and South Carolina. In these states politics is significantly shaped by tradition and history (an argument about the official recognition of Confederate flags, for example, can be a major election-year issue in such states). Like the settlers of individualistic states, those who settled the South sought personal opportunity. The pre-industrial, agrarian economy of the South, however, led to a culture that was little more than a variation of the feudal order of the European Middle Ages. As far back as the 1830s, French aristocrat and writer Alexis de Tocqueville noted that, "as one goes farther south . . . the population does not exercise such a direct influence on affairs . . . The power of the elected officials is comparatively greater and that of the voter less." [23]

Few states today are considered "pure" cultures. In other words, most states have elements of two of the cultures or of all three. For example, a number of traditionalistic states like Florida and Georgia have seen a huge influx of people from northern states, people who often are not from traditionalistic cultures. The Deep South is also considerably more urban than it used to be. Such changes tend to mix elements of moralistic and individualistic cultures into the traditionalistic mix.

Even with such changes, however, for most states one of Elazar's three political cultures is likely to be dominant, as Map 1-2 shows. Numerous studies have found that the dominant political culture shapes politics and policy in important ways. Policy change and innovation, for example, are more likely in moralistic states. Individualistic states are more likely to offer businesses tax breaks. Traditionalistic states tend to commit less public money to areas such as education.[24] Faced with similar problems, the Texas and Wis-

MAP 1-2 Dominant Political Culture by State

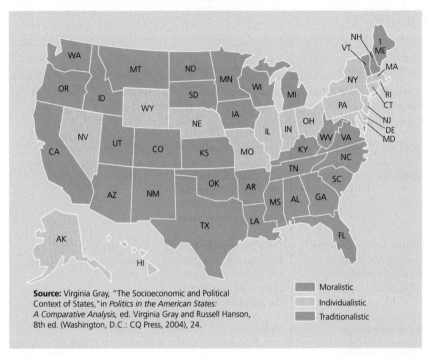

Source: Virginia Gray, "The Socioeconomic and Political Context of States," in *Politics in the American States: A Comparative Analysis,* ed. Virginia Gray and Russell Hanson, 8th ed. (Washington, D.C.: CQ Press, 2004), 24.

Moralistic
Individualistic
Traditionalistic

consin state legislatures may propose radically different policy responses. These differences are at least partially a product of the political cultures that still distinguish each state. In other words, culture and history matter.

These cultural differences certainly are apparent when it comes to supporting higher education. Moralistic states commit considerably more resources to higher education than governments in individualistic and traditionalistic states. They spend about 13 percent more per capita on colleges and universities than states in the other two cultures. Since moralistic states are those in which attitudes support higher levels of commitment to the public sector, these spending differences make sense in cultural terms. Why do some states provide more support to higher education than others? Apparently, another part of the answer is that some political cultures see higher education in more communal than individual terms.

Economy

The relative size and health of a state's economy has a huge impact on its capacity to govern and provide public services. The per capita gross state product—the state equivalent of the gross national product—varies from about $26,000 in Mississippi to $64,000 in Delaware.[25] (See Map 1-3.) This means government in Delaware has the ability to tap greater

TABLE 1-2

Political Cultures at a Glance

	Elazar Classification		
	Moralistic	**Individualistic**	**Traditionalistic**
Role of Government	Government should act to promote the public interest and policy innovation.	Government should be utilitarian, a service provider.	Government should help preserve the status quo.
Attitude of Public Representatives	Politicians can effect change; public service is worthwhile and an honor.	Businesslike. Politics is a career like any other, and individual politicians are oriented toward personal power. High levels of corruption are more common.	Politicians can effect change, but politics is the province of the elites.
Role of Citizens	Citizens actively participate in voting and other political activities; individuals seek public office.	The state exists to advance the economic and personal self-interest of citizens; citizens leave politics to the professionals.	Ordinary citizens are not expected to be politically involved.
Degree of Party Competition	Highly competitive	Moderate	Weak
Government Spending on Services	High	Moderate; money goes to basic services but not perceived "extras."	Low
Political Culture	Strong	Fragmented	Strong
Most Common in . . .	Northeast, northern Midwest, Northwest	Middle parts of the country, like the Mid-Atlantic; parts of the Midwest, like Missouri and Illinois; parts of the West, like Nevada and California	Southern states, rural areas

resources than government in Mississippi. The difference in wealth, in effect, means that if Delaware and Mississippi were to implement identical and equivalent public services, Mississippi would have a considerably higher tax rate. This is because Mississippi would have to take a greater proportion of its smaller resources compared to Delaware. These sorts of differences also are visible at the local level. Wealthy suburbs can enjoy lower tax rates and still spend more on public services than economically struggling urban or rural communities.

Regional economic differences do not just determine tax burdens and the level of public services. They also determine the relative priorities of partic-

MAP 1-3 **Economy by State**

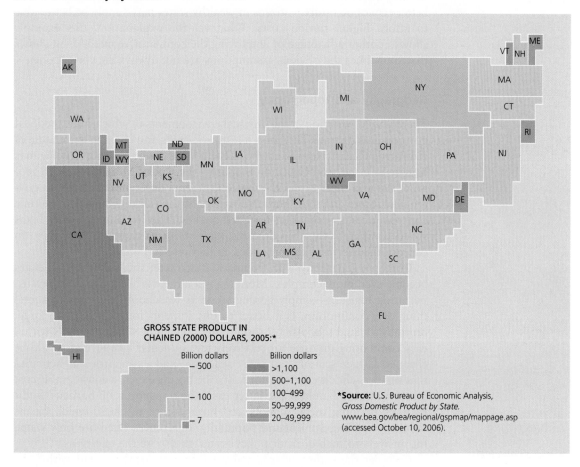

GROSS STATE PRODUCT IN
CHAINED (2000) DOLLARS, 2005:*

Billion dollars
— 500
— 100
— 7

Billion dollars
>1,100
500–1,100
100–499
50–99,999
20–49,999

*Source: U.S. Bureau of Economic Analysis,
Gross Domestic Product by State.
www.bea.gov/bea/regional/gspmap/mappage.asp
(accessed October 10, 2006).

ular policy and regulatory issues. Fishing, for example, is a sizable industry in coastal states in the Northeast and Northwest. States like Maine and Washington have numerous laws, regulations, and enforcement responsibilities tied to the catching, processing, and transporting of fish. Regulating the economic exploitation of marine life occupies very little government attention and resources in places such as Kansas and Nevada, although agriculture in the former and gambling in the latter create just as many policy challenges and demands for government action.

Regardless of the basis of a state's economy, greater wealth does not always translate into more support for public programs. States with above average incomes actually tend to spend *less* per capita on higher education. Why would less wealthy states concentrate more of their resources on higher education? There are a number of possible explanations. Education is a critical component of a post-industrial economy, so states that are less well-

The relative size of state economies is measured in terms of gross state product. Notice how big states with small economies (Montana and Alaska) compare to small states with big economies (New Jersey and Massachusetts).

off may direct more of their resources into education in hopes of building a better economic future. Citizens in wealthy states may simply be better able to afford higher tuition costs. Whatever the explanation, this example shows another advantage of employing the comparative method—it shows that sometimes the obvious assumptions are not always the correct ones.

Geography and Topography

There is wild variation in the physical environments in which state and local governments operate. Hawaii is a lush tropical island chain in the middle of the Pacific Ocean, Nevada encompasses a large desert, much of Michigan is heavily forested, and Colorado is split by the Rocky Mountains. Such geographical and topographical variation presents different challenges to government. State and local authorities in California devote considerable time and resources to preparing for earthquakes. Their counterparts in Texas spend comparatively little time thinking about earthquakes, but they do concern themselves with tornadoes, grass fires, and hurricanes.

Combine geography with population characteristics and the challenges become even more complex. Montana is a large, rural state in which transportation logistics—simply getting students to school—can present something of a conundrum. Is it better to bus students long distances to large, centrally located schools? Or should there be many, smaller schools within easy commuting distance for relatively few students? The former would be cheaper. Larger schools can offer academic and extracurricular activities that smaller schools cannot afford. But the busing exacts a considerable cost on students and families. The latter eases the transportation burdens, but it requires building more schools and hiring more teachers, which means more taxes. Geographical and population differences often not only shape the answers to such difficult policy issues, they pose the questions.

Consider the variety of seasonal weather patterns that occur within the enormous geographical confines of the United States. In Wisconsin, snow removal is a key service provided by local governments. Road clearing crews are often at work around the clock during bad weather. The plows, the crews, and the road salt all cost money. They all require a considerable investment in administration and coordination to effectively do the job. In Florida, snow removal is low on local governments' lists of priorities for good reason—it rarely snows in the Sunshine State. On the other hand, state and local authorities in Florida do need to prepare for the occasional hurricane. Less predictable and less common than snow in Wisconsin, it only takes one hurricane to create serious demands on the resources of local authorities.

And, yes, even basic geography affects your tuition bill, especially when combined with some of the other characteristics discussed here. Many large public colleges and universities are located in urban centers because central geographical locations serve more people more efficiently. Delivering higher education in rural areas is a more expensive proposition simply because there are fewer people in the service area. States with below average population densities tend to be larger and more sparsely populated. They also tend to spend more on higher education. Larger government subsidies are necessary to make tuition affordable.

Recognizing the Stakes

The variation across states and localities offers more than a way to help make sense of your tuition bill, or to explain why some public school systems are better funded, or to understand why taxes are lower in some states. These differences also serve to underline the central role of states and localities in the American political system. Compared to the federal government, state and local governments employ more people and buy more goods and services from the private sector. They have primary responsibility for many of the issues that people care about the most, including education, crime prevention, transportation, healthcare, and the environment. Public opinion polls often show that citizens place more trust in state and local governments than in the federal government. These polls frequently express citizens' preference for having the former relieve the latter of a greater range of policy responsibilities.[26] With these responsibilities and expectations, it should be obvious that state and local politics are played for high stakes.

High stakes, yes, but it is somewhat ironic that state and local governments tend to get less attention in the media, in private conversation, and in curriculums and classrooms than their federal counterpart.[27] Ask most people to think about American government and chances are they will think first about the president, Congress, Social Security, or some other feature of the national government. Yet most American government is state or local. Five hundred and thirty-five elected legislators serve in the U.S. Congress. Thousands of legislators are elected at the state level, and tens of thousands more serve in the legislative branches of local government.

In terms of people, state and local governments dwarf the federal government. The combined civilian workforce of the federal government (about 2.7 million) is less than half of the number of the number of people working for a single category of local government—more than six million people work for public elementary and secondary schools.[28] Roughly five million state employees and more than thirteen million local government employees punch the time clock every day. (See Map 1-4.) In terms of dollars, state and local governments combined

> Compared to the federal government, state and local governments employ more people and buy more goods and services from the private sector. They have primary responsibility for many of the issues that people care about the most, including education, crime prevention, transportation, healthcare, and the environment.

represent about the same spending force as the federal government. In 2002, state and local government expenditures combined totaled approximately $2.7 trillion.[29]

The size of state and local government operations is commensurate with their twenty-first-century role in the political system. After spending much of the twentieth century being drawn closer into the orbit and influence of the federal government, states and localities have become much more aggressive in asserting their independence during the past thirty years. This maturing of nonfederal, or subnational, government has made its leaders and its policies—not to mention its differences—among the most important characteristics of our political system. What is at stake in state and local politics turns out to be not just what *you* are interested in, but just about anything that anyone is interested in.

Consider Hurricane Katrina, which devastated a massive swath of the Gulf Coast in 2005, flooding large sections of New Orleans, Louisiana, and

States that are more densely populated have fewer employees per resident than states that are more sparsely populated. Why? Relatively fewer people are required to serve densely settled populations than to assist populations scattered over large areas.

MAP 1-4 **Number of Government Employees by State**

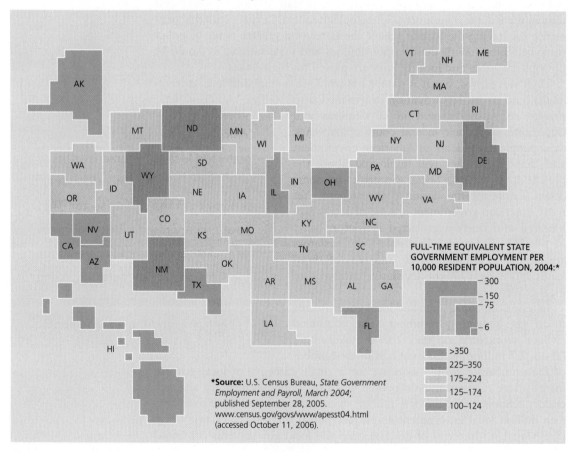

FULL-TIME EQUIVALENT STATE GOVERNMENT EMPLOYMENT PER 10,000 RESIDENT POPULATION, 2004:*

- 300
- 150
- 75
- 6

- >350
- 225–350
- 175–224
- 125–174
- 100–124

*Source: U.S. Census Bureau, *State Government Employment and Payroll, March 2004*; published September 28, 2005. www.census.gov/govs/www/apesst04.html (accessed October 11, 2006).

Governing States and Localities

literally wiping some communities off the map. The storm not only created an immediate need for emergency first responders, it also created a long-term recovery problem. Debris needed to be cleaned up, transportation and utility infrastructures needed to be repaired, public services such as education needed to be reestablished, public buildings such hospitals needed to be reopened, and public and private reconstruction had to be carried out—the list is almost endless. While the federal government certainly is involved in these, it is the state and local governments—such as the administrations of Louisiana governor Kathleen Blanco and New Orleans mayor Ray Nagin—that must shoulder the most responsibility for these efforts.

The context of the federal system of government, and the role of state and local governments within that system, is given more in-depth coverage in chapter 2. Nonetheless, it is important to recognize now that governance in the United States is more network than hierarchy. The policies and politics of any single level of government are connected and intertwined with the policies and politics of the other levels of government in a complex web of interdependent relationships. The role of states and localities in these governance partnerships has changed considerably in the past few decades.

What states and localities do, and how they go about doing it, turns out to shape national life overall as well as the lives of individual citizens. Given what is at stake at the state and local level, no citizen can fully comprehend the role and importance of government without understanding subnational politics.

Laboratories of Democracy: Devolution and the Limits of Government

U.S. Supreme Court justice Louis Brandeis famously described the states as **laboratories of democracy**. This metaphor refers to the ability of states—and, to a lesser extent, localities—to experiment with policy. Successful experiments can be replicated by other states or adopted by the national government. In an era in which states have greater responsibilities, capabilities, and levels of autonomy, they are more willing to accept the risks of innovation. For much of the past twenty years, state-federal relations have been characterized by **devolution**, or the process of taking power and responsibility away from the federal government and giving it to state and local government. As a result, it is the states, not just the federal government, that are aggressively promoting new ways to solve old problems in such high-profile policy areas as welfare, gun control, and education. These issues and others are addressed in depth in later chapters.

How state and local governments decide to exercise their independent decision-making authority is dependent upon a number of factors. Some of these factors are external. The U.S. Constitution, federal laws and regulations, nationwide recessions, and the like constrain what states and localities can and cannot do. Increasingly, however, it is the characteristics of a

LABORATORIES OF DEMOCRACY

A term used for the states that emphasizes their ability to engage in different policy experiments without interference from the federal government.

DEVOLUTION

The process of taking power and responsibility away from the federal government and giving it to state and local governments.

particular state—not the firm hand of the federal government—that limits what the state decides to do.

The "big three" of these limits are wealth, the characteristics of the state's political system, and the relative presence of organized interest groups, those individuals who organize to support policy issues that concern them. Public programs cost money. Wealth sets the limits of possible government action. Simply speaking, wealthier states can afford to do more than poorer states. Political system characteristics are the elements of the political environment that are specific to a state. States in which public opinion is relatively conservative are likely to pursue different policy avenues than states in which public opinion is more liberal. States in which Republicans dominate government are likely to opt for different policy choices than states in which Democrats dominate. States with professional, full-time legislatures are more likely to formulate and pursue sustained policy agendas than are states in which legislators are part-timers who only meet periodically. States in which the governor perceives an electoral mandate to reform government are more likely to be innovative than are states in which the government perceives an electoral mandate to retain the status quo.[30] Organized interest group activity helps determine what sort of policy demands government responds to. Governments in states with powerful teachers' unions, for example, experience different education policy pressures than governments in states in which teachers' unions are politically weak. These factors constitute the basic ingredients for policymaking in the states. Specifics vary enormously from state to state, and the potential combinations in this democratic laboratory are virtually infinite.

Localities face more policymaking constraints than states do because they typically are not sovereign governments. This means that, unlike states, local governments get their power from the level of government above them, rather than directly from citizens. The states have much greater control over local governments than the federal government has over the states. Yet while local governments are much more subordinate to state government than state government is to the federal government, they do not simply take orders from the state capitol. Many have independent taxing authority and broad discretion to act within their designated policy jurisdictions.

These policy jurisdictions, however, are frequently subject to formal limits. The authority of school districts, for example, extends only to funding and operating public schools. State government may place lids on districts' tax rates and set everything from minimal employment qualifications to maximum teacher-to-pupil ratios. Yet even within this range of tighter restrictions, local governments retain

School districts contract out a wide range of services, hiring private companies to do everything from running cafeterias to providing student transportation. School districts often do this to save money, but there are downsides. Rancho Cordova, California, school bus driver Jill Marchuk is a school employee who fears losing her job if the district contracts out transportation services.

Local Focus: **The Federal City**

Riddle me this: It is a city. It is sort of a state. It is ruled by Congress. What is it? It is the District of Columbia, otherwise known as Washington, D.C. It is also the nation's capitol, and it is surely the most unusual and unique local government in the country.

Technically, Washington, D.C., is a federal city. Article I, Section 8, Paragraph 17 of the U.S. Constitution gives Congress the power to rule over an area not to exceed ten square miles that constitutes the seat of national government. Yet it has never been quite clear what that means in terms of governance. Should Congress rule the city directly? Should citizens of the city be given the right to elect a representative government? If they do this, should the government be subordinate to Congress, or should it be counted as an equivalent to a state and be free to make any laws that do not violate the U.S. Constitution?

Throughout its history, these questions have been answered very differently. In the early 1800s the district was a strange collection of cities and counties, each governed by different means. Washington City and Georgetown were municipalities run by a chief executive (a mayor) and a legislature (a council). Depending on the time period, however, the mayors were sometimes appointed by the federal government and sometimes elected. In addition to the two cities, there were also two counties. Maryland laws governed Washington County. Alexandria County followed the laws of Virginia.

In the 1870s, Washington City, Georgetown, and Washington County were combined into a single governmental unit, a federal territory with a governor appointed by the president and a legislature elected by territorial residents. This eventually became the District of Columbia, or Washington, D.C. For most of its history, commissioners appointed by the federal government governed the district. It was not until 1974 that the residents of Washington, D.C., gained home rule and the right to elect their own mayor and council.

This mayor/council arrangement, however, is unlike any other municipal government in the United States. The laws passed by the council have to be reviewed and approved by Congress. The laws that govern federal-state relationships treat the district as a state, even though it is not a state and cannot operate like one. The mayor is not considered the head of a federal agency, but he or she is expected to act like one when seeking appropriations from Congress.

This odd hybrid of local, state, and federal government is reflected in the unique electoral status of Washington, D.C., voters. Voters in the district have a local vote, but only half of a federal vote. They can vote for the president, but not for a member of Congress. They can vote for a mayor and council, but they have no voting representative in Congress. Yet Congress has the power to overturn laws passed by the council. The district now has three electoral votes. Prior to 1963 it had none, and D.C. voters could not cast a ballot for president.

All this makes Washington, D.C., the nation's most unusual local government. It is the only municipality that is a creature of the United States rather than of a state constitution, and as such it is the only really national city in the country.

Source: Select material from Council of the District of Columbia, "History of Self-Government in the District of Columbia," 1997. www.dccouncil.washington.dc.us (accessed September 23, 2003).

considerable leeway to act independently. School districts often decide to contract out cafeteria and janitorial services, cities and counties actively seek to foster economic development with tax abatements and loan guarantees, and police commissions experiment with community-based law enforcement. During the past two decades many of the reforms enthusiastically pursued at all levels of government—reforms ranging from innovative new management practices to outright privatization of public services—have had their origins in local government.[31]

What all this activity shows is that states and localities are not only the laboratories of democracy, but also the engines of the American republic. States and localities are not just safe places to engage in limited experimentation, they are the primary mechanisms connecting citizens to the actions of government. As the specifics of these connections vary considerably, the comparative method is an intuitive way to impose order on and make sense of politics and policy at the subnational level.

> States and localities are not just safe places to engage in limited experimentation, they are the primary mechanisms connecting citizens to the actions of government.

Conclusion

While pursuing the nuances and details of politics and government is not of primary interest to the typical college student, there are good reasons for developing a curiosity about state and local government. State politics determine everything from how much you pay for college to whether your course in state and local government is required or elective. Above and beyond understanding its impact on your own life and interests, state and local government is important to study because of its critical role in the governance and life of the nation. Subnational, or non-federal, government employs more people than the federal government and spends as much money. Its responsibilities include everything from pothole repair to education to homeland security. It is difficult, if not impossible, to understand government in the United States and the rights, obligations, and benefits of citizenship without first understanding state and local government.

This textbook fosters such an understanding through the comparative method. This approach involves looking for patterns in the differences among states and localities. Rather than advocating a particular perspective on state and local politics, the comparative method is predicated, or based, on a systematic way of asking and answering questions. Why is my tuition bill so high? Why does Massachusetts send mostly Democrats to the U.S. House of Representatives? Why are those convicted of capital crimes more likely to be executed in Texas than in Connecticut? Why are sales taxes high in Alabama? Why is there no income tax in South Dakota? Each of these questions can be answered by comparing states and looking for systematic patterns in their differences. The essence of the comparative method is to use one difference to explain another.

The study of state and local politics has been organized into three distinct sections. The first section consists of four chapters designed to set the basic framework, or context, for studying state and local politics. Included here are chapters on federalism, state constitutions, political participation, and political parties and interest groups. The second section covers the institutions of state and local government: legislatures, executives, courts, and bureaucracy. Although elements of local government are discussed in all of these, there are also two chapters in this section devoted solely to local politics and government. The final section covers a series of distinct policy areas: budgets and taxes, education, healthcare, and crime. These chapters not only cover areas of substantive policy interests, but also offer concrete examples of how a broad understanding of the context and institutions of state and local government can be combined with the comparative method to promote a deeper understanding of the politics of states and localities.

Key Concepts

comparative method (p. 7)
devolution (p. 21)
individualistic (p. 12)
laboratories of democracy (p. 21)
moralistic (p. 12)
political culture (p. 11)
sociodemographics (p. 9)
traditionalistic (p. 14)
variance (p. 8)

Suggested Readings

Elazar, Daniel. *American Federalism: A View from the States.* New York: Crowell, 1966. The classic work on political culture in the states.

Gray, Virginia, and Russell Hanson, eds. *Politics in the American States: A Comparative Analysis.* 8th ed. Washington, D.C.: CQ Press, 2003. One of the better-known comparative studies of state politics and policies. Periodically updated.

Hovey, Kendra A., and Harold A. Hovey. *CQ's State Fact Finder 2007: Rankings across America.* Washington, D.C.: CQ Press, 2007. Comprehensive reference on all aspects of the states. Good source for comparative research.

Van Horn, Carl, ed. *The State of the States.* 4th ed. Washington, D.C.: CQ Press, 2005. Thorough overview of the trends in state politics and in political institutions.

Suggested Web Sites

http://cspl.uis.edu/InstituteForLegislativeStudies/SPPQ/. Web site of *State Politics & Policy Quarterly,* an academic research journal devoted to studying state-level questions. Includes links to a publicly accessible database on state politics and policy.

www.census.gov/statab/www/ranks.html. Bureau of the Census Web site that lists state rankings on such measures as population, per capita income, employment, poverty, and other social and economic indexes.

www.csg.org/csg/default. Web site of the Council of State Governments (CSG), an organization that represents elected and appointed officials in all three branches of state government. Publishes on a wide variety of topics and issues relevant to state politics and policy.

CHAPTER 2

Federalism
The Power Plan

It was never clear who was navigating the government's response to Hurricane Katrina, and federal, state, and local governments often seemed lost. Relations between the administrations of President George Bush (center), Louisiana governor Kathleen Blanco (to Bush's right, in red), and New Orleans mayor Ray Nagin (to Bush's left) became strained as each level of government blamed the other for failing its responsibilities. As the three executives toured the aftermath of the storm, it became clear that effective responses to big policy challenges require, first and foremost, effective coordination of the federal system.

2

What are the advantages and disadvantages of federalism?

Why does the federal government seem to be gaining power while the states lose it?

Why would some businesses prefer to be regulated by the federal government rather than state governments?

By the evening of September 1, 2005, the time for diplomacy had passed for Ray Nagin, the mayor of New Orleans, Louisiana. Three days earlier, Hurricane Katrina—the worst natural disaster in the history of the United States—had hit the Gulf Coast and left 80 percent of the Crescent City under water. Tens of thousands of the city's poorest residents were stranded in squalid conditions in the city's convention center and the Superdome. Armed looters roamed the city. The hurricane had passed, but the political storm was in full swing. The response to the disaster was stymied by disagreements among local, state, and federal government agencies about their responsibilities.

On local radio station WWL-AM that Thursday night, amid criticism of his own government's preparedness for the storm, Nagin lashed out at President George W. Bush and Louisiana governor Kathleen Babineaux Blanco. "I don't know whose problem it is," he said. "I don't know whether it's the governor's problem. I don't know whether it's the president's problem, but somebody needs to get their ass on a plane and sit down, the two of them, and figure this out right now." [1]

Just a year earlier, some three hundred local, state, and federal emergency response officials had participated in a tabletop exercise—dubbed Hurricane Pam—that had simulated a Category 3 hurricane hitting New Orleans. It was difficult after Katrina, however, to discern what agreements or arrangements the exercise had finalized. Relationships among the Federal Emergency Management Agency (FEMA), Louisiana, and New Orleans were informal; fingers could be (and were) pointed in all directions. [2]

Little more than a week after Nagin's on-air explosion, the water began to recede, FEMA director Michael Brown was fired, and Vice Admiral Thad Allen was installed as the federal government's Hurricane Katrina point man. But the experiences left scars, with officials at all levels pledging to forge better relationships. And it wasn't just the people directly involved with the Katrina response who learned about the push and pull of American government; people across the country—and the world—did, too. Yes, virtually all nations have local or regional units of government, and even the most authoritarian political system has to distribute at least some power and policy responsibilities among them.

But Hurricane Katrina demonstrated that the United States is somewhat unusual. Its subnational governments—states and localities—play a central policymaking role and enjoy a high degree of independence from the central government. It is this independence that allows many of the differences across states and localities to exist and makes the comparative method a useful approach to studying them. This importance and independence are products of **federalism**. Federalism is a political system in which national and regional governments share powers and are considered independent equals. In the case of Katrina, this led to confusion about who should take charge of rescue and relief efforts. Although Gulf Coast residents likely would have welcomed order of any sort, Blanco and Mississippi governor Haley Barbour rebuffed Bush's proposal to shift the command of their National Guard units to the federal government.[3]

This system of shared powers is critical to understanding the politics of states and localities and the central role they play in the U.S. political system. The question at the heart of it all is: Who—the federal government or the state governments—has the power to do what? In the words of noted University of Chicago law professor Cass Sunstein, the debate over the distribution of powers between the state and federal levels holds "the ultimate fate of measures safeguarding the environment, protecting consumers, upholding civil rights, protecting violence against women, protecting endangered species, and defining criminal conduct in general and banning hate crimes in particular."[4]

This chapter provides a basic understanding of federalism, its history and evolution in the United States, and its implications for politics and governance for states and localities.

FEDERALISM

Political system in which national and regional governments share powers and are considered independent equals.

Systems of Power

Generally speaking, a nation organized under a single sovereign government, that is, a government that depends on no other government for its political authority or power, can distribute power and responsibility throughout its political system in any of three ways. (See Figure 2.1.) One is to concentrate power in the central government. Nations in which legal authority is held almost exclusively by a central government are known as **unitary systems**. Unitary systems typically have regional or local governments, but these can only exercise the powers and responsibilities granted them by the central government. The United Kingdom is a good example of a unitary system. Although the United Kingdom has a strong tradition of local government, and has set up regional legislatures in Scotland and Wales and (intermittently) in Northern Ireland, power is concentrated in the nation's Parliament. If it so chooses, Parliament can expand or contract the powers and responsibilities of its lower governments or even shut them down entirely, which has happened periodically in Northern Ireland.

> The central question at the heart of it all is: Who—the federal government or state governments—has the power to do what?

UNITARY SYSTEMS

Political systems in which power is concentrated in a central government.

FIGURE 2-1 How It Works: Systems of Government

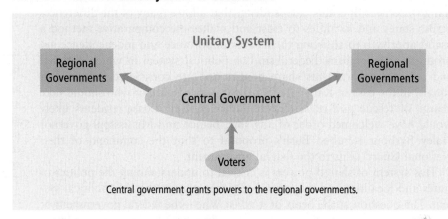

Unitary System

Regional Governments

Central Government

Regional Governments

Voters

Central government grants powers to the regional governments.

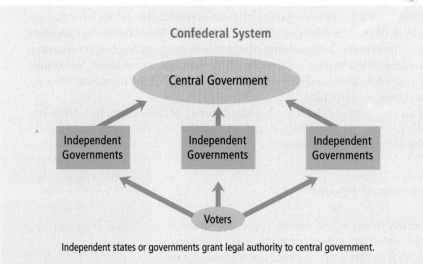

Confederal System

Central Government

Independent Governments

Independent Governments

Independent Governments

Voters

Independent states or governments grant legal authority to central government.

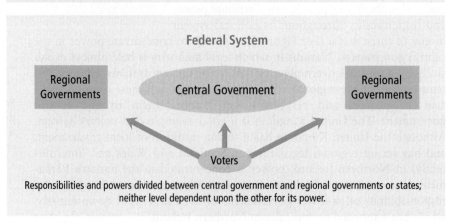

Federal System

Regional Governments

Central Government

Regional Governments

Voters

Responsibilities and powers divided between central government and regional governments or states; neither level dependent upon the other for its power.

In contrast to unitary systems, confederal systems concentrate power in regional governments. A **confederacy** is a voluntary association of independent states or governments. The central government is dependent upon the regional governments for its legal authority. The United States has experimented with a confederal system twice during its history. The Articles of Confederation was the first constitution of the United States. It organized the U.S. political system as an agreement of union among sovereign states. The national government consisted of a legislature in which all states had equal representation. There was no national executive branch, such as the presidency, and no national judiciary, such as the Supreme Court.

This confederal system was adopted during the Revolutionary War and remained in effect for more than a decade. Many of the nation's founders saw its many flaws, however, and wrote its replacement at the Constitutional Convention of 1787 in Philadelphia. The product of that gathering—the U.S. Constitution—was ratified in 1788 and replaced the Articles of Confederation as the basis of the U.S. political system.[5]

The second experiment with confederacy began in 1861 at the onset of the Civil War. Those southern states that sought to secede from the Union organized their political system as a confederacy. All of this ended with the South's surrender in 1865 and the return of the seceded states into the Union.

Federal systems operate in a middle range between unitary systems and confederacies. Responsibilities in a federal system are divided between the two levels of government, and each is given the appropriate power and legal authority to fulfill those responsibilities. The system's defining feature is that neither level of government is dependent upon the other for its power. Within their defined areas of responsibility, each is considered independent and autonomous. In the United States, states are equal partners with the national government and occupy a central role in the political system.

Why Federalism?: The Origins of the Federal System in the United States

There are a number of reasons why the United States is organized as a federal system and not as a unitary system or a confederacy. The framers of the Constitution rejected a confederal system largely because of their experiences with the Articles of Confederation. The national government was so weak under the Articles that prominent figures, such as James Madison and George Washington, feared it doomed the newly independent republic to failure.

These fears were not unfounded. Following the successful conclusion of the Revolutionary War in 1783, the new United States found itself in the grip of an economic recession, and the central government had little power to address the crisis. Indeed, it actually contributed to the problem by con-

CONFEDERACY

A political system in which power is concentrated in regional governments.

stantly threatening to default on its debts. Independence had brought political freedom, but it also meant American-made products now were in head-to-head competition with cheap, high-quality goods from Great Britain. This made consumers happy but threatened to cripple American businesses. The economic difficulties pitted state against state, farmer against manufacturer, and debtor against banker, while the central government could do little but stand by and hope for the best.

As internal tensions mounted within the United States, European powers still active in the Americas threatened the nation's very sovereignty. Spain shut down shipping on the Mississippi. The British refused to withdraw from some military posts until the U.S. government paid off its debts to British creditors. George Washington believed the United States, having won the war, was in real danger of losing the peace. He said that something had to change in order "to avert the humiliating and contemptible figure we are about to make on the annals of mankind." [6]

For a loose coalition of the professional classes that called themselves Federalists, that "something" was obviously the central government. This group of lawyers, businessmen, and other individuals drawn mostly from the upper social strata began to agitate for a new constitution to replace the Articles. Their primary goal was to create a stronger and more powerful national government. Americans, however, were not particularly enthusiastic about handing more power to the central government, an attitude not so different from today. Most recognized that the Articles had numerous flaws, but few were ready to copy the example of the British and adopt a unitary system.

Two events in the fall of 1786 allowed the Federalists to overcome this resistance and achieve their goal of creating a more powerful national government. The first was the Annapolis Convention. This meeting in Maryland's capital convened to try to hammer out an interstate trade agreement. Few states sent delegates. Those who did show up had strong Federalist sympathies. They took advantage of the meeting and petitioned Congress to call for a commission to rewrite the Articles of Confederation.

The second event was Shays's Rebellion, named after its leader, Daniel Shays, a hero of the recently won Revolutionary War. The rebellion was an uprising of Massachusetts farmers who took up arms in protest of state efforts to take their property to pay off taxes and other debts. It was quickly crushed, but with further civil unrest threatening to boil over into civil war and with mounting pressure from powerful elites within the Federalist ranks, the Continental Congress was pushed to call for states to send delegates to Philadelphia in the summer of 1787. The purpose for the meeting was the rewriting of the Articles of Confederation.

The delegates formed what is now known as the Constitutional Convention. Representatives largely consisted of Federalist notables such as Washington and Madison. Once convened, the group quickly abandoned their mandate to modify the Articles of Confederation and decided to write an entirely new constitution. In doing so, the Federalists who dominated the convention rejected confederacy as an adequate basis for the American political system. Their experience under the Articles had taught them that a central government subordinate to the states was not much of a government at all. What they wanted was a government capable of effectively dealing with national problems, and this meant a government independent of the states.

While some Federalists, most notably Alexander Hamilton, were attracted to the idea of a unitary government, such a system was never seriously considered. For one thing, there was strong popular sentiment against a unitary system. Remember that the Revolutionary War had been fought in no small part because of the perceived arrogance and abuse of a unitary system. For another, any new constitution would have to be ratified by the states, and it was highly unlikely the states were going to voluntarily agree to give up all of their powers to a national government. Federalism remained as the only practical option. Thus the establishment of a federal system of government is the central feature of the Constitution of the United States.

A federal system, however, represented more than the price that had to be paid to achieve a stronger national government. The Founders were attempting to construct a new form of **representative government**, a form of government in which citizens exercise power indirectly, on the basis of a paradox. Convention delegates wanted a more powerful national government, but at the same time they did not want to concentrate power for fear it would lead to tyranny. Their solution to this problem was to create a system of separated powers and checks and balances. They divided their new and stronger national government into three branches—legislative, executive, and judicial—and made each branch partially reliant on the others to carry out its own responsibilities. This made it difficult for any single group to gain the upper hand in all three divisions of government and gave each branch the power to check the excesses of the other branches.

A similar set of goals was achieved by making state and national governments co-equal partners. By letting states remain independent decision makers in a wide range of policy arenas, power was divided between the national and subnational levels of government. The national government was made more powerful by the new constitution, but the independence of the states helped set clear limits on this power.

The Advantages and Disadvantages of Federalism

Dividing power between state and local units of government helped the Founders achieve their philosophical aims of dispersing and separating power. The newly adopted federal system overcame the immediate political challenge of getting the states to agree to a stronger national government. It

REPRESENTATIVE GOVERNMENT

A form of government in which citizens exercise power indirectly by choosing representatives to legislate on their behalf.

also bequeathed a further set of advantages and disadvantages that have benefited and bedeviled the American political system for more than two centuries.

There are four key advantages to the federal system. First, it keeps government closer to the people. Rather than have the federal government impose a "one size fits all" policy, states have the freedom and authority to match government decisions to local preferences. This freedom also results in the local variance in laws, institutions, and traditions that characterize the U.S. political system and provide the comparative method with its explanatory strength.

Second, federalism allows local differences to be reflected in state and local government policy and thereby reduces conflict. Massachusetts, for example, tends to be more liberal than, say, Alabama. California has a much more ethnically and culturally diverse population than Nebraska. Rather than have the various interests and preferences that spring from state-to-state differences engage in a winner-take-all policy struggle at the federal level, they can be accommodated at the state level. This reduces the friction among interests and lowers conflict.

Third, independent subnational governments allow for flexibility and experimentation. The states, as Supreme Court justice Louis Brandeis famously put it, are "the laboratories of democracy." Successful policy innovations in one state can be adopted by other states and copied by the federal government.

Fourth, independent subnational governments make it easier to achieve at least some national goals. For example, although homeland security became a national policy priority following the terrorist attacks of September 11, 2001, the federal government was ill equipped to create emergency response plans for potential attacks in every state and every locality. It did not have the infrastructure, the resources, or the legal authority. While the national government struggled to put together an overall blueprint for homeland security, state and local governments took matters into their own hands by incorporating terrorism into their ongoing emergency response planning operations. One group, the Mid-America Regional Council (MARC), an association of 144 cities and 8 counties in the Kansas City metro area, already had a well-established arrangement that allowed local governments to cooperatively respond to emergencies.

State and local organizations like MARC were well positioned to become immediate and effective terror-response agencies. The federal government simply piggybacked on these existing resources by making funds available to maximize state and local capability to combat terrorism. Rather than create the needed emergency response infrastructure from scratch, the federal government cooperated with existing state and local organizations to achieve the broader goal of national security.

Along with its benefits, however, federalism also confers a set of disadvantages. First, while allowing local differences does keep government closer to the people, it also creates complexity and confusion. For example, if you own a nationwide business, you have to deal with state *and* federal regulations—fifty-one sets of regulations in all. That means, among other things, fifty-one tax codes and fifty-one sets of licensing requirements. And many communities also have their own restrictions and requirements to meet as well.

Second, federalism can increase conflict as easily as reduce it. The Constitution is very vague on the exact division of powers between state and federal government. This results in a constant struggle—and a lot of litigation—in an effort to resolve what level of government has the responsibility and legal authority to take the lead role in a given policy area. For example, who should challenge drug companies that make false or misleading claims about their products? In January 2007, thirty states settled with the Bayer Corporation for $8 million over safety concerns about a cholesterol-reducing drug that had since been pulled from the market. But just weeks earlier, the makers of four purported weight-loss drugs agreed to pay $25 million to settle allegations by the Federal Trade Commission that they had made unproven claims about the effectiveness of their products. Similar cases, but one was ruled on at the state level and the other at the national level.

Third, while federalism promotes flexibility and experimentation, it also promotes duplication and reduces accountability. Local, state, and national governments, for example, have all taken on law enforcement responsibilities. In some areas, this means there may be municipal police departments, a county sheriff's department, and the state patrol, plus local offices of the Federal Bureau of Investigation and the U.S. Drug Enforcement Agency. The responsibilities and jurisdictions of these organizations overlap, which means taxpayers end up paying twice for some law enforcement activities. When these agencies are unsuccessful or ineffective it also is hard to figure out who is responsible and what needs to change. Hurricane Katrina provides a good example of this; almost as soon as the storm hit the coast it was clear that government response was ineffective. What was less clear was who was at fault and how things should be changed.

Fourth, the federal system can make it hard to coordinate policy efforts nationwide. Organizations like MARC offer a well-trained, ready solution to terrorism preparedness efforts, but these efforts are not uniformly duplicated in other states and other urban areas. Police and fire departments on opposite sides of a state border, or even within adjacent jurisdictions in the

Emergency services in Richmond, Missouri, take advantage of the scheduled demolition of a middle school to train for incidents involving explosions and mass casualties. Such training is crucial to help first responders from different agencies learn how to work effectively with each other.

TABLE 2-1

Advantages and Disadvantages of Federalism

Advantages	Disadvantages
Allows for flexibility among state laws and institutions.	Increases complexity and confusion.
Reduces conflict because states can accommodate citizens' interests.	Sometimes increases conflict when jurisdictional lines are unclear.
Allows for experimentation at the state level.	Duplicates efforts and reduces accountability.
Enables the achievement of national goals.	Makes coordination difficult.
	Creates inequality in services and policy.

same state, may have different communication systems. It is hard to coordinate a response to a terror attack if the relevant organizations cannot talk to each other, and the federal government cannot force state and local governments to standardize radio equipment.

Finally, a federal system creates inequality in services and policies. The quality of public schools and welfare services, for example, depends heavily on the choices state and local governments make. This inevitably means that some states offer better educational opportunities and do more for the needy than others.

The Constitutional Basis of Federalism

The relationship between national and state governments is something of a sibling rivalry. It is hard to imagine either level of government getting along without the other, yet because each is independent and focused on its own interests, conflict is common. The ink was barely dry on the newly ratified Constitution before the federal government and the states were squabbling over who had the power and authority in this or that policy area. In writing the Constitution, the Founders recognized that differences between states and the federal government were likely to be a central and lasting feature of the political system. Accordingly, they attempted to head off the worst of the disputes—or at least provide a basis for resolving them—by making a basic division of powers between the national and state governments.

The Constitution grants the federal government both enumerated and implied powers. **Enumerated powers** are grants of authority explicitly given by the Constitution. Among the most important of these is the **national supremacy clause** contained in Article VI, section 2. This states that the

Policy in Practice: Preemption: The Gorilla that Swallows State Laws

Lamar Alexander, former governor of Tennessee and presidential candidate, arrived in the U.S. Senate in 2003 ready to promote states' rights. Instead, he found neither conservatives nor liberals interested in advancing devolution, and he admits that the ability of state and local governments to protect even local tax and spending priorities is slipping.

States are feeling somewhat disrespected by the feds. In recent years, the federal government has exerted power in numerous policy areas previously left to the states, including healthcare, the environment, and public safety. The No Child Left Behind Act is perhaps the most high-profile example of this trend. It imposed federal rules on two-hundred-year-old state and local education systems, but left those governments to pay for tens of billions in program costs. What's more, Congress continues to underfund special education and security programs it insisted upon.

For all the states' bellyaching, they've recently been successful in implementing solutions that the federal government has not, particularly in the areas of clean air, patients' rights, and in some cases, the regulation of utilities like gas and electricity. Congress stepped in with its versions of do-not-call and do-not-spam lists only after dozens of states already had passed their own. Some government observers see this not as a dismantling of federalism, but as a new pattern: States advance policy, then Congress follows by writing federal law based on state solutions. Some state initiatives

are diminished, but many of their creative ideas are preserved.

The continued power of states is found most clearly in the offices of the state attorneys general. Since forty-six of these players brokered a multibillion-dollar settlement with tobacco companies in 1998, they've become increasingly active, asserting their influence to limit carbon dioxide emissions, filing actions against mutual funds and insurance companies, and pursuing pharmaceutical companies that market drugs illegally.

Their clout has sent the business community in search of relief from the federal government. Michael Greve of the American Enterprise Institute's Federalism Project long argued against federal government regulation of the economy, but he now argues that federal preemption is needed to protect businesses from conflicting state laws. Why did he change his tune? It is not because the states are victims in the federal system, but instead because the free markets don't like the actions that state attorneys general have taken.

The three-way tussle among state preferences, national power, and the agendas of special interests has produced an ironic result. In the first 200 years of its existence, Congress preempted roughly 250 state laws. In the past two decades—the era of New Federalism and devolution—it has roughly doubled that number. While devolution may have loosened federal leashes on the states, it clearly has not caged the preemption gorilla.

Sources: Adapted from Alan Greenblatt, "The Washington Offensive," *Governing* magazine, January 2005; Alan Ehrenhalt, "States' Not-So-Dire Straits," *Governing* magazine, March 2005; and Jonathan Walters, "Save Us from the States," *Governing* magazine, June 2001.

Constitution "shall be the supreme law of the land; and the judges in every state shall be bound thereby." In other words, federal law takes precedence over all other laws. This allows the federal government to preempt, or override, areas regulated by state law. In recent decades the federal government has aggressively used this power to extend its authority over states in a wide range of policy issues. So much so that **preemption** has been called "the gorilla that swallows state laws." [7]

PREEMPTION

The process of the federal government overriding areas regulated by state law.

Other enumerated powers are laid out in Article I, section 8. This part of the Constitution details a set of **exclusive powers**—grants of authority that belong solely to the national government. These include the power to regulate commerce, to declare war, and to raise and maintain an army and navy. Article I, section 8 also confers a set of **concurrent powers** to the national government. Concurrent powers are those granted to the national government but not denied to the states. Both levels of government are free to exercise these prerogatives. Concurrent powers include the power to tax, borrow, and spend.

Finally, this same section of the Constitution gives the national government **implied powers**. The basic idea behind implied powers is that the authors of the Constitution realized they could not possibly list every specific power the national government would require to meet the needs of a developing nation. Accordingly, they gave Congress the flexibility to meet unforeseen challenges by granting the federal government a set of broad and largely undefined powers. These include the **general welfare clause**, which gives the federal government the authority to provide for "the general welfare of the United States," and the **necessary and proper clause**, the ability for Congress "to make all laws which shall be necessary and proper" to carry out its responsibilities as defined by the Constitution. (See Table 2-2 for an explanation of these and other provisions.)

The Constitution says a good deal about the powers of the federal government but very little about the powers of the states. The original, unamended Constitution spent much more time specifying the obligations of the states than it did defining their power and authority. The obligations list includes Article IV, section 2, better known as the **full faith and credit clause**. The clause requires all states to grant "full faith and credit" to each other's public acts and records. This means that wills, contracts, and marriages valid under one state's laws are valid under all. Under the **privileges and immunities clause**, states are prohibited from discriminating against citizens from other states. The idea here was to prevent people traveling across states or temporarily residing in a state because of business or personal reasons from becoming the target of discriminatory regulation or taxation.

The Constitution also sets out an often criticized system of electing the nation's president and vice president. The presidency goes not to the candidate who wins the most votes but rather to the one who wins the most states. Article II, section 1 charges the states with appointing electors—one for each of the state's U.S. senators and representatives—who actually choose the president based on the winner of the state's popular vote. (If the Republican candidate gets the most popular votes, the state's delegation is made up of Republican Party loyalists who vote for the Republican nominee.) A presidential candidate needs a majority in the electoral college, which requires the votes of at least 270 of the 538 state electors, to be named the winner.

Other than these responsibilities and explicitly granting the states the right to enter into compacts, or binding agreements, with each other on matters of regional concern, the Constitution is virtually silent on the powers of the states. This lopsided attention to the powers of the federal government was a contentious issue in the battle to ratify the Constitution. Opponents of the document, collectively known as Anti-Federalists, feared that states would become little more than puppets of the new central government. Supporters of the Constitution sought to calm these fears by arguing that states would remain sovereign and independent and that the powers not specifically granted to the federal government were reserved for the states. As James Madison put it, in writing the Constitution the Federalists were seeking "a middle ground which may at once support due supremacy of the national authority," but would also preserve a strong independent role for the states.[8]

Madison and his fellow Federalists offered to put these assurances in writing. In effect, they promised that if the Constitution were ratified, the first order of business for the new Congress would be to draft a set of amendments that spelled out the limits of central government power and specified the independence of the states. Although Anti-Federalist skepticism remained, the Federalists kept their promise. The First Congress formulated a series of changes that eventually became the first ten amendments to the Constitution and are collectively known as the **Bill of Rights**.

Most of these amendments set specific limits on government power. The aim was to guarantee certain individual rights and freedoms, and at least initially, they were directed at the federal government rather than state governments. The **Tenth Amendment**, however, finally addressed the power of the states. In full, the Tenth Amendment states: "The powers not delegated to the United States by the Constitution, nor prohibited by it to the states, are reserved to the states respectively, or to the people." This provided no enumerated, or specific, powers to the states, but those implied by the language of the amendment are considerable. The so-called reserved powers encompass all of the concurrent powers that allow the states to tax, borrow, and spend; to make laws and enforce them; to regulate trade within their borders; and to practice eminent domain, which is the power to take private property for public use. The reserved powers also have been traditionally understood to mean that states have the primary power to make laws that involve the health, safety, and morals of their citizens. Yet the powers reserved for the states are more implied than explicit, and they all rest in an uneasy tension with the national supremacy clause of Article VI.

After the Tenth Amendment, the **Fourteenth Amendment** is the most important in terms of specifying state powers. Ratified in 1868, the Fourteenth Amendment is one of the so-called Civil War Amendments that came in the immediate wake of the bloody conflict between the North, or the Union, and the South, or the Confederacy. The Fourteenth Amendment prohibits any state from depriving individuals of the rights and privileges of citizenship and requires states to provide due process and equal protection guarantees to all citizens. The Supreme Court has used these guarantees to

FULL FAITH AND CREDIT CLAUSE

Requires states to recognize each other's public records and acts as valid.

PRIVILEGES AND IMMUNITIES CLAUSE

Prohibits states from discriminating against citizens of other states.

BILL OF RIGHTS

The first ten amendments to the Constitution that set limits on the power of the federal government and set out the rights of individuals and the states.

TENTH AMENDMENT

Guarantees a broad, but undefined, set of powers be reserved for the states and the people.

FOURTEENTH AMENDMENT

Prohibits states from depriving individuals of the rights and privileges of citizenship and requires states to provide due process and equal protection guarantees.

TABLE 2-2

U.S. Constitution's Provisions for Federalism

What It Is . . .	What It Says . . .
Article I, section 8 (Commerce Clause)	The Congress shall have Power . . . To regulate Commerce with foreign Nations, and among the several States, and with the Indian Tribes. . . .
Article I, section 8 (Necessary and Proper Clause)	The Congress shall have Power . . . To make all Laws which shall be necessary and proper for carrying into Execution the foregoing Powers, and all other Powers vested by this Constitution in the Government of the United States, or in any Department or Officer thereof.
Article IV, section 3 (Admission of New States)	New States may be admitted by the Congress into this Union; but no new State shall be formed or erected within the Jurisdiction of any other State; nor any State be formed by the Junction of two or more States, or Parts of States, without the Consent of the Legislatures of the States concerned as well as of the Congress.
Article IV, section 4 (Enforcement of Republican Form of Government)	The United States shall guarantee to every State in this Union a Republican Form of Government, and shall protect each of them against Invasion; and on Application of the Legislature, or of the Executive (when the Legislature cannot be convened) against domestic Violence.
Article VI (Supremacy Clause)	This Constitution, and the Laws of the United States which shall be made in Pursuance thereof; and all Treaties made, or which shall be made, under the Authority of the United States, shall be the supreme Law of the Land; and the Judges in every State shall be bound thereby, any Thing in the Constitution or Laws of any State to the Contrary notwithstanding.
Tenth Amendment	The powers not delegated to the United States by the Constitution, nor prohibited by it to the States, are reserved to the States respectively, or to the people.
Fourteenth Amendment	All persons born or naturalized in the United States, and subject to the jurisdiction thereof, are citizens of the United States and of the state wherein they reside. No state shall make or enforce any law which shall abridge the privileges or immunities of citizens of the United States; nor shall any state deprive any person of life, liberty, or property, without due process of law; nor deny to any person within its jurisdiction the equal protection of the laws.
Sixteenth Amendment	The Congress shall have the power to lay and collect taxes on incomes, from whatever source derived, without apportionment among the several States, and without regard to any census or enumeration.
Seventeenth Amendment	The Senate of the United States shall be composed of two Senators from each State, elected by the people thereof, for six years; and each Senator shall have one vote. . . . When vacancies happen in the representation of any State in the Senate, the executive authority of each State shall issue writs of election to fill such vacancies: Provided that the legislature of any State may empower the executive thereof to make temporary appointments until the people fill the vacancies by election as the legislature may direct.

apply the Bill of Rights to state governments as well as to the federal government and to assert national power over state power in issues ranging from the desegregation of public education to the reapportioning state legislatures.

The implied powers of the federal government, the limitations set on states by the Fourteenth Amendment, and the undefined "leftovers" given to the states by the Tenth Amendment mean that the scope and the author-

Gives Congress the right to regulate interstate commerce. This clause has been broadly interpreted to give Congress a number of implied powers.

An implied power giving Congress the right to pass all laws considered "necessary and proper" to carry out the federal government's responsibilities as defined by the Constitution.

Allows the U.S. Congress to admit new states to the union and guarantees each state sovereignty and jurisdiction over its territory.

Ensures that a democratic government exists in each state and protects states against foreign invasion or insurrection.

States that federal law takes precedence over all other laws.

Guarantees a broad, but undefined, set of powers be reserved for the states and the people, as opposed to the federal government.

Prohibits any state from depriving individuals of the rights and privileges of citizenship and requires states to provide due process and equal protection guarantees to all citizens.

Enables the federal government to levy a national income tax, which helped further national policies and programs in subsequent years.

Provides for direct election of Senators, rather than election by each state's legislature.

ity of both levels of government are, in many cases, dependent upon how the Constitution is interpreted. The Constitution, in other words, provides a basic framework for solving the sibling rivalry squabbles between the states and the federal government. It does not provide, however, an unambiguous guide to who has the primary power, responsibility, and authority on a broad range of policy issues. This, as we shall see, means that the U.S.

FIGURE 2-2 Powers of National and State Governments

National Government Powers

Coin money

Regulate interstate and foreign commerce

Tax imports and exports

Make treaties

Make all laws "necessary and proper" to fulfill responsibilities

Make war

Regulate postal system

Powers Denied

Tax state exports

Change state boundaries

Impose religious tests

Pass laws in conflict with the Bill of Rights

Concurrent Powers

Tax

Borrow money

Charter banks and corporations

Take property (eminent domain)

Make and enforce laws and administer a judiciary

State Government Powers

Run elections

Regulate intrastate commerce

Establish republican forms of state and local government

Protect public health, safety, and morals

All powers not delegated to the national government or denied to the states by the Constitution

Powers Denied

Tax imports and exports

Coin money

Enter into treaties

Impair obligation of contracts

Enter compacts with other states without congressional consent

Source: Adapted from Samuel Kernell and Gary C. Jacobson, *The Logic of American Politics,* 2d ed. (Washington, D.C.: CQ Press, 2003). 75, Figure 3-2.

Supreme Court is repeatedly thrust into the role of refereeing power disputes between national and state governments.

The Development of Federalism

Disagreements about the scope and authority of the national government broke out shortly after the First Congress convened in 1789. The issue of a national bank was one of the most controversial of these early conflicts and the one with the most lasting implications. Alexander Hamilton, secretary of the treasury under President George Washington, put together a broad program designed to get the newly empowered national government to address the nation's economic woes. Part of this program was the proposed creation of a national bank. The problem was that although Hamilton believed a central bank was critical to stabilizing the economic situation, there was nothing in the Constitution that specifically granted the federal government the authority to create and regulate such an institution.

Lacking a clear enumerated power, Hamilton justified his proposal by using an implied power. He argued that the necessary and proper clause implied the power to create a national bank because the bank would help the government manage its finances as it went about its expressly conferred authority to tax and spend. Essentially, Hamilton was interpreting necessary as "convenient" or "appropriate." Secretary of State Thomas Jefferson objected, arguing that if the Constitution was going to establish a government of truly limited powers, the federal government needed to stick to its enumerated powers and interpret its implied powers very narrowly. He thus argued that the "necessary" in the necessary and proper clause should be properly interpreted as "essential" or "indispensable." Hamilton eventually won the argument, and Congress approved the national bank. Still, the issue simmered as a controversial—and potentially unconstitutional—expansion of the national government's powers.

The issue was not fully resolved until 1819 when the Supreme Court decided the case of *McCulloch v. Maryland*. This case stemmed from the state of Maryland's attempts to shut down the national bank, which was taking business from state chartered banks, by taxing its operations. The chief cashier of the national bank's Baltimore branch refused to pay the tax, and the parties went to court. The Supreme Court, in essence, backed Hamilton's interpretation of the Constitution over Jefferson's. This was important above and beyond the issue of a national bank. It suggested that the Constitution gave the national government a broad set of powers relative to the states. Key to this early affirmation of the federal government's power was U.S. Chief Justice John Marshall, whose backing of a broad interpretation of implied powers laid the foundation for later expansions in the scope and authority of the federal government.

The full impact of *McCulloch v. Maryland*, however, would not be felt for some time. For the most part, the federal government began to feel its way into the gray areas of its constitutional powers pretty cautiously. Federalism went on to develop in four distinct stages—dual federalism, cooperative federalism, centralized federalism, and new federalism—and the first of these stages leaned toward the more limited role of the federal government favored by Jefferson.

Dual Federalism (1789–1933)

Dual federalism is the idea that state and federal governments have separate jurisdictions and responsibilities. Within these separate spheres of authority, each level of government is sovereign and free to operate without interference from the other. It represents something of a middle ground in the initial interpretations of how the Constitution divided power. On one side of the debate were Federalists like Hamilton, who championed a nation-centered view of federalism. They wanted to interpret the Constitution as broadly as possible to give the national government supremacy over the states.

On the other side were fierce **states' rights** advocates like John Calhoun of South Carolina, who served as vice president in the administrations of

DUAL FEDERALISM

The idea that state and federal governments have separate and distinct jurisdictions and responsibilities.

STATES' RIGHTS

The belief that states should be free to make their own decisions with little interference from the federal government.

John Quincy Adams and Andrew Jackson. Supporters of states' rights wanted the federal government's power limited to the greatest possible extent and saw any expansion of it as an encroachment upon the sovereignty of the states. In the 1820s and 1830s Calhoun formulated what became known as the **compact theory** of federalism. The idea was that the Constitution represented an agreement among sovereign states to form a common government. It interpreted the Constitution as essentially an extension of the Articles of Confederation, meaning that the United States was more a confederal system than a federal one.

The compact theory argued that since sovereignty ultimately rested with the states, the states rather than the Supreme Court had the final say in how the Constitution should be interpreted. The states also had the right to reject federal laws and make them invalid within their own borders. This process was known as **nullification**, and the compact theory took it to an extreme. Calhoun argued that states could reject the entire Constitution and choose to withdraw, or secede, from the Union. In the 1820s national policies—especially a trade tariff—triggered an economic downturn in the southern states, which created wide support for nullification and **secession** arguments. These extreme states' rights views were not completely resolved until the Union victory in the Civil War ended them for good.

Dual federalism walked the line of moderation between the extremes of **nation-centered federalism** and **state-centered federalism**. Basically, dual federalism looks at the U.S. political system as a layered cake. The state and federal governments represent distinct and separate layers. To keep them separate, advocates of dual federalism sought to limit the federal government to exercising only a narrow interpretation of its enumerated powers. If the Constitution was to be interpreted broadly, that interpretation should favor the states rather than Congress. This became the central operating philosophy of the U.S. Supreme Court for much of the nineteenth century and is most closely associated with the tenure of Chief Justice Roger B. Taney, who served from 1836 to 1864. Unlike his predecessor John Marshall, Taney was much less sympathetic to arguments that interpreted the federal government's powers broadly.

The dual federalism doctrine gave rise to some infamous, not to mention downright notorious, landmark decisions on the powers and limitations of the federal government. Perhaps the best-known expression of the philosophy came in *Scott v. Sandford* (1857). Dred Scott was a slave taken by his master from Missouri, a slave state, to Illinois, a free state, and on into what was then called the Wisconsin Territory, where slavery was outlawed by the Missouri Compromise of 1820. This federal law stipulated which new states and territories could and could not make slavery legal. After his master's death, Scott sued for his freedom, arguing that his residence in a free territory had legally ended his bondage. Scott's case was tied to the Missouri Compromise, which the Supreme Court subsequently ruled unconstitutional. Their justification was that Congress did not have the enumerated, nor the implied, power to prohibit slavery in the territories. Thus Scott remained a slave, although his owners voluntarily gave him his freedom shortly after the Supreme Court decision. He died of tuberculosis in 1858, having spent only one of his nearly sixty years as a free man.

Cooperative Federalism (1933–1964)

In theory dual federalism defines and maintains a clear division between state and national governments and sets a clear standard for doing so: If the federal government has the enumerated power to take the disputed action or make the disputed law, it has supremacy over the states in the particular case. If it does not have the enumerated power, then the Tenth Amendment reserves that power for the states and state preferences take precedence.

The problem was that its clarity in theory rarely matched the complex realities of governance in practice. State and national government have shared interests in a wide range of issues, from education to transportation. To cleanly divide these interests into separate spheres of influence was not only difficult, in many cases it was not even desired. Even at the height of the dual federalism era, states and the federal government were collaborating as much as they were fighting. The federal government, for example, owned vast tracts of land in the Midwest and West, and it made extensive grants of these lands to the states to help develop transportation and education systems. Many of the nation's best-known state universities got their start this way as land-grant colleges.

In the nineteenth century the federal government also gave out cash grants to support Civil War veterans housed in state institutions, gave money to the states to support agricultural research, and loaned federal manpower—primarily U.S. Army engineers—to help state and local development projects.[9] Rather than a layered cake, some experts believe a more appropriate metaphor for federalism is that of a marble cake with the different levels of government so thoroughly mixed with each other that they are impossible to separate. (See Figure 2-3.)

Certainly as the nation became increasingly industrialized and more urban, state and federal interests became increasingly intertwined. As the nineteenth century drew to a close and the twentieth century began, the federal government undertook a significant expansion of its policy responsibilities. In 1887 it began to regulate the railroads, a policy with enormous significance for the economic development of states and localities. In economic and social terms this was roughly equivalent to the federal government of today announcing comprehensive regulation of the Internet and software manufacturers. By fits and starts, dual federalism gradually fell out of favor with the Supreme Court. The Court instead

> The theoretical clarity of dual federalism rarely matched the complex realities of day-to-day government.

began to interpret the powers of the federal government very broadly and to allow the jurisdictions of state and national governments to gradually merge.

Several events accelerated this trend. In 1913, the Sixteenth Amendment was ratified, giving the federal government the ability to levy a nationwide income tax. The new taxing and spending authority helped further national policies designed during the next decades.[10] The First World War (1914–1918) resulted in a significant centralization of power in the federal government. The Second World War (1939–1945) centralized that power even further. The need to fight global conflicts pushed the federal government to assert the lead role on a wide range of economic and social issues.

Even more important to the long-term relationship between state and national governments was the Great Depression of the 1930s, a social and economic catastrophe that swept aside any remaining vestiges of dual federalism. State and local governments were ill equipped to deal with the problems created by the Great Depression. They simply did not

The Sixteenth Amendment gave the federal government the power to levy an income tax. It does not require long lines at the post office every April, although it can seem that way. The last-minute rush to file tax returns ahead of the April 15 filing deadline can mean long lines at post offices like this one in Guilderland, New York.

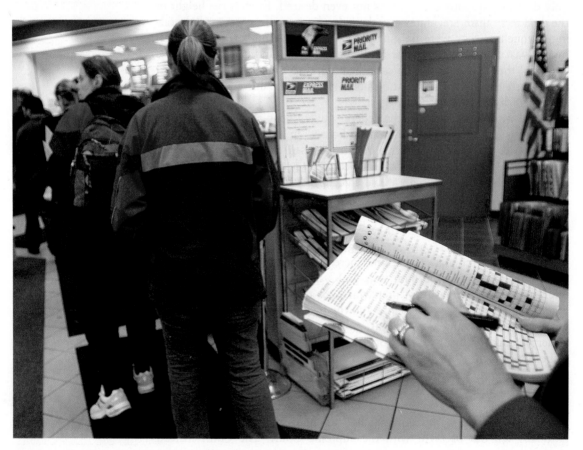

Governing States and Localities

have the resources and, at first, the federal government was simply reluctant to act.

The catalyst for a fundamental change in the nature of state-federal relations was the election of Franklin Delano Roosevelt to the presidency in 1932. In an effort to combat economic and social malaise, Roosevelt aggressively pushed the federal government into taking a lead role in areas traditionally left to the states. The federal government in the 1930s became deeply involved in regulating the labor market, creating and managing welfare programs, and providing significant amounts of direct aid to cities. The general approach of Roosevelt's so-called New Deal agenda defined the central characteristics of **cooperative federalism**—use the federal government to identify the problem, set up the basic outline of a program to address the problem, make money available to fund that program, then turn over much of the responsibility for implementing and running it to the states and localities. This arrangement dominated state and federal relations for the next three decades.

Centralized Federalism (1964–1980)

Having all levels of government addressing problems simultaneously and cooperatively paid dividends. It combined the need to attack national problems with the flexibility of the decentralized federal system. Cooperative federalism, however, also signaled a significant shift in power away from the states and toward the federal government. The key to this power shift was money, specifically federal **grants-in-aid**, which are cash appropriations given by the federal government to the states. An ever-increasing proportion of state and local budgets came from federal coffers. At the beginning of the nineteenth century, federal grants constituted less than 1 percent of state and local government revenues. By the middle of the 1930s, federal grants accounted for something like 20 percent of state and local revenues.[11]

For the next thirty years, the federal government continued to rely on grants to administer programs, including the 1950s construction of the federal highway system Americans drive on today. The 1960s marked a shift, though. **Centralized federalism**, ushered in with Lyndon Baines Johnson's presidency, further increased the federal government's involvement in policy areas previously left to state and local governments. It is commonly associated with Johnson's Great Society program, which used state and local governments to help implement such national initiatives as the Civil Rights Act and the War on Poverty. Sometimes it is referred to as "picket-fence federalism," due to its many crosscutting regulations.

Those initiatives meant more money—and more regulations—for states and localities. The federal government aggressively began attaching strings to this money through **categorical grants**. Federal-state relations evolved into a rough embodiment of the Golden Rule of politics—he who has the gold, gets to make the rules.

COOPERATIVE FEDERALISM

The notion that it is impossible for state and national governments to have separate and distinct jurisdictions and that both levels of government must work together.

GRANTS-IN-AID

Cash appropriations given by the federal government to the states.

CENTRALIZED FEDERALISM

The notion that the federal government should take the leading role in setting national policy, with state and local governments to help implement the policies.

CATEGORICAL GRANTS

Federal grants-in-aid given for specific programs that leave states and localities with little discretion on how to spend the money.

FIGURE 2-3 The Varieties of Federalism

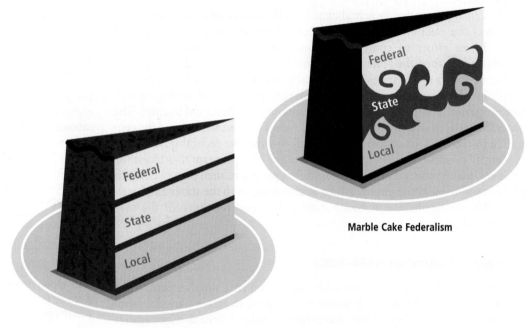

Layer Cake Federalism

Marble Cake Federalism

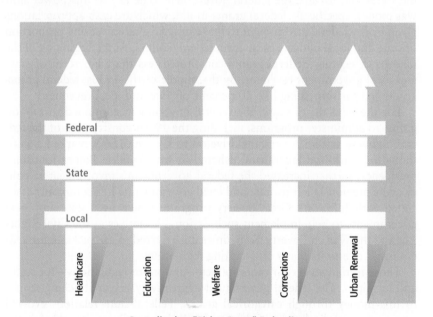

Centralized or "Picket Fence" Federalism

Governing States and Localities

FIGURE 2-4 Key Dates in the History of American Federalism

Revolutionary War starts	1775		
		1776	Declaration of Independence adopted
Articles of Confederation ratified	1781		
		1783	Revolutionary War ends
Annapolis Convention	1786	1786	Shays's Rebellion
Constitutional Convention drafts new constitution	1787		
		1788	U.S. Constitution ratified
First Congress adopts Bill of Rights	1791		
McCulloch v. Maryland establishes that the federal government has a broad set of powers over the states	1819		
Roger Taney sworn in as chief justice; adopts dual federalism as model for federal-state relations	1836	1832	South Carolina attempts to nullify federal law
		1857	*Scott v. Sanford* demonstrates the limits of the federal government
Southern states experiment with confederacy as Civil War starts	1861	1860	South Carolina secedes from the Union in December; hostilities between North and South begin a month later
		1865	Civil War ends with Union victory; Thirteenth Amendment abolishes slavery
Fourteenth Amendment passes	1868		
		1887	Federal government regulates the railroads
Sixteenth Amendment passes	1913		
Great Depression	1930	1933	Franklin Delano Roosevelt takes office; Era of cooperation federalism begins
Era of centralized Federalism begins	1964		
		1972	Richard Nixon begins revenue sharing
Election of Ronald Reagan and emergence of New Federalism	1980		
Supreme Court decides *Bush v. Gore;* George W. Bush receives Florida's contested electoral votes and becomes president	2000	1986	William Rehnquist becomes chief justice; Supreme Court begins to look more favorably on states rights arguments

Richard Nixon's administration took a slightly different tack: It cut some strings but continued to increase the number of grants doled out by the federal government.[12] In the late 1960s, the administration pioneered the idea of **general revenue sharing grants**, federal funds turned over to the states and localities with essentially no strings attached. Although popular with states and localities—from their perspective it was "free" money—this type of grant-in-aid had a short life span; it was killed by the Reagan administration in the early 1980s.

Federal grants, strings or no strings, do not sound so bad on the surface. Money is money, and a government can never have too much. The problem was that the grants were not distributed equitably to states and localities, and a central feature of cooperative federalism was the often fierce competition to control and access these revenues. The politics became complex. One form of these politics was between the states and the federal government over what type of grant should be used for a particular policy or program. States and localities favored federal grants with fewer strings. Congress and the president often favored putting tight guidelines on federal money, since this allowed them to take a greater share of the credit for the benefits of federal spending.

Perhaps the most important dimension of the politics of grants-in-aid, however, was the federal government's increasing desire to use its purse strings to pressure states and localities into adopting particular policies and laws. Beginning in the 1960s and 1970s, cooperative federalism began a new, more coercive era with the rise of ever more stringent grant conditions. These included **crosscutting requirements**, or strings that applied to all federal grants. For example, one condition to receive virtually any federal government grant is an assessment of the environmental impact of the proposed program or policy. Accordingly, most state and local governments began writing—and defending—environmental impact statements for any construction project that involved federal funds.

The federal government also began applying **crossover sanctions**. Crossover sanctions are strings that require grant recipients to pass and enforce certain laws or policies as a condition of receiving funds. An example is the drinking age. The federal government requires states to set twenty-one as the minimum legal drinking age as a condition of receiving federal highway funds.

Increasingly, the strings came even if there were no grants. State and local governments were issued direct orders, essentially commanded, to adopt certain laws or rules, such as clean water standards and minimum wage laws.[13] These **unfunded mandates** became a particular irritant to state and local governments. Even when there was broad agreement on the substance of the mandate, subnational governments resented the federal government's taking all the credit while leaving the dirty work of finding funds and actually running the programs to the states and localities.

Congress eventually passed a law banning unfunded mandates in the mid-1990s, but it is full of loopholes. For example, the law does not apply to appropriations bills—the laws that actually authorize the government to spend money. In fiscal year 2006 the National Conference of State Legislatures estimated the federal government shifted $22.5 billion in costs onto the states. Despite the law, Congress continues to pass laws that subnational governments must obey and pass on the costs of these to the states.[14]

New Federalism (1980–Present)

Centralized federalism's shift of power toward the national government always faced opposition from states' rights advocates, who viewed the growing influence of the national government with alarm. By the end of the 1970s centralized federalism also was starting to face a practical crisis—the federal government's revenues could not keep up with the demand for grants. With the election of Ronald Reagan in 1980, the practical and ideological combined to create pressure for a fundamental shift in state and federal relations.

Reagan was not the first president to raise concerns about the centralization of power in the national government. A primary reason for Nixon's support of general revenue sharing, for example, was the attraction of giving states more flexibility by cutting the strings attached to federal grants. It was not until Reagan, however, that a sustained attempt was made to reverse the course of centralized federalism. Reagan believed the federal government had overreached its boundaries, and he wanted to return power and flexibility to the states. At the core of his vision of state-centered **New Federalism** was the desire to reduce federal grants-in-aid. In return, states would be given more policymaking leeway with the money they did get through **block grants**.

Reagan's drive to make this vision a reality had mixed success. The massive budget deficits of the 1980s made cutting grants-in-aid a practical necessity. Reducing the federal government's influence over states and localities turned out to be another matter. Reagan, like many conservatives, was a modern heir to a states' rights perspective that dated back to the Anti-Federalist movement. This meant he believed that government should be as close to the voters as possible—in the city hall or the state capitol—rather than far away in Washington, D.C. Yet believing that government should be closer to the people in the abstract is far different from putting that belief into practice. Taking power from the federal government did advance a core philosophical belief of the Reagan administration, but it also created problems for Reagan supporters, who were not shy about voicing their displeasure.

Such core conservative constituencies as business and industry quickly realized that dealing with one government was much less of a headache than dealing with fifty governments. They almost immediately began to put counterpressure on the movement toward expanded state policymaking

NEW FEDERALISM

The belief that states should receive more power and authority and less money from the federal government.

BLOCK GRANTS

Federal grants-in-aid given for general policy areas that leave states and localities with wide discretion on how to spend the money within the designated policy area.

A Difference that Makes a Difference: States Seeing Green

Within a single ninety-day period in 2004:

- New Mexico joined the Chicago Climate Exchange, a market in which companies and governments pledge to reduce their emissions or buy credits from other participants;
- Seattle City Light became the first U.S. utility company to reduce its greenhouse-gas emissions to zero; and
- the (then) seven states that comprise the Regional Greenhouse Gas Initiative (RGGI) announced an agreement to reduce carbon dioxide emissions from power plants.

These moves are but a fraction of the environmental policy being made by states and localities. Since the federal government refused to ratify the international Kyoto Protocol, which would have rolled back greenhouse-gas production to 7 percent less than 1990 levels by 2012, state and local governments have stepped forward to fill the void. Most of their efforts are centered on limiting carbon dioxide emissions produced by burning fossil fuels such as oil, natural gas, and coal. Among the approaches being tried are greater reliance on renewable energy, increased investment in mass transit, and new regulations on industry. "The states have been the leaders in climate change and will continue to be the leaders," says Joanne Morin, a New Hampshire environmental administrator involved in RGGI.

Three initiatives stand out within the state and local green movement. California's limit on carbon dioxide emissions from new cars and light trucks dates back to 2004 and is perhaps the most controversial of the plans. The standards have yet to be implemented; they're being challenged in court, and California must get the U.S. Environmental Protection Agency's approval before enforcing them. Despite the debate, ten other states have pledged to adopt the same standards if California prevails.

Farther north, Seattle, Washington, mayor Greg Nickels has garnered the support of more than two hundred other mayors in his effort to participate in the Kyoto Protocol at the city level. If each city meets the goal, as many as 15 percent of the nation's residents will be living in Kyoto-abiding localities in 2012. At the state level, the ten states in the RGGI—Connecticut, Delaware, Maine, Maryland, Massachusetts, New Hampshire, New Jersey, New York, Rhode Island, and Vermont—promised to cut power plant emissions by 10 percent by 2019.

These efforts reflect frustration at the state and local level about the lack of federal action, and the proponents of the state and local plans readily admit that they're trying to affect national policy. Because there are limits on what these governments can achieve on their own, they're hoping that their successes might spur federal-level action. "All of the states involved in RGGI would love to see a national model," says Frank Litz, a New York state environmental official. "You have to start somewhere."

Source: Adapted from Josh Goodman, "Greenhouse Gumption," *Governing* magazine, May 2005.

authority. The result was something of a push-and-pull, with the Reagan administration trying to shove power off onto the states with one set of legislative priorities and yank it back to the federal government with another.

Ultimately, Reagan did succeed in cutting grants-in-aid. He consolidated fifty-seven categorical grants into nine new block grants. General revenue sharing and another sixty categorical grants were eliminated entirely. This reduced the amount of money sent to the states while increasing their ability to act independently.[15] Yet Reagan also engaged in a number of fairly aggressive preemption movements and backed a number of unfunded mandates. This reduced the independence of states and forced them to fund programs they did not necessarily support.

The seeds of New Federalism had a hard time taking root at the national level, but its roots sank fast and sank deep at the state and local levels. States were caught between the proverbial rock of a cash-strapped federal government and the hard place of the demand for the programs traditionally supported by federal funds. They slowly and often painfully worked themselves out of this dilemma by becoming less reliant on the federal government. States aggressively began pursuing innovative policy approaches to a wide range of social and economic problems.

Both subnational governments and conservative constituencies had their reasons for wanting New Federalism to just dry up and blow away, but their wish was not to be. "New federalists" who emerged from the 1980s included prominent Democrats and Republicans whose desire to get the states out of the federal government's shadow became a well-organized and coordinated movement. Groups such as the National Governors Association and the National Conference of State Legislatures gave a powerful voice to state concerns, a voice that had an increasingly sympathetic ear in the White House. None of the first six presidents following World War II— Harry Truman, Dwight Eisenhower, John F. Kennedy, Lyndon Johnson, Richard Nixon, and Gerald Ford—had gubernatorial experience. Four of the next five—Jimmy Carter, Ronald Reagan, Bill Clinton, and George W. Bush—all had served as governors. This meant that the state perspective was in many ways the White House perspective. There was, as one author put it, "a developing agreement among state and national political elites that states should have greater authority and flexibility in operating public programs." [16]

Political elites were not alone in their increasing desire to push power from the federal government. Public opinion polls consistently show that Americans place more trust in state and local governments and express a greater confidence in their ability to effectively manage a broad range of policies and programs compared to the federal government.[17] In the 1990s the Clinton administration picked up the pace of an orderly transition of power from the federal to the state level, an extension of New Federalism that was termed devolution. Although devolution essentially sought to reverse the trend of centralizing power in the federal government, the primary characteristic of the state-federal relationship remained grants-in-aid.

Clinton did follow Reagan's lead and shifted authority to the states by consolidating categorical grants and federal entitlement programs into block grants. Probably the best-known example of this is the Personal Responsibility and Work Opportunity Reconciliation Act of 1996, popularly known as the law that "ended welfare as we know it." The law, which Clinton signed under Republican pressure during the 1996 presidential campaign after vetoing it twice, ended Aid to Families with Depen-

Michigan was the first state to plow its roads and to use the yellow dividing line on its highways.

dent Children (AFDC) and replaced it with a block grant. In essence, the law reduced the federal government's financial commitment to social welfare programs and turned over primary policymaking responsibilities in this area to the states.

Like its parent, New Federalism, the devolution revolution faced strong resistance, often from an old enemy. Conservatives, at least rhetorically, still were the strongest states' rights advocates. Yet when states' rights conflicted with key portions of the conservative political agenda, conservative groups still fought tenaciously for federal supremacy over the states, just as they had during the 1980s. An example of this contradiction in behavior is the 1996 Defense of Marriage Act. This federal law was proposed in the wake of movements in Hawaii and Vermont to legalize same-sex unions. Now, remember, the full faith and credit clause means that a contract made under the laws of one state is legally recognized and binding in all states. So, if one state made same-sex unions legal, it raised the possibility that the other forty-nine would have to recognize civil unions as the legal equivalent of marriage. There was a strong push from many traditional states' rights advocates for the federal government to, in essence, grant states exceptions from their full faith and credit obligations. The Defense of Marriage Act did this. It also put the federal government into the business of defining what constitutes a marriage, an area traditionally left to the states.[18]

This was not enough to stop some states and localities from moving toward legalizing same-sex unions under their own laws. In 2003 the Massachusetts Supreme Court ruled that legally prohibiting same-sex marriages violated the state's constitution. This cleared the way for homosexual couples to marry. In the same year, the city of San Francisco began issuing marriage licenses to same-sex couples until it was ordered to stop by the California Supreme Court. Some viewed these developments with alarm. Many conservatives began to call for a constitutional amendment banning gay marriage, a proposal that President George W. Bush publicly supported. The Senate, however, rejected the proposed amendment in 2006. Such an amendment would be in many ways the ultimate form of federal preemption.

Conservatives have not limited their calls for federal dominance of policymaking to gay marriage. In the past few Congresses, conservatives also have pushed the federal government to preempt state authority in a broad array of other policy areas that range from electric utility deregulation to property rights.

The mixed commitment to New Federalism is perhaps best exemplified by the presidency of George W. Bush. Bush came to the White House from the Texas governor's mansion and at least on the surface was a strong supporter of the principles of New Federalism. He established the Interagency Working Group on Federalism shortly after being inaugurated and charged it with finding ways to cut through the regulatory red tape that often accompanies grants-in-aid. The group also was asked to identify additional federal programs that could be turned over to the states. Once again, the federal government was making it easier for the states by reducing grant application hassle while making it harder for them by giving them more programs to support. Reuben Morales, former director of the federal Office of Intergovernmental Affairs, summarized the Bush administration's approach to federalism, "[F]ederalism is no longer just about which level of government does what. Services and programs are more integrated than ever before ... [and] the federal government must find ways to be a better partner with states and localities." [19]

Three things blunted Bush's plans to accelerate New Federalism: recession, war, and his own agenda. Throughout the history of the United States, power has centralized in the national government during times of crisis—it simply is better equipped to deal with national economic challenges or international conflict. The Bush administration found itself struggling with a soft economy while also committing the nation's resources to a global war on terrorism in response to the devastating attacks of September 11, 2001. Both problems pretty much required that the federal government take a lead policy role, one that both the White House and Congress continue to hold tightly.

Key parts of Bush's agenda specifically called for a stronger federal role in areas that were the traditional responsibility of states and localities. In 2005, as the nation continued to struggle with closing the loopholes that allowed the September 11 terrorists into the United States, Congress passed the REAL ID Act, which requires states to adopt national driver's license standards by December 31, 2009. If the states fail to comply, their residents' licenses will not be accepted for federal identification purposes—something that no doubt would lead to longer security lines at airports and other facilities. States fiercely opposed the REAL ID Act, estimated to cost $11 billion to implement, and continued to appeal for revisions after its enactment.[20]

Where two decades earlier the Reagan administration proposed abolishing the U.S. Department of Education, the Bush administration's education policy centered on the No Child Left Behind Act (NCLB), which forced states to administer achievement tests and demonstrate "adequate yearly progress." In 2005, several states pushed back. Utah's Republican governor, Jon Huntsman Jr., signed into law an act that requires state education law to take precedence over NCLB. That same year, Connecticut's attorney general filed suit against the U.S. Department of Education, alleging that the federal government inadequately compensated states for the additional expenses incurred in administering the program.[21]

All of this has conspired to make some argue that the first decades of the twenty-first century are likely to be characterized by what some have called **ad hoc federalism** rather than a continued commitment to the core principles of New Federalism.[22] Ad hoc federalism describes the process of choosing a state-centered or nation-centered view of federalism on the

AD HOC FEDERALISM
The process of choosing a state-centered or nation-centered view of federalism on the basis of political or partisan convenience.

basis of political or partisan convenience. In other words, the issue at hand, not a core philosophical commitment to a particular vision of federalism, determines a policymaker's commitment to state or federal supremacy.

The Supreme Court: The Umpire of Federalism

Article VI, the national supremacy clause of the Constitution, declares that the Constitution, laws passed by Congress, and national treaties are the "supreme law of the land." This does not mean that the states are always subordinate to the national government. Don't forget—the Tenth Amendment also counts as part of that supreme law. However, it does mean that federal courts often have to referee national-state conflicts. Since it has the final say in interpreting the Constitution, the Supreme Court is, in effect, the umpire of federalism. Its rulings ultimately decide the powers and limitations of the different levels of government.

The Rise of Nation-Centered Federalism on the Court

Throughout U.S. history the Supreme Court has cycled through trends of state-centered and nation-centered philosophies of federalism. As already seen, the early Supreme Court under Chief Justice John Marshall pursued a fairly broad interpretation of the federal government's powers in such cases as *McCulloch v. Maryland*. Marshall's successor, Roger Taney, took the Court in a more state-centered direction by establishing dual federalism as the Court's central operating philosophy. The shift from dual federalism to cooperative federalism required a return to a more nation-centered judicial philosophy. Although the Court initially took a more nation-centered track in its rulings following the Civil War, it was not until the Great Depression and Roosevelt's New Deal that a decisive tilt in its rulings cleared the way for the rise of cooperative federalism and the centralization of power in the national government.

A number of New Deal programs—including the Agricultural Adjustment Act, which provided federal subsidies to struggling farmers—at first were struck down by the Court. In a series of 5–4 rulings, the Court declared these programs to be unconstitutional expansions of federal power. In 1937 a frustrated Roosevelt proposed "packing" the Court as a way to prod it into fully accepting cooperative federalism. Under this plan, every time a justice turned seventy and did not retire, the president could appoint an additional judge to the Court. Roosevelt's scheme would have allowed him to alter the balance of power on the Supreme Court by packing it with up to six more members.

Reaction to the plan was largely negative. The proposed law reached Congress pretty much dead in the water—and it is remembered today as one of the Roosevelt presidency's few public relations disasters. Law or not, however, the court-packing plan had the desired effect. As it became apparent that Roosevelt was serious about pursuing a significant shake-up, the Supreme Court switched direction and began to rule in favor of key New Deal proposals. This included upholding the constitutionality of the first Social Security Act.

The shift toward a liberal interpretation of the federal government's powers dominated the Supreme Court's operating philosophy for much of the next sixty years and is exemplified by *United States v. Darby Lumber Co.* (1941). The substantive issue at stake was whether the federal government had the power to regulate wages. The Supreme Court said yes, but the decision is of more lasting interest because of the majority opinion's dismissive comment on the Tenth Amendment. Supposedly the constitutional lockbox of state power, the Court viewed the amendment as doing little more than stating "a truism that all is retained which has not been surrendered." In other words, the Tenth Amendment was simply a basket for the "leftover" powers the federal government had not sought or did not want.

During and after the New Deal era, the Supreme Court also accelerated a trend of broadly interpreting Congress's powers to regulate interstate commerce. It did this through its interpretation of the **interstate commerce clause**. In *Wickard v. Filburn* (1942), the Court ruled that the clause gave Congress the power to regulate what a farmer can feed his chickens. In *Heart of Atlanta Motel v. United States* (1964) and *Katzenback v. McClung* (1964), the justices ruled that it gave Congress the power to regulate private acts of racial discrimination.

A series of such decisions over the course of more than fifty years led some judicial scholars to conclude that the Supreme Court had essentially turned the concept of enumerated and reserved powers on its head. In effect, the assumption now seemed to be that the federal government had the power to do anything the Constitution did not specifically prohibit.[23] The states and localities were drawn ever closer into subordinate satellite roles in orbit around the federal government. This situation continued until just before the turn of the twenty-first century. At that point the Court once again began siding with the states over the federal government.

A Tenth Amendment Renaissance or Ad Hoc Federalism?

By the mid-1990s, the Supreme Court was dominated by justices appointed by new federalists. Reagan, who had campaigned on his intention to nominate federal judges who shared his conservative philosophy, appointed four. He also elevated a fifth, William Rehnquist—originally appointed by Nixon—to the position of chief justice. Reagan's vice president and presidential successor, George Bush, appointed two more justices. The end result was a Supreme Court chosen largely by conservative Republican presidents

INTERSTATE COMMERCE CLAUSE

The constitutional clause that gives Congress the right to regulate interstate commerce. This clause has been broadly interpreted to give Congress a number of implied powers.

who wanted limits set on the federal government's powers and responsibilities. The justices obliged.

In a series of narrow—mostly 5–4—decisions in the 1990s, the Court began to back away from the nation-centered interpretation of the Constitution that had dominated its rulings during the era of cooperative federalism. *United States v. Lopez* (1995) was a significant victory for states' rights and a clear break from a half century of precedent. This case involved the Drug Free School Zone Act of 1990, which made it a federal crime to possess a firearm within one thousand feet of a school. Following a good deal of precedent, Congress justified its authority to regulate local law enforcement by using a very liberal interpretation of the interstate commerce clause. The Supreme Court disagreed and argued that the commerce clause granted no such authority.

Similar reasoning was used by the justices in *United States v. Morrison* (2000) to strike down the Violence Against Women Act (VAWA). Congress had passed this law in 1994 out of concern that the states, although having primary responsibility for criminal law, were not adequately dealing with the problem of violence against women. The key provision of the VAWA gave assault victims the right to sue their assailants in federal court. Congress argued that it was authorized to pass such a law because fear of violence prevented women from using public transportation or going out unescorted at night. Such fears, the reasoning went, placed limits on economic opportunities for women. This argument made the connection to commerce and Congress's constitutional authority. The Supreme Court again rejected this broad interpretation of the commerce clause.

At the same time that it was narrowly interpreting the Constitution to limit federal power, the Supreme Court after 1990 began to interpret the Constitution broadly to expand state power. Notably, the Court made a series of rulings that broadly interpreted the Eleventh Amendment's guarantee of **sovereign immunity** to the states. Sovereign immunity is essentially "the right of a government to be free from suits brought without its consent."[24] In cases such as *Seminole Tribe of Florida v. Florida* (1996) and *Alden v. Maine* (1999), the Supreme Court adopted an interpretation of the Eleventh Amendment that limited the right of citizens to sue states for violations of federal law. These rulings not only lessened the power of the federal government over the states, they arguably gave the states more power over their own citizens.

Although these and other rulings resurrected the Tenth Amendment and underlined the independent power of the states, there has been an element of inconsistency to Supreme Court decisions since 1990. In *Bush v. Gore* (2000), the Supreme Court seemed to abandon its commitment to states' rights by overruling the Florida Supreme Court and ordering a halt to the contested recount of presidential ballots. Democratic presidential nominee Al Gore indisputably won the popular vote in 2000, but the outcome of the presidential election was decided by Florida's electoral votes. Gore and

SOVEREIGN IMMUNITY

The right of a government to not be sued without its consent.

Bush ran neck and neck in this state, the decision so close that a series of controversial and hotly contested recounts were undertaken with the approval of Florida courts. In effect, the U.S. Supreme Court overturned the state court's interpretation of state law—which allowed the recounts—and decided the presidency in favor of George W. Bush. Another decision that favored federal power over state power came in *Lorillard Tobacco Co. v. Reilly* (2001). Here, the Court overturned a Massachusetts law that regulated the advertising of tobacco products. The Court argued that federal law—specifically, the Federal Cigarette Labeling and Advertising Act— legitimately preempts state law on this issue.

More recently, the Court trumped ten states that have legalized marijuana for medical purposes. In *Gonzales v. Raich* (2005), the Court, led by its more liberal justices, ruled that federal law enforcement officers, prosecutors, and judges can prosecute and punish anyone possessing marijuana.

TABLE 2-3

Key U.S. Supreme Court Rulings Regarding Federalism, 1995–2006

United States v. Lopez (1995)	Court strikes down a federal law prohibiting possession of firearms near public schools. State claim upheld.
Seminole Tribe of Florida v. Florida (1996)	Court rules Congress cannot allow citizens to sue states in a federal court except for civil rights violations. State claim upheld.
Printz v. United States (1997)	Court strikes down federal law requiring mandatory background checks for firearms purchases. State claim upheld.
Alden v. Maine (1999)	Court rules that Congress does not have the power to authorize citizens to sue in state court on the basis of federal claims. State claim upheld.
United States v. Morrison (2000)	Court strikes down federal Violence Against Women Act. State claim upheld.
Reno v. Condon (2000)	Court upheld a federal law preventing states from selling driver's license information. State claim overturned.
Bush v. Gore (2000)	Court overrules Florida Supreme Court action allowing hand recounts of contested election ballots. State claim overturned.
Alabama v. Garrett (2001)	Court rules that state employees cannot sue their employees in federal court to recover monetary damages under the provisions of the Americans with Disabilities Act. State claim upheld.
Lorillard Tobacco Co. v. Reilly (2001)	Court strikes down Massachusetts laws regulating the advertising of tobacco products. State claim overturned.
Kelo v. City of New London (2005)	Court rules that government can seize private property for public purposes, including economic development. State claim upheld.
Gonzales v. Oregon (2006)	Court rules U.S. attorney general overstepped his authority by threatening to eliminate prescription-writing privileges for doctors who follow state law allowing physician-assisted suicide. State claim upheld.

CLOSED CAPTIONING PROVIDED FOR THE HEARING IMPAIRED.

Most observers agree that, in purely democratic terms, the 2000 presidential election was pretty much a turkey. The loser of the popular vote won, claiming victory only after a contested Florida ballot in which the intentions of voters are a matter of disagreement to this day. About the only thing that is not up for debate about the election's outcome is the preeminent role of states and localities in making the nation's most important decision—choosing who sits in the White House.

The ruling weakened the states' laws; however, it did not overturn them, for state and local officials need not participate in the efforts to seize medical marijuana.[25] Just six months later, though, the Court upheld a state law related to serious illnesses when it ruled in *Gonzales v. Oregon* (2006) against the federal government's challenge of Oregon's law that allows physician-assisted suicide.

Some scholars argue that these sorts of inconsistencies have long been characteristic of the Supreme Court's federalism rulings. It is ideology—not a firm commitment to a particular vision of state-national relations—that ultimately decides how a justice rules in a particular case.[26] Therefore, a Court dominated by conservative appointees will occasionally depart from the state-centered notion of federalism if a nation-centered view is more ideologically pleasing, whereas a Court dominated by liberal appointees will do the opposite. The Supreme Court, like the president, also finds it hard to resist the temptations of ad hoc federalism.

Conclusion

The Constitution organizes the United States into a federal political system. This means that the states are powerful, independent political actors that dominate important policy areas. Many of these policy areas are those with the most obvious and far-reaching roles in the day-to-day lives of citizens. Education, law enforcement, utility regulation, and road construction are but a handful of examples. The independence they are granted under the federal system allows states a broad leeway to go their own way in these and many other policy areas.

The resulting variation has a number of advantages, such as making it easier to match local preferences with government action and allowing states and localities to experiment with innovative programs or policies. There are also a number of disadvantages. These include complexity and difficulty in coordinating policy at the national level. The interests of state and national governments overlap in many areas. Because of this and because the Constitution does not clearly resolve the question of who has the power to do what in these arenas of shared interest, conflict is inevitable.

What is the future of federalism? Whether the states' rights perspective embedded in New Federalism will evolve into the guiding principle of future state-federal relations or give way to the less predictable whims of ad hoc federalism remains to be seen. Over the past decade or so, Congress and the president have exhibited a very mixed commitment to devolution. The federal government has pushed for greater state authority in such areas as welfare and Medicaid while simultaneously pursuing aggressive preemption of state laws in such areas as crime and the environment.[27]

Broader social trends and world events also are complicating the drive to allow the states more independence. The burden of homeland security, for example, falls heavily on states and localities. Yet the federal government is directing and, with mixed success, taking the lead in coordinating these efforts.

Or consider the battle over gay marriage, which has upended traditional states' rights allegiances. Even as many states have legally prohibited same-sex unions, either through statutes or amendments to state constitutions, the drive for recognition of these unions is gaining ground in other states. Vermont has allowed civil unions, which confer many of the same rights and benefits as marriage, since 2000, and New Jersey followed suit in February 2007. In 2004 Massachusetts became the first state to legalize gay marriage. The obligations of other states to recognize such unions is intensely debated, and many who would normally consider themselves states' rights advocates are pressuring for federal dominance. The idea is to eliminate any possibility that gay marriages will become legally portable across state borders through the full faith and credit clause of the Constitution. There have been several attempts to introduce constitutional amendments banning same-sex marriage at the federal level. These efforts have largely been initiated by conservative Republicans who traditionally have been the strongest supporters of states' rights.

Finally, the states spent much of the first four years of the twenty-first century in a severe budgetary bind, even as they were asked to take on more responsibility by the federal government. What can be seen from all of this is not a gradual flow of power from Washington, D.C., to state capitals, but an inconsistent give and take, with the supporters of national or state dominance shifting with the issue.

The federal system has evolved into a complex web of intergovernmental relationships that recognizes the practical necessity of cooperation among the various levels of government. All of this creates a situation ripe for continued conflict between state and federal governments, conflicts that in many cases will have to be resolved by the Supreme Court. The Court recently has exhibited some inconsistency in its own commitment to favoring states' rights in resolving state-federal conflicts. Observers will be watching new justices to see how they will shape the Court's record in the years to come. Yet regardless of how these conflicts are ultimately resolved, the future undoubtedly will find states and localities continuing to play a central role in the U.S. political system, both as independent policymakers and as cooperative partners with the federal government.

Key Concepts

Suggested Readings

Ellis, Richard E. *The Union at Risk: Jacksonian Democracy, States' Rights, and the Nullification Crisis.* New York: Oxford University Press, 1990. A history of the states' rights movement and the nullification crisis of the 1820s and 1830s.

Kendall, Douglas T. *Redefining Federalism: Listening to the States in Shaping "Our Federalism."* Washington, D.C.: Environmental Law Institute, 2004. An examination of recent federalism cases before the U.S. Supreme Court from the Community Rights Counsel, a nonprofit law firm that assists state and local governments in health and welfare cases.

Peterson, Paul E. *The Price of Federalism.* Washington, D.C.: Brookings Institution, 1995. Overview of how federalism operates in the United States; documents how federal-state relations have evolved.

Storing, Herbert J., and Murray Dry. *What the Anti-Federalists Were For.* Chicago: University of Chicago Press, 1981. Explains why the Anti-Federalists opposed the U.S. Constitution and fought for the Bill of Rights.

Walker, David B. *The Rebirth of Federalism: Slouching toward Washington.* 2nd ed. Washington, D.C.: CQ Press, 1999. Comprehensive history of federalism in the United States and an assessment of current problems and issues.

Suggested Web Sites

www.federalismproject.org. Web site of the Federalism Project, a program sponsored by the American Enterprise Institute that promotes New Federalism ideas.

www.ncsl.org/statefed/statefed.htm. Web site sponsored by the National Conference of State Legislatures that is dedicated to state-federal issues.

www.nga.org. Web site of the National Governors Association that includes a section devoted to state-federal relations.

www.oxfordjournals.org/our_journals/pubjof/index.html. Web site of *Publius,* a scholarly journal dedicated to the study of federalism.

www.supremecourtus.gov. Web site of the U.S. Supreme Court; includes text of the Court's opinions.

CHAPTER 3

Constitutions
Operating Instructions

Unlike the U.S. Constitution, state constitutions are changed on a regular basis, often to accommodate highly specific laws and policies. In 2000 a majority of Florida voters approved a constitutional amendment that required the state government to build a high-speed rail system. The state government refused to fund it. In 2004 an even bigger majority of Florida voters repealed the amendment. It is hard to conceive of such rapid changes in the U.S. Constitution, especially on such issues as whether or not to build a railway.

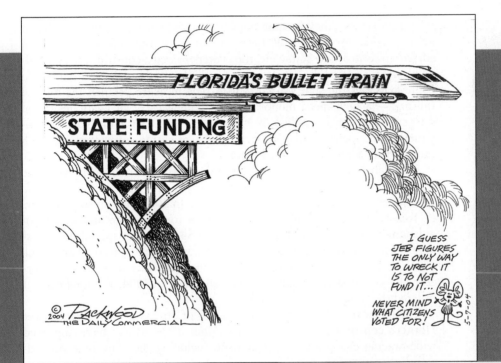

What impact do state constitutions have on our lives?

Why do state constitutions differ?

How do constitutions determine what state and local governments can and cannot do?

In 2000, Floridians boarded a bullet train to nowhere.

That November they became notorious nationwide for voting in almost even numbers for George W. Bush and Al Gore. But another ballot item stirred up controversy statewide, too. Voters passed a constitutional amendment that mandated the construction of a high-speed rail system that would connect five of the state's largest cities. The measure detailed the type of railroad—"a high-speed monorail, fixed guideway, or magnetic levitation system"—and set a deadline of November 1, 2003, for the start of construction, but left out the project's pesky price tag, estimates of which ranged from $6 billion to $22 billion.

Gov. Jeb Bush vowed to fight the rail program. True to his word, he repeatedly vetoed budget allocations to fund the bullet train, and the November 1, 2003, deadline came and went. In 2004, he and state treasurer Tom Gallagher spearheaded a movement to repeal the high-speed rail amendment. Opponents of the train raised $4 million to spread their message. Their campaign resonated with voters, who were concerned about the train's cost after an especially destructive hurricane season. In 2000, 53 percent of voters passed the bullet train amendment; in 2004, about 64 percent ordered the train back to the station.[1]

The bullet train back and forth was one of dozens of fights waged over Florida's constitution in recent years. Since 1976, voters have approved wide-ranging changes to the document, including the "Sunshine Amendment" that widened access to government meetings and documents, a controversial measure limiting class sizes, and an amendment that made it unconstitutional to use fishing nets that could trap turtles.[2] In many cases, they have battled over measures that in other states might have been proposed statutes, not constitutional amendments. But in Florida, citizens interested in affecting state government through **direct democracy** must petition for changes to the constitution. State law blocks them from proposing statutes, even though it would be easier to undo a statute if opinions change or the state runs short of cash.

State constitutions have an enormous impact on state governments and policymaking—and on us. They affect the education we receive, the employment opportunities we enjoy, the political culture of the states in which we live, and the rights we do—or don't—have, as the case may be.

DIRECT DEMOCRACY

The means for citizens to make laws themselves, rather than relying on elected representatives.

State constitutions and the rights and powers they provide also vary widely. The constitution of Alabama preserves the state's use of eminent domain to seize private property for public use. In 2006, nine states, including Arizona and Nevada, passed initiatives to prohibit the practice.

This chapter explores how the role state constitutions allow citizens to play significantly affects governing. California's constitution embraces the idea of direct democracy. The **electorate**, or those individuals who can vote, can make its opinions known at the voting booth. Ballot initiatives and referendums allow voters to override the decisions of the state's elected officials—or even remove the officials entirely—with ease. New York's constitution does not. Its politicians are famously insulated from voters' demands, and decisions are made by a handful of senior elected officials.

What explains the tremendous variation among state constitutions? A state's constitution reflects its historical experiences, its political culture, its geography, and its notions of what makes good government. Alabama's constitution, for instance, was drafted in 1901 by a small group of wealthy planters and reflected their fears that rapid industrial development would threaten the "best" form of government—that is, planter government. Although some resisted it at the time, the state's generally traditional political culture made these ideas broadly acceptable.[3] As time passes and a constitution becomes more entrenched, it begins to shape a state's culture and determine the range of political possibilities. Alabama remained a traditional state at least in part because its constitution thwarted industrialization and modernization; although it has been amended more than six hundred times, the state has resisted changing many of those features. And Alabama is not alone in this regard. Many of the differences in subnational politics can be traced directly to state constitutions.

In recent years, state constitutions have become more important, not less. Since the 1990s, the U.S. Supreme Court has handed down a number of decisions, some of which have strengthened state governments at the expense of the federal government, whereas others have trumped state law. The Court's insistence on determining the boundaries of federalism and evaluating state laws and regulations—a form of activism sometimes referred to as **judicial federalism**—even gained former Chief Justice William Rehnquist the nickname "Governor Rehnquist."[4]

State supreme courts also are becoming more assertive. In 1977, Supreme Court justice William Brennan, a former New Jersey state supreme court justice, wrote a famous article for the *Harvard Law Review* that noted that state constitutions afford their citizens another layer of rights above and beyond the rights protected in the U.S. Constitution. He urged state courts to pay more attention to these rights and to assert themselves more forcefully. They have. In the past two decades, for example, twenty state supreme courts have found school financing systems "unconstitutional." (See box on page 70.) State governments have become even more powerful actors in the U.S. political system, and ever more assertive courts have

ELECTORATE
Individuals who can vote.

JUDICIAL FEDERALISM
The idea that the courts determine the boundaries of state-federal relations.

FIGURE 3-1 How It Works: Alabama's State Constitution: The More Things Change, the More They Stay the Same

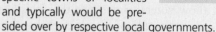

Since 1819, Alabama has adopted six different constitutions. The most recent was ratified in 1901 and consists of more than 360,000 words. The bulk of this comes from the 772 amendments that make it the world's longest operating constitution. It was the product of a constitutional delegation comprised of 155 white males who, like convention president John Knox, were mostly large planters. They wished to hold back the industrialization that had recently left the state in great debt. Knox, however, described its primary purpose as "secur[ing] white supremacy." African American voters were stripped of voting rights, and interracial marriage was forbidden. Civil rights advocate Booker T. Washington, among others, condemned the document. Many of these provisions are now defunct or have been retracted.

Some still persist, however. For instance, the constitution still contains a statute that calls for racially segregated education. (A call in 2004 to remove the provision was narrowly defeated in the state legislature.) Other provisions allow the continuing disfranchisement of many citizens, delay of economic development, and denial of governing powers to localities. The constitution is accused of encouraging unproductive government action; the state legislature spends nearly 70 percent of its time debating issues that have only local relevance. Roughly 40 percent of bills deliberated pertain only to specific towns or localities and typically would be presided over by respective local governments.

Over time, six different governors have tried to change the existing 1901 document. In each case, they met resistance from the legislature, the state supreme court, or powerful planters and industrialists.

Is Alabama's constitution set in stone forever? How can it change? There are two ways: a constitutional convention or article-by-article amendments.

In 2006 and 2007, there seemed to be some headway toward reform. Rep. Demetrius Newton sponsored a bill that would have allowed voters to convene a citizens convention. Supporters wore shirts proclaiming, "We're unhappy because our constitution is crappy" and rallied outside the state capital during House debates. Newton, however, withdrew the bill in early May 2007, citing a lack of votes from fellow legislators, who had likely been swayed by . . . a group called the Alabama Farmer's Federation.

Constitutional Convention

State legislature proposes constitutional convention. → Voters approve. → Convention begins; legislature may not interfere with the convention's decisions.

State legislature selects delegates for constitutional convention.

New constitution ratified by popular vote.

Article-by-Article Amendments

State legislature proposes amendments; may propose more than one at the same time. → Amendments must be approved by popular vote and may not be part of entirely new constitutional document.

found new rights in state constitutions. This means that the documents that reflect and determine what state and local governments can and cannot do have become even more important to understanding politics in the United States.

What State Constitutions Do: It's Probably Different than You Think

Mention "the constitution," and chances are good that your listener will think instantly of the U.S. Constitution. The Founders have gotten more than 225 years of good press for their work in 1787. Schoolchildren memorize, "We the People of the United States, in order to form a more perfect Union . . ." and venerate the document's wisdom. Yet the U.S. Constitution is only half of the story. As residents of the United States we live under a system of **dual constitutionalism,** in which the federal government and state governments are co-sovereign powers. Both run in accordance with the rules laid out in their respective constitutions. Despite the important role state constitutions play in establishing our rights and organizing our local and state governments, most people know very little about them.

The U.S. Constitution and all state constitutions share some common functions: They all set forth the roles and responsibilities of governments, describe the basic institutional structure of the government, and establish procedures for these institutions to operate by. Most state constitutions reflect the influence of the U.S. Constitution. They create three primary branches of government (legislative, executive, and judicial) and provide a general governmental framework. Like the U.S. Constitution, they all contain something roughly equivalent to a bill of rights that spells out the rights of citizens and places specific limits on governmental powers. Most state constitutions place these rights firmly in the context of **natural law,** also known as **higher law,** a tradition that holds that these rights are not political creations but divine endowments. Such **constitutional amendments,** or changes, are meant to ensure these rights for citizens.

Yet in many ways it is misleading to compare state constitutions with their better-known federal counterpart. Consider these important differences:

Permanence. The U.S. Constitution is widely seen as the document that created the United States—the embodiment of the Founders' wisdom. As such, politicians and the public alike hold it in the highest regard. It has lasted more than two centuries and has been formally changed only twenty-seven times. In contrast, state constitutions are amended and even replaced much more frequently. Most states have replaced their original constitutions at least once. California is currently on its second constitution. New York is on its fourth. Louisiana is on its eleventh. In fact, one political scientist has estimated that the average state constitution lasts for only about seventy years.[5]

DUAL CONSTITUTIONALISM

A system of government in which people live under two sovereign powers. In the United States this is the government of their state of residence and the federal government.

NATURAL, OR HIGHER, LAW

A set of moral and political rules based on divine law and binding on all people.

CONSTITUTIONAL AMENDMENTS

Proposals to change the constitution, typically enacted by a supermajority of the legislature or through a statewide referendum.

A Difference that Makes a Difference:
State Constitutions, Educational Equity, and the New Judicial Activism

Robert Frost once began a poem by proclaiming New Hampshire to be one of the two best states in the Union. He said Vermont was the other. Frost is one of the few people in history who have ever been fond of both states. For virtually everyone else, it is one or the other.

To much of New Hampshire, Vermont represents a failed experiment in socialism, a onetime dairy state in which social workers now outnumber cows. To much of Vermont, New Hampshire is an enclave of wacky and irresponsible libertarians, one small step above a gun-toting militia. Just how different these two states are can be seen by their very different reactions to court rulings made in each state in the late twentieth century.

Within a ten-month period in 1997, the supreme courts of New Hampshire and Vermont both declared that the finance systems of their respective states violated their state constitutions. The reasoning differed, but the demand was the same: change the system.

Vermont's case is an "equity" case similar to those in many of the two dozen states that have been placed under school finance court orders in the past two decades. At the time of the decision, the poorest 5 percent of Vermont school districts were spending $3,732 per pupil per year. The richest 5 percent were spending $5,964—60 percent more. "Children who live in property-poor districts," the court said, "should be afforded a substantially equal opportunity."

New Hampshire had disparities just as bad as those across the border, but the court decision there didn't focus on equity. It focused on "adequacy." Although the decision made reference to tax burdens that were four times as high in some towns as in others, its fundamental point was that, in the poorest communities, the public schools were not meeting the test of "a constitutionally adequate education to every educable child." For instance, the mostly blue-collar residents of Franklin, a central New Hampshire mill town, were taxing themselves at a rate much higher than the residents of nearby Gilford, a property-rich town near Lake Winnipesaukee. Despite its tax burden, Franklin was able to spend barely half the amount Gilford could spend and was saddled with obsolete buildings and equipment, the highest student-teacher ratios in the state, and an inexperienced staff that turned over at a rate of 25 percent a year.

In recent years, more state school systems have been invalidated on grounds of adequacy than on grounds of equity. Kansas, Kentucky, New Jersey, Ohio, Texas, West Virginia, and Wyoming are all struggling, as is New

Length. The federal constitution is a relatively short document. At about 7,400 words, it is shorter than most chapters in this book. In contrast, state constitutions tend to be much longer—about twenty-six thousand words on average. Some are much, much longer. New York's constitution and California's ruling document are each roughly fifty thousand words long. The longest state constitution, Alabama's, is more than forty-five times the length of the U.S. Constitution.[6]

Specificity. Why are state constitutions so much longer than the federal constitution and so much more likely to change? Part of the answer has to do with the different functions of the federal constitution versus those of state constitutions. The U.S. Constitution is primarily concerned with setting up the basic structures and procedures of government. State constitutions do these things too. However, state constitutions often set forth procedures and address policies in much greater detail than the federal constitution. Where-

Hampshire, to meet a court-declared adequacy standard—although the definition of that standard can be difficult to determine.

Equity cases are easier to deal with than accountability cases in one key respect: just reshuffle enough tax money and the requirement is met. In contrast, under the terms of the New Hampshire supreme court's ruling, politicians there had to come up with a spending plan that not only ensured that pupils were literate and numerate but also provided them with "knowledge of his or her mental and physical wellness" and "sufficient grounding in the arts . . . to appreciate his or her cultural and historical heritage."

The Vermont legislature moved promptly to comply with the ruling of its highest court. New Hampshire politicians did not, and the battle over school funding became a long-running soap opera. Many Republicans proposed responding to the ruling, which was based on the state constitution, by passing an amendment that would strip the supreme court of its jurisdiction over school finance. Such an amendment would, in effect change the constitution that was, after all, the basis of the New Hampshire court's ruling. Democrats proposed

complying by passing a broad-base sales or income tax or a statewide property tax, as Vermont did, and then pumping much of the revenue into education. The statewide property tax won out after years of acrimonious debate, only to be deemed unconstitutional itself in 2001. In 2006, the school funding conundrum persisted, with the state supreme court once again considering the constitutionality of a revised funding plan.

For Vermonters, New Hampshire's saga was a sign of its distorted priorities. "I look across," said longtime state legislator Nancy Chard, D-Windham, "and feel sorry for them. They haven't been able to accept the court decision. There has never been in New Hampshire the kind of human concern for the citizens that Vermont has had."

For New Hampshire citizens, however, Vermont was the sad spectacle. "New Hampshire people look at Vermont," observes former Keene school district assistant school superintendent Dean Haskell, "and say, 'We'd rather be here. We like local control. We can actually do things that make sense, rather than just worrying about state regulations.' "

Sources: Adapted from Alan Ehrenhalt, "SCHOOLS+TAXES+POLITICS=CHAOS," *Governing* magazine, January 1999; Dennis Farney, "Insufficient Funds," *Governing* magazine, December 2004.

as the federal constitution creates a framework for government, state constitutions often get into the policy details. South Dakota was one of several states that once sanctioned its state prison to produce twine and cordage. Oklahoma's constitution, for instance, mandates that home economics be taught in school. Maryland's regulates off-street parking in Baltimore. Louisiana's provides instructions on how to build pipes. Political scientist Christopher Hammonds has estimated that 39 percent of the total provisions in state constitutions are devoted to specific matters of this sort. In contrast, only 6 percent of the U.S. Constitution deals with such specific issues.[7]

Embrace of Democracy. The U.S. Constitution creates a system of representative democracy; it purposefully rejects direct democracy as a basis for governance. The Founders went to great pains to check "the whimsies of

State constitutions contain provisions on everything from free speech to parking fees, from how to organize a government to how to build a pipe. Oklahoma's constitution requires schools to offer courses in the "domestic sciences," and South Dakota's once provided for the construction of a twine and cordage plant at its state penitentiary. Unsurprisingly, state constitutions tend to be considerably longer than the U.S. Constitution.

the majority" by designing a system of checks and balances that deliberately keeps policy-making at arm's length from the shifting winds of popular opinion. During the Progressive Era in the early 1900s, many states revamped their constitutions to do just the opposite. This was particularly true of the newer western and midwestern states in which old school politics were less entrenched and political cultures tended toward the moralistic or individualistic.

Progressive reformers believed old constitutional arrangements were outmoded and that citizens should have an opportunity to participate directly in making laws. Moreover, they worried that state legislatures had been captured by wealthy special interests. In other words, they thought that representative democracy was working for the benefit of a few rather than for the benefit of all. Their solution was to give the people the ability to amend their constitutions and pass laws directly through the use of referendums and ballot initiatives. Thus, in many cases, state constitutions champion direct democracy in a way that the U.S. Constitution purposefully does not.

Finances. Congress and the executive branch can run up as much national debt as they can persuade bond buyers to swallow. In contrast, thirty-two state constitutions require the legislative and executive branches to balance their budgets. Another seventeen states have statutes that mandate balanced budgets. Only Vermont can run up debt like the feds. Even state constitutions that do not require a balanced budget take a much more proscriptive, or restrictive, view of budget matters than does the U.S. Constitution. California's constitution, for instance, mandates that at least 40 percent of the state budget go toward education, a requirement that has often constrained legislators' options when faced with budget shortfalls.

Other state constitutions mandate a specific style and format for the laws that allow the transfer of money to the executive branch. These are known as **appropriations bills.** During the 1990s, some states, including Arizona, Colorado, Nevada, Oklahoma, and South Dakota, amended their constitutions to require supermajorities—two-thirds or three-fifths of the electorate—instead of simple majorities of the legislature to increase revenues or taxes.[8] Sometimes the constitutions get more specific still, prohibiting legislators from attaching "riders" to appropriations bills and requiring a single subject for each bill. Riders are amendments or additions unrelated to the main bill. Not surprisingly, state legislators sometimes try to evade these strict requirements. As a result, state judges tend to be much more involved in monitoring the budget process than their federal counterparts. In 2004, for instance, the Ohio Supreme Court reminded legislators that it would strike down any laws passed in violation of the state's single-subject rule.

There's another important and surprising difference between the U.S. Constitution and state constitutions—the scope of the documents. The U.S. Constitution's original purpose was to organize a federal government with sharply limited powers. In contrast, state governments have a wider field of activities. As the Tenth Amendment of the U.S. Constitution makes clear, all powers not expressly delegated or forbidden to the federal government are reserved for the states. In other words, the range of responsibilities patrolled by state governments is much larger than the federal government's. Given this fact, it is not surprising that state constitutions change more quickly and tend to be longer, more detailed, and more varied.

> While the federal constitution creates a framework for government, state constitutions often get into the policy details. Oklahoma's constitution, for instance, mandates that home economics be taught in school.

APPROPRIATIONS BILLS
Laws passed by legislatures authorizing the transfer of money to the executive branch.

The Evolution of State Constitutions

The first state constitutions were not technically constitutions at all. Rather, they were **colonial charters** awarded by the king of England. These charters typically were brief documents giving individuals or corporations the right to establish "plantations" over certain areas and govern the inhabitants therein. King James I of England granted the first charter in 1606. It created the Virginia Company of London, which in 1607 established the first English settlement in North America at Jamestown in what is now the state of Virginia.

COLONIAL CHARTERS
Legal documents drawn up by the British crown that spelled out how the colonies were to be governed.

As the colonies expanded, many of these charters were amended to give the colonists "the rights of Englishmen." Just what those rights were, however, was not entirely clear. Britain's constitution was not (and is not) a written document. It is a tradition based on the Magna Carta of 1215 and on a shared understanding of what government should and should not do. From the start, some colonies took an expansive view of their rights and privileges. The Massachusetts Bay Colony, like other English settlements in North America, was organized as a corporation and controlled by a small group of stockholders. But whereas the charters of the other companies remained in England within easy reach of the British courts, Puritan leader John Winthrop took his colony's along when he sailed for the New World in 1630. This made it difficult for the English government to seize and revoke the charter if the company misbehaved or operated illegally, which it soon did. The Puritans excluded nonchurchgoers from local governments, punished people who violated their sense of morals, and generally behaved like an independent polity. This misbehavior eventually incurred the displeasure of King Charles II, who revoked the charter in 1691. Massachusetts then received a new royal charter that provided for a royal governor and a general assembly—a form of governance that lasted until the Revolutionary War nearly a century later.[9]

When the colonies won their independence, it was clear that colonial charters had to be replaced or at least modified. It was less clear what should replace them. Some colonial leaders believed that the Continental Congress should draft a model constitution that every state should adopt. Richard Henry Lee, a Virginia politician, explained the idea in a letter to John Adams in May 1776: "Would not a uniform plan of government, prepared for America by the Congress, and approved by the colonies, be a surer foundation of unceasing harmony to the whole?" [10]

Adams thought not. While he liked the idea of uniform state constitutions in principle, Adams worried about what would happen in practice. He believed that effective government required a strong executive. The colonists' experience dealing with royal governors, however, had created an aversion to executive power. Adams feared that the Continental Congress would create governments dominated by powerful **unicameral legislatures** or even do away with governors altogether and create a special committee of legislators to handle the everyday business of governing. This would violate what he saw as the wise precautionary principle of the **separation of powers.**

Ultimately, despite being a unicameral body itself, the Continental Congress rejected that particular idea. Instead, it passed a resolution that urged the thirteen colonies to reorganize their authority solely "on the basis of the authority of the people." [11] This set the stage for the states to create their own varied blueprints for government.

After independence was declared and secured, states convened special assemblies to draft new constitutions. Most adopted lightly modified ver-

UNICAMERAL LEGISLATURES

Legislatures that possess only one chamber. Nebraska is currently the only state with a unicameral legislature.

SEPARATION OF POWERS

The principle that government should be divided into separate legislative, executive, and judicial branches, each with its own powers and responsibilities.

sions of the old colonial charters. References to the king of England were deleted and bills of rights added. In most of the new states power was concentrated in the legislative branch to diminish the possibility of tyrannical governors appearing in the political arena.

The First Generation of State Constitutions

This first generation of state constitutions created powerful **bicameral legislatures**—with a few exceptions. Georgia, Pennsylvania, and Vermont opted for unicameral legislatures. Governors and state judiciaries were clearly subordinate in most cases. In fact, legislatures often appointed both the governor and judges. No one envisioned that one day a state supreme court would have the power to overrule the acts of a legislature on the grounds that its laws were unconstitutional. Indeed, the states that did provide for a constitutional review entrusted that function to a special "council of revision" or to "councils of censor."

Nor did the early state constitutions embrace the now commonplace idea of "one person, one vote." Every early state constitution except Vermont's restricted voting access to white males who met certain minimum property requirements. Vermont gave the vote to every adult male. Supporters of a limited **franchise** defended these limitations as essential to the new republic. Without property qualifications, John Adams warned,

> There will be no end to it. New claims will arise; women will demand a vote; lads from 12 to 21 will think their rights are not enough attended to; and every man who has not a farthing will demand an equal voice with any other, in all acts of the state. It tends to confound and destroy all distinctions, and prostrate all ranks to one common level.[12]

Indeed, Adams wanted to restrict the franchise even further by setting still higher property requirements.

In practice, the actual requirements necessary to achieve the right to vote varied widely. Some states, such as New Hampshire, let all white male taxpayers vote. This reflected the fact that New Hampshire was a state of small landowners with a fairly egalitarian political culture. However, even this fair state had a higher threshold of property ownership to meet should a man wish to hold office. In Virginia, a state with a more hierarchical political culture dominated by a small group of wealthy landowners and planters, property qualifications were stiff. Only white males who owned at least twenty-five acres and a twelve-foot by twelve-foot house, or fifty acres unsettled, or a town lot with a twelve-foot by twelve-foot house could vote. It is not entirely clear how many people met these qualifications. Most scholars, however, believe that in the more democratic northern states 60 percent to 80 percent of white males could vote. Needless to say, women and minorities could not.

BICAMERAL LEGISLATURES

Legislatures that possess two chambers, typically a house of representatives, or assembly, and a senate.

THE FRANCHISE

The right to vote.

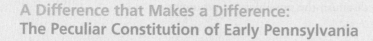

A Difference that Makes a Difference: The Peculiar Constitution of Early Pennsylvania

The original American colonies were established for very different purposes. The Massachusetts Bay Colony, for example, started off as haven for a persecuted religious sect. The Puritans were determined to create, in the words of Massachusetts's first governor, John Winthrop, "a city upon a hill" to serve as an example of a holy community for all people. Other colonies, such as Virginia, began as business ventures. Still others, including Pennsylvania, were both.

Pennsylvania's first colonial charter reflected the colony's dual purposes as a religious settlement and an investment. It illustrates how state constitutions or charters were created to serve very particular goals—and how "rights" that Americans now take for granted, such as the right to self-governance, were by no means obvious to this country's founders.

The colony started out as a business venture. In 1681, William Penn received a proprietary interest—the controlling share—in what is now the state of Pennsylvania as repayment for a debt that England's King Charles II owed Penn's father. Penn was already deeply involved in land speculation in North America. He and eleven other investors already owned East Jersey (present-day New Jersey). Soon after buying into Pennsylvania, they acquired a lease on Delaware.

Penn, however, wasn't just a businessman. He was also a devout Quaker, a member of a peace-loving religious group that was often at odds with the official Church of England. Pennsylvania was to Penn "a holy experiment"—a unique chance to found a province dedicated to Quakerism's unique vision of equality and religious freedom.

William Markham, Penn's deputy, was sent in 1681 to establish a seat of government for Penn's new colony. Penn also instructed his representative to construct a "City of Brotherly Love"—Philadelphia. One year later, Penn himself arrived in his fledgling colony.

His first major action was to draw up a constitution, or charter, for his new colony, which he called "the Frame of Government." His second major act was to establish friendly relations with American Indians in the area—an unusual action that reflected his pacific religious beliefs.

In many ways, the Frame of Government echoed Quakerism's progressive dogmas. Penn's constitution guaranteed religious freedom to everyone who believed in God. It also set forth a humane penal code and encouraged the emancipation of slaves. In contrast, the early settlers of Massachusetts were interested not in individual religious freedom but in establishing a just Puritan society. As a result, the functions of local churches and town governments were intertwined in early Massachusetts. Indeed, the colony was governed as a virtual theocracy for its first two hundred years.

However, the Pennsylvania model was not a uniform triumph of humane liberalism. Penn did use his charter to protect his business interests. While the Frame of Government provided for an elected general assembly, it also concentrated almost all power in the executive branch of government, which was controlled by Penn and the other proprietors.

It was not long before colonists began to chafe at some of the less progressive features of William Penn's early constitution. He was forced to return to Pennsylvania in 1701 and issue a new constitution, the Charter of Privileges, which granted more power to the provincial assembly. However, the conflict between proprietary and antiproprietary forces did not diminish until 1776. That year, noted revolutionary Benjamin Franklin led a convention to assemble and approve a new constitution for the state as it struggled for independence from Great Britain.

Over the course of the nineteenth century, the franchise was expanded gradually, although in a very uneven and often unjust fashion. A number of southern states, for example, rewrote their constitutions to allow minorities to vote as part of the price for readmission to the Union after the Civil War. African American rights also were enshrined in the Fourteenth Amendment of the U.S. Constitution. Yet despite these protections, gains for African Americans proved short-lived. In the last decade of the 1800s, African Americans' ability to vote and to participate in all aspects of society were harshly limited by the passage of **Jim Crow laws**. These laws provided for the systematic separation of races and sharply restricted access to the franchise, and they permitted the outright intimidation of African Americans.

Women fared only slightly better. Wyoming began to allow women the vote in 1869. By 1912, only thirteen states had followed suit. It took the Nineteenth Amendment, ratified in 1920, to secure the right to vote, or suffrage, for all women nationwide. This was also the culmination of the Suffrage Movement of the nineteenth century.

The limitations on the franchise imposed by many early state constitutions did little to promote good governance. State legislatures quickly developed an impressive record of corruption and fiscal extravagance, because some of the men who had the legal right to vote also had money to influence politicians, an easy task in many states. But the era of unlimited legislative power did not last very long. New territories entering the Union, such as Indiana and Mississippi, opted for elected governors, as did older states that began to revise or replace their constitutions in the 1820s. The intention was to create more balance among the branches of government and allow all voters (not just the rich ones) more of a voice in deciding who would run a state. By 1860, South Carolina was the only state with a governor selected by the legislature.[13] In hindsight, the nineteenth century would be seen as a period of tumultuous constitutional change.

Formal Constitutional Changes

Every state constitution provides a method for making changes. Fourteen states actually require citizens to periodically vote on whether or not they want to convene a **constitutional convention**. Voters can decide if they want to amend or replace their state's constitution.[14]

In the early nineteenth century, suggesting such change could be an exciting—and dangerous—business. In 1841 a patrician attorney and renegade lawmaker by the name of Thomas Wilson Dorr convened an illegal constitutional convention. Its task was to replace Rhode Island's colonial charter with a more modern and progressive constitution. The aged document still limited the franchise to voters owning land valued at $134 or more at a time when other states had long since abandoned such requirements. Dorr's supporters elected him "governor" the following year on a platform that pro-

JIM CROW LAWS

Measures passed in the last decade of the nineteenth century that sought to legally and systematically separate blacks and whites.

CONSTITUTIONAL CONVENTION

An assembly convened for the express purpose of amending or replacing a constitution.

MAP 3-1 Number of Constitutions per State

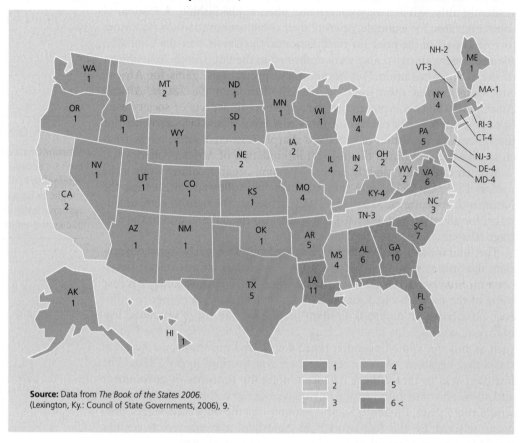

WA 1
MT 2
ND 1
MN 1
OR 1
ID 1
WY 1
SD 1
WI 1
MI 4
NH-2
VT-3
ME 1
NY 4
MA-1
RI-3
CT-4
PA 5
NV 1
NE 2
IA 2
IL 4
IN 2
OH 2
NJ-3
DE-4
MD-4
CA 2
UT 1
CO 1
KS 1
MO 4
WV 2
VA 6
KY-4
NC 3
AZ 1
NM 1
OK 1
AR 5
TN-3
SC 7
MS 4
AL 6
GA 10
AK 1
TX 5
LA 11
FL 6
HI 1

Legend:
1
2
3
4
5
6 <

Source: Data from *The Book of the States 2006*.
(Lexington, Ky.: Council of State Governments, 2006), 9.

posed allowing all white males—even Catholic immigrants, a group viewed with great suspicion—to vote, which caused the sitting governor to order him arrested and tried for treason. Thus began the Dorr War, or Dorr's Rebellion. His supporters then attempted to seize the arsenal in Providence but were repelled when their cannons failed to discharge. A month later, Dorr and his followers tried again. This time a force of militiamen and free blacks from Providence repelled them.[15] Still, Rhode Island's establishment got the hint. A new, more liberal constitution was quickly enacted.

The amendment process has since become a bit more routine in most states. Amending or replacing a state constitution is typically a two-step process. First, a constitutional amendment or a new constitution must be proposed and meet a certain threshold of support. Then it must be ratified.

There are four primary ways to propose changes to state constitutions: legislative proposals, ballot initiatives or referendums, constitutional conventions, and constitutional commissions.

More than 2,200 initiatives have been included on state ballots since 1904. Oregon leads the nation, with 341 initiatives presented by December 2006.

MAP 3-2 Number of Amendments Adopted per State

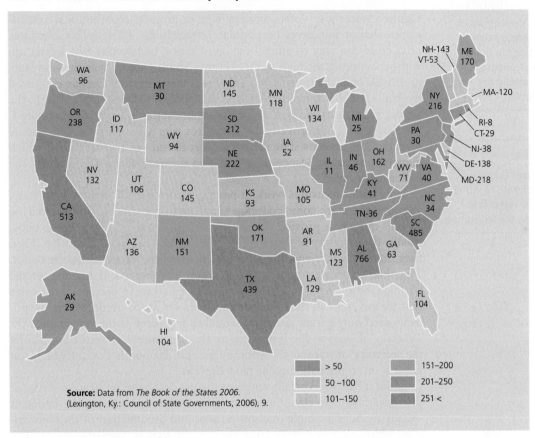

Source: Data from *The Book of the States 2006.*
(Lexington, Ky.: Council of State Governments, 2006), 9.

Legend:
> 50
50–100
101–150
151–200
201–250
251 <

Legislative Proposal

Most attempts to change a state's constitution begin with a legislative proposal. Forty-nine state constitutions allow the state legislature to propose constitutional amendments to the electorate as a whole.[16] In seventeen states, a majority vote in both houses of the legislature suffices to send a constitutional amendment on for **ratification**. However, most states require a supermajority for a constitutional amendment to go into effect. Some states set the bar even higher. The constitutions of eleven states—Delaware, Indiana, Iowa, Massachusetts, Nevada, New York, Pennsylvania, South Carolina, Tennessee, Virginia, and Wisconsin—require their legislatures to vote for a constitutional amendment in two consecutive sessions before it can be ratified.[17] In principle, some state legislatures also can propose completely new constitutions to voters. However, no state legislature has successfully proposed a wholesale constitutional change since Georgia did so in 1982.

RATIFICATION

A vote of the entire electorate to approve a constitutional change, referendum, or ballot initiative.

BALLOT INITIATIVES

Process through which voters directly convey instructions to the legislature, approve a law, or amend the constitution.

REFERENDUMS

Procedures that allow the electorate to either accept or reject laws passed by the legislature.

Ballot Initiatives and Referendums

Eighteen states give voters another way to propose constitutional amendments—**ballot initiatives** or popular **referendums**. These ballot measures offer citizens a way to amend the constitution or to enact new legislation without working through the legislature. South Dakota was the first state to provide ballot initiatives, in 1898, but it was only after Oregon embraced them in 1902 that the push for direct democracy really got underway. In the sixteen years that followed, nearly two dozen states followed Oregon's lead. The last state to approve ballot initiatives was Mississippi in 1992, some seventy years after its state supreme court tossed out its first ruling, which allowed initiatives.[18] Since then, just two measures have qualified for the ballot. Both failed.

How ballot measures work in practice varies widely from state to state, although there are some common elements to the process. In most states, citizens must first provide the text of their proposal to an oversight body, usually the secretary of state's office or a legislative review committee. Then they need to gather enough signatures to place the proposal on the ballot. This threshold varies widely among states: Wyoming and Arizona set the bar high, requiring a number of signatures equal to 15 percent of the votes cast for governor in the last election. It's easier in Colorado, where proponents need only gather signatures equal to 5 percent of the votes tallied for secretary of state in the last election. The signatures are verified, again by the secretary of state or the attorney general. Proposals that pass each test make it on to the ballot at the next election.

Ballot measures typically combine the proposal and ratification stages of the amendment process. Once a proposed amendment is on the ballot, it usually requires a simple majority to pass and become part of the constitution, although some state constitutions do require supermajorities. The practical result is laws without lawmakers; the initiative is commonly employed to seek policy changes that, for whatever reason, are not being considered or undertaken by the legislature.

Constitutional Conventions

The most freewheeling approach to changing or replacing a state constitution is to convene a constitutional convention. Massachusetts, whose constitution was drafted in 1780 and is the nation's oldest, was the first state to adopt a constitution via a convention. Most other states quickly followed. Currently, the only states that make no provisions for changing their constitutions through the use of constitutional conventions are Arkansas, Indiana, Mississippi, New Jersey, North Dakota, Pennsylvania, and Texas. A constitutional convention typically begins when a state legislature passes a resolution that calls for a statewide referendum on whether a convention should be held. If a majority of the electorate votes in favor of the proposal, then the next step is to hold elections for convention delegates. In most states, a law is passed that provides for the election of convention members from local election districts. Of course, there are exceptions. The legislatures of Georgia, Louisiana, Maine, South Carolina, South Dakota, and Virginia can call a constitutional convention without the approval of the electorate. Iowa holds an automatic constitutional assembly every ten years, and Alaska's lieutenant governor can propose a constitutional convention through a ballot question if one has not occurred within the last decade.

Once delegates are selected, a constitutional convention can convene. Members are free to amend, revise, or even replace their state's constitution. A constitutional convention has virtually unlimited discretion to make such changes. It can change the existing document in any way it sees fit or write an entirely new constitution. Ultimately, its handiwork goes before the electorate as a whole to be voted in or cast out.

Or it can do nothing at all. In 1974, Texas convened a convention to rewrite its creaky 1876 constitution. Members spent several months drafting a new constitution, but when it came time to vote on their handiwork, a majority of the delegates unexpectedly came out against it. The next year the state legislature voted to put the constitution the convention had drafted to the public anyway as a referendum. The voters turned it down.[19]

> State legislators tend to be wary of constitutional conventions, which can reexamine any and all aspects of state and local government. Lawmakers might end up initiating a process that leads to more far-reaching changes than they'd expected.

State legislators tend to be wary of constitutional conventions and rarely convene them. The reason for this caution is that once convened, a constitutional convention theoretically can reexamine any and all aspects of state and local government. Lawmakers who approve a convention might end up initiating a process that leads to more far-reaching changes than they had expected. Increasingly, the average voter seems to share this skepticism. In 2002, Alabama governor Don Siegelman's plan to call a convention to draft a new constitution was derailed when Siegelman lost his reelection bid. Voters in Alaska, Montana, and New Hampshire also rejected referendums that would have provided for constitutional conventions. In fact, the last constitutional convention was held in 1986 in Rhode Island.[20]

Constitutional Revision Commissions

If constitutional conventions are for the bold and trusting, then **constitutional revision commissions** are often the cautious technocrat's prefer route to constitutional change. Constitutional revision commission cally consist of a panel of citizens appointed by the governor, by th legislature, or by both. The commissions suggest—but cannot manda changes to their state constitutions. Between 1990 and 2000, seven states

Alaska, Arkansas, California, Florida, New York, Oklahoma, and Utah—convened constitutional commissions.

Two states go even further in their enthusiasm for constitutional commissions. Florida's constitution requires that a constitutional revision commission convene every twenty years. It also gives this commission a unique power—the right to present proposed changes directly to voters for their approval or rejection. Florida's last constitutional revision commission met in 1998. It recommended thirteen changes to the state constitution, including a proposal to allow local governments to expand the background checks and waiting period requirements on gun sales. That led the head of Florida's chapter of the National Rifle Association (NRA) to decry the proposal as a power grab and to issue a warning that gun owners might vote down all constitutional changes, even changes with universal support, should the proposal pass.[21] The commission refused to back down. Six months later, more than 70 percent of voters supported the measure.

The other state with an unusual constitutional revision commission is Utah, the only state whose commission is permanent. Utah Constitutional Revision Commission members are appointed by the governor, the leaders of both houses of the legislature, and by sitting commission members. Unlike Florida's commission, Utah's commission can only issue its recommendations in the form of a public report to the governor.

Ratification

Once an amendment has been proposed and found acceptable, it must be ratified before it can go into effect. In most states, this is a straightforward process. First, the proposed constitutional amendment or new constitution is put before the voting public in the next statewide election. Then the electorate either approves or rejects it. Two states do add a twist to this process. In South Carolina, a majority of both houses of the state congress must vote to approve a constitutional amendment—after the successful popular referendum—before the amendment can go into effect. In Delaware, approval by a two-thirds vote in two successive general assemblies gets a constitutional amendment ratified. As already discussed, the ballot initiative essentially combines the proposal and ratification stages. Once a proposed amendment is qualified for the ballot, it usually requires only a simple majority to become part of the constitution.

Informal Methods for Changing Constitutions

In recent years, voters and legislators nationwide have generally resisted making major changes to their states' constitutions. However, many state constitutions have changed dramatically in informal ways. The most common route of informal constitutional change is via state supreme courts. For instance, this is the case when a court interprets an existing constitution in a way that creates a new right, such as the right to an adequate or equitable education discussed earlier in the feature box, "State Constitutions, Educational Equity, and the New Judicial Activism."

Sometimes constitutional changes also come about from **judicial review**. In December 1999, the Vermont Supreme Court directed the state legislature to pass a law that provided for civil unions. Its rationale? The court found that because the state constitution was "instituted for the common benefit, protection and security of the people," the state government could not refuse to provide the benefit of marriage to gay people. To those who objected that the state constitution, which was enacted in 1793 and is a model of brevity at 8,200 words, said nothing about gay marriage, the court explained that its job was "to distill the essence, the motivating idea of the framers," not to be bound by eighteenth-century notions of jurisprudence.[22] In November 2003, the Massachusetts Supreme Court took a step further when it declared the state's ban on same-sex marriage unconstitutional, which prompted efforts nationwide to amend the U.S. Constitution to explicitly define marriage as the union between a man and woman.

State constitutions also can change when other branches of government successfully lay claim to broader powers. For example, Rhode Island's legislature has used its strong constitutional position—a clause in the state constitution says the General Assembly "can exercise any power" unless the constitution explicitly forbids it—to take control of functions that most states delegate to governors. That means that in Rhode Island legislators not only sit on the boards and commissions that oversee a range of state agencies, they also dominate the board that sets the salaries for high-ranking executive branch officials. Not surprisingly, this has given the legislature a great deal of power over executive branch decisions. In short, Rhode Island has just the type of government that John Adams feared.

Southern states such as Florida, Mississippi, and Texas also tend to have constitutions that provide for weak governors. In these cases, this arrangement is a legacy of the post–Civil War **Reconstruction** period. During Reconstruction the victorious Union Army forced most of the former Confederate states to replace their constitutions. Reconstruction ended in 1876, and the Union troops withdrew. With the exception of Arkansas, North Carolina, and Tennessee, most southern states abandoned their revised constitutions in favor of new ones that greatly weakened gubernatorial powers.[23] Part of the reasoning for this was that weak governors could be kept from enacting policies that the federal government encouraged but that were contrary to the norms of these traditionalistic states. This is what had happened during Reconstruction, when the governors of the states that had seceded from the Union were replaced by individuals sympathetic to the federal government in Washington or were forced to

JUDICIAL REVIEW
The power of courts to assess whether a law is in compliance with the constitution.

RECONSTRUCTION
The period following the Civil War when the southern states were governed under the direction of the Union Army.

Procedures for Constitutional Amendment by Legislature

MAP 3-3 Legislative Vote Required for Proposal

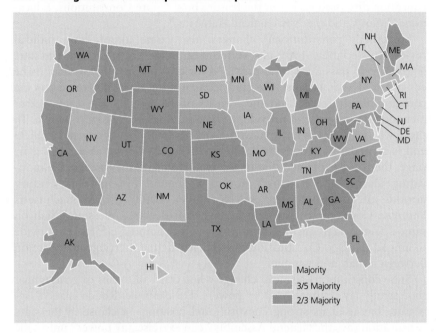

Majority
3/5 Majority
2/3 Majority

MAP 3-4 Consideration by Two Sessions Required

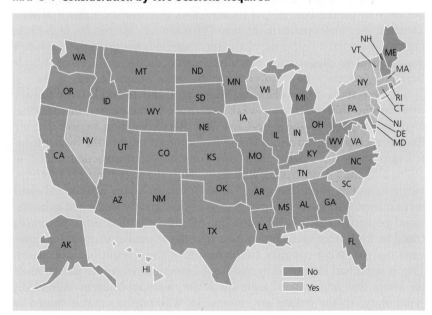

No
Yes

Note: Connecticut, Hawaii, and New Jersey follow different rules for legislative consideration that involve a second session if a supermajority is not achieved in the first session.

Governing States and Localities

MAP 3-5 Vote Required for Ratification

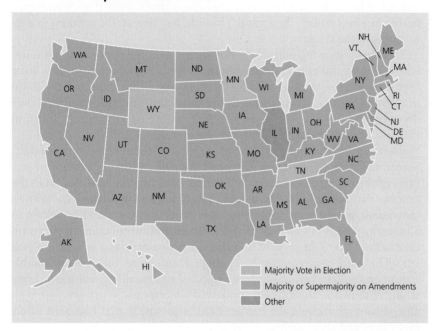

Majority Vote in Election

Majority or Supermajority on Amendments

Other

MAP 3-6 Limitation on Number of Amendments Submitted at One Election

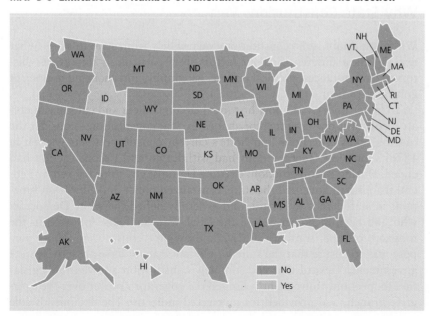

No

Yes

Source: Data compiled from *The Book of the States, 2006* (Lexington, Ky.: Council of State Governments, 2006), 11–12.

cooperate with federal policy in regard to such issues as African American rights. For example, in 1885 Florida passed a constitution that took away the governor's right to appoint his own cabinet. Members were elected instead. Although it has been amended many times since, that constitution is still in effect today. As a result, Florida has one of the weakest governorships in the country.[24]

Of course, state legislatures do not always gain the upper hand. In states whose constitutions give governors the edge, some chief executives have been very aggressive in expanding their powers. While their techniques do not involve written amendments to the state constitutions themselves, they do affect the distribution of powers within state government—a function that is a primary concern of state constitutions.

There is another way to change state constitutions—simple neglect. Sometimes state governments just stop enforcing obscure or repugnant sections of their state constitutions, effectively changing the constitution in the process. No politician today would dare to argue for denying the vote to individuals simply because they are poor or do not own land or belong to a minority group, yet until 1999 Texas's constitution contained a provision that limited the right to vote to citizens who owned land and paid a poll tax. The state government had stopped enforcing these objectionable requirements long before but had neglected to actually repeal them. Likewise, Alabama's constitution outlawed interracial marriages until an amendment overturned the ban in 2000, a provision that had been informally dropped years earlier.

Why State Constitutions Vary

Without a doubt, state constitutions vary widely from state to state. What explains these differences? Four factors seem particularly important—historical circumstances, political culture, geography, and changing notions of good government.

To better understand how historical circumstances and culture can create a constitution—and then be shaped by that constitution—consider the case of Texas. The Lone Star State's current constitution was written in 1876, soon after federal troops had withdrawn and Reconstruction had ended. During Reconstruction, a strong Unionist governor backed by Federal troops had governed the state, centralized police and education functions in state hands in Austin, and generally defied the white Democrats who had been in power before the Civil War. So Texas followed in the footsteps of other southern states and drew up a constitution whose purpose was to ensure that the state would never again have an activist state government. Toward that end, the new constitution allowed the legislature to meet only infrequently, limited the governor's power over the executive branch, and provided for an elected judiciary. The document's sole progressive feature was a provision that for the first time allowed women to continue to own their own property after they were married.[25]

White Democrats' antipathy to Reconstruction explains much of the content of Texas's 1876 constitution. The state's political culture explains why its constitution has endured to the present. Political scientist Daniel Elazar classified Texas as a "traditionalistic/individualistic" state that, in his words, "places a premium on limiting community intervention" and "accepts a natural hierarchical society as part of the ordered nature of things."[26] While Elazar's categories have blurred in recent years, state constitutions continue to bear out his categories. In short, Texas's constitution is well suited to its political culture—a culture that views strong, activist government with suspicion.

In contrast, a constitution that allowed the legislature to meet only every other year would suit a moralistic state poorly. Not surprisingly, moralistic states like Michigan, Minnesota, and Wisconsin allow their legislatures to meet far more frequently than does Texas. Because they envision fairly robust styles of governance, constitutions in these states allow their legislature to meet throughout the year, creating what are, for all intents and purposes, full-time professional legislatures.

> Of course, history, political culture, and geography aren't the only factors that determine the kind of constitution a state will have. Another important factor is the changing sense of what works best.

New England's propensity for short, framework-oriented constitutions is a variation based noticeably on geography. One political scientist has hypothesized that such a variation may reflect the fact that New England states are small and relatively homogenous and that their citizens are thus less inclined to fight to include policies they support in their states' constitutions.[27]

Of course, history, political culture, and geography aren't the only factors that determine the kind of constitution a state will have. Another important factor is the changing sense of what works best. In the early nineteenth century, many states concluded that a system in which the legislature operates with unbridled power simply did not work well. So they changed their constitutions in ways that strengthened the chief executive. Eighty years ago, groups like the National Municipal League argued that state constitutions should be more like the federal constitution—that is, that they should be much shorter documents that provided a framework for governance rather than long documents that get into the details of the policies. That argument gave rise to the **model constitution**, a kind of ideal that states interested in "improving" could adopt. During the 1960s and 1970s, many states did revise their constitutions in ways designed to make their governments more effective, although the last edition of the model constitution was written in 1968.

MODEL CONSTITUTION

An expert-approved generic or "ideal" constitution that is sometimes used by states as a yardstick against which they can measure their existing constitutions.

Since the mid-twentieth century, however, some political scientists have questioned the assumptions behind the model constitution movement. To these revisionists, the fact that most state constitutions outside of New England are long and policy rich is actually a good thing—a healthy sign of an engaged electorate. Revisionists argue that while Americans have essentially left it to the U.S. Supreme Court to interpret and on occasion to change the federal constitution, citizens have defended their right to participate by shaping their state constitutions.[28]

How State Constitutions Differ

The most obvious ways in which state constitutions differ involve their length and ease of amendment. These are not simply cosmetic differences. Rather, they almost always reflect the different functions state constitutions serve. Vermont has the shortest state constitution. Like the U.S. Constitution, its goal is primarily to establish a framework for effective government. This is true to a lesser extent of other states in New England as well.

In contrast, constitutions in other regions of the country tend to be longer and more specific in their policy prescriptions. Voters and interest groups in most states who want to accomplish a goal like increased state spending on education will lobby the governor or the legislature. In California, a state with a long, policy-specific constitution that provides for a high degree of direct democracy, people often attempt to amend the constitution instead. While the majority of political scientists wring their hands about this tendency, it undeniably gives Californians a role in shaping their constitution that voters in regions of the country like New England lack.

Operating Rules and Selection for Office

State constitutions create varying organizational structures and operating rules for the constituent elements of state government. They establish different methods and requirements for serving in state politics. Some of these differences reflect the historical differences among states, as well as different political cultures and geography. Other differences reflect different notions of what makes good government. Sometimes these notions can be quite quirky. Consider the following, for example. To serve as the governor of Oklahoma, a state of 3.4 million people, you must be at least thirty-one years old. In contrast, to lead California's population of thirty-four million, the chief executive need only be eighteen. You can lead one of the nation's largest states, but don't try to get a beer or a glass of wine at your fund-raisers!

In addition, state constitutions differ widely in how many statewide elected positions they create and how those positions are filled. One of the most important such differences has to do with the judiciary. At the feder-

Virginia's executive mansion is the oldest continuously occupied governor's residence in the United States. It has been the home of Virginia's governors since 1813.

al level, judges are selected by the president and approved by the U.S. Senate. Things work very differently in the states. Most give their governors the right to nominate state supreme court justices, often from a list of names chosen by a judicial screening commission. Eighteen states—Arkansas, Georgia, Idaho, Illinois, Kentucky, Louisiana, Michigan, Mississippi, Missouri, Nevada, North Carolina, North Dakota, Ohio, Oregon, Pennsylvania, Texas, Washington, and West Virginia—select their supreme court justices and lower level judges in elections.

Many states use a hybrid of appointment and elections called the Missouri Plan to select and retain judges. Named after the state in which it was first adopted, the plan calls for a governor to appoint a judicial nominating commission. This commission then recommends candidates to fill vacancies on the bench. It presents a list of three carefully vetted, or selected, candidates to the governor, who selects one to fill the vacancy. The nominee assumes the office, but first must be approved by the voters, usually during the next general election. Once approved, the judge faces periodic retention elections. As long as the voters approve, the judge retains office.[29]

Seemingly small institutional differences can have a big impact on how state governments work. A governor with strong veto powers, for example, may have an easier time getting a recalcitrant legislature to consider the executive's point of view on a particular piece of legislation than one who does not. Elected judges are more likely to uphold the death penalty in capital crimes than those more insulated from the ballot box.[30] In short, the different operating rules embedded in state constitutions lead to very different types of governance.

Distribution of Power

State constitutions make very different decisions about where power should reside. While all state constitutions make at least a bow toward the principle of the separation of powers, in actuality, many have given one branch of government a preponderance of power. Under some state constitutions, the reins of government are clearly in the hands of the legislature or general assembly. Other states have amended their constitutions in ways that give their governors the upper hand.

As previously discussed, some state constitutions clearly give the state legislature an advantage over the governor in the struggle for preeminence. Rhode Island is the classic example. Yet while strong state legislatures still may be the norm, in recent decades, constitutional changes in many states have bolstered their governors' powers. More than forty state constitutions now give governors the important power of the **line-item veto**, the ability to veto certain portions of appropriations bills while approving the rest. Exactly what counts as an item, and thus what is fair game for a governor's veto pen, is often unclear. As a result, line-item veto court cases have become a common part of the legal landscape.

LINE-ITEM VETO

The power to reject a portion of a bill while the rest remains intact.

Former Wisconsin governor Tommy Thompson looks more like Evel Knievel than Vanna White on his Harley Davidson Road King. A Harley is fitting, though, and not just because the motorcycles are made in Wisconsin. His use of Vanna White veto powers—the ability to strike single words from bills—gave him a reputation for riding over the wishes of the state legislature.

Some states go even further. Twelve states allow governors to reduce spending by striking a digit from the amount appropriated. Wisconsin's state constitution even allows a governor the power to strike out an appropriation entirely and write in a lower figure. Former Wisconsin governor Tommy Thompson pushed the power of the partial veto to strike passages and even individual words from bills that came to his desk. In some cases, Thompson would strike individual letters from bills to create entirely new words and meanings and change the entire meaning of the legislation. Critics came to call Thompson's creative writing "the Vanna White veto." In one case, Thompson used the Vanna White veto and his Scrabble skills to transform a piece of legislation from a bill that set the maximum detention period for juvenile offenders at forty-eight hours into one that allowed for a ten-day detention period, a move that enraged the Democratic legislature.[31] Voters later amended the constitution to prohibit that particular veto maneuver. Yet despite the controversies that surrounded such actions, during his record fourteen-year reign, none of Thompson's more than 1,900 budget vetoes were ever overturned by the legislature.[32]

The power structures set up by the constitutional systems of some states resist easy classification. Take Texas. The fact that the legislature meets for only five or six months every other year might lead one to think that power in Texas would reside primarily with the governor. Not so. In fact, the Texas constitution arguably makes the office of lieutenant governor the most powerful in the state. In Texas, the lieutenant governor presides over the senate, appoints senate committees and assigns bills, and chairs the powerful Texas Legislative Council, which is responsible for researching and drafting bills. Indeed, many observers attribute George W. Bush's two successful terms as governor to his close relationship with his lieutenant governor, Bob Bullock, a Democrat.

Rights Granted

State constitutions not only create different mechanisms of governance and give governments different sets of constraints and powers, they also confer different rights to citizens. For example, the U.S. Constitution does not explicitly create a right to privacy, although the U.S. Supreme Court did define a limited right to privacy in *Griswold v. the State of Connecticut* (1965). In contrast, Montana's constitution states that "the right to individual privacy is essential to the well-being of a free society and shall not be infringed without the showing of a compelling state interest." [33] As a result, courts in Montana—and Kentucky and Tennessee—have interpreted their state constitutions to protect adults' freedom to engage in consensual oral or anal sex that until quite recently were illegal in many other states. [34]

Representative Government vs. Direct Democracy

One of the most striking differences among state constitutions is the degree to which they have or have not embraced direct democracy. Most Americans celebrate the United States as a democracy, but the Founders believed that they were establishing something somewhat different—a representative democracy. This is a form of government in which qualified representatives of the public make the decisions. Direct, or pure, democracy was viewed with suspicion by most of the Founders. "[A] pure democracy, by which I mean a society consisting of a small number of citizens, who assemble and administer the government in person, can admit of no cure for the mischiefs of faction," warned James Madison, one of the primary authors of the U.S. Constitution, in his famous argument for the document in *The Federalist,* No. 10:

> A common passion or interest will, in almost every case, be felt by a majority of the whole . . . and there is nothing to check the inducements to sacrifice the weaker party or an obnoxious individual. Hence it is that such democracies have ever been spectacles of turbulence and contention; have ever been found incompatible with personal security or the rights of property; and have in general been as short in their lives as they have been violent in their deaths. [35]

In other words, Madison believed that entrusting a simple majority with the power to carry out its will would lead to fickle and tyrannical behavior and a government that teetered between anarchy and autocracy.

The U.S. Constitution's solution to the problem of pure democracy was to create a representative government or, as Madison saw it, government by a small group of elected officials "whose wisdom may best discern the true interest of their country." [36] In accordance with this belief, the U.S. Constitution created an upper chamber—the Senate—whose members would be selected by state legislatures from among their eminent men. The document also created an electoral college to elect the president. Both of these decisions were made to insulate the federal government from the whims of the majority. The Constitution makes no provision for direct democratic processes. There is not a single federal office *directly* elected by the entire nation. Indeed, as we saw in 2000 with the election of George W. Bush, the electoral college system can result in a candidate winning the presidency after losing the popular vote.

The creators of the federal government took great care to ensure it was insulated from direct democratic processes. Many states decided to do just the opposite during the Progressive Era. By giving their citizens the chance to make laws and change their constitutions directly, the Progressives sought to circumvent legislatures and executives they viewed as beholden to wealthy special interests. As Robert M. La Follette, a leader of the Progressive Party in Wisconsin and later a governor and senator from the state, put it:

> The forces of the special privileges are deeply entrenched. Their resources are inexhaustible. Their efforts are never lax. Their political methods are insidious. It is impossible for the people to maintain perfect organization in mass. They are often taken unaware and are liable to lose at one stroke the achievements of years of effort. In such a crisis, nothing but the united power of the people expressed directly through the ballot can overthrow the enemy. [37]

For politicians like La Follette, direct democratic mechanisms, such as the ballot initiative and the referendum, represented the general populace's best hope for breaking the power of political bosses and moneyed interests. Between 1902 and 1918, direct democracy enjoyed a great vogue in the states. Sixteen states adopted the ballot initiative in that fourteen-year period. After the First World War, ballot initiatives lost some of their luster as popular enthusiasm for Progressive ideas waned. Only five states—Alaska (1959), Florida (1968), Wyoming (1968), Illinois (1970), and Mississippi (1992) have amended their constitutions to allow for ballot initiatives since the end of the Progressive Era. [38] What's more, note where these states are located. The majority of the states that allow direct democracy lie west of the Mississippi River, where the practice fits with much of the West's populist history. [39]

For much of their existence, initiatives and referendums were used sparingly. Then came Proposition 13 in California. In the 1970s, taxpayer activist Howard Jarvis and retired real estate salesman Paul Gann launched what at first seemed a foolishly impractical campaign to roll back California property taxes and cap the rate at which they could grow. Their campaign struck a chord with many Californians. The state's booming economy had sent property values skyrocketing. Higher property assessments led to higher real estate taxes, which created a huge revenue boom for state and local governments. Indeed, at the time the state government had a $5 billion annual surplus. Yet despite the public outcry for relief from rising property costs, Gov. Jerry Brown and the politicians in Sacramento could not agree on a tax reduction plan.

In 1978, California voters passed Proposition 13 and took the decision out of their hands. It directed the state to roll back real estate taxes to 1975 levels and decreed that property assessments could not increase by more than 2 percent a year, regardless of inflation. Most localities previously had reassessed real estate taxes every two years. Proposition 13 decreed that property could only be reassessed when it was sold. The legislation also cut property tax receipts in half and marked the beginning of a nationwide "taxpayer revolt." The revolt culminated in the election of former California governor Ronald Reagan to the presidency two years later.

For California's political establishment, the passage of Proposition 13 was viewed with great trepidation. Politicians worried that it would cripple their ability to pay for the schools and infrastructure that had contributed so much to California's post–Second World War successes. These fears proved well founded. In the wake of Proposition 13, California went from having one of the best funded public school systems (in the top third in terms of per pupil spending) to having one of the worst (in the bottom third). The proposition put such draconian limits on the ability of local government to raise revenues that municipalities and counties became increasingly dependent on the state for their funding—so much so that ten years later, in 1988, California teachers' unions would push through Proposition 98, which mandated that 40 percent of California's general revenue go to education.[40]

Besides complicating government finances and drastically reducing the flexibility of lawmakers in California, the success of Proposition 13 revived interest in ballots in the twenty-four other states in which they were permitted. In the three decades from 1940 through 1970, there was an average of nineteen ballot initiatives per two-year election cycle in the United States. In the 1980s, that number shot up to fifty initiatives in the average election cycle. In the 1990s, it hit seventy-six ballot initiatives per election cycle.[41] Many of these initiatives were proposed constitutional amendments. Their sheer numbers indicate that states with the initiative are now engaged in an almost continuous cycle of changing their constitutions. These changes are increasingly less about broad questions of good governance and more about pushing narrow agendas.

Qwest Field, home of the Seattle Seahawks, was made possible by a ballot initiative that provided $300 million in public financing for construction of the stadium. The team's owner, billionaire and Microsoft cofounder Paul Allen, financed the successful ballot initiative.

In the past two decades, ballot initiatives have been used to push through some of the most controversial political issues in the entire country. Oregon voters used a ballot initiative to narrowly—51 percent to 49 percent—approve physician-assisted suicide in 1994. In California, voters have used initiatives to impose some of the nation's strictest term limits on elected officials (Proposition 140), to end affirmative action (Propositions 209 and 96), to deny education and health benefits to families of illegal immigrants (Proposition 87), to spend $3 billion on stem-cell research (Proposition 71), and to recall a sitting governor and replace him with an action movie star.

The initiative process has become big business. In 2004, more than $200 million was spent waging battles over California's ballot measures alone.[42] Several companies are devoted to gathering signatures and getting issues placed on the ballot for anyone who can afford their services. To those who have used them successfully, ballot initiatives are a nifty way to circumvent a hostile legislature and act on the will of the majority. But most political scientists and close observers of state politics have a different viewpoint. To them, ballot initiatives only reinforce the wisdom of the Founders in their decision to keep direct democratic processes out of the U.S. Constitution. A number of those who have examined initiatives conclude that they have been hijacked by those with deep pockets and individuals who use them to further their own self-interests.

Veteran *Washington Post* political reporter David Broder describes ballot initiatives in scathing terms:

> At the start of a new century—and millennium—a new form of government is spreading in the United States. It is alien to the spirit of the Constitution and its careful system of checks and balances. Though derived from a reform favored by Populists and Progressives as a cure for special-interest influence, this method of lawmaking has become the favored tool of millionaires and interest groups that use their wealth to achieve their own policy goals—a lucrative business for a new set of political entrepreneurs.[43]

Exploiting the public's disdain for politics and distrust of politicians, interest groups with deep pockets now have a mechanism to literally rewrite state constitutions to advance their own agendas. For example, in 1997 Microsoft cofounder and Seattle Seahawks owner Paul Allen made an end-run around a balky state legislature and spent $6 million on a ballot initiative that required the state to foot much of the cost for a new stadium for his team. It proved to be a good investment; the initiative passed by 51 percent. While this was welcome news for many football fans, most political scientists probably see it as an illustration of the very problem Madison identified in *The Federalist* No. 10. In some ways the initiative has created a very odd form of governance where citizens live under laws that are often resisted by their elected governments. With its ability to make sweeping changes in state constitutions, the initiative process threatens to radically change the American system of government in the next few decades.

In some cases, state-level initiatives may even affect national elections. Through 2006, twenty-three states had passed constitutional amendments that banned gay marriage, prompted in part by the Massachusetts Supreme Court's 2003 decision supporting same-sex marriage. (Arizona has been the only state where a same-sex marriage ban has failed to pass.) Observers speculated that such a measure on the Ohio ballot in 2004 boosted turnout among conservative voters, helping to deliver a second term for President George W. Bush, although scholars say more research is needed to determine the indirect effects of direct democracy.[44]

Constitutions for Local Government?

For the most part, substate governments, or **special districts,** such as school districts, counties, and many municipalities, are considered subordinate arms of the state. They may seem like autonomous political units, but they in fact operate under state constitutions and at the discretion of state governments. The courts generally have viewed only the federal government and the states as sovereign entities with the right to determine how their authority should be exercised. The authority and power of local governments is largely confined, if not outright dictated, by the states.

There are some exceptions to this rule. The **municipal charter** is a key example. In a rough sense, these charters are similar to the charters that served as the governing documents for the original colonies. Legally, most municipalities are corporations, and their charters describe the purposes of the municipality and the processes for achieving these objectives. A charter is not a constitution, but rather a grant of authority derived from a constitution or from state law. Some states have **home rule**, which allows municipalities the right to draft and amend their own charters and to regulate local matters within their jurisdictions without interference from the state. There are states that have municipal home rule provisions in their constitutions. Others grant municipal home rule through legislation. Municipal home rule means that some local governments are operated by charters that "can take on many characteristics of a constitution."[45] Even in the most liberal home rule states, however, state constitutions and state law generally take precedence over municipal charters.

SPECIAL DISTRICTS
Entities created by state legislatures that enjoy some attributes of government.

MUNICIPAL CHARTER
A document that establishes operating procedures for local governments.

HOME RULE
A form of self-governance granted to towns and cities by the state.

Conclusion

Even though you rarely read about them in the newspaper—much less hear about them on the evening news—state constitutions play *the* critical role in defining the possibilities of politics in most states. All state constitutions set the basic structure of government, apportion power and responsibilities to particular institutions and political actors, and determine the rights and privileges of citizenship. State constitutions reflect states' distinctive political cultures and, in time, reinforce or alter those traditions.

Yet beyond this common core of shared functions, state constitutions vary greatly. Some protect and extend the rights of the individual beyond the guarantees of the U.S. Constitution; others do not. Perhaps the single biggest difference among state constitutions is the degree to which they serve as a venue for policymaking. In western states, whose constitutions provide for a high degree of direct democracy, advocates and interest groups often attempt to enshrine their policy positions in the state constitution. As a result, these states have long, detailed constitutions. In contrast, the constitutions of the eastern states, particularly in New England, more closely resemble the U.S. Constitution.

State constitutions tend to have a bad reputation with political scientists, for understandable reasons. While many function well, in more than a few instances, they play an outright disruptive role. In states like Alabama and Texas, antiquated state constitutions have made it difficult for state governments to promote economic development—a function that most people believe the state government should play. In California and other states, interest groups have used the constitution to ensure that the state's general revenues flow toward the programs they support. In the process, they have greatly reduced the ability of elected officials to make spending decisions on their own.

But as political scientist Christopher Hammonds has argued from another perspective, the fact that constitutions continue to be a contentious venue for politics in many states is not necessarily all bad. While it is still theoretically possible to change the U.S. Constitution, for all practical purposes, we as a society have given that right over to the U.S. Supreme Court. It takes an extraordinarily contentious issue, such as reproductive rights, to provoke talk about changing the federal constitution. In contrast, citizens continue to exercise their right to tamper with and tweak their state constitutions. Is that all bad?

Key Concepts

appropriations bills (p. 73)

ballot initiatives (p. 80)

bicameral legislatures (p. 75)

colonial charters (p. 73)

constitutional amendments (p. 69)

constitutional convention (p. 77)

constitutional revision commissions (p. 81)

direct democracy (p. 66)

dual constitutionalism (p. 69)

electorate (p. 67)

the franchise (p. 75)

home rule (p. 95)

Jim Crow laws (p. 77)

judicial federalism (p. 67)

judicial review (p. 83)

line-item veto (p. 89)

model constitution (p. 87)

municipal charter (p. 95)

natural law, or higher, law (p. 69)

ratification (p. 79)

Reconstruction (p. 83)

referendums (p. 80)

separation of powers (p. 74)

special districts (p. 95)

unicameral legislatures (p. 74)

Suggested Readings

Book of the States. Lexington, Ky.: Council of State Governments. The single best source of information on state constitutions. Updated yearly, it includes a chapter written by a leading researcher with the latest state constitution news.

Matsusaka, John. *For the Many or the Few: Initiative, Public Policy, and American Democracy.* Chicago: University of Chicago Press, 2004. Examines the effect of special interests on the initiative process.

Tarr, G. Alan. *Understanding State Constitutions.* Princeton, N.J.: Princeton University Press, 1998. Offers the most detailed look at state constitutions and avoids the tendency to view them as inferior versions of the federal constitution.

Suggested Web Sites

www-camlaw.rutgers.edu/statecon. Web site for Rutgers University Center for State Constitution Studies.

www.iandrinstitute.org Web site for the Initiative and Referendum Institute at the University of Southern California, a clearinghouse for information about the initiative and referendum processes of the states.

CHAPTER 4

Political Attitudes and Participation

Venting and Voting

Citizen participation is the key to getting government to be attentive to citizen interests. In democracies, government pays the most attention to citizens who get involved in the political process and make their views known. Citizens can exercise their right to get involved in many ways, but the most common is voting. Here, voters in Little Rock, Arkansas, wait to cast their ballots on the last day of early voting in October 2006.

4

Early Vote

Waiting Time Appx: 2 Hours

What causes some states or localities to change party preferences?

How do state regulations affect voting?

How do politicians tune into what citizens are thinking?

When it comes to party preferences—and we're not talking raves versus house parties, but Democratic or Republican—states aren't as monolithic as you may think. Although some states have historically supported Republican candidates and others have been more loyal to Democrats, these types of outcomes are in flux across the political landscape right now. This is despite the fact that, according to current popular culture, the political preferences of individual states are set in stone—or at least in their color palette choices.

Appearing on someone else's cable television show a month after the last presidential election, *Daily Show* host Jon Stewart had some thoughts about the way the political habits of American voters are classified. By 2004, the red state-blue state divide had become part of the mythos of the country, which Stewart thought was way too simplistic. "You know, I never thought there would be a way to reduce the nuanced differences between people in this country to something easier than Republican-Democrat, or liberal-conservative," Stewart said. "They've actually literally found a way to reduce it to just primary colors." [1]

The whole concept of states being either "red," meaning they tend to support Republicans, or "blue" (Democratic) is still relatively new. It used to be that TV networks mixed up the colors they used to show how states had voted, for instance, using red to indicate the incumbent party's states and blue for the other party's. Occasionally, one of them might even throw in a splash of yellow. In 1980, *Time* magazine called the mostly blue map that showed Republican Ronald Reagan's historic win "Lake Reagan." [2] One way or another, there was no great logical underpinning for the color scheme. But starting on election night in 2000, all the networks standardized their palettes.

That year's color coding stuck and became short-hand for all kinds of differences between states—not all of them political—in part because the 2000 election was so close and its outcome remained in dispute for weeks. Red states were not only more conservative, but they were said to have more churches and NASCAR fans, whereas residents of liberal blue states listened to NPR on their way to trying out the latest Thai restaurant. [3]

These demographic differences were more than skin deep. In December 2006, newly attained Democratic control of the U.S. Senate appeared at risk because of health problems suffered by Tim Johnson just after the election.

Johnson is a Democratic senator from the "red" state of South Dakota whose replacement would be named by the state's Republican governor. One medical reporter wrote, "It is no small irony that the political balance between red states and blue states . . . hangs at the junction of red and blue blood vessels in the brain of ailing Sen. Tim Johnson." [4]

But are states really so predictable politically that not only their voting patterns but their eating, movie-going, and procreating proclivities can be summed up according to a choice of one of two colors? It is true that only three states switched their presidential votes between 2000 and 2004, with New Mexico and Iowa turning red and New Hampshire going blue. Even when it comes to politics, however, states are a lot more complicated than the red-blue divide suggests.

For one thing, just because a state regularly votes one way for president does not mean its residents will stick with the president's party for other offices. Kansas has not backed a Democrat for president since 1964 nor sent a Democrat to the U.S. Senate since the 1930s, yet Democratic governor Kathleen Sebelius won reelection easily in 2006, carrying other Democrats into statewide and congressional offices. In fact, no fewer than fifteen states that had voted for President Bush in 2004 were home to Democratic governors following the 2006 elections, whereas six states that supported Democrat John Kerry for president had Republican governors. Although one party or the other tends to dominate the political landscape in many states—Republicans in Idaho and Utah, Democrats in Maryland and Hawaii—candidates today from either party are able to win any given office in just about every state.

State political cultures do evolve over time. In response to the growing influence of the South's conservative political culture on the Republican Party, many areas that were traditionally Republican, but were more moderate or liberal, have become fertile ground for Democrats. This is especially true in the northeastern part of the United States. Massachusetts now is considered one of the bluest of the blue states—the only state that allows gay couples to marry—and New England as a whole now has just one Republican member of Congress. But Massachusetts elected Republican governors in every election from 1990 until 2006, and heavily Democratic Vermont and Rhode Island continue to have Republican governors.

The truth is that at any given moment in time virtually all states are home to a mix of political voting habits. The coasts may be more liberal than the interior, but within each state there generally are marked differences between, for instance, rural areas and major cities. This split within states was perhaps most famously summed up by Democratic political consultant James Carville, who described Pennsylvania—considered to be a swing, or "battleground," state in presidential voting—as "Philadelphia on one end, Pittsburgh on the other, with Alabama in the middle." [5]

Political professionals recognize these differences. The biggest buzzword of the 2006 election cycle was "microtargeting." In the old days, candidates and parties targeted their messages according to precincts—groups of several hundred voters who showed a tendency over time to support one party or the other. Now technology and demographic breakdowns borrowed from commercial marketers, such as guessing voter preferences according to the types of magazines a person subscribes to, are used to microtarget individuals. The goal is to crack open each subdivision and make a good guess about which residents are liberal and which ones are conservative—even when the bulk of their neighbors vote in the opposite way. Rather than sending out six or seven pieces of mail to an entire state legislative or congressional district, a campaign now may send twenty different mailings directed at individuals who are part of five entirely different groups, such as veterans, seniors, or gun owners.

The reason for this, of course, is that if it is not safe to predict how people will vote based on where they live, it is probably a safer bet to predict their preferences based on the issues they care about and the interest groups they belong to. Interest groups, as discussed at greater length in Chapter 5, are organizations that attempt to influence policymakers. There are so-called single-issue interest groups, such as the National Rifle Association, which is concerned with gun owners' rights. There also are organizations that address a wider range of issues, such as the U.S. Chamber of Commerce, which cares about such issues as tax policy, business regulation, education, legal issues, and immigration. Although most people will rarely, if ever, call or write to members of Congress or state officials, many of them will belong to some group or other that makes a case for a particular position on an issue.

The squeakiest wheels get the grease, and interest groups can bring resources to a campaign in return for attention to their issues by candidates. But not everybody belongs to an interest group—or thinks of themselves as part of one—and politicians know that their careers depend on more than financial contributions from these organized interests. Come election time, they need the support of the vast majority of people who do not belong to such groups and who do not pay close attention to politics on a regular basis.

Given all of this, how do politicians figure out what the voters back home are thinking, when it seems that the only people they hear from at the capitol or city hall are part of some organized group? How can they pay attention to the needs and desires of the majority of constituents who do not speak out and do not subscribe to *TV Guide,* much less to their local paper?

This chapter answers those questions, and also looks at how voters maintain or change the political cultures and preferences of their states and districts over time. Some of the mechanisms for change discussed include elections and the avenues for direct democracy, such as ballot initiatives and referenda. Public opinion—and how and whether politicians respond—is another factor that influences political outcomes.

Elections

Unquestionably, we have created an odd paradox as a nation. We like elections—we hold more of them than any other country on earth—yet we consistently score one of the lowest voter turnout rates of any democracy in the world.

State political cultures are reflected and sustained through elections, when a majority, or **plurality**, of voters elects officials who more or less reflect that majority's political beliefs. Elections for public office are the fundamental process of representative democracies. More bluntly, they are the main way that the will of the people connects to and influences the actions of government. Each state must determine what constitutes a valid vote. Election laws are set and controlled by the states. There is much variation between them as to how easy or how hard it is for citizens to vote. Some of those differences have been smoothed away in recent years by federal laws and court decisions. Differences do remain, however, and they are largely reflective of the types of political cultures that Elazar described and that were outlined in previous chapters.

These differences, in turn, affect national politics. The way that people vote in their own state—the type of access that they have to the ballot—helps determine the success or failure of presidential candidates and the makeup of Congress. For about one hundred years after the Civil War, for example, Republicans were not a true national party. They had next to no presence in the South, which still resented Republican intrusions during the Civil War and Reconstruction in support of abolition, suffrage, and equal opportunity for African Americans. That is one reason Democrats held the region for decades. In fact, the Republican Party of the nineteenth century bore a closer resemblance in some ways to the Democratic Party of today than to its twenty-first-century Grand Old Party descendant. Times and political parties change, however. These days, the South is one of the pillars of Republican strength. The region's continuing conservatism now fits well within the GOP.

Southern states and the less populous, rural states in the Mountain West tilt toward Republican interests and form a bloc that helps elect presidents through its disproportionate share of the electoral college. Each state's electoral college votes are equal to the size of its congressional delegation. As each state is guaranteed at least two U.S. senators and one U.S. representative, the electoral college gives a minimum of three votes to each state, regardless of population. This means that the voting power of smaller states in the electoral college is disproportionately larger than their population, whereas the voting power of bigger states is disproportionately lower.

For example, in 2004, California had fifty-five electoral votes to represent a population of roughly thirty-four million. In that presidential election, then, each of California's electoral college votes represented about

PLURALITY

The highest number of votes garnered by a candidate for a particular office but short of an outright majority.

FIGURE 4-1 How It Works: Elections Procedures in Oregon, 2006

Think voting is complicated? Try running an election. In Oregon, as elsewhere, these are complicated affairs, requiring hundreds of pages of rules and regulations—305 pages, to be exact—designed to ensure fairness and preserve democratic processes. Oregon's 2005–2006 "Election Laws" codebook covers everything from voter registration to recall procedures. And that's just the start. There's a good chance that in the run up to the 2006 elections, every major party candidate for state office in Oregon reluctantly cracked open the 41-page candidate's manual, which detailed the hoops and hurdles facing them and no doubt whetted their appetite for the 184-page campaign finance manual. Anyone interested in sponsoring an initiative or referendum got a 69-page primer. Voters themselves were treated to a 2-volume, nearly 200-page voter's pamphlet. This timeline reveals only a fraction of the process leading up to election day.

Anytime prior to election	**Prospective initiative or referendum petition may be filed.** Petitioners are urged to leave ample time to draft the initiative, gather signatures, face possible appeals, and receive certification. Deadlines for each part of the process depend upon the date upon which the prospective initiative was first filed. Signatures for referendum petitions must be filed for verification no later than the ninetieth day after the legislature adjourns.
September 8, 2005	**Deadline by which prospective candidates for state office must have registered** to vote as a member of the party they plan to represent.
March 7, 2006	**Candidate filing deadline.** Candidates may file to run for office either by declaration or by nomination. Most candidates for state office form a candidate committee by opening a campaign account and filing a Statement of Organization for Candidate Committee (SEL 220) and Campaign Account Information form (SEL 223) with the Elections Division.
	Candidates filing by nomination for statewide office must gather signatures from active registered voters in at least seven counties. Signatures must be from at least 5 percent of the precincts from each of these counties.
March 9	**Voter's pamphlet filing deadline for the primary election.** Candidates submit material for inclusion in the voter's pamphlet. Required documents include: three copies of the Candidate's Statement for State Voters' Pamphlet, a Statement of Endorsement, a list of phone and fax numbers for contacts, the filing fee, and two identical 5 x 7 black and white photos.
March 10	**Deadline for withdrawing a candidacy or nomination.** Second thoughts? The deadline is 5 p.m.
March 20	**Corrections on an insufficient Voter's Pamphlet filing due.**
March 31–May 12	**Campaign contribution and expense reports.** Candidates receiving more than $2,000 in contributions before the primary election must file contribution and expenditure reports. The first report is due no later than March 31, and all subsequent filings, including supplements, must be filed no later than May 12.
April 1	**Ballots mailed to long-term absent voters (overseas and military).**
April 17	**Ballots mailed to out-of-state voters.** Qualified absentee voters include those absent on business, senior citizens, disabled persons, those prevented by employment from registering, out of state and out of precinct residents, those absent for religious reasons, students, and those temporarily out of jurisdiction.
April 19–21	**Voters' pamphlets are mailed.**
April 25	**Voter registration deadline for the primary elections.**
April 28–May 2	**Ballots mailed to voters, other than long-term and out-of-state.** Oregon voters are allowed to vote by mail. Ballots are due by 8 p.m. on election day.
May 16, 2006	**Primary election held.**

Governing States and Localities

FIGURE 4-1, continued

June 5, 2006	County Elections Officials deliver abstract of votes for the primary election.
June 15	Elections Division must complete primary post-elections procedures and by which candidates must have filed post-elections campaign contributions and expenses reports.
July 7	Signatures for ballot measures and amendments due. Statutory measures require 75,630 valid signatures, and constitutional amendments require 100,840.
August 29	Candidate filing deadline for the general election.
August 29	Voters' pamphlet filing deadline for the general election.
September 1	Deadline for withdrawing a candidacy or nomination.
September 7	Elections division certifies the state measures to be voted on to each county elections official for placement on the official ballot by this date.
September 8	Deadline to provide corrections on an insufficient Voter's Pamphlet filing.
September 23	Ballots mailed to long-term absent voters (overseas and military)
October 2– November 3	Campaign contribution and expense reports for the general election must be filed between these dates.
October 9	Ballots mailed to out-of-state voters
October 17	Voter registration deadline (21 days before election) for the general election.
October 20–24	Ballots mailed to voters other than long-term and out-of-state voters
November 7	General election held. Oregon does its voting by mail. Other states open their doors as early as 6 a.m. and some close as late as 9 p.m.
November 27	Deadline for county elections officials to deliver abstract of votes for the general election.
December 7	Deadline by which the Elections Division must complete post-elections procedures and by which candidates must file post-election campaign contribution and expense reports.
January 5	Last date to file supplements to the post-election campaign contribution and expense reports.

618,000 people. Contrast that to Wyoming, which had the minimum of three electoral college votes, but only had a population of about 495,000. Each of Wyoming's electoral college votes, in other words, represented about 165,000 people. Political analyst Steven Hill, director of the political reform program at the New America Foundation, calls this "affirmative action for low-population states."[6] This is one reason why George W. Bush could win the presidency in 2000 despite losing the popular vote.

The Mountain West also may be shifting. The region retains its traditional libertarian response to government in that it wants to be left alone by a federal government that owns the vast majority of the land in many western states. However, some libertarian-leaning westerners have been put off by the national Republican Party's intrusion into private matters, such as the attempt in 2005 to keep Terri Schiavo, a brain-damaged Florida woman, on life support against her husband's wishes. This resistance to government intervention in private affairs has given Democrats an opportunity to capitalize on social issues that Republicans frequently have championed. There were no Democratic governors in eight western states in 2002, today there are five. Colorado, which was long dominated by Republicans, now has both a Democratic governor and legislature. How these states will vote for president in 2008, along with the upper Midwest states that remain up for grabs, most likely will determine that election's outcome.

Elections may be how citizens can speak out for their beliefs, and they may give states a voice in national politics, but you wouldn't know it from the interest they generate in the general public. The franchise appears to be a diminished thing, with the act of voting on the decline. People do not feel well connected to government. Some hate it. Fewer than half of the voting age population cast ballots in presidential elections. In elections in which congressional or statewide offices are at the top of the ticket, the percentage drops to less than 40 percent. For municipal elections, turnout rates are generally less than 20 percent.

Voting does tend to pick up for competitive races—when voters feel like they have a genuine choice and might make a real difference. The major political parties, however, have reconciled themselves to the reality that millions of people feel their vote does not count. (Sometimes they are even accused of suppressing turnout and using negative ads and other means to sour people who might vote for the other side.) Turnout rates are particularly abysmal for traditional college students and other young people. In an online chat in 2003, political analyst Stuart Rothenberg wrote,

> All non-voters are irrelevant and unimportant, and I am skeptical about efforts by the right, left, or radical center to motivate large numbers of non-voters. It seems that every election we talk about bringing new people into the system, but the 2004 contest is likely to be about which party motivates its base and sways swing voters.[7]

That attitude was the prevailing wisdom for several years. It was the doctrine of Karl Rove, President Bush's lead political adviser. Upset that an estimated four million evangelical Christians did not vote in 2000, Rove designed a reelection campaign that would motivate these voters through use of such issues as limitations on stem-cell research and bans on gay marriage. Other issues would be used to appeal to other blocs of voters, but Bush's reelection campaign was designed primarily to motivate his "base" voters rather than reach across the political spectrum to appeal more broadly. The strategy worked, at least in the short run.

The idea that voters are most easily motivated by appealing to a few core issues also has promoted the growing use of ballot initiatives as a means of promoting turnout. For instance, Ohio's vote in favor of a constitutional ban on gay marriage in 2004 is said to have helped turn out conservatives who in turn helped Bush carry that year's most contested state. Two years later, liberals, looking for weapons of their own, ran minimum wage increases on half a dozen state ballots. Some political scientists have found evidence that controversial ballot initiatives do increase turnout, particularly in nonpresidential election years.[8]

But the idea that most voters are motivated by a single issue, or a handful of issues, oversimplifies things in much the same way as the red-state, blue-state divide flattens our perception of actual electoral behavior. It is true that the majority of voters remain loyal to one party or the other throughout most of their voting lives. They can be convinced to cast votes—or even convinced to change their votes—by any number of factors. The state of the economy or the health of a state's budget, or corruption scandals or the course of a military conflict may change minds and voting habits. "Each election forces one to revisit such topics as to what's effective in voter mobilization or who you aim at," says independent political analyst Rhodes Cook. "White evangelicals and moral values were the story after 2004, while independents and moderates seem to be the story of 2006."[9]

State Supervision of Elections

It seems obvious, but elections are fundamental to democracy. They are the source of authority for governmental decisions and power. On these occasions a majority of eligible citizens presumably give their blessing to office-holders who will determine the course of policy. Elections are the main conduit for citizens to express their pleasure or displeasure with governmental decisions. If voters are unhappy with the decisions their elected officials have made, they can turn them out of office during the next election. For all the system's faults, politicians and parties have to win approval from voters at regularly scheduled intervals if they are to remain in power.

The U.S. Constitution gives states the authority to determine "the times, places and manner of holding elections." In nearly every state, the secretary of state has the practical duty of running elections—setting dates, qualifying candidates, and printing and counting ballots. In a few states, the lieutenant governor or a state election board may oversee these chores. The states, in turn, rely on counties or, in some cases, cities to run the polls themselves. The localities draw precinct boundaries and set up and supervise polling places. In many cases they have the main responsibility for registering voters. Following the election, county officials count up the ballots and report the results to the appropriate individual, such as the secretary of state, who then tabulates and certifies the totals.

The style of ballots varies. California currently uses a random alphabet system to decide the order in which candidate names will appear and rotates the starting letter of that alphabet in each state assembly district. The **office group ballot**, also known as the **Massachusetts ballot**, lists candidates' names, followed by their party designation, under the title of the office they are seeking (governor, state representative, etc.). The other major type of ballot is called the **party column ballot**, or the **Indiana ballot**, which

OFFICE GROUP (MASSACHUSETTS) BALLOT

Ballots in which candidates are listed by name under the title of the office they are seeking.

PARTY COLUMN (INDIANA) BALLOT

Ballots in which the names of candidates are divided into columns arranged according to political party.

Policy in Practice: Automation Frustration: Electronic Voting Still Has Some Bugs

Fifty-five freshman members were sworn into the U.S. House in 2007. All but thirteen were Democrats. The fact that one particular Republican had won a seat, however, was controversial. Vern Buchanan claimed Florida's 13th District seat with a margin of just 369 votes, while more than 18,000 votes had gone missing, meaning voters had made selections for lower-ballot races, but not for Congress. Most of the missing votes were in the most Democratic county in Buchanan's congressional district. But rather than any fraud or cheating, the botched vote appeared to have been a case of simple mechanical error.

That's how it's gone with electronic voting machines. For all the horror stories about how hackers can break into them and change results, the real problems have been caused through plain old error. In the few years since many states and counties began adopting ATM-style voting machines—prodded by the federal Help America Vote Act (HAVA) of 2002—most of the problems have been caused through ordinary machine error or human error.

There's been plenty of human error. During elections in 2006, voters in major cities such as Denver, Cleveland, Chicago, and Baltimore experienced long delays or other problems simply because poll workers hadn't been instructed properly on how to operate the machinery. "You're dealing with a population of poll workers that is fairly stagnant, that is aging, that is generally not familiar with the latest and greatest in technology," says Dan Seligson, editor of Electionline.org.

Lawrence Norden, a voting expert at New York University's Brennan Center, says that many of the problems have resulted from the fact that governments switched so rapidly to electronic voting systems. Since the kinks are still being worked out, numerous states, and the federal commission that advises them on voting rules, are leaning toward requiring some form of paper printout of votes, so that recounts are more feasible in situations such as the Florida 13th race.

There was some irony to the fact, after all, that Buchanan had succeeded Katherine Harris, who had

Many states and localities have shifted to high-tech, electronic voting machines in the past few election cycles. The results have been mixed, and some criticize the machines for being overly vulnerable to hackers. The machines also suffer from some very low-tech drawbacks. Here a touch-screen ballot machine is temporarily out of service in a very busy polling place . . . because it ran out of paper.

presided over Florida's controversial presidential voting in 2000 as the state's chief election officer. It was the myriad problems with thousands of paper ballots—in a race that George W. Bush won by just 537 votes after the U.S. Supreme Court put an end to the lengthy recount process—that triggered the mass move to electronic voting in the first place.

Although the new systems have problems, Norden points out that there are some upsides. There is less doubt about voter intent—who they meant to vote for—than there had been with paper ballots that were not properly "punched." Votes now are also easier to count than in the old days. "Electronic voting machines are an improvement over the old punch cards and lever machines, primarily because they're easier to use," says David Kimball, a political scientist at the University of Missouri–St. Louis.

But, he adds, "One of the unfortunate things is that there was this rush among some states and local governments to quickly switch to a new voting system without maybe carefully considering what that new system was and how it worked and what the potential problems might be."

Source: Original piece reported and written for this text by Alan Greenblatt.

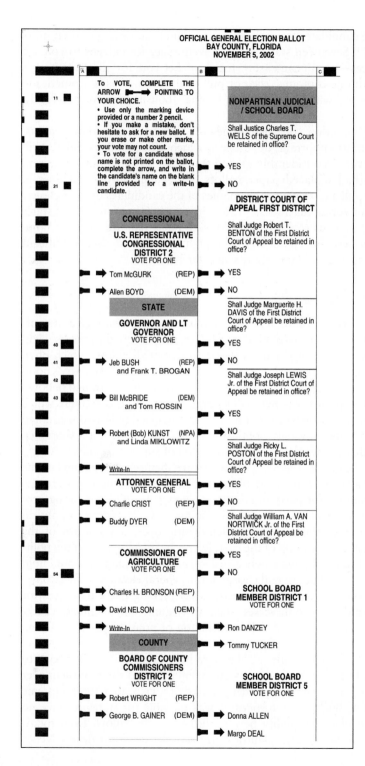

OFFICIAL BALLOT, GENERAL ELECTION
BARBOUR COUNTY, WEST VIRGINIA
NOVEMBER 5, 2002

REPUBLICAN TICKET	DEMOCRATIC TICKET	MOUNTAIN TICKET

STRAIGHT TICKET VOTERS: "IF YOU MARKED A STRAIGHT TICKET: When you mark for an individual candidate in a different party, that vote will override your straight party vote for that office."

NATIONAL TICKET	NATIONAL TICKET	NATIONAL TICKET
FOR U.S. SENATOR (Vote For ONE)	FOR U.S. SENATOR (Vote For ONE)	FOR U.S. SENATOR (Vote For ONE)
JAY WOLFE Salem Harrison Co.	JAY ROCKEFELLER Charleston Kanawha Co.	
FOR U.S. HOUSE OF REPRESENTATIVES 1st Congressional District (Vote For ONE)	FOR U.S. HOUSE OF REPRESENTATIVES 1st Congressional District (Vote For ONE)	FOR U.S. HOUSE OF REPRESENTATIVES 1st Congressional District (Vote For ONE)
	ALAN B. MOLLOHAN Fairmont	

STATE TICKET	STATE TICKET	STATE TICKET
FOR STATE SENATOR 14th Senatorial District (Vote For ONE)	FOR STATE SENATOR 14th Senatorial District (Vote For ONE)	FOR STATE SENATOR 14th Senatorial District (Vote For ONE)
SARAH M. MINEAR Davis Tucker Co.	JAMES A. HAUGHMAN Philippi Barbour Co.	
FOR MEMBER OF HOUSE OF DELEGATES 40th Delegate District (Vote For ONE)	FOR MEMBER OF HOUSE OF DELEGATES 40th Delegate District (Vote For ONE)	FOR MEMBER OF HOUSE OF DELEGATES 40th Delegate District (Vote For ONE)
LONNIE L. MOORE, SR. Belington Barbour Co.	MARY M. POLING Moatsville Barbour Co.	
FOR FAMILY COURT JUDGE 21st Family Court Circuit (Vote For ONE)	FOR FAMILY COURT JUDGE 21st Family Court Circuit (Vote For ONE)	FOR FAMILY COURT JUDGE 21st Family Court Circuit (Vote For ONE)
	BETH LONG Barbour Co.	

COUNTY TICKET	COUNTY TICKET	COUNTY TICKET
FOR COUNTY COMMISSIONER (Vote For ONE) Not more than one resident of any magisterial district may be elected	FOR COUNTY COMMISSIONER (Vote For ONE) Not more than one resident of any magisterial district may be elected	FOR COUNTY COMMISSIONER (Vote For ONE) Not more than one resident of any magisterial district may be elected
TIM McDANIEL Philippi North Dist.	GERALD (Bucky) GAYNOR Philippi North Dist.	

BALLOT OF CONSTITUTIONAL AMENDMENTS

AMENDMENT #1 – "COUNTY AND MUNICIPAL OPTION ECONOMIC DEVELOPMENT AMENDMENT"

"To amend the State Constitution to permit the Legislature by general law to authorize county commissions and municipalities to use a new economic development tool to help create jobs. This tool will permit county commissions and municipalities to assist in financing economic development or redevelopment projects by redirecting specific new property tax revenues from an approved project to assist and districted. These redirected revenues will be used to pay-off revenue bonds or other obligations issued to finance some or all of the cost of the project. This amendment authorizes the financing of some or all of the cost of qualified economic development and redevelopment projects through issuance of county and municipal revenue bonds or other obligations, payable from property taxes assessed on the enhanced value of property located in the economic development or redevelopment project area or district. This proposed amendment does not apply to taxes from excess levies, bond levies or other county levies. Upon payment-in-full of the bonds or other obligations, the property tax revenues revert to the appropriate ... during the term of the bonds or other obligations may not exceed thirty years."

☐ FOR THE AMENDMENT

☐ AGAINST THE AMENDMENT

AMENDMENT #2 – "EQUALIZING NUMBER OF YEARS OF EXCESS LEVIES AMENDMENT"

"The purpose of this amendment is to allow county and municipal governments to propose excess levies for the same time periods as board of education, which is up to five years."

☐ FOR THE AMENDMENT

☐ AGAINST THE AMENDMENT

The two main types of ballots are the office group ballot and the party column ballot. These sample ballots from elections in Florida and West Virginia show the differences between the two basic approaches to ballot design. The West Virginia ballot exemplifies the party column ballot, which lists the candidates in columns that indicate their party designation. The Florida ballot, on the other hand, emphasizes office rather than party. This is the key feature of the office group ballot, which lists candidates by name and party under the title of the office they are running for.

"arranges the candidates for each office in columns according to their party designation." [10] Seventeen states make it even easier for citizens to vote for party nominees—voters can cast a **straight ticket** vote for all of the party's nominees with one computer click or pull of the lever. This is a practice in decline, however, with several states having abolished it—most recently, Missouri, in 2006. [11]

Each state's election code determines the specific details about ballots, and perhaps most important, the order in which offices and candidates will appear. This varies considerably among states. By 1992, about 80 percent of the states had replaced paper ballots with punch cards, machines in which voters pull a lever next to the names of the candidates of their choice, or optical scan voting machines. [12] Voters in an increasing number of states use electronic systems resembling ATMs. All but a handful of states tabulate votes for write-in candidates, although victories or even significant showings by such candidates are few and far between.

Regulating the Parties

A state's authority to print ballots or purchase voting software gives it enormous control over what parties and candidates get presented to voters. Until the late nineteenth century, parties themselves printed ballots, which obviously encouraged voters to select a straight ticket of their chosen party's nominees. The advent of the **secret ballot**—also known as the **Australian ballot**—led the states to print their own ballots and, therefore, to determine which parties should appear on ballots. "From there," writes Kay Lawson, a retired San Francisco State University political scientist, "it seemed but a short step to requiring that parties show a minimum level of support to qualify." [13]

The Republican and Democratic parties are themselves regulated at the state level by a bewildering array of varying state laws. Some states provide detailed regulations for party organization, activities, and nominating procedures. Others are silent on many specific matters. According to political scientist V. O. Key, the traditional Democratic one-party control of the South, although now a thing of the past, led to the introduction of the political primary. Primaries gave voters a real say in who ultimately would hold an office, since they had no real choice in the general election. [14] These days, nearly every state holds primary elections for picking party nominees for state offices, although some states, such as Virginia, still nominate candidates at party conventions. A fuller discussion of political parties is found in Chapter 5.

Major parties may not like all the state ballot regulations they have to comply with, but the rules in many states seem designed to favor them over new or minor parties and independent candidates. Prior to a 1968 Supreme Court decision, *Williams v. Rhodes,* it was possible for states to have no mechanism in place to qualify new parties for their ballots. Even today, according to Richard Winger, editor of the newsletter *Ballot Access News,* new parties in eleven states cannot qualify for the ballot before they have picked their candidates, who must be listed on their ballot access petition— the collection of voters' signatures.[15]

The Court's decision meant that a state no longer could require a certain percentage of signatures be collected in each county. But that did not mean states could not erect new roadblocks to keep out aspiring parties or candidates. Nine states changed their laws to require signatures be collected in each congressional district. This kept ballot access elusive for candidates or parties who had most of their support in a particular city or region. Fifteen states also placed time constraints on when signatures can be collected— California and Ohio require new parties to qualify even before the election year begins. Virginia blocks petitioners from gathering signatures outside of their home congressional district. In Texas, voters who participated in major party primaries are not allowed to sign a petition to get a new party on the ballot. The state also requires citizens to know and affix their voter registration numbers next to their signatures on petitions. Similarly, Alabama, Arkansas, New York, and Virginia require signers to supply their precinct numbers. Quick—what's your precinct number?

In a 1971 decision, *Jenness v. Fortson*, the Supreme Court upheld a Georgia law that requires minor parties or independent candidates to collect signatures that represent 5 percent of the total number of votes cast in the last election for the office. Independent or minor party candidates for governor in 2006 had to accrue 101,295 signatures to qualify for the gubernatorial ballot. That is a lot of signatures for a new political player, and it is more than double the amount of votes the one minor party candidate for the office received in 2002. Not surprisingly, no new minor party or independent candidate has qualified for the ballot in Georgia since 1964.[16]

The Supreme Court ruling emboldened several other states to erect strict barriers against access to the ballot. States such as Alabama, North Carolina, Oklahoma, and West Virginia have the most difficult requirements for parties and candidates to get around. In West Virginia, for instance, the law requires circulators who are trying to collect signatures to tell everyone they approach, "If you sign my petition, you can't vote in the primary." That happens to not be true—but it is the law. Why make a law requiring circulators to fib to voters? Well, the fib benefits the major parties by keeping out the competition, and the major parties write the laws.

For third parties and independent candidates, it can be a real challenge to gain access to the ballots on any of the states discussed here. Given what we know about Elazar's theory about southern, or traditionalistic, states, and their hierarchical attitude toward politics, it should not surprise us that these states have the most restrictive ballot access laws. That does not mean that hundreds of minor party and independent candidates have not overcome all these hurdles and more to win spots on statewide ballots. A couple of them have even won election as governor—for instance, in Minnesota in 1998 and Maine in 1994 and 1998. Their place on a ballot one year, however, is no guarantee that members of their parties will qualify the next time around. Alabama requires that a minor party poll at least 20 percent of the vote for governor in order to win automatic qualification for the next ballot. Half a dozen other states require at least 10 percent. Given all the restrictions, Lawson concludes, "The laws have been effective in keeping minor parties off the ballot in election after election." [17]

Why all the restrictions? Keeping minor parties off the ballot naturally helps the two major parties. Those who are in power control the rules that keep them in power. In Georgia, bills to loosen the state's restrictions have been introduced at least seven times over the last twenty years. They have always failed.

Restricting Voters

States do not just regulate the access of parties to the ballot. They also regulate the interaction of citizens with that ballot. They determine who can register to vote and how they can register. Changes in federal law over the years have removed many of the initial barriers states had imposed that restricted voting rights based on property ownership, literacy, race, sex, and age. But there are still differences among states in terms of how easy they make it for citizens to register—a necessary step toward having the chance to vote in every state except North Dakota, which does not require voter registration.

In the early years of the nation, most eastern states required citizens to own property in order to vote. Those requirements diminished over time, in large part because the western frontier states lacked the type of class structure that reinforced them. The eastern states, however, soon came up with the idea of imposing literacy tests. New immigrants had to demonstrate knowledge of the state constitution or other complex issues to the satisfaction of the local election official.[18] Native whites who were illiterate often were exempted from this requirement. Southern states took up literacy testing as a means of keeping African Americans from voting, since they generally received inadequate educations in schools segregated by race. Literacy tests remained a part of the southern legal landscape until the federal Voting Rights Act of 1965 barred them. (See box on page 114.)

Several amendments to the U.S. Constitution expanded voting rights to include minorities and women. The Fifteenth Amendment was passed following the Civil War and was meant to end discrimination against black men seeking to vote. Until the civil rights movement of the 1960s, however, it was effectively bypassed for a century through literacy tests, intimidation, and other means. The Voting Rights Act of 1965 gave the federal government authority to review state requirements for registration and voting. In 1964, the Twenty-Fourth Amendment banned the use of poll taxes meant to keep blacks and other poor people from voting. Women received the right to vote with the ratification of the Nineteenth Amendment in 1920. The voting age was lowered to eighteen by the Twenty-Sixth Amendment in

1971. In 1993, Congress passed a law known as "motor voter" registration, which requires states to allow citizens to register to vote when they take tests to receive their driver's licenses.

Why all of the effort to get people registered to vote? The purpose of registering voters is to prevent fraud. It prevents people from voting more than once or outside of their home jurisdictions. This makes sense, but throughout the nation's history, many states have used registration laws as a means of making voting inaccessible to some.

About 19 percent of the total number of registered voters in Minnesota—590,242— registered to vote on election day in 2004. Minnesota is one of just six states to allow same-day registration.

Voter Turnout

It has never been easier to register and to vote, yet fewer and fewer people are actually doing either. Motor voter produced an initial spike in registration, but had little or no effect on the numbers of people voting. According to Curtis Gans of the Committee for the Study of the American Electorate, **voter turnout** rates have declined by about 25 percent over the last forty years.[19] Turnout did spike for the hotly contested 2004 presidential race, but dropped again in 2006. There are countless reasons why voter turnout has declined, including a general disaffection with politics and government, a measurable decline in civic education and newspaper reading, a weakening of such civic-minded institutions as student government and unions, and the changing role of political parties away from engaging and educating voters and toward raising money and providing services to candidates.

Turnout rates are in decline, but they are not declining uniformly across the states. There are many reasons why some states have turnout rates 20 percentage points higher than others, but most of these differences are explained by political culture, demographics, and party competition. The variations in voter registration laws have relatively little effect at this point.

In general, the closer you live to Canada, the more likely you are to vote. The states with the turnout rates of more than 70 percent for the 2004 presidential election, including New Hampshire, North Dakota, and Wisconsin, are all in the northern tier of the country. The states with lower turnout rates, including Arkansas, Hawaii, Nevada, and Tennessee, are in the South or far West. (See Table 4-1.) What explains the difference? Culture, for one thing. Elazar's theory about moralistic states appears to hold up, at least as far as voter turnout goes. "You're talking about states with fairly vigorous political parties, communications media that do cover politics and an educational system more geared toward citizen engagement than other parts of the country," says Gans. A big state like California has a mix of cultures—individualistic and moralistic—according to Elazar.

The moralistic states also tend to be homogenous in terms of demographics. People are more likely to vote if they are better educated, if they are elderly, and if they are white. "In states with high percentage of minorities, you're going to have low turnout," says Steven Hill of the New Ameri-

The percentage of eligible citizens who register to vote and do vote.

A Difference that Makes a Difference: How Some States Discourage Voters

Thirty years ago, a political scientist named Robert H. Blank came up with a formula for ranking states according to how easy they made it for their citizens to vote. He came up with fifteen different criteria, including whether they allowed people to vote by absentee ballot for any reason (which was true of thirty-six states); whether they kept polls open for a uniform twelve hours across the state (twenty-nine states); whether they allowed people to register to vote within one month of an election (thirty-five states); and whether they required people to establish residency in the state for more than a year before they could register to vote (twelve states).[a]

According to Blank's scale, traditionalistic states, such as Alabama, Arkansas, and Mississippi, made it hardest for people to vote. These states typically tried to maintain a hierarchical political structure in which white, non-elite citizens—and all African Americans—were discouraged from playing an active role. Obviously, attempting to disenfranchise people (keep them from voting) was the most blatant way possible to limit access to political decision making. Conversely, the states that did the most to make it easier to register and to vote, such as Idaho, Michigan, and Minnesota, were moralistic states that encouraged political participation among the widest number of people possible. Raymond E. Wolfinger and Steven J. Rosenstone found that voting participation was highest in individualistic states in which government is seen as a marketplace for advancing self-interest among people who have direct interest access to government jobs and contracts.[b]

Since Blank's survey, many of the differences in voting and registration laws among the states have been done away with because of federal intervention. A federal court ruled in 1972 that states could not cut off registration any sooner than thirty days before an election. This effectively eliminated longer state residency requirements. In 1995 the federal government adopted a "motor voter" law, based on a

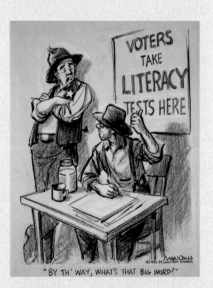

"BY TH' WAY, WHAT'S THAT BIG WORD?"

Although once a common voting requirement, literacy tests always flunked Democracy 101. States that required literacy standards used them mainly as a way to disenfranchise minorities. Whites, literate or not, were often exempt, and the standards were unevenly applied. The white male test taker in this cartoon has a much higher chance of passing the test than a minority even though he obviously is not qualified. In addition to literacy tests, voters were required to complete lengthy registration forms, like the four-page example seen here from 1950s

law pioneered in Michigan, to allow citizens to fill out a registration form whenever they applied for a driver's license. Previously, some states had restricted registration so that prospective voters had to show up at a county registrar's office during limited business hours.

There are still differences among the states, though. North Dakota does not require voters to register at all, while some states, including Minnesota, allow voters to register to vote on election day itself. Since 1998, Oregon has conducted all of its elections exclusively by mail, which means that citizens do not need to leave their homes to vote and do not have to vote on one specific day. No question, the states that make it easier for their citizens to vote tend to have the highest voter turnout.

Given the many changes in election laws in recent decades, however, the difference in turnout rates has become less pronounced. Voting in southern states still lags behind the rest of the country, but by a much smaller amount than in the days of poll taxes and literacy tests. And some of the reforms have not made that much difference. Motor voting produced a surge in registration of about five percentage points during the first two years of its operation, but did not lead to higher voter turnout rates in subsequent elections.

States that make registration harder do discourage voters—but then, their entire political cultures are based on limiting participation. The reverse is true of states with high voter turnouts. Differences in registration laws do not explain their higher levels of political participation as well as their generally inclusive cultures. People tend to vote when they are given a choice—when they think their vote matters. This is why more people vote in states that have healthy competition between the major parties, rather than being dominated by just one of them. Other factors explain voting turnout rates as well. People who are better educated, have higher incomes, are white, or are older vote more than people who are young, poor, poorly educated, or members or minority groups.

[a] Robert H. Blank, "State Electoral Structure," *Journal of Politics* 35, no. 4 (November 1993): 988–994.

[b] Raymond E. Wolfinger and Steven J. Rosenstone, *Who Votes?* (New Haven, Conn.: Yale University Press, 1980).

Alabama. These forms asked such questions as, "Give names and addresses of two persons who know you and can verify the statements made above by you relative to your residence in this state, county, and precinct, ward or district." and "Are you a college student? If so, where?" Compare that to the simple one-page Alabama voter registration form of today. The form can be printed out, completed, folded, and mailed like a postcard.

TABLE 4-1

Percentage of the Voting Age Population Casting Ballots in the 2004 Presidential Election

Rank	State	Percentage of Total Voting Age Population	Elazar Classification	Rank	State	Percentage of Total Voting Age Population	Elazar Classification
1	Minnesota	76.7	Moralistic	25	Nebraska	61.3	Individualistic
2	Wisconsin	73.0	Moralistic	26	Illinois	61.0	Individualistic
3	Maine	72.0	Moralistic	27	New Mexico	60.9	Traditionalistic
4	North Dakota	70.8	Moralistic	28	Mississippi	60.7	Traditionalistic
5	Oregon	70.6	Moralistic	29	Kansas	59.7	Moralistic
6	Montana	69.9	Moralistic	29	Maryland	59.7	Individualistic
7	New Hampshire	68.9	Moralistic	30	Oklahoma	59.2	Traditionalistic
8	Iowa	68.8	Moralistic	31	Idaho	58.7	Moralistic
9	South Dakota	67.0	Moralistic	32	Connecticut	58.5	Individualistic
10	Missouri	66.3	Individualistic	33	Virginia	58.4	Traditionalistic
11	Wyoming	66.2	Individualistic	34	North Carolina	58.2	Traditionalistic
12	Vermont	65.6	Moralistic	35	New Jersey	57.6	Individualistic
13	Alaska	65.0	Individualistic	36	Rhode Island	57.4	Individualistic
14	Ohio	64.8	Individualistic	37	Indiana	57.3	Individualistic
15	Michigan	64.7	Moralistic	38	West Virginia	57.2	Traditionalistic
16	Massachusetts	63.7	Individualistic	39	Arkansas	56.7	Traditionalistic
17	Kentucky	63.4	Traditionalistic	40	Florida	56.1	Traditionalistic
18	Louisiana	63.1	Traditionalistic	41	Arizona	54.3	Traditionalistic
19	Delaware	62.9	Individualistic	42	New York	53.1	Individualistic
20	Utah	62.7	Moralistic	43	Tennessee	52.7	Traditionalistic
21	Pennsylvania	62.5	Individualistic	44	Georgia	52.6	Traditionalistic
22	South Carolina	62.0	Traditionalistic	45	Nevada	51.3	Individualistic
22	Washington	62.0	Moralistic	46	Texas	50.3	Traditionalistic
23	Alabama	61.8	Traditionalistic	47	California	49.1	Individualistic
24	Colorado	61.7	Moralistic	48	Hawaii	46.2	Individualistic

Source: U.S. Census Bureau, Table 406, "Persons Reported Registered and Voted, by State: 2000 to 2004," *Statistical Abstract,* 2007. www.census.gov/compendia/statab/tables/07s0406.xls (accessed January 16, 2007).

ca Foundation. "States with higher voter turnout, such as Minnesota and Maine, tend to be fairly white states." [20] The moralistic states historically also have bred strong two-party competition. This tends to increase turnout. Citizens in states or districts dominated by one party or the other tend not to vote as eagerly. Their candidate of choice is certain to win—or to lose—if they are "orphaned" voters whose party is weak in their home state.

Voter turnout rates actually have increased in the South, where many of the historical impediments against registration and voting have declined. There also is more competition between the major parties than has been the case for more than one hundred years. But the region has merely stabilized at a slightly lower turnout rate than the rest of the country. Its high proportion of African Americans and its historical legacy of suppressing their votes and the votes of some whites keep its turnout rates sluggish even though African Americans do tend to vote more than other minorities, such as Hispanics.

Hispanics have long been considered the "sleeping giant" of American politics because of their failure to vote in numbers commensurate with their share of the population. They cast just 6 percent of the ballots in the United States in 2004, barely half as many as blacks, even though they comprise a larger share of the national population. The standard explanation is that this group simply lacks the well-established political organizations needed to encourage registration and turnout. But other factors are involved as well. Once you subtract noncitizens, the percentage of voting age Hispanics who went to the polls in 2004 was just less than 50 percent—less than for blacks and non-Hispanic whites but by a relatively small margin. Ruy Teixeira, a Democratic polling expert, says, "People who look at the overall size of the Hispanic population and look at the vote think, 'Oh my God, what if these people ever get mobilized?' ... But so many of these people can't vote anyway." [21]

Then there's age. The median age of Hispanics in the U.S. is just twenty-seven, compared with thirty-nine for non-Hispanic whites. A much higher percentage of Hispanics do not vote because they are simply too young. That will change. About 750,000 Hispanics will turn 18 every year for the next 20 years. It could mean that Hispanic voting rolls will swell enormously—or it could mean that young Hispanics, just like young Americans of every race, will fail to exercise their right to vote in great numbers. Hispanics, in other words, already behave pretty much like everybody else. Given a sufficiently dramatic cause, however, they will turn out.[22] That proved to be the case in 2006 when, according to some estimates, the Hispanic share of the total vote approached 9 percent in a year when immigration became a front-burner political issue.

As previously mentioned, there are many other factors that determine rates of voter turnout. Elderly people tend to vote a lot—which is one reason why Social Security and Medicare are always important political issues. Young people, by contrast, rarely vote. People who are wealthy also tend to vote more than the poor, whereas people with higher levels of education vote much more regularly than people with limited educations. These are some of the reasons why a high-income state with an educated population, such as Connecticut, has much higher turnout rates than a low-income state where the population is poorly educated on the whole, such as Hawaii.

A competitive election will draw a crowd even in a state that normally has low voter turnout. When people feel like they have a real choice, they are more likely to make the effort to vote. A close, three-way race for governor, as took place in Minnesota in 1998, will produce record turnout, whereas a yawner between a popular incumbent and a no-name opponent will make people sit on their hands. Some states tend to have consistently competitive elections because the two major parties are matched fairly evenly, each getting a roughly equal share of support from the electorate. Other states are "one-party states," with Republicans or Democrats dominant. One-party states rarely have competitive elections—but when they do, voter turnout is certain to go up.

In his bestselling 2000 book, *Bowling Alone,* Robert Putnam notes that moralistic states such as Minnesota and the Dakotas have much higher rates of volunteering, attendance at public meetings, and "social trust," as measured by polls, than traditionalistic states. In other words, voter turnout is just one indication of the overall sense of civic engagement in a place. States with strong "socializing institutions"—anything from membership organizations to news media that still cover politics—are more likely to be places where people are engaged enough to vote.

What Elections Are Used For

Forty-nine states elect a governor and two sets of state legislators—senators and members of a state House of Representatives, Delegates, or Assemblymen. Nebraska, the only exception, elects a governor and a one-chamber legislature. Beyond that, there is quite a bit of variation among the states in what they allow people to vote for. Some states allow voters to pick a number of statewide officeholders, such as attorney general and secretary of state, whereas in a few places these are appointed positions. Judges are the product of the voting booth in most places but not in about a dozen states. Roughly half the states allow voters to make policy decisions directly through ballot initiatives and referendums.

A look at state elections shows that states have quite different rules about who gets to vote for whom. That in turn can affect how a state makes policy. A governor who can appoint his entire cabinet is likely to have better success at pushing through his own policies than one who has to contend with a group of elected officials each with his own agenda.

All this is putting aside local elections, which also vary considerably. Most large cities, such as Chicago and San Francisco, allow voters to elect a mayor directly. Many smaller cities have what is called a council-mayor format. The city council picks one of its own members to serve as mayor, while the city is administered by a city manager, who is not elected. The same holds true for counties. In some places a county commission will pick its own leader, whereas in others voters may pick a county executive on their own. Local elections are, for the most part, **nonpartisan**. Candidates do not run under a party label—but, again, there are exceptions, such as the highly partisan elections for mayor of New York City.

Electing the Executive Branch

In New Jersey, voters elect only their governor among all of their statewide officeholders. This has helped create one of the most powerful governorships in the country. It wasn't always so. For centuries, New Jersey governors were much weaker players than the legislature. They were limited to a single term with weak veto and appointment powers. County officials in the state also were quite powerful, at the expense of state officials. That all changed, however, beginning with the new state constitution of 1947. The constitution was pushed through by reformers of the moralistic strain that was always present, although usually not dominant, in New Jersey politics. The reformers got new powers for the state's governors, including the ability to succeed themselves, authority to appoint not just cabinet officials but also about five hundred board and commission members, and broad authority to reject legislation. New Jersey's governors now can veto all or part of many bills and can issue a conditional veto, meaning a governor can reject portions of a bill while suggesting new language for it.[23]

Compare all of that influence with the limited powers of the governor of Texas. In Texas, the governor is only one of twenty-five elected statewide officials—and is not even the most powerful one among them. That distinction belongs to the lieutenant governor. In most states, the lieutenant governor holds a purely symbolic office, with little to do but wait around for something crippling to befall the governor. (New Jersey did not even bother with the office of lieutenant governor, but following a string of gubernatorial vacancies, voters created the position in 2005, which will take effect following the 2009 elections.) In Texas, the lieutenant governor is the president of the state Senate and therefore wields tremendous influence over the course of legislation.

Meanwhile, the governor of Texas can recommend a budget, but he has no authority to make the legislature grapple with it seriously. Compare that to Maryland, in which legislators can only accept or defeat the governor's spending proposals but make no fresh additions of their own. The Texas governor gets to appoint the secretary of state and members of many boards or commissions, but many of the latter serve staggered terms. This means that the governor has to work with people who were appointed by his predecessor.

As recently as a government reorganization bill debated in 2003, efforts have been put forth to provide the governor with more power. Generally, they have gone nowhere. The state's so-called **plural executive system** illustrates the desires of the framers of the 1876 state constitution to keep too much power out of the hands of any one person or institution. They

NONPARTISAN ELECTIONS

Elections in which candidates do not have to declare party affiliation or receive a party's nomination; local offices and elections are often nonpartisan.

PLURAL EXECUTIVE SYSTEM

A state government system in which the governor is not the dominant figure in the executive branch, but instead is more of a first among equals, serving alongside numerous other officials who were elected to their offices rather than appointed by the governor.

believed in a separation of powers not just between branches of government but also within the executive branch.[24] The weakened powers of the governor are a reflection of the distrust Texans had for strong government, in keeping with their constitution's many restrictions on raising taxes.

A couple of other southern and traditionalistic states, such as Alabama and Georgia, also divide power within the executive branch. In 1999, Alabama Democrats in the state Senate sought to strip control of their chamber along with other powers from Republican lieutenant governor Steve Windom. They could have done it if only he had left the Senate floor. Windom refused. To stay present and to keep control of the chamber for that day, and thus for the rest of his term, he urinated into a plastic jug in the chamber.[25]

Other states chart more of a middle-of-the-road course, electing a handful of statewide officials. In most states, voters elect a lieutenant governor, treasurer, secretary of state, and attorney general. A few states elect other officers as well, such as an insurance commissioner. Some observers believe that appointed officials are removed from political concerns and can make decisions without regard to partisan interests. Others believe that having individual officers answer directly to the public makes them more responsive. Regardless, the fact that many statewide officeholders run for office independently of the governor gives them a power base of their own.

Attorneys general, treasurers, or other statewide officials often have aspirations of becoming governor themselves one day. This leads inevitably to conflict with the sitting governor. During the 1980s in Texas, for example, Democratic attorney general Mark White frequently sparred with Republi-

The heads of many state executive agencies are independently elected rather than appointed by the governor. This can lead to friction, as agency heads may not agree with gubernatorial policy and may harbor ambitions to hold the chief executive's office themselves. Texas State Comptroller Caroline Keeton Strayhorn (shown here with members of her family), for example, ran an independent campaign against gubernatorial incumbent Rick Perry in 2006. Even though Strayhorn and Perry were both Republicans, they frequently clashed on policy matters, and Strayhorn unsuccessfully sought Perry's job.

can governor Bill Clements and eventually unseated him. Today in Texas every statewide officeholder is Republican, but that has not put an end to squabbling within the executive branch. Caroline Keeton Strayhorn, the state comptroller, has frequently provoked the governor and lieutenant governor, accusing them of using dishonest budget numbers and raising fees excessively. "Sounds like the primary started early this year," Lieutenant Governor David Dewhurst said in 2003.[26] Strayhorn ran unsuccessfully for governor as an independent in 2006.

Legal Offices

Voters pay comparatively little attention to candidates running for some executive branch offices. Races for, say, state treasurer or secretary of state are just, for the most part, not seen as all that exciting. Most often, the party that wins the governorship takes the lion's share of the secondary executive branch offices anyway, so there is not much mystery. These are offices often pursued by legislators or other politicians looking to move up the political ladder. They hope these second-tier positions will firm up their resumés during future bids for prominent offices such as governor.

One office for which the majority-party-takes-all dynamic no longer holds is that of attorney general, the chief law enforcement officer in the state. For many years, Democrats completely dominated these positions. That began to change in the late 1990s. For one thing, the job came to be seen as a more important stepping stone to the governorship than in the past; in 2007 seven former state attorneys general were serving as governors. (See Map 4-1.) Republicans, understandably, became increasingly unwilling to concede this important gateway to the chief executive's office. For another, state attorneys general, who traditionally had concentrated on law enforcement or consumer protection disputes within their states, had joined in a series of "multistate" settlements that represented an important challenge to corporate interests. They forced a series of settlements in 1998, for instance, that pushed the major tobacco companies to change their marketing strategies and pay states an estimated $246 billion over twenty-five years.

Some Republicans believed that these activist attorneys general were engaging in "government lawsuit abuse"—not targeting criminal behavior but instead going after companies to achieve changes in policy and regulation that could not be accomplished in the legislative arena. They founded the Republican Attorneys General Association (RAGA) as a campaign wing to elect members of their party to the office and funneled contributions from businesses and conservative interest groups that were threatened by the new activism to their candidates. "Historically . . . attorney general races were off most business people's radar screens," according to Bob LaBrant of the Michigan Chamber of Commerce. In the new environment, he says, "there's greater incentive to get involved in an attorney general race because

MAP 4-1 States Attorneys General: Party Affiliation, 2007

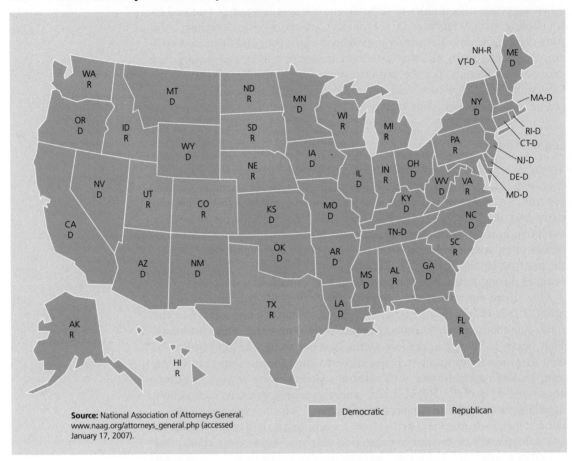

Source: National Association of Attorneys General. www.naag.org/attorneys_general.php (accessed January 17, 2007).

of the increased involvement of attorneys general across the country in litigation against the business community." [27]

Such interest group money and influence does make a difference. In 2002, the Law Enforcement Alliance of America, an arm of the gun lobby, ran an estimated $1.5 million late-season ad campaign that helped keep the Texas attorney general's office in Republican hands. This was an expanded version of the U.S. Chamber of Commerce's effort in Indiana in 2000, when a $200,000 ad campaign was widely viewed as a leading factor in driving an incumbent Democrat out of office.[28] All told, Republicans have improved their numbers since RAGA's founding from just twelve attorneys general in 1999 to twenty in 2003. (After the GOP lost a couple of seats in 2006, the number of Republican attorneys general stood at nineteen.) Both parties now believe that campaigns for attorney general will remain more expensive and competitive than they had been historically.

A related phenomenon is affecting judicial elections, which traditionally were sleepy affairs. All but eleven states hold some type of election for judicial posts. This may mean direct election by voters or retention elections used by voters to grant another term to justices appointed by the governor or the state legislature. Until the mid-1990s, judicial campaigns were cheap and fairly ho-hum. What campaign contributions candidates did receive mainly came from trial lawyers, along with unions and other constituencies allied with the Democratic Party. As with the attorney general office, however, all of that began to change during the 1990s. Republicans and their business allies grew weary of seeing their legislative victories in areas such as tort law and workers' compensation overturned by high courts. In 2000, candidates in supreme court races in twenty states raised a total of $45.5 million dollars—a 61 percent increase over the previous record. The average cost of winning a judicial election jumped 45 percent between 2002 and 2004, while individual races also kept breaking records, with one Illinois contest nearing the $10 million mark in 2004.[29] Elections for individual lower-level court races have broken through the million-dollar barrier also.

Direct Democracy

In addition to electing officials to state and local offices, voters can participate in certain forms of **direct democracy**. In about half the states, voters can pass legislation on their own through ballot initiatives or referendums, which also are available in hundreds of municipalities across the country. In twenty-four states, citizens can petition to place a piece of legislation or a constitutional amendment on the ballot for approval or rejection by voters. Also in twenty-four states—mostly the same states—citizens can petition to review a law passed by the legislature and the governor, which they then can accept or reject. (See Table 4-2.)

When citizens or groups other than elected officials put a measure on the ballot to become a law, that is called a popular initiative. When citizens put a measure on the ballot to affirm or reject an action of the legislature or other political actor, this is called a popular referendum. When the legislature places a measure on the ballot to win voter approval, it is called a legislative referendum. Some referendums are nonbinding—expressing the will of the people but not becoming law—but most are binding and do have the force of law once passed.

In all fifty states, the legislature or other government agencies can refer a proposition to the ballot for voter approval. This may consist of a constitutional amendment, bond issue, or other matter. This is the legislative referendum just mentioned.

In the decades following independence, citizens in several northeastern states ratified new constitutions. Congress subsequently made legislative referendums for constitutional amendments mandatory for all new states

DIRECT DEMOCRACY

The means for citizens to make laws themselves, rather than relying on elected representatives.

entering the union after 1857.[30] As discussed in Chapter 3, the notion of popular referendums and initiatives really took root after the efforts of reformers from the Populist and Progressive movements. These individuals sought to give citizens more influence over state political systems that they saw as dominated by moneyed interests such as banks, railroads, and mining companies. A majority of the states that have adopted the popular initiative process, under which citizens can collect a certain number of signatures to place issues directly on the ballot, did so in the late 1800s and early 1900s. Most of these states are in the West or Upper Midwest, which had political cultures that welcomed the idea of populist control. Much of the opposition in the eastern and southern states grew out of racist concerns that to give people direct authority for making laws would give too much power to African Americans or new immigrants such as the Irish.

Recent ballot initiatives and referendums have covered a wide range of topics, from legalizing marijuana and allowing physician-assisted suicide to making sure that pregnant pigs are housed in large enough pens—an amendment to the Florida constitution approved by voters in 2002. Many initiatives have to do with tax and spending issues. Sometimes voters send contradictory signals. For instance, in Washington State, voters in recent years have approved limitations on property and other taxes, while at the same time approving such expensive programs as teacher pay increases and class size limitations.

> Recent ballot initiatives and referendums have covered a wide range of topics, from legalizing marijuana and allowing physician-assisted suicide to making sure that pregnant pigs are housed in large enough pens—an amendment to the Florida constitution approved by voters in 2002.

Those who favor the initiative process say that it gives voters a chance to control government directly. Voters know that they are voting for an environmental safety program or a campaign finance law, as opposed to voting for candidates who say that they favor these things but who act differently once in office. Initiative states do tend to have lower state spending per capita, but that gap generally is bridged by local spending, which tends to run higher in initiative states.[31]

Critics of the initiative process say that it creates more problems than it solves. Since voters are presented with a straight "yes" or "no" choice about spending more on, say, elementary and secondary education, they are not taking into account other competing state priorities, such as transportation or colleges, the way legislators must. Voters can say, as in Washington, that they want both lower taxes and more services and leave legislators and governors few tools for balancing the budget or responding to economic recessions.

Those opposed to initiatives also say that the idea that they express the popular will better than elected representatives can sounds good in theory but is flawed in practice. In many states—particularly California—initiatives have become big business. They are not necessarily expressions of grassroots ideals any more. Instead, they are proposed and paid for by wealthy individuals or interest groups, such as teachers' unions or gambling casinos.

Far and away the most famous and influential modern ballot initiative was Proposition 13, approved by California voters in 1978, which limited property tax rates and made other changes to the state's tax and spending laws (this was discussed in Chapter 3). The initiative was copied successfully in Michigan and Massachusetts, and most states soon placed limitations on their own property tax rates. The success of the proposition fueled the modern initiative movement. There were only eighty-seven statewide initiatives proposed during the entire decade of the 1960s. Since 1978, however, there have been about three hundred initiatives proposed per decade. Ninety-three statewide initiatives were placed on ballots in 1996 alone. That appears to have been the peak year, with supporters of the initiative process complaining since then that state legislatures have placed new restrictions on ballot access and signature collection.

Another piece of evidence of the power of initiatives is the idea of legislative term limits, which exist in nearly every state that allows ballot initiatives but in only a couple of states that do not. Term limits, after all, were imposed in virtually every case by voters through ballot measures, rather than by legislators themselves.

Congressional term limits were a popular idea during the 1990s and were approved in a number of states, but the U.S. Supreme Court ruled in 1995 that states cannot unilaterally alter constitutional requirements for holding federal office. State legislators are subject to term limits in fifteen states, but the defeat of a term-limits initiative in Oregon in 2006 signaled the likely end of that movement.

Rather than looking to expand term limits, legislators and many others concerned with the effects of term limits on good governance have been seeking to expand the length of time legislators may serve. Term limits are still too popular to repeal, but some people believe allowing legislators ten to twelve years in a chamber, as opposed to six to eight, will make them more expert in grappling with the complex policies they must address. Even these efforts, however, have proven to be tough sells.

Ballots have become regular battlegrounds for a number of other issues. Limitations on reproductive rights, such as parental notification requirements to obtain an abortion, have been debated by voters in many states, as have smoking bans and property rights protections. Although many ballot measures seek to put restraints on government, by limiting state spending, for instance, or by holding judges more accountable for their decisions, voters in recent cycles have rejected these ideas. Public officials were able to make the case that these sometimes rigid restrictions would have tied their hands even in emergency situations. Perhaps surprisingly, their arguments were echoed in many states by organized business groups who, although conservative fiscally, were concerned that artificial limits on government would affect their own priorities, such as higher education and transportation projects.

Since 2004, perhaps the most prominent measure on many ballots has been a ban on gay marriage. Many states already had defined marriage as the union of a man and a woman, but following a Massachusetts court decision that found gays had a right to marry, twenty-seven states have changed their constitutions to ban same-sex marriage. Arizona became the first state to oppose a ban in 2006. As noted earlier, some political scientists have suggested that high-profile initiatives do lead more people to vote. Given the attention given to a gay marriage ban in Ohio in 2004, when that state's electoral votes ultimately decided the presidency, there was much coverage in the media that looked at the question of whether the initiative helped President Bush by encouraging social conservatives to vote. "I'd be naïve if I didn't say it helped," Robert T. Bennett, chair of the Ohio Republican Party, told the *New York Times*. "And it helped most in what we refer to as the Bible Belt area of southeastern and southwestern Ohio, where we had the largest percentage increase in support for the president." [32]

Not surprisingly, liberals decided to jump on this particular bandwagon, finding causes, such as minimum wage increases and stem-cell research support, to place on ballots in hopes that more progressive voters would turn out as well. But there is a school of thought that argues that they need not have bothered. Simon Jackman, a statistician at Stanford University, has shown that same-sex marriage initiatives boosted turnout by about 3 percent in the eleven states that had them on the ballot in 2004. On examining data from all of Ohio's counties, however, he concluded that that state's initiative did not boost support for Bush. [33]

Others have noted that it is not an accident that high-profile initiatives tend to appear in closely contested states. "The list of [presidential] battleground states almost exactly matches up with the list of controversial ballot measures this year," said Jennie Drage Bowser, who tracks initiatives for the National Conference of State Legislatures, in 2004. [34]

Beyond initiatives and referendums is perhaps the ultimate expression of popular dissatisfaction—the **recall**. Recalls of local officials are allowed in thirty-six states and 61 percent of U.S. municipalities—more local governments than allow initiatives or referendums. Like ballot initiatives, recall laws are mainly byproducts of the intention of early twentieth-century reformers to make state governments more responsive to average citizens. Recalls of state officials are allowed in eighteen states. The most famous example of a recall took place in 2003, when California governor Gray Davis was recalled and replaced by Arnold Schwarzenegger.

Before that election, recalls were fairly common at the local level but rare at the state level. Over the past one hundred years, there have been fewer than two dozen recall elections involving state officials, including legislators. [35] The only governor to be recalled before Davis was Lynn Fra-

RECALL

An occasion for citizens to collect signatures and then vote on the ouster of an incumbent politician prior to the next regularly scheduled election.

TABLE 4-2

Avenues for Direct Democracy

State	Popular Referendum	Ballot Initiative	Constitutional Amendment by Initiative	Recalls of State Officials
Alabama	No	No	No	No
Alaska	Yes	Yes	No	Yes
Arizona	Yes	Yes	Yes	Yes
Arkansas	Yes	Yes	Yes	No
California	Yes	Yes	Yes	Yes
Colorado	Yes	Yes	Yes	Yes
Connecticut	No	No	No	No
Delaware	No	No	No	No
Florida	No	Yes	Yes	No
Georgia	No	No	No	Yes
Hawaii	No	No	No	No
Idaho	Yes	Yes	Yes	Yes
Illinois	Yes	Yes	No	No
Indiana	No	No	No	No
Iowa	No	No	No	No
Kansas	No	No	No	Yes
Kentucky	Yes	No	No	No
Louisiana	No	No	No	Yes
Maine	Yes	Yes	No	No
Maryland	Yes	No	No	No
Massachusetts	Yes	Yes	Yes	No
Michigan	Yes	Yes	Yes	Yes
Minnesota	No	No	No	Yes
Mississippi	No	Yes	Yes	No
Missouri	Yes	Yes	Yes	No
Montana	Yes	Yes	Yes	Yes
Nebraska	Yes	Yes	Yes	No
Nevada	Yes	Yes	Yes	Yes
New Hampshire	No	No	No	No
New Jersey	No	No	No	Yes
New Mexico	Yes	No	No	No
New York	No	No	No	No
North Carolina	No	No	No	No

TABLE 4-2, **continued**

State	Popular Referendum	Ballot Initiative	Constitutional Amendment by Initiative	Recalls of State Officials
North Dakota	Yes	Yes	Yes	Yes
Ohio	Yes	Yes	Yes	No
Oklahoma	Yes	Yes	Yes	No
Oregon	Yes	Yes	Yes	Yes
Pennsylvania	No	No	No	No
Rhode Island	No	No	No	Yes
South Carolina	No	No	No	No
South Dakota	Yes	Yes	Yes	No
Tennessee	No	No	No	No
Texas	No	No	No	No
Utah	Yes	Yes	No	No
Vermont	No	No	No	No
Virginia	No	No	No	No
Washington	Yes	Yes	No	Yes
West Virginia	No	No	No	No
Wisconsin	No	No	No	Yes
Wyoming	Yes	Yes	No	No
Total # of States with	25	24	18	18

Sources: Data compiled from the Initiative and Referendum Institute at the University of Southern California, www.iandrinstitute.org/statewide_i&r.htm (accessed January 17, 2007); and the National Conference of State Legislatures, www.ncsl.org/programs/legman/elect/recallprovision.htm (accessed January 17, 2007).

zier of North Dakota back in 1921. Frazier, the state attorney general, and the agricultural commissioner each lost his office after a grassroots movement swelled against scandals in Frazier's ranks. The only other governor who has ever faced a scheduled recall election was Evan Mecham of Arizona, until the legislature saved voters the trouble by removing him from office in 1987.

California makes the recall process pretty easy, requiring fewer signatures as a percentage of the number of people who voted in the last election for the office than in other states. California only requires 12 percent, whereas most states require 25 percent and Kansas requires 40 percent. Gray Davis was unpopular, having won reelection the year before by a small plurality. He also had come to be blamed for the state's $38 billion deficit and electricity crisis.

The idea of a recall took on some currency in 2007 for Nevada governor Jim Gibbons. Soon after taking office, Gibbons became the subject of a federal investigation into allegations that he had accepted improper gifts or payments from a military contractor while a member of Congress. Gibbons denied any wrongdoing. In Nevada, officials can not be recalled until they have held office for six months, so a Web site called VoteGibbonsOut.com displayed a countdown clock alerting citizens to exactly how many days— and seconds—they had left until they could begin the recall process. "It might actually be easier to raise money in Nevada today for a recall than for Gibbons' legal defense," wrote a *Las Vegas Review-Journal* columnist in March 2007.[36]

Public Opinion

Randall Gnant, the former president of the Arizona Senate, says that there is quite a contrast between the politics of today and those of the 1800s. Back then, he says, "It seemed that everybody took part in the political process—there were torchlight parades, party-run newspapers for and against candidates." Today, "We're into sort of a reverse kind of period. Now, almost nobody participates in the electoral process—voter turnout rates are abysmally low." But that does not mean that citizens are not paying any attention to the political process. Given the importance of talk radio, the Internet, and other media that quickly spread public opinion— at least a share of it—the old idea that voters agree to a sort of contract with politicians whom they elect to a two-year or four-year term is rapidly becoming dated. Voters are more than willing to express their displeasure about a given policy well before the next scheduled election day. "Try to get somebody interested in electing a candidate and they just don't want to get involved," Gnant points out. "But they are perfectly willing to get involved if somebody does something they don't want them to do."[37]

Citizen opinion usually does not register loudly enough to result in a recall or other formal protest. On most issues that come before policymakers at the state level, citizen opinion hardly seems to exist or be formulated at all. After all, how many citizens are going to take the time to follow—let alone express an opinion about—an obscure regulatory issue concerning overnight transactions between banks and insurance companies?

This lack of interest, or at the very least, this lack of time, begs an important question. If citizens do not or cannot make their feelings known on every issue addressed in the hundreds of bills that wend through the average state legislature each year, how can legislators know that their votes will reflect the will of their constituents? After all, as V. O. Key once wrote, "Unless mass views have some place in the shaping of policy, all the talk about democracy is nonsense."[38]

Responding to Opinion

Doug Duncan served for a dozen years as county executive of Montgomery County, Maryland, before giving up the job in 2006. Like many veteran officeholders, he found that one of the biggest changes in his job came in the area of communications. "Doing it is half the job," he says, "and the other half is telling people about it so they know how you're spending their money."[39] The old outlets for government officials making announcements or responding to criticism—local daily newspapers and evening TV news broadcasts—have declined in audience or even gone away completely in some cases. Meanwhile, there are more information sources than ever with the growth of the Internet. "The information's there," Duncan says. "It's just a question of how you make it available."

E-mail, listservs, and Web sites devoted to neighborhood concerns or services such as libraries have made it easier for public officials to know what their constituents are thinking—at least, those constituents who are motivated enough to make their opinions known on a given issue. But let's be realistic—state officials, in particular, cannot know what majority opinion is in their district about every issue they confront. On most issues, they do not hear from any constituents at all. A few high-profile concerns, such as tax increases or legalizing casino gambling, may lead a newspaper or an interested party to conduct a statewide poll—but even on the rare occasions in which there are polls on a state issue, these polls will not break down opinion in each legislative district. Given the absence of specific information each legislator or gubernatorial aide has about how constituents view a particular area, public officials have to rely on a series of clues.

Some political scientists have taken data from various nationwide polls, broken it down by state, and seen how well elected officials have reflected the general ideology and desires of the public in their states.[40] What they found is that average state opinion does seem to get reflected in the policy decisions made in individual states. What does average state opinion mean? It is the type of things discussed earlier when talking about Daniel Elazar's classifications of the states. Some states tend to be more liberal overall, whereas others are more conservative. The average citizen's desire—whether in a conservative state like Texas or a more liberal one like Vermont—tends to be pretty well reflected by state laws on issues that range from restrictions on abortion services to welfare spending, the death penalty, environmental protections, and gay rights.[41]

How does this happen? For one thing, elected officials devote an enormous amount of time trying to gauge how opinion is running in their districts. They may not hear from constituents on every issue, but they pay close attention to those concerns that are registered through letters and phone calls. They go out and seek opinion by attending religious services and civic events where they can hear the concerns of constituents direct-

A Difference that Makes a Difference: Town Hall, Version 2.0

You don't usually need to book a convention center to hold a civic meeting. But recently in Washington, D.C., two thousand people filled a large room in the cavernous space for a give-and-take with the mayor and city officials. They were able to give City Hall a piece of their collective mind because technology was used to gather their ideas, distill them, and flash them on large screens, allowing participants to vote with key-pads on their top priorities. Other cities around the country are now running electronic town hall meetings with a similar objective: extracting the opinions of citizens in a comprehensive fashion.

The whole business of citizens trying to contact governments, and of governments wanting to relay good information to citizens, has always been a creaky process. New tools such as blogs, wikis, and public comment software are smoothing things out a little and allowing governments to enhance some of the traditional ways of communicating with the public.

Carole Brown, who's at the Chicago Transit Agency, started a blog in 2005, after feeling frustrated by negative newspaper reports on what was happening at the CTA. When Brown read letters to the editor of the newspaper, she realized that readers, angry at the CTA, didn't understand the complexities behind public transportation funding. So Brown blogged away, offering details that riders weren't getting from the press. Today, her blog serves many purposes, from straightening out misconceptions that riders get from other sources to allowing the agency to communicate early and often with transit riders. "My blog is an incredible tool," says Brown. "We're using it to focus on issues most important to our riders, and they have no problem telling us what those are."

At electronic town hall meetings, city officials bring people together in groups of eight or ten at a table with one laptop computer and a trained facilitator. As citizens give their opinions on issues, someone types them up and forwards them to a team of people that gathers and distills the ideas by theme. Concepts that crop up over and over are then flashed on large overhead screens. Eventually those are whittled down to a handful of top priorities by the participants who vote on them by keypad.

Such a distillation was helpful to San Francisco mayor Gavin Newsom at his first electronic town hall meeting. He already had plenty of information about what lobbyists and professional advocates wanted. What the mayor hoped to find out was what the rest of the city wanted. "The average resident is not typically asked to come or doesn't have time or an entrée to attend a three-hour meeting with the mayor to offer opinions," says Jennifer Petrucione, the mayor's spokeswoman. The virtual town hall was a novel, and helpful, way to find out.

Source: Adapted from Ellen Perlman, "The Missing Link," *Governing* magazine, March 2006.

ly. They use surrogates—such as newspaper articles and interest groups— as ways of determining what is on their constituents' minds. Susan Herbst, a political scientist now at the State University of New York at Albany, spent some time a few years back hanging out with legislators in Springfield, Illinois. She found that the media were important in shaping public opinion by giving a voice to average people in their stories. The media also shaped the terms of debate. Herbst noted that people in the capital thought that lobbyists often were good indicators of how people felt about an issue: "Staffers seem to think that the nuances and intensity of public opinion are best captured in the communications of interest groups." [42]

Elected officials do not just have to address the issues they campaigned on, respond to views expressed at the ballot box, deal with the demands of special interest groups, and be attentive to the expectations of political parties. They also have to be prepared to deal with the unexpected. Hurricane Katrina was a dramatic example of this, but other kinds of emergencies, natural or otherwise, happen all the time. Here, Nebraska governor Dave Heineman (right, in blue), and state senator Deb Fisher survey the damage done by a wildfire that destroyed homes in the city of Valentine. State and local emergency agencies were required to control the fire, and other agencies helped deal with the aftermath.

That is not to say that using interest groups as surrogates can't be misleading sometimes. The National Rifle Association, for example, may call upon its state members to send letters to legislators in numbers that dwarf those mustered by gun control advocates—even in places where a majority favors gun control. "Intense minorities can come off potentially sounding like majorities when in fact they're not," says Illinois Wesleyan University political scientist Greg Shaw.[43] Legislators like to think that they have a pretty good sense of whether a mail-writing campaign has sprung up spontaneously or shows signs of having been organized—everyone signing their name to the same form letter, for example—but sometimes this is easier said than done.

Formal interest groups do not represent every constituent. Some people may favor environmental protection, but not give money to the Sierra Club or the World Wildlife Fund. Some older people actually resist the invitations to join AARP at cheap rates. Still, legislators do gain some sense of how active such groups are in their states and whether they seem to have favorable support at home. A lot of this is inexact, but legislators learn from talking to people whether their constituents are most upset about crime or transportation problems. They are convinced that if they vote for things that voters broadly support, such as mandatory sentencing guidelines for drug offenders or limits on welfare benefits, they will be rewarded politically.

Conversely, a legislator's major fear is of being punished politically. Not getting reelected can be the death knell of a political career. It is important to note, however, that if legislators or governors did not broadly reflect the wishes of the populace that elected them, they would never have won their positions in the first place. In this age of computer-assisted **redistricting**, legislative districts in particular are shaped according to a local political culture

REDISTRICTING

The drawing of new boundaries for congressional and state legislative districts, usually following a decennial census.

that tends to lean in one ideological direction or another. A liberal is not going to get elected to a conservative district, ninety times out of a hundred.

Once elected, legislators who want to get reelected are careful not to stray too far from public opinion in their districts, as best as they can perceive it. They cannot know what public opinion is about the specifics of every bill—but the fact that not every individual is paying close attention to state politics does not mean that legislators can do whatever they want. Political officials recognize that lobbyists and other interested parties are watching their voting records carefully and can use such information against them, if necessary. "Legislators aren't worried about what their constituents know—they are worried about what an opponent might do with their record in the next election," says Paul Brace, a Rice University political scientist. They act, therefore, as if there is someone or some group out there who has a chance of using a potentially unpopular record against them. "Legislation is written in minutiae, but you know if you vote for it, you'll get an opponent who can dumb it down and use it against you in the next election, and you won't do it." [44]

Some states offer less opportunity for using a politician's record against him. In a moralistic state such as Minnesota, there are more daily newspapers paying close attention to state policy matters than in, say, individualistic Wyoming. There are more public interest groups and state-level think tanks closely monitoring St. Paul than there are monitoring Cheyenne. Citizens in states with higher levels of civic engagement are more likely to be able to keep their politicians "honest"—reflecting voters' overall policy desires—than citizens in less-engaged states.

In a state like Idaho or Maryland, one party so completely dominates state politics that only rarely are politicians voted out of office because their records do not reflect public opinion. But even Idaho Republicans or Maryland Democrats can lose—if only in the party primary—if voters sour on their records. All of the state capitals have engendered enough of an echo chamber that examines and discusses the work of legislators and other elected officials for an overall sense of their records—conservative or liberal, sellout or crusading—to be known to people who care enough about politics to vote. If those records do not reflect local opinion, the job will go to someone else in the next election.

Conclusion

This is a highly partisan era, with little civility or cooperation, it seems, between Republicans and Democrats. But the war between the red and the blue will never be as heated as the war between the blue and the gray—the colors of the North and South during the Civil War. Although voters are divided, they are not as deeply divided as they have been at moments in the country's past, such as the Civil War or Watergate.

That fact is reflected in the recent series of contentious but ultimately narrowly won presidential contests, and on down through other levels of government. As with Congress and the electoral college, state legislatures have been closely divided, with the two main parties switching leads in total number of seats nationwide throughout the early twenty-first century. The lead among governorships has switched around, too, with Democrats currently up.

The outcome of recent elections is reflecting the divided public mood. State and local officials have less ability to control who participates in the political process because of the many changes in voting laws passed at the federal level. They do still maintain a lot of control over whom citizens can vote for through their regulation of political parties and their ability to decide who deserves to get their names onto ballots.

Which officials citizens get to vote for differs depending on where they live. In most states, citizens vote for several statewide officials such as governor, attorney general, and secretary of state. In others, they might vote only for the governor. Similarly, in some localities, citizens elect the mayor directly whereas in others the mayor is chosen by the city council from among its own membership. Some states allow people to vote directly for judges, while judges are appointed to office in other states. Some localities allow people to vote for school boards. In others, these positions are appointed.

In general, citizens vote for enough officeholders with the authority to control policies that the majority's will generally becomes law. However, since polling is done far more often at the national level than it is at the local or even state level, officeholders sometimes have only an anecdotal sense of what their constituents are thinking. They do pay close attention to what clues they are given and monitor opinion as closely as they can. If they do not create the types of policies that most people want, they are well aware that they are not going to stay in office for long.

Key Concepts

direct democracy (p. 123)

nonpartisan elections (p. 119)

office group (Massachusetts) ballot (p. 107)

party column (Indiana) ballot (p. 107)

plural executive system (p. 119)

plurality (p. 103)

recall (p. 126)

redistricting (p. 132)

secret (Australian) ballot (p. 110)

straight ticket (p. 110)

voter turnout (p. 113)

Suggested Readings

Abramowitz, Alan. *Voice of the People: Elections and Voting in the United States.* New York: McGraw-Hill, 2004. A recent look at voting behavior and partisan preferences that suggests some reasons for voter disengagement.

Patterson, Thomas. *The Vanishing Voter.* New York: Knopf, 2002. A political scientist seeks to explain why voter turnout is falling.

Wolfinger, Raymond, and Steven Rosenstone. *Who Votes?* New Haven, Conn.: Yale University Press, 1980. A classic study of voter participation in the United States.

Suggested Web Sites

http://fairvote.org. Web site of the Center for Voting and Democracy, which promotes voting and advocates instant runoffs and abolition of the electoral college.

www.lwv.org. Official Web site of the League of Women Voters. Provides a wealth of voter education information.

www.nass.org. Official Web site of the National Association of Secretaries of State. Secretaries of state typically serve as chief election officials, and their offices have primary responsibility for recording official election outcomes.

CHAPTER 5

Parties and Interest Groups

Elephants, Donkeys, and Cash Cows

Interest groups can influence policymakers in a number of different ways. They can make campaign contributions, directly lobby lawmakers, or mount a public pressure campaign. The latter approach was taken by teachers' unions in Florida in an attempt to increase education's share of the state budget. They gathered more than four hundred thousand petitions supporting their view, presented them to the state legislature, and called a press conference on the steps of the state capital.

Let's stop cheating our children!

RECLAIM EDUCATION'S SHARE

5

Why are political parties weaker than they used to be?

Why are political parties stronger in some states than in others?

How do interest groups influence policymakers?

Colonel Aureliano Buendia was a young man when he learned the difference between his country's Liberals and Conservatives in the Gabriel Garcìa Màrquez novel *One Hundred Years of Solitude.* Liberals, his father explained, fight the authority of the church and the central government and recognize the rights of illegitimate children. Conservatives are defenders of public order and morality.

POLITICAL PARTIES

Organizations that nominate and support candidates for elected offices.

Buendia grew up to lead the Liberal revolutionary forces, without success, in nearly twenty years of civil war. Eventually, his political advisers suggest that he renounce the party's longstanding fight against clerical influence and the rest of the Liberal platform he had been introduced to years before. One adviser, however, speaks against the idea. He points out that they are merely adopting the Conservative platform because it is more popular, even though it represents everything they have fought for so long. Buendia sees things differently. What it means, he says, is "that all we're fighting for is power." [1]

This is the classic cynical view of **political parties**, those organized groups that hope to win power by controlling a variety of elective offices, such as mayor or governor. They shift with the winds and pursue whatever policy stances bring them power—even if these stances directly contradict what the parties stood for during the last election. Both major parties have had moments in recent years when it seemed they had clung to power long after they had run out of guiding ideas. Democrats admitted as much after losing control of Congress in the 1994 elections, and Republicans made similar noises after losing it back in 2006. "Every revolution begins with the power of an idea and ends when clinging to power is the only idea left," wrote *Time* magazine reporter Karen Tumulty during the 2006 election season. [2]

Ever since George Washington warned against "the baneful effects of the spirit of party" in his farewell address, many Americans have taken his words to heart. Political disaffection—the feeling that voting really does not make a difference—is why more than half the adult populace of voting age does not do so, whether they are registered or not. "People feel disconnected from parties and think there's no difference between the parties, despite our rhetoric being different," said Royal Masset, a consultant and former political director of the Texas Republican Party. [3]

Real, non-rhetorical differences do exist between the Democratic Party and the Republican Party. Without dwelling too much on specific points, this chapter explains the role of parties in American politics. It looks at how parties—including minor, or third, parties—have evolved; how parties function at the state and local levels; and how their influence differs from state to state. In addition, it takes a look at **interest groups**—individuals, corporations, or associations who seek to influence the actions of elected and appointed public officials on behalf of specific companies or causes.

Political parties are not as dominant in American life as they once were. From roughly the 1820s until the 1940s, parties were a prime organizing force in this country. They provided citizens not only with a political identity, but also were a major source of social activity and entertainment—and, in many cases, jobs. Today, parties are not as effective at getting people out to vote or even at organizing them around an issue. However, they do remain important to candidates as a kind of "brand name" identification and as fund-raisers.

Although there are two major national parties, they play larger roles at the state level than they do as national forces. Their respective strength varies widely from state to state and is affected by such factors as the different ways states regulate parties, the differences in the historical roles that parties played within each state, and the amount of competition between the major parties within a given state. In general, the more closely balanced the two main parties are in a state, the more likely that they will have well-funded and well-organized party organizations.

A Primer on Political Parties

Political parties recruit candidates for offices and provide them with support for their campaigns. They give candidates money or help them to raise it and offer logistical and strategic assistance. Just as important, they help coordinate a candidate's message with those of other candidates running for other offices under the party's banner.

Since the 1850s, the vast majority of candidates have run as members of either the Democratic or the Republican Party. Democrats as we know them today evolved from **factional splits** in the earliest days of the American republic. The country started without a two-party system, but factions soon developed. The Federalists, led by Alexander Hamilton, favored a strong central government with power rooted in the industrial North. The Democratic Republicans, led by Thomas Jefferson, emerged as the party opposing the Federalists. They argued for states' rights against a "monarchical" rule by the aristocracy and declared that farmers, craftspeople, and shopkeepers should control their own interests without interference from the capitol.

Jefferson's party, which eventually morphed into the Democratic Party, dominated politics throughout the first half of the nineteenth century. That same time period saw the creation of numerous parties—Whigs, Know-

INTEREST GROUPS

Individuals, corporations, or associations who seek to influence the actions of elected and appointed public officials on behalf of specific companies or causes.

FACTIONAL SPLITS, OR FACTIONS

Groups that struggle to control the message within a party; for example, a party may be split into competing regional factions.

Nothings, Barnburners, Softshells, Hunkers, and Free Soilers. They all had some success, but the Democratic Party of Jefferson and Andrew Jackson dominated so completely that, as the main source of political power, the party split into factions, with northern and southern Democrats arguing over the expansion of slavery. That argument created an opening for a new major party.

The Republican Party was formed in 1854 in opposition of slavery. It soon replaced the Whig Party, which had been formed in 1834 to protest the spoils system politics of Andrew Jackson. The Republicans, also known as the "Grand Old Party" (GOP), quickly enjoyed congressional success. Following the election of Abraham Lincoln in 1860, they dominated the presidency for decades to come. Their antislavery stance, however, guaranteed that they were practically nonexistent in the South until the civil rights era of the 1950s and 1960s. Democrats reemerged as the nation's dominant party in the 1930s, when Republicans were forced to take the blame for the Great Depression. The Democrats' New Deal coalition of Southerners, union workers, African Americans, the poor, and the elderly drove American politics well into the 1960s but fragmented after that, resulting in a loss of political control.

Since then, longstanding Democratic majorities at the congressional and state levels have eroded (the party's majorities following the 2006 elections still do not match those of forty years ago), whereas Republicans have held the presidency for most of the past thirty years. In 2002, Republicans gained a majority of seats in state legislatures for the first time in fifty years—but their majorities were not overwhelming and were soon lost to the Democrats. Democrat Al Gore won a plurality of the presidential vote in 2000, even as he lost the electoral college vote to Republican George W. Bush. But in 2004 Bush became the first presidential candidate since 1988 to win a majority—51 percent—of the popular vote. Basically, the two parties have spent the past decade at roughly equal strength.

It is no secret that contemporary politics is highly competitive. Neither side enjoys a consistent advantage nationally. Candidates from either party are capable of winning statewide offices in nearly every state. Overall support for the parties is, however, split along regional lines, with Democrats enjoying more support along the West Coast and the Northeast, whereas Republicans are dominant in the South and the Plains states. The Upper Midwest and parts of the Mountain West have become the most competitive regions. (Ironically, for a party created to oppose slavery, today the GOP's greatest support is from those areas where slavery once was legal.)

While people are familiar with the Republican and Democratic parties, political parties actually take many different shapes. When people refer to Democrats or Republicans, they are really referring to officials belonging to two umbrella groups that cover a wide variety of parties. Each of the national parties is in reality a consortium of state parties. Party chairs and other representatives from the state parties dominate national party committees. State parties, in turn, are consortiums of local parties. In some states, local parties are defined by counties. In others, they are defined by congressional districts. Although both the Democratic and Republican parties are active in every state, some state and local parties are more active than others. Parties in densely populated states such as Florida and California are well-funded, professionally run organizations. In less-populated states like Montana or Idaho, the parties have very small full-time staffs and take on more help just during the few months leading up to an election.

Particular states may have particular dominant political parties, but overall, most other Western-style democracies have much stronger political parties than those in the United States. For example, in the United States, party leaders are not able to nominate candidates of their own choosing. Most candidates are now chosen directly by the voting public through primaries. In fact, even a party's top nominee—its presidential candidate—may not have been the first choice of party leaders. This is much different than is the case in, say, Great Britain. There, political parties are much more centralized. Leadership within the party translates more cleanly into leadership in government. The party, not voters, selects the party's nominee for prime minister.

Here, the national Republican and Democratic parties essentially are made up of state parties. The Republican National Committee, for instance, is made up almost exclusively of state party chairs and one male and one female representative from each state. Representatives from the territories—Puerto Rico, Guam, and the U.S. Virgin Islands, among others—form the rest of the body. U.S. political parties tend to be regulated at the state level. The ways in which they raise and spend money, their organizational structures, and the rules they follow to nominate candidates and place them on ballots all are subject to differing state regulations. How much power the national parties have in relation to the state party shifts over time, as we shall see.

That is not to say that parties are not collections of interests. They are conglomerations of people who share some overlapping ideology, or set of political, economic, and social beliefs. These days, Democrats are supported by prochoice groups and gun control advocates. Environmentalists, trial lawyers, labor union members, and African Americans also tend to be Democrats. Republicans gain support from corporate and small businesses and social conservatives. Party members tend to advocate respect for private property and protection of rights for gun owners. Republicans are also more likely to regularly attend church than are Democrats. These differences, though, are far from absolute. For many people partisanship represents a psychological attachment to a political party—a sort of "brand loyalty"—rather than a rational assessment of personal beliefs and party stance.

After Ronald Reagan and other Republicans chipped into Democratic support among certain groups in the New Deal coalition, the Democrats

FIGURE 5-1 How It Works: Democratic and Republican Party Organization in Ohio and Cuyahoga County

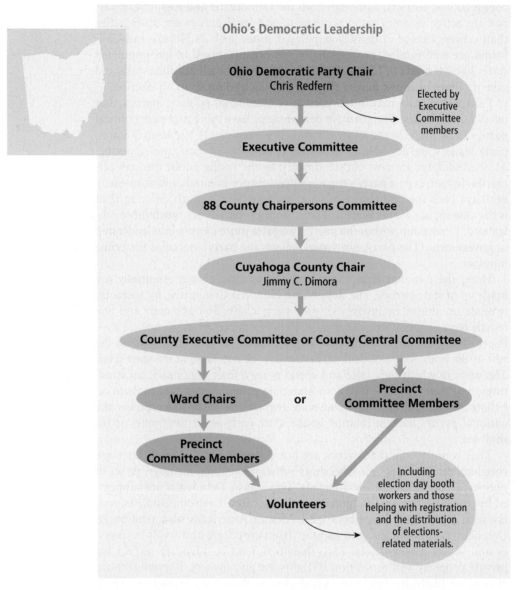

Ohio's Democratic Leadership

Ohio Democratic Party Chair
Chris Redfern

Elected by Executive Committee members

Executive Committee

88 County Chairpersons Committee

Cuyahoga County Chair
Jimmy C. Dimora

County Executive Committee or County Central Committee

Ward Chairs   or   Precinct Committee Members

Precinct Committee Members

Volunteers

Including election day booth workers and those helping with registration and the distribution of elections-related materials.

became a famously argumentative group, with various factions within the party finding it hard to find a common cause with one another. As recently as 2006, a Democratic strategist wrote about "the Democratic Party's well-deserved reputation for being a fractious coalition of infighting special interests."[4] But following their poor showing in that year's elections, Republicans began to argue more loudly among themselves about which ideas

FIGURE 5-1, continued

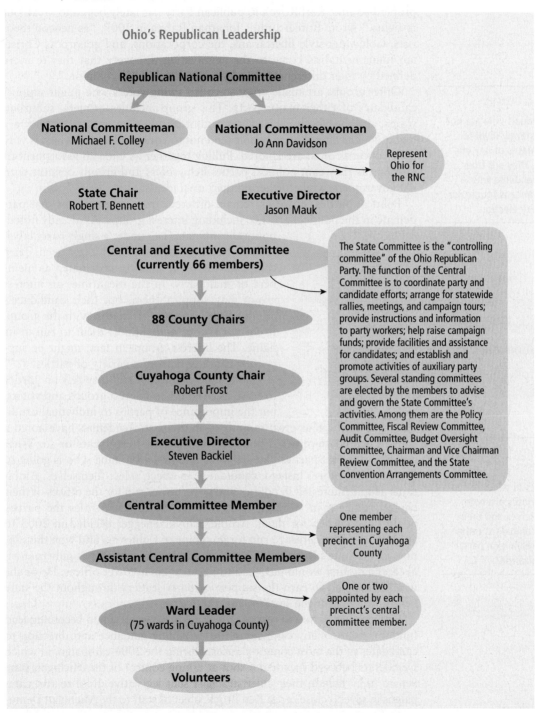

Ohio's Republican Leadership

Republican National Committee

National Committeeman
Michael F. Colley

National Committeewoman
Jo Ann Davidson

Represent Ohio for the RNC

State Chair
Robert T. Bennett

Executive Director
Jason Mauk

Central and Executive Committee
(currently 66 members)

The State Committee is the "controlling committee" of the Ohio Republican Party. The function of the Central Committee is to coordinate party and candidate efforts; arrange for statewide rallies, meetings, and campaign tours; provide instructions and information to party workers; help raise campaign funds; provide facilities and assistance for candidates; and establish and promote activities of auxiliary party groups. Several standing committees are elected by the members to advise and govern the State Committee's activities. Among them are the Policy Committee, Fiscal Review Committee, Audit Committee, Budget Oversight Committee, Chairman and Vice Chairman Review Committee, and the State Convention Arrangements Committee.

88 County Chairs

Cuyahoga County Chair
Robert Frost

Executive Director
Steven Backiel

Central Committee Member

One member representing each precinct in Cuyahoga County

Assistant Central Committee Members

One or two appointed by each precinct's central committee member.

Ward Leader
(75 wards in Cuyahoga County)

Volunteers

should prevail within the party. "Like so many parties that go on past their proper bedtime, Karl Rove's Republican Party has lately begun to break out in fights," wrote British author Jonathan Raban in 2007, "as neocon theorists, Goldwater-style libertarians, the corporations, and grassroots Christian fundamentalists come to the aggravating discovery that they're more defined by their differences than by what they hold in common."[5]

Other groups are made up of so-called **swing voters** who might support candidates of either major party. This group includes farmers, suburban voters, and the elderly. Their votes cannot be taken for granted, so they are highly sought after. Young people tend not to vote much at all, which is why their concerns often are ignored. Pulling together as wide an assortment of interests as they can, political parties help voters and groups connect with the government while furthering their own ideals.

Political parties, however, remain different from other groups that participate in the political process, including interest groups. As already noted, political candidates run under a single party label, such as Republican, Democratic, or Green. They campaign for office and are nominated as members of that party. In the meantime, an interest group may support them, but their candidacies are not based on their affiliation with the group. It did not recruit and support them to run in its name. The interest group, in fact, might be supporting candidates from a variety of parties.

These same candidates still may rely on parties to serve as conduits to interest groups and voters, but the importance of parties to individual candidates has not been as great recently as in the past. Academics have noted a shift to **candidate-centered politics** over the past thirty years or so. What they mean is that parties play less of a role in determining who is going to run for what office. Instead, candidates, in effect, select themselves. Ambitious people interested in politics and government run for the offices of their choice, rather than working their way up the ranks in roles the parties might have chosen for them. Arnold Schwarzenegger decided in 2003 to give up his acting career to run for governor of California and won the support of the state's Republican Party. In the old days, a party's gubernatorial candidate first would have had to put in years in lower offices. He or she would have had to earn the support of party leaders throughout the state before running for the state's highest office.

Parties have started to reassert themselves, however, again becoming lead fund-raisers for many campaigns and providing guidance and direction to candidates in the most contested races. During the 2006 campaign, in which Democrats believed they had a shot at taking control of the Michigan state Senate (they failed), their chief strategist sent legislative aides to run campaigns in several close races. Ken Brock, chief of staff to the Michigan Democratic Senate Campaign committee, paid homage to the idea that candidates

SWING VOTERS

Individuals who are not consistently loyal to candidates of any one party. They are true independents whose allegiance is fought for in every election.

That is not to say that parties are not collections of interests. They are conglomerations of people who share some overlapping ideology, or set of political, economic, and social beliefs.

CANDIDATE-CENTERED POLITICS

Politics in which candidates promote themselves and their own campaigns rather than relying on party organizations.

with a good feel for local issues were crucial. But he was equally interested in "educating our candidates" about the resources, messages, and tactics he believed would work for them. Lansing strategists provided the list of voters that candidates should try to contact. Brock summed up his reasoning: "The way I see it is that they're all highly competent people, but they haven't had the experience of running in an expensive, marginal contest." [6]

Parties are also a primary mechanism for the organization of government. Except for Nebraska, which is nonpartisan, all other state legislatures are organized by party. If the Democrats have a majority of the seats in the Maine House of Representatives, for example, the Speaker and other top leaders will be Democrats, and the party will control each committee as well. Not everyone supports this system. George Norris, a U.S. senator from Nebraska who promoted many changes to his home state's political system during the 1930s, argued that state politicians should be nonpartisan. That way, he claimed, they would be judged on their records dealing with issues at home, rather than on the question of whether they adhered to positions taken by national parties.

Some things have changed, however. Once the dominant force in U.S. politics—deciding who would get to run for what office and with how much support—today's political parties are such loose conglomerations of differing interests that they might be better described as marketing organizations. They are brand names that individual candidates choose to apply as a shortcut to identification in the marketplace. For example, to say that you are a Democratic candidate provides voters with a fairly reliable indication that you are for abortion rights legislation. Republicans—those who run for office, if not all rank-and-file party members—nearly always feel the opposite. In other areas, however, such as crime, welfare, and some trade issues, the distinction between party officials is less clear.

Given the overall decline of strong **voter identification** with either major party, today's politics generally centers more around individual candidates than around party politics. Parties have found a new role as support organs. They offer consulting and fund-raising services to self-selected aspirants. They have become "basically what you might call holding companies," says Walter Dean Burnham, a political science professor at the University of Texas. "They organize cash and spread it around." [7] But now parties are being forced to adapt to legal restrictions on those functions as well. A federal campaign finance law passed by Congress in 2002 and upheld by the Supreme Court in 2003 makes it more complicated for parties to spend money on activities designed to register voters or encourage them to vote. (The Supreme Court agreed to revisit the issue in 2007.) Although parties still play important roles, often candidates are raising their own money, producing their own TV ads, and creating their own campaign organizations.

This does not mean political parties have become any less important to state and local politics. What they do and how they do it has changed considerably, but democratic politics—and this certainly includes politics in

VOTER IDENTIFICATION
When a voter consistently identifies strongly with one of the parties and can be considered, for example, a Democrat or Republican.

states and localities—is virtually unthinkable without political parties. As a
theoretical ideal, or baseline, political scientists use the **responsible party
model** as a way to measure and assess political parties. The responsible
party model holds that political parties should present clear policy options
to voters, that voters will cast ballots based on the options they favor the
most, that while in office parties try to create and implement the programs
they promise, and that in the next election the parties will be judged by their
performance in delivering these programs. In short, this model views political parties as connecting the wishes of citizens to government programs
and policies, organizing the government to deliver on those wishes, and acting as the agents used to hold government accountable for delivering on
what it promises. These are all highly valuable services to democratic politics, and despite all their changes, political parties have always served these
roles, and still do.

Of course, how well parties serve these functions varies from state to
state. To have some semblance of a responsible party model you need at
least two competitive political parties offering voters clear choices on policies and programs. You also need parties that actually try to deliver on these
policies and programs once they secure a controlling influence in government. Finally, you need voters who pay attention to what the party in power
is doing and vote accordingly. States in which only one party is competitive
at the polls or where there is consistently low voter turnout are less likely
to fulfill the promises of the responsible party model.

What Parties Were Like

In their early years, political parties in the United States were a lot more
than just brand identifiers and fund-raisers. Many of the social services now
provided by local governments, such as food assistance and job placement
services, were the province of political parties throughout much of the nineteenth century. For all of the contemporary complaints about the "liberal
media," one-sided bloggers, or the domination of talk radio by conservative
hosts, today's nonpartisan media is a far cry from the newspapers of the late
nineteenth century, which were often openly affiliated with a particular
party. The pro-Republican *Chicago Tribune,* upon learning that a Democrat had won the 1876 presidential election, ran a headline that read: "Lost.
The Country Given Over to Democratic Greed and Plunder." [8] Such an
openly partisan statement is unimaginable in the mainstream media of
today, if not so unlikely on blogs.

People's party loyalties were so strong because so many of their livelihoods revolved around party interests. Party machines doled out jobs, government contracts, and other benefits to their workers and supporters. The
idea was that "offices exist not as a necessary means of administering government but for the support of party leaders at public expense," as one political scientist wrote of nineteenth-century party cliques in New York State. [9]

Politics in many cities and some states was totally dominated by these usually indigenous party machines. In Rhode Island, the Democratic Party was dominant through much of the twentieth century, and party leaders accepted little dissent. Only a handful of free-agent candidates were able to pry nominations away from those who had been endorsed by the party. In Providence, the state capital and largest city, only three individuals held the office of mayor from 1941 until 1974. Two of those men were state Democratic Party leaders. Over the same thirty-year period, only two chairs headed the Providence Democratic Party. Both of them doubled as head of the city's Department of Public Works. Party leaders controlled 2,800 jobs, doling them out roughly equally among the various wards, or political districts, within the city.[10]

The close links connecting control of jobs, government spending, and party activity were hardly unique to Rhode Island. Chicago; Nassau County on Long Island, New York; and Pennsylvania were all home to legendary **political machines**, which were also called party machines. A longstanding joke about Chicago politics held that, because they were kept on election rolls, as many dead people voted as living ones. In Oklahoma, the state gave control of most government jobs—the decision-making power over hiring and firing workers—to individual officeholders. These individuals were not afraid to exploit such control for their own benefit. "I have 85 employees— garage men, road workers, janitors, elevator operators—and they work for me when I need them," said a county commissioner. "These people care if I stay in office."[11]

The machine system was self-perpetuating, with control of jobs and power and offices feeding off of one another. "Each succeeding election was viewed not as a separate contest involving new issues or new personalities," writes political scientist Joel Sibley, "but as yet another opportunity to vote for, and reaffirm, an individual's support for his or her party and what it represented."[12] Party machines and rival factions ran "slates," or specific lists, of endorsed candidates for different offices and lent their backing to favored candidates. Sometimes this support came at a price. For instance, contenders for the West Virginia General Assembly once had to pay between $250 and $400 for the honor of being listed on one of the various slates in Kanawha County, in which the state capital of Charleston is located.

Given party contacts and contracts with private sector entities, party control of jobs often extended well beyond the borders of government. Sometimes—as was the case in Jersey City, New Jersey—the machines would charge an automatic kickback of, say, 3 percent of public employee salaries. Such trimmings were not always enough to satisfy machine lead-

POLITICAL MACHINES
Political organizations controlled by a small number of people and run for partisan ends; controlled party nominations for public office and rewarded supporters with government jobs and contracts.

"I have 85 employees—garage men, road workers, janitors, elevator operators—and they work for me when I need them," said a county commissioner. "These people care if I stay in office."

Huey Long was nicknamed "Kingfish," and the implication of royalty was fitting. He served as governor of Louisiana from 1928 to 1934, went on to serve in the U.S. Senate, and was considering a presidential run before his assassination in 1935. The head of one of the most powerful political machines of the twentieth century, as a political boss he controlled Louisiana politics with an iron fist and a mix of populist appeal and demagoguery.

ers. Clear cases of corruption, such as extorting union funds, running gambling operations, and taking kickbacks on government contracts, often led to the election of reform candidates for mayor and other city and state offices.

There were other backlashes against such obvious corruption. In New Orleans, a Democratic Party political machine called the Old Regulars ruled the city from the 1890s until the mid-1930s. By then, they were the only political force left in Louisiana outside the control of the Populist governor, Huey Long. In 1934 and 1935, Long concentrated all of his powers on changing the machine's management. He limited local control over jobs and triggered a police investigation. He even sent the National Guard into New Orleans. In the end, the machine had no choice but to accept a new city leader and get on board the Long bandwagon.[13]

Breaking up the machines usually took less extreme effort. For one thing, in many states, such as Alabama, Florida, and Michigan, there was little **patronage**—the ability of elected officials or party leaders to hand out jobs to their friends and supporters, rather than hiring based on qualifications. Therefore, there was little motivation to build up a machine. In some places, like Texas, nineteenth-century political parties were weak. They helped administer election code and tried to remain acceptable to all candidates. In other places, disgust over corruption in politics led to antimachine statutes, such as the imposition of civil service requirements on many government jobs and tougher anticorruption laws. The widespread use of **nonpartisan ballots** for municipal offices is the direct result of reforms imposed in reaction to political machines. These ballots, which do not list candidates by political party, are designed to separate city government from party voting.

California may be the best example of a state that had such a progressive reaction against machines. The state was hostile toward parties, lacked any type of patronage system, and held nonpartisan elections. Precinct and ward organizations were weak, whereas individual candidates were assertive.[14] Party organizations were once banned from endorsing candidates in primary contests. The law also limited state party chairs to two-

PATRONAGE

The ability of elected officials or party leaders to hand out jobs to their friends and supporters, rather than hiring based on merit.

NONPARTISAN BALLOTS

Ballots that do not list candidates by political party; still often used in local elections.

year terms and required the rotation of chairs on a geographical basis every two years. In 1989 the U.S. Supreme Court threw out the statute and declared it unconstitutional.[15]

California was the exception to the rule. Throughout the 1800s, most states essentially treated parties as private associations and chose not to regulate them. This remains the position of many other countries today. But during the twentieth century that all changed in the United States. States began to regulate parties as though they were public utilities. Such state regulation of political parties is examined later in this chapter.

Parties in the Twentieth Century

At the dawn of the twentieth century, political machines were generally locally based, and local parties were much more important political actors than state parties in states where there were powerful, big-city machines. Elsewhere, state parties often were funded and controlled by corporate interests—in many cases by just one interest, such as the DuPont Corporation in Delaware or the Anaconda Copper Company in Montana. Following the Progressive Era reforms in states such as California, state parties became little more than empty shells. As late as the 1970s, many state parties lacked permanent headquarters and were run out of their chairs' homes.[16]

State parties lost much of their ability to influence **primary elections**. Such elections had been used to determine a party's nominees for offices in **general elections** against other parties' nominees. It used to be that parties picked their nominees through **party conventions**—meetings of a few hundred party officials or supporters. Party leaders closely controlled most votes. In primaries, by contrast, the general public has a chance to cast a secret ballot. This gives party officials less direct control of the nominating process. Some states, such as Virginia, still allow for the option of nominating candidates by party conventions, but every state now has a system in place to nominate candidates by primaries. Every party holds a statewide convention, and many hold conventions at the local or district level as well. Nowadays, practically anyone who cares to attend a state or local convention can do so. But it still takes some effort or connections to attend a national party convention, especially as a voting delegate.

Direct primaries allow rank-and-file voters to choose nominees for public office through means of a direct ballot. This contrasts with the convention system in which the role of voters is indirect—voters choose delegates to a convention, and the delegates choose the nominee. At the state level, there are three basic types of direct primaries. **Closed primaries** allow only registered party members to vote in the party's primary, meaning that you must be a registered Democrat to vote for the Democratic nominee for office or a registered Republican to vote for the Republican nominee. This

PRIMARY ELECTIONS

Elections that determine a party's nominees for offices in general elections against other parties' nominees. Participation in primary elections is sometimes limited to voters registered as members of that particular party.

GENERAL ELECTIONS

The decisive elections in which all registered voters cast ballots for their preferred candidates for a political office.

PARTY CONVENTIONS

Meetings of party delegates called to nominate candidates for office and establish party agendas.

CLOSED PRIMARIES

Nominating elections in which only voters belonging to that party may participate. Only registered Democrats can vote in a closed Democratic primary, for example.

CROSSOVER VOTING

When members of one party vote in another party's primary. This practice is not allowed in all states.

OPEN PRIMARIES

Election races that are open to all registered voters regardless of their party affiliation.

BLANKET PRIMARIES

Elections in which all voters may cast ballots for any candidate for any office regardless of party.

RUNOFF PRIMARY

An election held if no candidate receives a majority of the vote during the regular primary. The two top finishers face off again in a runoff to determine the nominee for the general election. Such elections are held in some states, primarily in the South.

type of primary helps prevent **crossover voting**, which is when the member of one party votes in another party's primary—a Democrat voting in a Republican primary, for instance. This practice is not allowed in all states. **Open primaries** allow independents—and in some cases members of both parties—to vote in any primary they choose. **Blanket primaries** list all candidates from all parties on a single ballot and allow voters in effect to mix and match which primary they participate in. Voters can vote in one party's primary for a particular office, then switch to another party's primary for another office. In 2000 the Supreme Court invalidated blanket primaries in *California Democratic Party v. Jones*. The only blanket primary now remaining is Louisiana's, which is a nonpartisan blanket primary. If no candidate wins an outright majority in the primary, the two top vote getters—regardless of party—go on to a general election face-off. A **runoff primary** sometimes occurs in other states if no candidate receives a majority of the vote. In that case, the top two candidates face off. Map 5-1 shows the state-by-state breakdown of the three main types of primaries.

In contrast to the relative openness of primaries is the "smoke-filled room"—an area at a convention that is closed off to the public in which party barons, some puffing on big cigars, choose a candidate of their liking. It is one of the classic images in American politics. Examples of such cronyism abound. At the 1912 Republican national convention, President William Howard Taft had to stave off a challenge from his predecessor, Theodore Roosevelt. Roosevelt had been able to demonstrate his popularity among the party's rank-and-file by winning every primary that year, save the Massachusetts primary. At the time, however, only a dozen states even held primaries. Taft retained the support of the national party machinery and dominated delegate selection in nonprimary states. Ultimately, he controlled the convention. Taft was renominated, but not reelected. Roosevelt bolted the party, angrily maintaining that Taft's nomination thwarted the will of the "honestly elected majority" of GOP delegates. The split within Republican ranks was enough to elect Woodrow Wilson, only the second Democrat at that point to win the White House since the Civil War.[17]

As late as 1968, party officials had selected about 600 delegates out of 2,600 to the Democratic Party—almost 25 percent—two to four years ahead of the party's national convention. Senator Eugene McCarthy had made such a surprisingly strong showing in the New Hampshire primary that he drove President Lyndon Johnson from the race. But Johnson's backing was still enough to help his vice president, Hubert H. Humphrey, win the support of delegates controlled by party officials. McCarthy believed party rules had cheated him, so he proposed that all delegates be chosen through "procedures open to public participation" in the same year in which the nominating convention took place.

Humphrey recognized that McCarthy and Senator Robert F. Kennedy, both of whom had campaigned on anti-Vietnam platforms, had taken 69 percent of the primary vote. Respectful of what that number meant, he want-

MAP 5-1 Party Affiliation Requirements for Voting in Direct Primaries

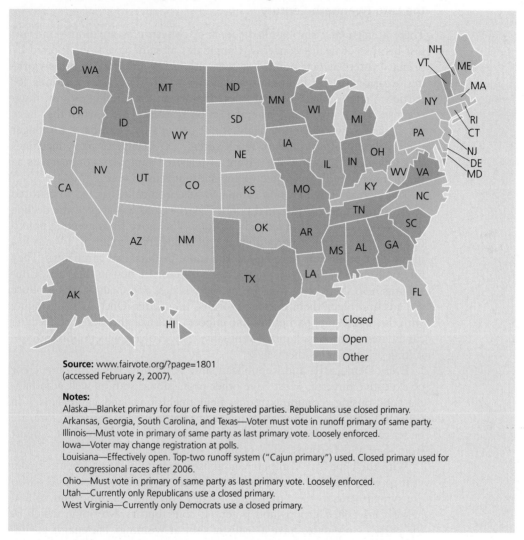

Closed
Open
Other

Source: www.fairvote.org/?page=1801
(accessed February 2, 2007).

Notes:
Alaska—Blanket primary for four of five registered parties. Republicans use closed primary.
Arkansas, Georgia, South Carolina, and Texas—Voter must vote in runoff primary of same party.
Illinois—Must vote in primary of same party as last primary vote. Loosely enforced.
Iowa—Voter may change registration at polls.
Louisiana—Effectively open. Top-two runoff system ("Cajun primary") used. Closed primary used for congressional races after 2006.
Ohio—Must vote in primary of same party as last primary vote. Loosely enforced.
Utah—Currently only Republicans use a closed primary.
West Virginia—Currently only Democrats use a closed primary.

ed to reward their followers with a consolation prize. So Humphrey coupled McCarthy's changes with one proposed by Senator George McGovern. McGovern wanted to see delegations demographically match—or at least reflect—the composition of the states they represented. More and more states threw up their figurative hands as they tried to meet each of these new requirements. Taking the path of least resistance, they decided that the easiest thing to do was to hold a popular vote primary. There had been only fifteen Democratic primaries in 1968, but by 1980 there were thirty-five. Conventions were reduced to little more than coronation ceremonies.[18]

How State Parties Recovered: Campaign Reform in the Late Twentieth Century

There aren't many smoke-filled rooms at conventions anymore—and not just because of health concerns. Candidates already have been selected by primary voters at that point. Yet conventions are still important networking occasions for officeholders and activists. They provide occasions for parties to change their internal rules. The action for candidates now, however, is in the primary and general election seasons. This is when they have the chance to woo voters directly, if not personally. Candidates no longer need hierarchical machines to reach voters. The decline of party machines was followed in time by the advent of televised campaign commercials as the dominant mode for trying to persuade citizens to vote.

The increasing reliance on campaign ads, ironically, has led to restored strength for state and national political parties and has spelled the decline of local party strength in federal elections. The move from greeting potential voters in person at party dinners and county fairs to airing TV ads has meant that politicians have had to run more professional campaigns. They hire pollsters to figure out what issues will resonate best in their ads. Consultants help shape their message on these issues, and media gurus produce the ads and place them during favorable time slots. Once more changing with the times, state parties became important clearinghouses in connecting candidates with consultants. Eventually, they evolved into important consulting organizations themselves.

Every Democratic and Republican state party now has a full-time chair or executive director. Most have other professional staff as well who handle fund-raising, communications, field operations, and campaigns.[19] In general, Republican state parties tend to be better funded and, therefore, are better run. Democratic state parties, however, often gain equivalent support from their allied groups, such as public sector unions.

With their massive computer databases, maintained and updated from year to year, political parties help candidates target and reach voters who are sympathetic to their messages. Parties also play an important role in helping interested groups and potential contributors determine which of the party's candidates have a realistic shot at winning. The major parties are not the voter organizers they were in the machine days, when individuals were encouraged to vote "early and often." Parties, however, do still contact up to 25 percent of the electorate in any election cycle. Individuals contacted by parties have a much higher tendency to vote than people who are not contacted, possibly because they feel like the party thinks their votes matter and that's why they were called, or maybe just due to the helpful reminder. While the national parties typically play a greater role in polling and developing issues, "local and state parties [are] particularly important for registering voters and conducting get out the vote campaigns."[20]

One state chair of the 1950s exemplified the move parties made toward professionalized consulting services. Ray Bliss took over the Ohio Republican Party after it suffered an electoral drubbing in 1948. He immediately began to identify and recruit better candidates. He also looked at ways to encourage citizens to vote, noting that in 1948, 140,000 rural Republicans did not vote and 150,000 potential Republican voters in urban areas were not even registered. Following Bliss's registration and get out the vote drives, Ohio Republicans in 1950 reelected a U.S. senator, won three statewide offices, and regained control of the state legislature.[21]

For years, Republicans in Ohio were so dominant that they controlled every statewide office and both chambers of the state legislature. The Democratic candidate for state attorney general in 2002 tried to turn this hegemony into a campaign issue, complaining, "What has happened in Ohio is that in many ways we have turned government over to the business community with this one-party rule."[22] That kind of complaint became more salient in 2006, when a series of scandals involving GOP officials and their cronies led to the election of a Democratic governor for the first time in twenty years.

Minority party members enviously keep close tabs on the governing party, and they alert the public and the press to every perceived misstep and abuse. It also is important for minority parties not to get demoralized and to continue to offer voters alternative choices, so that candidates from their parties will be in place once the public is ready for a change. For instance, conservative Republicans dominated the Arizona Senate during the late 1990s. It seemed certain that Arizona Speaker of the House Jeff Groscost would join their ranks in 2000, since he was running in a Senate district that heavily favored the GOP. Late in the campaign season, however, Groscost was implicated in a scandal surrounding a massive tax break that aided SUV owners—including a Groscost friend who sold the vehicles—and cost the state hundreds of millions of dollars. Groscost was beat by his previously unknown Democratic challenger, and the Senate ended up operating under divided control between the parties.

The two parties remain so closely competitive nationally today that political scientists refer to a period of **dealignment**, meaning that neither party is dominant. In earlier periods of American history, one party or another generally dominated politics, meaning it held most of the important offices. The two major examples are Republican dominance from the time of the Civil War into the 1920s and the Democratic New Deal coalition, which held power from the presidential election of 1932 into the 1960s. The 1932 election of Franklin D. Roosevelt was the best example of a **realignment**. This means that popular support switched from one party to another. Neither party has pulled off a similarly lasting realignment since then as voters seem about equally supportive of both major parties. Indeed, Republican hopes of creating a "permanent majority" following Bush's 2004 win look illusory at this point.

DEALIGNMENT

When no one party can be said to dominate politics in this country.

REALIGNMENT

When popular support switches from one party to another.

State Party Regulation and Finance

It is important to note that the parties, although they are most active during the campaign season, do not dry up and blow away once an election is over. Not only is there planning for the next election . . . and the one after that . . . and the one after that, in perpetuity, but parties also play an important role in actual government operations. Granted, parties no longer are able to run government strictly to perpetuate their own power, as was true to a certain extent in the machine era. But they still help their most important supporters maintain access to officeholders and other officials.

Most municipal governments are organized on a nonpartisan basis like the Nebraska state legislature. Every other state legislature is organized by party. In other words, if the Democrats hold a majority of the seats in a state's House of Representatives, they not only control the leadership, schedule, and agenda of the House, but other Democrats chair House committees as well. There are exceptions and examples of shared power, particularly when partisan control of a legislature is tied, but these are rare. The more normal state of affairs is for the majority party to rule.

State Party Regulation

Remember that states did not regulate political parties until the beginning of the twentieth century, when the progressive backlash against machine abuse led states to intervene. Political scientists now refer to parties as equivalent to public utilities, such as water and electricity, in which the public has a sufficient interest to justify state regulation.[23] Political parties, after all, are the main conduit for contesting elections and organizing government. The legal justifications states have used to regulate parties revolve around registration requirements—twenty-seven states register voters by party—since party names are printed alongside those of their candidates on ballots.

Thirty-eight states regulate aspects of the structure of their state and local parties, often in explicit detail, in order to avoid antidemocratic, machine boss control.[24] A state sometimes determines, for instance, how the members of a state party's central committee should be selected and how often that committee will meet. It can specify what party organization can name a substitute candidate if a nominee dies or withdraws prior to an election. Such regulation is practiced whether it is in regard to a state party in Minnesota or a local party in Pennsylvania.

A relatively limited number of state parties have challenged the laws in their states in the wake of the 1989 Supreme Court decision, mentioned previously. The Court ruled that the state of California did not have the authority to dictate how political parties are organized. The major parties in New Jersey did adopt a number of changes in party structure, but for the most part the parties seem satisfied with the way things are being run under the systems imposed on them by the states.

Governing States and Localities

Nineteen eighty-nine was not the first time nor the last time the U.S. Supreme Court weighed in on the political party issue. The nation's highest court has issued a number of other decisions in recent years to clarify the legal rights of parties. In a series of cases emanating from Illinois during the 1970s and 1980s, the Court made it clear that "party affiliations and support" are unconstitutional bases for the granting of a majority of government or public jobs, except at the highest levels.[25] In 1986, it ruled that the state of Connecticut could not prevent independents from voting in Republican Party primaries, if the GOP welcomed them.[26] This precedent, which allowed the parties rather than the state to determine who could participate in a party's primary, was later followed in several other states. The parties have not always gotten their way, however. In 1999 the Court determined that states have the constitutional right to regulate elections and prevent manipulation. The ruling blocked a new party in Minnesota from "fusing" with the state's Democratic Party by nominating candidates for election that the Democrats already had nominated.[27]

A total of $5,903,658 was contributed to Hawaii's Democratic and Republican parties in 2005—with $4,031,829 of that going to Democrats.

Campaign Finance

In 1996, the U.S. Supreme Court lifted federal limits on how much parties could spend. Under the new rules, a party could spend as much as it liked to support a candidate, as long as the candidate did not approve the party's strategy or ads or have any say over what the party was doing. The Court decided that no one had the right to restrict **independent expenditures,** or those activities that are run without the candidate's knowledge or approval. "We do not see how a Constitution that grants to individuals, candidates, and ordinary political committees the right to make unlimited independent expenditures could deny the same right to political parties," wrote Justice Stephen G. Breyer.[28] A decade later, the Court tossed a Vermont law that sought to limit fund-raising and the amounts that could be spent by candidates on state campaigns.

In addition to this legal windfall, state parties already had been exempted from a number of federal campaign finance limits. In 1974 and 1976, Congress enacted laws that limited the amount of money candidates could collect from individuals and **political action committees,** or PACs. Congress revised the law in 1979 after complaints from party leaders that the new laws almost completely eliminated state and local party organizations from participating in presidential campaigns. The old law, party leaders contended, put too many restrictions on how parties could spend money during a presidential election year. The revised law lifted all limits on what state and local parties could raise or spend for "party building" activities. These included purchasing campaign materials, such as buttons, bumper stickers, and yard signs, and conducting voter registration and get-out-the-vote drives.[29]

It quickly became clear that the more lax restrictions were broad enough to allow for the purchase of TV ads and other campaign-related activities

INDEPENDENT EXPENDITURES

Ad campaigns or other political activities that are run by a party or an outside group without the direct knowledge or approval of a particular candidate for office.

POLITICAL ACTION COMMITTEES

Groups formed for the purpose of raising money to elect or defeat political candidates. They usually represent business, union, or ideological interests.

A Difference that Makes a Difference:
That Clean-All-Over Feeling: Maine's Public Financing of Campaigns

Many people believe politics is inherently corrupt. This belief is compounded by the fact that campaign funding comes from individuals, corporations, and unions with a direct interest in the policies and decisions elected officials make once in office. For this reason, the public financing of campaigns has long held appeal for reformers. "I think it's a very freeing feeling," says Maine state representative Marilyn Canavan, who helped draft a public finance law as head of the state ethics commission. "It means I can make decisions that are right for the people of Maine, and not be concerned in the least whether any campaign contributions are forthcoming."[a]

Through a ballot initiative, Maine has set up a voluntary system of public campaign finance for state legislative offices.[b] Anyone who wishes to pursue any state office is granted enough free money to run a credible campaign, as long as a sufficient number of $5 contributions are received upfront to show the candidate's serious intent. In 2006 more than 80 percent of Maine's candidates for the legislature renounced private funding in favor of taking the public money.

But whether Maine has really succeeded in lessening the role of special interests in state politics is a more complicated question. Since there are no restrictions on what the parties can spend—even on behalf of publicly financed candidates—there are those who see the new law as likely to attract more special interest money, not less. Among those skeptics is a former Maine governor, Angus King. The so-called clean elections law, he says, "has a gigantic loophole that really bothers me. You're running as a clean candidate, but the party can spend a million dollars on your behalf. To me, that undermines the whole premise. What you've really done is add a layer of public money to the old system." As if to prove his point, legislative leaders in Maine—even some who initially opposed the clean elections law—have been building up political action committees that raise hundreds of thousands of dollars they can spend supporting candidates of their choice.

A number of other states have enacted partial public finance laws of one sort or another during the past three decades. Some have achieved modest success. Candidates in Minnesota, for instance, tend to abide by spending limits and receive some public financing in return. More commonly, however, public financing has been a failure and largely for one reason. The money available—usually from voluntary tax checkoffs, in which taxpayers designate a few dollars from their tax returns to be spent on campaign finance—is insufficient to pay for the campaigns it is supposed to cover. Wisconsin, for example, became a pioneer when it enacted a public financing law in the late 1970s. But spending limits in Wisconsin have not been raised since 1986, and participation in the voluntary tax checkoff has fallen to less than 10 percent. That means that the amount of public financing grants has dropped to the point where no serious legislative or gubernatorial candidates are willing to choose them instead of taking private contributions.

Maine's law allows for inflationary adjustment, and the state has a small population and a low-key political system with a tradition of informal personal campaigning. A clean elections budget of $20,000 comes closer to full funding of a state senate election in Maine than it would almost anywhere else in the country.

Still, the state's lobbyists and pressure groups are adapting to the law, changing the way they interact with candidates seeking office. Rather than treating candidates like charities, writing out checks and declaring themselves done, interest groups are recruiting candidates themselves and then running issue ads to support them. Such ads do not fall under the clean elections law limits. "People are changing strategies to do the same things they've always done," says Ed McLaughlin, president of the Maine Economic Research Institute. "I expect as time goes by and people get savvy about what they can and cannot do, you're going to see more money come into campaigns. I think part of the intent of the public in passing this law was to take money out of politics. It ain't gonna happen."

[a] Adapted from Alan Greenblatt, "That Clean All-Over Feeling," *Governing* magazine, July 2002, 40.
[b] Arizona has a similar system; five other states have limited programs.

with so-called **soft money** donations, which were nominally meant to support party building. Restrictions on how parties spent soft money, which was raised in increments of $100,000 and more from corporations, unions, and wealthy individuals, were nearly meaningless—as long as the parties did not coordinate directly with candidates. Parties violated the spirit, if not the letter of the law, with state parties acting as virtual soft money laundering machines for the national parties and for each other. In 2002, Congress revisited the issue and enacted the McCain-Feingold campaign finance law, which blocked the national parties from collecting soft money donations.[30]

Meanwhile, the state parties themselves are no slouches at raising money, as is seen in Figure 5-2. Democrats and Republicans at the state level raised a total of $735 million during the 2004 election cycle—which represented a slight dip because of the loss of federal party transfers under McCain-Feingold.[31] But no matter what limitations are placed on campaign finance, money finds its way into the system, because the U.S. Supreme Court has held that political expenditures are equivalent to free speech. Says University of Virginia government professor Larry J. Sabato,

> There is no way to stop the flow of interested money and there will always be constitutional ways around the restrictions enacted into law. What is so fundamental is that politics and government determine the allocation of goods and values in society. Those goods and values are critical to the success or failure of hundreds of interest groups and millions of individuals. Those groups and individuals are going to spend the money to defend their interests, period.[32]

Party Competition: Why Some States Are More Competitive than Others

The Republican Party came out of the 2002 elections with control over many of the nation's political institutions. Republicans held the White House, the U.S. House of Representatives, and they regained control of the Senate. They defied predictions and held onto a majority of governorships. For the first time since 1952, the party came out ahead in the total number of state legislative seats. Yet their victories did not represent political breakthroughs that they could necessarily bank on. All of the Republican majorities were quite narrow, reflecting the level of parity between the two major parties that has kept both of them from firm political dominance for a decade.

Just how narrow were some of the margins? Republicans had only two more governorships than Democrats. Both congressional chambers were nearly tied. Following the 2002 elections, Republicans held 49.6 percent of

FIGURE 5-2 State Party Fund-raising over Time

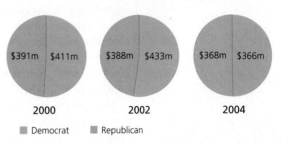

Democrat   Republican

Source: Reprinted by permission from the Center for Public Integrity. www.publicintegrity.org/partylines/report.aspx?aid=690 (accessed March 14, 2007).

SOFT MONEY

Money that is not subject to federal regulation that can be raised and spent by state parties. A 2002 law banned the use of soft money in federal elections.

the nation's 7,400 legislative seats, whereas Democrats trailed just slightly with 49.4 percent of the seats. Republicans held a slight edge in the number of state chambers and legislatures they controlled, but the margins often were slim. In fact, a vacancy in any of a dozen legislative chambers could have resulted in a change of party control.[33] Things got even tighter after the 2004 elections, when the two parties ended up essentially tied in the total number of seats they controlled nationwide.

Democrats not only regained control of Congress in 2006, but made impressive gains at the state level as well. Following that year's elections, Democrats held twenty-eight of the fifty state governorships—their first majority in a dozen years. In addition, Democrats emerged with a 660-seat advantage in state legislative seats. But a swing of less than 5 percent of the total number of seats could leave the two parties essentially tied once again.

Historically, most state political cultures have heavily favored one party or the other, as shown in Map 5-2. A well-known example of this is the old Democratic "Solid South." For more than a century, most Southern voters were "yellow dog" Democrats, meaning they would sooner vote for a yellow dog than for a Republican. From 1880 to 1944, all eleven states of the old Confederacy voted for Democrats in every presidential election—with a couple of exceptions in 1920 and 1928—elected only Democrats and a few independents governor, and elected only Democrats to the U.S. Senate after popular voting for senators began in 1916.[34] The Democratic hegemony in the South began to break up with the civil rights era that began, roughly, with the elections of 1948.

Today, either party starts out with a fair chance of winning statewide elections in just about every state. That is actually a big change. Republicans are now about even—or dominant—politically in the South, but they have lost their edge in the Northeast, which is now one of the more Democratic sections of the country. Republicans hold the advantage in many states of the Mountain West, but Democrats are stronger along the Pacific Coast. All of this was perhaps most noticeable in the 2002 gubernatorial elections, when old party strangleholds finally broke. Georgia elected a Republican governor for the first time since 1868, ending the longest drought for either party in any state before or since. The GOP also took the governor's mansion in other states that had traditionally gone Democratic. These states included Maryland, which elected a Republican for the first time since 1966, and Hawaii, which chose the Grand Old Party for the first time since 1959. Democrats, meanwhile, won in Illinois, Maine, Michigan, and Wisconsin for the first time in well over a decade. They seated governors in Arizona, Kansas, Oklahoma, and Wyoming—states that had been supporting mostly Republicans in recent years.[35] Of the twenty-four new governors elected in 2002, twenty wrested control from a governor of another party. In 2006, most of the Democratic gains at the gubernatorial level came in states Republicans had left vacant due to term limits or retire-

MAP 5-2 Interparty Competition, 1999–2003

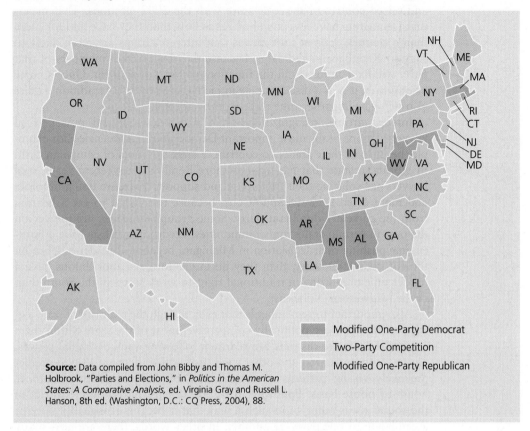

Modified One-Party Democrat

Two-Party Competition

Modified One-Party Republican

Source: Data compiled from John Bibby and Thomas M. Holbrook, "Parties and Elections," in *Politics in the American States: A Comparative Analysis,* ed. Virginia Gray and Russell L. Hanson, 8th ed. (Washington, D.C.: CQ Press, 2004), 88.

ment; Maryland governor Bob Ehrlich was the only incumbent Republican who was defeated.

Why the decline of one-party dominance in nearly every state? One factor is the increased mobility of the American population. People once put down roots and perpetuated the political culture of their families, whereas today the country's population is constantly shifting. The many Northeasterners who have moved into the South, for example, do not hold the same cultural memory of the Civil War that kept many conservatives from supporting Republicans. Immigrants to California have made the state more Democratic—Republicans politically misplayed their hand with California Hispanics by pushing an anti-immigrant ballot initiative during the 1990s (a pattern that may have been repeated at the national level in 2006 when House Republicans supported a bill to deport illegal aliens). But the departure of many conservative voters who moved to other Western states such as Nevada and Utah has made the Golden State more Democratic as well.

All of that said, there are still plenty of places that are dominated by a single party. Republicans currently control every statewide office in Texas and seized control of the legislature with the 2002 elections. That means that Democrats have less power in Texas now than they have had for more than a century. This in turn means that interest groups are more likely to support Republican candidates, because they believe that members of that party will have more say in the function of state government. Once a party loses power, it is at a disadvantage in recovering power. Its traditional allies also will have a harder time pushing their agenda.

Interest groups recognize the fluid nature of political power. Trial lawyers are one of the most important Democratic constituencies, for example, because of their ability to contribute large amounts of campaign cash. In Florida, a state that has become more Republican in recent years, trial lawyers are splitting their donations and support. They are lining up more and more often behind Republicans, because they want to get a hearing from the currently dominant party. Some groups, however, are forever on the outs in certain states and communities. Environmentalists have a harder time pushing their legislation in Michigan, because of its dependence on the automotive industry, than they do in California. Labor unions have a harder time organizing in traditional right-to-work states in the South than in the Midwest or Northeast.

Also important to remember is that even though the majority of state legislative chambers are politically competitive, most of the seats within them are not. Legislative districts are redrawn following each decennial census. Given computerization and other tools, political leaders are able to predict the likely voting patterns of people on a block-by-block or sometimes house-by-house basis. Following the 2000 census, nearly every district in the country was redrawn in such a way that it became reasonably safe for a candidate of one party or another. In other words, there are now many safe Democratic districts and safe Republican districts, but not a lot of districts that are competitive. That means that most of the competition for a seat will take place in the primary race of the dominant party. If a district looks likely to support a Republican, several qualified candidates might run for the GOP nod. The Democratic nomination probably will not stimulate as much competition.

Effect of Parties on Political Culture

Democrats are generally more liberal, favoring governmental solutions to social problems. Republicans are generally more conservative, preferring a limited role for government. These are not hard and fast rules, but they are true most of the time and have been true for many decades. As a result, the dominance of one party over the other has had an effect on the political culture of many states. Where there have been successful efforts to mobilize low-income voters through class-based appeals, in places such as Louisiana and Minnesota, government has gotten bigger. If these individuals put someone into office, they expect the support and social programs they were promised.

It is equally unsurprising that politicians who have come to power promising not to raise taxes have kept government growth in check. In New Hampshire, William Loeb, the editor of the Manchester *Union Leader,* came up with the idea of challenging political candidates to sign a no tax pledge. The pledge became embedded in the state's political culture. Within thirty years New Hampshire was transformed from a relatively high revenue state, one that could depend upon gaining adequate monies from taxes to fund public programs, to a low revenue state.[36] The result? Among other things, New Hampshire was the only state in the country not to offer universal kindergarten classes as recently as 1997.

What may be surprising is the fact that when the parties *really* held real sway—when the machines were more important than any individual office-holder—they were not much interested in expanding government either. Machine politicians wanted to maintain their grip on the government jobs and contracts they already had. This would seem to make sense for a conservative machine, like that run by Sen. Harry Byrd in Virginia from the 1920s to the 1960s. After all, Byrd and his acolytes shared a respect for balanced budgets and a small public sector. But party machines in general, even progressive ones, usually were not expansionistic. In the machine era, party officials squabbled more over who got control of what government jobs than about changing the number or nature of those jobs. They certainly did not present new government-based solutions to problems. Keeping jobs tied to political loyalties discouraged the creation of a professionalized bureaucracy.

In the meantime, the public did not want corrupt machine politicians to control any more of their money than necessary. Interest groups, such as unions, that might have wanted an expansion of government programs, did not hold enough influence to promote them.[37] As the parties and political machines weakened, however, candidates, party activists, and interest groups became free agents, free to promote all manner of new programs and government expansion.

Party Factions and Activists

Parties are no longer able to reward their followers directly with jobs or other payoffs. Decisions handed down by the U.S. Supreme Court have made it clear that party affiliation is not a constitutional basis to decide government hires. Kentucky governor Ernie Fletcher learned that the hard way in 2006, when he and several other top state officials were indicted for hiring supporters. Fletcher had been the first Republican elected to run the state in more than thirty years, and members of his administration were apparently too eager to hire party loyalists for government positions, disregarding the state's merit-hiring law in some instances.

Without party leaders being able to dispense prizes such as jobs, activism and party tasks have become largely volunteer activities. And since people seldom work for free unless they believe in something very strongly, political volunteers have become more ideological. People work for candidates and parties because they believe in specific causes, such as handgun legislation or protections for small business owners.

Just because jobs are no longer the parties' golden eggs does not mean that politicians and parties do not seek to pluck favors from their constituents through policies or promises. Both major parties court the elderly with assurances of healthcare benefits, such as providing prescription drugs through Medicare. The reason is that senior citizens vote and thus are worth courting. Young people, by contrast, do not vote. Only 13 percent of all people aged eighteen to thirty voted in the November 2002 elections.[38] The young did vote in greater numbers in 2004 and 2006, energized by issues such as the war in Iraq. But their turnout remained fairly anemic. About 24 percent of Americans thirty years of age and younger voted in 2006, which was the best midterm showing for the young in twenty years.[39]

Each party has its main constituent groups, but that does not preclude both parties from trying to poach supporters from the other side. Democrats have been at pains in recent years to present a friendly face to business interests, while Republican president George W. Bush has courted Teamsters and building trade unions. Remember, however, that each party is a kaleidoscope of interest groups and can only appeal so much to any one group before it risks alienating support among other groups.

It is obvious that you cannot simultaneously support higher pay for teachers and cutting educational budgets. That is why politicians must perform the neat trick of motivating the true believers within party ranks to support their candidacy during a primary election without pinning themselves down so much that they do not appeal to members of the other party and independents during the general election. Overall, the more contentious the issue, the more a party will try to blur its differences with the other party. Candidates do not want to promise so much to their core supporters—known as the "base"—that they cannot reach other voters. If you promise a lot of money for public transportation, for instance, that might help you in the city but hurt you in the suburbs.

Both major parties try to appeal to as much of the populace as possible. But their supporters sometimes care more about promoting an issue than they do about winning elections. Interest groups now raise their own funds and use them freely to promote their issues in campaigns. We'll talk about how interest groups lobby governments a little later in this chapter, but it is worth examining quickly the type of role they can play in contemporary politics.

A 1998 special election for a vacant congressional seat based in Santa Barbara, California, demonstrated the difficulty that the parties have in maintaining discipline in message and candidate selection. Congressional Republican leaders, both in Washington and in Southern California, favored a state representative who was a liberal on social issues. They thought he had the right profile to win in the liberal-leaning district. Local and national conservative activists, however, were unwilling to accept this candidate. Two conservative Christian groups, the Catholic Alliance and the Christian Coalition, each distributed one hundred thousand voter guides at churches and other venues in the days leading up to the special primary in support of a more conservative candidate. That candidate won the GOP nomination but lost the general election.[40]

Numerous interests took an active role in that particular general election campaign that fall, including groups that favored term limits, antiabortion and prochoice advocates, labor unions, environmental organizations, and antitax groups. In fact, the amount of money the candidates spent on their own campaigns was dwarfed by the amount spent by these and other outside groups. This has become more the rule and less the exception in recent years. In Wisconsin, political races often are dominated by issue ads run by the Wisconsin Manufacturers and Commerce and the Wisconsin Education Association Council (WEAC). Because these groups care so much about, respectively, taxes and education, these issues dominate many races. Politicians and parties have no control over such ads, so they cannot control the agenda. Anything else the candidates might want to emphasize is likely to be drowned out. Nobody disputes that taxes and schools are important, but making them the only subjects detracts from other issues.[41]

By the 1980s, it appeared that candidates were fairly free agents. They were rid of the old party machine apparatus and able to set their own agendas and spread their own messages, largely through broadcast ads. Twenty years later, times have changed again. Yes, candidates are more independent, presenting themselves for party nomination and spending sums they have raised to get into the public eye. Campaigns, however, have become such big business that these funds and this self-motivation often are not enough. Plus, candidates need votes, and to get these votes they must join ranks with party officials and interest groups who tend to take the candidate's ball and run away with it. Candidates become mere pawns in campaigns that have been overtaken by deep-pocketed interest groups. They stand on the sidelines and watch as parties or other groups run the greater volume of ads, redefining their campaigns for them.

It is easy to become confused about who is the most powerful—candidates, interest groups, or political parties—and in which situations they hold that power. What is important to remember is that all three are vital parts of the political process and that their relative importance varies depending on the time and place. It is impossible to illustrate every variation, but none of them are ever either nothing or everything. Their roles are entwined.

Pragmatism vs. Idealism

Interest groups, just like parties, are most likely to play a prominent role in races that are closely contested or that can tip the partisan balance in a legislature. Redistricting at both the federal and state legislative levels, however, has grown so sophisticated—with so much emphasis placed on making districts safe for incumbents—that relatively few of these races are closely contested. Much of the action takes place in primary contests. But in true "swing" districts, where either party has a shot at winning, both major parties and all of their allies will spend as much money as they can muster to win.

In these cases, party leaders grow frustrated when interest groups trumpet issues that do not appeal to a wider public, as was the case in the California congressional race just discussed. The main goal of parties is to win elections, so they are much more interested in fielding candidates who fit the profile of the office in contention than they are in promoting a specific ideology. The Republican National Committee, for example, defeated an attempt in 1998 to pass a party resolution that would have blocked the party from giving any money to candidates opposed to a ban on late-term abortions. Social conservatives were angry that the national committee had spent $760,000 supporting the reelection effort of New Jersey governor Christine Todd Whitman, who had vetoed a state ban on the procedure. "I'm about as pro-life as anybody," said Bob Hiler of Indiana's national committee, "but I just cannot accept a situation in the Republican Party where there is a litmus test if you want to join or be a candidate. I respect the decisions of our national party leaders to place money where it needs to go to ensure that we win that seat." [42]

With just two broad-based national parties, neither can afford to preach an unyielding gospel on any single issue. The people most interested in politics may be motivated by their investment in a particular issue, but if they hang around long enough, they come to realize that no one can win all the time. Perversely, the parties that are best able to keep their troops in line and satisfied with less than perfect ideological purity are the parties currently out of power. In other words, the desire to get back into the White House or to hold majority control of a legislature is often strong enough to convince all the quarreling factions to back someone who looks like a winner—even if that candidate is not "perfect" on all of the issues.

But the fact that both parties spend a good deal of time blurring their positions on the most important issues of the day to try to appeal to the most people while alienating the fewest number has made a lot of voters sour on them. As Colonel Aureliano Buendia discovered in *One Hundred Years of Solitude,* many Americans believe that politicians do not stand for anything and are more interested in preserving power than doing the right thing. That is a major reason why voters have become more independent in recent decades and have refused to give lifelong allegiance to one party or the other in the same way that their grandparents did. "It probably would have been better for the parties if the public had become more negative rather than more neutral toward them," writes political scientist Martin Wattenberg. "Negative attitudes can easily be turned into positive attitudes by better performance or a change in policies. To induce people to care about political parties once again may well be more difficult." [43]

Third Parties and Independents

Since millions of people are disenchanted with the Republican and Democratic parties, for a variety of reasons, why isn't there more of a movement toward establishing a viable third, or minor, party as an alternative? After all, in most other democracies, there are numerous parties with strong support. In countries such as Israel and Italy, the leading party typically does not have enough seats in parliament to construct a government on its own and has to enter into a coalition with other parties.

That has never been the case in the United States for a number of reasons. Democrats and Republicans, as we have been exploring, have established wide networks of contacts and supporters—individuals and groups who have long loyalties to one party or the other. They have officeholders at all levels who can help with strategy and fund-raising.

The major parties also have many institutional advantages. For one thing, the United States favors a winner-takes-all system in which the highest vote getter in a district wins. In some countries, seats are distributed on a percentage basis, so that if a party gets 5 percent of the vote it receives about 5 percent of the total seats available. But if a party only took 5 percent of the vote across the United States, it probably would not win a seat anywhere. In 1992, Texas computer billionaire Ross Perot, the most successful third party presidential candidate in decades, took 19 percent of the vote but did not carry a single state.

For the 1996 presidential race, Perot established the Reform Party, which he called his gift to the American people. Perot used that gift himself, running for a second time but not doing nearly so well. He had a hard time getting on the ballot in some states—the rules differ in many places and are often complicated. In the state of New York, for instance, a candidate must collect a certain number of signatures from each of the congressional districts to get on the ballot. Many candidates with less financial means than Perot have had difficulty gaining access to ballots. Perot himself was excluded from the presidential debates. The commission running the debates—composed of officials from the Democratic and Republican parties—decided he was not showing enough strength in the polls to warrant being included.

Excluded though he was, Perot nevertheless took 8 percent of the vote in 1996. This was enough to guarantee the Reform nominee in 2000 a spot on all fifty state ballots, as well as $12 million in federal campaign funds. With Perot out of the running, however, the Reform nomination dissolved into chaos. Two separate conventions nominated two separate candidates. The states were left having to decide which candidate deserved the spot on the ballot. "There are no statutes to guide us," said Mike Cooney, Montana secretary of state. "The Reform Party needed to resolve this issue before it got to this point. It's an internal party problem that has been foisted upon the states and put us all in a bad situation." The eventual Reform nominee proved not to be as much of a factor in the race as Green Party nominee Ralph Nader. The Reform Party seemed to have self-destructed. Several of the old minor parties that had taken up its banner, such as Minnesota's Independence Party, soon returned to their original names.

Difficulties of Building Support

Many Democrats blamed Nader for the defeat of their candidate, Al Gore. Gore won more popular votes than Republican George W. Bush but was defeated in the electoral college. Some people believe that a third party candidate will never be anything more than a "spoiler" who deprives major party candidates of needed votes. Others believe that third parties help present a real and needed alternative to the Democrats and Republicans. Unless the major parties are challenged, the thinking goes, they will never change.

The major parties, however, have proven quite adept at co-opting the most popular ideas presented by third party candidates. Both Democratic and Republican candidates of the 1990s took the idea of a balanced federal budget more seriously because Perot had raised the issue. During the 1930s, Franklin D. Roosevelt lifted many of the ideas of Socialist candidate Norman Thomas. When faced with the rare strong minor party challenge, a major party candidate can argue that he offers the best vehicle for presenting any shared ideals—and stands a better chance of beating the other major party candidate. As noted earlier, Perot's 1992 showing was the best by a third party candidate since Theodore Roosevelt's in 1912—and neither one of them came close to winning.

Minor party candidates have enjoyed more success running for lower offices, but not much. Within a state or a legislative district, there is a better chance that an individual will enjoy enough personal popularity to equalize the playing field against Democrats and Republicans who typically are better funded and connected. Still, there have been only five governors elected during the last fifty years who were not either Democrats or Republicans. Two of those five—Walter Hickel of Alaska and Lowell Weicker of Connecticut—had earlier won statewide office as Republicans. Another two were elected in Maine, a state noted for the independent-mindedness of its electorate. The fifth, Jesse Ventura of Minnesota, served only one term, and the would-be successor from his Independence Party finished a distant third in 2002.

At the legislative level, things are just as grim for third party candidates. Following the 2006 elections, there were only 18 third party or independent state legislators in the United States (not counting nonpartisan Nebraska), out of a total of 7,400. Each of these candidates had dedicated followers. But from a pragmatic perspective—say, as a voter or an interest group interested in seeing your agenda becoming law—it probably makes better sense to support a Democrat or Republican who has a chance of serving in the majority party than it does to pull for a person who will hold just one vote.

A few minor parties have enjoyed a period of success in certain states, such as the Progressive Party during the 1920s in Wisconsin and the Farmer-Labor Party during the 1930s in Minnesota. Over time, though, these parties have been unable to survive the loss of early, popular leaders or have been absorbed by one of the major parties. For example, the official name of Minnesota's Democratic Party is still the Democratic Farmer-Labor Party, in reference to its merger with the defunct minor party. The Liberal Party of New York boasted a New York City mayor in the 1960s named John Lindsay. New York is one of the few states that allow candidates to be listed multiple times on a ballot, as the nominee of, for instance, both the Liberal and the Republican parties. In 1980, U.S. senator Jacob Javits was denied the nomination of the state's Republican Party and ran on the Liberal line. He succeeded only in splitting the votes of liberals, moderates, and Democrats and helping to elect a more conservative Republican. The Liberal Party disbanded in 2003 after failing to garner enough votes in the previous year's gubernatorial contest to maintain its guaranteed spot on state ballots. "Parties, I suppose, have a life span," said Dan Cantor, executive director of the Working Families Party. "They had their heyday in the [19]50s and [19]60s. It looks like they have come to a full stop." [44]

Ultimately, it is the states that print the ballots and have the authority to decide which parties' nominees are going to be listed on them. It is the states that grant ballot access to parties based on their having won a minimum percentage of the vote in a previous statewide general election. The threshold varies from 1 percent in Wisconsin to as much as 20 percent in Georgia. Such high institutional barriers make minor parties' complaints about two-party dominance of American politics about as fruitless as trying to hold back the tide.

Major Party Support

One other reason minor parties have trouble gaining traction is that people are not, in the main, terribly unhappy with the major parties. The major parties, after all, do devote themselves to appealing to as broad a range of citizens as possible. That said, voter identification with the parties has declined. Some states once allowed voters to vote a straight ticket, meaning they could pull one lever to vote for all the Democratic or Republican candidates on the ballot. Such procedures are now considered quaint. Voters are more and more willing to divide their ballots, a practice called **ticket splitting**. One voter joked, "I vote for the man for president, and give him a Congress he can't work with."

In 1960, the Gallup Organization found that 47 percent of respondents identified themselves as Democrats, 30 percent as Republicans, and just 23 percent as independents or members of other parties. By the 1990s, those numbers had converged. Polling by the Pew Research Center for the People and the Press over a fifty-four-month period in the mid-1990s found an average of 33 percent of the respondents called themselves Democrats, 29 percent Republicans, and 33 percent independents, with a handful naming other specific parties.[45] A poll released by the Pew Research Center in early 2007 found that Democrats had picked up strength, but other contemporary polls found a continuing three-way division.

Most self-identified independents are not true independents, however. What this means is that their preferences generally do lean toward one major party or the other. "Partisan loyalties in the American populace have rebounded significantly since the mid-1970s, especially among those who actually turn out to vote," concluded political scientist Larry M. Bartels in 2000.[46] Pure independents, those who do not lean toward either party, peaked at 16 percent in 1976. Twenty years later, true independents were just 9 percent of the populace.[47]

The Republicans and Democrats have dominated American politics for 150 years. They have met every challenge—both ideological and structural—and found a way to preserve their near-total control. As political scientist Jeff Fishel puts it,

> If there's any lesson of history about the two major parties in American politics, it is that they're incredible adaptive survivors. They lost the monopoly they had, particularly on candidate recruitment and finance. That certainly does not mean that they're going out of business, just that they have to compete with other groups.[48]

Interest Groups and Lobbies

If many citizens are cynical about political parties, they're even more cynical about interest groups. It's true that lobbyists representing big companies or unions often push for legislation to promote or protect their own narrow interests. But lobbying is how citizens and private companies make their views known to policymakers between election seasons. Sometimes, people even lobby for altruistic reasons, rather than self-interest.

Consider Daniel Millenson. He was a freshman at Brandeis University who grew alarmed about stories of genocide taking place in the Darfur region of Sudan. Being Jewish and having a "cultural memory" of the Holocaust, he decided he wanted to do something.[49] Millenson established the Sudan Divestment Task Force, which aims to persuade public entities, such as universities and state pension systems, from selling any stock in companies that provide revenues or weaponry to the Sudanese government.

Millenson's task force became the leading group coordinating this effort, but other students across the country got involved in similar ways. A handful of students from the University of California, Los Angeles met in a Westwood living room to talk about the issue starting in 2004 and, as each invited friends, the meetings soon outgrew the living room. Over the next couple of years, hundreds of students got involved. Following a march that included students and film actor Don Cheadle, the University of California's regents agreed to divest from Sudan in 2006. The state of California's public pension systems soon followed. By the start of 2007, six other states had similarly divested, with legislation pending in about twenty other states.

Millenson and his peers had seen a need to address an issue and created their own interest groups to fill the void. Most interest groups are standing organizations that allow constituencies to petition governments about the decisions that affect them. They are the vehicle for people who are not policymakers, but who are affected by policy, to influence the political process.[50]

As should be apparent by now, interest groups have always been important sources for candidates—both of money and of volunteers and other services. They are those organizations that take a direct interest in political activity—both in terms of supporting candidates during an election season and lobbying elected and appointed government officials over policy and spending matters. They differ from parties in that politics and elections are not their whole reason for being. As political scientist Frank J. Sorauf notes, "The American Medical Association devotes only part of its energies to protecting its interests through political action. Not so the political party. It arises and exists solely as a response to the problems of organizing the political process."[51] In other words, the American Medical Association (AMA) may spend millions of dollars annually trying to affect elections and legislation, but it devotes more of its energy to educating its members, promoting good health techniques, and other private activities.

Interest groups basically come in five flavors. One is a membership group, like the AMA or Sierra Club, made up of individual members. A second type is the trade association, which represents individuals or organizations in a particular industry or field, such as the National Restaurant Association or the Alliance of Automobile Manufacturers. The third group is the individual institutions themselves, such as Microsoft and General Motors. The larger groups are bound to have lobbyists on staff or devote a significant portion of their executives' time to lobbying. A fourth would be government lobbyists (sometimes called legislative liaisons)—those who represent the interests of one branch of gov-

Policy in Practice:
Lobbying for the Environment in the "Old Line" State

Despite growing concerns about climate change, consensus on environmental issues has been impossible to reach in recent years in Washington. Consequently, green groups have been pushing their ideas for controlling emissions from cars and power plants at the state level—and doing so with some success.

Maryland is home to several large coal-fired power plants. Environmentalists had tried for years to convince legislators to require these plants to invest in improved filtration of such toxins as mercury, sulfur dioxide, and nitrogen. But they could not overcome the opposition of the power companies and the administration of Gov. Bob Ehrlich, which sent several cabinet members to testify against such legislation in 2005.

"Ain't the beer cold!" boasted Ehrlich's deputy environmental secretary, a former energy company lobbyist, in an e-mail to department colleagues after the bill died in committee.[a]

But circumstances changed as the year wore on. Most significantly, the federal Environmental Protection Agency came out with a long-awaited clean air rule that made it clear that Maryland would not meet limitations on health-related pollutants. States that are not in "attainment" with federal clean air regulations will have significant brakes put on future development.

In response, Ehrlich issued new clean air rules addressing the power plants. He didn't go as far as environmentalists hoped, but the fact that his rules would cost the plants significant amounts of money—which had been the main argument used against previous legislation—made the groups' selling job a lot easier.

The power companies still hoped to stall the "healthy air" bill. They used familiar means, such as campaign contributions to influential legislators, as well as broadcast ads that sought to tie the proposed regulations to a recent hike in electricity costs in some Maryland jurisdictions.

To combat such messages, several state and national environmental groups decided to work together on the issue, coordinating events and their messages to members and the media. They held an environmental summit at the capital in Annapolis early in the 2006 legislative session to highlight this issue, while hosting several town hall meetings around the state that were attended by legislators and the general public. They commissioned studies from outside analysts showing that the proposed changes wouldn't cost as much as the power companies claimed and held press events to trumpet such findings.

ernment in front of another. Executive branch officials have aides designated to lobby Congress or a legislature on their behalf, whereas cities, counties and states hire lobbyists to make their cases in Washington. A fifth small category is made up of private individuals who lobby on their own behalf, whether for a pet project or against a policy that they find reprehensible.[52]

People and organizations have a constitutional right to petition the government for redress of grievances. That means that they have the right to complain to lawmakers and regulators about their disagreements with laws and how they are enforced. That's what lobbying is. It is worth noting that government runs some of the most active lobbies. The White House maintains a lobbying shop to try to persuade Congress of the wisdom of its policies. Municipal governments hire lobbyists and associations to protect their

Like many interest groups, the environmental organizations concentrated their strength by having hundreds of members come to the capital for a "lobby day," fanning out to meet legislators and their staffs, and making their issue prominent through their presence. Groups that host lobby days can seem to swarm all over a capital, with people wearing buttons or lapel stickers so everyone can see just what concerns them.

The environmentalists also pursued a lobbying strategy that has become common, reaching beyond their own ranks and turning to others for help in promoting their message. In this case, they received significant aid from healthcare professionals, including both doctors' and nurses' groups, as well as from the religious community. "We formed an ad hoc group called the Healthy Air Coalition," said Ed Osann, a consultant to nonprofit groups, including the Natural Resources Defense Council.[b]

Even with all of these efforts, compromises had to be made to insure the bill's passage. One key legislator whose district was home to a power plant—and who had received big campaign donations from energy companies—insisted on softening the penalties for noncompliance. The governor sought to remove greenhouse gases from the list of pollutants covered by the bill, but he was ignored. Once both legislative chambers had passed the bill by veto-proof margins, Ehrlich surprised everyone by going ahead and signing it.

Having tasted success, the environmentalists returned in early 2007 with a "clean cars" bill designed to follow California's strict vehicle emissions standards. Since this bill would affect individual citizens more directly than the power-plant regulations, environmentalists took their message not only to the capital but also to many more citizens to build support for it. One hundred volunteers working with the Chesapeake Climate Action Network placed an estimated twenty thousand "tickets" under the windshield wipers of SUVs across the state. These tickets included postcards addressed to Martin O'Malley, who had defeated Ehrlich in November 2006, to urge his support for clean cars legislation.[c]

[a] Tom Pelton, "Clean Air Law Enacted," *Baltimore Sun,* April 7, 2006, 1A.
[b] Phone interview with author, March 1, 2007.
[c] Julie Scharper, "Just the Ticket for a Gas-Guzzler," *Baltimore Sun,* December 10, 2006, 3B.

interests in their state capitals. There are about forty thousand lobbyists working in state capitals, and the number of associations and related groups has quintupled over the last fifty years.[53] Lobbying in the states is now a billion-dollar business.[54]

It has become easier to track which interest groups are active in which states. Open up a Web browser and type in the name of a state and "lobbying registration" and you'll be taken to an ethics commission or other state board with which all lobbyists must register. The National Institute on Money in State Politics (followthemoney.org) and the Center for Public Integrity (publicintegrity.org) also offer detailed information about campaign finance and lobbying activity in the states, as well as studies about overall trends.

But looking at raw numbers—who is spending what where—tells only part of the story. It is often difficult to find out which group has influenced the outcome of a specific piece of legislation. Some interest groups play a very public game, like the Sudan Divestment Task Force, but others are more secretive, playing an insider game in which influence is a matter of quiet access to legislators.

That's why many interest groups hire a **contract lobbyist**. This is usually a lawyer or former government staffer or elected official who is valued for possessing valuable insider knowledge and contacts within a particular state capital. Contract lobbyists generally have a number of clients, as a lawyer would. About 20 percent of lobbyists registered to ply their trade in a given capital are contract.[55] They use their relationships and contacts to convince legislators that they should or should not pass a bill. And while lobbyists ignore the executive branch at their peril, since spending decisions and regulatory action are carried out there, more lobbying activity happens in the legislative arena. "You don't change their minds," said a California lobbyist. "You find ways of making them think they agreed with you all along."[56]

Alan Autry, once an actor on the *Dukes of Hazzard* who later served as mayor of Fresno, came to Washington one day in 2003 to ask for money for his city. He met with members of Congress and a senator who represented his area—who nevertheless needed reminding about Fresno's need for funds for law enforcement and an industrial park. Autry was thrilled

CONTRACT LOBBYIST

A person who works for different causes for different clients in the same way that a lawyer will represent more than one client.

Alan Autry (right) is known to many as Capt. Bubba Skinner from the television show *In the Heat of the Night.* He went on to become the mayor of Fresno, California. As chief executive of a city, Autry understands the importance of lobbying Congress for various municipal projects and programs. That's why he hired Len Simon (left), a contract lobbyist paid a handsome fee to make sure members of Congress know the views of Autry's administration.

when Sen. Barbara Boxer looked him in the eye and pledged her support for a $500,000 study that was the first step toward a major mass transit system in the San Joaquin Valley. "When you sit face to face to get a commitment, that's huge," he said.[57]

But if Autry saw the value of coming to "beg" in person, he recognized that most of his time was spent back in Fresno, running the city day to day. That's why he hired Len Simon, a lobbyist for several Western cities, to keep track of his projects and build support—for a fee of $24,000 a year. Simon walks the corridors of the capitol, reiterating the same points to the same members of Congress, staff members, and executive branch bureaucrats, because it is an article of faith in any capital that legislators respond to repetition—if an interest group keeps asking about a project, it must really want it.

Legislators often rely on lobbyists to provide them with information, whether it is simply data about an industry's economic outlook or their opinions about whether a bill would cost jobs in legislators' districts. Legislators are always grappling with many issues at once—the state budget, education, the environment, and so on. It is up to lobbyists to keep legislators and their staffs apprised of who favors a particular bill, and who would benefit from or be hurt by it. Lobbyists build up relationships with legislators over time, and legislators come to trust some of them for reliable information, even if they hold a differing position on an issue.

Standing in contrast to a contract lobbyist such as Simon is a **cause lobbyist** who promotes a single-issue agenda, such as medical marijuana or campaign finance reform. A cause lobbyist often plays an outsider's game, using the media to sway public opinion and pressure public officials. Groups who do not have an economic interest in legislative outcomes are able to get away with that tactic because their ideological position is clear for all to see. Someone like Len Simon engages in **direct lobbying**, dealing directly with legislators in hopes of persuading them. The students trying to get public officials to divest from Sudan were taking an **indirect** approach, building support for their cause through the media, through rallies, and through other ways of influencing public opinion, hoping that legislators will be swayed by the resulting buzz.

Using the media effectively can be trickier for private corporations and other entities directly affected by legislation. The media nearly always portray this third type of lobbyist in a negative light. If a politician sponsors a bill favoring a particular industry and individuals in that industry have made substantial donations to his campaign treasury, there are bound to be stories written about that money trail. Numerous states, including Kentucky, Massachusetts, and Minnesota, have passed ethics laws in recent years that preclude lobbyists who used to wine and dine legislators from giving them anything of value, even a cup of coffee.[58]

Today, many interest groups try to combine the direct and indirect approaches, hitting up legislators in private meetings for favors while also

CAUSE LOBBYIST

A person who works for an organization that tracks and promotes an issue, for example, environmental issues for the Sierra Club or gun regulation for the National Rifle Association.

DIRECT LOBBYING

A form of lobbying in which lobbyists deal directly with legislators to gain their support.

INDIRECT LOBBYING

A form of lobbying in which lobbyists build support for their cause through the media, rallies, and other ways of influencing public opinion with the ultimate goal of swaying legislators to support their cause.

MAP 5-3 Spending by Lobbyists, 2005

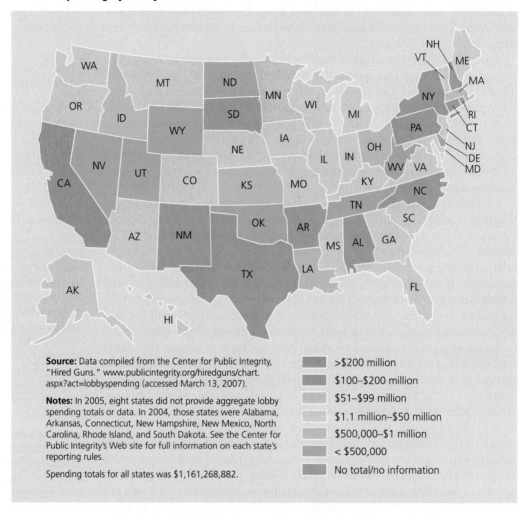

Source: Data compiled from the Center for Public Integrity, "Hired Guns." www.publicintegrity.org/hiredguns/chart. aspx?act=lobbyspending (accessed March 13, 2007).

Notes: In 2005, eight states did not provide aggregate lobby spending totals or data. In 2004, those states were Alabama, Arkansas, Connecticut, New Hampshire, New Mexico, North Carolina, Rhode Island, and South Dakota. See the Center for Public Integrity's Web site for full information on each state's reporting rules.

Spending totals for all states was $1,161,268,882.

>$200 million
$100–$200 million
$51–$99 million
$1.1 million–$50 million
$500,000–$1 million
< $500,000
No total/no information

running public relations campaigns through the media. Groups also are likely to join together in coalitions, hoping that a united front will not only present a more coherent and persuasive message, but also hoping that the company of others will prevent any individual group from looking like it is pleading out of a narrow self-interest. Interest groups often look for surprising allies who will plead their case. For instance, groups looking to increase funding for afterschool programs will enlist sheriffs to argue that the programs help cut crime by giving young people something constructive to do.

As mentioned earlier, some interest groups tend to be loyal to one party or the other, particularly groups with ideological agendas. But interest groups as a whole do not give most of their support to candidates of a particular party. They give most their support to *incumbents* of either party. There are a number of reasons for this. One is that incumbents are reelected the vast majority of the time, so betting on their victory is pretty safe. It makes more sense, pragmatically speaking, to curry favor with someone who possesses power than with someone who does not. Even if the incumbent does not subscribe to an interest group's entire program, the group may find it is able to work with the individual on an issue or two.

Another reason that interest groups favor incumbents is because their campaign contributions are based more on rewarding public officials for positions they already have taken than they are based on trying to persuade them to take new positions altogether. In other words, if a legislator already has demonstrated support for gun owners' rights, the NRA will be inclined to support him. The group does not give donations to gun control advocates in hopes of changing their minds. The money follows the vote, in most cases, rather than the other way around.

The adoption of gift bans and other ethical restraints has done nothing to retard the lobbying industry or deter interest groups. Too much is at stake in too many state capitals for corporations, unions, or cause activists not to play an active role. At the beginning of the twentieth century, one or two powerful home-state companies dominated many state political cultures. State capitals remained old boys' clubs, where just a few powerful interests typically held sway, until about World War II. Since then, states have come to rival Washington in terms of the buzz of activity among competing interests.

About 1,100 different occupations are regulated by states today, and fighting among those industries is neverending. Art therapists, for instance, want their profession recognized by more state legislatures so that they will be guaranteed reimbursement from insurance companies. Mental health counselors, on the other hand, do not want the added competition and oppose such recognition. Orthopedic surgeons and podiatrists face off over who gets to treat ankle injuries and force legislators to debate whether the ankle is part of the foot. (The Colorado legislature decided it was, opening up the field to podiatrists.) Dog groomers fight veterinarians for the right to brush canine teeth.[59]

TABLE 5-1

Top Ten Most Influential Interests in the States, 2002

Ranking	Organization
1	General business organizations
2	Schoolteacher organizations (National Education Association and American Federation of Teachers)
3	Utility companies and associations (electric, gas, water, telephone/telecommunications)
4	Insurance: general and medical (companies and associations)
5	Hospital/nursing home associations
6	Lawyers (predominantly trial lawyers, state bar associations)
7	Manufacturers (companies and associations)
8	General local government organizations (municipal leagues, county associations, elected officials)
9	Physicians/state medical associations
10	General farm organizations (state farm bureaus, etc.)

Source: Data compiled from Clive S. Thomas and Ronald J. Hrebenar, "Interest Groups in the States," in *Politics in the American States: A Comparative Analysis,* 8th ed., eds. Virginia Gray and Russell L. Hanson (Washington D.C.: CQ Press, 2004), 119.

TABLE 5-2

Most Active Lobbying Organizations, 2000

Ranking	Organization	Number of States Registered in
1	Anheuser-Busch Companies Inc.	50
2	American Insurance Association	48
3	Brown & Williamson Tobacco Corporation	47
4	Lorillard Tobacco Company	46
5	AT&T Corporation	45
6	UST Public Affairs, Inc.	43
7	MCI WorldCom Inc.	43
8	Pfizer Inc.	43
9	National Federation of Independent Businesses	42
10	RJ Reynolds Tobacco Company	41
11	Motion Picture Association of America	41
12	Health Insurance Association of America	40
13	Variable Annuity Life Insurance Company	40
14	Pharmacia & Upjohn Company	40
15	American Cancer Society	40
16	State Farm Insurance Companies	38
17	Glaxo Wellcome Inc.	38
18	Alliance of American Insurers	37
19	Merck & Co. Inc.	37
20	Wyeth-Ayherst Laboratories	37
21	National Rifle Association Institute for Legislative Action	37
22	AFLAC Inc.	36
23	Eli Lilly and Company	36
24	Smokeless Tobacco Council Inc.	35
25	National Association of Independent Insurers	35

Beer is regulated at the state level, which is why Anheuser-Busch hires lobbyists in all fifty states. Insurance also is regulated at the state level. Many more industries, in fact, are turning their attention to the states because that is where the federal government and the courts have sent more power. The states have assumed authority over issues such as securities regulation and have taken the lead on issues that have not progressed in Congress. The federal government has failed in recent years to regulate health maintenance organizations, but over the last decade more than forty states have passed bills addressing the topic.

TABLE 5-2, continued

Ranking	Organization	Number of States Registered in
26	Wine Institute	35
27	Teachers Insurance & Annuity Association/ College Retirement Equities Fund (TIAA-CREF)	34
28	Dehart & Darr Associates Inc.	34
29	AARP	34
30	Household Financial Group Ltd	32
31	3M Company	32
32	American Council of Life Insurance	31
33	General Motors Corporation	31
34	Philip Morris Management Corp	30
35	Allstate Insurance Company	30
36	American Heart Association	30
37	Distilled Spirits Council of the US (DISCUS)	30
38	Golden Rule Insurance Company	29
39	Enron Corp	28
40	Pharmaceutical Research & Manufacturers of America	28
41	Alliance of Automobile Manufacturers	28
42	GTECH Corporation	27
43	Johnson & Johnson	26
44	Novartis Pharmaceutical Corporation	26
45	United Transportation Union	26
46	West Group	25
47	American Petroleum Institute	25
48	Waste Management Inc.	25
49	American Express Company	25
50	Prudential Insurance Company of America	25

Source: Center for Public Integrity, "Fourth Branch State Project," 2000. www.publicintegrity.org (accessed June 4, 2004).

The active role of the state in regulating economic and social activity has induced some industries, such as pharmaceutical companies, to maintain lobbies that are just as powerful in the states as they are in Washington. Others, such as the oil industry, have a major presence at the federal level but are weaker players in most states, because state politics largely don't affect them. National companies that are not based in a particular state are likely to hire local contract lobbyists to lend clout to their causes. The consumer products company Johnson & Johnson has its own lobbyists but also maintains memberships in its home state in the New Jersey Chamber of Commerce, the state's Business and Industry Association, and the New Jersey Health Products Company Group. It also belongs to industry associations in California, Illinois, Massachusetts, and elsewhere. At the national level, Johnson & Johnson belongs to the Pharmaceutical Research and Manufacturers of America, the Health Care Industry Manufacturers' Association, and still more groups.[60]

When an industry has relatively little credibility, it often will turn to allies to represent the public face of its cause. Tobacco companies favor hiring lobbyists who have earned the respect of state legislators as former colleagues or by working for other, less controversial clients. They also seek other groups to take the lead on a lot of their fights. When a state considers legislation that will regulate smoking in public places, for example, the most public opponents are more likely to be restaurant groups rather than the tobacco industry. "We're going to participate in a very upfront way," said a Philip Morris spokesman. "But like any other industry, we're going to look to people who share that point of view on any given issue" to take a role as well.[61]

As in the case of tobacco companies fighting smoking bans, lobbyists spend the majority of their time playing defense, trying to kill bills they believe would harm their companies or clients. Still, interest groups and their desires stir up much of the activity in state capitals. "Frankly, the legislature in New Jersey exists for the lobbyist," said one lobbyist there.[62] What he was suggesting was that the governor may want five or six bills passed during a session, while individual legislators may want one or two of their own passed as well. The remaining 99 percent of the thousands of bills introduced in a given year are a wish list of wants and needs by the lobbyists and the interests they represent.

That is why interest groups are an important part of the political landscape in every state. Certain groups play a disproportionate role in particular states—gambling in Nevada or the poultry industry in Arkansas.[63] But the full range of interest groups have crucial influence over the workings of every state. Clive S. Thomas and Ronald H. Hrebenar, two political scientists who have been studying interest group activity in the states for decades, rank the states according to which have policies that are most influenced by interest groups. In no state are interest groups "subordinate," meaning they are consistently out-gunned by other policy players, such as governors or political parties.

Those players are stronger in some states than in others. The relative weakness of political parties lead Thomas and Hrebenar to argue that interest groups are most powerful in a few states in the South and West, such as Alabama, Nevada, and West Virginia.[64] Certain interest groups may hold greater sway at any given time. The importance of environmental issues, in particular, seems to ebb and flow over time. But Thomas and Hrebenar note that in the majority of states, the influence of interest groups as a whole remains fairly constant—and fairly strong.

The influence of interest groups is difficult to measure, but it's nonetheless quite apparent, part of the very air that policymakers breathe. Some groups may score a victory here and there—dentists looking for a regulatory change or animal rights' activists looking to ban cockfighting. Other groups comprise a permanent part of the landscape, such as business lobbies concerned with taxes, transportation, and education.

There are some interest groups that are powerful everywhere because their members are everywhere. Groups such as teachers' unions, car dealers, restaurant owners, and Realtors hold particular sway because they have members in every legislative district, and legislators are more likely to be persuaded by individuals or employers from their home districts. Most Realtor lobbying, for example, is handled by volunteer members and state association staff, rather than by hired contract lobbyists, because realtors tend to be well connected in their communities. They also make it a point to have particular members of their professional community get to know individual legislators from their districts and keep them up to date about their issues of concern. Realtors, like other professions affected at the state policy level, also seek office themselves in part-time legislatures. During the 2005–2006 session, no fewer than twenty-two people who made their living in real estate also served as members of the

Realtors are known for having well-organized and effective lobbying organizations. The payoff can be a sweet ride. Tennessee Realtor Cindy Jasper, pictured here, uses a Hummer as her eye-catching business vehicle. Because she uses these mammoth SUVs for her business, she is eligible to deduct the purchase price—up to $100,000—as a business expense on her taxes.

Utah legislature—including the president of the National Association of Realtors.[65]

Taken together, interest groups are the means through which individual citizens and private companies, as well as governmental bodies, influence the policy decisions that affect their lives or ways of doing business.

"I don't believe there are some states where interest groups are stronger and others where they're weaker," says Alan Rosenthal, an expert on state politics at Rutgers University. "In every state, interest groups are important. That's the way interests are represented, through groups."[66]

Conclusion

The essential job of political parties is to nominate candidates for public office. They no longer control many government jobs, but despite changes in campaign finance laws, they have maintained their positions as leading fund-raising organizations. They also perform many other functions in American democracy. They aggregate and articulate political interests and create and maintain majorities within the electorate and within government. They are not the dominant organizing forces they once were, in part because voters and candidates have become more independent than they were a century ago. Parties, however, do still play important roles in recruiting political candidates, supporting them financially and logistically, and helping them market themselves to like-minded voters.

For the past 150 years, two major parties—the Democrats and the Republicans—have dominated politics in the United States. Few candidates not belonging to either of these parties have won office at any level of government. In most cases, their victories were based on personal appeal rather than support for the third party they represented. The Republican and Democratic parties have been able to adapt to changing times and tastes in ways that have kept them in power, if not always in perfect favor.

With states regulating more industries, interest groups have proliferated so that there are now far more lobbyists than elected officials. Interest groups help push agendas subscribed to by individuals or corporations. Other interest groups push back. Their primary mission is winning as many political offices as possible, so the parties, with varying success, collate and mute the ideological agendas of their interest group allies. Parties cannot afford to have any one group's ideas play such a prominent role that it alienates other groups or voters. It is a difficult balancing act between trying to appeal to the majority of voters at any given time, while also standing for clear enough principles that most people are willing to support them.

Governing States and Localities

Key Concepts

blanket primaries (p. 150)

candidate-centered politics (p. 144)

cause lobbyist (p. 173)

closed primaries (p. 149)

contract lobbyist (p. 172)

crossover voting (p. 150)

dealignment (p. 153)

direct lobbying (p. 173)

factional splits, or factions (p. 139)

general elections (p. 149)

independent expenditures (p. 155)

indirect lobbying (p. 173)

interest groups (p. 139)

nonpartisan ballots (p. 148)

open primaries (p. 150)

party conventions (p. 149)

patronage (p. 148)

political action committees (p. 155)

political machines (p. 147)

political parties (p. 138)

primary elections (p. 149)

realignment (p. 153)

responsible party model (p. 146)

runoff primary (p. 150)

soft money (p. 157)

swing voters (p. 144)

ticket splitting (p. 168)

voter identification (p. 145)

Suggested Readings

Black, Earl, and Merle Black. *Divided America: The Ferocious Power Struggle in American Politics.* New York: Simon and Schuster, 2007. The twin political scientists show that while one of the two major parties is dominant in most regions, neither can claim a permanent governing majority nationwide.

Gould, Lewis. *Grand Old Party: A History of the Republicans.* New York: Random House, 2003. An excellent recent history of the Republicans from Abraham Lincoln to the present day.

Jewell, Malcolm E., and Sarah M. Morehouse. *Political Parties and Elections in the American States.* 4th ed. Washington, D.C.: CQ Press, 2000. Shows how and why political parties vary at the state level.

Rosenthal, Alan. *The Third House: Lobbyists and Lobbying in the States,* 2nd. ed. Washington, D.C.: CQ Press, 2001. A primer on how interest groups operate in and influence state legislatures.

Witcover, Jules. *Party of the People: A History of the Democrats.* New York: Random House, 2003. Companion to Lewis Gould's *Grand Old Party,* that traces the Democratic Party from its Anti-Federalist antecedents to Bill Clinton.

Suggested Web Sites

http://politicsorg.com/Lobbying. This Web site provides links to dozens of lobbyists and associations in Washington, D.C., and in the states.

www.dnc.org. Web site of the Democratic National Committee.

www.followthemoney.org. Web site of the National Institute on Money in State Politics, which tracks political donations and lobbying in all fifty states.

www.irs.gov/charities/political/article/0,,id=109644,00.html. The IRS's Political Organization Disclosure

www.opensecrets.org. Web site for Open Secrets

www.politicalmoneyline.com. Congressional Quarterly's Political Money Line.

www.politics1.com/states.htm. Provides links to candidates for most major offices in all the states.

www.publicintegrity.org. The Center for Public Integrity produces reports on campaign finance and lobbying activity in the states and Washington, D.C.

www.rnc.org. Web site of the Republican National Committee.

CHAPTER 6

Legislatures

The Art of Herding Cats

Running a legislature is often like herding cats. In some cases it's like herding cats in the hat. Here, a group of Wisconsin legislators (they're the ones in the hats) participate in Read Across Wisconsin Day by sharing a Dr. Seuss book with grade schoolers.

6

Why do so many citizens think that legislatures accomplish so little—or accomplish the wrong things altogether?

What constraints do legislatures face in making effective laws?

Why are some legislators more powerful than others?

State legislatures operate in complex ways, especially when it comes to how members negotiate with their colleagues as they attempt to make laws. Their basic dynamics, however, are fairly similar to how you and your friends decide what movies to rent.

Let's say—for the sake of argument—that a group of your women friends wants to rent a chick flick, while the guys insist on watching $100 million worth of things blowing up. If there are six women and five men and all votes are counted as equal, then you'll be watching a DVD featuring Drew Barrymore and a wedding. Similarly, if Democrats hold fifty-three seats in the Indiana House of Representatives and Republicans have only forty-seven, most of the time the Democrats are going to get their way. This is called **majority rule**.

But bills do not always pass according to predictable partisan majorities. Let's change our movie-rental scenario. Now it is just you (a young woman), your roommate (also a woman), and your boyfriend. You would like to watch that Drew Barrymore movie, but your roommate wants to watch a thriller. Betraying you, you feel, your boyfriend agrees with her! Something similar happens regularly in legislatures, when some members abandon their fellow Democrats or Republicans to vote with the opposing party. For instance, most Democrats might want to pass stricter gun control laws, but some of their rural, more conservative Democratic colleagues might block them by joining with the GOP. This is called **coalition building**.

By the next night, though, your boyfriend might have come to the realization that it is not smart policy for him to favor your roommate's taste over yours. In his heart, he would rather watch what the roommate wants to watch, but he knows he is better off in the long run if he agrees to watch your favorites. In much the same way, legislators often vote for bills that they do not particularly like in order to win support for other priorities. They might want to curry favor with their party leaders, or they might simply want to earn a colleague's help in the future by voting for the colleague's pet bill now. This is called trading votes, or **logrolling**.

Or maybe you have learned that you cannot count on your boyfriend to stick up for you when it's time to head out for the video store. You know you are going to end up renting a movie—it's a Sunday, and your whole suite is bored from reading about state and local government. So you go around to all your pals in the dorm and plant the idea that what would really be fun tonight would be watching one of the old *Matrix* movies. Legisla-

MAJORITY RULE

The process in which the decision of a numerical majority is made binding on a group.

COALITION BUILDING

The assembling of an alliance of groups to pursue a common goal or interest.

LOGROLLING

The practice in which a legislator will give a colleague a vote on a particular bill in return for that colleague's vote on another bill to be considered later.

Governing States and Localities

tors—and other people concerned with what legislators are up to—do this all time. They try to solicit support from people who are going to vote long before a vote actually takes place so that the result will come out the way they want. This is called lobbying and is similar to the kind of lobbying interest groups do, as we saw in Chapters 4 and 5.

But let's say while you are busy polling your friends that one of them unexpectedly says that she hates *The Matrix* worse than poison, that she refuses to watch *The Matrix*. What's more, since her DVD player is the only one on the floor that's hooked up to a decent screen, there is no way you are going to watch *The Matrix* at any point this semester. This sort of thing often happens in legislatures. If there is a bill to increase state spending for abortion clinics, for instance, you can bet that one or more legislators will do everything in their power to block that spending.

There are many ways that an adamant opponent can stop a hated piece of legislation, including **filibusters**—endless debates in the Senate. Another way is to attach unwanted amendments, or **riders**, to a bill. The road to a bill's passage into law is twisty and sometimes full of unexpected hurdles. John Dingell, the longest-serving member of the U.S. House of Representatives, perhaps best described the strange relationship between the actual substance of a bill and how it moves through the House when he said in 1984, "If you let me write procedure and I let you write substance, I'll screw you every time."

In all fairness, legislatures were not designed to be simple. The congressional system was designed to be difficult enough to prevent new laws that have not been properly thought through and debated from bothering everybody. "The injury which may possibly be done by defeating a few good laws will be amply compensated by the advantage of preventing a number of bad ones," wrote Alexander Hamilton in *Federalist Paper*, No. 73. Most state legislatures share the basic structure of the U.S. Congress, with a House chamber and a Senate chamber that each must approve a bill before it can go to the governor to be signed into law. That means that even if a bill makes its way through all the circuitous steps of getting passed by the House, including **committee** fights and winning a majority in the chamber, it can easily die if the Senate refuses to sign off on an identical version. To use our video renting comparison one more time, this is like finally getting every member of your family to agree to rent some animal movie, but then having your neighbors refuse to watch it because they're in the mood to watch something with Will Ferrell. Getting the 150 or so legislators who serve in every state to agree on anything is one of the toughest tricks in politics.

The consequence of this complexity is a grave misperception by the general public about how well legislatures work and how competent individual legislators are. Legislators work hard. Thousands of bills and constituent complaints are addressed every year, but the institutional structures of legislatures make it difficult for them to respond quickly to the issues of the

FILIBUSTERS

Debates that under Senate rules can drag on, blocking final action on the bill under consideration and preventing other bills from being debated.

RIDERS

Amendments to a bill that are not central to its intent.

COMMITTEE

A group of legislators formally tasked with considering and writing bills in a particular issue area.

day. The early part of the twenty-first century also finds the electorate split politically in most states, as well as nationwide, so it is especially difficult to reach an agreement that pleases everyone.

The fact is, legislators are mostly working harder to address more complicated problems than in the past. But the public's perception is that they are not getting the job done. Recent studies show that the average person is not in touch with what his or her legislature is up to, considers the legislature to be unnecessarily contentious, and thinks legislators are guilty of talking when they should be acting. Many people believe that legislators are too cozy with the interest groups that provide them with campaign contributions and perhaps other favors. Voters wonder why their representatives do not simply vote the "right" way and go home.

The problem is that there is no one "right" way. Many cross currents blow through every legislature. Some legislators represent liberal **districts**— others represent conservative areas. Some represent cities, while others represent farmlands grappling with entirely different, nonurban issues. Legislators acting in good faith will come to different conclusions about what is the right approach to take on any number of issues, from education and transportation to job creation and taxes. All sides get to present their most convincing arguments, but only rarely can a majority of members of a legislature come to an agreement that pleases them all. In their disagreement, they reflect the different opinions of their **constituents**, the citizens back home—which is precisely the way the system is supposed to work.

Let's say that you and your friends are still arguing about the chick flick versus the action picture. Only this time, each movie has an even number of fans. In the end, you decide that you will watch something entirely different, an old comedy you have all seen but are willing to watch again. None of you is thrilled—none of you gets to watch exactly the kind of movie you were hoping for—but all of you can live with the choice. This is called **compromise**, and it is the kind of agreement legislators make more than any other. This chapter will give you a sense of how legislators come to their decisions, who they are, what they do, and how they organize themselves in their institutions. Localities—city and county governments—typically have some form of legislature as well. These are covered in Chapter 10.

The Job of Legislatures

You may have heard of the Segway. It is a device that was introduced with much hype and fanfare on national television at the end of 2001 and moves individuals around at speeds of up to twelve miles per hour. The device is undoubtedly cool, with its five gyroscopes and ten onboard computers to keep its rider balanced and to change directions with the simplest weight shift. But it cannot do anybody much good unless it can be ridden on sidewalks. At the time the product was unveiled, motorized vehicles were

DISTRICTS

Geographical areas represented by members of a legislature.

CONSTITUENTS

Residents of a district.

COMPROMISE

The result when there is no consensus on a policy change or spending amount but legislators find a central point on which a majority can agree.

banned from sidewalks in all but three states. Segway LLC, the maker of the device, decided to change all that.

The company had a hot product, which it incorporated into a lobbying strategy—legislators were allowed to take rides on the machine at capitol receptions. Seeing how easy the Segways were to ride and to stop, legislators could not think of any reason they should not allow the devices on their state's sidewalks. In fact, they thought these machines might alleviate all sorts of transportation problems. Segways would cut down on air pollution, revitalize downtowns where parking cars is a problem, and provide easily accessible mobility to the elderly and handicapped. Safety advocates, who worried about the possibility of sixty-nine-pound machines barreling into pedestrians, were hardly heard. Segway bills passed through several legislatures without hearings or substantive debate. By the summer of 2004, forty states had passed bills to allow Segways on sidewalks. By the following year, all but six had laws in place to allow people to scoot along on their Segways.[1]

> The consequence of this complexity is a grave misperception by the general public about how well legislatures work and how competent individual legislators are. Legislators work hard. Thousands of bills and constituent complaints are addressed every year, but the institutional structures of legislatures make it difficult for them to respond quickly to the issues of the day.

It was a remarkable achievement, especially for a new company. It was also a classic example of how legislatures are *not* supposed to work. A special interest group—a single company, in fact—was able to use a $1 million public relations and lobbying campaign to work its will with legislators all across the country. Usually attempts to get states to pass uniform laws sputter along, with perhaps only a handful of states taking up an issue during any given session. The federal Centers for Disease Control and Prevention (CDC), for instance, crafted model legislation in 2002 for states to strengthen their public health response to terrorist attacks and many other emergencies. By the middle of the year, the bill had been introduced in only nineteen states and enacted into law in just six.[2]

Fairly or not, the differing fates of the Segway and the public health laws are examples of how the public gets its negative opinion of legislatures. Segway was able to curry favor through private receptions and joyrides. Meanwhile, in the face of a dreaded public health threat, legislatures could not even agree on the powers they wanted to give their governors in case of a biological emergency. They were not able put aside their differences to serve the public good.

This caricature represents a commonly held sense of how "politics as usual" works but it also baldly overstates the problems with legislatures and unfairly maligns them. A lot more goes on than the public realizes or sees, and this creates a very skewed view. As a case in point, the Segway bills

Texas legislators approved a bill that would allow for random drug testing of thousands of high school athletes in an effort to stamp out steroid use.

Lobbyists are sometimes seen as taking legislators for a ride, but perhaps not quite so literally as this. As part of its lobbying effort to make sure its premier product was not regulated off of city sidewalks, the maker of the Segway gave state legislators across the country a chance to try out the unique personal transportation system. This was an effective tactic and headed off the regulatory threat. Here Connecticut state senator George Gunthor puts the Segway through its paces.

were actually an example of legislators happy to help out a new technology they believed was safe, would create jobs, and would help correct other problems. And the success of the Segway blitzkrieg really was quite unusual. The fate of the CDC bill, by contrast, was quite typical. However, while the exact legislation initially proposed was not widely embraced by many states, legislatures across the country did pass other, specially tailored laws to deal with public health risks unique to their situations. Hawaii's legislature, for example, passed a plan to create a nursing branch in its public health department that could respond to hurricanes and tsunamis (tidal waves). (The governor did not agree with the legislators and vetoed the program.) Connecticut's General Assembly—as the state's entire legislature is called—passed separate laws that ensured that the state could respond to a catastrophic event at its nuclear power facility and that make special plans for children and youth in the event of an emergency.

What Legislatures Do

All state legislatures share three basic purposes:

- They pass laws and create policy for their states.
- They provide representation for the citizens in their districts in state government—including offering personalized constituent service to help residents sort out their problems with the state government.
- They oversee the governor and the executive branch and some private businesses through public hearings, budget reviews, and formal investigations.

State legislatures might all address similar issues, including taxes, budgets, and a broad range of other matters such as regulating office safety and requiring sex offenders to register their place of residence with police. Differences in timing, state history, and political culture, however, may cause one state's laws on a topic to differ widely from those of other states. Occasionally, legislatures are pressured to pass uniform laws—as when the federal government insisted that the states raise their legal drinking ages to twenty-one or risk losing highway funding. Louisiana, with its proud tradition of public drinking, resisted the longest.

More often than not, laws are adapted to the local scene and are not easily molded to match other states' versions. Large insurance companies are regulated at the state level. They would love to have their agents qualified to sell in every state rather than having to take fifty different qualifying exams. But only a few states have acted on the proposal. "I'm still not sure what happens if Michigan says you can be an insurance agent if you can sign your name with your eyes shut, and New York says you've got to take a three-year course," said Alexander Grannis, chair of the insurance committee in the New York Assembly. "What happens if someone screws up—if we cancel a Michigan guy's license to practice here for malpractice, does that mean Michigan can retaliate and cancel a New Yorker's right to practice there?" [3]

Within a given state, the media and the public manage to register many failures of a legislature while not giving the institution enough credit for its successes in balancing all the competing interests within the state. Ethics scandals generally receive greater coverage than substantial debates, yet legislators debate and pass laws that cover everything from levels of Medicaid health insurance funding to clean water protections to aid for local governments to workers' compensation payments to the price of milk. In most legislatures, 90 percent of the bills receive almost no media attention and are of interest only to those they directly affect. The media—and with it, the voting public—pay attention only when issues that affect the broadest range of people are considered, such as increases, or cuts, in property tax rates. Legislators do not have the luxury of tuning out when complex and boring but important issues crop up.

State senators and representatives fight their biggest fights over budgets. Most of their power is derived from the fact that with the approval of the governor they can set fiscal policy, including tax rates. How much the state devotes to each of its programs is a way of revisiting all the problems that never go away. How much is enough to spend on education? How much of that education tab should the state pick up? While public schools traditionally were funded by local property taxes, most states now pick up one-third of the bill or more. How much money for healthcare? Should all children be covered, regardless of income? How big an investment should the state make in roads or public transportation? How much can be spent overall before the state is taxing individuals and businesses too highly? Practically every state has a constitutional requirement to balance its budget every year, so legislators cannot spend what they do not take in from tax receipts. State legislatures annually address hundreds of such issues, large and small.

> State senators and representatives fight their biggest fights over budgets. Most of their power is derived from the fact that with the approval of the governor they can set fiscal policy, including tax rates. How much the state devotes to each of its programs is a way of revisiting all the problems that never go away.

Lawmaking

Legislatures tend to be reactive institutions. Early in 2005, Jessica Marie Lunsford, a nine-year-old Florida girl, was raped and buried alive by a convicted sex offender. By the end of 2006, half the states had passed a version of "Jessica's Law," which required longer sentences for sex offenders and electronic tracking of their whereabouts following their release from prison. Jessica's Law was just one among hundreds of laws passed by states in recent years in reaction to high-profile sex crimes against children—and the attention they received from programs such as Bill O'Reilly's show on Fox News Channel and NBC's *To Catch a Predator.*

Most issues attract far less attention. The New York state legislature grappled with nearly 21,000 bills in 2006,[4] and even much mellower Montana takes up about 1,500 a year.[5] Despite this amount of activity—or perhaps because of it—legislators generally do not go looking for issues to address. The typical bill is introduced for one of several reasons. It is a bill that has to be considered, such as the annual state budget. It is a bill dealing with a common problem modeled after another state's legislation. Or, it is something that an individual or a group outside of the legislature wants considered. These outside influences include constituents, the governor, and lobbyists.

It may not always seem like it, but constituents can have a lot of influence in government. In Massachusetts, for instance, legislators are obliged to consider petitions to introduce bills on any topic a state resident wants. During the debate over same-sex marriages in 2004, for instance, various groups petitioned the legislature with the approaches they favored. They effectively filed their own amendments. Governors and the executive branch are also powerful players in the legislative process. They promote ideas they want legislators to work on. These can be bills designed to quickly address relatively small-scale problems, such as the $4 million program to combat wasting disease in deer that the Wisconsin legislature approved in 2002, or larger issues that might be debated for years.[6]

For example, the legislature in Washington State has battled for several years over funding for transportation projects in the Puget Sound area and elsewhere. In 2001, legislators failed to agree to Gov. Gary Locke's proposal to spend $9 billion more on roads, despite Locke calling them into three special sessions. That was in part because Republicans and Democrats had a hard time coming to agreement on changes in contracting laws that require workers to be paid a union wage in rural areas.[7] Legislators and Christine Gregoire, Locke's successor, finally agreed on a transportation package and a gas-tax increase that voters upheld in 2005. But in 2007, Seattle voters sent them partway back to the drawing board by rejecting two different proposals for the package's centerpiece project.

Finally, lobbyists representing a client such as Segway LLC often will promote draft legislation in hopes that a member of the legislature or General Assembly—as legislatures are known in Colorado, Georgia, Pennsylvania, and several other states—will sponsor it as a bill.

Remember, however, that a string of wins such as Segway enjoyed is unusual. Lobbyists may promote bills, but they also devote an enormous amount of energy trying to kill other bills. The state acts as a sort of referee between a lot of competing interests. Any change in state law that someone views as a positive step is likely to adversely affect—or at least frighten—someone else. What gun control advocates want, the gun owners' rights groups will try to stop.

Legislators react most strongly to bills in which they have a personal stake or that they know will affect their constituents directly. Let's say that environmentalists are concerned about a river's water quality and want to require new water filters at a paper mill. The mill's owners, concerned that the cost of the filters will be exorbitant, warn that they will have to lay off three hundred employees if the bill goes through. A legislator from that area will have to worry about whether creating a healthier environment is worth being accused of costing people their jobs. Other legislators who live clear across the state from the river and its mill, though, will hold the deciding votes. The people directly affected—the company, the workers, downstream residents worried about pollution—will all try to portray themselves as standing for the greater good. If no side is clearly right, and favoring one side or the other can do political damage, the bill easily could die. Legislators could then be accused of doing nothing, but they will merely be reflecting the lack of statewide consensus about how to solve the problem.[8]

Representation

The bulk of the work legislators do involves formulating the law and trying to keep an eye on the executive branch, but their primary responsibility is to provide **representation** for their constituents. Basically, they ensure the interests of those they speak for are properly considered as part of decision making at the state level. Sometimes legislators address issues because their constituents are having problems that only a change in the law can address. Medicaid is a shared federal-state program that provides health insurance to the poor. It is an entitlement program, which means that anyone who meets its eligibility requirements is supposed to receive help. But not everyone who is eligible receives that help. In 2001, Garnet Coleman, a Democrat who represented parts of Houston in the Texas House of Representatives, decided to try to change that. The state at that time required as many as fourteen different forms from parents before their children could enroll in Medicaid, and they had to be recertified every few months. Coleman sponsored legislation to reduce all that paperwork to a single four-page form. That change alone was expected to put one-third of the state's 1.4 million uninsured children on the Medicaid rolls.[9]

Coleman simply wanted to change current rules to make it easier for people who were eligible to be able to apply. Except that Texas, with its tradition of fiscal conservatism, was not about to vote to expand its Medicaid

Local Focus: Taking on the Law in the Land of the Free . . . and the Home of the Silly

Rich Smith, a British journalism student, spent one Christmas Day playing board games. He came across reference to an obscure law in Florida that made it illegal for divorced women to go parachuting on Sundays. Enchanted by this and a treasure trove of other dumb American laws, he decided to spend the summer after graduation driving all across the United States, breaking every outdated or just plain absurd law he could find. "Tying giraffes to lampposts seemed a funnier way in which to become a felon," than arson or murder, Smith writes in his book about the spree, *You Can Get Arrested for That.* *

Smith and a friend attempted to break two dozen laws in all, succeeding in most cases. Many of the laws concerned personal behavior. Traveling east from San Francisco, Smith's first successful crime was to peel an orange in a hotel room, which is illegal throughout California.

He then drove to Globe, Arizona, where it is illegal to play cards on the street against an American Indian, and did just that. He made sure to order plenty of garlic bread along with his pizza in Indianapolis, because that city makes it illegal to enter a theater within three hours of eating garlic. He also broke the law by eating watermelon in a cemetery in Spartanburg, South Carolina, and by sleeping on top of a refrigerator in Pennsylvania.

The fashion police have made it illegal to wear a goatee in Massachusetts, so Smith grew one in plenty of time for his visit to that state. He also broke several laws concerning fishing, including his attempt to hunt down marine mammals in a lake in Utah and, of course, his blatant disregard for Chicago's ban on fishing while wearing pajamas. But he lacked sufficient skill to violate Tennessee's stricture against catching a fish with a lasso.

If Smith managed to break numerous laws, several others defeated him. He failed to find a bathtub to carry illegally across the village green in Longmeadow, Massachusetts, and couldn't persuade a woman in Iowa to kiss him for longer than five minutes (or at all).

Several of his crimes were witnessed by police or private security guards, but perhaps it's in the nature of "dumb" laws that they aren't rigorously enforced. The only time Smith and his buddy got into serious trouble was when they drove ninety-seven miles-per-hour in a seventy-five-mile-per-hour zone in Wyoming. That time, they got nailed.

*Published by Three Rivers Press, New York, 2006.

program. Other states with histories of greater governmental generosity had expanded their Medicaid programs throughout the 1990s in order to widen the pool of people eligible for coverage. Vermont, for example, vastly enlarged its Medicaid program so that all children in families with incomes under 300 percent of the poverty line—about $50,000 for a family of four—would be eligible. As state budgets turned sour around 2002, many states cut back on their Medicaid coverage. But as the budget picture improved in 2006 and 2007, while the numbers of the uninsured continued to grow, nearly half the states again proposed major expansions in their health programs, including attempts at universal coverage in Massachusetts and California.

If a problem is real and persistent enough, a state's legislature will address it eventually. Sometimes there is a general recognition that such a long-festering problem just needs to be fixed once and for all. That does not mean the fix is going to be easy. Some states, including Kansas, Ohio, and Pennsylvania, have had to tweak their school funding formulas continually in response to state supreme court decisions that found their education systems inadequate. And numerous states, including Mississippi, Pennsylvania, and West Virginia, have changed their tort laws, laws that cover damages to individuals, in the last couple of years. They have done this in order to help their doctors and trauma centers afford medical malpractice insurance. Addressing medical malpractice issues is difficult in part because trial lawyers object to any limitations on punitive damages that people can receive from lawsuits after suffering as a result of medical negligence.

The reason that this objection by trial lawyers is important is that trial lawyers are influential in Democratic politics. This is perhaps especially true in the Deep South, which has a reputation for hefty jury verdicts. States like Alabama and Mississippi traditionally have been hostile to trade unions, with "right to work" laws that have made it difficult for the unions to organize. Elsewhere, in the Midwest and Northeast, where unions are active, they are important donors to Democratic candidates. But where unions are weak, trial lawyers have become the major source of funding for Democrats. The role of such interest groups was discussed in Chapter 5.

Legislatures often finish their work on an issue not because of outside pressure but because of internal changes. New leaders in the Arizona Senate in 2001 brought with them solutions to longstanding issues that included understaffing in the state's highway patrol, underfunding in the state's mental health system, and provisioning for water through new contracts. Legislators even managed to repeal antiquated sex laws that made it a crime for unmarried couples to live together.[10]

States with stagnant leadership or long-term control by one party or the other have a harder time making breakthroughs. New York is a prime example. Republicans have long controlled the Senate, Democrats have long controlled the Assembly, and the two refuse to agree on certain issues. The Senate majority leader for years has refused to allow a vote on a gay rights bill, while the Assembly Speaker will not permit a vote on banning late-term abortions. Legislators in one chamber regularly refuse to allow votes on the other chamber's versions of bills—even on issues that the Senate and Assembly do agree on, including a stricter drunk driving law.[11]

Before a bill can even get far enough to be debated, the idea for it must be developed. To get ideas for bills, legislators turn to each other, to staff, to colleagues in other states, and to outside sources, whether it is a company with a cause of its own, like Segway, or a think tank interested in pushing change. Minnesota has an unusually fertile landscape when it comes to ideas for the legislature. More than 750 foundations are active in the state's public life. During the mid-1990s, thirty of them matched funds with the legislature to help nonprofit groups plan for federal budget cuts and changes in welfare law.[12]

FIGURE 6-1 How It Works: A One-Eyed Frog's View of the Legislative Process, or How a Bill *Really* Became a Law in Minnesota

The mechanisms by which a bill becomes a law at the state level are similar to the mechanisms at work at the federal level. And we've all seen the flowcharts that outline the ins and outs: a bill goes in one side, gets debated, marked-up, reported out, and then comes out the other side as a real life law to be implemented, or it gets returned to the legislature for an override, or it gets "killed." You'd be forgiven for thinking that beneath that abstraction lay a more complex and interesting process.

You'd be right. Below is a different flowchart, this one fleshing out what actually happened when a group of Minnesota teens brought to light the fact that the frog population in their area was turning up with extra limbs and missing eyes. About eight months and $151,000 later, the frogs were in much better shape.

> In the summer of 1995, Henderson, Minnesota, students discover deformed frogs during a field trip near the Minnesota River. Their findings make headlines in the area.

> These headlines prompt the Minnesota Pollution Control Agency to ask for more state funding to research the problem.

> Four days later a similar bill is introduced in the Senate by Steven Morse of Dakota.

> On January 25, 1996, Rep. Willard Munger of Duluth introduces a bill in the House that would give the Pollution Control Agency $50,000 to fund research into the cause of the deformities.

> Students from the Henderson school appear at the state capitol in St. Paul to testify in front of the twenty-four-member House Environment and Natural Resources Committee in support of the proposal. They share photos of the deformed frogs, and tell legislators about what such deformities might indicate about the pollution hazards for the human population.

> A similar process takes place in the Senate.

> As a result of the testimony, Rep. Virgil Johnson of Caledonia adds an amendment to the House bill requesting an additional $28,000 to fund surveys and public outreach, bringing the requested amount up to $78,000.

Source: Minnesota House of Representatives Public Information Office, "Capitol Steps: How Six Bills Became Law." www.house.leg.state.mn.us/hinfo/How6bil.pdf (accessed April 13, 2007).

Governing States and Localities

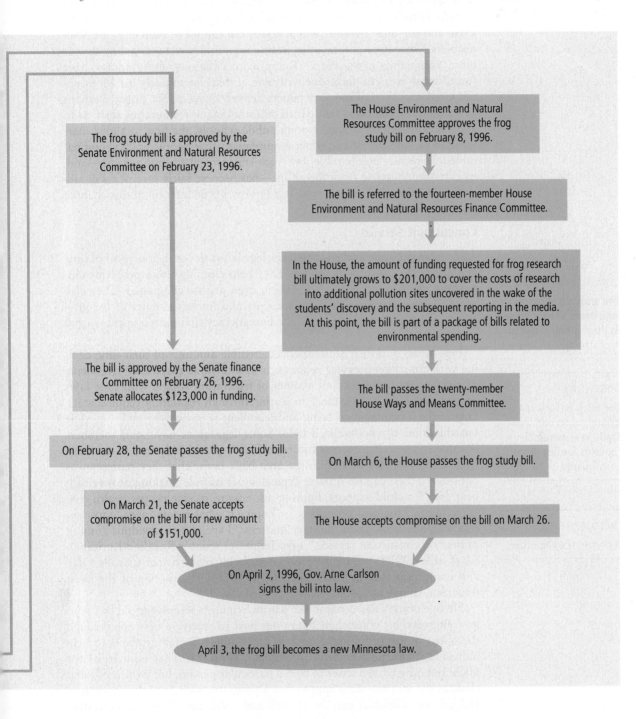

The House Environment and Natural Resources Committee approves the frog study bill on February 8, 1996.

The frog study bill is approved by the Senate Environment and Natural Resources Committee on February 23, 1996.

The bill is referred to the fourteen-member House Environment and Natural Resources Finance Committee.

In the House, the amount of funding requested for frog research bill ultimately grows to $201,000 to cover the costs of research into additional pollution sites uncovered in the wake of the students' discovery and the subsequent reporting in the media. At this point, the bill is part of a package of bills related to environmental spending.

The bill is approved by the Senate finance Committee on February 26, 1996. Senate allocates $123,000 in funding.

The bill passes the twenty-member House Ways and Means Committee.

On February 28, the Senate passes the frog study bill.

On March 6, the House passes the frog study bill.

On March 21, the Senate accepts compromise on the bill for new amount of $151,000.

The House accepts compromise on the bill on March 26.

On April 2, 1996, Gov. Arne Carlson signs the bill into law.

April 3, the frog bill becomes a new Minnesota law.

In addition, the state capitol of St. Paul has the now-unusual benefit of being able to mine two major metropolitan daily newspapers—the *Pioneer Press* and the *Star Tribune,* which serves the capitol's "twin city" of Minneapolis. Once upon a time, numerous communities were served by two or more competing newspapers. Today, consolidations and foldings have forced most areas to make due with one, if that. Fortunately for Minnesota's legislators, both Twin City papers actively cover public policy. Perhaps as a result, the state was the first to ban smoking in restaurants, the first to allow schoolchildren choice among public schools, the first to allow charter schools, and the first to enact requirements that people holding comparable jobs receive comparable pay. Such engagement from the media—and, by extension, interest from the public—has become fairly rare. We will talk about how the media cover state legislatures a little later on in this chapter.

Constituent Service

Aside from debating and passing laws, legislators devote a good deal of time and energy to **constituent service.** They help clear up those problems citizens are having with public agencies or even private companies. They also act as liaisons between their constituents and unelected parts of the government in the executive branch, the bureaucracy that everyone knows and loves to hate.

Legislators and their staffs spend incredible amounts of their time dealing with constituent service requests, also known as **casework.**[13] Residents of a state may experience all manner of frustration coping with state laws or may merely want assistance in sorting through regulatory requirements. One of the advantages of being an **incumbent** is having the ability to dole out this kind of personalized help. Some legislators have staff members devoted solely to helping constituents. This is particularly true in their district offices—offices located in the area back home that they represent, as opposed to their capitol offices. Typical issues include tracking down deadbeat dads for child support, figuring out how to receive proper health coverage under Medicaid programs, or knowing what federal agency to contact with questions about military matters. "I spend a tremendous amount of time on constituent service," says Tennessee senator Rosalind Kurita, D-Clarksville. "When we are in session, I probably make five or six calls a day and easily that many emails and letters. To me, that is one of the most important things we do." [14]

No one objects to a senator like Kurita helping a seven-year-old boy who has outgrown his wheelchair figure out how to receive a new one through the state's health insurance program. The problem is that attempts to help individuals sometimes morph into policy decisions. That is, a legislator might not only write a letter to help a particular person, but write a bill that changes the way the state approaches a program, such as health insurance. Helping an individual may be all well and good, but changing the system

Constituency service, or casework, is an important part of any elected official's job, even if it's not necessarily the most exciting part. Here, Beaufort County (S.C.) councilwoman Margaret Griffin talks to one of her constituents.

based on the personal story of one person is not necessarily the best way to change policies that will affect thousands.

Undoubtedly, it is important for legislators to hear about the real-world experiences of their constituents. Since they cannot meet with everybody, however, they need to rely on reports and studies to get a complete picture. They otherwise might be swayed too greatly by personal interactions. The danger of the increased need for politicians to raise significant finance treasuries is not so much that their votes can be bought, but that they are much more likely to meet with the people or interest groups who give them campaign contributions. Campaign donors often give money simply so that they can have access to a legislator when they hand over the check. That means that people who do not or cannot give money may not get heard.

Oversight

Under the U.S. system of checks and balances, legislatures are charged with **oversight**, the task of making sure that the governor and the executive branch agencies are functioning properly. The executive branch is called that because it executes the laws written by the legislature. Legislators are only doing their job when they call governors and executive branch agencies to account through hearings, investigations, and audits for how they are carrying out those laws. Unfortunately, the most ubiquitous form

OVERSIGHT

The role the legislature takes in making sure that the implementation of its laws by the executive branch is being done properly.

Local Focus: Constituent Service: Going the Extra Mile

When John Medinger was a member of the Wisconsin State Assembly, he worked back-breaking hours to do his job—and to make sure that his constituents knew he was doing his job. He needed to let people know how seriously committed he was to representing them and their interests, because Medinger is a Democrat who represented a Republican district.

He drove the 137 miles to the capitol in Madison and the 137 miles back home to La Crosse three times a week, even when the legislature was not meeting. When he was in La Crosse, he was in perpetual motion. "If I don't have anything to do at home," he said, "I go sit in a coffee shop and shoot the breeze. I might be home two nights a week to tuck my kids in. I go to every pancake breakfast and every rummage sale. I am always looking for something to do. If there's nothing else, I go to a basketball game and mingle with the crowd."

All that work paid off politically. One year, Medinger got a perfect 100 rating from the AFL-CIO but was rated at 29 by the Wisconsin Association of Manufacturers. The La Crosse chamber of commerce endorsed him for reelection anyway. As Medinger once said, "There are some Republicans in my district who could run against me and make my life miserable. . . . But the Republicans can't come up with candidates who will put in 100-hour weeks. So they don't make it."[a] The

fact is, no one who interacts with legislators doubts that they work hard. They keep long hours meeting with colleagues, constituents, lobbyists seeking a favor for their clients, and business leaders from their districts and across the state.

For all of the clear evidence that politicians work hard, some people still question whether all of the meeting and studying and debating those legislators do actually accomplish anything. "A politician's day is long," says satirist P. J. O'Rourke. "He gets into the office early, reads newspaper clippings with his name highlighted, submits to a radio interview with Howard Stern, goes to a prayer breakfast and an ACLU lunch, checks opinion polls, meets with an NRA delegation, makes a friendly call to Al Sharpton, sits in the Inland Waterways Committee hearing room drawing pictures of sailboats and seagulls on a notepad, proposes National Dried Plum Week, votes "yea" (or is it "nay"?) on something or other (consult staff), exercises with the president, recovers from a faked charley horse after being lapped on the White House jogging track, watches the signature machine sign letters to constituents, returns a corporate campaign contribution to WorldCom, speaks at a dinner supporting campaign-finance reform, goes home, gets on the phone, and fundraises until all hours."[b]

[a] Quoted in Alan Ehrenhalt, *The United States of Ambition* (New York: Times Books/Random House, 1991) 133.
[b] P. J. O'Rourke, "No Apparent Motive," *Atlantic Monthly,* November 2002, 34.

of oversight is a legislator intervening with administrative agencies on behalf of constituents or constituent groups in ways that are "episodic and punitive."[15]

For example, several years ago, the Arkansas Livestock and Poultry Commission filed suit against a livestock sales barn for failure to meet state regulations of an infectious livestock disease called brucellosis. The senator from that district placed language to weaken those regulations on the bill to fund that commission, which prompted the commissioner to resign.[16] The commissioner had taken the funding cut as a signal that his authority was being undermined, so he quit. That kind of scattershot approach—helping a particular constituent at the expense of the public good—is by its nature inequitable. The point of bureaucratic norms is to make sure that regulations and laws are applied fairly and evenly across the board.

Unfortunately, oversight is pretty far from the minds of most legislators. Staff aides regularly perform audits and evaluations, but legislatures only make sporadic use of them. Most oversight comes in a less systematic way, through budget reviews and occasional committee hearings. In states that impose limits on the number of terms that legislators can serve, there is even less opportunity to perform oversight. Members have less time to become expert in a particular area and so they often rely more heavily on expert testimony from the very executive branch that they are meant to oversee.

Organization and Operation of Legislatures

The U.S. system of representative democracy was designed to be messy. One recent book argued that the institutions of democracy should be more popular because they work pretty well, but conceded, "The American political system was not designed for people to understand." [17] Legislatures were created because, even in colonial days, this country was too large and its problems too complex to be addressed by its vast numbers of individual citizens. We elect legislatures in our republican form of government to argue out our problems in a single time and space in sessions at the capitol. The ranks of the legislature have become far more diverse over the last thirty years. Although the average state legislator is still a white male, there are twice as many African Americans and nearly six times as many women serving in legislatures today than there were in 1970. Also over the past thirty years or so, legislatures have become better equipped to do their job by hiring better staff and receiving more professional training. None of these changes, however, have made state legislatures any more popular with the public.

Bicameralism

Legislatures are not, of course, random groups of people hanging around a dorm and picking movies to watch. Every state has a constitution that describes a body that can pass state laws. In every case but Nebraska, which has a unicameral (or one-house) legislature, legislatures are bicameral, or divided into two houses, pretty much like the U.S. Congress. As mentioned earlier in this chapter, one chamber is normally called either the House of Representatives or Assembly and the other is called the Senate. The Tenth Amendment of the U.S. Constitution reserves all powers not given to the federal government for the states, and state legislatures can write any state law that does not interfere with federal laws.

The House, or Assembly, is considered more of a "people's house," with its members representing fewer people for shorter terms than their colleagues in the Senate. The House always has more members, known as state

TABLE 6-1

Total Number of State Legislators (House and Senate), 2007

State	Senate Members	House Members	Total Members
Alabama	35	105	140
Alaska	20	40	60
Arizona	30	60	90
Arkansas	35	100	135
California	40	80	120
Colorado	35	65	100
Connecticut	36	151	187
Delaware	21	41	62
Florida	40	120	160
Georgia	56	180	236
Hawaii	25	51	76
Idaho	35	70	105
Illinois	59	118	177
Indiana	50	100	150
Iowa	50	100	150
Kansas	40	125	165
Kentucky	38	100	138
Louisiana	39	105	144
Maine	35	151	186
Maryland	47	141	188
Massachusetts	40	160	200
Michigan	38	110	148
Minnesota	67	134	201
Mississippi	52	122	174
Missouri	34	163	197
Montana	50	100	150
Nebraska	49	n/a	49
Nevada	21	42	63
New Hampshire	24	400	424
New Jersey	40	80	120
New Mexico	42	70	112
New York	62	150	212
North Carolina	50	120	170
North Dakota	47	94	141
Ohio	33	99	132

TABLE 6-1, continued

State	Senate Members	House Members	Total Members
Oklahoma	48	101	149
Oregon	30	60	90
Pennsylvania	50	203	253
Rhode Island	38	75	113
South Carolina	46	124	170
South Dakota	35	70	105
Tennessee	33	99	132
Texas	31	150	181
Utah	29	75	104
Vermont	30	150	180
Virginia	40	100	140
Washington	49	98	147
West Virginia	34	100	134
Wisconsin	33	99	132
Wyoming	30	60	90
Total	**1,971**	**2,619**	**7,382**

Source: National Conference of State Legislatures, "Current Number of Legislators, Terms of Office and Next Election Year, January 2007." www.ncsl.org/programs/legismgt/about/numoflegis.htm (accessed April 12, 2007).

representatives, than the Senate. There are 163 representatives in the Missouri General Assembly, for example, but only 34 senators. There are some exceptions, but often senators serve four-year terms, whereas House members have to be reelected every two years. The two chambers operate independently, with separate leaders, committees, and agendas, although both chambers have to pass the same version of a bill before it can be sent to the governor to be signed into law or vetoed. Nebraska, with its unicameral legislature, is the one exception.

Legislative Leadership

Most legislatures have essentially the same leadership structure, at least for their top positions. Before the beginning of a session, each House votes in its Speaker. This is generally someone picked beforehand by a **caucus**, or meeting, of members of the majority party. The majority leader and the minority leader rank just below the Speaker of the House. "Majority" and "minority" refer to the respective strengths of the major parties. Either the Democratic or Republican Party may hold the majority of seats in a chamber. Less than 1 percent of all state legislators are independent or members of so-called third parties. In the Senate, the top

CAUCUS

All the members of a party—Republican or Democrat—within a legislative chamber. Also refers to meetings of members of a political party in a chamber.

leader is known as the president, president pro tem, president pro tempore, or the majority leader.

Certain aspects of the leadership positions remain constant across all the states. For example, a Speaker will typically preside over daily sessions of the House or Assembly, refer bills to the appropriate committees, and sign legislation as it makes its way over to the Senate or the governor's desk. Leaders appoint committee chairs—in some states, all the members of committees—set or change committee jurisdictions, and offer staff or legislative help to rank-and-file members. They also often help with campaigns, including financial help.

The amount of power invested in the office of Speaker or Senate president does vary by state, however. In the Texas Senate, leadership powers are invested in the office of lieutenant governor. Lieutenant governors normally do not possess much formal power, but in Texas, they appoint committees and committee chairs in the thirty-one-member body and decide which bills are considered and when. In some older legislatures, such as those in New Jersey and Massachusetts, the Senate president performs all of those functions, presides over debates, counts votes, and ensures member attendance. In California, those powers rest with the Senate president pro tem. But regardless of how the formal duties are divided up, usually there is one individual who emerges as holding the most power and speaking for the chamber in negotiating with the other chamber and the governor.

With the exception of Nebraska, where parties are actually banned from the nonpartisan unicameral legislature, legislatures are divided along party lines. Not only does the majority party get to pick the top leader, it gets to fill virtually all of the important committee chairs as well. A party majority is worth much more than the comfort of knowing that your fellow Democrats or Republicans will help you outvote the opposition on most bills. To hold the leadership and chair positions means that the majority party gets to set the agenda—deciding which bills will be heard for a vote. Democrats from the 1950s into the early 1990s held a two-to-one edge in number of legislative seats and controlled many more chambers than the GOP. In recent years, however, Republicans have pulled into near-ties both in terms of raw numbers of legislators and in how many chambers they control. At the end of World War II, all but seven of the forty-eight states had united governments, meaning one party controlled the governorship and both legislative chambers. By 1986, only twenty-one of fifty states had united governments.[18] The increasingly competitive nature of legislative politics has meant that every election cycle since 1984 has resulted in at least one tied chamber somewhere.[19]

Some leaders hold their positions for decades, although this is exceptional. Jimmy Naifeh has been the Speaker of the Tennessee House since 1991. Mike Miller started his run as president of the Maryland Senate back in 1987. Voters unhappy with the status quo often will unseat top leaders in symbolic decapitations. That happened in 2006 to Bob Garton, who had

MAP 6-1 Partisan Control of State Government, 1954

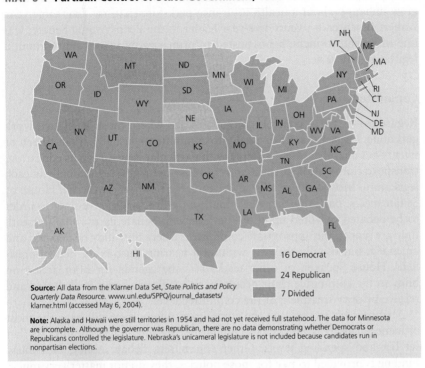

16 Democrat

24 Republican

7 Divided

Source: All data from the Klarner Data Set, *State Politics and Policy Quarterly Data Resource.* www.unl.edu/SPPQ/journal_datasets/klarner.html (accessed May 6, 2004).

Note: Alaska and Hawaii were still territories in 1954 and had not yet received full statehood. The data for Minnesota are incomplete. Although the governor was Republican, there are no data demonstrating whether Democrats or Republicans controlled the legislature. Nebraska's unicameral legislature is not included because candidates run in nonpartisan elections.

MAP 6-2 Partisan Control of State Government, 2007

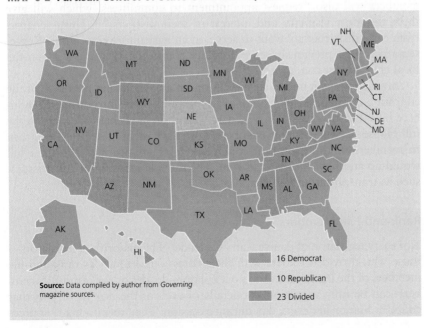

16 Democrat

10 Republican

23 Divided

Source: Data compiled by author from *Governing* magazine sources.

Legislatures

led the Indiana Senate for twenty-six years but lost his seat when voters grew unhappy about a health insurance perk for senators. That same year, Robert Jubelirer, a twenty-five-year leader in the Pennsylvania Senate, was one of seventeen incumbents ousted in primaries by voters angry about a legislative pay raise.

Committees

Regardless of party control, committees are where most legislative work gets done. Legislators are divided into committees—usually about fifteen or twenty per chamber—that grapple with particular issues, such as education, transportation, or taxes. Thousands of bills are introduced annually in each legislature. Most of these bills never reach the floor where the full House or Senate meets. Basically, they never make it past the committee stage in order to be debated or voted upon by the House or Senate as a whole. Instead, they are sent to the appropriate committee, where they may be debated and amended, but usually they die without a hearing. Just as the Senate president, House Speaker, or other leader sets the agenda for floor action on bills, so the committee chair decides which bills are going to be heard and receive priority treatment at the committee level.

Members try to serve on the committees where they will have the most influence. The most prestigious committees are the budget committees that set tax and spending levels. Other committees debate policy, but unless funding is provided to pay for those policies, they do not matter very much. Seats on a finance or appropriations committee are highly sought after, but members will also "request appointment to committees, which will give them the most visibility and interest in their districts." [20] Thus, senators from rural districts may want to serve on an agriculture committee. Representatives who previously served on city councils may want seats on the local government committee.

Any member can introduce legislation on any topic, but members of the education committee, for example, are more likely to introduce and influence bills that affect schools. When an education bill is being debated in the full House or Senate, other members, who have other specialties, will turn to members of the education committee for guidance about what a bill would do and how they should vote. The same holds true for other issues, such as transportation and healthcare.

Rank-and-File Members

Not every legislator, of course, can be a leader. The majority of legislators—those who provided leaders with their votes—are known as **rank-and-file members** of the legislature. And no legislator—leader or rank-and-file member—can be fully versed on the details of each of the dozens of bills that confront him or her every day during a session. They turn to many sources for information on how to vote. There is a classic notion, posited by political philosopher and statesman Edmund Burke, that divides legislators into **delegates**, who vote according to the wishes of their districts, and **trustees**, who vote according to their own consciences.[21] Given the proliferation of legislation, however, members never hear from a single constituent on probably 90 percent of the bills they must consider. Instead, they rely for guidance on staff, other legislators, interest groups and lobbyists, executive branch officials, foundations, think tanks, and other sources.

The fact that legislators cannot rely solely on their own judgment to vote is the source of many people's sense that legislators' votes can be bought—or at least rented. This is ironic, considering that political scientists note that most of the time most legislators are extremely attentive to their districts and vote according to their sense of their desires. Their primary goal, after all, is to win reelection. In addition, most states have made it tougher for lobbyists to get lawmakers' attention. It is difficult under the new ethics rules for a lobbyist to spring for a legislator's cup of coffee, much less treat for lunch. In Kentucky, for example, there are fewer of the nightly receptions that once kept Frankfort well fed, and lobbyists are prohibited from making any personal contributions to candidates for the legislature. "A lot of the principal lobbyists are still here, so folks have had to learn to adapt," says Bobby Sherman, head of the Kentucky legislature's nonpartisan research staff. "It's more work for them. They have to build relationships in a different way, and information delivery is much more important." [22]

All of this is necessary because, as with most things, times have changed. It used to be that rank-and-file members voted pretty much the way they were instructed by their party leaders. In Connecticut, the legislature of the early 1960s was an assemblage of party hacks—members beholden to the party chair for patronage. This meant that most of the legislature's important decisions were made in small meetings to which the public—and even most rank-and-file members—were not invited.

Examples do still exist of members caving in to party or leadership pressure. In his book *Experiencing Politics,* former state representative John McDonough, a Democrat, recounts one afternoon in the fall of 1995 when he was sitting on the floor of the Massachusetts House of Representatives. The chamber was preparing to vote on a huge tax break for Raytheon, a locally based defense contractor. McDonough thought the tax break was a terrible idea. He considered it a form of corporate blackmail. So he pushed the little red button on his desk and voted against it. Then the majority whip—the party's head vote-counter—came over to see him. "The Speaker wants a green [light] from you on this," the whip said. That did not make any sense to McDonough. The tax break was passing easily. His vote was not needed. The whip did not answer his question as to why the Speaker needed his vote. "He just does," she said. So, McDonough tells us, he caved. A few months down the road, he had his own favorite bill coming up, and he wanted the Speaker's help. He did not want to take any chances.

Legislators who primarily see their role as voting according to their constituents' beliefs as they understand them.

TRUSTEES

Legislators who believe they were elected to exercise their own judgment and to approach issues accordingly.

He walked right back to his desk and switched his vote. It was a classic example of trading votes. "Was my switch," he asks, "an example of naked, opportunistic self-interest or of a hard trade-off necessary to achieve a higher good? Anyone can characterize my action either way. The most honest answer is that both perspectives contain some degree of truth." [23]

Such practical decisions are made all the time. Nevertheless, leaders today carry much less weight with members than they did even a generation ago. Leaders these days are no stronger than members want them to be; they often lead by listening. Consider two examples from about a decade ago. Connecticut House Speaker Irving Stolberg was considered a brilliant legislator, but he was heavy handed as a leader. When he met with his lieutenants, it was not to consult them on strategy but rather to tell them what the strategy would be. Many of the Democrats under him thought he abused his power, so they coupled their votes in 1989 with House Republicans and drove him out. [24]

Compare this to a story from across the country the next year. In May 1990, months of work on a workers' compensation reform package threatened to go to waste during a meeting in the office of Oregon House Speaker Vera Katz. Bob Shiprack, chair of the labor committee, grew impatient as the conversation got stuck on the topic of how chiropractors would be treated under the law, so he stormed out. Katz, rather than ordering him to get back to work, ran after him and mothered him, soothed him, and sympathized with his exhaustion. "It disarmed me," Shiprack said. "Vera loves to disarm." Katz's tactic worked, and the workers' compensation package went though. [25]

Leaders cannot bully their way through the way they did a generation ago for two reasons. One is that members do not rely as extensively on party leaders any longer to manage or fund their campaigns. Legislative leaders still control massive amounts of money. The Senate president in Maine, for example, raised more than $450,000 in 2006, in a state where legislative races still can be won with a few thousand dollars. But today's rank-and-file member has greater access to expert advice for hire and separate sources of money, whether from political action committees (PACs) run by industries or labor unions or elsewhere.

We have already touched upon the other factor—members do not have to rely on leaders as much as they once did for information about bills or for help writing legislation. The proliferation of lobbyists and the **professionalization** of legislatures have meant that members have their own resources to draw upon. [26] We will talk more about what it means for a legislature to become more professional in the next section of this chapter.

Apportionment

One more issue that profoundly affects all legislators is **apportionment**. Following the U.S. census, which occurs every ten years, each state draws new

PROFESSIONALIZATION

The process of providing legislators with the resources to make politics their main career, such as making their positions full-time or providing them with full-time staff.

APPORTIONMENT

The allotting of districts according to population shifts. The number of congressional districts a state has may be reapportioned every ten years.

Compared to earlier generations of legislative leaders who could dictate to the party's rank and file, their contemporary counterparts, like Maine Senate president Beth Edmonds, have to rely more on persuasion and negotiation. For the most part, party leaders in state legislatures no longer have the absolute power to dictate policy and tactics to the legislature's rank and file.

lines for its legislative districts. In states with more than one member of Congress, congressional districts are redrawn as well. The **redistricting** process is the most naked exercise of political power in the states. The incumbent party will do everything it can to preserve its hold or, preferably, increase its numbers. Each party will seek to draw the maximum number of districts possible that are likely to elect members of its own party. The two major parties will fight each other as best they can to make certain that the other side does not gain the upper hand. "Just like there are no atheists in foxholes, there are no nonpartisans in redistricting," says Paul Green, director of the School of Policy Studies at Roosevelt University in Chicago. "You use whatever leverage you can." [27]

We've already discussed how Democrats control New York State's Assembly and Republicans hold the reins in the Senate. Both sides must like things that way, because they continually draw district maps to preserve that status quo. But New York has been losing population—relative to other states—for decades. This translates into a lost congressional seat or two every ten years. In 2001 the legislature came up with a map that sliced and diced counties and towns in an effort to create new districts that balanced competing political interests in the state. Monroe County, which includes Rochester, was home to 735,000 residents following the 2000 census, more than enough to earn its own congressional seat. Instead, the county was cut into four different congressional districts, including one that stretches one hundred miles in a thin strip along the Niagara River and the Lake Ontario shore to link parts of Buffalo and Rochester and their Democratic precincts.

REDISTRICTING

The drawing of new boundaries for congressional and state legislative districts, usually following a decennial census.

Political maps that link disparate communities or have odd shapes that resemble earmuffs or moose antlers are known as **gerrymanders,** after Elbridge Gerry, an early nineteenth-century governor of Massachusetts. **Malapportionment** occurs when districts violate the principle of equal representation. In the past, some state legislative districts could have many times the number of constituents as other districts. Votes in the smaller districts, in effect, counted for more. Relatively few people in, say, a sparsely populated rural district would have the same amount of representative clout in the legislature as an urban district with many times the rural area's population.

Legislatures draw the maps in most states, but there are exceptions. Since the 1980s, Iowa's political maps have been created by the nonpartisan Legislative Services Agency. The agency instructs its computers to draw one hundred House districts and fifty Senate districts according to rules that keep population as equal as possible, avoid splitting counties, and keep the districts compact. In contrast to legislature-drawn maps, the agency does not consider party registration, voting patterns, or the political territory of incumbents. Largely as a result, partisan control of the Iowa legislature flips just about every ten years. Other states use other commission models. In New Jersey, a bipartisan commission composed of six Democrats and six Republicans is charged with the task of coming up with a plan that can command a majority. If it cannot—which is typical—the chief justice of the state supreme court appoints a thirteenth member to the committee as a tiebreaker. In 2001, the new maps landed the Democrats a majority, and they were able to retake control of the Assembly for the first time in a decade and also pulled into a tie in the Senate.

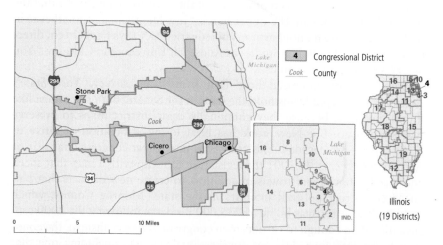

Illinois's Fourth Congressional District is a classic example of a gerrymandered political jurisdiction. It consists of two strips of land running east-west on Chicago's north and south sides. These strips are connected only by a stretch of Interstate 294. The district was drawn this way to capture two majority Hispanic sections of the Chicago area.

The idea that redistricting needs fixing has become a kind of grail among reformers, but attempts to make redistricting less partisan by taking it out of the hands of legislators themselves have gotten nowhere. Voters in California and Ohio soundly defeated ballot measures in 2005 that would have given redistricting powers to a panel of retired judges or a commission, respectively.

Partisanship is the primary concern of redistricting, but it is not the only one. Issues of representation also play a big part. African Americans are overwhelmingly Democratic, but some blacks joined with Republicans following the 1980 and 1990 censuses to create black majority districts, especially in the South. For African Americans, their deal with the GOP offered the advantage of creating districts in which blacks were likely to be elected. It wasn't that they *joined* the Republican Party, they simply allied themselves with the GOP to draw **majority-minority districts**, which guaranteed the election of more African Americans but also made neighboring districts more likely to elect Republicans. An additional benefit for Republicans was that concentrating African American voters into relatively few districts weakened Democratic chances in neighboring districts. Following the Voting Rights Act of 1982, the federal Justice Department encouraged state legislators to create majority-minority districts whenever possible, until a series of U.S. Supreme Court decisions during the 1990s put an end to the practice. In a confusing and often contradictory series of rulings, the Court ruled that race could not be the "predominant" factor in redistricting.[28]

In most state legislatures, the major goal of redistricting following the 2000 census seemed to be protecting incumbents. Members of the two major parties colluded to draw few competitive districts, preferring to know they would run in "safe" Republican-leaning or Democratic-leaning districts. Drawing districts that were politically safe for current officeholders necessarily meant creating fewer new districts that were likely to elect minorities. That was true even for Hispanics, who were the fastest-growing minority group in the United States during the 1990s, accounting for 60 percent of the population growth in Texas and 80 percent of the growth in California.[29] Nevertheless, the California legislature and the Texas judicial panel that drew that state's maps did not go out of their way to draw new Hispanic-majority districts. Hispanics held only about two hundred state legislative seats in 2001, and their number did not rise appreciably in the 2002 elections.

As we have seen, incumbents usually get their job security taken care of, but the results for everyone else are pretty mixed. In part because of the uncertainty caused by the Supreme Court's decisions, black legislators after the 2000 census devoted more energy to preserving the districts they had won than to trying to create new African American–dominated districts. Hispanics, for their part, did not follow the "strange bedfellow" coalition strategy blacks had pursued with Republicans and chose instead to push for more Hispanic-majority districts through a series of mostly unsuccessful lawsuits that challenged the new political maps.

MAJORITY-MINORITY DISTRICTS

Districts in which a minority group, such as African Americans or Hispanics, make up a majority of the population or electorate.

State Legislators

If you were to make a composite drawing of the average state legislator, he—and it would be a he—would be white and in his forties or fifties. He would have had at least some college education, an income topping $50,000, describe himself as moderate or conservative, and would have lived in the community he is representing for at least ten years.[30] There are many, many exceptions to all of the aspects of this composite. The type of person who runs for state legislative office has changed a good deal over the past thirty years—there are far more women and African Americans in office and fewer lawyers—but nonetheless, the type of middle-to-upper-middle-class American male described above still predominates.

The nation's 7,382 state legislators come from all manner of backgrounds, particularly in the states where the House and Senate meet only for part of the year. In the full-time legislatures, such as California and Pennsylvania, the legislators tend, not surprisingly, to be career politicians who have served in local or other elected office or perhaps as members of a legislative staff. In part-time legislatures, like Arkansas and Indiana, members come from many different walks of life, devoting perhaps one-third of their working hours to politics while earning their living through some other means.

Professional Background

Some employers encourage the political hopes of their employees because they know legislative service can be good for business. This holds true especially for professions most directly affected by state lawmaking, such as big business. Buddy Dyer kept up his law practice while serving in the Florida Senate and in 2002 had to respond to complaints that his bills would have protected industrial company clients from fines and lawsuits. His defense? "Probably not a bill that goes through the Legislature" did not affect one of his firm's clients.[31]

Consider public education. Teachers' unions are usually among the most effective lobbying groups in any state, but schools do not necessarily have to rely on outsiders to influence the legislature. Teachers themselves are often members of legislatures, and employees of other institutions of higher learning also may serve. Harold Moberly is chair of the Kentucky House Appropriations Committee, which helps determine spending levels for all state agencies, but for years he also wore another hat as director of student judicial affairs for Eastern Kentucky University. His dual role gave his home campus a big say in legislative arguments about higher education funding. He was just one of a half-dozen legislators in the state who work for public colleges and universities.[32] In Maine, state law requires that teachers be granted leave if they want to run for office. Maine's legislature meets for only one-half of the year, every other year. But even that chunk of time is enough to play havoc with a person's work schedule, and there's a good deal of concern in the state that retirees are coming to dominate the legislative chamber.

The reality is that retired persons account for only about 15 percent of state legislators nationwide. About the same number of legislators are lawyers—a big decline from past decades. In New York, 60 percent of the Assembly and 70 percent of the Senate used to be made up of lawyers.[33] Nowadays, the dominant group in legislatures nationwide are people with business backgrounds. They make up about 30 percent of today's legislators. The remaining half or so come from education, healthcare, real estate, insurance, or agriculture.

Demographic Diversity

The number of women legislators has risen dramatically since the "second wave" feminist era of the late 1960s and early 1970s, but their numbers are still far from reflecting the female share of the overall population. In 1970, women held just 4 percent of all state legislative seats.[34] Their numbers doubled quickly, to 8 percent of all legislators by 1975, and they climbed to 18 percent by 1991. Their ranks held steady at just over 20 percent for about a dozen years before spiking to 23.5 percent after the 2006 elections. Still, even then, only six states—Arizona, Colorado, Maryland, Minnesota, New Hampshire and Vermont—could brag in 2007 that a third or more of their legislators were women.[35]

The number of women entering state legislatures may not be growing exponentially, but the type of women holding House and Senate offices has changed. In the old days of the 1970s—about a decade before most readers of this book were born—most women running for office came to politics later in life than men. They had not been tapped to run by party professionals or other "queenmakers." Instead, they jump-started their own careers, drawn into the policy realm out of concerns about their children's schools or their local communities. Men may know from the time they are in school that they want to run for office, says Barbara Lee, who runs a foundation dedicated to helping women run for office, but women often find out later in life that it is important to enter the game because of their specific concerns and experiences.[36] This dynamic has changed to some extent. Women now enter politics at ages comparable to men. Many still tend to care about a set of issues—education, healthcare, and the environment—that are noticeably different from the top priorities of men—taxes and budgets. But sometimes they address such issues because they still find it harder to get onto the more powerful finance committees in representative numbers.

Back in the 1970s, when the first relatively large numbers of women legislators entered the capitols, they tended to be less politically ambitious and less likely to enter the ranks of legislative leadership than men. They devoted more attention to constituent service matters and tended to serve on education, health, and welfare committees. They also tended to have less education and come from jobs that were not as good as those held by their male counterparts. During the 1980s, the average socioeconomic status of women legislators improved, and they served on a broader range of committees, but they mostly still focused on issues of women, family, and children. By the 1990s, women legislators held about 15 percent of all legislative leadership positions but were still unlikely to serve on tax committees.[37] Their backgrounds had become more varied, but they had become more conservative—although they still were more liberal than men—and they were also significantly more likely to initiate legislation than their male colleagues.[38] Women are also more likely than men to successfully get their priority bills through the legislative process.[39]

Women, however, do not alter the fundamental political dynamics in legislatures, perhaps because they remain a fairly tiny minority in most states. For example, women legislators, by and large, favor reproductive rights, but they do not have an especially powerful impact on a given state's policy regarding this issue. Whether a state devotes much funding toward abortion programs or places a number of restrictions on such programs, including requiring parental notification, depends more on whether the state's overall political culture is liberal or conservative than on whether women make up a large minority of legislative caucuses.[40]

Still, women legislators do tend to bring up issues and concerns that are not going to be raised by an all-male legislature. This fact is even more true of issues of concern to minorities. African Americans have made gains similar to women in legislatures over the past thirty-five years, growing from a microscopic minority to a larger minority, albeit one still not reflective of their overall share of the population. Their numbers have doubled to about 610—less than 10 percent of all the legislators nationwide.

Although it is both dangerous and wrong to generalize about any group, the interests of African Americans as a whole have long been fairly stable and predictable. "On questions of public policy, ideology, and candidate choice," writes Kerry L. Haynie in his 2001 book on black state legislators, "African Americans have been the most cohesive and consistent policy subgroup in United States politics."[41] The timing of the increase in numbers of black state legislators was fortunate. Since the 1970s, decisions about issues of importance to African Americans, including Medicaid, student aid, school lunch, community development, welfare, and environmental protection, have devolved from the federal level to the states.[42] In his study of how representatives in Arkansas, Illinois, Mississippi, New Jersey, and North Carolina acted in three different sessions, Haynie found that 55 percent to 82 percent of African American legislators introduced bills that addressed issues of particular interest to blacks. White legislators, by contrast, almost never introduced such legislation. In only one of the three years that Haynie studied (1969, 1979, and 1989) did more than a quarter of nonblack legislators introduce even one bill of interest to blacks.[43] It may sound obvious, but black issues are much more likely to be addressed when African Americans are serving in state legislatures.

More African American legislators does not mean changes in voting trends, however. Voting remains polarized along racial lines. Whites will support African American incumbents but are often reluctant to vote for black newcomers. The main reason for the growth in the number of black legislators, therefore, has been the creation of majority-black districts.[44]

Professional vs. Citizen Legislators

Legislatures, which were strictly white male playgrounds in the past, have become more inclusive of women and minorities and more attentive to their concerns. But the biggest changes in legislatures over the past thirty-five years have come in the very ways that they do business. Where once legislatures were sleepy backwaters in which not much got done—and even less got done ethically—now many chambers are highly professional operations. Most legislatures used to meet for a short time every other year. These days all but a handful meet every year and, in a few cases, nearly year-round. "No single factor has a greater effect on the legislative environment than the constitutional restriction on length of session," two leading legislative scholars wrote long ago.[45]

The most pronounced differences among states are between "professional" legislatures that meet full-time, pay members a high salary, and employ large numbers of staff, and "amateur," or "citizen," legislatures that meet part-time, have members who usually hold other jobs, and have smaller staffs. To some extent, all legislatures have become more professional. Even "amateur" legislators devote a third of their time to legislative work. In the early 1940s, only four states—New Jersey, New York, Rhode Island, and South Carolina—met in annual sessions, but that number has climbed continuously.[46] Today, only six states do not meet in regular annual sessions. Expenditures per legislator have increased in nearly every state above the rate of inflation, and today, the most professional legislatures have resources that rival those of the U.S. Congress.[47]

There are many variations among states as to how professional their legislatures are, which profoundly affects their effectiveness, how much institutional strength they have compared to governors, and how popular they are with the public. Some disagreement still exists about whether professional legislators really do a better job than their citizen-legislator cousins. Typically, however, the more professional a legislature is, the more effective it is at the essential jobs of drafting and passing laws and overseeing the governor and the executive branch. Most of the more populous states, except Texas, have highly professional legislatures. These professional legislatures are able to provide more resources to their chambers. This allows these chambers to keep up with the wider variety of interests that more

TABLE 6-2

State House Demographic Diversity: Total Numbers and Percentages of Legislators Who Are Women, African American, and Hispanic, 2007

State	Total Number of Legislative Seats	Total Women State Legislators	Percentage of Total Seats	Total African American State Legislators	Percentage of Total Seats	Total Hispanic State Legislators	Percentage of Total Seats
Alabama	140	18	13%	34	24%	0	0%
Alaska	60	13	22%	1	2%	0	0%
Arizona	90	31	34%	2	2%	17	19%
Arkansas	135	28	21%	15	11%	0	0%
California	120	34	28%	9	8%	28	23%
Colorado	100	34	34%	3	3%	5	5%
Connecticut	187	53	28%	19	10%	6	3%
Delaware	62	19	31%	5	8%	1	2%
Florida	160	38	24%	25	16%	17	11%
Georgia	236	46	20%	56	24%	3	1%
Hawaii	76	25	33%	0	0%	1	1%
Idaho	105	24	23%	0	0%	1	1%
Illinois	177	49	28%	29	16%	11	6%
Indiana	150	28	19%	13	9%	1	1%
Iowa	150	34	23%	3	2%	0	0%
Kansas	165	48	29%	6	4%	4	2%
Kentucky	138	17	12%	7	5%	0	0%
Louisiana	144	25	17%	29	20%	0	0%
Maine	186	57	31%	0	0%	0	0%
Maryland	188	62	33%	42	22%	4	2%
Massachusetts	200	49	25%	8	4%	5	3%
Michigan	148	29	20%	19	13%	3	2%
Minnesota	201	70	35%	1	> 1%	3	1%
Mississippi	174	24	14%	42	24%	0	0%
Missouri	197	38	19%	12	6%	1	1%
Montana	150	38	25%	0	0%	1	1%
Nebraska	49	10	20%	1	2%	1	2%
Nevada	63	19	30%	7	11%	3	5%
New Hampshire	424	154	36%	1	> 1%	2	<1%
New Jersey	120	23	19%	10	8%	5	4%
New Mexico	112	33	30%	2	2%	44	39%
New York	212	50	24%	43	20%	17	8%
North Carolina	170	42	25%	26	15%	2	1%

TABLE 6-2, continued

State	Total Number of Legislative Seats	Total Women State Legislators	Percentage of Total Seats	Total African American State Legislators	Percentage of Total Seats	Total Latino State Legislators	Percentage of Total Seats
North Dakota	141	25	18%	0	0%	0	0%
Ohio	132	23	17%	16	12%	0	0%
Oklahoma	149	19	13%	6	4%	0	0%
Oregon	90	28	31%	3	3%	1	1%
Pennsylvania	253	37	15%	21	8%	1	<1%
Rhode Island	113	22	20%	1	1%	3	3%
South Carolina	170	15	9%	28	17%	1	1%
South Dakota	105	18	17%	0	0%	0	0%
Tennessee	132	21	16%	12	9%	1	1%
Texas	181	37	20%	14	8%	36	20%
Utah	104	18	17%	0	0%	2	2%
Vermont	180	67	37%	1	1%	0	0%
Virginia	140	24	17%	17	12%	1	1%
Washington	147	48	33%	3	2%	3	2%
West Virginia	134	19	14%	0	0%	0	0%
Wisconsin	132	30	23%	8	6%	1	1%
Wyoming	90	21	23%	0	0%	2	2%
TOTAL	**7382**	**1,734**	**23%** (average)	**600**	**6%** (average)	**238**	**4%** (average)

Sources: Center for American Women and Politics (CAWP), "Women in State Legislatures 2007," www.cawp.rutgers.edu/Facts/Officeholders/stleg.pdf (accessed April 12, 2007); National Black Caucus of State Legislators; and NALEO Educational Fund, 2006 NALEO National Directory of Latino Elected Officials. Los Angeles, Calif., 2006.

Note: Percentages are rounded to the nearest whole number.

densely populated states must deal with compared to most of their less populous neighbors. Legislatures in some states, such as Pennsylvania and California, meet essentially year-round, whereas Arkansas's part-time legislature meets for only ninety days only in odd-numbered years.

More populous states have the money to invest in the full-time legislatures that are necessary to keep on top of issues facing their more complicated and developed economies and diverse populations. The reason that Texas, with a population second only to California's, has a part-time legislature is that state's general dislike or distrust for government in general. Texas is one of only nine states that do not impose an income tax, so a legislature that meets only part-time every other year is in keeping with its general low-tax, low-service point of view. Other states have a tradition of embracing more expansive government. States with strong progressive traditions, such as Michigan and Wisconsin, have long utilized full-time, professional legislators with substantial staffs at their command. The Northeastern states have maintained their traditional interest in hands-on government, which grew out of their old practices of self-government, including town hall meetings and the like. These states boast some of the largest legislatures. The New Hampshire House is the most extreme example, with 400 members, each representing about 3,400 people. California's legislature is one of the best equipped and most professional in the country. It has to be, considering that each member of the Assembly has more than 423,000 constituents.

Some states impose severe restrictions on the meeting times of their legislatures. In Colorado, the state constitution limits the House and the Senate to no more than 120 days per year. Sometimes such limits are honored mostly in the breach. The governor may insist that the legislature meets in special session to address a budget crisis or other issue that cannot wait until the next regular session. Or the legislature may simply carve out a little more time for itself, as happened in 2002 in North Carolina. House rules require that the chamber be shut down by 9 P.M., so members stopped the clock one night at 8:50, essentially "freezing time," so they could continue debate until 3:35 A.M. and finish a session that had run for months longer than expected.[48]

Just like most of us, legislators feel intensely the pressure to get their work done on time. The fact that they have deadlines—for passing budgets or for adjournment—usually keeps them focused—in much the same way that a final exam will make college students finally hit the books at term's end. Newspapers, however, routinely write stories that criticize legislatures for missing their budget deadlines. The reality is that a legislature is pretty cheap to operate—in no state does its cost top much more than one-half of 1 percent of the state budget—but elected officials know that their overtime does not play well with voters.[49] The *Orlando Sentinel,* for instance, ran a pretty typical piece in 2002 criticizing the Florida legislature for meeting in special session at a cost of about $25,000 a day to the state. That amount, the paper said, was almost enough to pay a teacher's salary for a year.[50] Such stories are one reason why legislatures, as they get more professional and better at their jobs, remain unpopular with the public. Map 6-3 shows the breakdown of full-time, hybrid, and part-time legislatures among the states.

The Citizen's Whipping Boy: Legislators and Public Opinion

Thirty or forty years ago, legislatures were, to put it bluntly, sexist, racist, secretive, boss-ruled, malapportioned, and uninformed. Alabama's legislature was an extreme but representative case. In 1971 it ranked fiftieth out of the fifty state legislatures in independence, fiftieth in accountability, and forty-eighth in overall performance in a Ford Foundation study. Yet, just

MAP 6-3 Full-time, Hybrid, and Part-time Legislatures

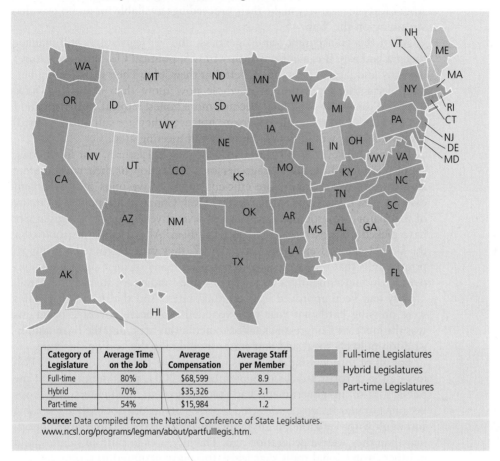

Category of Legislature	Average Time on the Job	Average Compensation	Average Staff per Member
Full-time	80%	$68,599	8.9
Hybrid	70%	$35,326	3.1
Part-time	54%	$15,984	1.2

Full-time Legislatures
Hybrid Legislatures
Part-time Legislatures

Source: Data compiled from the National Conference of State Legislatures. www.ncsl.org/programs/legman/about/partfulllegis.htm.

three years earlier, 65 percent of the respondents in a statewide poll judged the institution favorably. By 1990, the legislature had freed itself of its institutional racism, secrecy, and malapportionment and was fully equipped to gather information and operate in a new, state-of-the-art legislative facility. That year it got an approval rating of 24 percent.[51]

Performance and approval ratings and other information about legislators and what they are up to is out there in the open for all to see. Legislatures are much more transparent institutions than the other branches of government and certainly are more open about what they are doing than are private sector businesses or unions. This is not to say that many legislative decisions are not still made behind closed doors, but they are acted upon out in the open. Interested citizens can find out how their legislators have represented them by paging through their voting records on the Web, by reading the newsletters their representatives and senators mail to them, and, in twenty-eight states, by watching the legislature in action on TV. About forty legislatures make their proceedings available for audio or video streaming on the Web.[52]

All of this transparency and openness, and yet legislatures still manage to get a bad rap. It is a curious reality of U.S. political life. State legislatures have, by and large, gotten much better at their jobs. Their membership better reflects the population as a whole now more than ever. They have reformed themselves and have become more honest, ethical, and competent in the process. To the average person, however, they are still out-of-control institutions that would do less harm by not meeting at all.

By now, however, it should be evident that legislatures, just like books, cannot be judged by the average person's perception of their covers. State legislatures have become more efficient and effective units of government over the past thirty years. At the federal level, Congress has punted on many of the major domestic issues of the last several years, but state legislatures have picked up those balls and run with them. After Democrats took over the U.S. House of Representatives in 2007, they proudly touted a group of priority bills that they were able to pass. Yet many of their signature initiatives, including a minimum wage increase and funding for stem-cell research, already had been approved in numerous states. And the reason that states were pressing hard that year for expanded healthcare coverage programs was the fact that Congress has failed to act in this area, and the Bush administration publicly suggested that states should take the lead on the issue.

For all of this, legislatures are as unpopular as they have ever been. Following the terrorist attacks of September 11, 2001, polls indicated that the public's faith in government had been restored. Firefighters and cops became popular figures, but elected representatives did not bask in the same sort of glow for very long. If anything, legislators have become more unpopular than they were a generation ago. The increases in staff, in salaries, and in other professional tools that legislators have acquired in recent decades probably have made them better at their jobs. But as they have become more professional, legislatures also have become greater targets of disdain for a public that believes it has little or no use for professional or career politicians. Amateur legislatures hold a stronger appeal to deeply rooted American desires for limited government and limited governmental power.

To a large extent, the general public does not view large staffs and good salaries as ways of ensuring that the legislature does its job in a professional manner. Instead, these increases in legislative resources are seen as yet more proof that politicians want to exploit their offices for personal gain. More than policy issues, the public is quick to anger over such ethical questions as legislative pay raises or other perks for elected officials. "The public does not want the same thing out of a legislature that you think they might want," says John Hibbing, a University of Nebraska political scientist who has written about the unpopularity of legislatures. "The public wants a legislature whose members are not in a position to feather their own nests."[53]

Legislators have done a poor job of selling the idea that what they do is important and necessary in a democracy. And the media is more concerned with dramatizing conflicts than explaining what are sometimes awfully dry policy matters; therefore, it has not helped legislators to make their case. A primary job of the media in a democracy is to report on what the government is up to, but less and less media attention is devoted to legislatures. Books about such media failings are even more tiresome, if you can believe it, than books about state and local government. But a few points are worth making here.

One such point is that ever since Watergate, the scandal that forced President Richard Nixon to resign in 1974, the press has taken an adversarial position toward government. People in government, including legislators, are not very good in the first place at getting out the good news about what they are doing or publicizing their successes. Reporters are by their nature skeptics and are good at covering scandals and mistakes. "Skepticism is not just a personality quirk of journalists," says one reporter. "It's a core value, the wellspring of all our best work." [54] The media have made boo-boo coverage practically the mainstay of government reporting. This is not true in 100 percent of the cases, of course, but the press's general attitude toward government was summed up well a few years ago by a reporter in Pennsylvania who told a public official, "Your job is to manage the public business and mine is to report when you do it wrong." [55]

Reporters may be too cynical about what legislators are up to, but a bigger problem might be that there are so few reporters watching them. An *American Journalism Review* survey in 2002 found that there were only 510 daily newspaper reporters covering state capitols—about one-sixth the number of journalists who cover the Super Bowl. That is an average of about ten reporters per state, but Nevada, for instance, had only five full-time statehouse reporters. The number of capitol reporters in some other states, such as Michigan, had dropped by nearly half in the previous decade or so. The numbers are even weaker for television coverage. [56]

Earlier we touched briefly upon how unusual it was that each of Minnesota's Twin Cities had a daily newspaper. Well, one effect of fewer newspapers can be fewer reporters to cover more areas. Another is intense competition for readership, and quite honestly, "sex sells." At least that is what the media argue. You may have heard this "chicken or the egg" argument. On the one hand, the media claim that people want to read about scandals and wrongdoing and not about state legislatures and policy issues. So, the media give the public what it wants. The people, on the other hand, claim that they are sick of reading about dirty politicians. They say they do not read about state legislatures and policy issues because the media seldom cover these topics. Which claim actually came first? Which is actually right?

Fewer reporters translate into fewer stories about what legislators are doing to earn their taxpayer-financed livings. The more populous states, such as New York and Florida, still boast a relatively sizable capitol press corps, but even in these states the legislatures lose out because their stories get lost in the clutter of other news. The South Dakota legislature, when it is in session, is a major source of news in that underpopulated state, but the Illinois General Assembly loses out to coverage of other activities in Chicago and the surrounding area.[57] As a result of diminished coverage, says Gary Moncrief, a political scientist at Boise State University, "I'm not sure the American public is very attuned to the inner workings of legislatures and the fact that they probably do work better today than thirty or forty years ago."[58]

Some of the slack has been taken up by bloggers—nearly every capital is covered by at least a handful. The Texas blogging corps includes political junkies, college students, the producers of a talk-radio show, mainstream journalists, and a couple of state representatives who blog directly from the House floor. Of course, nothing is perfect, and a common complaint about statehouse bloggers, like all bloggers, is that their coverage tends toward the snarky. "We live in a pretty cynical age and the blogs are pretty cynical," said a press aide to the lieutenant governor. "The more critical they are, the more readers they get. There are no lines any more between what's fair game and what's not."[59]

Many blogs are merely updated political pamphlets, aping and expressing a party line. Of course, some bloggers do more than comment and provide real reporting and fresh information. Some devote attention to specialized topics, such as the environment or criminal justice. But, unfortunately, most of the best material is read only by an insider audience made up of people who follow the legislature or track an issue for a living, leaving the general public relatively uninformed.

In 2006, however, the potential power of bloggers on the legislative process was amply demonstrated in Louisiana. A blogger who had been a long-time legislative counsel said that a bill to provide legislators with heavily discounted health premiums, which had passed the legislature but received virtually no attention from traditional media outlets, sounded like a bad idea that the governor ought to veto. Blog attention prompted talk radio attention, which prompted angry calls to the governor's office. Three days

Many state legislatures now have a dedicated core of bloggers who report and comment on the activities of the legislature. Some of these bloggers include the legislators themselves. This is a screen shot of Illinois representative John Fritchey's "Open House" blog.

later, Kathleen Blanco, the governor, issued a statement saying she'd heard the people loud and clear and would in fact veto the bill. What's more, legislators changed their votes—as they're allowed to do in Louisiana—and both major parties, which had endorsed the bill, came out in opposition.[60]

All of this mostly negative attention means that amateur legislatures are much more popular with their constituents than more professional chambers. The urge to return legislatures to their more humble but lovable position as citizen institutions has been the main driver behind the term limits movement. Limits on the number of terms an individual may serve in the House or Senate have been approved in most of the states that allow ballot initiatives. As of 2007, there were fifteen states with term limits. The limits range from a low of six years of service per legislative chamber in states such as Arkansas and Maine to twelve years service in Nevada, Oklahoma, and Utah.

Term limits are especially strict in states where the public thinks there was not enough turnover in the legislature. "The lower the existing turnover rate in the legislature," a pair of political scientists concluded in 1996, "the harsher the term limits they tend to adopt."[61] In California, for example, Assemblyman Willie Brown became the poster child for a term limits initiative because of his fourteen years as Assembly Speaker. That state now has term limits that match the strictest limits in the nation. In 1990 California voters sent an even stronger message. Even as they limited terms, they also cut the legislature's budget and staffing levels by 40 percent—the third cut in six years. The same year, Colorado voters imposed eight-year term limits on legislators and limited sessions to no more than 120 days a year.

Professional or part-time politician, voters like people who cut through the clutter surrounding issues and offer solutions. The public's attitude is often one of "just the facts, ma'am, and spare me the details." Think about how much ridicule Al Gore received during his presidential campaign in 2000 for being a wonk who knew too much about congressional bill numbers and specific policy decisions. Policy competence in legislators is often similarly viewed as a negative. The idea is that if they are too distracted by details and special interest wishes, they will never shut up and actually do something to serve the common good.[62] Political nominees are eager to appeal to this public sentiment. "I just want to get things done," one candidate said in 2002 in a typical statement. "Hewing to the party line—any party's line—does not interest me."[63]

The problem with this worldview is that there is no such thing as an easily defined common good. No one likes Osama bin Laden, but agreement stops soon after that. Like terrorism, gun control is another such hot-button topic. After each shooting spree in a school, such as the one that occurred in April 2007 at Virginia Tech in Blacksburg, Virginia, there are calls for stricter gun control laws. Yet a large proportion of the public does not want gun owners' rights trampled on. There is no consensus on this

Policy in Practice: Outwit, Outlast, Outplay: Who Really Got the Best Deal with Term Limits?

The biggest change to hit state legislatures over the last quarter century has been the advent of term limits. In the fifteen states with term limit laws—which were almost all approved by voters sick of career politicians via ballot initiatives—legislators are limited to serving no more than six, eight, or twelve years in either the House or Senate. Although that may sound like a long time, it turns out not to be enough for most legislators to master all the complexities of understanding and formulating a wide range of policy.

Term limits have failed the public's goal of bringing in more "citizen legislators." Instead, legislators are constantly seeking their next political job, rather than carving out a career in one chamber for decades. Term limits also have failed to bring in the anticipated and hoped-for substantial numbers of women and minorities to the legislative ranks. The total number of women legislators is up nationwide, but their ranks have actually been slower to grow in states that impose term limits.[a]

But if they haven't fulfilled all their promises, term limits have not been quite the disaster their opponents predicted, either. One of the most common predictions—that with members serving so briefly, lobbyists hoarding institutional and policy knowledge would accrue all the power—appears to have missed the mark. Term limits pretty much have been a mixed bag for lobbyists, who must introduce themselves to a new, skeptical set of legislators every couple of years, rather than relying on cozy relations with a few key committee chairs. "I don't know one lobbyist who thinks it's a good thing," said Rick Farmer, who wrote about term limits as an academic before going to work for the Oklahoma House. "If term limits are such a good thing for lobbyists, why do so many lobbyists hate them?"

It does seem clear, however, that legislators in term-limited states have lost power to the executive branch—the governors and their staff who actually know how to operate the machinery of government. "Agency heads can outwait and outlast anyone and everyone on the playing field and they have consolidated their power," said one southern legislator-turned-lobbyist.

Academic studies in term-limit states, including California, Colorado, and Maine, have found that legislators make far fewer changes to governors' budgets than they used to, representing many billions of dollars in legislative discretion that is no longer exercised. "The crumbling of legislative power is clear across states," said Thad Kousser, a political scientist at the University of California, San Diego, and author of a book about term limits. "There's no more clear finding in the research than a shift in power where the legislature is becoming a less than equal branch of government."

For all that, it's become common to hear governors and other executive branch officials complain about term limits, because the laws mean they lack negotiating partners whose knowledge and expertise they can count on. It seems that no one who works in a state capital—or in the law and lobbying shops that surround any capital—likes term limits.

But there is one group that still finds them attractive—the voting public. Polls suggest that about 75 percent of the public favors them. "With new people in office, you have people with real world experience," says Stacie Rumenap, president of U.S. Term Limits, a group that advocates limits. "Under term limits, you might have a schoolteacher sitting on the education committee."[b]

That sort of suggestion often is made about term limits—you get rid of the professional politicians and get people who know what the real problems are because they themselves are real. And while legislatures in Idaho and Utah have repealed their limits, efforts to extend or weaken term limits have been rejected several times by voters since 2002 in Arkansas, California, Florida, and Montana.

The main effects of term limits, after all, are procedural. It's difficult to make a convincing case that they have made any one particular policy worse, let alone imperiled the quality of life in any state that observes them. The underlying complaint of term limits opponents, that they make legislatures less powerful, is one reason why many people supported them to begin with.

Source: Adapted from Alan Greenblatt, "The Truth about Term Limits," *Governing* magazine, January 2006, 24.
[a] Peter Slevin, "After Adopting Term Limits, States Lose Female Legislators," *Washington Post,* April 22, 2007, A4.
[b] Interview with Stacie Rumenap, October 4, 2002.

National Conference on State Legislatures's Term Limits Poll: Survey Results, 2003

Do you support term limits for legislators?

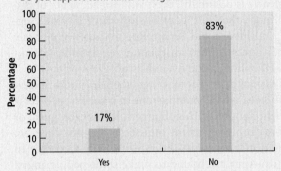

As a result of term limits, do you think your legislature is...

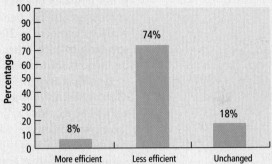

As a result of term limits, are legislative committees in your state...

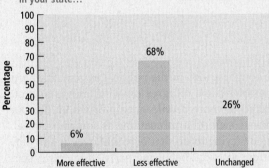

As a result of term limits, do you think the members of your state legislature are...

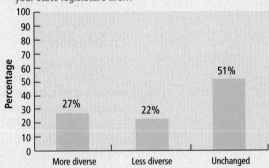

As a result of term limits in your state, do legislative staff exert...

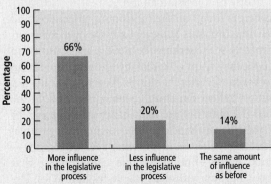

As a result of term limits in your state...

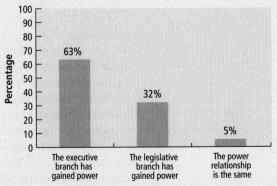

Source: www.ncsl.org/programs/legismgt/about/survrslt.htm (accessed April 25, 2007).

Note: In 2003, the National Conference on State Legislatures surveyed 134 state legislators, legislative staff members, lobbyists, and others in states with term limits for legislators. The results of a few of the survey questions are shown here.

issue, just as there is no consensus on whether SUVs should be banned to save the environment or whether the best way to address a state budget deficit is to cut funding for health coverage or to raise taxes.

The American electorate is clearly divided, as reflected by the tied presidential election of 2000, an evenly divided U.S. Congress, and the near parity in total numbers of Republican and Democratic legislators. Even in states in which one party clearly is dominant, there still can be plenty of disagreement. To cite one example, the GOP controlled both of Florida's legislative chambers in 2002, but House and Senate Republicans were barely speaking to each other after fights about redistricting, regulation of banking and insurance, and a $10 billion battle over sales tax exemptions.[64]

If there is no agreement in your dorm room about whether to rent *Spider-Man* or *Pirates of the Caribbean,* why should anyone in a society as diverse as ours expect easy agreement about taxation, budgets, healthcare, guns, or the environment? Legislators simply reflect the messiness of public opinion. No matter which way they decide an issue—even if it is only to decide to maintain the law as it stands—they are bound to make some people angry. People would prefer decisions to be neat and simple and harmonious. Maybe that is why no one likes legislatures.

Conclusion

Legislatures have one of the toughest jobs in the political system. It's hard enough trying to get a group of friends to agree on what movie to rent. Imagine trying to get a hundred or more people—many of whom flat out oppose your preferred choice—to sign off on something as controversial as, say, a welfare bill. Now imagine trying to do that over and over again: putting in the research; negotiating; meeting; balancing partisan interests, special interests, and constituent interests; and finally, hammering out an agreement that no one is fully satisfied with and everyone is willing to criticize. That gives some idea of the reality of a legislator's job.

Historically speaking, legislators today do their jobs more effectively and more fairly than at any other time. For this achievement, they are mistrusted and disliked. Why? Ultimately it is perhaps because a legislature can never give the people everything they want. Democracy is simply not set up to do this because people want very different things. Legislatures do not really create conflict, they simply reflect the disagreements that exist in the electorate. Or at least they do if legislators are reasonably effective at representing the preferences of their constituencies. What democracy promises, and what state legislatures largely deliver, is not what everyone wants—on most issue no such option exists—but reasonable compromises that most people can live with. Like a group with differing tastes in movies, legislatures are successful when they can agree on second best.

Key Concepts

apportionment (p. 206)

casework (p. 196)

caucus (p. 201)

coalition building (p. 184)

committee (p. 185)

compromise (p. 186)

constituents (p. 186)

constituent service (p. 196)

delegates (p. 205)

districts (p. 186)

filibusters (p. 185)

gerrymanders (p. 208)

incumbent (p. 196)

logrolling (p. 184)

majority-minority districts (p. 209)

majority rule (p. 184)

malapportionment (p. 208)

oversight (p. 197)

professionalization (p. 206)

rank-and-file members (p. 204)

redistricting (p. 207)

representation (p. 191)

riders (p. 185)

trustees (p. 205)

Suggested Readings

Kurtz, Karl T., et al. *Institutional Change in American Politics: The Case of Term Limits.* Ann Arbor: University of Michigan Press, 2007. A group of academics and legislative advisers present case studies about the effects of term limits, "the most significant institutional change in American legislatures" since the 1970s.

Loomis, Burdett A. *Time, Politics, and Policies: A Legislative Year.* Lawrence: University Press of Kansas, 1994. A year in the life of the Kansas state legislature.

Rosenthal, Alan. *The Decline of Representative Democracy: Process, Participation, and Power in State Legislatures.* Washington, D.C.: CQ Press, 1998. A political scientist's comprehensive look at the work of state legislatures and how that work is changing.

———. *Heavy Lifting: The Job of the American Legislature.* Washington, D.C.: CQ Press, 2004. This book argues that the success of state legislatures is best measured by the effectiveness of their processes, not by the specific product of their legislation.

Rosenthal, Alan, et al. *Republic on Trial: The Case for Representative Democracy.* Washington, D.C.: CQ Press, 2002. After examining the many flaws of legislators, as well as other political leaders, the authors conclude that these leaders still do a pretty good job representing the public's interest.

Suggested Web Sites

http://governing.typepad.com/13thfloor/. Governing's 13th Floor blog provides coverage of state issues, as well as links to prominent blogs covering governments in every state.

http://ncsl.typepad.com/the_thicket/. The National Conference of State Legislatures's blog, The Thicket offers coverage of state issues.

http://stateline.org. A foundation-sponsored news service that provides daily news about state government.

www.alec.org. Web site for the American Legislative Exchange, an influential conservative organization that drafts model legislation. Both legislators and private sector interests are members.

www.csg.org. Web site for the Council of State Governments, which provides training and information to state government officials.

www.ncsl.org. Web site of the National Conference of State Legislatures that includes a wealth of information about legislative structures and procedures as well as the major issues faced by legislators.

CHAPTER 7

Governors and Executives

There Is No Such Thing as Absolute Power

The evolution of man? Not exactly, but these wax figures certainly represent the evolution of one man's career. Arnold Schwarzenegger is not the first actor to turn politician, but he may be one of the first to make such effective use of a changing political environment. In 2003, California's voting public turned against recently reelected governor Gray Davis and demanded that he leave office. Schwarzenegger used his powerful personal connections to fellow Republicans, including President George H. W. Bush, and his links to America's royal family, the Kennedys, through his wife, Maria Shriver (a Kennedy relative), to beat out more than 130 other candidates running for the newly opened governor's seat.

7

Governor Schwarzenegger

Terminator Schwarzenegger

Schwarzenegger the Barbarian

How did governors get to be such powerful players, when for much of American history their offices were weak?

Why do some states still give their governors more pomp than power?

Arnold Schwarzenegger, who was an international movie star before entering politics, has shown a deft understanding of how to use the media and the star power of his office as governor of California. He has unquestionably set and dominated the state's political agenda over the last several years. Yet he has learned the hard way that even a popular governor can't succeed entirely on his own.

Schwarzenegger was elected in an unusual recall election at the end of 2003. During his first year in office, Schwarzenegger, a Republican, showed himself to be a savvy negotiator. He outmaneuvered the Democrats who dominated the legislature, making unusual alliances with various groups to get his way on such major issues as an overhaul of the state workers' compensation insurance law and a series of budget packages. He knew how to use his celebrity to focus attention on a problem, win a victory, and then carry that momentum forward into the next fight.

That was his first year. But he lost his way during his second year. He took to calling Democrats "girlie men" for not supporting his priorities and vowed to take his proposals directly to the public in the form of ballot initiatives. Schwarzenegger ended up doing just that. He called a special election in 2005 to determine the fate of his proposals to limit state spending and weaken his opponents through changes in redistricting and campaign spending. How did his gamble pay off? Every one of his proposals went down to defeat, and his own approval ratings slipped to 38 percent. Early polling in 2006 suggested Schwarzenegger would lose his bid for reelection.

Instead, Schwarzenegger staged an amazing comeback. He began cooperating with legislators, rather than calling them names. Together, they passed some $40 billion worth of infrastructure projects and a landmark bill to address global warming. Schwarzenegger won a decisive reelection victory and began his second term with ambitious proposals to change the state's prison and sentencing systems and offer all Californians health coverage.

What the actor-turned-politician had learned is that, although the governor calls the tune, he needs other players to join his band to accomplish anything. "Where he has gotten so much of his recent star power is in his ability to work compromises with the legislature," Mark Baldassare, director of research for the Public Policy Institute of California, said early in 2007. "His popularity is derived from working both sides of the aisle to come to a compromise. That's what he's going to have to do, or he will see his star power diminish." [1]

That's what all governors have to do. Historically, governors in U.S. politics have held more token prestige than real governmental strength. Today they command enormous power, but they still can get hardly anything done without the cooperation of others. They can't pass laws without legislators, they can't implement policy without assistance from state agencies, and they can't create jobs without the private sector.

Still, governors are the prime political actors in virtually every state. Some are notably more successful than others, but all are seen as leaders. In most states, the governor sets the agenda, largely determining what policy issues will be pursued and how the state budget will look. They are unique among state-level politicians in terms of the media attention they can attract. This helps them promote their causes, but they must rely on other institutional players if they are going to accomplish more than making speeches.

Recently, governors have become a lot better equipped to control the rest of the executive branch. For more than one hundred years after the founding of the American republic, governors were strong in title only, with little real power. In fact, they were hardly more than figureheads. Throughout the last decades of the twentieth century, however, governors were given more and more formal control over the machinery of government at the same time that the federal government shifted greater control of many programs, including welfare, to the states. They have longer terms than they once did and enjoy greater authority to appoint the top officials in virtually every government agency. (Only New Hampshire and Vermont still have two-year gubernatorial terms. The rest of the states have four-year terms. Only Virginia limits its chief executive to a single consecutive term—although two-term limits are common among the states.) These changes were the result of changes in laws in many states that were specifically designed to strengthen the office of governor in hopes of creating greater accountability and coherence in government. They are now, with few exceptions, not just the most famous politicians in their states but also the most powerful.

Governors are expected to be the leading cheerleaders for their states. They are expected to attract business and jobs, to set the political tone, to manage state affairs. They serve as the primary face and voice of government during natural disasters or other crises. With this much power, of course, comes a great deal of expectation. If a state is not doing well—if it is losing more jobs than its neighbors during a recession, for example, or is running a budget deficit—voters and the media will hold the governor responsible. That is why Kathleen Blanco, the Democratic governor of Louisiana, announced in 2007 that she would not run for reelection, following the failure of her "Road Home" reconstruction program after Hurricane Katrina.

Governors are like mini-presidents in each state. Like the president, the governor commands the lion's share of political attention in a state, is generally seen as setting the agenda for the legislative branch, and is basically the lead political actor—the figure most likely to appear on television on a regular basis. As with the president, governors tend to receive the blame or enjoy the credit for the performance of the economy.

And, like the president, a governor shares responsibility for running the government—implementing laws; issuing regulations; and doing the work of building the roads, maintaining the parks and other public functions—

> Governors are like mini-presidents in each state. Like the president, the governor commands the lion's share of political attention in a state, is generally seen as setting the agenda for the legislative branch, and is basically the lead political actor—the figure most likely to appear on television on a regular basis. As with the president, governors tend to receive the blame or enjoy the credit for the performance of the economy.

with the help of a cabinet. Presidents appoint their cabinet officials to run the Departments of Defense and Agriculture and the like. Governors have no foreign policy responsibilities, of course, but they do have help in running state-level departments of agriculture, finance, environmental protection, and so on. In most cases, in most states, the governor appoints officials to head these departments. But some other statewide officials, such as attorneys general, often are elected on their own and may even represent another party. We will explore the roles of these other executive branch officials in this chapter.

And this chapter also will answer these questions: How did governors get to be such powerful players, when for much of U.S. history their offices were weak? Why is this so? How is it even possible? Why do some states still give their governors more pomp than power? We will look at how the office of governor has changed over the years. We will examine the types of power governors can command by virtue of the office and which powers they must create out of the force of personality. We'll look at what sorts of people get elected governor and how they get elected. Finally, we will survey some of the other important statewide offices, such as lieutenant governor and attorney general.

The Job of Governor

Following the American Revolution, governors had very little power for one simple reason—distrust. Colonial governors, appointed by the British, had imposed unpopular taxes and exploited their positions to make themselves rich. Americans did not want to invest too much power into individuals who might turn into mini-dictators. There was no national president, after all, under the original Articles of Confederation. In the states, most of the power was disbursed by giving it to many individuals holding office in legislatures and on state boards and commissions. Governors in all but three of the original states were limited to one-year terms. While in office, they were not given control over state departments and agencies. Separately elected individuals, boards, or commissions ran these instead. After his state's constitutional convention, one North Carolina delegate said that the governor had been given just enough power "to sign the receipt for his salary." [2]

The number of agencies grew as government became more complex toward the end of the nineteenth century. Lack of central control over these agencies, however, meant that states had difficulty functioning coherently. The U.S. Constitution had done much to improve the political structure in the United States—but not for governors. Governors still lacked the authority to perform in a way that the public expected given their position at the top of the political pyramid. This problem persisted well into the twentieth century.

Lynn Muchmore, a political scientist, summed up the sort of frustrations governors had as late as the 1980s in terms of getting various parts of government to act as they wished. Muchmore laid out a theoretical case of a governor elected on a platform of promoting growth in the state's rural areas and documented the difficulties he had in making good on those promises. In this scenario, the new governor finds that the highway department, which is run by a separate commission, had decided a decade ago to complete urban segments of the state's road system. This decision siphoned money away from plans to develop better roads in rural areas. The board that oversees public colleges and universities has a policy of phasing out satellite campuses in favor of investing in three urban campuses. The state's department of commerce will not work in any county that does not have a local economic development corporation. Many rural counties lack such corporations because they do not have the population or tax base to support them. The state legislature has passed restrictions that deny new businesses breaks on rural utility rates.[3] Despite his promises, the governor's battle to help rural areas was an uphill one.

Not every scenario is so extreme, but it is often the case that state agencies not headed by people appointed by the governor—and therefore not answering to him or her—will have their own constituencies and concerns. They will not have in mind the big picture of how the different parts of state government can best work together to promote the general good. Only the governor sees the whole field in that way.

In recent decades, governors have been granted greater powers in hopes that states will function more efficiently. They now have much more power over appointments than they once did. This means that they are able to put their own teams in place to carry out their policies. They have become important symbols of the state not only at home but also as ambassadors who promote their states to businesses that they hope to attract in other states and abroad.

Terry Sanford, a former governor of North Carolina, summed up the job of the contemporary governor well:

The governor by his very office embodies his state. He must . . . energize his administration, search out the experts, formulate the programs, mobilize the support, and carry new ideas into action. . . . Few major undertakings ever get off the ground without his support and leadership. The governor sets the agenda for public debate; frames the issues; decides on the timing, and can blanket the state with good ideas by using his access to the mass media. . . . The governor is the most potent political power in the state.[4]

Governors must be multitaskers. They propose legislation, which has to win approval from the legislature. They can implement regulations that help clear up how those laws actually are applied to individuals, businesses, and other groups. Increasingly, in recent years, governors have become the strongest advocates and public relations people for their states, traveling to promote tourism and help close deals with out-of-state trading partners who might locate offices or operations in their states. We will explore all these roles in some detail.

Chief Legislator

Just as the president does not serve in Congress, governors do not sit as members of state legislatures. Like the president, however, they have enormous influence over the work legislatures do. Governors outline their broad proposals in inaugural and annual state of the state addresses. They and their staffs then work with individual legislators and committees to translate these proposals into bills.

Some governors are better at getting what they want from legislatures than others. Why? Part of it is personal charm, but a lot of it has to do with the powers granted to a governor in a given state. In Texas, for instance, most of the influence that the executive branch holds over legislation is given to the lieutenant governor, not the governor. Governors all vary in terms of how much authority they have in blocking bills they do not like through use of the **veto,** or rejection of the bill. Those variations in authority help to determine how much clout a governor has in the legislature.

Governors never get everything they want from state legislatures, but governors do have a great deal of impact on what bills become laws. There are a number of reasons for this. In every state, bills almost never become law without the governor's signature. Governors can veto them. Legislators can get around a veto, but that often means that they have to pass the bill again by a **supermajority vote.** Supermajority votes are usually votes of two-thirds or more. Since it is hard enough to get both legislative houses to agree on a bill in the first place, such a large vote in support rarely happens. If you can't pass a law without the governor's approval, it stands to reason that you will want to work with him in order to create a version of the bill that will win such approval.

Another factor that makes governors enormously influential in the legislative process is their command of state budgets. In nearly every state, the

VETO

The power to reject a proposed law.

SUPERMAJORITY VOTE

A legislative vote of much more than a simple majority, for instance, two-thirds of a legislative chamber voting to override a governor's veto.

main responsibility for creating a state budget rests in the office of the governor. The governor proposes budgets that detail the amount of money that will go to every state agency, welfare program, highway department, and school district. There are often restrictions on how a state must spend much of its money from year to year, whether because of old laws or federal requirements. But a governor gets the first crack at deciding how most of the state's money is going to be spent.

Maryland's governor is the nation's most powerful in terms of setting a state budget, the result of changes prompted by a serious deficit in 1916 for which the legislature took the blame.[5] There, once the chief executive lays out the budget, the legislature cannot add any more money to fund individual departments or programs or shift money among those programs. Legislators *can* reduce the size of appropriations, but cannot create programs of their own. In the other states, legislators have more power to tinker. In New York State in 2003, the legislature passed its own budget by overriding the governor's veto. Usually, however, the governor's blueprint gets passed, with legislators only making changes here or there. "As far as legislators are concerned," one political scientist wrote, "the ability to create the budget is so powerful that it becomes *the* major tool for a governor in achieving his legislative programs."[6]

Governors might get to decide, for instance, whether bridges are going to be built in particular districts. In order to get those bridges—or any other goodies they might want—legislators often have to give governors what they want in terms of passing their major initiatives. "Any legislator who says he needs nothing from the governor's office is either lying or stupid,"

Maryland governor Martin O'Malley uses a farm tour to tout his new budget, which includes funds to help farmers promote environmentally friendly practices. While most governors exercise considerable influence over budgets, the Maryland governor has more power than most. A number of legal restrictions make it difficult for the Maryland legislature to make major changes to the budget proposed by the governor.

according to one observer of the Alabama political scene.[7] Legislators who belong to the governor's party are inclined to help out anyway, because they will be perceived as part of the same team when facing voters in the next election.

Some governors choose only to focus on a few big issues and leave many small matters to the prerogative of the legislature. Others tackle a wide range of problems. How much success a governor enjoys varies greatly according to his or her individual abilities and skills. Yet there is no question that a governor is the most likely person to set the main agenda for the legislature and the state.

> "Any legislator who says he needs nothing from the governor's office is either lying or stupid," according to one observer of the Alabama political scene.

Head of State Agencies

Governors at one time had very little control over who ran their states' departments. This meant that people with other agendas could set policy over taxes or healthcare or other issues. Even today, for instance, Texas voters elect twenty-five different statewide officials. Texas governors cannot hire their own choices for such positions as comptroller (the state's chief financial officer), agriculture commissioner, or state supreme court justices.

In most states, that has changed in recent times. Only about half of the governors chose their own cabinet officials in 1969, but nearly all of them do today.[8] In fact, the current trend is to try to merge even large departments so that they do not work at cross purposes or duplicate work. In 1998, Florida voters decided to shrink the state's cabinet and put more power directly in the governor's office. In Massachusetts, Gov. Mitt Romney created a "supercabinet" position in 2003 that oversaw the state's economic, consumer affairs, and labor departments in hopes of coordinating their budgets and activities. His other attempts to consolidate more power in the governor's office through a major reorganization of the government structure were rejected by the legislature, however.

The power to appoint people to run state departments offers obvious benefits for governors. They can pick their own people who they know will pursue their policy preferences. If they fail, they can be fired. How much influence a governor has over state education policy, say, or environmental protection still depends on the amount of energy and time the governor can afford to devote to these issues, as opposed to everything else that must be done. One Arkansas governor said that a governor "will spend almost as much time keeping his staff and his cabinet and the people around him happy as he does keeping his constituency happy."[9]

In other words, governors who can appoint their own people to run the government cannot count on accomplishing the administration's major goals. Just like any other boss, governors may be disappointed in the performance of the people working for them. The ability to hire and fire people, however, as well as the ability to determine how much money their departments are going to get, means that governors are truly the leaders of the executive branch of government.

Chief Spokesperson for the State

Mississippi governor Haley Barbour is the first to credit the countless government workers who helped southern Mississippi cope with Hurricane Katrina, which devastated the Gulf Coast in 2005. But a major crisis such as Katrina also demands a strong leader who can communicate calm to the public and provide "a central decision-making point for when things get balled up or go sideways, which they do," as Barbour says. He excelled at both. Barbour was straight with the facts about the utter devastation in the area, but his own demeanor in public appearances suggested that the state would summon the will to rebuild.[10]

A governor acts as the chief spokesperson and public face of a state's government, in good times as well as bad. New Mexico governor Bill Richardson has worked hard to send signals that the state government wants to be as friendly as possible to business growth. New Mexico had the forty-seventh lowest per capita income in the country, so Richardson didn't even wait until his inauguration in January 2003 to begin his sales pitch for his programs and for the state. The day after his election, he got on a plane to talk to executives in California's Silicon Valley in hopes of persuading them to set up operations in New Mexico.

Since then, he has lured movie shoots to the state with an $85 million investment fund. Richardson helped double the state's trade with Mexico during his first year in office, and used his international connections from his days as UN ambassador to begin a relationship with Mexican president Vicente Fox. Richardson proudly boasts he calls CEOs on a daily basis and "sucks up to them big time."

Other governors perform similar chores. Former Wisconsin governor Tommy Thompson used to host business executives from Minnesota at the opening of fishing season to show off the state's outdoor activities and to try to convince them to locate new facilities there. In order to combat a significant decrease in travel and tourism in the months following the terrorist attacks of September 11, 2001, Florida governor Jeb Bush wrote letters of thanks to every group that agreed to hold its convention in the state. Governors regularly send out press releases about their role in helping to land new jobs and companies through tax incentives, the creation of cooperative biotechnology ventures, or other economic development activities.

Basically, their main role as chief face of the state is now in sales. They promote their states' benefits to economic interests. They pitch the virtues of low tax rates, good roads and transportation systems, livable communities, well-educated workforces, or anything else they can think of that might seem attractive to individuals scouting potential business sites. Their desire to have good packages to sell has had an effect on their policies, with most governors afraid to make any moves that might be perceived as unfriendly to business.

That proved to be the case for Colorado governor Bill Ritter. In early 2007 the state legislature swiftly passed a bill that would have made it easier for organized labor to unionize workplaces. Ritter had campaigned with union support and had pledged to union members that he would support such a move. But he surprised everyone by vetoing the bill, deciding that he could not afford to alienate business interests so early in his term when he would need their help on other issues, such as higher education and transportation. "I recognize how deeply disappointed my friends in organized labor will be with this decision," Ritter wrote in his veto message. But he was more worried "about the impact this change would have on our ability to attract new business to Colorado, to create new economic opportunity for all.[11]

Governors do speak out in other roles as well. They appear in tourism brochures. Sometimes they get criticized for this, as some see it as promoting their own images at state expense. During the 2006 campaign season, the Maryland legislature called a halt to ads featuring Gov. Bob Ehrlich, who was running for reelection. "If he's really the state's best attraction for tourists, pity Ocean City," commented the Washington Post in an editorial.[12]

When their teams are in major bowl games or the World Series, governors are sure to let the media know that they have bet some celebrated state product against those of other governors. More substantively, governors have become important lobbyists in Washington, seeking more federal money for their states. They are the only people that lobby in the nation's capitol who can be sure that members of Congress and cabinet officials will meet with them directly, rather than having them meet with staff.

Party Chief

Governors are also the leading figures in their party within their states. U.S. senators arguably might be more influential figures, but governors are more important politically at home. Governors command more foot soldiers. They may be able to call on thousands of state workers, whereas a senator's staff numbers in the dozens at most. Not all of a governor's workers will be loyal members of the same party—in fact, changes in patronage laws and the creation of a civil service system mean that governors appoint far fewer state employees than they did some decades ago. Governors, however, will have more people whose jobs depend on them than will any other elected official.

Governors often pick state party chairs of their liking. They help to recruit and raise money for candidates for other statewide offices and the legislature. They use the media attention they attract to campaign for those they support. For all this, state parties are not as important as they were forty years ago, so governors now devote less energy to political activities than to the nuts and bolts of their own jobs. This does not mean they do not have to pound the political pavement. They are still the titular heads of the party in their states, and no modern politician (who isn't already rich) can avoid the duties of raising campaign contributions.

In their role as head of state, governors often are seen as the building blocks toward putting together a winning electoral map in presidential races. Unquestionably, having a popular governor on your side won't hurt you politically. It is taken as an article of faith among pundits and other political experts that governors can help swing their states toward the presidential nominee of their choice through their media presence and ability to sway some percentage of their states' votes. This doesn't always turn out to be the case, however. George W. Bush, then the governor of Texas, did receive a major boost toward capturing the Republican presidential nomination in 2000 when every other Republican governor endorsed him. To the surprise of some, however, they did not help him much in the general election. Republicans then held eight out of the ten largest states, but Bush only carried three of them.[13] Bush did a little better in 2004, carrying four out of the five large states that had Republican governors by then.

Commander-in-Chief of the National Guard

Even in this country's earliest days, when governors had few powers, each governor's military position was strong, "with all states designating him as commander-in-chief."[14] Southern governors perhaps most famously used their power to control the National Guard in resisting desegregation during the 1950s and 1960s. The National Guard in each state is a state agency, but the president has the power to federalize it, calling up units to perform federal service. That happened in the civil rights era, when the Guard was ordered to work for the feds against governors resisting integration. Today's National Guard is more likely to fight alongside federal soldiers in such places as Iraq.

Governors do not use the Guard as their private armies, however. Instead, they can call out units to respond to natural disasters or riots. Milton Sharp, governor of Pennsylvania during the 1970s, remembered his years in office in terms of emergency response to floods, a pair of hurricanes, droughts, ice storms, fires, and a gypsy moth infestation rather than in terms of lawmaking and policy agenda setting.[15]

Still, the question of who controls the National Guard has become a politically potent one in recent years. The federal government pays for troop training and many of their operations and the Supreme Court has found that the feds—not governors—have the final say over where units are deployed.[16]

Governors complain that because of this they have been caught short during times of disaster, such as Hurricane Katrina. Fortunately, they have generally been able to make up for these shortfalls in home state personnel through agreements with other states that send spare troops. Then in 2006 Congress passed a law that made it easier for the White House, rather than the state house, to take command of the Guard during times of disaster. All fifty governors signed a letter protesting an earlier version of the law. "We see this as an expansion of the president's authority, a change to allow the possibility that the National Guard would be federalized," said David Quam, a lobbyist with the National Governors Association.[17]

Most governors naturally hope to avoid having their tenure defined by the natural disasters and other factors beyond their control that Milton Sharp felt shaped his tenure. Governors have to attend to many political tasks during their time in office. How much success they have in setting their own courses depends on the amount of power they command. That power, in turn, varies a good deal by state and depends not just on the **formal powers** of the office but also on the amount of power individuals in that office can create for themselves.

The Powers of Governors

Anyone who follows sports understands that natural ability does not necessarily translate into success. Some players look great on paper—they're strong, they can run fast, they have whatever skills should help them dominate their sport. But for whatever reason, players like that sometimes squander their talent and are shown up by weaker athletes who nevertheless have a greater understanding of the game, work harder, or simply find a way to win.

It is the same with governors. Some of them look incredibly strong on paper, and their states' constitutions give them powers that their neighbors can only envy. Nevertheless, states that have set up the governor's office to be strong sometimes end up with weak governors. Conversely, states in which the governor's official powers are weak sometimes can have individuals in that office who completely dominate their states' politics. They are able to exploit the **informal powers** of their office—they have managed to create personal powers, as opposed to relying on relatively weak institutional powers.

When we talk about the powers of governors, we obviously do not refer to an ability to cast spells or turn back armies with their wands. If you want to understand why some governors are considered successful or powerful and why others are quickly forgotten even by their supporters, there is an obvious place to start. You need to look at what sorts of power governors are given by right of taking that office. If they do not have the tools to influence policy, they will have a much harder time winning political victories.

FORMAL POWERS

The powers explicitly granted to a governor according to state law, such as vetoing legislation or appointing heads of state agencies.

INFORMAL POWERS

The things a governor is able to do, such as command media attention or persuade party members, based on personality or position, not on formal authority.

Yet every governor, even those whom state law does not grant much authority, has enough stature to expect success.

Let us outline the different types of powers that governors actually do have, both the formal—the roles that come as part of the necessary equipment of the office—and the informal powers that these individuals create for themselves by using their office as a platform.

Formal Powers

Most governors have a wide variety of formal powers granted to them by state constitutions or other laws. Among the most important of these are appointing officials to run state agencies, the power to veto legislation, the power to craft budgets, the power to grant pardons, and the power to call legislatures into session. Each of these aspects of a governor's job description is examined in this section.

The Power to Appoint. As mentioned earlier, the first governors in this country lacked **appointment powers**. They could not pick their own people to run state agencies, which made those agencies more independent. Nowadays, governors can pick their own teams, which gives them greater authority to set policy. When John Engler served as governor of Michigan during the 1990s, for example, he put in place a series of appointees with a strong ideological commitment to limited government. These appointees helped him carry out his desire to shrink the state's government. His contemporary, Ann Richards of Texas, set out to change the face of state government by changing the faces of the people within it—appointing women, blacks, and Hispanics to replace the white men who had always run things in Austin.

Since governors cannot run their states alone, they must rely on the work of people they appoint to help carry out broad policy desires. If a governor wants to offer people living in public housing more opportunities to buy their homes, she will have a better chance of succeeding if she can appoint a housing director who shares those views, as opposed to governors with the same philosophy who have to work with housing directors who answer to independent commissions that oppose privatizing public housing.

Having loyal foot soldiers on your team rather than free agents is important for governors who want things done their way. This is not the only benefit the power of appointment carries with it, however. Governors get to appoint dozens and sometimes thousands of people to full-time government jobs and to commissions and boards. For instance, if you are attending a public college, chances are that the governor appointed the board of governors of your school or university system. These are considered plum jobs and giving them out is a way for a governor not only to influence policy but also to reward campaign contributors or other political allies.

Of course, there is a downside to the power of appointment, which is the risk of picking the wrong people. Earlier, we talked about former Pennsyl-

APPOINTMENT POWERS

A governor's ability to pick individuals to run state government, such as appointing cabinet secretaries.

Texas governor Rick Perry (left) is introduced to by Texas lieutenant governor David Dewhurst. Although technically the second-ranking executive in the Texas state government, Dewhurst actually may wield more power. Texas governors have very few formal powers. The lieutenant governor, however, presides over the state Senate, sets the agenda, and appoints senators to the committees. This makes Dewhurst the executive with the most direct influence over the legislature.

vania governor Milton Sharp, who remembered his administration mainly as a time of dealing with natural disasters. It is little wonder he prefers to remember his time in office that way, as many of his appointments turned into disasters of his own making. His secretary of property and supplies was sent to prison for contracting irregularities. The same fate befell a member of his turnpike authority. Other members of his administration came under ethical shadows as well. Even though Sharp himself was never touched by scandal, subsequent candidates—including the man who would succeed him as governor—ran campaigns against corruption. They won office by pledging to clean up Harrisburg.[18]

Still, the ability to appoint the heads of departments that run such areas as correctional facilities, educational institutions, highways, and utilities helps define a governor's overall power and influence. In some states, governors can pick their own top people without needing the approval of the legislature. In other states, they do need such approval, although the strength of the legislature hold over this area varies. Rhode Island voters in 2004 strengthened the governor's appointment powers and weakened the legislature's reach into the executive branch through a ballot referendum that banned legislators from serving on boards and commissions. Conversely, in Texas, a legislative attempt to strengthen the governor's weak appointment powers was defeated in 2003. The primary reason for this was that legislatures and governors often have adversarial relationships—each can be the enemy of the other. Within the political system, all players are reluctant to surrender power to those in another branch or institutional position.

Governing States and Localities

Policy in Practice: Governors with Gumption: Policy Innovation and Interstate Influence

Governors are the masters of their political domains—their own states. Sometimes, however, they have an effect that reaches far beyond their own state boundaries. Their ideas can spread to be emulated by their colleagues and can even affect federal policy.

In a political era that considers governors in general to be great lobbyists in Washington, there are some who stand out. Few have had an impact equal to that of Tommy Thompson. Thompson served as Wisconsin's governor from 1987 until President George W. Bush put him in charge of the Department of Health and Human Services (HHS) in 2001. While governor, Thompson had petitioned the HHS for waivers from federal welfare law requirements. One of his first acts upon taking office had been to bring together a group of welfare mothers to tell him their stories. He wanted to learn about the obstacles that made it difficult for them to get and keep jobs.

Using these personal stories as motivation, he created a program called Wisconsin Works. The program requires virtually all welfare recipients to work, either at regular jobs that the government has subsidized or in community service. The state increased its spending on child care, healthcare, transportation, and other support services. The combination of Wisconsin's welfare reforms and a healthy economy helped the state cut its welfare caseload by about 65 percent during Thompson's first decade in office, saving more than $1 billion.*

One of Thompson's main pulpits for spreading his gospel of reform and renewal was the National Governors Association (NGA). The association is designed as a clearinghouse for governors from throughout the country to exchange information, as well as to lobby on behalf of the states in Washington. Thompson's experi-

ments were imitated elsewhere. The innovations that he and other governors came up with formed the backbone of the 1996 federal welfare law. The restructured law put time limits on how long a person could stay on welfare and imposed new work requirements.

In 2001, Maryland governor Parris Glendening—one of Thompson's successors as NGA chair—used the position to push a very different agenda. Glendening was tired of seeing farmland and open fields in his state torn up in favor of development. He thought that new houses and businesses should be built near existing houses and businesses, rather than sprawling across the countryside. The excessive development only led to long commutes and environmental degradation.

His Smart Growth Act, which became Maryland law in 1998, is designed to steer the state's money toward the expansion of roads and other infrastructure in such a way as to discourage sprawl and encourage development and redevelopment in settled communities. It does not prevent builders or local governments from creating new projects on virgin land. It merely says that the state no longer subsidizes such projects.

The idea took root, at least for a while. Other governors initially followed Glendening's example. Within a few years, however, sprawl had become a high-profile issue in at least thirty states. Nearly a dozen of these previously had passed sprawl control measures more or less similar to Maryland's.

Thompson's changes in welfare law were an example of moving the national debate by influencing Congress. Glendening's story is about having an impact by providing a model for—and offering guidance to—other states. In both cases, governors of relatively uninfluential states were able to promote big ideas that changed people's lives across the country.

*Ellen Perlman, "The Welfare Risk-Taker," *Governing* magazine, December 1997, 32.

Power to Prepare State Budgets. The most powerful tools governors have may be their ability to shape a state's budget. It gives them enormous influence in their dealings with the legislature. The same is true in terms of their ability to maintain control over state agencies. In most states,

TABLE 7-1

Formal Powers of the Governors by State

State	Budget Power		Line-Item Veto Power	Authorization to Reorganize through Executive Order	Power to Appoint Leaders of the Bureaucracy
	Full Responsibility	Shared Responsibility			
Alabama	Yes		Yes	Yes	Yes
Alaska	Yes		Yes		Yes
Arizona	Yes		Yes	Yes	Yes
Arkansas		Yes	Yes	Yes	Yes
California	Yes		Yes		Yes
Colorado	Yes		Yes		Yes
Connecticut	Yes		Yes		Yes
Delaware	Yes		Yes	Yes	Yes
Florida	Yes		Yes		Yes
Georgia	Yes		Yes	Yes	Yes
Hawaii	Yes		Yes		Yes
Idaho	Yes		Yes		Yes
Illinois		Yes	Yes	Yes	Yes
Indiana		Yes		Yes	Yes
Iowa	Yes		Yes		Yes
Kansas	Yes		Yes		Yes
Kentucky	Yes		Yes		Yes
Louisiana		Yes	Yes		Yes
Maine	Yes				Yes
Maryland	Yes		Yes		Yes
Massachusetts	Yes		Yes	Yes	Yes
Michigan		Yes	Yes	Yes	Yes
Minnesota	Yes		Yes	Yes	Yes
Mississippi		Yes	Yes	Yes	Yes
Missouri	Yes		Yes	Yes	Yes
Montana		Yes	Yes	Yes	Yes
Nebraska		Yes	Yes		Yes
Nevada	Yes				Yes
New Hampshire	Yes				Yes
New Jersey	Yes		Yes		Yes
New Mexico	Yes		Yes		Yes
New York		Yes	Yes		Yes
North Carolina	Yes			Yes	Yes

TABLE 7-1, **continued**

State	Budget Power		Line-Item Veto Power	Authorization to Reorganize through Executive Order	Power to Appoint Leaders of the Bureaucracy
	Full Responsibility	Shared Responsibility			
North Dakota	Yes		Yes	Yes	Yes
Ohio	Yes		Yes		Yes
Oklahoma		Yes	Yes		Yes
Oregon	Yes		Yes		Yes
Pennsylvania	Yes		Yes		Yes
Rhode Island	Yes				Yes
South Carolina		Yes	Yes		Yes
South Dakota	Yes		Yes	Yes	Yes
Tennessee	Yes		Yes	Yes	Yes
Texas		Yes	Yes		Yes
Utah	Yes		Yes		Yes
Vermont	Yes			Yes	Yes
Virginia	Yes		Yes	Yes	Yes
Washington	Yes		Yes		Yes
West Virginia	Yes		Yes		Yes
Wisconsin	Yes		Yes		Yes
Wyoming	Yes		Yes		Yes

Source: Adapted from *The Book of the States 2003* (Lexington, Ky.: Council of State Governments, 2003), 188–189.

agencies and departments submit their budget proposals to a central budget office that works as part of the governor's team. The governor's ability to deny them funds or shift money among departments helps make sure that agencies remain focused, at least to some extent, on the governor's priorities.

A governor can use the budget process to override old agency decisions, to make sure that the transportation department, for example, fully funds bike trails that previously had been ignored. Even when an agency has some independence about how it spends its money, a governor can persuade its officials to fund other priorities—a new law school at a state university, for example—by threatening to withhold some percentage of its overall budget.

Power to Veto. In talking about the governor as chief legislator, we touched upon the governor's ability to veto legislation in every state. (North

Carolina's governor was the last to win this power, in 1997.) Legislators can override vetoes, but that rarely happens because of supermajority vote requirements. Members of the governor's own party usually are reluctant to vote to override a veto. That means that if the governor's party holds just one-third of the seats in a legislative chamber, plus one, a veto is likely to be sustained—meaning the governor wins.

Legislators, therefore, try to work with governors or their staffs in order to craft a version of a bill that the governor will sign. There is little point in passing a bill if you know it is going to be rejected. Of course, legislatures sometimes pass a bill just to get it vetoed, making the governor's opposition official and public. That happened often when Gary Johnson was governor of New Mexico during the 1990s. Johnson would not support any bill that increased the size of government, and so he ended up vetoing more than seven hundred bills. Legislators sent him bills that would increase funding for popular programs, such as education, in hopes that his vetoes would make him look bad. Whether that happened or not, Johnson almost always won the procedural battle. Not only was the legislature unable to override his vetoes except in one instance, but he also was reelected to a second term.

All but seven governors—those in Indiana, Maryland, Nevada, New Hampshire, North Carolina, Rhode Island, and Vermont—have a power known as the line-item veto, meaning that they can reject just a portion of a bill. If there is a bill funding education, for example, the governor can accept all of it except for an increase in funding for a school in the district of a legislator who is a political enemy. Governors can use the line-item veto to try to cut spending, as when New York governor George Pataki eliminated spending for more than one thousand items from the state budget in 1998. The governor's ability to cut legislators' pet projects out of the budget forces most to support that governor's major initiatives. Congress tried to give the president line-item veto authority, but the U.S. Supreme Court ruled the practice unconstitutional in 1998.

When Tommy Thompson was governor of Wisconsin during the 1990s, he used the line-item veto to an unusual degree. Some governors can strike not only projects from bills, but individual words and letters as well. Thompson became notorious for vetoing just enough letters to completely alter the meaning of a bill. The courts upheld his right to do so, but that power was soon curbed. However, in 2005, Jim Doyle, the state's Democratic governor, was able to strike out 752 words from a budget bill in order to cobble together a new, twenty-word sentence that shifted $427 million from transportation to education.[19]

Power to Grant Pardons. One clichéd motif of old movies and television was to depict a prisoner about to be put to death, only to be spared by a last-minute pardon from the governor. Governors, like the president, can forgive crimes or commute (change) sentences if they feel a person has been convicted unfairly. They sometimes act on the recommendations of pardon boards, but the decision to pardon is theirs alone and not reversible.

A famous example of the use of pardon power happened in Illinois in 2003. During his last week in office, Gov. George Ryan pardoned 4 prisoners condemned to death and commuted the sentences of the other 167 death-row prisoners to life in prison. Ryan had grown concerned that the number of death row cases that were being overturned because new evidence, such as DNA lab work, indicated that the death penalty was being unfairly and inequitably assigned. He appointed a commission to study the application of the death sentence and became convinced that the state could not impose the death penalty with such absolute certainty that innocent people would not be put to death. The move gained Ryan international celebrity among death penalty opponents but was criticized by prosecutors and others at home.

Not all governors use their pardon powers in such a high-minded way. In Tennessee in 1979, Lamar Alexander was sworn in as governor three days early to prevent outgoing governor Ray Blanton from commuting the sentences of any more prisoners. Blanton already had granted fifty-two last-minute pardons, and the FBI already had arrested members of his staff for extorting money to sell pardons, paroles, and commutations.

The Power to Call Special Sessions. Most legislatures meet only part-time and generally have fixed session schedules. When necessary or desired, however, every governor has the power to call legislatures into special session. Nearly half the nation's governors have the ability to set the agenda of a special session. This means that legislators can deal only with those issues that the governor wants addressed.

Special sessions can be useful for governors who want to deal with an issue right away. In recent years, many governors have called special sessions when the state's revenues have fallen short so that the legislatures can help them cut spending. Sometimes, special sessions allow legislators to focus on a complex issue, such as changing medical malpractice liability laws. Such issues might get lost in the shuffle of a regular session, when most attention is devoted to passing a budget.

Although governors can call special sessions, they typically will not enjoy success unless they can work out deals on their pet bills in advance. "If a governor calls a special session without knowing what the outcome's going to be," said former Mississippi House Speaker Tim Ford, "it's chaos for everybody." Working without a deal already in place, legislators will sit around reading newspapers and eating snacks while their leaders try to hammer out an agreement with the governor. They resent having to give up time from their regular jobs to sit idly in the capitol.

And governors may be able to call legislators into special session, but they cannot necessarily make them do anything. In Iowa in 2002, Gov. Tom Vilsack called the legislature back in hopes they would increase funding for

As powerful as they are, there are some things governors may not be able to control. The weather is one. The insurance industry may be another. Florida's Republican governor Charlie Crist tackled both in his first term as he worked behind the scenes and in front of the cameras to pass legislation to stem rising insurance costs in the state.

THE PROBLEM. The disastrous 2004 and 2005 hurricane seasons left many of Florida's homeowners with more than just flattened roofs: it landed them with crushing insurance bills. The cost of insuring a home more than doubled in 2006, and many residents considered leaving the state altogether. Joining a chorus of voices advocating for a host of insurance reforms, Governor Crist urged Floridians to stay put and promised to work with lawmakers to help bring down insurance rates.

That's no small feat. Insuring property in a state that saw nearly $36 billion in storm damages in one year alone is an expensive business—and regulating that industry is the state's responsibility. Even the industry's harshest critics understand that the premiums homeowners pay on a regular basis to insure their homes must keep pace with the amounts that agencies anticipate will be paid out in future claims. That's basic math. But, critics say, insurers' profits have soared in recent years. Some agencies have adopted such misleading or unfair practices as creating differently named subsidiary companies that offer different rates than their parent agencies. Others offer restricted insurance plans to Floridians (for example, they offer auto but not homeowners insurance). Still others refused to offer policies in that state, leaving many without coverage.

In their wake stands Citizens Property Insurance, a state-run agency created in 2002 by the Florida legislature as an insurance "safety net." Under its original rules, homeowners were allowed to switch to Citizens only if they had been denied coverage by a national company or if their premiums were quoted at more than 25 percent higher than Citizens's rates. By 2006, however, Citizens was set to become the insurer for more than half of all of Florida's homeowners—about 1.3 million policyholders—making it the state's largest insurance company rather than the agency of last resort.

With so many homeowners forced to pay exorbitant rates or cut loose from national policies altogether and Citizens stepping in to fill the gap, Governor Crist and Florida's lawmakers were made to reconsider the role that Citizens should (or could) play in wholesale insurance reform.

THE PROCESS. In January 2007 Crist called a week-long special legislative session to try to hammer out a plan. Crist himself brought several aggressive measures to the table, including recommendations to lower threshold requirements for homeowners to get coverage through Citizens, to cap the agency's ability to raise rates, and to crackdown on subsidiaries. He also asked for the power to appoint the company's director. But the hallmark of his plan was to make Citizens more competitive with private insurers. After the special session, the legislature continued the reform debate during its regular session.

Early predictions of Crist's likelihood of success were not good. The insurance lobby came on strong, as did a handful of legislators from his own party, who warned the public that increasing the role of the state-sponsored Citizens was tantamount to socialism and potentially could bankrupt the state. But having once been a state legislator himself, Crist knew how to work the ropes. His main advantage was his stratospheric popularity: he had plenty of political capital, and he wasn't shy about spending it.

To promote his plan, Crist put in rare appearances before several House and Senate committees and stumped to persuade homeowners that the promised rate relief wasn't an illusion. He also traveled to Washington, D.C., to help Florida lawmakers appeal for a national disaster relief fund to help defray costs to that state's homeowners.

Crist and his staff continued to work behind the scenes, too, with the governor's staff "buttonholing" legislators. State senator J. D. Alexander reported that "there had been some political arm-twisting," adding, "You don't go against a governor with a 77-percent approval rating." [a]

Both the House and Senate took up bills that included a number of Crist's original proposals; by the end of their regular session, they'd reached resolutions.

[a] Paige St. John, "Crist Still Pushing for Property-insurance Legislation," *Tallahassee Democrat.* www.tallahassee.com/apps/pbcs.dll/article?AID=2007705030346 (accessed May 3, 2007).

[b] S. V. Date, "Sessions End More Like Recess Than Finale," Palm Beach Post.com. www.palmbeachpost.com/state/content/state/epaper/2007/05/05/m1a_XGR_session_0505.html (accessed May 7, 2007).

THE OUTCOMES. Crist got a lot of what he wanted. Legislators agreed to freeze Citizens's rates at 2006 levels through 2009. Policyholders will be allowed to choose coverage through Citizens if they receive quotes from national insurers that are more than 15 percent higher than Citizen's annual premiums. Other provisions also are in place to allow the agency to be more competitive with private insurers.

"You put the nail in the coffin this afternoon on the industry that was hurting our people. That's right and just fair and important, and you did it, and God bless you for fighting for the people of Florida," Crist told legislators. "I hear some groans from insurance lobbyists? Tough. That's right. We work for the people, not them." [b]

But Crist didn't get everything he asked for. Legislators killed an amendment giving him the power to appoint Citizens's director. Also rejected was a proposal that would have allowed the agency to write policies for auto, theft, and fire insurance that would have made it better able to amass greater financial reserves and offer lower premiums.

education and health, but the legislature adjourned after a single day without debating any bill. "We just came in and went home," said House Majority Leader Christopher Rants. Vilsack then signed a package of budget cuts he had accepted in meetings with legislators and went on to call a second special session later in the month.[20]

Sometimes, the fact that governors have to resort to the use of such powers as calling special sessions or issuing vetoes is a sign of weakness. What it may show is that they could not get what they wanted from their legislatures during the regular course of business.

Informal Powers

The powers just outlined are spelled out in state constitutions and statutes. Governors either have line-item veto authority or they do not. Much of the outcome of a governor's program, however, depends on a governor's individual ability to wield informal powers—the ability to leverage the power and prestige of the office into real influence in a way that may not be replicated by successors. Governors may be personally popular, have a special gift for working with legislators, or have some other skills that help them do their jobs well but that are not based on any authority that the state granted.

Popular Support. One thing that will always help a governor is popular support. A governor who wins with 51 percent of the vote has all of the same formal powers as a governor who wins with 73 percent, but the more popular governor is clearly going to have an edge. Legislators and other officials will accept more readily the need to go along with a popular governor's program because they believe that program is what most voters in the state want. This is especially true if the governor ran strong in their districts. In a case like this, "[l]egislators cannot fail to be impressed," according to political scientist Alan Rosenthal, "for if there is one thing they are sensitive to it is the number of votes candidates receive."[21]

It is a long time between gubernatorial elections—four years in most cases—so in order to maintain and build on their popularity, governors do all sorts of public relations work. They never fail to alert the press to all their good deeds, they appear in other forums—TV shows, groundbreakings, dedications, state fairs, church socials—where they can impress the public, and they propose legislation that they believe will be popular. The fortunes of governors rise and fall with the health of the economy of their states, but individual governors can make themselves more or less popular depending on how well they appear to address the problems of the day.

Party Support in the Legislature. Having members of their own party dominate the legislature certainly helps governors get their agendas passed. Governors can be successful if the other party controls the legislature, but

TABLE 7-2

Ranking of the Institutional Powers of Governors, 2007

State	Separately Elected Executive Branch Officials	Tenure Potential	Appointment Powers	Budgetary Powers	Veto Powers	Party Control	Total Score	Rank
Massachusetts	4	5	3.5	3	5	5	4.3	1
Alaska	5	4	3.5	3	5	4	4.1	2
Maryland	4	4	2.5	5	5	4	4.1	2
New Jersey	5	4	3.5	3	5	4	4.1	2
New York	4	5	3.5	4	5	3	4.1	2
West Virginia	2.5	4	4	5	5	4	4.1	2
Utah	4	5	3	3	5	4	4.0	7
Colorado	4	4	3.5	3	5	4	3.9	8
North Dakota	3	5	3.5	3	5	4	3.9	8
Illinois	3	5	3	3	5	4	3.8	10
Iowa	3	5	3	3	5	4	3.8	10
Nebraska	4	4	3	4	5	3	3.8	10
Pennsylvania	4	4	4	3	5	3	3.8	10
Tennessee	4.5	4	4	3	4	3	3.8	10
New Mexico	3	4	3	3	5	4	3.7	15
Arkansas	2.5	4	3	3	4	5	3.6	16
Connecticut	4	5	2.5	3	5	2	3.6	16
Florida	3	4	2.5	3	5	4	3.6	16
Maine	5	4	3.5	3	2	4	3.6	16
Michigan	4	4	3.5	3	5	2	3.6	16
Minnesota	4	5	2.5	3	5	2	3.6	16
Missouri	2.5	4	3	3	5	4	3.6	16
Ohio	4	4	3.5	3	5	2	3.6	16
Washington	1	5	3.5	3	5	4	3.6	16
Delaware	2.5	4	3.5	3	5	3	3.5	25
Montana	3	4	3	3	5	3	3.5	25
Oregon	2	4	3	3	5	4	3.5	25
Wisconsin	3	5	2	3	5	3	3.5	25
Arizona	2.5	4	4	3	5	2	3.4	29
Hawaii	5	4	2.5	3	5	1	3.4	29
Louisiana	1	4	3.5	3	5	4	3.4	29
Idaho	2	4	2	3	5	4	3.3	32
Kansas	3	4	3	3	5	2	3.3	32
Kentucky	3	4	4	3	4	2	3.3	32
California	1	4	4	3	5	2	3.2	32

(Table continues on next page)

TABLE 7-2, **continued**

State	Separately Elected Executive Branch Officials	Tenure Potential	Appointment Powers	Budgetary Powers	Veto Powers	Party Control	Total Score	Rank
Georgia	1	4	2	3	5	4	3.2	32
New Hampshire	5	2	3	3	2	4	3.2	32
Texas	2	5	1	2	5	4	3.2	32
Virginia	2.5	3	3.5	3	5	2	3.2	32
Wyoming	2	4	3.5	3	5	1	3.1	40
Nevada	2.5	4	3.5	3	2	3	3.0	41
South Carolina	1	4	2	2	5	4	3.0	41
South Dakota	1	4	2	2	5	4	3.0	41
Indiana	3	4	2.5	3	2	3	2.9	44
Mississippi	1.5	4	2	3	5	2	2.9	44
North Carolina	1	4	3.5	3	2	4	2.9	44
Alabama	1	4	3	3	4	2	2.8	47
Oklahoma	1	4	1	3	5	3	2.8	47
Rhode Island	2.5	4	3	3	2	1	2.6	49
Vermont	2.5	2	3.5	3	2	2	2.5	50

Source: Thad Beyle and Margaret Ferguson, "Governors and the Executive Branch," in *Politics in the American States,* Ninth edition, Virginia Gray and Russell L. Hanson, eds. (Washington, DC: CQ Press, Forthcoming).

Separately Elected Executive Branch Officials: 5 = only governor or governor/lieutenant governor team elected; 4.5 = governor or governor/lieutenant governor team, with one other elected official; 4 = governor/lieutenant governor team with some process officials (attorney general, secretary of state, treasurer, auditor) elected; 3 = governor/lieutenant governor team with process officials, and some major and minor policy officials elected; 2.5 = governor (no team) with six or fewer officials elected, but none are major policy officials; 2 = governor (no team) with six or fewer officials elected, including one major policy official; 1.5 = governor (no team) with six or fewer officials elected, but two are major policy officials; 1 = governor (no team) with seven or more process and several major policy officials elected. [Source: CSG, The Book of the States, 2007 (2007): forthcoming].

Tenure Potential: 5 = 4-year term, no restraint on reelection; 4.5 = 4-year term, only three terms permitted; 4 = 4-year term, only two terms permitted; 3 = 4-year term, no consecutive election permitted; 2 = 2-year term, no restraint on reelection; 1 = 2-year term, only two terms permitted. [Source: CSG, The Book of the States, 2007 (2007): forthcoming].

Appointment Powers: in six major functional areas, including corrections, K-12 education, health, highways/transportation, public utilities regulation, and welfare. The six individual office scores are totaled and then averaged and rounded to the nearest .5 for the state score. 5 = governor appoints, no other approval needed; 4 = governor appoints, a board, council or legislature approves; 3 = someone else appoints, governor approves or shares appointment; 2 = someone else appoints, governor and others approve; 1 = someone else appoints, no approval or confirmation needed. [Source: CSG, The Book of the States, 2007 (2007): forthcoming].

Budget Power: 5 = governor has full responsibility, legislature may not increase executive budget; 4 = governor has full responsibility, legislature can increase by special majority vote or subject to item veto; 3 = governor has full responsibility, legislature has unlimited power to change executive budget; 2 = governor shares responsibility, legislature has unlimited power to change executive budget; 1 = governor shares responsibility with other elected official, legislature has unlimited power to change executive budget. [Source: CSG, The Book of the States, 2007 (2007): forthcoming and NCSL, "Limits on Authority of Legislature to Change Budget" (1998).

Veto Power: 5 = governor has item veto and a special majority vote of the legislature is needed to override a veto (3/5's of legislators elected or 2/3's of legislators present); 4 = has item veto with a majority of the legislators elected needed to override; 3 = has item veto with only a majority of the legislators present needed to override; 2 = no item veto, with a special legislative majority needed to override a regular veto; 1 = no item veto, only a simple legislative majority needed to override a regular veto. [Source: CSG, The Book of the States, 2007 (2007): forthcoming].

Party Control: The governor's party - 5 = has a substantial majority (75% or more) in both houses of the legislature; 4 = has a simple majority in both houses (under 75%), or a substantial majority in one house and a simple majority in the other; 3 = split control in the legislature or a nonpartisan legislature; 2 = has a simple minority (25% or more) in both houses, or a simple minority in one and a substantial minority (under 25%) in the other; 1 = has a substantial minority in both houses. [Source: NCSL webpage].

Score: total divided by six to keep 5-point scale.

it is a lot tougher. The reasons are fairly obvious. Republican legislators want to see a Republican governor succeed, and the same holds true, obviously, for Democratic legislators serving under Democratic governors. Voters perceive politicians belonging to the same party as being part of the same team. Therefore, the political fortunes of these politicians will be tied to one another's during the next election. Members of the same party are likely to hold similar positions on such issues as taxes, levels of social service spending, and the environment. "Governors are far more likely to influence legislators from their own party," a pair of political scientists concluded in 2002.[22] Each party naturally is going to try to strengthen the power of the institution it controls and weaken the one it does not, but a party that controls both the executive and legislative branches is going to be able to push through legislation in a cooperative fashion.

Governors are more likely to grant favors to legislators of their own party or raise money for them. This, in turn, makes those legislators more likely to support their programs. Some governors curry favor with legislators because they used to be legislators themselves and still have friends in the House or Senate. One-time Tennessee governor Ned McWherter, for example, was a long-time legislator before taking the top office. He concentrated his attention on a few pet initiatives, such as a major overhaul of the state Medicaid system, and went along with whatever his pals in the legislature were thinking on most other matters.

Unified control of government is no guarantee of success for the governor, however. Just as some governors have become unpopular with members of their own party in the state legislature, there certainly have been plenty of others who were able to work well with legislatures controlled by the other party. But having to do so only made their jobs tougher. Governors need at least a large enough minority of their own party to sustain their vetoes. This is the only definite way to ensure real influence over the legislative process.

Unfortunately for governors, divided control of state governments has become common. Voters are more likely to split their tickets and vote for nominees of different parties for different offices. Divided government is likely to make the governorship more difficult, since governors must try to convince political competitors to get with their programs. Cooperation becomes consorting with the enemy.

Political scientists have built on the work David R. Mayhew has done in studying divided power between Congress and the White House to examine divided power in the states. It was once commonly thought that divided power necessarily meant that less work got done. That does not appear to be the case. What it may mean is that different types of bills become law. In other words, a Democratic governor might work with a Republican-controlled legislature to create lots of laws, but the nature of these laws might be very different from what it would have been if the governor had worked with a Democratic legislative majority. A Democratic governor working with a Democratic-controlled legislature should be able to pursue legislation more in keeping with party's principles and desires than a Democratic governor who has to compromise with a GOP-controlled legislature.

"[E]ach party attempts to strengthen the institution it commands and to weaken the institution controlled by the opposition," noted one political scientist.[23] In other words, if Republicans hold the governorship, they will try to make that office more powerful at the expense of a Democratic legislature and vice versa. But because power is so often shared these days under divided government, the two parties cannot just attack each other's programs. If they share power, they also share responsibility in the eyes of the voters, and so they have to work together to forge compromises on central issues such as the budget.

Conflict is more likely if the party in opposition to the governor's holds both legislative chambers, which should not be all that surprising. If each party controls one chamber, the governor is much more likely to claim victory.[24] It is all a matter of leverage and pressing the advantages your party has.

Ability to Communicate. We have already touched upon the advantage governors have over legislators in regard to media exposure. There is no law that says newspapers and TV stations have to pay more attention to pronouncements from the governor—but that is what happens anyway. Pretty much anything legislators say and do takes a back seat. The governor is a single, well-known individual who is important to every voter in the state. A legislator, by contrast, even a powerful one, is just an individual legislator among 120 or 150 legislators and represents a district that is only a fraction of the state.

Smart governors are aware of the power of the mass media in helping to spread their messages. Contemporary governors have large public relations staffs that deal exclusively with the media and make sure that their governors' faces appear on television regularly. A governor's fame adds to the grandeur of the office, making the officeholder appear more potent to legislators, to aides, and to other people who deal with the governor. Power builds on power, in the sense that a governor who becomes famous for pushing through a landmark change in law becomes a more formidable presence in the state in the next policy battle.

Governors have to play both an "inside" game and an "outside" game. They have to appeal both to capital insiders and to the public at large. A governor who makes every move based on the ability to turn it into a press release or who appeals to the public by bashing the "corruption" in the capital may score points with the media and the public but soon will have few friends in the legislature. In Illinois, Rod Blagojevich was elected governor by railing against the corruption of state government and did not change his theme song once he took office. He refused even to establish a permanent residence in the state capital of Springfield, commuting from his home in Chicago. "We're going to keep fighting to reform and change the system and give the people a government that stops spending their money like a bunch of drunken sailors," he said toward the end of his first year in office. Needless to say, the legislators whom Blagojevich had likened to drunken sailors were not eager to cooperate with him any more than they had to—even though his own party had a majority in both chambers.

Blagojevich is not alone in his criticisms. Many governors have bashed the legislature. What they have found is that although it made them popular with the public it did not help them get their agendas passed. That was the lesson Arnold Schwarzenegger learned. As discussed in the opening vignette, when he was elected governor of California in 2003, Schwarzenegger continually threatened to take his agenda directly to the people through ballot initiatives and referenda if the legislature refused to go along for his ride. Yet even the Man Who Was the Terminator could not convince voters about items he could not get passed in the legislature.

Merging Formal and Informal Powers

Roy Barnes, who served one term as governor of Georgia from 1999 until 2003, said back during his days in the state legislature, "When you are called down to the governor's office, it is a very impressive office, you're talking to the governor, and you know that he controls things that could be good or ill for your district. He controls grants, he controls roads, and other things." [25] In other words, the formal powers of the governor—the ability to control projects—merge with the informal powers—the mystique of the office—to influence legislators and other supplicants.

When Carroll Campbell became governor of South Carolina in 1987, that state's governor's office was among the weakest in the nation. The state's government consisted of seventy-nine separate administrative agencies, and the governor had sole appointment power in only ten of them. Campbell spent three years arguing that the modern executive needs more power to run a state well. He devoted nearly all of his attention to the office, using all of his informal powers—including the ability to persuade and the ability to keep an issue in front of voters and legislators through use of the media—to increase his formal powers. In the end, he won. In 1993, the legislature restructured the government. They consolidated the administration into seventeen departments and gave the governor the power to appoint the directors of twelve of them.

The importance of being dealt such a fine political hand of cards cannot be stressed enough. Governors with constitutional authority to set the budget, to appoint their own people to spend that budget and implement their plans, and to line-item veto to keep legislators intimidated are going

TABLE 7-3

Ranking of the Personal Power of Governors, 2007

State	Governor	Electoral Mandate	Position on Ambition Ladder	Personal Future	Job Performance Rating in Public Opinion Polls	Personal Powers Index Score	Rank
Arkansas	Mike Beebe	5	5	5	na	5.0	1
Colorado	Bill Ritter	5	5	5	na	5.0	1
Connecticut	M. Jodi Rell	5	5	5	5	5.0	1
Nebraska	Dave Heineman	5	5	5	5	5.0	1
Vermont	Jim Douglas	5	5	5	5	5.0	1
Ohio	Ted Strickland	5	5	5	4	4.8	6
Arizona	Janet Napolitano	5	5	3	5	4.5	7
Indiana	Mitch Daniels	5	5	5	3	4.5	7
Kansas	Kathleen Sebelius	5	5	3	5	4.5	7
Alaska	Sarah Palin	4	3	5	5	4.3	10
California	Arnold Schwarzenegger	5	5	3	4	4.3	10
Iowa	Chet Culver	4	5	5	3	4.3	10
Mississippi	Haley Barbour	4	5	4	4	4.3	10
Montana	Brian Schweitzer	3	5	4	5	4.3	10
New York	Eliot Spitzer	5	3	5	4	4.3	10
West Virginia	Joe Manchin III	5	3	4	5	4.3	10
Wisconsin	Jim Doyle	4	5	5	3	4.3	10
Alabama	Bob Riley	5	3	3	5	4.0	18
Idaho	C.L. "Butch" Otter	4	3	5	na	4.0	18
Kentucky	Ernie Fletcher	4	5	4	3	4.0	18
Michigan	Jennifer M. Granholm	5	5	3	3	4.0	18
New Hampshire	John Lynch	5	1	5	5	4.0	18
New Mexico	Bill Richardson	5	3	3	5	4.0	18
Oklahoma	Brad Henry	5	3	3	5	4.0	18
Oregon	Ted Kulongoski	4	5	3	4	4.0	18
South Dakota	Mike Rounds	5	3	3	5	4.0	18
Florida	Charlie Crist	4	2	5	5	4.0	18
Delaware	Ruth Ann Minner	5	5	1	4	3.8	28
Georgia	Sonny Perdue	5	3	3	4	3.8	28
Hawaii	Linda Lingle	5	2	3	5	3.8	28

TABLE 7-3, continued

State	Governor	Electoral Mandate	Position on Ambition Ladder	Personal Future	Job Performance Rating in Public Opinion Polls	Personal Powers Index Score	Rank
Illinois	Rod Blagojevich	4	3	5	3	3.8	28
Maryland	Martin O'Malley	4	2	5	4	3.8	28
New Jersey	Jon Corzine	4	2	5	4	3.8	28
Tennessee	Phil Bredesen	5	2	3	5	3.8	28
Texas	Rick Perry	2	5	5	3	3.8	28
Utah	Jon Huntsman	5	1	4	5	3.8	28
Massachusetts	Deval Patrick	5	1	5	3	3.5	37
Minnesota	Tim Pawlenty	2	3	5	4	3.5	37
Missouri	Matt Blunt	2	5	4	3	3.5	37
North Dakota	John Hoeven	4	1	4	5	3.5	37
Pennsylvania	Edward Rendell	5	2	3	4	3.5	37
South Carolina	Mark Sanford	4	3	3	4	3.5	37
Wyoming	Dave Freudenthal	5	1	3	5	3.5	37
North Carolina	Michael Easley	3	5	1	4	3.3	44
Louisiana	Kathleen Blanco	3	3	4	2	3.0	45
Virginia	Tim Kaine	3	1	3	5	3.0	45
Washington	Chris Gregoire	2	2	4	4	3.0	45
Maine	John Baldacci	2	3	3	3	2.8	48
Nevada	Jim Gibbons	3	1	5	1	2.5	49
Rhode Island	Don Carcieri	2	1	3	4	2.5	49

Source: Thad Beyle and Margaret Ferguson, "Governors and the Executive Branch," in *Politics in the American States*, Ninth edition, Virginia Gray and Russell L. Hanson, eds. (Washington, DC: CQ Press, Forthcoming).

Notes:

Governor's electoral mandate: 5 = landslide win of 11 or more points; 4 = comfortable majority of 6 to 10 points; 3 = narrow majority of 3 to 5 points; 2 = tight win of 0 to 2 points or a plurality win of under 50%; 1 = succeeded to office. [Source: Author's data - www.unc.edu./~beyle]

Governor's position on the state's political ambition ladder: 5 = steady progression; 4 =former governors; 3 = legislative leaders or members of Congress; 2 = substate position to governor; 1 = governorship is first elective office. [Source: Individual governors' websites in each state and author's data].

The personal future of the governor: 5 = early in term, can run again; 4 = late in term, can run again; 3 = early in term, term limited; 2 = succeeded to office, can run for election; 1 = late in final term. [Source: CSG, The Book of the States, 2007 (2007): forthcoming and author's data.]

Gubernatorial job performance rating in public opinion polls: 5 = over 60% positive job approval rating; 4 = 50 to 59% positive job approval rating; 3 = 40 to 49% positive job approval rating; 2 = 30 to 39% positive job approval rating; 1 = less than 30% positive job approval rating; na = no polling data available. [Source: Author's data]

Governor's personal powers' index score: the sum of the scores for EM, AL, PF, GP divided by 4 and rounded to the nearest .#, except for those states without a governor's job performance rating where the sum is divided by 3 and rounded to the nearest .#.

to have a lot easier time than their neighbors who lack some or all of those tools. One of those neighbors may be a more skilled politician and ultimately may have more success. People today expect the governor to be a powerful figure in the state and, in most cases, the governors have the tools to be just that. If only because of the power and prestige of the office and the ability to command media attention, a governor holds enormous influence in determining what issues are brought to the forefront and how they are handled.

Becoming Governor and Staying Governor

This chapter has described governors as the most powerful and important political actors in their states. It should come as little surprise then, given the history of politics in this country, that middle-aged white males have dominated the job. Women are being elected governor with greater frequency, but there are still plenty of states that have yet to elect a woman for the top job. In 2007, nine women served as governor, the highest number to ever serve at one time. In 1873, P. B. S. Pinchback, the black lieutenant governor of Louisiana, was elevated to the post of acting governor for forty-three days, but only two African Americans have ever been elected as governor of any state.[26] Douglas Wilder of Virginia held the job during the first half of the 1990s; Deval Patrick was elected to the office in Massachusetts in 2006. There have been a handful of Hispanic and Asian governors, including Bill Richardson of New Mexico and Gary Locke of Washington State, respectively.

> Governors with constitutional authority to set the budget, to appoint their own people to spend that budget and implement their plans, and to line-item veto to keep legislators intimidated are going to have a lot easier time than their neighbors who lack some or all of those tools.

Many nonpoliticians have been elected governor, including Arnold Schwarzenegger, former wrestler Jesse Ventura of Minnesota, and business executives Mark Warner of Virginia and John Lynch of New Hampshire. Most governors, however, have had a good deal of previous government experience. They have served in the U.S. Congress, the state legislature, or other statewide positions such as lieutenant governor and attorney general or even state supreme court justice. Only a handful of independent or third party candidates have been elected governor in recent years, including Ventura in 1998 and Angus King of Maine in 1994 and 1998.

One qualification for modern governors is quite clear—they must have the ability to raise money. Gubernatorial campaigns have become multimillion dollar affairs, particularly in heavily populated states in which television ads are expensive to run because the media markets are competitive and costly. The total campaign costs for the thirty-six governors races in 2002 was $840 million—a jump of 63 percent over the campaigns conducted only four years earlier. Those numbers were a bit skewed by two wealthy candidates in Texas and New York who spent a combined $140 million on their own races. But overall gubernatorial campaign spending was up to about $800 million in 2006, even without such free-spending, self-funding contenders.

Factors Driving Gubernatorial Elections

Like the Winter Olympics, gubernatorial elections in most states have been moved to the second year of the presidential term in what are called "off-year" elections. Thirty-four states now hold their gubernatorial elections in the off-year. Another five states—Virginia, New Jersey, Kentucky, Mississippi, and Louisiana—hold their elections in odd-numbered years. Nine states—Delaware, Indiana, Missouri, Montana, New Hampshire, North Carolina, North Dakota, Utah, and Vermont—hold their elections at the same time as the presidential contest. In addition, New Hampshire and Vermont, the only states that have clung to the old tradition of two-year terms, hold elections for governor every even-numbered year.

The majority of governors are elected in an even-numbered off-year because states want to insulate the contests from getting mixed up in national issues. They want voters to concentrate on matters of importance just to the state instead of diverting their attention to federal issues brought up in presidential campaigns. This was the desire and the intent. But the plan has not been a 100 percent success. Elections for governors are often the biggest thing on the ballot, so voters use the races as a way of expressing their opinions about who is *not* on the ballot. In 1994, when antipathy was running high against Democratic president Bill Clinton, Republicans not only took control of both houses of Congress but also won a majority of the governorships for the first time in more than a decade. In 2002 and 2003, when Republican president George W. Bush was generally popular, Republicans did better than had been expected in gubernatorial contests. But as Bush's popularity sank, so did the ranks of Republican governors. Democrats in 2006 regained the majority of governorships for the first time since 1994, holding twenty-eight states, compared with the GOP's twenty-two.

Overall, however, governors races are still less prone to follow national trends than, say, elections for the U.S. Senate. The reason? Voters understand that the governor's position is important in and of itself. They consider state-level issues carefully when choosing a governor. The dominant concern in most gubernatorial contests is the state economy. Even the most powerful politicians have only limited control over the economy at best, but voters tend to reward or punish the incumbent party based on the econom-

TABLE 7-4

Who's Who among U.S. Governors, 2007

State	Governor	Party	Education (highest degree obtained)	First Elected In...	Previous Political Life
Alabama	Bob Riley	Republican	University of Alabama	2002	Member, U.S. House of Representatives
Alaska	Sarah Palin	Republican	University of Idaho	2006	Councilmember for Wasilla City Council
Arizona	Janet Napolitano	Democrat	University of Virginia (JD)	2002	Elected AZ Attorney General
Arkansas	Mike Beebe	Democrat	University of Arkansas (JD)	2006	Arkansas state senator
California	Arnold Schwarzenegger	Republican	University of Wisconsin	2003	Started at the top as governor; previously major movie star
Colorado	Bill Ritter	Democrat	University of Colorado (JD)	2006	Elected District Attorney for Denver
Connecticut	M. Jodi Rell	Republican	Attended Old Dominion University and Western Connecticut State University	2006	Member, CT House of Representatives
Delaware	Ruth Ann Minner	Democrat	GED	2000	Worked to top state position from first political job stuffing envelopes
Florida	Charlie Crist	Republican	Cumberland School of Law (JD)	2006	State director for U.S. Senator Connie Mack
Georgia	Sonny Perdue	Republican	University of Georgia (DVM)	2002	Houston Country Planning and Zoning Board
Hawaii	Linda Lingle	Republican	California State University, Northridge	2002	Maui County Councilmember
Idaho	C.L. "Butch" Otter	Republican	College of Idaho	2006	Member, ID House of Representatives
Illinois	Rod Blagojevich	Democrat	Pepperdine (JD)	2002	Member, IL House of Representatives
Indiana	Mitch Daniels	Republican	Georgetown (JD)	2004	Chief of staff, Richard Lugar
Iowa	Chet Culver	Democrat	Virginia Tech	2006	Elected Secretary of State
Kansas	Kathleen Sebelius	Democrat	University of Kansas	2002	Elected KS Insurance Commissioner
Kentucky	Ernie Fletcher	Republican	University of Kentucky	2003	Member, KY House of Representatives
Louisiana	Kathleen Blanco	Democrat	University of Louisiana	2003	Member, LA House of Representatives
Maine	John Baldacci	Democrat	University of Maine, Orono	2002	Member, Bangor City Council
Maryland	Martin O'Malley	Democrat	University of Maryland (JD)	2006	State field director for Barbara Mikulski's 1986 campaign
Massachusetts	Deval Patrick	Democrat	Harvard University (JD)	2006	Appointed Assistant Attorney General for Civil Rights by Bill Clinton
Michigan	Jennifer M. Granholm	Democrat	Harvard University (JD)	2002	Elected Michigan's Attorney General
Minnesota	Tim Pawlenty	Republican	University of Minnesota (JD)	2002	Eagan City Council Member

TABLE 7-4, continued

State	Governor	Party	Education (highest degree obtained)	First Elected In...	Previous Political Life
Mississippi	Haley Barbour	Republican	University of Mississippi (JD)	2003	Director, White House Office of Political Affairs
Missouri	Matt Blunt	Republican	United States Naval Academy	2004	Member, MO General Assembly
Montana	Brian Schweitzer	Democrat	Montana State University (MS)	2004	Appointed to the USDA Farm Service Agency Committeews
Nebraska	Dave Heineman	Republican	United States Military Academy	2005	Office Manager, Fremont Area, Congressman Doug Bereuter
Nevada	Jim Gibbons	Republican	Southwestern University (JD)	2006	Member, NV state legislature
New Hampshire	John Lynch	Democrat	Georgetown University (JD) Harvard University (MBA)	2004	Appointed to NH's University System Board of Trustees, then chair
New Jersey	Jon Corzine	Democrat	University of Chicago (MBA)	2005	U.S. Senator
New Mexico	Bill Richardson	Democrat	Tufts University	2002	Member, U.S. House of Representatives
New York	Eliot Spitzer	Democrat	Harvard University (JD)	2006	State Attorney General
North Carolina	Michael Easley	Republican	North Carolina Central University (JD)	2000	District Attorney
North Dakota	John Hoeven	Republican	Northwestern University (MBA)	2000	Started at the top as governor; previously president and CEO of the Bank of North Dakota
Ohio	Ted Strickland	Democrat	University of Kentucky (PhD)	2006	Member, U.S. Congress
Oklahoma	Brad Henry	Democrat	University of Oklahoma (JD)	2002	State senator
Oregon	Ted Kulongoski	Democrat	University of Missouri (JD)	2002	Member, OR House of Representatives
Pennsylvania	Edward Rendell	Democrat	Villanova University (JD)	2002	Elected District Attorney, Philadelphia
Rhode Island	Don Carcieri	Republican	Brown University	2002	Started at the top as governor; previously CEO Cookson America
South Carolina	Mark Sanford	Republican	University of Virginia (MBA)	2002	Member, U.S. Congress
South Dakota	Mike Rounds	Republican	South Dakota State University	2002	State senator
Tennessee	Phil Bredesen	Democrat	Harvard University	2002	Mayor, Nashville TN
Texas	Rick Perry	Republican	Texas A&M University	2000	Member, TX House of Representatives
Utah	Jon Huntsman	Republican	University of Pennsylvania	2004	White House staff assistant to Ronald Reagan
Vermont	Jim Douglas	Republican	Middlebury College	2002	Member, VT House of Representatives
Virginia	Tim Kaine	Democrat	Harvard University (JD)	2005	Richmond City Councilmember
Washington	Chris Gregoire	Democrat	Gonzaga University (JD)	2004	Elected State Attorney General
West Virginia	Joe Manchin III	Democrat	West Virginia University	2004	Member, state legislature
Wisconsin	Jim Doyle	Democrat	Harvard University (JD)	2002	District Attorney, Dane County
Wyoming	Dave Freudenthal	Democrat	University of Wyoming (JD)	2002	Appointed U.S. attorney, WY

Source: National Governors Association, "Governors of the United States, Commonwealths and Territories, 2007." www.nga.org/Files/pdf/BIOBOOK.pdf (accessed April 30, 2007).

ic performance. If a state is faring poorly or doing considerably worse than its neighbors, the incumbent party is likely to struggle.

Economic matters certainly play a role in elections if the state budget is in trouble. Voters consider budget crises a sign of bad management and will take their anger out on the governor in many instances. In 2002, most state budgets were suffering shortfalls as revenues dipped due to a recession. Only a dozen governors were reelected that year, whereas a record two dozen freshman governors took office. Of those new governors, fully nineteen succeeded a governor of another party or an independent. In other words, voters in many states were ready for a change and blamed the incumbent party for the state's money problems. The dynamics were a little different in 2006. Although Democrats gained a net of six governorships that year, most of their wins came in states where Republican governors were retiring or forced out by term limits. They defeated only one incumbent that year, Bob Ehrlich of Maryland.

For most of the twentieth century, Democrats dominated gubernatorial contests, but they lost their edge to Republicans starting in 1994. Yet, in general, momentum over the last several years has swung back and forth between the parties. In 2002, the two parties showed that they are each competitive in nearly every state. Republicans were elected governor for the first time in decades in states such as Georgia, Hawaii, and Maryland. Democrats, on the other hand, were elected in places where their party had struggled for years to win a statewide office, including Kansas, Oklahoma, and Wyoming. The Democrats' 28–22 margin following the 2006 elections was the exact opposite of where things had stood before election day, when it had been the GOP controlling twenty-eight states.

Since gubernatorial elections attract a great deal of media attention, voters are more likely to vote for the person rather than the party. Indeed, voters more often use party as a guide in lower-profile contests such as state legislative races. Voters are better informed about individual gubernatorial candidates. One reason is greater news coverage of the races. Another important factor is the amount of money that candidates for governor spend to publicize themselves. Candidates create extensive organizations that promote their campaigns and use all the modern techniques of political consultants, polling, and media buys. Voters are far more likely, even in less-populous states, to get to know the candidates through TV ads and brochures than through speeches or other personal appearances. In 2002, New York governor George Pataki spent $44 million to win a second term. Even so, he still was outspent by a third party candidate who spent more than $75 million of his own money. The Democratic candidate in Texas, Tony Sanchez, spent $76.3 million in his losing effort. California governor Gray Davis spent $64 million winning reelection that year.[27] In the 2006 gubernatorial election in Michigan, Dick DeVos, heir to the Amway fortune, spent $35 million of his own money. That helped to make it the most expensive governor's race in Michigan history, but didn't help DeVos any; he lost by a fourteen-point margin, each of his votes having cost him, on average, $22 apiece.

Keeping and Leaving Office

For all of the potential upsets, the office of governor is a pretty stable one these days. States used to change governors just about every chance they got, but that is no longer the case. According to political scientist Thad Beyle, states changed governors by an average of more than two times apiece during the 1950s. By the 1980s, though, turnover occurred on average just over once a decade. During the 1990s, the rate climbed back up a bit, so that the average state changed governors 1.4 times.

It is not unusual to see governors get reelected by vote margins that top 70 percent. Not only are they in charge of setting policy, but they also actually get things done. They educate children, build roads, respond with help when miners get trapped. Translation? They generally are viewed more favorably than legislators. From a constituent's standpoint, what do legislators do, after all, except vote, and their votes tend to be highly partisan. Governors, on the other hand, have to compromise because of the number of people they must deal with. Of course, there are governors who are polarizing figures, but in the main they are less contentious figures than legislators or members of Congress.

Governors are rarely booted out of office prematurely. In June 2004, Connecticut governor John Rowland resigned after being investigated by the legislature for accepting gifts from a contractor with business before the state. Faced with possible **impeachment** and a federal criminal investigation, Rowland, one of the nation's longest serving governors at the time, chose to step down. In 2003, Gray Davis was the first governor forced to leave office by a **recall election** since Lynn Frazier of North Dakota was booted more than eighty years earlier on charges of corruption. Voters felt that Davis had dug California into such a deep hole financially that the state would take years to recover. His liberal views on such issues as gay marriage also had stirred up controversy. Arnold Schwarzenegger won the special election held on the same day as Davis's recall.

Arizona governor Evan Mecham was impeached and convicted in 1987 for impeding an investigation and lending state money to a car dealership that he owned. The previous conviction dated back to 1929, when Henry Johnston of Oklahoma was removed for general incompetency by a legislature with possible political motives. A few governors, including Fife Symington of Arizona (1997), Jim Guy Tucker of Arkansas (1996), and Guy Hunt of Alabama (1993), have resigned following criminal convictions. In early 2007, Jim Gibbons of Nevada was under federal investigation for allegedly having taken illegal gifts and payments from a friend who had won secret government contracts while Gibbons was a member of Congress.

IMPEACHMENT

A process by which the legislature can remove executive branch officials, such as the governor, or judges from offices for corruption or other reasons.

RECALL ELECTION

A special election allowing voters to remove an elected official from office before the end of his or her term.

TABLE 7-5

Recall Rules

State	Grounds for Recall	Specific Signature Requirement	Petition Circulation Time	Election for Successor
Alaska	Yes	25%	Not specified	Successor appointed
Arizona	No	25%	120 days	Simultaneous (5)
California	No	12%	160 days	Simultaneous (6)
Colorado	No	25%	60 days	Simultaneous (6)
Georgia	Yes	15% (1)	90 days	Separate special
Idaho	No	20% (1)	60 days	Successor appointed
Kansas	Yes	40%	90 days	Successor appointed
Louisiana	No	33.3% (1)	180 days	Separate special
Michigan	No	25%	90 days	Separate special
Minnesota	Yes	25%	90 days	Separate special
Montana	Yes	10% (1)	3 months	Separate special
Nevada	No	25%	60 days	Simultaneous (5)
New Jersey	No	25% (2)	320 days (4)	Separate special
North Dakota	No	25%	Not specified	Simultaneous (5)
Oregon	No	15% (3)	90 days	Separate special
Rhode Island	Yes	15%	90 days	Separate special
Washington	Yes	25%	270 days	Successor appointed
Wisconsin	No	25%	60 days	Simultaneous (5)

Source: Adapted from the National Conference of State Legislatures and Alan Greenblatt's, "Recall Rules," in "Total Recall," *Governing* magazine, September 2003, 26.

Note: Signature requirement is % of votes cast in last election for official being recalled. Exceptions: (1) % of eligible voters at time of last election; (2) % of registered voters in electoral district of official sought to be recalled; (3) % of total votes cast in officer's district for all candidates for governor in last election; (4) applies to governor or U.S. senator; all others 160 days; (5) recall ballot consists of a list of candidates for the office held by the person against whom the recall petition was filed. The name of the officer against whom the recall was filed may appear on the list; and (6) recall ballot consists of two parts: The first asks whether the officer against whom the recall petition was filed should be recalled. The second part lists candidates who have qualified for the election. The name of the officer against whom the recall was filed may not appear on this list.

A more common threat to gubernatorial staying power is term limits. Governors in thirty-six states are limited to two terms or two consecutive terms in office. The governor of Utah can spend no more than three terms in office. The only two states that have two-year terms instead of four-year terms—Vermont and New Hampshire—place no limits on the number of terms a governor may serve. Howard Dean served five full terms as governor of Vermont before running for president in 2004.

So what do governors do once they leave office? Several of them, like Dean, run for higher offices like the presidency or Senate. Four out of the last five presidents, in fact, were governors in their last jobs before winning the White House (see box on page 264). Not surprisingly, once in office, these former governors appoint other governors to positions in their administrations. They realize that these individuals know and understand what it means to lead and how to delegate and get things done. Former Texas governor George W. Bush appointed five former governors to cabinet positions and an ambassadorship after moving into the Oval Office in 2001. Governors also regularly run for the U.S. Senate. Eight senators and one representative serving in 2007 previously had been governors.

Entering the Senate or serving as a cabinet official generally is considered a step up the professional ladder from being a governor. Many politicians, however, find that being governor—able to make and implement decisions, with a large staff and all the machinery of state government at their disposal—is the best job they'll ever have. Dirk Kempthorne, who gave up a Senate seat to run for governor of Idaho in 1998, said that many of his colleagues regretted having to give up the governorship to come to Washington and be just one more legislative voice among many. "They all said that being governor is the best job in the world," Kempthorne said upon taking office. "I'm ready to find out." [28] Kempthorne left the governorship just before his term limit ran out, taking the job of running the federal Environmental Protection Agency in 2006.

Other Executive Offices

Only the president is elected to the executive branch of the federal government. The vice president is the president's running mate and is elected as part of a package deal. The heads of all the cabinet departments—Defense, Transportation, Energy, Agriculture, and so on—are appointed by the president, subject to Senate approval. Voters do not get to say who gets in and who stays out.

Things work differently at the state level. The governor is the only statewide official elected in every state. Most states, however, also have several other statewide officials elected in their own right. This is a holdover from earlier times when the governor was not invested with much power and authority was distributed among a number of officeholders. Texas still has two dozen officials elected statewide, whereas New Jersey only elects the governor. (That will change in 2009, when Garden State voters will elect a lieutenant governor for the first time.) Most states have a handful of officials elected statewide, and we'll outline the responsibilities of a few of them here.

Lieutenant Governor

The office of lieutenant governor traditionally has been seen as something of a joke. Lieutenant governors, it's been said, have nothing to do but wait

A Difference that Makes a Difference: From State House to White House: Translating a Governorship into a Presidency

How big of an advantage is it to run for the presidency as a sitting governor as opposed to some other position? About as big as they come. For more than a quarter of a century, every occupant of the White House except one has come to the presidency fresh from the governor's seat.

Four out of the last five presidents were previously governors—Jimmy Carter, Ronald Reagan, Bill Clinton, and George W. Bush. The one exception was Bush's father, George H. W. Bush, who came to the Oval Office after serving as Reagan's vice president. Very early in the 2004 presidential campaign season, it looked as though two former governors—Bush of Texas and Howard Dean of Vermont—were destined to go head to head.

That ended up not happening, as Dean's campaign imploded. Still, despite the fact that the large presidential fields in 2008 most likely will be dominated by senators, many governors and ex-governors believed that their stature as chief executives at the state level provided the best qualifications for the job of president—or at least floated such an idea. Among their number were Mitt Romney of Massachusetts, Bill Richardson of New Mexico, Mike Huckabee of Arkansas, and Mark Warner of Virginia.

No wonder so many were eager. Compare the record of governors to holders of other offices: no sitting U.S. senator has been elected president since 1960. No member of the U.S. House has been elected since James Garfield, all the way back in 1880.

What makes governors such attractive candidates for the nation's most powerful office? And what makes legislators so *unattractive*?

For one thing, governors are the only other politicians who have run governments that are anywhere near as complicated as the federal government. Given the complex nature of some state governments, it may even be a toss-up sometimes as to which is the more difficult—ruling one state or ruling all fifty. True, governors do not formulate foreign policy, but they do have to become experts in running departments that cover everything from taxes and education to public health and public safety. Governors have to run things. Members of Congress just vote. "Because the presidency is no place to begin to develop executive talents, the executive careerist clearly is preferable to the legislator," writes political scientist Larry J. Sabato.[a]

Furthermore, legislators have to vote "yes" or "no" on thousands of issues, so they leave a long paper trail. This trail is a clear record bound to contain more controversial elements than any governor's list of bridges built and budgets balanced. Legislators' records often are distorted in smear campaigns that

for their governors to resign or die so that they can accrue some real power. That situation has changed just over the last few years. Some states, such as Georgia and Virginia, responded to budget shortfalls of recent years by slashing the budgets and limiting the powers of their lieutenant governors' offices. More states, however, have expanded the purview of the office, recognizing that security demands created by the terrorist attacks of 2001 mean that there is plenty of work to go around and the skills of the second-in-command should be utilized more fully.

In Nebraska, for example, Gov. Mike Johanns appointed Lieutenant Governor Dave Heineman to head all of the state's homeland security

make use of attack ads and mudslinging. Their vote for a $300 billion bill becomes defined by one tiny provision it contained.

Congress is a major part of "official" Washington, and legislators hardly can say they have no connection with what occurs there. Conversely, governors running for the White House can always claim they are Washington "outsiders" who are going to sweep in and clean up the town. Former governor-turned-president Clinton reportedly advised Sen. Joseph Biden, D-Del., that senators had to overcome big handicaps to run for president. Not only did they have their records to explain, but they also had forgotten how to speak the language of the average person. "When you get to Washington, the only people you talk to are the elites: elites in the press, elites among the lobbyists, elites that you hire on your own staff," Clinton told Biden. "You're not regularly talking to ordinary, everyday people."[b] Biden ultimately didn't listen to Clinton, launching his second bid for the presidency in 2008. But then, neither did Clinton's wife—Sen. Hillary Rodham Clinton of New York.

Senator Clinton did understand what her husband was saying, though, beginning her presidential campaign with a "listening tour." Her initial campaign slogan, "Let the Conversation Begin," was roundly ridiculed on *The Daily Show* and by bloggers.[c]

Governors are able to advertise the fact that they have to talk to "real people" every day. By contrast, the out-of-touch image of Congress and Washington in the public mind hampers members of Congress seeking national office. "It could probably be shown by facts and figures that there is no distinctly native American criminal class except Congress," Mark Twain wrote. Governors running for national office invariably present themselves as fresh alternatives to the tired habits of Washington, promising to change the culture and tone of the nation's capital.

That they fail to do so is almost a given. That opens up the field for the next fresh face from the state of California or Arkansas or Texas. Do not forget that all of the recent governors turned presidents came from the South or West—reflecting the growing populations and political power of these regions.

[a] Larry J. Sabato, *Goodbye to Good-Time Charlie,* 2nd ed. (Washington, D.C.: CQ Press, 1983), 33.
[b] E. J. Dionne Jr., "Govs 4, Senators 0. Tough Odds," *Washington Post,* January 4, 2004, E4.
[c] Linda Feldmann, "Hillary Clinton Targets Women's Vote," *Christian Science Monitor,* February 1, 2007, 1.

efforts immediately after the September 11 attacks. Minnesota's lieutenant governor Carol Molnau was given charge of the state's Department of Transportation after her election in 2002 and saved the state the $108,000-a-year expense of hiring a separate transportation secretary. Similarly, right after the 2003 election, Kentucky's new lieutenant governor, Stephen Pence, was named secretary of the Department of Justice, which put him in charge of public safety, corrections and law enforcement, the state police, and vehicle enforcement. "It's rare that the lieutenant governor doesn't have some specific duties," says Julia Hurst, director of the National Lieutenant Governors Association.[29]

In the cases cited here, power was granted to the lieutenant governor because of the desire of the governor. The next person to hold the office may have very different responsibilities or nothing to do at all. In many states, though, the lieutenant governor's responsibilities are laid out by law. In Indiana, for example, the lieutenant governor's portfolio includes the departments of commerce and agriculture. In half the states, the lieutenant governor presides over the state Senate and has varying degrees of authority in each of these states. In Texas and Mississippi, lieutenant governors play much more than a ceremonial role. Not only do they preside over the Senate, but they also set the agenda and appoint senators to committees. In both states, the lieutenant governor often is referred to as the most powerful figure in the state, with authority in both the executive and legislative branches.

Twenty-four states elect their governors and lieutenant governors as part of the same ticket. In eighteen other states, the two are elected separately. The other eight states—Arizona, Maine, New Hampshire, New Jersey, Oregon, Tennessee, and Wyoming—don't elect lieutenant governors, although in Tennessee the Speaker of the Senate is given the title. (As noted earlier, New Jersey soon will begin electing lieutenant governors, a change voters approved in 2005 after a series of recent gubernatorial vacancies.) Electing the governor and lieutenant governor separately can be a cause of mischief, especially if the people elected are not from the same party. Lieutenant governors often assume the powers of the governors when their bosses are out of the state. During the 1970s, Republican Mike Curb of California had a lot of fun appointing judges and issuing **executive orders** while Democratic governor Jerry Brown was busy out of the state doing, among other things, his own presidential campaigning.

Attorney General

Perhaps the statewide office that has undergone the greatest transformation in recent years is that of attorney general. Always referred to as the top law enforcement officer in the state, the duties of the attorney general sometimes have been quite minimal, with most criminal prosecutions being taken care of at the county level. But attorneys general have become major political players, finding new power by banding together in multi-state consumer protection cases against Microsoft, financial firms, toymakers, drug companies, and shoemakers Reebok and Keds, among many other examples.

The granddaddy of all such cases were the lawsuits filed against the tobacco companies during the mid-1990s. The attorneys general argued that the cigarette makers had engaged in fraud and caused a great deal of sickness and health conditions that the states ended up paying to treat through Medicaid and other programs. An initial agreement with the industry was not ratified by Congress. Instead, in 1998 the attorneys gen-

EXECUTIVE ORDERS

Rules or regulations with the force of law that governors can create directly under the statutory authority given them.

eral settled their lawsuits with the companies on their own. The tobacco companies agreed to pay the states an estimated $246 billion over twenty-five years. More recently, as attorney general of New York, Eliot Spitzer got as much attention as any other state official and has been featured prominently in *Time* and *Newsweek*, among other national media outlets, for pursuing cases against brokerage firms and mutual funds. Spitzer went on to be elected governor in 2006.

Not surprisingly, there has been a backlash against these newly powerful officials. In part, this was based on the fact that for Spitzer and many other attorneys general the job has been a successful launching pad toward the governorship. But the fight over control of the office has largely been ideological. One of the great philosophical divides in U.S. politics lies between those with opposing views of how business should be regulated. There are those who believe that businesses have a right to conduct their affairs with a minimum of interference from state governments, which only can hinder their productivity and profits. Others believe just as strongly that conducting business in a state is a privilege that confers with it a number of responsibilities that the state has the duty to enforce. The majority of state attorneys general over the past few years have acted as if they were members of the "privilege" camp, and that has fueled the rise of groups designed to combat what the business sector sees as excessive regulatory activism.

New York governor Eliot Spitzer takes the oath of office in January 2007. Prior to winning the governor's race, Spitzer was a crusading state attorney general who made headlines prosecuting high-profile cases dealing with everything from securities fraud to pollution. His record as attorney general served as the springboard for his successful gubernatorial bid.

Attorneys general have traditionally been Democrats, their campaigns funded by trial lawyers. In recent years, the U.S. Chamber of Commerce and many business groups have spent millions trying to defeat "activist" attorney general candidates. "Historically . . . attorney general races were off most business people's radar screens," says Bob LaBrant of the Michigan Chamber of Commerce. Today, "there's greater incentive to get involved in an attorney general race because of the increased involvement of attorneys general across the country in litigation against the business community." [30] The Republican Attorneys General Association was found-

TABLE 7-6

The Powers of the Offices

In many states, Lieutenant Governors . . .	Secretaries of State . . .	Attorneys General . . .
Preside over the senate	File and/or archive state records and regulations; other corporate documents	Institute civil suits
Appoint committees	Administer uniform commercial code provisions	Represent state agencies and defend and/or challenge the constitutionality of legislative or administrative actions
Break roll-call ties	Publish state manual or directory, session laws, state constitution, statues, and/or administrative rules and regulations	Enforce open meetings and records laws
Assign bills	Open legislative sessions	Revoke corporate charters
May be assigned special duties by governor	Enroll and/or retain copies of bills	Enforce antitrust prohibitions against monopolistic enterprises
Serve as cabinet member or a member of an advisory body	Register lobbyists	Enforce air, water pollution, and hazardous waste laws in a majority of states
Serve as acting governor when the governor is out of state		Handle criminal appeals and serious statewide criminal prosecutions • Intervene in public utility rate cases • Enforce the provisions of charitable trusts • Enforce open meetings and records laws

Sources: Compiled from the National Lieutenant Governors Association, www.nlga.us/Members.htm (accessed May 13, 2004); *The Book of the States 2003* (Lexington, Ky.: Council of State Governments, 2003), 215, 221, and 224; and the National Association of Attorneys General, www.naag.org/ag/duties.php (accessed May 13, 2004).

ed in 1999 to elect candidates who believe that their colleagues have gone too far in pursuit of business regulations and the revenues such cases can generate. Their strategy appeared to work—the number of GOP attorneys general climbed from twelve in 1999 to twenty by 2003, but slipped to nineteen by 2007.

When any institution of government extends its power, there is the likelihood of a counter-reaction by some other part of government or by the media or other private sector forces against it. And the main battleground is always the ballot box. Voters elect those candidates they feel will get the most done for them and for the state.

Other Offices

Every state elects its governor and most states elect a lieutenant governor and attorney general. In terms of what other offices are held by elected officials—as opposed to officials appointed by the governor or boards and commissions—the states vary widely. The theory behind electing many officials directly is that it gives the public a greater voice in shaping a variety of state programs, instead of just selecting a governor and leaving it all up to him or her.

In 2003, New Mexico governor Bill Richardson convinced voters to approve a referendum that gave him the power to name the state's top education official directly. Richardson knew he would receive the credit or blame for running the schools anyway, so he wanted to have the power to shape policy in that office by being the boss of the person who ran it.

Only a few states, including Georgia, Montana, and Oregon, elect a state superintendent of education. In Nebraska, a state board of education is elected and the board in turn selects a superintendent. Several states, mostly in the South, directly elect their secretary of agriculture. An increasing number of states allow citizens to vote for an insurance commissioner. Most states elect a secretary of state who, in turn, regulates elections in those states. Many states structure their executive branches similarly—if there isn't an elected agriculture secretary there is certain to be an appointed one.

Some believe, however, that electing separate department heads makes too much of government political. A state treasurer who has to worry about getting reelected might not make politically unpopular but fiscally necessary decisions to make sure that the state's books are balanced. The other trouble with electing officials is that the departments they head will squabble over money and power instead of being part of a team that is working together to promote the greater good.

Conclusion

How did governors become the most important political figures in their states? Over the years, their offices have become the center of state power, with more and more authority given to them. The power of governors now matches, in most cases, the prestige they have always enjoyed. It is always a balancing act when trying to weigh the interests of direct citizen selection of their leaders versus the need to have professional people appointed to pursue a coherent policy promulgated by a single, accountable leader. Currently, the pendulum is swinging in favor of investing more power within the office of the governor.

Once weak, unable to set policy or budgets, governors have become unquestioned leaders. They are able to select cabinets that run most of the state agencies according to the governors' priorities. Sometimes their staff picks prove to be embarrassments, but they are able to fire bad people in hopes of seeing their agendas pushed forward by more eager replacements. Many positions are designed with staggered terms so that governors cannot appoint their own people to every position. Strong governors, though, are able to combine their power of appointment with their ability to command attention from the mass media in order to set the terms of political issues and their direction in their states. That clout extends to the judicial branch, with many governors able to appoint most state judges.

Their control of budgets and veto authority provides governors with enormous sway over the legislative branch as well. While they never get everything they want from their legislatures, they almost always get more of what they want than any individual legislator.

The unrivalled power of governors and their ability to command attention from the media and political donors makes them the leading political actors at the state level. Their ability to put people to work in shaping policy and campaigns, as well as their ability to raise money, makes them players in political races ranging from local and legislative contests all the way, in many instances, to the presidency.

Governors, in short, are the top dogs in the states.

Key Concepts

appointment powers (p. 239)

executive orders (p. 266)

formal powers (p. 238)

impeachment (p. 261)

informal powers (p. 238)

recall election (p. 261)

supermajority vote (p. 232)

veto (p. 232)

Suggested Readings

Behn, Robert D., ed. *Governors on Governing.* New York: Greenwood Press, 1991. Sixteen sitting governors talk about what they do.

Cannon, Lou. *Governor Reagan: His Rise to Power.* New York: Public Affairs, 2003. A thorough recounting of the future president's two terms in California.

Congressional Quarterly's Guide to U.S. Elections, 4th ed. Washington, D.C.: CQ Press, 2001. Part Four contains records of all gubernatorial primary and general elections since 1776 as well as a host of other data pertaining to governors.

Herzik, Eric B., and Brent W. Brown, eds. *Gubernatorial Leadership and State Policy.* New York: Greenwood Press, 1991. A collection of essays by political scientists on the roles and powers of governors.

Rosenthal, Alan. *Governors and Legislatures: Contending Powers.* Washington, D.C.: CQ Press, 1990. An examination of the role of governors and their relations with the other policymaking branch of government.

Sabato, Larry J. *Goodbye to Good-Time Charlie,* 2nd ed. Washington, D.C.: CQ Press, 1983. An overview of the role of governors and how it has changed since World War II.

Suggested Web Sites

http://library.cqpress.com. CQ Press's Electronic Library has an online voting and elections collection with a component for gubernatorial elections.

www.csg.org. Web site of the Council of State Governments, a forum for state officials to swap information on issues of common concern, such as drugs, water, and any number of other policy matters.

www.naag.org. Web site of the National Association of Attorneys General, which has become increasingly prominent as state attorneys general have banded together on a number of high-profile cases.

www.nga.org. Web site of the National Governors Association, which shares information among governors and also lobbies the federal government on their behalf.

www.stateside.com. Web site of Stateside Associates, a lobbying firm that keeps close tabs on policies and actions in the states.

CHAPTER 8

Courts

Turning Law into Politics

Judges who make decisions in
high-profile, politically charged cases
increasingly find themselves under
pressure from all parts of the political
system. When Florida judges allowed
the death of Terry Schiavo,
a brain-damaged woman, in 2005
it prompted demonstrations from
pro-life groups and threats from then
U.S. House of Representatives
Majority Leader Tom DeLay.

8

Why are some states' judges elected and some appointed?

Why are some states' courts more likely to impose the death penalty than others?

Angry political rhetoric and personal attacks have intruded upon the once quiet hallways of state courts in a big way. **"Activist judge!"** has become a rallying cry for politicians from the president on down against those members of the judiciary who do not immediately rubberstamp their political and legislative goals. Republican senator Orrin Hatch of Utah wrote that judges have "become the most dangerous branch" of government. Organizations decry "runaway courts" and judges "run amok" or "subverting the laws."

ACTIVIST JUDGE

A judge who is said to act as an independent policymaker by creatively interpreting constitutions and statutes.

Of course, railing against judges is nothing new. In 1954, when the U.S. Supreme Court, under Chief Justice Earl Warren, ordered an end to the practice of segregating schools by race, "Impeach Earl Warren" signs popped up along roadsides in many states. But former Supreme Court Justice Sandra Day O'Connor writes that today the "breadth of rage currently being leveled at the judiciary may be unmatched in American history."[1]

The complaint that activist judges create new laws to fit their personal political beliefs is particularly common among conservatives. But the expression is frequently used on both ends of the political spectrum, so it is not always clear what—if anything—is meant by it beyond not being happy with the outcome of a case. Such judges are accused of "legislating from the bench" rather than interpreting the law. Critics assert that power is taken away from democratically elected state legislatures when courts overturn or block legislation. If, however, a willingness to overturn democratically passed legislation is the definition of activist, a 2005 study of the U.S. Supreme Court found that it was the most conservative members of the court who voted to strike down the greatest number of congressional regulations, whereas those generally considered more liberal struck down the smallest number.

This is not to say that liberals do not also complain about activist judges. In May 2005, when Massachusetts senator Edward (Ted) Kennedy was challenging the record of California Supreme Court justice Janice Rogers Brown, who was up for a federal judgeship, he called her a "judicial activist who will roll back basic rights."[2] According to this view, conservative activists are hostile to government programs to provide civil rights, workers' rights, or consumer protections. Environmental protections could be undermined by a judicial holding that required compensation to property owners for changes in value to their property stemming from land-use regulations. Opponents of the current U.S. Supreme Court assert that it could limit the sweep of federal clean water legislation, or find that the government does not have the authority to address global warming issues.

Unpopular opinions also tend to involve such hot-button issues as gun control, immigration, criminal sentences, zoning laws, and school vouchers. Conservative columnist George Will wrote with disgust when the Florida Supreme Court sided with the teachers' union to hold unconstitutional a school voucher program that allowed children to transfer out of troubled schools:

> The court's ruling was a crashing non sequitur: that the public duty to provide something (quality education) entails a prohibition against providing it in a particular way (utilizing successful private educational institutions). The court's ruling was neither constitutional law nor out of character, and it illustrates why the composition of courts has become such a contentious political issue.[3]

When Florida judges allowed the death of a brain-damaged woman, Terri Schiavo, in 2005, outraged conservative politicians threatened everything from budget cuts to impeachment. Then U.S. House of Representatives Majority Leader Tom Delay swore that the judges would be made to "answer for their behavior," and Sen. John Cornyn, also of Texas, suggested a link between well-publicized, sometimes lethal attacks on judges and their politically charged decisions.

Beyond overturning laws based on state constitutions, judges also are called activist when they impose mandates so specific that they look a lot like legislation. Nobody likes being told what to do, and legislatures in particular do not like being dictated to about how to correct constitutional deficiencies.

Case in point: The extremely polarizing issue of gay marriage has caused considerable frustration among social conservatives who fear that no matter what laws are passed, the final say will be from state courts interpreting state constitutions. The first state and still the only state to require a state legislature to recognize gay marriages is Massachusetts. The ruling was handed down in 2003, and it may be no coincidence that the judges who did so were appointed to the bench and entitled to serve until their seventieth birthday without ever facing an election. Since then, more than eight thousand gay marriages have taken place in Massachusetts.

Following that decision was a period of losses for those advocating gay marriage. Court rulings in California, New York, and Washington State all essentially rejected the claims of gay couples to the benefits of marriage, although California does permit same-sex couples to enter into civil unions. (Other states that permit civil unions are Connecticut, Hawaii, Maine, New Jersey, and Vermont, in addition to the District of Columbia.) Twenty states amended their state constitutions to expressly ban gay marriage, thus taking the issue out of the purview of state judges entirely. Many others passed statutory bans, which are still potentially subject to being held unconstitutional by state judges. In the 2006 elections, another seven states passed antigay marriage amendments, although Arizona became the first state to reject such an amendment.

Just before those elections, the highest court in New Jersey, another state with appointed judges, ruled that "the unequal dispensation of rights and benefits to committed same-sex partners can no longer be tolerated under our state constitution." The court stopped short of finding a fundamental right to same-sex marriage. Instead, it gave the legislature 180 days to provide gay couples the benefits and rights of marriage, such as tuition assistance, survivor's benefits, and criminal spousal privilege. Whether to call this relationship "marriage" was left up to the legislature. The court's decision was 4–3. The minority would have gone further, granting gay couples the right to marry, but the majority held that such decisions must come from the legislature. The court was criticized by conservative groups for "trading judicial robes for legislative pens."

In the 2006 elections, a handful of western states voted on ballot initiatives that were designed to rein in these "out of control" judges. The most extreme was in South Dakota, where a group called "JAIL 4 Judges" advocated a state constitutional amendment to create special grand juries to punish judges for unpopular decisions. Other initiatives would have subjected judges to lawsuits or recalls because of their decisions, imposed retroactive term limits on higher court judges, and required that judges be elected from the districts they live in. None of these initiatives passed, but they reflect a frustration among many with unpopular state court decisions.

Anti-judge rhetoric and threats, whether they cross the line into intimidation or not, clearly put political pressure on judges to pay more attention to the potential political fall-out of their decisions. In states that elect judges, this just adds to an already extremely political climate in which judges must campaign and solicit sometimes enormous sums of money, often from political parties, to run the kinds of TV ads we are used to seeing from politicians. Interest groups fund high-cost campaigns. After all, what is the point of getting legislation passed if a judge throws it out as unconstitutional?

And in a closely divided political climate, courts increasingly find themselves in the middle of the most overtly political decisions possible: deciding who won an election. Most notably, in 2000 the U.S. Supreme Court decision on recounting ballots pretty much handed the presidential election to Bush, then the Texas governor, over then Vice President Al Gore. Less visibly, this same type of decision is made in political contests across the country. In Montana, the court intervened in a close 2004 election to give a state House seat to Democrat Jeanne Windham and thus decided control of that chamber.

Increasingly, judges themselves are objecting to being used as political punching bags and are arguing for the importance of an independent judicial branch. They emphasize that part of a judge's job is to provide a check on the other two branches of government and to protect minority rights, notwithstanding the political sentiments of the day. Both of these vital roles will at times anger a majority of people, and they cannot be fulfilled by judges who fear either for their jobs or their lives, either figuratively or literally. Again, former U.S. Supreme Court Justice Sandra Day O'Connor, who has been speaking out about the importance of judicial independence, framed the significance of the issue. "It takes a lot of degeneration before a country falls into dictatorship," she said, "but we should avoid these ends by avoiding these beginnings." Those angriest with judges tend to frame the issues in terms of accountability and democratic values, rather than independence. They are outraged when judges interfere with what they regard as the political arena.

When it comes to all of this, it quickly becomes obvious that there is no single "right way" in which judges, justices, and courts operate. Each of the fifty states, the District of Columbia, and Puerto Rico has its own unique court system. Sometimes it seems as if every county in every state has its own way of doing things. From judicial selection to sentencing reform, states have organized their justice systems to meet the needs of their unique political pressures and social dynamics.

All of this is of the utmost importance because it may affect public confidence in state courts, institutions with a tremendous amount of power. This chapter provides an introduction to state court systems. First, the different types of courts and the different ways these courts are structured are examined. Then the focus turns to the different ways state court judges are chosen and retained and the controversy these processes create. Many issues surround each of the players in the state justice system, from prosecutors and defenders to victims and jurors, and these are explored before the discussion looks at some possible areas of reform.

At the apex of most state court systems is a supreme court. State supreme court justices, such as Mississippi supreme court justices Jess Dickinson (left) and Michael Randolph (right), typically have the final say on appeals from lower courts.

The Role and Structure of State Courts

When people complained on old TV shows about how they felt abused or ripped off by their friends, those friends would often say, "Don't make a federal case about it." In the real world of crime and legal conflict, there are actually relatively few federal cases, since those must involve violations of federal law, federal constitutional rights, or lawsuits that cross state borders. With the exception of celebrity trials like the O. J. Simpson murder case, state courts operate largely below the public's radar.

Yet they are enormously important institutions. The federal U.S. district courts hear several hundred thousand cases a year. By comparison, close to one hundred million cases are filed in the lowest state courts every year. These courts have the awesome responsibility to resolve the vast majority of the nation's disputes. If you crash your car or your landlord evicts you, if you get divorced and fight for child custody, if your neighbor's tree lands in your yard, or if your employer won't pay you, then you'll find yourself in a state court. State courts are also where virtually all criminal cases are tried, from drunk driving to murder, misdemeanors to capital offenses. If you get a serious enough traffic ticket, you will find yourself in a state court.

There are two basic kinds of court cases—**criminal cases** and **civil cases**. Criminal cases involve violations of the law, with the government prosecuting the alleged perpetrator, or criminal. Those found guilty usually go to jail. By contrast, civil cases involve disputes between two private parties, such as a dry cleaner and a customer with badly stained pants. In civil cases, individuals sue each other, usually for financial judgments. Both types of cases start out in **trial court**. If the parties in a case cannot reach agreement through a **settlement** or a **plea bargain**, they go to trial.

Inevitably every trial has a winner and a loser. Those unhappy with the trial's outcome can file an **appeal**. Most states have two levels of courts that hear appeals from trial court judgments. The appeal first goes to an **intermediate appellate court**, which reviews the original trial's record to see if any errors were made. After the appellate court has ruled, parties who still are not satisfied can attempt to appeal to the highest state court of appeals, usually called the **state supreme court**. In most states, this court does not automatically have to take an appeal, but can pick and choose among cases, typically choosing those whose resolutions will require a clarification of the law. Such resolutions could set a **precedent** that has consequences well beyond the specifics of the case being appealed.

A state supreme court is the highest legal body in the state court system. This gives it the ultimate power to interpret the state constitution. Its decisions are almost always final. Only the U.S. Supreme Court outranks the highest state courts. Even the nine justices in Washington, D.C., however, cannot review—that is, come up with a new decision for—a state supreme court judgment unless it violates the U.S. Constitution or federal law.

When such federal issues are involved, there is no question that state courts must follow the rulings of the federal courts. The chief justice of the Alabama Supreme Court, Roy S. Moore, learned this lesson in 2003 after placing a two-and-a-half ton monument to the Ten Commandments in the rotunda of the state supreme court building. Federal judges ordered him to move it, ruling that such a display violated the First Amendment's separation of church and state. He refused and ultimately was removed from office for having tried to place himself above the law. In 2006 his former colleague on the court, Justice Tom Parker, expressed anger at other justices for following the U.S. Supreme Court precedent that prohibits the use of the death penalty for crimes committed by minors. Justice Parker unsuccessfully urged his colleagues not to follow Supreme Court opinions "simply because they are precedents."[4]

Trial Courts

Almost one hundred million cases were filed in state courts in 2004, about one case for every three citizens. These numbers have stayed remarkably constant over the last ten years. More than half of the cases involved traffic offenses. The number of civil and criminal cases was roughly equal—16.9 and 20.7 million cases, respectively—and there were 7.8 million domestic and juvenile cases.[5] The vast majority of these millions of cases were resolved through plea bargains or settlements. Only a small minority ever went to trial.

When parties do go to trial, they appear before a state court judge in what is often referred to as a **court of first instance**. In this court, nothing has been determined, nothing is a "given." The trial is a blank canvas on which the parties can introduce documentary and physical evidence, such as fingerprints or DNA. Witnesses can testify as to what they saw or heard, and experts can try to help explain complex evidence.

The judge presides over the introduction of evidence; rules on objections, which occur when either of the parties thinks that the other party has said or done something wrong, and issues of admissibility, or whether or not it is all right for specific evidence or facts to be included in the trial; and instructs the jury as to the relevant laws. The judge further instructs the jury that they must apply the laws as stated to the facts as they find them. It is the jury, however, that must decide what the facts are. (In **bench trials**, this is done by the judge.) The jury or the judge must decide who and what to believe and what happened. Unless this decision is based on a legal mistake, such as improper evidence, hearsay testimony (testimony based on rumor), or a misleading statement of the relevant law, the result typically will be upheld on appeal. The business of the trial court is to examine the facts to resolve the dispute. Subsequent appellate courts review the trial court's application of the law to those facts.

INTERMEDIATE APPELLATE COURT

A court that reviews court cases to find possible errors in their proceedings.

STATE SUPREME COURT

The highest level of appeals court in a state.

PRECEDENT

In law, the use of the past to determine current interpretation and decision making.

COURT OF FIRST INSTANCE

The court in which a case is introduced and nothing has been determined yet.

BENCH TRIALS

Trials in which no jury is present and a judge decides the facts.

A Difference that Makes a Difference:
The New Judicial Federalism

A century ago, state supreme courts were described as so quiet, "you could hear the justices' arteries clog." [a] No one says this today, and the New Judicial Federalism is one big reason why.

This doctrine describes a newfound reliance on state constitutions to protect those rights not covered by the U.S. Constitution. Under the principles of federalism, each state has its own justice system—distinct from those of its neighbors and from the federal system—and its own constitution. The U.S. Constitution is the supreme law of the land, and no state court can interpret its own state's constitution in a way that limits rights secured by the federal charter. States are free, however, to interpret their own constitutions any way they like, except for that single proviso.

For most of the country's history, state constitutions were overlooked. Rarely were they relied on to overturn state laws, especially on the basis of civil rights. But starting in the early 1970s, state supreme courts increasingly began to use state constitutions as independent sources of rights. By 1986, Justice William J. Brennan characterized the "[r]ediscovery by state supreme courts of the broader protections afforded their own citizens by their state constitutions [as] . . . probably the most important development in constitutional jurisprudence in our time." [b]

In many legal areas, the actual impact of judicial federalism on civil liberties has not been all that sweeping. It is still true that most state court judges continue to interpret state constitutions in lockstep with interpretations of the U.S. Constitution. One commentator found, however, that in approximately one out of every three constitutional decisions, state courts extended rights beyond federal levels. [c] In some areas, such as the interpretation of rights to exercise religion freely and in search and seizure rulings, state courts, relying on their own constitutions, have continued to grant rights after the U.S. Supreme Court's interpretation of the Constitution took a more conservative and restrictive turn.

In other cases, state courts rely on unique constitutional provisions. For instance, state constitutions, unlike the federal document, often commit state governments to the achievement of particular policy ends. New Jersey's constitution requires a "thorough and efficient system of free public schools," Illinois requires the state to "provide and maintain a healthful environment for the benefit of this and future generations," and the New Mexico constitution requires bilingual education. Relying on explicit provisions like these, state supreme courts have ordered legislatures to restructure the way they finance public education when inequalities are so extreme they rise to the level of constitutional violation.

Today, the new judicial federalism is well established, with more and more cases raising state constitutional issues, sparking a renewed interest in these once overlooked documents. State supreme court justices are more likely now to take a fresh look at their own constitutions than to slavishly follow the interpretations of the U.S. Supreme Court. Activists also have focused more attention on state constitutions, mounting campaigns to amend them to either extend or curtail rights.

[a] G. Alan Tarr, "The New Judicial Federalism in Perspective," *Notre Dame Law Review* 72 (1997): 1097.

[b] William J. Brennan, *National Law Journal,* September 29, 1986, S–1.

[c] James N.G. Cauthen, "Expanding Rights under State Constitutions: A Quantitative Appraisal," *Albany Law Review* 63 (2000): 1183, 1202.

The key distinction among state courts is between **general jurisdiction trial courts** and **limited,** or **special jurisdiction, trial courts.** A general jurisdiction trial court hears any case not sent to a special court whether it is civil or criminal. The kinds of cases that can be tried in special jurisdiction courts are statutorily limited. Some are limited to cases of less seriousness, such as misdemeanors or civil cases that involve small amounts of money. Others are limited to the types of parties involved, such as juvenile offenders or drug abusers.

Not all states make this distinction between trial courts. Illinois has no limited jurisdiction courts. On the other hand, New York, the state with the largest number of judges, is also the state that relies most heavily on limited jurisdiction courts. More than 3,000 of the state's 3,645 judges sit on limited jurisdiction courts.[6] (See Figure 8-1.) The majority of these limited jurisdiction courts over which most of these judges preside are "town and village courts" or "justice courts." A lengthy 2006 exposé in the *New York Times* documented decades of criticism of these courts as outmoded, unsupervised, and unfair. It stated that elected judges are rarely lawyers, that they are sometimes illiterate, that they are given no training or supervision, and that they run their courts like "little fiefdoms."[7] In light of these accusations, New York's court officials have recently requested $50 million over the next five years to revamp this system.[8] In states that do not rely on limited jurisdiction courts, appeals go directly to appellate courts. In states that make the distinction, some issues can be appealed from limited jurisdiction courts to general jurisdiction courts.

Appeals Courts: Intermediate Appeals and Courts of Last Resort

When one of the parties in a trial is dissatisfied with the outcome, that party can challenge the result by filing an appeal. As a general rule, an appeal cannot be based on mere dissatisfaction with the trial's result. Appellants do not get a free second chance to try their whole case. Appellate courts do not decide issues of guilt or innocence or ensure that trials were conducted perfectly. Instead, an appeal must state that there were legal errors in the original trial. But it is not enough to say that an error occurred. Courts also require the error to be **prejudicial.** That is, the error had to have affected the outcome of the case. Appellants have to argue that there was a good chance the result would have been different if the error had not been made. This often is a very challenging argument to make.

To cite just one example, in 2006 the defense attorney representing the convicted murderer of an Indiana University freshman asked that the sentence should be thrown out, arguing that jurors may have been drinking during legal proceedings. Some of the male jurors in the trial painted their toenails and raced down a hotel hallway in a bailiff's backless high heels. "Two men with heels on, painting their toenails, it is not a normal activity unless they are intoxicated," he said. The judge ruled against him, say-

GENERAL JURISDICTION TRIAL COURTS

Courts that hear any civil or criminal cases that have not been assigned to a special court.

LIMITED, OR SPECIAL JURISDICTION, TRIAL COURTS

Courts that hear cases that are statutorily limited by either the degree of seriousness or the types of parties involved.

PREJUDICIAL ERROR

An error that affects the outcome of a case.

FIGURE 8-1 How It Works: State Court Structure in Illinois and New York

At a glance, it's easy to see why New York State's court system has been called Byzantine—just compare it to Illinois's (left). Although it encompasses 22 circuits with more than 850 justices, Illinois's single trial court system (its general jurisdiction courts) looks like a model of clarity and simplicity stacked against New York's 10 different trial courts (the courts of general and limited jurisdiction). But the differences run deeper than what a simple organizational chart can reveal. New York's 300-year-old town and village justice court system, in particular, has been subject to loud and persistent criticism for cronyism, corruption, fiscal mismanagement, and plain old inefficiency. According to *New York Times* reporter William Glaberson, "the [town and village justice] courts have survived in part because the justices—most of them not even lawyers—have long-standing and deep ties to the upstate political system, and because of the substantial cost of replacing them with more professional courts."[a] With 2,300 justices involved at that level, that would indeed be a tall order.

What can be done? New York's chief judge Judith S. Kaye, the state's top advocate for court reform, has made a number of recommendations that, according to her "Action Plan," would fall "across four broad areas: court operations and administration; auditing and financial control; education and training; and facility security and public protection."[b] A few of these proposed changes could be imple-

Illinois's State Court Structure

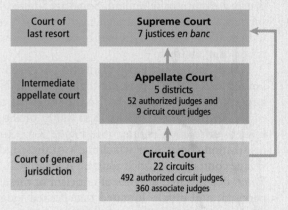

mented right away, including requiring word-for-word records of court proceedings—a bona fide court transcript—to ensure fairness, and the purchasing of recording equipment to make that possible. Other changes would require more sweeping institutional modifications. Judge Kaye called for state funds to help support the town and village justice courts, which are currently funded and operated locally. This change would require legislative approval. Her most aggressive recommendation—to simplify the trial court structure itself into a more common two-tiered organization—actually would require an amendment to the state's constitution.

ing there was no indication of drunkenness in court or during actual deliberations.[9]

There is no one way that all of the states decide how to hear appeals from the trial courts. States have made different decisions about how many levels of review to grant an appeal, how to choose which cases can be appealed, and how many judges will hear an appeal. These decisions combine to form different appellate court structures.

Not all states, for example, have both an intermediate appellate court and a supreme court. Back in 1957, only thirteen states had intermediate appellate courts. Today, eleven states and the District of Columbia still

New York State's Court Structure

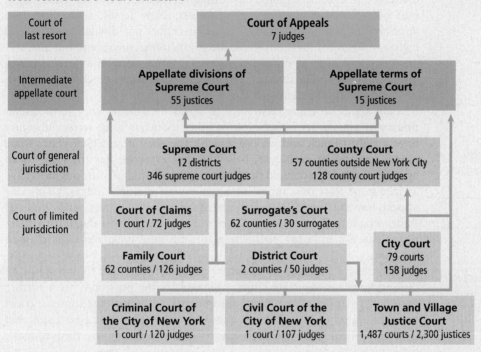

Court of last resort		**Court of Appeals** 7 judges		
Intermediate appellate court		**Appellate divisions of Supreme Court** 55 justices	**Appellate terms of Supreme Court** 15 justices	
Court of general jurisdiction		**Supreme Court** 12 districts 346 supreme court judges	**County Court** 57 counties outside New York City 128 county court judges	
Court of limited jurisdiction	**Court of Claims** 1 court / 72 judges	**Surrogate's Court** 62 counties / 30 surrogates		
	Family Court 62 counties / 126 judges	**District Court** 2 counties / 50 judges	**City Court** 79 courts 158 judges	
	Criminal Court of the City of New York 1 court / 120 judges	**Civil Court of the City of New York** 1 court / 107 judges	**Town and Village Justice Court** 1,487 courts / 2,300 justices	

[a] William Glaberson, "Justice Courts in Small Towns to Be Upgraded," *New York Times,* November 22, 2006.

[b] Judith S. Kaye and Jonathan Lippman, "Action Plan for the Justice Courts," November 2006. See www.courts.state.ny.us/publications/pdfs/ActionPlan-JusticeCourts.pdf (accessed May 2, 2007).

resolve all of their appeals with only one level of review. These states, including Delaware, Montana, North Dakota, Rhode Island, South Dakota, Vermont, and Wyoming, are less populous—eight have populations of less than one million—and thus tend to have fewer cases to resolve. Smaller populations give rise to relatively more manageable caseloads.

The sheer volume of appeals makes it impossible in the majority of states for one appellate court to hear and resolve every appeal. To deal with burgeoning caseloads, most states have created another tier of review. In these states, appeals go first to an intermediate appellate court. Only after they have been reviewed at this level can they move on to the court of last resort, usually the state supreme court. The intermediate court makes it possible for the state judicial system to hear many more appeals and creates the possibility of a second level of appeal.

Intermediate appellate courts range in size from three judges in Alabama, Alaska, Hawaii, and Idaho, to ninety-three judges in California. States with the most judges at the intermediate appellate level usually divide their jurisdictions into specific regions. California, for example, divides these judges into nine appellate divisions. By contrast, New Jersey, with thirty-two appellate judges, has the largest appellate court not divided into judicial regions.[10] Regional divisions make the courts more convenient, but also create a danger. All these different courts may come up with different rulings on the same or similar issues. This has the potential to set different, possibly conflicting, precedents for future litigation.

State appellate courts also vary in terms of whether they have **discretionary** or **mandatory jurisdiction**. In other words, in some states the courts have a right to pick and choose which cases they hear. Other states force judges to consider each case, believing that everyone has the right to an appeal. It is widely accepted that losers in a single-judge court ought to have a right to at least one appeal to a court with multiple judges.[11] This one appeal, however, is generally considered sufficient to correct any prejudicial errors made in the trial courts. Even in states in which the court of last resort has discretionary jurisdiction, capital punishment appeals may be mandatory.

Two tiers of appellate courts allow petitioners the right to one appeal to the intermediate appellate court, followed by the possibility of a further appeal to the court of last resort. Such a structure allows the supreme court or other courts of last resort to choose whether or not to hear cases that might have relevance beyond the parties in the case, allowing them to make the law clear to others.

One more variable in the state court system structure involves the number of judges at each level who hear a particular appeal. At either the appellate court level or at the court of last resort level, judges may hear an appeal *en banc*, or all together, or they may sit in smaller **panels**, typically of three judges. Sitting in panels may be more convenient, since courts sit simultaneously in different locations. This allows more appeals to be heard and makes the courts more convenient to the parties. However, like regional divisions, this may lead to similar problems of unifying doctrine created by various courts at the same level.

States that use panels have a variety of techniques to limit divergence among panels. These include conferencing drafts of opinions *en banc*. This means that the panel's draft opinions are circulated among all the judges, even those not on the panel. Two states have created two supreme courts with different subject matter jurisdiction, rather than have one supreme court sit in panels. Texas and Oklahoma have one supreme court with largely civil jurisdiction and one court of last resort that hears only crimi-

DISCRETIONARY JURISDICTION

The power to decide whether or not to grant review of a case.

MANDATORY JURISDICTION

Occurs when a court is required to hear every case presented before it.

EN BANC

Refers to appeals court sessions in which all of the judges hear a case together.

PANELS

Groups of (usually) three judges who sit to hear cases in state courts of appeal.

nal appeals. Each of these courts sits *en banc*. In Texas, the intermediate appellate court has both civil and criminal jurisdiction. In Oklahoma, the intermediate appellate court has only civil jurisdiction—all criminal appeals go directly to the court of last resort for criminal cases. A few states have created intermediate appellate courts with differing subject matter jurisdictions and then a single court of last resort.

States have mixed and matched all these variables to come up with different ways to organize the appellate court review process. The most common pattern, adhered to by half the states, involves making an intermediate appellate court, sitting in panels, consider all appeals. The decisions of these panels are then subject to review by a court of last resort, such as a supreme court, sitting *en banc*. Usually, this court can hear just the cases it sees fit to hear. States without an intermediate court of appeals often make their courts of last resort hear all the cases that are sent to them. However, two such states, New Hampshire and West Virginia, hear all appeals through a supreme court with discretionary review. The supreme courts in these two states get to pick and choose their cases. In the District of Columbia, all appeals are heard by a court of appeals with nine justices who often sit in panels of three.

In other words, if you lose your case, you will have at least one chance—and usually more than one chance—to get your appeal heard. But you will face a legal labyrinth that involves variations of courts and judges and panels and rules. All of these variations add up to one more reason to hire a good lawyer.

Selecting Judges

How judges are selected is a significant political decision. Historically, such decisions have generated tremendous controversy, and the controversy continues today. Why is there no clear consensus on such an important issue? Controversy is perhaps inevitable. The judiciary is one of the pillars of the U.S. political system, but at the same time, we want to believe that judges are above politics. We like to think that they are independent and will rule only as justice requires, based on the specific facts presented and the applicable law. Of course, judges are only human. That's why we want them held accountable for their decisions. These competing values—independence and accountability—tug judges in different directions. Focusing on independence leads to the appointment of judges for lifetime tenures similar to those of judges in the federal system. Focusing on accountability supports the public elections of judges. How a state structures its courts and chooses its judiciary may impact the types of decisions made by individual judges.

Almost no two states select judges the exact same way. The states can, however, be roughly divided into two camps of almost equal size. The first group includes states that choose judges through popular elections, either partisan or nonpartisan. In partisan elections, judicial candidates first run in party primaries and then are listed on the ballot with a designation of their political party. Candidates in nonpartisan elections run on the ballot without any party label. States in the second group have appointed, rather than elected, judges. Under the appointment model, the governor or the legislature may appoint judges. In some states the choice of whom to appoint is limited to choosing from names advanced by a nominating committee.

To make matters even more confusing, many states use different methods to choose judges at different levels of their judiciaries. States might, for example, choose trial judges by popular election but appoint supreme court justices. What's more, many states employ different methods by region. In Arizona, for example, trial courts in counties with a population greater than 250,000 choose judges through merit selection. Less populous districts rely on nonpartisan elections. Indiana holds partisan elections in a portion of its judicial districts and nonpartisan elections in others. Finally, some states that generally elect their judges fill mid-term judicial vacancies by appointment.

How states choose their judges has been historically volatile. Movements to change the methods for judicial selection rise up, gain popularity, and then, eventually, are supplanted by the next big reform movement. How a state originally chose its judges had much to do with which reform was in vogue at the time the state entered the Union and ratified its constitution. No single judicial reform ever succeeded in completely replacing earlier methods, however, and so, there is tremendous variation among the states in the way they select judges.

Under the U.S. Constitution, the president, with the advice and consent of the Senate, appoints all federal judges. Similarly, the original thirteen states chose to appoint judges, giving the appointment power to one or both houses of the legislature, and less commonly to the governor, either alone or with the consent of the legislature.[12]

Then, in the mid-1800s, during the presidency of Andrew Jackson—a period marked by distrust of government and movement toward increased popular sovereignty—the appointive system came under attack. Every state that entered the Union between 1846 and 1912 provided for some form of judicial elections.[13] At the dawn of the twentieth century, concern that judges were selected and controlled by political machines led to a movement for nonpartisan elections. By 1927, twelve states employed this practice.[14]

During the second half of the twentieth century, judicial reformers focused on persuading states to adopt a new method of choosing judges, referred to as merit selection. The variations of merit selection systems are discussed in detail in the following section on appointment. Basically, though, a merit system is a hybrid of appointment and election. It typically is based on a bipartisan judicial nominating commission whose job is to create a list of highly qualified candidates for the bench. The governor appoints judges from this list, who must then face a retention election. The retention election for a newly appointed judge is usually set to coincide with the next general election, and it provides voters with a simple choice: to keep or not to keep the judge on the bench. If the vote is for retention, the judge stays on the bench. If the vote is against retention (this is rare), the commission goes back to work to come up with another list of candidates for the post.

Under some merit systems all judges, not just newly appointed ones, must face periodic retention elections, although the length of term and other specifics vary from state to state. Missouri became the first state to adopt such a judicial selection method in 1940, which is why judicial merit selection is sometimes referred to as "the Missouri Plan." The movement enjoyed considerable success from the 1960s to the 1980s. The number of states that embraced merit selection for choosing supreme court justices grew from three in 1960 (Alaska, Kansas, and Missouri) to eighteen by 1980.[15]

Recently, however, this movement appears to have lost momentum. Approximately half of the states still rely on merit selection to choose some or all of their judges, and no merit selection state has returned to selection through elections. However, since 1990, most states that have considered adopting merit selection, whether for trial courts or appellate level courts, have rejected it. In Florida, for example, a 2000 initiative for the merit selection of trial court judges appeared on the ballot and was soundly defeated in every county.[16] A poll taken in early 2007 showed that an overwhelming majority of Pennsylvanians opposed changing the method of selecting judges from election to appointment.[17] Each method for selecting judges and the issues they raise will be addressed at length in the sections that follow. (See Map 8-1 for the systems of selection for each state.)

The merit selection of judges originated in Missouri and was prompted by a power struggle between Gov. Lloyd Stark (left) and Tom Pendergast (right) over who got to select judges. Pendergast ran one of the most powerful (and corrupt) political machines in the country, and his attempt to gain control of judicial selection in the late 1930s caused a backlash that led to the creation of the merit selection system.

Popular Elections

Why do some states elect judges? Elections allow greater popular control over the judiciary and more public accountability for judges. Proponents argue that such elections are compatible with this country's democratic traditions and that voters can be entrusted to make choices for judges that are as good as those that legislators or mayors would make. To these support-

MAP 8-1 Initial Judicial Selection, by Type of Court

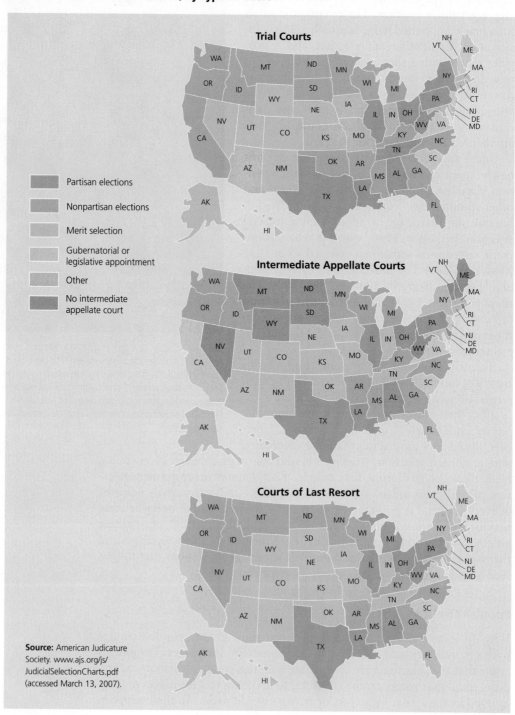

Trial Courts

Intermediate Appellate Courts

Courts of Last Resort

Partisan elections

Nonpartisan elections

Merit selection

Gubernatorial or legislative appointment

Other

No intermediate appellate court

Source: American Judicature Society. www.ajs.org/js/JudicialSelectionCharts.pdf (accessed March 13, 2007).

ers, the appointment of judges smacks of elitism and there is a worry about old-boy networks—judges getting appointed because they are the cronies or political allies of elected officials.

Some argue that electing judges can increase the representation of women and minorities on the bench. Several studies have found no correlation between selection method and diversity, although one recent researcher did find a slightly lower proportion of minorities selected through merit selection than the proportion of minorities on state courts across the country.[18] Nationwide, as of 2002, 22 of the 365 state supreme court justices were African American and 97 were women.[19] In the judicial elections of November 2006, diversity was a big winner. In twelve states, male and female candidates faced each other for state supreme court seats, and in two-thirds of these elections the women won.[20]

Those on the other side of the argument are critical of judicial elections in general, whether partisan or nonpartisan. They focus on what they see as a threat to the independence of the judiciary posed by the introduction of politics into the selection process. The tone of judicial elections has deteriorated substantially and in a manner that some fear could damage the image of the judiciary. Qualified candidates for office could choose to opt out.

It is a debate about more than academic ideas, however. How a state chooses judges has a very real political impact, with consequences for judicial impartiality, campaign fund-raising, the role of interest groups, and the character of judicial campaigning. Some point to these problems as reasons to move away from selecting judges through judicial elections and toward a merit selection system. Others argue that the problems can be addressed without abandoning elections altogether, but rather by tinkering with them. Die-hard supporters of elections see the increased politicization of judicial elections as positive because greater competitiveness translates into more meaningful choices for voters.

Before jumping into the consequences of elections, it is important to remember that elections for state court judges, when they are held, can be either partisan or nonpartisan. Most or all of the judges in eight states—Alabama, Illinois, Louisiana, Michigan, Ohio, Pennsylvania, Texas, and West Virginia—are selected through partisan elections. Another five states (Indiana, Kansas, Missouri, New York, and Tennessee) select some of their judges this way.[21] Nonpartisan elections are held to select most or all judges in thirteen states—Arkansas, Georgia, Idaho, Kentucky, Minnesota, Mississippi, Montana, Nevada, North Carolina, North Dakota, Oregon, Washington, and Wisconsin—and some judges in another seven states—Arizona, California, Florida, Indiana, Michigan, Oklahoma, and South Dakota.[22] In some cases labeling a popular election partisan or nonpartisan may be a distinction without a difference. All Ohio judges and Michigan Supreme Court justices run without party labels on ballots, but the candidates are chosen through party primaries or conventions, and the parties are heavily involved in judicial campaigns.[23]

The legislative and executive branches are clearly political. Representatives of the people are chosen and held accountable through elections. Why shouldn't judges be elected like other powerful players in the political system? Because the judge's role is designed to be different. Judges decide specific cases and controversies based on hearing the evidence. They are supposed to rely only on statutes, case precedent, constitutional law, and the unique facts presented by each case. They are not supposed to rule based on the wishes of those who elect them or with the next election in mind.

A lot rides on the public's belief that a judge will be neutral and impartial. That belief underpins the willingness to bring disputes to the courts and to abide by the results—the keys to both economic and political stability. Judges cannot, as political candidates do, make campaign promises about future decisions without undermining respect for the impartiality and independence of the judiciary. For the same reasons, judges cannot represent specific interest groups or constituents or even the will of the majority. There are times when all judges, doing their jobs properly, are compelled by the law to make unpopular judgments or to protect the rights of those without political power.

In 1999, U.S. Supreme Court Justice Anthony Kennedy pointed out in an interview that there are times for every judge when the law requires the release of a criminal whether the judge likes it or not. To characterize a judge in that case as "soft on crime" betrays a misunderstanding of the judicial process and the constitution.[24] In the same television interview, Justice Stephen Breyer also expressed concerns about the way judicial elections require judges to court public opinion. He asked, "Suppose I were on trial. Suppose somebody accused me. Would I want to be judged by whether I was popular? Wouldn't I want to be judged on what was true as opposed to what was popular? . . . We have a different system. And our system is based upon . . . neutrality and independence."[25]

Is this how it really works? Or only how it is *supposed* to work? The highly charged issue of capital punishment makes a useful test case. Why are some courts more likely to impose the death penalty than others? Some research indicates that state supreme court justices facing reelection in states in which capital punishment is particularly popular are reluctant to cast dissenting votes. Researchers Paul Brace and Melinda Gann Hall found that—among politically comparable states—rulings to uphold death sentences are more likely in states with elected judges.[26] Not only that, but the closer supreme court justices are to reelection, the more likely they are to support capital punishment.[27]

Texas and Florida share at least one thing in common—hundreds of inmates on death row and a high volume of death penalty appeals. But the similarity stops there. Texas justices are elected in partisan elections, and they almost never reverse a death sentence. In Florida, however, supreme court justices are merit selected, and the court has one of the nation's highest reversal rates.[28] It is not misguided for a judge facing reelection to fear reversing a death sentence. There are numerous examples of state supreme court justices who were labeled as soft after opposing the imposition of capital punishment in a particular case and were voted off the bench. This occurs even when the unpopular opinions are later held to be correct by the U.S. Supreme Court.[29]

The effects of judicial selection ripple out beyond those cases that tackle politically volatile issues like capital punishment and raise issues of improper influence on the judiciary. Professor Steven Ware reviewed all arbitration decisions made by the Alabama Supreme Court from 1995 to 1999. Justices there are selected through partisan elections, and this period encompassed a shift in the court majority from Democrats to Republicans. In virtually every case—even those that involved bland issues of law that appeared ideologically neutral—Ware found a direct correlation between voting and campaign contributions.[30] The Democrats, funded mostly by lawyers who worked for the plaintiffs, opposed arbitration. The Republicans, financed primarily by business interests, favored it. In 2006, the *New York Times* published the results of an examination of campaign financing over twelve years in regard to the Ohio Supreme Court, finding that justices routinely sat on cases after receiving campaign contributions from the parties involved or from groups that filed supporting briefs. The article found that justices, on average, voted in favor of contributors 70 percent of the time, with one particular justice voting for his contributor 91 percent of the time.[31]

OK, so this all sounds somewhat shady, but candidates running for judicial office must raise money. Frequently, this money comes from the very people who have a vested interest in the outcome of cases that are or will be before a judge. Describing judicial fund-raising, Justice Paul E. Pfeifer, a Republican member of the Ohio Supreme Court, said, "I never felt so much like a hooker down by the bus station in any race I've ever been in as I did in a judicial race." [32] The funds required to run a campaign have been skyrocketing, particularly in state supreme court races. In 2006, many judges raised more than $2 million. The most expensive supreme court race was in Alabama, where the incumbent chief justice raised $4.5 million and his successful challenger raised $1.9 million.[33] Much of this money comes from lawyers, litigants, and other groups with an interest in the outcome of litigation.

> The funds required to run a campaign have been skyrocketing, particularly in state supreme court races. In 2006, many judges raised more than $2 million.

Why do these groups contribute so much money to judicial elections? As with any other political donation, there is at least some truth to the cynic's sense that campaign contributions are a good investment. The president of the Ohio state bar concluded, "The people with money to spend who are affected by court decisions have reached the conclusion that it's a lot cheaper to buy a judge than a governor or an entire legislature, and he can probably do a lot more for you." [34]

When judicial reform organization Justice at Stake surveyed 2,428 state court judges, roughly half said that campaign contributions influenced their decisions. Even if justices do not allow campaign contributions to affect their decisions, the appearance of a conflict already has been created. A 2001 survey found that eight out of ten people believe campaign contributions to judges influence decisions.[35]

Single-issue interest groups may target a judge for a specific ruling on a topic such as capital punishment, abortion, or same-sex marriage. Groups may criticize or praise the judge, taking the case completely out of its legal context. Such groups have joined together in the type of coalitions formed in other partisan political contests. Given the power of interest groups, Santa Clara University law Professor Gerald Uelmen has observed that judicial independence is most endangered in states with growing death row populations without any executions, states with laws requiring parental consent for abortions by minors, and states that allow statutory enactments or constitutional amendments by initiative.[36] In two states, Ohio and Kentucky, these three judicial landmines have come together. Both states elect supreme court justices in highly partisan and expensive races on a recurring basis.

Prior to 2002, judges' campaigns generally were subject to codes of judicial conduct that placed tight restrictions on campaigning to prevent judges from discussing topics that may later come before them on the bench. In *Republican Party of Minnesota v. White* (2002), however, the U.S. Supreme Court struck down such restrictions as violations of judges' free speech rights. Since then, interest groups such as the Christian Coalition of Georgia have asked judicial candidates to complete questionnaires, pressuring them to reveal their views on hot-button issues. The groups then target specific "bad" judges for removal. Some candidates themselves have run outspoken campaigns stating opinions on such issues as school funding that will clearly appear before the court.

Campaigns increasingly rely on thirty-second TV spots, which can do little more than offer simplistic sound bites about complicated issues. According to Justice at Stake, in 2002 only one in ten of these TV spots was negative—that number had risen to more than one in five by 2004. In the 2000 elections for the Michigan Court of Appeals, the word "pedophile" ran in huge type near the name of the judge the GOP was accusing of upholding a light sentence for a pedophile. In that same race, the Democratic Party ran ads that declared that the incumbents had ruled "against families and for corporations 82 percent of the time"—a claim the *Detroit Free Press* found "border[ed] on the bogus." [37] These ads do seem to make a difference. In 2004, thirty-four judicial elections featured some form of television advertising, and in twenty-nine of them, the candidate with the most ad expenditures won.[38]

Added to this mix of expensive campaigns and thirty-second TV spots is the fact that ordinary citizens have very little information with which to make informed choices about judicial races. Voters commonly vote only for candidates at the top of the ticket, like governors or senators, and leave the ballots for judicial candidates incomplete.[39] Lack of voter participation undermines the public's ability to keep the judiciary accountable. It makes judges more vulnerable to single-issue groups.

In partisan elections, the additional danger is that the political parties may expect favors from the candidates they put forward. In 1976, the Michigan Supreme Court decided a redistricting case in a way that favored Republicans. In the next election, the Democratic Party refused to renominate the court's Democratic chief justice.[40] Thomas Phillips, a one-time chief justice of the Texas Supreme Court, has asked,

> When judges are labeled as Democrats or Republicans, how can you convince the public that the law is a judge's only constituency? And when a winning litigant has contributed thousands of dollars to the judge's campaign, how do you ever persuade the losing party that only the facts of the case were considered?[41]

Appointment

States in which judges are appointed rather than elected can be put into two general categories: **pure appointive systems** and merit selection systems that rely on a nominating committee.

Federal judges have always been selected through a pure appointive system. The president appoints judges who, if they are confirmed by the Senate, "shall hold their Offices during good Behavior." No state, however, employs precisely this method of judicial selection.

In four states—California, Maine, New Hampshire, and New Jersey—the governor appoints state court judges without a nominating commission. That is, these governors are not limited in their selections to a list of names provided by someone else.[42] Judges' nominations still require some kind of second opinion, however. In Maine, the governor appoints judges subject to confirmation by a legislative committee whose decision may be reviewed by the Senate. In New Jersey, the state Senate must confirm the governor's appointees, who then serve an initial seven-year term, after which the governor may reappoint them. A special five-member elected council confirms a judicial appointee in New Hampshire. California's governor appoints judges after submitting names to the state bar for evaluation. Unlike other judges in pure appointive systems, however, judges appointed in California serve short initial terms and then are subject to retention elections at the first general election and every twelve years after that.[43] In **retention elections**, judges run unopposed. The voter may only indicate either a simple "yes" or a "no" on the question of whether the judge should be retained.

Virginia is the only state in which the legislature appoints all state judges without a nominating committee. A majority vote of both houses of the Virginia General Assembly is required to appoint any judge.

PURE APPOINTIVE SYSTEMS

Judicial selection systems in which the governor appoints judges alone without a nominating commission.

RETENTION ELECTIONS

Judges run uncontested, and voters are asked to vote "yes" if they wish to retain a judge in office for another term or "no" if they do not.

A Difference that Makes a Difference: Indicting Politicians: Finding an Impartial Judge when Judges Are Partisan Politicians Themselves

Perhaps nobody knows the results of mixing politics with state courts quite as intimately as Tom DeLay. DeLay was a conservative Republican first elected to the U.S. House of Representative in 1984. Eventually, he rose to become majority leader. His nickname, "The Hammer," came from the brutal manner with which he enforced party discipline and brought retribution down on those who crossed him.

Meanwhile, back in Texas, Ronnie Earle ran for Travis County district attorney as a Democrat and won in the left-leaning capital city of Austin. In his twenty-seven years in the position, he developed a reputation for prosecuting Texan politicians, both Democrats and Republicans.

It took Earle three grand juries, but in 2005, he indicted DeLay for conspiring to violate Texas political fund-raising law and laundering money in violation of a state ban on the use of corporate money in local elections.

DeLay denied any involvement, calling the charges a sham. He argued that because Earle was a Democrat, he was pursuing the charges for political purposes, as part of a partisan vendetta. Nonetheless, Republican Conference rules forced DeLay to step down from his leadership position in the House. He managed to win his primary handily, and his hope was that he would be exonerated before the 2006 election. With his case still pending as the election neared, however, DeLay resigned from his seat in Congress and withdrew from the race. A judge ruled that his name had to remain on the general election ballot, even after he withdrew, and his seat ultimately was won by a Democrat, Nick Lampson.

DeLay's legal case was assigned initially to the court of district judge Bob Perkins, who had been elected to his post as a Democrat in a partisan election. DeLay objected to Perkins hearing his case because he was a Democrat and had contributed money to the liberal advocacy group MoveOn.org and to candidates such as 2004 Democratic presidential nominee John Kerry. After Perkins was removed from the case, administrative

In 2005, Travis County District Attorney Ronnie Earl (a Democrat) indicted U.S. House Majority Leader Tom DeLay (a Republican) on charges of violating Texas's laws on political fund-raising. Both sides in this dispute raised objections about the judges assigned to oversee the case. Judges in Texas are selected by partisan election, which put political loyalties at the center of the case.

judge B. B. Schraub, a Republican, was named to select a new judge. Now it was Earle's turn to complain—Schraub had made political contributions to Republican candidates. Schraub withdrew, asking state supreme court chief justice Wallace Jefferson to name the new judge. Even as Jefferson was selecting semi-retired senior judge Pat Priest of San Antonio, Earle was asking Jefferson to withdraw from the process as well because of entanglements with the Republican political action committee at the heart of the charges against DeLay.

In Texas, where partisan elections choose the judges, the prosecutors, and in DeLay's case, the defendant, everyone's politics may become relevant, paralyzing the state courts and throwing doubt on their ability to enforce the rule of law impartially. According to Charles Silver, a legal ethics professor at the University of Texas Law School, this kind of judicial wrangling "says that the judges who we elect can't be trusted to apply the law neutrally in cases that in some way, shape or form bear on their political beliefs. If that is true, we really need to revamp the whole system."*

*"Third DeLay Judge Appointed, but Confusion Remains," *USA Today,* November 4, 2005, available at www.usatoday.com/news/washington/2005-11-04-DeLay-Judge_x.htm?csp=34.

Merit selection, initially endorsed by the American Bar Association in 1937, was conceived as a way to limit the intrusion of politics into judge selection.[44] Most states that currently appoint judges rely on a method of merit selection through nominating committees. Twenty-four states and the District of Columbia rely on a merit selection plan for the initial selection of some or all judges. Another ten states use such plans to fill midterm vacancies at some or all levels of court.[45]

What puts the merit into merit selection? It is misleading to describe it as if it were a single method for selecting judges because the details vary considerably from state to state. At its core, it requires that the state assemble a nonpartisan nominating committee. This committee forwards a list of names from which either the governor or the legislature chooses a judge. How a partisan, distrustful legislature solves the problem of creating a nonpartisan committee differs in almost every state. Some require parity of political party affiliation for the commission members. Others have adopted extremely complex methods to assure the impartiality of nominating commissions.

A case in point is Tennessee. The fifteen commission members are chosen as follows: First, the Speaker of the Senate appoints three members from a list submitted by the Tennessee Trial Lawyers Association, three members from a list submitted by the District Attorney General Conference, and one nonattorney. Next, the Speaker of the House appoints two members from a list submitted by the Tennessee Bar Association—whose list may not contain personal injury or criminal defense attorneys—one member from a list submitted by the Tennessee Defense Lawyers Association, three members from a list submitted by the Tennessee Association of Criminal Defense Lawyers, and one nonlawyer. Finally, the speakers jointly appoint one nonattorney.[46]

Got all that? Even after the composition of the nominating commission is determined, states have different ways to choose its chair, the most influential position. In some states, including Maryland, New Hampshire, and Utah, the governor can exert considerable control over the commission through the ability to appoint its chair.[47] Other states, such as Alaska, Arizona, Colorado, and Utah, designate the chief justice of the state supreme court as chair. Some states allow the commission to choose its own chair, and, finally, New Mexico's constitution designates the dean of the University of New Mexico Law School as the chair of the state's judicial nominating commission.[48]

Usually, the governor chooses the judge from the list forwarded by the commission. In South Carolina and Connecticut, the nominating committee forwards a list of names to the legislature, which then meets in joint session, appointing judges by a majority vote.[49]

The ways in which judges are retained after being appointed initially also vary. In most states, judges appointed through merit selection serve shorter initial terms, usually one or two years. After that, they participate in retention elections. These special elections were conceived as a means to provide some public participation in the selection of judges while avoiding the intrusion of politics. In some states, notably California and Tennessee, this has backfired. Retention elections have become as fiercely partisan as popular elections.

Some merit selection states have dispensed with elections altogether. For instance, in Connecticut, Delaware, Hawaii, and New York, judges are reevaluated and reappointed by the judicial selection commission. In Vermont, after an initial appointment through merit selection, a judge receives an additional term as long as the General Assembly does not vote against it.[50]

Terms of Office

The length of a judge's tenure is another element in the balance between judicial independence and judicial accountability. In the federal court system, judges serve life terms, limited only by "good behavior." Judges can be removed only through an impeachment process for cause. This life tenure is considered an important element, perhaps the most important element, in insuring the independence of the federal judiciary.[51] There has never been a conviction of an impeached federal judge based solely on an unpopular judicial decision in the federal system.[52]

With only a few exceptions, state court judges serve fixed terms of office and must therefore seek reappointment or reelection. The rare exceptions include judges in Rhode Island, who serve life terms, and judges in Massachusetts and New Hampshire, who hold their positions until the age of seventy. Judges in states with fixed terms typically serve for less than ten years. New York judges serve the longest terms in the states—fourteen years—before mandatory retirement kicks in at age seventy. (See Tables 8-1, 8-2, and 8-3.)

Shorter tenures bring with them the increased danger that political interests and pressures will intrude upon judicial decision-making. Giving judges longer terms allows them to be judged on a more complete record. A judge can more easily put some distance between a particular controversial decision and the election. To look at this another way, research indicates that judges with longer terms of office are more willing to manifest partisanship than judges with shorter terms. For example, researchers Paul Brace and Melinda Gann Hall found that, out of all the judges studied, Democrats with long terms are least likely to support capital punishment, whereas Republicans with long terms are the most likely to support it. This led them to conclude "term length influences the willingness of individual justices to express their partisanship."[53]

TABLE 8-1

Courts of Last Resort: Terms and Methods of Reappointment by State, 2007

State	Name of Court of Last Resort	Initial Term (in years)	Subsequent Terms	Method of Reappointment	Geographical Basis for Selection
Alabama	Supreme	6	6	Reelection	Statewide
Alaska	Supreme	At least 3	10	Retention election	Statewide
Arizona	Supreme	At least 2	6	Retention election	Statewide
Arkansas	Supreme	8	8	Reelection	Statewide
California	Supreme	Until next gubernatorial election	12	Retention election	Statewide
Colorado	Supreme	At least 2	10	Retention election	Statewide
Connecticut	Supreme	8	8	Governor renominates; legislature reappoints	Statewide
Delaware	Supreme	12	12	Gubernatorial reappointment from judicial nominating commission; senate consents	Statewide
Florida	Supreme	At least 1	6	Retention election	Statewide
Georgia	Supreme	6	6	Reelection	Statewide
Hawaii	Supreme	10	10	Nominating commission retains	Statewide
Idaho	Supreme	6	6	Reelection	Statewide
Illinois	Supreme	10	10	Retention election	District
Indiana	Supreme	At least 2	10	Retention election	Statewide
Iowa	Supreme	At least 1	8	Retention election	Statewide
Kansas	Supreme	1	6	Retention election	Statewide
Kentucky	Supreme	8	8	Reelection	District
Louisiana	Supreme	10	10	Reelection	District
Maine	Supreme Judicial	7	7	Gubernatorial reappointment; senate confirms	Statewide
Maryland	Court of Appeals	At least 1	10	Retention election	Circuit
Massachusetts	Supreme Judicial	To age 70	NA	NA	Statewide
Michigan	Supreme	8	8	Reelection	Statewide
Minnesota	Supreme	6	6	Reelection	Statewide
Mississippi	Supreme	8	8	Reelection	District
Missouri	Supreme	At least 1	12	Retention election	Statewide
Montana	Supreme	8	8	Nonpartisan election	Statewide

TABLE 8-1, continued

State	Name of Court of Last Resort	Initial Term (in years)	Subsequent Terms	Method of Reappointment	Geographical Basis for Selection
Nebraska	Supreme	At least 3	6	Retention election	Statewide (chief justice); district (associate justices)
Nevada	Supreme	6	6	Reelection	Statewide
New Hampshire	Supreme	To age 70	NA	NA	Statewide
New Jersey	Supreme	7	To age 70	Gubernatorial reappointment; senate confirms	Statewide
New Mexico	Supreme	Remainder of unexpired term	8	Retention election	Statewide
New York	Court of Appeals	14	14	Gubernatorial appointment from nominating commission; senate consent	Statewide
North Carolina	Supreme	8	8	Reelection	Statewide
North Dakota	Supreme	10	10	Reelection	Statewide
Ohio	Supreme	6	6	Reelection	Statewide
Oklahoma	Supreme and Criminal Appeals	At least 1	6	Retention election	District
Oregon	Supreme	6	6	Reelection	Statewide
Pennsylvania	Supreme	10	10	Retention election	Statewide
Rhode Island	Supreme	Life	—	—	Statewide
South Carolina	Supreme	10	10	Legislative reelection	Statewide
South Dakota	Supreme	At least 3	8	Retention election	Statewide
Tennessee	Supreme	Until next general election	8	Retention election	Statewide
Texas	Supreme and Criminal Appeals	6	6	Reelection	Statewide
Utah	Supreme	At least 3	10	Retention election	Statewide
Vermont	Supreme	6	6	Vote of general assembly	Statewide
Virginia	Supreme	12	12	Legislative election	Statewide
Washington	Supreme	6	6	Reelection	Statewide
West Virginia	Supreme	12	NA	Reelection	Statewide
Wisconsin	Supreme	10	10	Reelection	Statewide
Wyoming	Supreme	At least 1	8	Retention election	Statewide

Sources: Data compiled from the American Judicature Society, www.ajs.org/js/select.htm (accessed December 28, 2006); and the National Center for State Courts' Courts Statistics Project, www.ncsconline.org/D_Research/Ct_Struct/Index.html (accessed December 28, 2006).

Note: NA = not available; — = not applicable.

TABLE 8-2

Intermediate Courts: Terms and Methods of Reappointment by State, 2007

State	Name of Intermediate Court	Initial Term (in Years)	Subsequent Terms	Method of Reappointment	Geographical Basis for Selection
Alabama	Civil Appeals; Criminal Appeals	6	6	Reelection	Statewide
Alaska	Appeals	At least 3	8	Retention election	Statewide
Arizona	Appeals	At least 2	6	Retention election	Division
Arkansas	Appeals	8	8	Reelection	District
California	Appeals	Until next gubernatorial election	12	Retention election	District
Colorado	Appeals	At least 2	8	Retention election	Statewide
Connecticut	Appeals	8	8	Governor renominates; legislature reappoints	Statewide
Delaware	No intermediate appellate court	—	—	—	—
Florida	District Courts of Appeals	At least 1	6	Retention election	District
Georgia	Appeals	6	6	Reelection	Statewide
Hawaii	Intermediate Court of Appeals	10	10	Nominating commission	Statewide
Idaho	Appeals	6	6	Reelection	Statewide
Illinois	Appeals	10	10	Retention election	District
Indiana	Appeals	At least 2	10	Retention election	District
Iowa	Appeals	At least 1	6	Retention election	Statewide
Kansas	Appeals	1	4	Retention election	Statewide
Kentucky	Appeals	8	8	Reelection	District
Louisiana	Appeals	10	10	Reelection	Circuit/District
Maine	No intermediate appellate court	—	—	—	—
Maryland	Special Appeals	At least 1	10	Retention election	Circuit
Massachusetts	Appeals	To age 70	—	—	Statewide
Michigan	Appeals	6	6	Reelection	District
Minnesota	Appeals	6	6	Reelection	Statewide
Mississippi	Appeals	8	8	Reelection	District
Missouri	Appeals	At least 1	12	Retention election	District
Montana	No intermediate appellate court	—	—	—	—
Nebraska	Appeals	At least 3	6	Retention election	District
Nevada	No intermediate appellate court	—	—	—	—

TABLE 8-2, **continued**

State	Name of Intermediate Court	Initial Term (in Years)	Subsequent Terms	Method of Reappointment	Geographical Basis for Selection
New Hampshire	No intermediate appellate court	—	—	—	—
New Jersey	Appellate Division of Superior Court	Appointed by chief justice of supreme court for fixed term	—	—	—
New Mexico	Appeals	Remainder of unexpired term	8	Retention election	Statewide
New York	Appellate Divisions of Supreme Court	5 years or through end of supreme court term, whichever is shorter	5	Governor reappoints from nominating commission	Statewide
North Carolina	Appeals	8	8	Reelection	Statewide
North Dakota	No intermediate appellate court	Cases assigned to the court of appeals by the supreme court are heard by three-judge panels.	—	—	—
Ohio	Appeals	6	6	Reelection	Appellate district
Oklahoma	Civil Appeals	At least 1	6	Retention election	District
Oregon	Appeals	6	6	Reelection	Statewide
Pennsylvania	Commonwealth and Superior	10	10	Retention election	Statewide
Rhode Island	No intermediate appellate court	—	—	—	—
South Carolina	Appeals	6	6	Legislative reelection	Statewide
South Dakota	No intermediate appellate court	—	—	—	—
Tennessee	Appeals; Criminal appeals	Until next general election	8	Retention election	Statewide
Texas	Appeals	6	6	Reelection	District
Utah	Appeals	At least 3	6	Retention election	Statewide
Vermont	No intermediate appellate court	—	—	—	—
Virginia	Appeals	8	8	Legislative reelection	Statewide
Washington	Appeals	6	6	Reelection	District
West Virginia	No intermediate appellate court	—	—	—	—
Wisconsin	Appeals	6	6	Reelection	District
Wyoming	No intermediate appellate court	—	—	—	—

Sources: Data compiled from the American Judicature Society, www.ajs.org/js/select.htm (accessed December 28, 2006); and the National Center for State Courts' Courts Statistics Project, www.ncsconline.org/D_Research/Ct_Struct/Index.html (accessed December 28, 2006).

Note: — = not applicable.

TABLE 8-3

Trial-Level Courts: Terms and Methods of Reappointment by State, 2007*

State	Name of Trial-Level Court	Initial Term (in years)	Subsequent Terms	Method of Reappointment	Geographical Basis for Selection
Alabama	Circuit	6	6	Reelection	Circuit
Alaska	Superior	At least 3	6	Retention election	District
Arizona	Superior	2 or 4, depending on population of county	4	Nonpartisan election; Retention election	County
Arkansas	Circuit	6	6	Reelection	Circuit
California	Superior	6	6	Reelection	County
Colorado	District	2	6	Retention election	County
Connecticut	Superior	8	8	Governor renominates; legislature reappoints	Statewide
Delaware	Superior	12	12	Governor reappoints from judicial nominating commission; senate consents	Statewide
Florida	Circuit	6	6	Reelection	Circuit
Georgia	Superior	4	4	Reelection	Circuit
Hawaii	Circuit and Family	10	10	Nominating commission	Island
Idaho	District	4	4	Reelection	District
Illinois	Circuit	6	6	Retention election	Circuit/County
Indiana	Superior and Circuit	6	6	Reelection	County
Iowa	District	At least 1	6	Retention election	District
Kansas	District	1 or 4 depending upon district	4	Retention election	District
Kentucky	Circuit and Family	8	8	Reelection	Circuit
Louisiana	District	6	6	Reelection	District
Maine	District and Superior	7	7	Governor reappoints; senate confirms	Statewide
Maryland	Circuit	At least 1	15	Nonpartisan election	County
Massachusetts	Superior	To age 70	—	—	Statewide
Michigan	Circuit	6	6	Reelection	Circuit
Minnesota	District	6	6	Reelection	District
Mississippi	Circuit	4	4	Reelection	District
Missouri	Circuit	6	6	Reelection	Circuit
Montana	District	6	6	Nonpartisan election	District
Nebraska	District	At least 3	6	Retention election	District
Nevada	District	6	6	Reelection	District
New Hampshire	Superior	To age 70	—	—	Statewide

TABLE 8-3, continued

State	Name of Trial-Level Court	Initial Term (in years)	Subsequent Terms	Method of Reappointment	Geographical Basis for Selection
New Jersey	Superior	7	To age 70	Governor reappoints; senate confirms	County
New Mexico	District	Remainder of unexpired term	6	Retention election	District
New York	Supreme and County Courts	14/10	14/10	Reelection/reelection	District/county
North Carolina	Superior	8	8	Reelection	District
North Dakota	District	6	6	Reelection	District
Ohio	Common Pleas	6	6	Reelection	County
Oklahoma	District	4	4	Reelection	District
Oregon	Circuit and Tax	6	6	Reelection	District and Statewide
Pennsylvania	Common Pleas	10	10	Retention election	District
Rhode Island	Superior	Life	—	—	Statewide
South Carolina	Circuit	6	6	Legislative reelection	Circuit and at-large
South Dakota	Circuit	8	8	Reelection	Circuit
Tennessee	District Courts	8	8	Reelection	Varies with court
Texas	District Courts	4	4	Reelection	District
Utah	District	At least 3	6	Retention election	District
Vermont	Family; Superior; District	6	6	Vote of general assembly	Statewide
Virginia	Circuit	8	8	Legislative reelection	Circuit
Washington	Superior	4	4	Reelection	County
West Virginia	Circuit	8	NA	Reelection	Circuit
Wisconsin	Circuit	6	6	Reelection	Circuit
Wyoming	District	At least 1	6	Retention election	District

* Information on trial-level courts refers to highest court at trial-level, for example, those with general, rather than limited, jurisdiction.
Source: Data compiled from the American Judicature Society. www.ajs.org/js/select.htm (accessed May 24, 2004).
Note: NA = not available; — = not applicable.

Judicial Compensation

In addition to selection and tenure, compensation is one of the bellwethers for assessing independence of the judiciary. How a state determines the salaries of its judges and whether those salaries can be reduced makes a difference. The U.S. Constitution forbids reducing federal judicial salaries as a protection for judges who make unpopular decisions. Not all state constitutions include this proscription. In Florida, for instance, the constitution does not prevent the legislature from amending state laws to reduce salaries to discipline judges for unpopular decisions.[54]

According to the National Center for State Courts, twenty states have created independent judicial compensation commissions to advise their legislatures on judicial salary levels. The goal of these commissions is to determine the amount necessary to retain and recruit qualified judges and to eliminate the need for judges to lobby for their own salaries. States without such commissions rely on a variety of methods to eliminate partisan bickering over judicial salaries. The District of Columbia links salary increases to those of federal judges. Judges' salaries in South Dakota are linked to annual increases of the salaries of other state employees. In Pennsylvania, salary increases are tied to increases in the Consumer Price Index. (See Table 8-4.)

Prosecution and Defense of Cases in State Courts

Criminal cases at the state court level most often involve a face-off between two state or county employees. The **prosecutor** pursues the case on behalf of the people and usually seeks incarceration of the accused. Little difference exists among the states in the selection of the chief prosecutor—an elected county official almost always fills the position. The individual often is politically ambitious and views the job of chief prosecutor as a stepping-stone to higher elected office. For this reason, the policies of prosecutors tend to reflect the specific wishes of the county voters.

PROSECUTOR

A government official who conducts criminal cases on behalf of the people.

TABLE 8-4

Associate Justices' Salaries, by Rank, 2006

Courts of Last Resort		Intermediate Appellate Courts		Trial Courts	
Top Five		**Top Five**		**Top Five**	
California	$182,071	California	$170,694	Delaware	$163,850
Delaware	179,670	Georgia	166,814	Illinois	152,930
Illinois	177,073	Illinois	166,658	California	149,160
District of Columbia	175,100	Michigan	151,441	District of Columbia	149,160
Michigan	164,610	Alabama	151,027	New Jersey	141,000
Bottom Five		**Bottom Five**		**Bottom Five**	
Montana	$100,884	New Mexico	$101,612	Montana	$94,093
North Dakota	103,087	Oregon	102,800	North Dakota	94,298
Idaho	104,168	Idaho	103,168	New Mexico	95,531
Oregon	105,199	Mississippi	105,050	Oregon	95,800
New Mexico	106,960	Oklahoma	108,336	Idaho	97,632

Source: Data from the National Center for State Courts, "Survey of Judicial Salaries" 30:2, January 1, 2006. www.ncsconline.org/WC/Publications/KIS_JudComJudSal010106Pub.pdf (accessed December 28, 2006).

PUBLIC DEFENDER

A government lawyer who provides free legal services to those accused of a crime who cannot afford to hire a lawyer.

Private attorneys defend those individuals who can afford their services. In many cases, however, a **public defender**, an attorney also on the public payroll, represents the accused. Public defenders fulfill the state's constitutional requirement to provide indigent defense services, that is, defense services for those who are poor. There is much more variety in how states organize their systems of indigent defense than in their systems of prosecution. Some are organized into statewide public defenders systems. Others have statewide commissions that set guidelines for local jurisdictions—sometimes distributing limited state funds to local programs that follow specific standards. Still others delegate the responsibility of how to provide and fund indigent defense entirely to the counties.

The competing values of state oversight and local control play out differently depending on the cultural and political realities of each state as well as any practical concerns involved. Even some states with statewide public defenders offices exclude rural areas where the case volume would make supporting such offices impracticable. In the current climate of runaway costs, increased caseloads, and widespread litigation-challenging programs, the trend has been toward more state oversight.

The Prosecutor

Commentators have gone so far as to say that the prosecutor has become the "most powerful office in the criminal justice system." [55] The prosecutor's office is run by an attorney referred to, depending on the state, as the chief prosecutor, district attorney, county attorney, commonwealth attorney, or state's attorney. Whatever the title, this lawyer represents the public in criminal and other cases. Most prosecutors are elected and typically serve four-year terms. It is a daunting job, particularly in major metropolitan districts, where the top prosecutor manages hundreds of lawyers and support staff, deals with horrific crimes, and balances the need to serve justice with the "unavoidable scrutiny of won-lost statistics that become a factor in re-election campaigns." [56]

Authority comes from the state, but prosecutors' offices are essentially local. Authority is over a specific jurisdiction—usually a county. County governments fund these offices, although close to half of them also receive some portion of their budgets from state funds. [57] Nationwide, there are more than two thousand state court prosecutors' offices, employing approximately seventy-eight thousand attorneys, investigators, and support staff. [58]

Most chief prosecutors serve jurisdictions with fewer than one hundred thousand people. About one-third of the chief prosecutors' offices have a total staff of four or fewer. [59] The top 5 percent of prosecutors' offices, however, serve districts with populations of five hundred thousand or more. They represent almost half the entire U.S. population. [60] In 2001, these large offices handled approximately 66 percent of the nation's serious crimes and had a median budget of more than $14 million.[61] The Los Angeles County district attorney's office has the largest staff, consisting of more than 2,700 people.[62] (See Table 8-5.) The types of cases handled by these offices have grown increasingly complex as prosecutors' offices encounter high-tech crimes, including identity theft and credit card fraud, and as they take on homeland security responsibilities.

A state's chief prosecutors have enormous discretion in the conduct of most of their responsibilities. The prosecutor makes all decisions as to whether or not to prosecute, whom to prosecute, and with what cause of action to prosecute. Discretion in charging is, in the words of one scholar, "virtually unchecked by formal constraints or regulatory mechanisms, mak-

TABLE 8-5

Statistics for State Prosecutors' Offices, 2006

Total number of offices	2,344
Total number of large offices[a]	42
Total number of medium offices[b]	213
Total number of small offices[c]	1,515
Total number of part-time offices	574
Total staff	78,000
Median total staff in large offices	419
Median total staff in medium offices	105
Median total staff in small offices	10
Median total staff in part-time offices	3
Median salary for chief prosecutor, all offices	$85,000
Median salary for chief prosecutor in large full-time offices	$149,000
Median salary for chief prosecutor in medium full-time offices	$125,000
Median salary for chief prosecutor in small full-time offices	$95,000
Median salary for chief prosecutor in part-time offices	$42,000
Median budget for prosecutorial functions, all offices	$355,000
Median budget for prosecutorial functions, large offices	$33,232,000
Median budget for prosecutorial functions, medium offices	$6,035,000
Median budget for prosecutorial functions, small offices	$389,000
Median budget for prosecutorial functions, part-time offices	$133,000
Median number of criminal cases closed by all state prosecutors' offices	1,100
Median number of criminal cases closed by large offices	42,953
Median number of criminal cases closed by medium offices	11,235
Median number of criminal cases closed by small offices	1,435
Median number of criminal cases closed by part-time offices	375

Source: Data compiled from Bureau of Justice Statistics Bulletin "Prosecutors in State Courts, 2005" by Steven W. Perry. www.ojp.usdoj.gov/bjs/pub/pdf/psc05.pdf (accessed December 28, 2006).

[a] Large offices are offices serving populations of 1 million or greater.
[b] Medium offices serve populations of 250,000 to 999,999.
[c] Small offices serve populations under 250,000.

ing it one of the broadest discretionary powers in criminal administration."[63] Charging decisions are enormously important, particularly in states in which statutory guidelines set minimum sentences or in which the same act can be subject to a number of different charges.

Several reasons exist for giving prosecutors such broad powers. One is the trend toward **legislative over-criminalization**. This is the legislative tendency to make crimes out of everything that people find objectionable.[64] By creating a large number of broadly defined crimes, legislatures have made it impossible to enforce all the criminal statutes even as they have made it possible to charge a single act under multiple, overlapping provisions.[65]

A second reason for a prosecutor's broad discretion is the need to individualize justice. Each case involves a unique set of facts and issues and requires careful weighing of the evidence. The severity of the crime must be balanced against the probability of sustaining a conviction to determine how best to spend limited resources. Prosecutors have been reluctant to publish general guidelines regarding their charging decisions. A Florida prosecutor stated that his office declines to prosecute drug cases when the amount of cocaine involved is deemed too small. But he refused to say just how much is too small. Understandably, he worried that drug smugglers would package their shipments in such a way to get under this arbitrary limit and escape prosecution.[66]

There are some limits to prosecutorial authority. For instance, the trial process itself. In many jurisdictions, the government first must obtain an **indictment**—or a formal criminal charge—from a **grand jury**. The U.S. Supreme Court has noted that the grand jury historically has been regarded as the primary protection for the innocent. However, only prosecutors and their witnesses appear before grand juries; no members of the defense are present. Prosecutors are able to offer their interpretation of the evidence and state the law and have no obligation to inform the grand jury of evidence of a defendant's innocence. Grand juries hear only one side of the case and thus almost always indict. For this reason, no discussion of grand juries is complete without including the immortal quip by former New York state judge Sol Wachtler that a grand jury could "indict a ham sandwich." It is also part of the reason that many states have abolished the grand jury and now rely instead on a preliminary hearing in which a judge decides if enough evidence exists to warrant a trial.

At trial, juries must determine guilt beyond a reasonable doubt. The possibility of **jury nullification** exists if the jury does not believe a case should have been brought to court. Trials, however, rarely come into play as a check on the discretion of prosecutors—few cases actually end up going to trial. Most are resolved through plea bargaining. Plea bargaining is another area in which prosecutors have broad discretion. Judges rarely question or second-guess plea bargains reached between the prosecutor and defendant. Prosecutors ultimately have to answer to voters, since more than 95 percent of all chief prosecutors are chosen through election.[67]

LEGISLATIVE OVER-CRIMINALIZATION

The tendency of government to make a crime out of anything the public does not like.

INDICTMENT

A formal criminal charge.

GRAND JURY

A group of between sixteen and twenty-three citizens that decides if a case should go to trial; if yes, an indictment is issued.

JURY NULLIFICATION

Occurs when a jury returns a verdict of "Not Guilty" even though jurists believe the defendant is guilty. The jury cancels out a law that it believes is immoral or was wrongly applied to the defendant.

There are positive and negative aspects to subjecting the prosecution of local crimes to the political process. On the positive side, the person deciding which laws to enforce and how to enforce them is answerable to the people of that district. More worrying is that political pressures—rather than the facts of a case—may guide the exercise of prosecutorial discretion. Prosecutors, for example, may choose not to charge politically connected friends. Some attributed the multibillion dollar savings and loan scandal of the 1980s and 1990s to the reluctance of prosecutors to subject friends and political allies to criminal indictment.[68] Discretion also can be misused when race enters the equation. Studies have shown that when the victim is white and the defendant is black, prosecutors are much more likely to seek the greatest possible punishment.[69]

Defense Attorneys

Anyone with even a casual acquaintance with TV crime dramas knows that after the police make an arrest they must inform the suspect of certain rights. One is that "you have the right to an attorney. If you cannot afford one, one will be appointed to you." This right derives from the Sixth Amendment of the U.S. Constitution: "In all criminal prosecutions, the accused shall enjoy the right . . . to have the assistance of counsel for his defense." In 1963, the U.S. Supreme Court found in *Gideon v. Wainwright* that this right to counsel is so fundamental and essential to a fair trial that the Constitution requires a lawyer be provided to the poor at state expense. Nine years after *Gideon,* the Court extended this right to counsel to all criminal prosecutions, state or federal, **felony** or **misdemeanor**, which carry a possible sentence of imprisonment. The Court also has made it clear that the Sixth Amendment guarantees "the right to the *effective* assistance of counsel." If an attorney was unprepared, drunk, or sleeping during a trial, that can be grounds for appeal.

FELONY

A serious crime, such as murder or arson.

No money came along with the constitutional mandate for counsel. And its scope is tremendous, since most criminal defendants in the United States cannot afford to pay for legal services. In 1991, about three-quarters of state prison inmates reported that they were represented by a court-appointed lawyer.[70] In 1999, in the nation's one hundred largest counties, criminal defense programs for the indigent received an estimated 4.2 million cases and spent an estimated $1.2 billion.[71] Sixty percent of this funding came from county governments. State governments paid 25 percent of the total funding.[72] Twenty-one states are funded almost exclusively by state sources, twenty use a combination of state and county funds, and nine use only county funds.[73] (See Tables 8-6 and 8-7.)

MISDEMEANOR

A less serious crime, such as shoplifting.

Not only did the mandate come with no funding, but it also lacked any specifications as to how indigent services must be provided. States and localities, as a consequence, have devised differing systems, with the quality of service provided varying tremendously. Three primary models have

TABLE 8-6

Maximum and Minimum Annual Salaries of Public Defenders and Supervisory Attorneys in State-Funded Systems, 1999

State	Assistant Prosecutor, entry level	Assistant Prosecutor, 5+ years experience	Supervisory Attorney
Alaska	$45,000 to 61,000	$55,000 to 75,000	$63,000 to 86,000
Colorado	$35,124 to 45,816	$54,480 to 73,008	$60,528 to 86,376
Connecticut	$41,612 to 46,808	$54,759 to 66,622	$57,217 to 100,406
Delaware	$36,000 to 43,000	$45,401 to 106,565	$— to 88,000
Iowa	$35,152 to 44,033	$44,033 to 68,286	$58,718 to 85,466
Massachusetts	$28,600 to 28,600	$42,000 to 42,000	$76,500 to 76,500
Missouri	$30,500 to —	$50,232 to —	$— to —
New Hampshire	$31,018 to 42,770	$48,204 to 52,754	$41,020 to 59,254
New Jersey	$40,965 to 47,873	$47,873 to 83,955	$63,198 to 91,000
New Mexico	$28,941 to 43,410	$44,834 to 67,253	$47,669 to 71,502
Rhode Island	$38,000 to 42,000	$42,000 to 46,000	$50,000 to 58,000
Vermont	$29,500 to 32,500	$39,000 to 42,000	$57,000 to —
West Virginia	$32,000 to —	$35,000 to 40,000	$55,000 to 78,000
Wisconsin	$37,087 to 93,108	$38,200 to 93,108	$42,829 to 98,850

Source: Adapted from Bureau of Justice Statistics. www.ojp.usdoj.gov/bjs/pub/pdf/sfids99.pdf (accessed May 25, 2004).

Note: Hawaii, Maine, Maryland, Minnesota, North Carolina, Oregon, and Virginia information not available.

— : Information not provided or not known.

ASSIGNED COUNSEL

Private lawyers selected by the courts to handle particular cases and paid from public funds.

CONTRACT ATTORNEYS

Private attorneys who enter into agreements with a state, a county, or a judicial district to work on a fixed-fee basis per case or for a specific length of time.

emerged throughout the nation, with most states employing public defender programs, **assigned counsel**, or **contract attorneys**, or some combination of these. The method chosen may vary from county to county in a state, or a state may rely primarily on one type and use either of the other types for casework overload or the inevitable cases involving a conflict of interest. Among the nation's one hundred most populous counties in 1999, public defender programs were operating in ninety counties, assigned counsel programs in eighty-nine counties, and contract programs in forty-two counties.[74] Public defenders usually serve metropolitan areas and assigned counsel programs or contract programs serve less populous regions.

Public defenders' offices draw on a salaried staff of attorneys. They provide criminal legal defense services either as employees paid directly by the government or through a public or private nonprofit organization. Large public defenders' offices generally employ attorneys who are trained and

TABLE 8-7

Statistics for State-Funded Public Defender Staff and Operations, 1999

State	Total Staff	Total State Indigent Defense Expenditures	Total Number of Cases Received	Chief Public Defender Appointed by	Salary of Chief Public Defender
Alaska	147	$11,460,400	29,983	Governor	$80,000
Colorado	380	31,394,830	64,179	Independent board or commission	90,590
Connecticut	348	25,095,150	56,327	Independent board or commission	110,524
Delaware	119	7,306,700	36,290	Governor	88,000
Hawaii	132	7,539,608	39,870	Governor	77,964
Iowa	199	30,720,729	61,232	Governor	75,000
Maine	—	6,999,820	—	—	—
Maryland	784	39,286,313	—	Board of Trustees	—
Massachusetts	190	62,200,000	7,143	Independent board or commission	95,760
Minnesota	636	46,400,000	178,175	Independent board or commission	89,627
Missouri	558	28,202,699	73,738	Independent board or commission	100,932
New Hampshire	127	10,667,700	15,522	Corporate board of directors	80,000
New Jersey	870	72,975,000	96,752	Governor	98,225
New Mexico	258	22,895,400	53,911	Governor	83,700
North Carolina	200	62,680,384	48,375	Judges	90,224
Oregon	—	32,564,390	—	—	—
Rhode Island	81	6,105,017	12,750	Governor	80,000
Vermont	68	5,829,246	12,703	Governor	62,000
Virginia	334	67,480,333	51,375	Independent board or commission	—
West Virginia	203	22,454,009	33,556	Independent board or commission	66,500
Wisconsin	—	61,590,139	124,171	Program advisory board	101,859

Source: Adapted from Bureau of Justice Statistics. www.ojp.usdoj.gov/bjs/pub/pdf/sfids99.pdf (accessed May 25, 2004).

Note: — : Information not reported or not known.

supervised and are supported by a staff of investigators, paralegals, and clerical staff.[75] The American Bar Association has observed, "When adequately funded and staffed, defender organizations employing full-time personnel are capable of providing excellent defense services."[76] In thirty states, a public defender system is the primary method used to provide indigent criminal defendants with lawyers.[77]

Another system is called assigned counsel—private attorneys are chosen and appointed either on a systematic or an *ad hoc* basis and are paid from

A 2005 survey of 2,485 Anchorage residents found that only 6.4% of respondents felt defense attorneys were excellent at treating people fairly. Prosecutors and judges fared little better, at 8% and 13.3%, respectively.

public funds. Depending on the state, individual judges, assigned counsel program offices, or the court clerk's office may make the appointments. In the oldest type of assigned counsel program, judges make *ad hoc* assignments of counsel. Sometimes the only basis for these decisions is whoever is in the courtroom at the time. These arrangements frequently are criticized for fostering patronage (the granting of jobs to political allies), particularly in less populated counties.

Most states appoint lawyers from a roster of attorneys available for assigned cases. These rosters are compiled in various ways. Generally, assigned counsel need do no more than put their names on a list to be appointed to cases. There is no review of their experience, qualifications, or competence. Some states, particularly those with organized plans administered by an independent manager, may require specific training before attorneys can be included on the roster. In Maine, all attorneys in the local bar are included on the roster unless they choose to be removed.[78] Assigned counsel generally are paid either a flat fee or an hourly rate, in some cases subject to an overall fee cap. Many are paid at very low rates, such that only recent law school graduates or those who were previously unsuccessful in the business of law will agree to take assignments.[79]

Contract attorney programs are another way to provide defense services. A state, a county, or a judicial district will enter into a contract for the provision of indigent representation. These contracts can be awarded to a solo attorney, a law firm that handles both indigent and private cases, a nonprofit organization, or a group of lawyers who joined together to provide services under the contract. The parties may agree to accept cases on a fixed-fee per case basis or to provide representation for a particular period of time for a fixed fee.

Fixed-fee contracts specify the total amount of compensation the lawyer will receive for work on all cases taken during a specified period of time. The contractor must accept all cases that come up during the duration of the contract. For this reason, they are viewed by some as quick fixes that allow the funding body to limit costs and accurately project expenses for the coming year. However, such contracts have been criticized severely by the courts and national organizations like the American Bar Association because to make a profit, the contracting attorney has to spend as little time as possible on each case. Few states rely on them to provide representation for all or even a majority of their indigent defense cases. Instead, they are more commonly used to handle public defender overload or conflicts. Sometimes, a public defenders office also will contract out a specific category of cases, such as juvenile or traffic offenses. Of the total amount spent on indigent criminal defense in the nation's one hundred largest counties, only 6 percent was spent on contract programs.[80]

Regardless of the model used by a county or state, all depend on adequate funding to successfully provide "effective assistance of counsel." Inadequate funding leads to lawyers carrying impossible caseloads. Over-

Local Focus: Phoenix's Flat Fees and the Death Penalty

You know you're in trouble when you're facing the death penalty and your lawyer would rather go to jail himself than work on your case. In the late 1990s, Phoenix attorney Mike Terribile represented convicted murderer Richard Rivas, but as the case entered the sentencing phase, he refused to do any more work. The reason? Terribile said the flat fee he had received from Maricopa County to handle the case as a contract attorney was not enough to cover his costs. He appealed the payment contract to a judge, saying he would refuse to prepare Rivas's defense if he was turned down, even if that meant being held in contempt and jailed.

As in many jurisdictions, the Maricopa County Public Defender's Office simply can't handle all the indigent cases they receive. To alleviate the problem, the county contracts with private attorneys to handle the overflow. The county generally pays about $64,000 for a set of eight cases. Maricopa County administrator David Smith says that's plenty. "If a case settles with just a few hours' work, they [still] get the $8,000," Smith says. He says that there is a provision in the contract that allows for extra compensation if a case gets complicated, but notes that 97 percent of the cases in the county are plea-bargained out. "We expect that it will all even out."

Terribile, who once chaired a statewide indigent-defense committee, said he hadn't taken on any more county cases, and he's not alone in refusing the work. Inadequate defense is a major reason why the American Bar Association has called for a death penalty moratorium. "You go to any death penalty state and start asking questions about counsel in those cases and, with very few exceptions, there are substantial problems," says Tye Hunter, of North Carolina's Indigent Defense Services Commission.

Source: Adapted from Alan Greenblatt, *Governing* magazine, March 2001. www.governing.com/archive/2001/mar/glimpses.txt (accessed May 28, 2004).

burdened lawyers make crucial decisions based on too little fact investigation and inevitably pressure clients to plead guilty.[81] Many indigent defense systems are plagued by lack of funding and resources, high attorney workloads, and little or no oversight over quality of services—problems that could result in the conviction of innocent people.[82] "Providing genuinely adequate counsel for poor defendants would require a substantial infusion of money and indigent defense is the last thing the populace will voluntarily direct its tax dollars to fund," writes attorney David Cole. "Achieving solutions to this problem through the political process is a pipe dream." [83]

Yet how secure would you feel if you were wrongly accused of a felony in Virginia, where your appointed lawyer could be paid only $395 to defend you? If you don't plead guilty quickly, your lawyer will lose money on your case. Recently, a wave of successful lawsuits by groups like the American Civil Liberties Union against underfunded and overburdened public defenders, assigned counsel programs, and contract attorneys have led legislators to enact reforms that "even the most skeptical observers admit have the potential to bring important changes to the process of criminal justice." [84] Some of these have led to successful injunctions or settlements, increased funding for indigent defense, and improved administration of such programs.[85] Furthermore, the defense community and organizations like the American Bar Association have been focusing on the need for standards for indigent criminal representation. The goal is to educate those policymakers who design the systems by which these legal services are delivered.

Juries

If you vote, pay a utility bill, or drive you may be called to jury duty at some point in your life. You may be asked to decide whether a defendant in a capital case lives or dies; whether someone spends the rest of his or her life in prison; whether a civil plaintiff, injured and unable to work, should be able to collect damages; or whether a civil defendant must be bankrupted by the large amount of damages ordered to be paid. Service on a jury may require spending days or weeks listening to intricate scientific evidence and expert testimony, listening to conflicting testimony, and deciding who is credible and who is not to be believed. Or, you may spend one day in a large room with other potential jurors, break for lunch, and go home at the end of that day without ever hearing a single case.

The right to a jury trial in state criminal proceedings is granted by the Sixth Amendment. Not all criminal prosecutions trigger the right to a jury trial—minor offenses involving a potential sentence of less than six months do not require juries. Neither do juvenile proceedings, probation revocation proceedings, or military trials.

The jury's role in a trial is that of fact-finder. The judge has to ensure a fair and orderly trial, but it is the jurors who must determine the facts of the case. In some instances, parties may agree to forego a jury trial and instead choose a bench trial in which the judge serves as both judge and jury. In a criminal bench trial, the judge alone decides guilt or innocence.

Differences and similarities in how judges and juries rule have been the subject of much research and review. Standard stereotypes might lead one to think that juries would be less able to separate emotion from reason than judges, or that they would decide cases more generously for injured plaintiffs and that grisly evidence in criminal cases may motivate them to decide based on passion or prejudice. Not so. For instance, research shows that civil plaintiffs in product **liability** and medical malpractice cases have more success before judges in bench trials.[86]

LIABILITY

A legal obligation or responsibility.

Historically, juries have been composed of twelve people who must come to a unanimous verdict. Since 1970, however, a series of U.S. Supreme Court decisions has allowed states to move away from this standard.[87] In state jury trials, whether unanimity is required depends on the size of the jury. A conviction by a twelve-member jury may be less than unanimous, whereas a six-member jury must have unanimity. A majority of states continue to require twelve-member juries to make unanimous rulings in felony criminal cases, but seven states use six-member or eight-member juries for noncapital felonies. Two states, Louisiana and Oregon, do not require a unanimous verdict in such cases.[88] Most states provide for civil juries of six members or eight members. Those that still require twelve members typically allow parties to agree to smaller juries. Unanimity is not required in most civil trials—instead, most states provide for verdicts based on a supermajority of either five-sixths or two-thirds.

States develop and maintain master lists from which they identify potential jurors. Their sources include driver's licenses, motor vehicle registrations, telephone directories, tax rolls, utility customer lists, voter registrations, and lists of actual voters. It is very hard to avoid ever being called in for jury duty. Jurors must be residents of the county in which the court sits and must generally be eighteen years old, although in Alabama and Nebraska the minimum age is nineteen and in Mississippi and Missouri it is twenty-one. States also usually have some sort of requirement regarding literacy and the ability to understand or communicate in English, or both. South Carolina requires at least a sixth-grade education, and Tennessee explicitly excludes those of "unsound mind" and "habitual drunkards." Most states also require that jurors not be convicted felons.

> Standard stereotypes might lead one to think that juries would be less able to separate emotion from reason than judges. . . . Not so. Research shows that civil plaintiffs in product liability and medical malpractice cases have more success before judges in bench trials.

The provisions for selecting a juror typically are the same for all the trial courts within a state, although some make distinctions between limited and general jurisdiction courts. The formal process of jury selection begins with a *voir dire* examination. This is the process by which prospective jurors are interviewed and examined. Some may be excused following a challenge by one of the attorneys in the case. The primary purpose of this is to impanel, or select, an impartial jury. If it appears during the questioning that a particular juror is biased or has a particular view of the case, that juror may be stricken **for cause**. There is no limit on the number of challenges a party can make for cause. In addition, each party receives a certain number of **peremptory challenges**, meaning the lawyers can kick off jurors for any reason other than race or gender.

Defendants' Rights vs. Victims' Rights

Crime typically involves at least two actors: a perpetrator and a victim. Traditionally, the criminal justice system in the United States interposes the ideal of public prosecution between the two. That is, all crimes are crimes against the state. The prosecutor, representing the public and not any particular individual, sees that justice is done objectively and fairly. The public's interest, under this system, is distinct from the victim's interest in retribution.

VOIR DIRE
The interviewing and examination of potential jurors.

FOR CAUSE CHALLENGE
Occurs when a lawyer asks the judge to excuse a potential juror because the individual appears to be biased or unable to be fair.

PEREMPTORY CHALLENGES
Used by lawyers to dismiss potential jurors for any reason except race or gender.

Numerous provisions in the Bill of Rights balance the rights of criminal defendants against the powers of the state. These "defendants' rights" include:

- the right to be presumed innocent until proven guilty,
- the right to be safe from arrest or searches and seizures unless the government has made a showing of probable cause,
- the right to a lawyer,
- the right to a jury trial,
- the right to confront witnesses,
- the rights to due process and the equal protection of laws, and
- if proven guilty, the right to punishment that is not cruel and unusual.

The Framers' concerns in creating these rights were of overreaching government power. They worried that innocent people otherwise might be railroaded into jail on charges they never had a chance to adequately defend themselves against. There is no mention of the rights of crime victims.

In the last two decades, this balance has undergone a radical transformation. Defendants still have all of the rights listed, but now state courts are increasingly balancing them against a new class of victims' rights. The movement advocating an increasing role for the victims of crime has become a formidable force and has achieved tremendous success in enacting legislation in all the states. The momentum started in 1982, when a president's task force on victims of crime described the United States justice system as "appallingly out of balance." That is not to say that victims were helpless—the number of state laws addressing victims' rights was already in the hundreds. By 1998, however, the number of crime victim-related statutes had soared to more than twenty-seven thousand. Twenty-nine states had passed victims' rights constitutional amendments.[89]

Today, every state has either a constitutional amendment or a statutory scheme that protects victims' rights. Some predict that the next amendment to the U.S. Constitution will be a victims' rights amendment. Supporters frequently argue that the justice system favors defendants over victims and that, without modification, the system itself constitutes a second victimization. On the other hand, civil rights organizations fear that some victims' rights laws upset the system of checks and balances in the nation's criminal justice system and undercut the basic due process protections designed to keep innocent people out of prison.

The specifics of victims' rights laws vary among the states. A variety of statutes or amendments guarantee that crime victims receive monetary compensation, notice of procedural developments in the case, protection from offender harm, and more attentive treatment from the justice system. The more controversial of such laws are directed toward providing victims with a significantly greater involvement in the actual prosecutions. This includes providing victims the right to confer with the prosecutor at all stages, including plea bargains; the right to attend all stages of the case, even if the victim will be called as a witness; and the right to introduce victim impact statements at the sentencing phase of the trial.

Perhaps the most controversial and interesting of the victims' rights laws concern victim impact evidence. This may be particularly true in capital cases in which impact statements have been described as

> highly emotional, frequently tearful testimony coming directly from the hearts and mouths of the survivors left behind by killings. And it arrives at the precise time when the balance is at its most delicate and the stakes are highest—when jurors are poised to make the visceral decision of whether the offender lives or dies.[90]

In 1991, the U.S. Supreme Court reversed itself and ruled that impact statements that detailed the particular qualities of the victim and the harm caused to the victim's family could be admissible in capital sentencing hearings.[91] Today, all states allow victims' impact evidence at the sentencing phase of the trial. Most of the states with the death penalty allow it in capital trials.

Sentencing

The state prison population has ballooned in the last twenty years, from less than 320,000 in 1980 to a total of two million today.[92] Corrections has been one of the fastest growing items in state budgets and averaged 7 percent of state budgets by 2000.[93] In most states, the judge holds a separate sentencing hearing after the jury finds the defendant guilty. In capital cases, the Supreme Court has held that only a unanimous jury, and not the judge, can sentence a defendant to death.[94] Thirteen states have provisions for a sentence of life without parole if the jury is unable to reach agreement.[95] In noncapital cases, by contrast, it is almost always the judge who sets sentence. Only in Arkansas, Missouri, Texas, and Virginia does the jury choose the sentence. In all states but Texas, the judge is free to disregard the jury's decision.

Sentencing policy involves the balancing of value judgments, such as the perceived severity of the crimes and the perceived severity of different punishments, with the relevance of mitigating circumstances. It must include considerations of the costs to taxpayers and to society of incarceration. Surveys indicate that attitudes on sentencing follow regional patterns, "with residents of New England demonstrating the greatest tendency to be lenient and residents of central southern states displaying the least leniency." [96] It is not surprising then that state sentencing laws vary and that the punishment a convict faces depends not just on what that person did but also on where the crime was committed. Voters in California and Oklahoma, for instance, view drug offenses differently. In California state courts, a cocaine dealer is subject to a two-year to four-year prison term. The same offense in Oklahoma brings a minimum of five years and a maximum of life imprisonment.[97]

The amount of discretion given to judges also varies from state to state. Depending on the type of crime or where the defendant is charged, the sentence can be a matter of "do the crime, do the time" or whatever the judge or parole board thinks is best.

A few decades ago, it was possible to talk of a predominant American approach to criminal sentencing. At all levels of the nation's criminal justice system, a concern for rehabilitation and deterrence led states to embrace **indeterminate sentencing**. Legislatures set very wide statutory sentencing margins within which judges had the discretion to impose sentence for imprisonment with little fear of appellate review. The sentence was indeterminate because the parole board, not the judge, had ultimate control over the actual release date. Under this system, the discretion of judges and parole boards was necessary to tailor punishment to the specific rehabilitative needs of the individual defendant. This practice led to wide discrepancies in the sentences imposed for those convicted of the same crime.

Indeterminate sentencing came under attack from several angles during the 1970s. The lack of guidance for judges led to the potential for discrimination in sentencing based on such factors as race, ethnic group, social status, or gender. There was also criticism of the ability of parole boards to successfully determine whether inmates had or had not been rehabilitated. Finally, rehabilitation lost favor as the country entered an era of tough-on-crime rhetoric and a "just desserts" theory of criminal sentencing.[98] Sentencing reform sought to replace indeterminate sentencing with **determinate sentencing**. This led to the adoption of federal sentencing guidelines—a structured system of binding sentencing rules that greatly limited judicial discretion in sentencing in the federal courts.

In contrast to the federal court system, there has been no single sweeping sentencing reform across all fifty states. Some states have made wholesale changes to determinate sentencing laws, but most continue to use indeterminate sentencing.[99]

Yet indeterminate sentencing does not necessarily mean more lenient sentencing. It just means that the actual amount of time served may vary depending on the judge or the findings of a parole board. For instance, before the charges were dropped, Los Angeles Lakers star Kobe Bryant was charged with felony sexual assault in Colorado. The sex offense statutes there are considered among the harshest in the country. Any sentence on a sex assault charge can mean the possibility of life imprisonment. In part, the severity of the sentence depends on the results of a battery of tests. These results are used by judges in sentencing and by parole boards to determine if the prisoner is a continued threat. They include plethismograph tests, which involve placing an electric band around the

INDETERMINATE SENTENCING

The judge sentences an offender to a minimum and a maximum time in prison. A parole board decides how long the offender actually will remain in prison.

DETERMINATE SENTENCING

The judge sentences an offender to serve a specific amount of time in prison depending on the crime.

penis in an attempt to measure deviant thoughts as the person is shown images of abusive behaviors. Described as "very Clockwork Orangish" by Don Recht, former head of the Colorado Defense Bar, the results are studied carefully nonetheless. Under Colorado's indeterminate sentencing, a convicted sex offender is released only when deemed safe to reenter society.

Most states still rely on indeterminate sentencing, but all states have adopted at least some features of determinate sentencing, although in greatly differing degrees. When it comes to sentencing reform, "the states have served as hothouses of experimentation during the last thirty years, with so much activity that the diversity of provisions among the states has become exceedingly complex." [100] Some of the major reforms adopted include sentencing guidelines, **mandatory minimum sentences** that are imposed for conviction of specified crimes, **habitual offender laws**, and **truth-in-sentencing laws**. With the implementation of these reforms, the time served in prison has been increasing as a percentage of the sentence imposed. In 1993, the percentage of a sentence an offender spent in prison was 31.8 percent; that percentage had increased to 43.8 percent by 1999.[101]

All fifty states and the District of Columbia have enacted some form of mandatory minimum prison sentencing.[102] These laws limit judicial discretion by requiring that individuals guilty of specific crimes must go to jail no less than a specified length of time. Such crimes include drug possession or trafficking, drunk driving, or sexual offenses. The mandatory sentencing laws also may take effect if certain acts enhanced the severity of the underlying crime, for instance, if weapons were involved. If a crime involved the use of a deadly weapon, New Mexico requires an additional year for the first offense or three additional years for a second offense. Use of a firearm to commit a crime in Nevada requires a doubling of the sentence for the underlying crime. In Ohio, use of a deadly weapon requires an additional term of three to six years.[103]

Habitual offender laws also are common among the states. These statutes impose more severe sentences for offenders who previously have been sentenced for crimes. California's "three-strikes" law was a prototype of this kind of legislation. The law states that if a defendant convicted of a felony has one prior conviction for a "serious" or "violent" felony, the sentence is doubled. Defendants convicted for a felony with two prior convictions for "serious" or "violent" felonies receive a life sentence without possibility of parole. The law has been severely criticized for its "unbending harshness," but has withstood constitutional challenges.[104] Twenty-four states have enacted some form of "two or three strikes" legislation. One such state is Michigan, in which the sentence is one and a half times the maximum sentence on the second conviction and twice the maximum sentence for a third conviction.[105]

MANDATORY MINIMUM SENTENCES

The shortest sentences that offenders may receive upon conviction for certain offenses. The court has no authority to impose a shorter sentence.

HABITUAL OFFENDER LAWS

These statutes impose harsher sentences for offenders who previously have been sentenced for crimes.

TRUTH-IN-SENTENCING LAWS

These laws give parole boards less authority to shorten sentences for good behavior by specifying the proportion of a sentence an offender must serve before becoming eligible for parole.

Another sentencing reform movement began in the 1990s. Known as truth-in-sentencing, these laws reduce the amount of discretion parole boards have to shorten sentences for good behavior. They do this by specifying the proportion of a sentence that offenders must serve before they may be considered for parole. Thirty-nine states have adopted some form of truth-in-sentencing laws.[106] Most, however, still have a parole board with some discretionary release authority and a system in which the incarcerated felons can accumulate "good time" under a specified formula. Arkansas, Louisiana, Vermont, and Wyoming are among the many states that provide for a day of "good time" for each day—or less—served. North Dakota grants five days of "good time" for every month served.

These formulas also can be complicated by the accumulation of work or education credits. Some states, like Illinois, have cut through the confusion by eliminating the good time credit for certain serious offenses. Others have eliminated it altogether. Michigan eliminated the concept of good time for all felony offenses committed after December 2000, and the District of Columbia has not offered it since 1994.[107]

As states reduce judges' discretion and increase time spent in prison, a considerable burden has been placed on the facilities and personnel of the prison system. In response to this, most states are exploring sentencing options for their less serious offenders that are less severe than imprisonment but more serious than ordinary probation.[108] One such option is house arrest. This requires the offenders to remain in their residences for the duration of their sentences. They often are required to wear electronic bracelets around the wrist or ankle that send a continuous radio signal to verify their location.

Many states rely on "intensive probation." This form of probation involves much closer supervision by parole officers with smaller caseloads than the norm. Parolees under these programs typically are required to hold a job, submit to urinalysis, pay restitution to victims, and perform community service. To alleviate prison overcrowding, some states release prisoners to "halfway" houses that assist with reintegration into the community. Young first-time offenders may be sentenced to "boot camps" for shorter periods and submitted to strict military discipline. Nonviolent offenders may be offered work release; weekend sentencing; alcohol, drug, or mental health treatment; or release subject to appearance at daily reporting centers.

Problems from the Lack of Sentencing Uniformity

Since the 1970s, sentencing reform movements have concerned themselves more and more with the sentencing disparities that occur when judges and parole boards have broad discretion in the sentencing of criminal offenders. Many states felt pressure to reform sentencing, but how they responded varies substantially. State sentencing guidelines, adopted by a minority of states, are not as rigid as new federal guidelines. State judges also tend to have more discretion than federal judges.

A parallel trend in criminal law has involved the increased federalization of crimes that were once the sole domain of the states. Many street crimes, such as low-level gun and drug offenses, are now federal offenses. Law enforcement officials have the choice of sending such cases to federal or state prosecutors and courts, and the cases are subject to the differing sets of sentencing guidelines. The trend away from discretion in sentencing has led to some uniformity nationwide in sentencing in federal courts. Ironically, however, the federal sentencing guidelines and the increased federalization of local crimes have increased the sense of randomness in sentencing within communities. Whether an offender is charged in state court or federal court for the same offense can lead to huge disparities in the sentence.

Nationwide, drug and weapons violations result in sentences that are an average of three times longer in federal courts than in state courts.[109] In some cases, the essentially random chance of being charged in federal court can lead to a death penalty, even where local voters have twice rejected capital punishment, as in the District of Columbia. In some areas, prosecutors have been suspected of "shopping" for either a state or federal trial depending on the race of the offender. In a region of Massachusetts in the late 1990s, white crack dealers were tried exclusively in state courts, whereas many black dealers were tried in federal courts.[110] When two members of the same community, who do the exact same thing, are subjected to drastically different treatment, it undermines confidence that justice is being done. This was one of the concerns that led to the passage of sentencing reforms in the first place.

The Case for Court Reform

How state courts are organized is not static or carved in stone. States constantly evaluate practices and modify procedures to adapt to demographic, economic, and political conditions. This section discusses some reforms being adopted or at least being discussed in most states. Specialized courts to handle drug offenses or family matters are currently in vogue to accommodate increasing caseloads, as are attempts to streamline and speed up court dockets. Given the controversy surrounding judicial elections, discussed in detail earlier, many states aren't waiting for major reforms to merit selection but instead are focusing on modifying elections to minimize the problems posed by the need for campaign contributions. Finally, this section addresses some of the pressures to reform that stem from the lack of uniformity across the country and within individual states.

The Problem of Increasing Caseload

Nationwide, violent crime rates are down. State courts nonetheless have found themselves on the frontlines dealing with the results of societal problems such as substance abuse and family violence since the 1980s. From 1984 to 1999, the U.S. population grew by only 12 percent. The number of juvenile cases grew by 68 percent during the same period, and the number of domestic relations cases grew by 74 percent. Criminal cases, mostly misdemeanors, grew by 47 percent.[111]

In reaction to such growth, many states have created "problem-solving courts." These include community courts, domestic violence courts, mental health courts, and drug treatment courts. Their purpose is to deal decisively with low-level nonviolent crimes. The solutions often involve closely monitored treatment plans meant to stop the revolving door of **recidivism**, or relapses into criminal behavior. Drug courts, with their focus on treatment for nonviolent drug-addicted offenders, contribute to the decline in violent crimes and save local and state governments millions of dollars annually from reduced incarceration rates.

States also have been experimenting with integrated family courts. These courts adopt a holistic approach to all the issues that affect a single family in a single court system. Such integrated courts can address issues more efficiently, especially in cases in which delays can leave children in foster care limbo. Many individuals who appear in such family courts traditionally have been forced instead to face multiple proceedings in multiple courts: assault in county courts, custody disputes in family courts, divorce issues in yet another court. The current trend is to put all of a family's problems before a single, informed judge to eliminate conflicting orders and multiple appearances. New York, with a pilot Integrated Domestic Violence Court, estimates that the court has slashed the number of cases from more than three thousand to less than nine hundred, reducing delay and duplication and increasing cost-effective case management.[112]

This increased focus on court administration and case management has not been confined to the criminal side of the court calendar. Until just a few years ago, crowded civil dockets and multiyear waiting periods were relatively common in many states. "Back in the 1980s, there was no incentive for an insurance company to settle a case for the first year," said Bill Sieben, who was then president of the Minnesota Trial Lawyers Association. "They knew the case wasn't even going to be nearing a trial for several years."[113] This is becoming less and less true as states focus on clearing their overcrowded and overly cumbersome civil dockets. Tom Phillips, former chief justice of the Texas Supreme Court, attributes faster-clearing caseloads primarily to the rise of the managerial judge.[114] Most trial judges may insist on a strong case-management system, but a generation ago, when caseloads were smaller and more manageable, not many of them did.

In recent years, not content with merely handing down verdicts, forceful judges have seized control of their courts and made it clear that things will

Since 2003, North Dakota has been one of twenty-eight states that, along with the District of Columbia, provides e-filing tools to those submitting materials to the courts.

run according to their schedules, not at the convenience of lawyers who never seem quite ready to go to trial. "A very strong component of civil cases is, just set a trial date and the case will go away," said Kevin Burke, formerly the chief judge of the Hennepin County Court in Minnesota. "Left to their own devices, lawyers aren't necessarily going to manage it to a speedy resolution."[115]

State initiatives to speed up dockets, or court case schedules, have included an increased reliance on **alternative dispute resolution**. In certain types of cases such resolutions now are mandated, and lawyers are required to inform their clients about alternatives to standard court fights. These alternatives usually involve hashing things out in front of an expert mediator. Some courts have been creative in finding appropriately authoritative experts. Hennepin County courts, for instance, refer dry cleaning disputes—stained pants, torn dresses, and busted buttons—to a retired owner of a dry cleaning business for speedy resolution. An accountant may resolve a financial dispute. These innovations increase the efficiency of the court system and free up trial judges for more complex cases.

Several states are experimenting with a **rocket docket** patterned after an innovation in a Virginia federal court. In essence, these fast-track dockets impose tight, unbending deadlines on lawyers in the handling of pre-trial motions and briefs. At the Vermont Supreme Court, the rocket docket applies to cases that present no novel issue likely to add to the body of case law. Rather than all five justices sitting *en banc* to hear these cases, each month they split and rotate through a smaller and less cumbersome panel of three that is able to reach consensus more quickly. The panel releases its decisions within twenty-four hours in 99 percent of the cases.

In Colorado, rapid population growth has led to mounting lawsuits, and courts increasingly have turned to **magistrates** to resolve less important cases. Often a local official or attorney hired on contract, these magistrates have helped the state to stay on top of an 85 percent increase in case filings despite only a 12 percent increase in the number of judges. The magistrates issue preliminary decisions that must then be upheld by a judge, but this is a formality in most cases. This modification is credited with enabling more routine cases to be handled efficiently and allowing more time for more complex cases, but some have complained to the Colorado bar that this reliance on contract attorneys to serve as magistrates decreases the accountability of the judges and does not yield sufficiently clear precedent to provide guidance to the attorneys who must practice before them.[116]

The Reform of Judicial Selection

Nationally, 87 percent of all state judges face partisan, nonpartisan, or retention elections or some mix of the above.[117] As discussed earlier, the trend in recent years has been for these elections to become more and more like elections for legislative and gubernatorial offices—loud, nasty, and

ALTERNATIVE DISPUTE RESOLUTION

A way to end a disagreement by means other than litigation. It usually involves the appointment of a mediator to preside over a meeting between the parties.

ROCKET DOCKET

Fast-track cases that often have limited, specific deadlines for specific court procedures.

MAGISTRATES

Local officials or attorneys granted limited judicial powers.

expensive. Some fear that this will lead to a blurring of the distinction between the judicial and political branches of government and throw into question the independent decision making of the judiciary.

Indeed, the U.S. Supreme Court's decision in *Republican Party of Minnesota v. White* (2002) may have brought politics closer than ever to the judicial elections process. A 5–4 majority ruled that the First Amendment did not allow the government "to prohibit candidates from communicating relevant information to voters during an election." This includes judicial candidates who wish to speak publicly about disputed legal matters. At the same time, the Court acknowledged the core responsibility of judges to "be willing to consider views that oppose [their] preconceptions, and remain open to persuasion when the issues arise in a pending case." Today, states that hold elections for judicial offices, such as Ohio, Pennsylvania, and Wisconsin, feature public debates among judicial candidates similar to those held for candidates for legislative office.

> Nationally, 87 percent of all state judges face partisan, nonpartisan, or retention elections or some mix of the above. The trend in recent years has been for these elections to become more and more like elections for legislative and gubernatorial offices—loud, nasty, and expensive.

The major reform movement of the latter half of the twentieth century was the merit selection of judges described previously. This movement initially was very successful but, after being adopted by roughly half the states, has stalled in recent years. Since 1990, all of the legislatures that have considered merit selection have rejected it. States seeking to adopt merit selection face both cultural and political obstacles. They face an ingrained cultural belief that elections are a critical part of our democracy not to be sacrificed without a fight. Combined with this is the political reality that in most states change to merit selection would require the legislative supermajority and public approval necessary for constitutional change.

Recognizing these barriers to adopting merit selection, reformers are focusing on improving popular elections to minimize the threat they pose to judicial independence and impartiality. For example, the unprecedented level of interest group activity in judicial elections has led to recommendations to require the disclosure of campaign contributions. This is an area with First Amendment implications that forces states to tread very carefully. Some states focus their reforms on the dangers inherent in campaign financing and are experimenting with public financing of judicial campaigns. They hope that this will reduce the potential of campaign contributions to influence or to create the appearance of influencing outcomes. In Wisconsin, revenue to publicly fund the campaigns of state supreme court candidates comes from a $1 state tax return check-off. In 2004, North Carolina became the first state to provide full public financing of elections for appeals court and supreme court candidates who accept spending limits.

Conclusion

State and local courts play a profound role in their state governments. They resolve civil disputes and hand out justice in criminal cases. They also protect the citizens of their states from unconstitutional behavior by the political branches of government. Despite the importance of this role, or perhaps because of it, judicial systems differ tremendously from state to state. There are organizational differences from initial trial to final appeal. Judges in some states are elected by voters and in others are appointed by the governor. Such differences reflect a state's unique orientation towards the values of politics, law, judicial independence, and accountability.

The focus in this chapter has been on the players involved as a case works its way through the judicial system. In a criminal case, the elected prosecutor has tremendous freedom to decide what charges to bring against an accused criminal. Anyone charged with crimes has the right to an attorney, and the state must provide attorneys to those unable to afford their own. Usually a public defender takes the case. If a plea bargain is not reached, the case goes to trial, and the fate of the accused rests in the hands of a panel of ordinary citizens who were called to jury duty. Potential jurors are selected from a pool of individuals who may have done something as simple as paying a utility bill. This does not mean, however, that there is anything simple about a jury's task. Often, this group holds the future of another individual in its hands.

If found guilty and sentenced to incarceration, the length of time an offender actually spends in jail depends a lot on how the values of rehabilitation, deterrence, and retribution have played out in a particular state's political system. Differences here can have enormous impact. One state may try a nonviolent drug offender in a special drug court that focuses on treatment. Another may try the same offense in a general trial court in which the judge has no choice except lengthy incarceration under rigid minimum sentencing guidelines.

None of the choices states make in structuring their courts are fixed and unchanging. States are always responding to altered societal or political realities, experimenting with what works, and adapting to political movements. Some of the areas of reform and change looked at in this chapter were triggered by the political rise of victims' rights movements, by the realities of changing caseloads, or by a perception that the selection of judges has become increasingly political.

Key Concepts

activist judge (p. 274)

alternative dispute resolution (p. 321)

appeal (p. 278)

assigned counsel (p. 308)

bench trials (p. 279)

civil cases (p. 278)

contract attorneys (p. 308)

court of first instance (p. 279)

criminal cases (p. 278)

determinate sentencing (p. 316)

discretionary jurisdiction (p. 284)

en banc (p. 284)

felony (p. 307)

for cause challenge (p. 313)

general jurisdiction trial courts (p. 281)

grand jury (p. 306)

habitual offender laws (p. 317)

indeterminate sentencing (p. 316)

indictment (p. 306)

intermediate appellate court (p. 279)

jury nullification (p. 306)

legislative over-criminalization (p. 306)

liability (p. 312)

limited, or special jurisdiction,
  trial courts (p. 281)

magistrates (p. 321)

mandatory jurisdiction (p. 284)

mandatory minimum sentences (p. 317)

misdemeanor (p. 307)

panels (p. 284)

peremptory challenges (p. 313)

plea bargain (p. 278)

precedent (p. 279)

prejudicial error (p. 281)

prosecutor (p. 303)

public defender (p. 304)

pure appointive systems (p. 293)

recidivism (p. 320)

Suggested Readings

Brace, Paul, and Melinda Gann Hall. "Studying Courts Comparatively: The View from the American States." *Political Research Quarterly* 48 (March 1995): 5–29. This study examines how politics and methods of judicial selection effect capital punishment decisions in state supreme courts. The authors conclude that party affiliation and whether judges are elected has an impact on how death penalty cases are decided.

Carp, Robert A., Ronald Stidham, and Kenneth Manning. *Judicial Process in America,* 7th ed. Washington D.C.: CQ Press, 2007. A comprehensive look at the state and federal court systems in the United States. Covers the foundations, history, organization, and processes of U.S. courts as well as other issues like policy implementation and judicial decision making.

Rottman, David, et al. *State Court Organization 1998* Washington, D.C.: Bureau of Justice Statistics, 2000. A basic overview of how the fifty states organize their state court systems. Includes everything from qualification requirements to selection methods to the number of courts and full-time judges serving in a state.

Ware, Steven. "Money, Politics and Judicial Decisions: A Case Study of Arbitration Law in Alabama." *Journal of Law and Politics* 15 (1999): 645. This article presents the results of a study of 106 decisions by the Alabama Supreme Court from January 18, 1995, through July 9, 1999. The study shows the correlation between campaign funding and judicial rulings.

Suggested Web Sites

www.abanet.org. Web site of the American Bar Association, the largest voluntary professional association in the world, with a membership of more than 400,000.

www.ajs.org. Web site of the American Judicature Society, a nonpartisan organization with a national membership that works to maintain the independence and integrity of the courts and increase public understanding of the justice system.

www.JusticeatStake.org. Web site of the Justice at Stake Campaign, a nonpartisan effort working to keep courts fair and impartial.

www.ncsconline.org. Web site of the National Center for State Courts, an independent non-profit organization that assists court officials to better serve the public.

retention elections (p. 293)

rocket docket (p. 321)

settlement (p. 278)

state supreme court (p. 279)

trial court (p. 278)

truth-in-sentencing laws (p. 317)

voir dire (p. 313)

www.ojp.usdoj.gov/bjs. Web site for the Bureau of Justice Statistics that includes information and statistics on a variety of areas, including courts, sentencing, crimes, and victims.

CHAPTER 9

Bureaucracy

What Nobody Wants but Everybody Needs

A Zamboni is not what usually springs to mind when you mention bureaucracy. Public agencies, however, come in many shapes and forms, including parks and recreation departments that are responsible for maintaining hockey rinks. Publicly run hockey rinks, believe it or not, fit right into the formal definition of a bureaucracy.

9

Why do we have so much bureaucracy?

How good—or bad—of a job does it really do?

How does technology enable more efficient and effective bureaucracy?

For Avigayil Wardein, setting up a lemonade stand was a way to earn a little pocket money and maybe learn a few business basics. She earned a little pocket money all right, but ended up learning more about bureaucracy than business.

In summer 2003, the six-year-old set up shop at the end of her mom's driveway in Naples, Florida. She quickly began attracting business from thirsty passersby. Within days, however, the police arrived to shut Avigayil down. In Naples, city regulations require a permit for all temporary businesses. Avigayil had not gone to the appropriate agency, filled out the necessary forms, and paid the required $35 permit fee. Since this temporary business permit expires as soon as a vendor shuts down for the day, complying with the rules meant Avigayil was faced with paying $35 a day to satisfy city hall bureaucracy. That was five dollars more than her record daily take.

A public agency ensnaring a six-year-old's lemonade stand in red tape and demanding a daily thirty-five bucks as the price of staying open? One more example, as if we needed it, of everything that is wrong with government bureaucracy, right? Bureaucracy is overbearing, interfering, and a needless complication in citizens' lives, right?

Wrong. In this story, bureaucracy turns out to be more the understanding hero than the heartless villain. Avigayil's lemonade stand was temporarily shut down as the result of a citizen complaint. A neighbor had called city hall and protested the illegal operation of a business. Technically, the complaint was accurate, and the city was legally obligated to respond. An officer was duly dispatched to shut down Avigayil, although he bought a glass of lemonade and was mostly apologetic about the whole process. The city then gave Avigayil a fistful of daily permits—more than enough to keep her business legal for the summer—and waived the fees. She was back in business.[1]

The permits are actually a reasonable rule. They are not designed to shut down lemonade stands run by entrepreneurial elementary school students, but rather to control temporary vendors like hotdog stands. Left unregulated, the latter could operate anywhere at any time, creating the potential for traffic problems, neighborhood nuisances, and unscrupulous business practices. Avigayil's story highlights bureaucracy's paradoxical nature. On the one hand, it does mean rules and red tape that are inconvenient at best and defy common sense at worst. Yet bureaucracy does not produce or enforce these rules just for kicks. Like it or not there are good reasons for the rules, and someone wants the bureaucracy to enforce them.

Bureaucracy represents what is perhaps the political system's greatest contradiction. We do not particularly like it, yet we seem unable to live without it. Like a trip to the dentist, bureaucracy often is inconvenient, involves too much paperwork, and can result in a certain amount of pain. Ultimately, however, it turns out to be good for us.

This chapter explores this workhorse of the U.S. political system—the state and local bureaucracies that implement and manage most public programs and services. We will try to understand what bureaucracy is and why it plays such an important role. Most important, we will try to use the comparative method to arrive at some explanation of why the American political system has so much bureaucracy when many citizens seem to value it so little.

What Is Bureaucracy?

For our purposes, **bureaucracy** is the public agencies and the public programs and services these agencies implement and manage. Thus, **bureaucrats** are simply the employees of the public agencies. These agencies—generically known as government bureaucracies—usually are located in the executive branches of state and local governments. Although these agencies are very different in terms of the programs and services they manage and deliver, the vast majority of them are organizationally very similar. There is a specific set of organizational characteristics associated with bureaucracy:

BUREAUCRACY

Public agencies and the programs and services they implement and manage.

BUREAUCRATS

Employees of public agencies.

Division of labor. Labor is divided according to task and function. Most large bureaucracies, for example, have separate technical, personnel, and financial specialists.

Hierarchy. There is a clear vertical chain of command. Authority is concentrated at the top and flows down from superiors to subordinates.

Formal rules. Bureaucracies are impartial rather than impulsive. They operate on the basis of rationally formulated guidelines and standardized operating procedures.

Maintenance of files and records. Bureaucracies record their actions.

Professionalization. Employees of bureaucratic organizations get their jobs on the basis of qualification and merit.[2]

PROFESSIONALIZATION

Bureaucratic employees earn their jobs based on qualifications and merit.

Virtually all large, complex organizations have these characteristics, not just government agencies. General Motors (GM) and IBM have these characteristics and can thus be considered bureaucratic organizations, even though they are private companies. What separates a public bureaucracy like the Department of Motor Vehicles or the local school district from a private bureaucracy like IBM is a difference in goals. In the end, what separates public bureaucracies from private bureaucracies is not what they are, but what they do.

What Does Bureaucracy Do?

Public bureaucracies play two fundamental roles in state and local political systems. First, they are the key administrators in the democratic process. They are charged with carrying out the decisions and instructions of elected public officials. This is the central focus of the academic discipline of public administration. Their second role is more controversial. Bureaucracies not only carry out the decisions of the democratic process, as it turns out, they have a fairly important say in what those decisions are.

Bureaucracy as Policy Implementer

POLICY IMPLEMENTATION

The process of taking the expressed wishes of government and translating them into action.

The first job of bureaucracy is to be the active manifestation of the will of the state. This is just a fancy way of saying that bureaucracy does what the government wants or needs done.[3] The whole process is known as **policy implementation**. Agencies implement policy by issuing grants and contracts, enforcing laws and regulations, or undertaking and managing programs directly. For example, when elected officials decide to build a new road, they do not adjourn the legislature to go survey land, drive bulldozers, and lay asphalt. It is a public agency that negotiates to buy and survey the land. It is the agency that either issues the contracts to build the road or takes on the job of construction using its own employees and equipment. This is what makes private and public bureaucracy different: IBM and GM exist to make money, whereas public agencies exist to serve the public interest by turning the decisions of elected officials into concrete reality.

It is a job staggering in its scope and complexity. Citizens ask government for a lot: roads, education, health benefits, safe drinking water, parks, reliable power grids ... the list is virtually endless. Governments respond by passing laws that create programs or policies, which then must be put into action and then managed or enforced. Governments respond, in other words, with bureaucracy. State and local bureaucracies manage not only state and local programs, but federal programs as well. The federal government relies on state and local agencies to implement the vast majority of its welfare, education, and highway programs.[4]

In their roles as implementers, managers, and enforcers, state and local government bureaucracies shape the day-to-day lives of citizens more than any other part of government.[5] The single largest form of bureaucracy in the United States is a fundamental part of virtually every community: public schools. Employing more than three million teachers, public schools serve almost fifty million students and have a combined budget of $388 billion.[6]

Other public agencies regulate and set licensing requirements for professions ranging from lawyers to bartenders. Think of the need to ensure that professionals are qualified to deliver the services they sell. Look around at all the public libraries, swimming pools, and parks that offer recreational and educational opportunities at little or no cost. Think of programs for garbage removal, law enforcement, and fire protection. From the barber who is licensed to cut our hair to the street sweeper who is hired to clean the paths we walk, bureaucracy literally covers us from our heads to our toes.

Inside Erie County, New York, there are: three cities, twenty-five towns, sixteen villages, twenty-eight school districts, and almost one thousand special fire, sewer, and lighting districts.

Bureaucracy as Policymaker

The second fundamental role of the bureaucracy is more controversial than its job as the government's agent of implementation. Public bureaucracies not only help translate the will of a government into action, in many instances they actually determine the will of the government. Put bluntly, bureaucracies do not just do policy—they also make it.[7] They do this in at least three different ways.

The first way is through what has been called the power of the street-level bureaucrat. **Street-level bureaucrats** are the lower-level public employees who actually take the actions that represent government law or policy. In many cases, street-level bureaucrats have the discretion, or ability, to make choices about what actions they do or do not take. In making these choices, they are essentially making policy. For example, the street-level bureaucrat associated with speed limits is the traffic cop. This public employee is actually on the highway with a radar gun making certain that motorists abide by the speed limits specified by state or local law. The legislature may have passed a law setting a maximum highway speed of sixty-five miles per hour, but if the traffic cop decides to go after only those motorists doing seventy-five miles per hour or faster, what really is the speed limit that motorists must obey? And who has set that limit? Arguably, it is not the legislature, but rather the street-level bureaucrat.[8]

This is not to suggest that street-level bureaucrats are power hungry tyrants. In many cases they have no choice but to make choices. On a road on which speeding is common, it may be impossible to stop every leadfoot. Does it not make more sense to concentrate on the most flagrant offenders who pose the most risks? Street-level bureaucrats have to balance the goals, laws, and regulations relevant to their agencies with the practical demands of the day-to-day situations they deal with. That often means making, not just implementing, policy.

STREET-LEVEL BUREAUCRATS

Lower-level public agency employees who actually take the actions that represent law or policy.

> From the barber who is licensed to cut our hair to the street sweeper who is hired to clean the paths we walk, bureaucracy literally covers us from our heads to our toes.

The second way in which bureaucracies make policy is through rulemaking. **Rulemaking** is the process by which laws or mandates approved by legislatures are turned into detailed written instructions on what public agencies will or will not do.[9] Rules are necessary because most laws passed by legislatures express intention. They do not specify the details of how to make that intention a reality. For example, the Nebraska state legislature created the Nebraska Games and Parks Commission to enforce a number of laws relating to hunting, fishing, wildlife preservation, and boating. The details of enforcing those laws—such as setting permit fees, determining bag limits for particular types of fish, and designating no-wake zones on lakes—are rules established by the commission rather than laws passed by the legislature. This makes sense. The legislature would quickly become bogged down if it had to delve into the myriad details that must be addressed to put a public program into action. These details are left to individual agencies.

Once a rule is approved, it typically becomes part of a state's administrative code, which is the bureaucratic equivalent of state statutes. These rules have the force of law—violate them and you could face fines. Just ask anyone who has ever been caught fishing without a license. Given this, rules are not left to the discretion of the street-level bureaucrat. Most state agencies have to follow a well-defined process for making rules. This process includes seeking input from agency experts, holding public hearings, and perhaps, listening to special interests. The Nebraska Games and Parks Commission is required to give public notice of any intention to create a rule and must hold a public hearing to allow interested parties to have their say. If this sounds a lot like the process of making laws in a legislature, it is. Rulemaking is probably the most important political activity of bureaucracy. In effect, it is a large lawmaking operation that most citizens do not even know exists.

Finally, bureaucracies also contribute to policymaking directly by pursuing political agendas. Street-level discretion and rulemaking are passive policymaking—in the sense that they involve bureaucrats responding or not responding to something such as a speeding car or a newly signed bill. Yet bureaucracies and bureaucrats also take *active* roles in politics. This is done in a number of ways. At the state and local level, the heads of many public agencies are elected. Such positions include everything from county sheriff to state attorney

Cutting Red Tape? Most people do not associate barbers or beauticians with bureaucracy. Yet most barbers must be licensed and regulated by state and/or local government.

general. As elected officials, these agency heads often make campaign promises, and once in office they try to get their agencies to deliver on them.

The visibility and importance of these elected state and local agency heads have increased with the rise of New Federalism. They now are widely recognized as critical players in the process of policy formulation, not just policy implementation.[10] Therefore, some agencies will be the tools used to deliver on a political agenda. It is also true that other bureaucrats, not just elected agency heads, try to influence policy. As shall be seen a little later, unions are powerful political actors in many states, lobbying for better pay and benefits and getting actively involved in election campaigns.

The implementation and political roles of bureaucracy make it a particular target for citizen concern and, at times, scorn. It is easy to see that we need some bureaucracy. Somebody has to manage all those programs and services we want from government. Yet government bureaucracy has a terrible reputation for inefficiency, incompetence, and mismanagement.[11] Many question whether we have too much bureaucracy, and still others are concerned about the powerful political role of what are mostly unelected officials. Why do we have so much bureaucracy? How good of a job does it really do? Could we not get by with less of it? Is there no better way to run public programs and services? Is there too much bureaucracy and too little democracy in state and local government? These are reasonable questions that the comparative method can help answer.

What Is "Enough" Bureaucracy?

Most people believe that whatever its merits, there is too much bureaucracy in government and in our lives. Undeniably, state and local government have a lot of bureaucracy. How much? Some insight into the size and scope of state and local agencies can be gleaned from Table 9-1, which lists the number of employees on state and local government payrolls by function. Combined, state and local governments have more than eighteen million full-time and part-time employees. Most of these—approximately thirteen million versus five million—are employees of local rather than state government. Local or state, the vast majority of these individuals work in what we would recognize as a bureaucracy.

The numbers contained in Table 9-1 confirm that there are a lot of state and local bureaucrats, but numbers alone give little insight into whether there is too much or too little bureaucracy. In reality, the size of the bureaucracy and the extent of its role in the day-to-day life of any given individual vary from state to state and locality to locality for two main reasons. First, in each locality, citizens make different kinds of demands on each state and local government agency. Some localities will need more of one particular resource, whereas others will need less. In Eden Prairie, Minnesota, the public will demand more cross-country ski trails, and in Yuma, Arizona, they

TABLE 9-1

State and Local Government Employment by Function

Function	Total Individuals (in thousands)	State Government (in thousands)	Local Government (in thousands)
Elementary and secondary education	7,480	64	7,416
Higher education	2,804	2,248	555
Hospitals	985	428	556
Police protection	962	106	856
Corrections	713	464	250
Streets and highways	569	249	320
Public welfare	532	234	298
Other government administration	454	60	394
Electric power and gas supply	92	4	88
Judicial and legal	432	164	268
Financial administration	423	173	250
Fire protection	394	0	394
Natural resources	208	164	44
Social insurance	93	93	0
State liquor stores	9	9	0
Other	2,499	583	1,917
All functions	18,649	5,043	13,606

Source: U.S. Census Bureau. *Statistical Abstract of the United States: 2006.*

will need more public swimming pools. As a result, the size and role of the public sector can vary significantly from place to place—more demand equals more bureaucracy.

Second, there is no universally agreed upon yardstick to measure what constitutes a "reasonably" sized bureaucracy. Where one person sees a bloated public sector over-regulating citizens' lives, a second sees the same set of agencies providing important public goods and services. At the very least, to compare the size of bureaucracy across states and localities we need to explore not just the total number of public employees, but also the size of a specific public sector relative to the size of the public it serves. Table 9-2 shows one way to do this. It lists the states with the five largest and the five smallest bureaucracies as measured by the number of government employees per every ten thousand citizens.

By this measure, the mostly large, urban, and populous states have the *smallest* bureaucracies. More rural, less populous states, conversely, have the *largest* bureaucracies. How can this be? Why would North Dakota have more bureaucracy than California? The answer is actually pretty simple. Fewer people do not necessarily mean less demand on government. Even the most rural state still needs an educational system, roads, and law enforcement. These are all labor-intensive propositions. Indeed, they may be even more labor intensive in rural states. For example, to serve a widely dispersed population, an educational system either has to build lots of small schools or figure out a way to transport lots of students over considerable distances to a smaller number of large schools. More urban, densely populated states can take advantage of the economies of scale that come with centralized locations. Basically, less bureaucracy is needed when the citizens being served are close by.

The same tale is told by using expenditures—in this case, the amount of money states spent for services—to measure the size of bureaucracy. Two of the five states with the largest bureaucracies as measured by number of employees—Alaska and Hawaii—also have the largest bureaucracies in terms of per capita expenditure. (See Table 9-3.) Not coincidentally, they are also the only noncontiguous states—Alaska neighbors Canada rather than the United States, and Hawaii is an island chain in the Pacific. Geographic isolation requires these states to do more for themselves, which means more bureaucracy.

Expenditures and employees tell us something about the size of the bureaucracy, but they do not tell us much about its influence or power over the daily lives of citizens. An undermanned bureaucracy with a small budget still can have considerable impact on the interests of an individual. If you have ever spent time in a university financial aid office, you probably already understand the point here—when people complain about bureaucracy being too big, they often mean the red tape and rules that come with it, not its budget or payroll. For the number of forms you fill out at the financial aid office, you may feel that the bureaucracy owes you a free meal, but there is only so much money in the pot. It is very easy to recognize this sort of thing as a central part of bureaucracy. It is very hard to measure it objectively. Lacking good measures of "red tape" or "rules" makes it hard to make comparisons. If there are no comparative measures, it is harder to use the comparative method to help show why some bureaucracies have more influence than others.

Despite this, there is little doubt that public bureaucracies in large, urban areas probably do have a more powerful role in the day-to-day lives of citizens than those in less populous rural areas. Why? It is not because bureau-

TABLE 9-2

States with the Most and the Least Bureaucracy by Number of Employees

State	State Employees (per 10,000 citizens)
Top Five	
Hawaii	460
Alaska	383
Delaware	299
North Dakota	285
New Mexico	247
Bottom Five	
Illinois	106
California	110
Florida	110
Nevada	110
Arizona	117

Source: U.S. Census Bureau. *Statistical Abstract of the United States: 2006.*

TABLE 9-3

States with the Most and the Least Bureaucracy by Expenditures

State	State and Local Expenditures (per capita)
Top Five	
Alaska	$13,172
New York	8,453
Wyoming	7,722
Connecticut	6,996
Hawaii	6,691
Bottom Five	
Arizona	4,641
Arkansas	4,829
New Hampshire	4,979
Tennessee	5,000
Idaho	5,066

Source: U.S. Census Bureau. *Statistical Abstract of the United States: 2006.*

cracy is more power hungry in cities, but rather because more concentrated populations require more rules. Building codes are more critical in urban areas because of the associated fire safety and health risks—a problem with one building can pose risks for those working or living in surrounding buildings. Building regulations thus tend to be more detailed, and enforcement of these rules tends to be a higher priority, in urban than in rural areas. In this sense, urban areas do have more bureaucracy than rural areas.

Measuring Bureaucratic Effectiveness: It Does a Better Job than You Think

So far, our application of the comparative method has given us a sense of how big bureaucracy is and why it is so big—because characteristics such as urbanization and geography result in different demands being placed on government. These different demands translate into different sized public agencies with varying levels of involvement in our day-to-day lives. What the comparative method has not told us is what sort of job public agencies do. The widespread belief is that they are, at best, mediocre managers of public programs and services.[12] Although this negative stereotype is held by many, for the most part it is wrong. Public agencies, as it turns out, are very good at what they do.

How good? Well, in many cases at least as good as, if not better than, their private sector counterparts. The assumption is that the private sector is more efficient and more effective than the public sector; however, numerous studies find this is based more on stereotypes than facts.[13] For example, in the early 1990s, officials in Fort Lauderdale, Florida, decided to shut down the city's pipe-laying operation and instead have the private sector bid on municipal pipe-laying jobs. The idea was to save the city money by getting competitive private sector bids and eliminating an entire public bureaucracy. A study undertaken by city engineers found that in-house costs for laying pipe were between $68 and $73 per linear foot. Much to everyone's surprise, the initial private sector bids were up to $130 per linear foot. The city undertook an extensive reorganization of its pipe-laying operations and managed to drop its costs to $43 per linear foot. The private sector responded by cutting its bids in half, into the $50 to $60 range. Even after these dramatic reductions, however, the private sector still could not do the job as cheaply as the "inefficient" public bureaucracy. More recently, audits of Florida and Texas's social service programs revealed that the millions of dollars in savings promised as a result of out-sourcing had failed to materialize.

This not only shows that the public sector can be as cost-effective and efficient as the private sector, it also provides a cautionary tale about the downside of the profit motive. It turns out that the private sector is quite willing to feed at the public trough to fatten its bottom line.[14] There is not much glamour associated with laying utilities, filling potholes, and running public transportation systems, but these are highly valued public services that consume a lot of tax dollars. And contrary to popular perception, public bureaucracies provide these services efficiently and spend these dollars effectively.

It is not just about overall performance. Public agencies come out equal to or better than the private sector on a wide range of employee characteristics used to identify an effective organization. Public and private sector employees are roughly equal in terms of their job motivation, their work habits, and their overall competence. Compared to the private sector, however, public employees tend to have higher levels of education, express a greater commitment toward civic duty and public service, abide by more stringent codes of ethical behavior, and be more committed to helping other people.[15] Various studies show that over the past thirty years state and local agencies have become more productive and more professional, and they have done so during an era when they have shouldered an increasing share of the burden for delivering programs and services from the federal government.[16]

There *is* wide variation between and within the states on how well public bureaucracies are managed. Good management has an enormous impact on the capacities and effectiveness of programs and agencies. States that engage in prudent, long-range fiscal planning are better positioned to deal with economic downturns, and they generally can deliver programs more efficiently. States that do a better job of attracting qualified employees with a strong commitment to public service almost certainly are going to be rewarded with more effective public agencies. States that make training their employees a priority are likely to enjoy similar benefits. The bottom line is that well-managed public agencies lower costs and improve results, whereas the reverse is true for badly managed agencies.[17]

Bureaucracies Put to the Test: Who Passes and Who Fails and Why

Which states and localities have the best run public agencies? The Government Performance Project (GPP) has devoted considerable resources to this question. A joint undertaking of the Pew Charitable Trusts, *Governing* magazine, and academic partners, the GPP holds state and local governments publicly accountable for the quality of management within their jurisdictions.[18] It does this by researching management practices and performances in four areas: money, people, infrastructure (roads, bridges, and construction), and information (how states gather, analyze, disseminate, and use information). The GPP then issues grades for performance in each

A Difference that Makes a Difference:
When the Government Performance Project Talks, Governors Listen

In 2003, Nevada was awarded the dubious distinction of having the worst state tax system in the country, according to a Government Performance Project report, published in *Governing* magazine. The so-called silver state—nicknamed for its silver mines—did few things well when it came to taxes, the vast majority of which were levied on sales and gaming. The system didn't generate enough revenue, was deemed regressive and unfair, and couldn't be adequately administered with the state's existing policies and technology. Nevada earned just one lousy star out of four possible stars for each of these three basic functions. Contrast that evaluation with the magazine's judgment of Hawaii, which received the highest rating for fairness and three of four possible stars in adequacy of revenue.

For Nevada, the report bolstered Gov. Kenny Guinn's push for an overhaul of the state's tax system. Although the legislature didn't enact Guinn's exact vision—he called for $1.1 billion in tax increases—later that year, the state House and Senate did approve an $836 million package that instituted state payroll taxes and real estate sales and raised alcohol and cigarette taxes.

For Alabama, also a one-star state, the road to reform was bumpier—and longer. Its rigid tax code, written into the state constitution, made it next to impossible to change the structure of the system, which provided nowhere near enough revenue to keep the state operating smoothly. What's more, the system was highly regressive, levying income taxes for a family of four beginning at just $4,600, nearly $15,000 below the federal poverty line.

Republican Gov. Bob Riley was new to his office when the report was issued, but he quickly began advocating for a massive $1.2 billion tax reform package. His plan would have reduced taxes for many of the state's poorest residents; however, it was overwhelmingly rejected by a two-to-one margin. The failure didn't deter Riley, who continued to tell whoever would listen about the "immorality" of the state's tax system. In 2006, he returned with a new, smaller tax reform package. This time, the state legislature agreed with the proposal and raised the state income threshold for a family of four to $12,600, the first time it had been raised since 1935. The cut would save Alabamians $60 million a year, with workers earning $20,000 or less annually receiving the bulk of the benefit. No one earning more than $100,000 would be eligible for the tax break.

As Riley was signing the bill into law, he was already gearing up for the next round in his tax fight: he plans to push the tax threshold even higher, to $18,000 for a family of four.

Sources: Adapted from Katherine Barrett and Richard Greene, Michele Mariani and Anya Sostek, "The Way We Tax," *Governing* magazine, February 2003; Sean Whaley and Jane Ann Morri, "Guinn Signs Record Tax Increase," *Las Vegas Review-Journal*, July 23, 2003; and David White, "Riley Signs Low-Income Tax Cut into Law," *Birmingham News*, April 13, 2006.

area (see box on this page). The result is an administrative report card for state and local governments, which is essentially an index of the relative performance of bureaucracy.

Table 9-4 shows the most recent grades issued to the states. The grades show that most state governments are doing at least an acceptable job, but that some are clearly doing better than others. These are differences that make a real difference. The quality of public schools and roads, and even the quality of the air we breathe, is dependent in no small measure on the effectiveness of public bureaucracies.[19] States with better-run bureaucracies provide the best and most effective services and make the most efficient use of taxpayer dollars.

Why are some state and local bureaucracies run better than others? Why does California rate a C-minus, whereas Virginia rates an A-minus? The answers to these questions are found not in the bureaucracy but rather in the broader political environment of the states. Ultimately, legislatures and governors are responsible for bureaucratic performance. This is not only because they set the laws that control personnel, management, and training practices. Their decisions on a wide range of policy issues have tremendous consequences even for a smoothly running agency. The most obvious example is budgets. States have gone through an extreme boom and bust cycle during the past ten years, with economic good times of the 1990s followed by a fiscal crisis shortly after the turn of the century. Some states practiced good fiscal management, with legislatures that resisted the temptation to spend excessively and enact large tax cuts. As the economy soured, these states also acted quickly to stabilize revenues.

Other states—like California—did the opposite. These states increased spending during the 1990s and then tried to put off the day of reckoning with creative accounting practices and by dipping into one-time revenue sources. The end result for California was a fiscal crisis that rocked the public sector, leaving it underfunded, understaffed, and a little shell-shocked—not exactly the ingredients for smoothly running public programs. The comparative method shows us that it is the states that avoided big tax cuts in the 1990s, states with divided governments in which the governor is from one party and the legislature is controlled by another, and states with powerful governors that are the states that spend less, have better financial management, and have public agencies with higher grades.[20]

> The real surprise is not that some bureaucracies are ineffective or poorly run, but that the vast majority of them, most of the time, manage to more or less serve the public interest. And they do so in spite of democratic institutions rather than because of them.

Many of the faults attributed to public bureaucracies actually can be traced to legislatures, which give agencies conflicting and confusing missions and often do not provide adequate resources to fulfill these missions. It is the legislatures that demand what is politically expedient, not what is effective or efficient, and then roundly and repeatedly criticize bureaucracy for not performing well. The real surprise is not that some bureaucracies are ineffective or poorly run, but that the vast majority of them, most of the time, manage to more or less serve the public interest. And they do so in spite of democratic institutions rather than because of them. At least one professional student of bureaucracy has suggested than any objective view of the joint performance of bureaucracy and representative democracy would lead to the conclusion that what we need is more bureaucracy and less democracy![21]

TABLE 9-4

Government Performance Project, Grades at a Glance, 2005

State	Money	People	Infrastructure	Information	Average Grade
Alabama	C	C+	D	C	C–
Alaska	C	C+	C+	C	C+
Arizona	B	B	B–	B–	B
Arkansas	B–	C	C+	C+	C+
California	D	C–	C	C	C–
Colorado	C–	C+	C+	C+	C+
Connecticut	C	B	C+	C–	C+
Delaware	A	B–	B+	B	B+
Florida	C+	B–	B+	B	B–
Georgia	B–	A	C+	B–	B
Hawaii	C	B	C–	D	C
Idaho	B+	B	C+	C+	B–
Illinois	B	C	C+	C+	C+
Indiana	C	C	B–	C	C+
Iowa	B+	B	B	B	B
Kansas	B+	B–	B–	B–	B
Kentucky	B+	B	B+	B	B+
Louisiana	B+	B	C+	A–	B
Maine	B–	B–	B	C+	B–
Maryland	B	B–	A–	C+	B
Massachusetts	C+	C+	C–	C+	C+
Michigan	B	B	B+	B+	B+
Minnesota	A–	B+	B	B+	B+
Mississippi	B–	C+	C+	C+	C+
Missouri	B	B–	B–	A–	B
Montana	C+	C+	B–	C	C+
Nebraska	B+	B–	B+	C+	B
Nevada	C+	C+	B+	B–	B–
New Hampshire	C	C+	C+	C–	C
New Jersey	C+	B	B–	C	B–
New Mexico	B	C+	D+	B	C+
New York	C+	B–	B+	C+	B–
North Carolina	B–	C+	C+	C+	C+
North Dakota	B–	B–	B–	C	B–

TABLE 9-4, continued

State	Money	People	Infrastructure	Information	Average Grade
Ohio	B+	B–	A–	C+	B
Oklahoma	B–	B–	C–	C	C+
Oregon	D	B–	B	B	C+
Pennsylvania	B+	B–	B+	B	B
Rhode Island	C+	D+	B–	C+	C+
South Carolina	B+	A–	C+	B	B
South Dakota	B+	B–	B	D	B–
Tennessee	B–	C–	B–	C+	C+
Texas	B	B	B–	B	B
Utah	A	B+	A	A–	A–
Vermont	B+	B	B–	B–	B
Virginia	A	A–	A–	A–	A–
Washington	A–	B+	B	A–	B+
West Virginia	B–	C	C	C+	C+
Wisconsin	B–	B	C	B–	B–
Wyoming	B	D+	C	C	C

Source: *Governing* magazine, February 2005.

That sentiment has taken real shape in some states in the form of increased performance auditing designed to improve the efficiency and effectiveness of government programs. "That's where you find out if money is being spent the way it is supposed to, or whether you're getting the most bang for the buck," says former Colorado state representative Brad Young.[22]

Past perceptions of auditors pegged them as glorified bean counters, but in some states, their independent reports carry significant weight. California's nonpartisan Legislative Analyst's Office has served as a model for other states,[23] and strong legislative support kept Florida's Office of Program Policy Analysis and Government Accountability operating despite multiple efforts by Gov. Jeb Bush to downsize the office.[24] In Washington State, even citizens see the benefits of performance audits: voters there approved a 2005 ballot initiative that increased the state auditor's authority to study state and local agency performance.

Is There a Better Way to Run Public Programs and Services?

Looking at bureaucracy comparatively, we learn how big it really is, why it is so big, and how well it performs. But is a traditional bureaucracy really the best way to run public programs and services? Do we really need less democracy and more bureaucracy? Do we really need eighteen million people on state and local government payrolls? The short answer is no. Public services and programs could be delivered through competitive bidding to the private sector. Public agencies could be staffed and run by political party loyalists or special interest supporters. Things could be done differently. Before abandoning the traditional public bureaucracy, however, it is worth considering why public agencies are so, well, bureaucratic.

Remember the key characteristics of bureaucratic organizations listed earlier? These turn out to be important advantages when it comes to running public programs and services. For one thing, bureaucracies tend to be impartial because they operate using formal rules, not partisan preference, bribes, or arbitrary judgment. If you need some form of license or permit, if your shop is subject to some form of environmental or business regulation, or if you are trying to receive benefits from a public program, it does not matter to the bureaucracy if you are rich or poor, liberal or conservative, an influential high roller or an average citizen. What matters to the bureaucracy are the rules that define the application process, eligibility, and delivery of the necessary service or program. Following bureaucratic rules can be maddening, but these rules do help ensure that public agencies are more or less impartial.

The bureaucratic characteristics of hierarchy and record keeping help hold public agencies accountable. Public agencies are expected to be answerable for their actions. They have to justify why they did what they did to legislatures, executives, the courts, and citizens.[25] An action at a lower level of bureaucracy almost always can be appealed to a higher level. Students at most colleges and universities, for example, can appeal their grades. In such appeals the bureaucrat responsible for issuing the grade—the instructor—is expected to justify to the appeals board and the dean why the grade represents a fair and reasonable application of the rules of the class and the grading policies of the university. Setting rules, requiring records, and setting up a clear chain of authority help ensure that bureaucrats and bureaucracies do not exceed their authority or act unfairly. If they do, these same factors provide a means for holding the bureaucrat or bureaucracy accountable.

Professionalization is another bureaucratic characteristic that is desirable in public agencies because it promotes competence and expertise. To get a job in most state and local bureaucracies, what you know is more important than who you know. Getting a job as a professor at a state university requires a specific set of professional qualifications. The same is true for an elementary school teacher, an accountant at the Department of Revenue, or a subway operator. Of course, setting and enforcing such qualifications as the basis for employment and promotion means another set of rules and regulations. These qualifications also help ensure that merit rather than partisan loyalty, family connections, or political influence is the basis for getting public sector employment. And as can be seen from Figure 9-1, there is a lot going on in the typical state bureaucracy—too much to be worrying about someone not being up to doing the job.

FIGURE 9-1 How It Works: Virginia's Bureaucracy: For This, You Get an A–

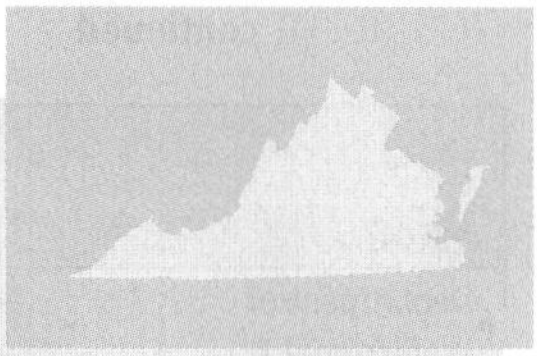

The Commonwealth of Virginia receives gold stars for its bureaucracy—it was one of the two top-ranked states (Utah was the other) in the most recent ratings conducted by *Governing* magazine's Government Performance Project. What puts Virginia at the top of the class? "There is little that Virginia does not do well in government management," the authors reported. "[I]t keeps looking for improvements, and very often finds them. . . . Virginia has an ethos of good management that has genuinely been institutionalized."* Part of that institution is the practice of holding the more than one hundred cabinet members and agency heads accountable to formal "executive agreements." These are reviewed by the governor and outline clear, measurable goals for each agency against which their performances are appraised. Public, yearly assessments of each agency are available online.

These scorecards evaluate performance in human resource management, government procurement, financial management, technology, performance management, and resource stewardship. In effect, this is an assessment of those agencies' leaders and their subordinates. This table shows only a portion of the scorecard for Virginia's executive agencies for 2007 and includes ratings for agencies in the Offices of Administration, Commerce and Trade, Education, Finance, and Health and Human Services. Overall, twenty-six of the sixty-five rated agencies met expectations in every category, nineteen were rated as needing to make progress in one area, and eighteen were rated as needing to make progress in two or more areas. No agencies were rated as operating below expectations.

Virginia's Executive Branch Agencies 2007 Scorecard

Legend:

● = Meets Expectations   ● = Progress toward Expectations   ● = Below Expectations   ● = Results Unavailable

Agency	Secretariat	Human Resource Management	Government Procurement	Financial Management	Technology	Performance Management	Resource Stewardship
Compensation Board	Administration	●	●	●	●	●	●
Department of Charitable Gaming	Administration	●	●	●	●	●	●
Department of Employment Dispute Resolution	Administration	●	●	●	●	●	●
Department of General Services	Administration	●	●	●	●	●	●
Department of Human Resource Management	Administration	●	●	●	●	●	●
Department of Minority Business Enterprise	Administration	●	●	●	●	●	●
State Board of Elections	Administration	●	●	●	●	●	●
Board of Accountancy	Commerce and Trade	●	●	●	●	●	●
Department of Business Assistance	Commerce and Trade	●	●	●	●	●	●
Department of Housing & Community Development	Commerce and Trade	●	●	●	●	●	●
Department of Labor & Industry	Commerce and Trade	●	●	●	●	●	●
Department of Mines, Minerals & Energy	Commerce and Trade	●	●	●	●	●	●

FIGURE 9-1, continued

Agency	Secretariat	Human Resource Management	Government Procurement	Financial Management	Technology	Performance Management	Resource Stewardship
Department of Professional & Occupational Regulation	Commerce and Trade	●	●	●	●	●	●
Virginia Economic Development Partnership	Commerce and Trade	●	●	●	●	●	●
Virginia Employment Commission	Commerce and Trade	●	●	●	●	●	●
Virginia Racing Commission	Commerce and Trade	●	●	●	●	●	●
Virginia Tourism Authority	Commerce and Trade	●	●	●	●	●	●
Department of Education	Education	●	●	●	●	●	●
Direct Aid to Public Education	Education	●	●	●	●	●	●
Roanoke Higher Education Authority	Education	●	●	●	●	●	●
Southern Virginia Higher Education Center	Education	●	●	●	●	●	●
Southwest Virginia Higher Education Center	Education	●	●	●	●	●	●
State Council of Higher Education for Virginia	Education	●	●	●	●	●	●
The Library of Virginia	Education	●	●	●	●	●	●
Virginia Commission for the Arts	Education	●	●	●	●	●	●
Virginia Museum of Fine Arts	Education	●	●	●	●	●	●
Department of Accounts	Finance	●	●	●	●	●	●
Department of Planning and Budget	Finance	●	●	●	●	●	●
Department of Taxation	Finance	●	●	●	●	●	●
Department of the Treasury	Finance	●	●	●	●	●	●
Comprehensive Services for At-Risk Youth and Families	Health & Human Resources	●	●	●	●	●	●
Department for the Aging	Health & Human Resources	●	●	●	●	●	●
Department for the Blind & Vision Impaired	Health & Human Resources	●	●	●	●	●	●
Department for the Deaf & Hard-of-Hearing	Health & Human Resources	●	●	●	●	●	●
Department of Health	Health & Human Resources	●	●	●	●	●	●

FIGURE 9-1, continued

Agency	Secretariat	Human Resource Management	Government Procurement	Financial Management	Technology	Performance Management	Resource Stewardship
Department of Health Professions	Health & Human Resources	●	●	●	●	●	●
Department of Medical Assistance Services	Health & Human Resources	●	●	●	●	●	●
Department of Mental Health, Mental Retardation, & Substance Abuse Services	Health & Human Resources	●	●	●	●	●	●
Department of Rehabilitative Services	Health & Human Resources	●	●	●	●	●	●
Department of Social Services	Health & Human Resources	●	●	●	●	●	●
Virginia Board for People with Disabilities	Health & Human Resources	●	●	●	●	●	●

Sources: Commonwealth of Virginia, "Organization of State Government," www.commonwealth.virginia.gov/StateGovernment/StateOrgChart/OrgChart2006-2007.pdf; "Virginia Performs: Management Scorecard Results, 2007," www.vaperforms.virginia.gov/agencylevel/src/ScoreCardResults.cfm. Both sites accessed March 26, 2007.

*Katharine Barrett and Richard Greene, "Grading the States, 2005," *Governing* magazine. www.governing.com/archive/2005/feb/gp5state.txt. (accessed March 27, 2007).

The great irony of public bureaucracy is that the very characteristics that help ensure neutrality, fairness, and accountability also produce the things that people dislike about it: red tape and inefficiency. Formal rules help guarantee equity and fairness but—as anyone who has spent time filling out forms and waiting in line can attest—they can be a pain. Enforcing rules, or "going by the book," may mean bureaucracy is fair, but it is not particularly flexible. Treating everyone the same is an advantage from an equity standpoint, but the fact is, not everyone *is* the same. Surely there are ways to make bureaucracy more responsive to the individual? Well, yes, there are. But the history of bureaucratic reform in the United States suggests that the cures are often worse than the problem. Although going through this history is not a particularly comparative exercise, it is necessary in order to understand why bureaucracy is the way it is.

The Transformation of State Bureaucracy: From Patronage to Professionalism

Public agencies have undergone a remarkably radical transformation during the past century. They have become more professionalized, more organized, and more able to shoulder a large share of the political system's responsibilities.

For much of the early history of the United States there was little in the way of state and local bureaucracy. State and local government functions we now take for granted, such as public schools, libraries, and fire protection, were left largely to the private sector. In most cases, this meant they did not exist at all or were available only to those who could afford them. Public education is the single largest public program undertaken by state and local governments. Yet public education in the contemporary sense did not exist until the last half of the nineteenth century, roughly a hundred years after the nation's founding. As the nation grew, however, so did the demands on government. Roads needed to be built, commerce regulated, streets cleaned, and crime curtailed. Taxes had to be collected to make all this happen. There was no centralized plan to expand public bureaucracy—it evolved in fits and starts as governments took on the jobs citizens wanted done.

At the federal level, staffing bureaucracy was initially a job for which only the educated elite were considered qualified. This example often was followed at the state and local levels. Public service was seen as an obligation of the aristocratic class of a community or state. This "gentlemen's" system of administration was swept away following the election of Andrew Jackson to the presidency in 1828.

SPOILS SYSTEM

The right of an electoral winner to decide who works for public agencies.

PATRONAGE

The process of giving government jobs to partisan loyalists.

Jackson believed in the **spoils system**, that is, the right of an electoral winner to control who worked for the government. The intent was to democratize government and make it more accountable by having regular citizens who supported the electoral winners run government agencies. This process of giving government jobs to partisan loyalists is called **patronage**.

Instead of producing a more democratic bureaucracy, the spoils system and patronage invited corruption. Following Jackson's example, the administrative arm of many state and local governments became a way for electoral winners to pay off political favors or reward partisan loyalty. Perhaps the most famous examples are the big city political "machines" that flourished well into the twentieth century and produced some of the most colorful characters ever to wield power in state and local politics. A political machine was an organization headed by a party committee or by a "boss." The committee or boss led a subset of ward or precinct leaders whose job it was to make sure voters in their district supported machine endorsed candidates. Supporters of the machine were in turn rewarded with government jobs and contracts. They also were often expected to contribute a set percentage of their salaries to the machine.[26] This created a well-regulated cycle, or machine—votes in one end, power and patronage out the other.

Machines dominated politics in many urban areas and even whole states in the nineteenth century and early twentieth century. They produced some of the most fascinating characters in U.S. political history: Boss Tweed of New York, Tom Pendergast of Kansas City, and Gene Talmadge of Georgia, to name just a few. These men wielded enormous power, aided in no small part by their ability to dole out government jobs and contracts. Some machines survived well into the twentieth century. Mayor Richard Daley of Chicago ran what many would recognize as a political machine well into the 1960s.

While the machines made for lively politics and brought almost unlimited power to their leaders, they were often corrupt. Machine politics meant that getting a government job was based on who you knew rather than what you knew. Job security only lasted as long as you kept in your political patron's good graces or until the next election. Understandably then, there was tremendous incentive to make the most of a government position. Kickbacks and bribery inevitably made their way into many state and local agencies.

The founders of the modern conception of government bureaucracy were progressive reformers of the late nineteenth and early twentieth centuries. They wanted a lasting solution to the gross dishonesty and inefficiency they saw in public administration. Toward this end, these reformers created a new philosophy. At its center was the idea that the administrative side of government needed to be more insulated from the political arena.[27] Reformers promoted the notion of **neutral competence,** the idea that public agencies should be impartial implementers of democratic decisions, not partisan extensions of whoever happened to win the election.

To achieve these ends, progressive reformers began to push for public agencies to adopt the formal characteristics of a bureaucratic organization. This was accomplished in no small part by lobbying for merit systems as an alternative to the spoils system. **Merit systems** are exactly that. They are systems in which jobs and promotions are earned on the basis of technical qualifications and demonstrated ability instead of given out as rewards for political loyalty. Merit systems also make it harder for public employees to be dismissed without due cause. This does not mean a guaranteed job. The idea is to create a system within which public employees can be fired only for failing to do their jobs and not because they missed a payment to a political boss. The overall goal was to make government bureaucracies less political and more professional.

The federal government shifted from the spoils system to the merit system in 1883 with the passage of the Pendleton Act. The main features of this merit system were: (1) competitive examination requirements for federal jobs; (2) security from political dismissals, meaning that people could not be fired simply because they belonged to the "wrong" party or supported the "wrong" candidate; and (3) protection from being coerced into political activities so that workers were no longer expected or required to contribute a portion of their salary to a political party or candidate. The

Political machines were powerful organizations that dominated many state and local governments for parts of the nineteenth and twentieth centuries. Their power was based on the ability to control government jobs, awarding these positions to supporters, or as the cartoon above suggests, to the highest bidder.

NEUTRAL COMPETENCE

The idea that public agencies should be impartial implementers of democratic decisions.

MERIT SYSTEMS

Systems in which employment and promotion in public agencies are based on qualifications and demonstrated ability, which blends very well with the organizational characteristics of bureaucracy.

basic principles of the merit system have since been expanded to include equal pay for equal work; recruitment, hiring, and promotion without regard to race, creed, national origin, religion, marital status, age, or disability; and protection from reprisal for lawful disclosure of lawbreaking, mismanagement, abuse of authority, or practices that endanger public health—so-called whistle-blower laws.

States and localities once again followed the example of the federal government and began shifting from spoils systems to merit systems. New York State was the first to do so, adopting a merit system in the same year that the Pendleton Act became law. In 1935, the federal Social Security Act made merit systems a requirement for related state agencies if they wished to receive federal grants. This stimulated another wave of merit-based reforms of state and local bureaucracies. By 1949, nearly half of the states had created merit-based civil service systems. Fifty years later, virtually all states and many municipalities had adopted merit systems. All of this helped professionalize state and local bureaucracies and turned what had been sinkholes of patronage and corruption or marginally competent good-old-boy networks into effective instruments of democratic policymaking.

Politics and the Merit System

Although using merit as the basis for public bureaucracy has effectively created agencies that are competent and professional, it has its drawbacks. Remember the two key roles of the bureaucracy—policy implementation and policymaking? Merit systems have positive and negative implications for both.

In some ways, merit-based bureaucracy is a victim of its own success. The whole idea of shifting to a merit system was to insulate public agencies and their employees from undue political influence. We want bureaucrats to work for the public interest, not for that of a party boss. We want bureaucrats to apply rules neutrally, not to interpret them through the lens of partisan prejudices. To a remarkable extent, merit systems have done exactly that. Rules are rules, and bureaucracies more or less competently and impartially enforce them regardless of which party controls the legislature or who sits in the governor's mansion. The merit system has undoubtedly been an enormous positive for the policy implementation role of bureaucracy.

The impact of merit systems on the policymaking, or political, role of bureaucracy is more open for debate. Merit systems did not eliminate the political role of the bureaucracy. They merely changed it. Under the spoils system, bureaucracy was an agent of a particular boss, party, or political agenda, and it favored the supporters of electoral winners. The merit system cut the connection between the ballot box and the bureaucracy. Distancing bureaucracy from elections, however, arguably makes it less accountable to the democratic process—a big concern if bureaucracy is policymaker as well as a policy implementer.

Once distanced from the ballot box, public agencies and public employees discovered their own political interests and began to pursue them with vigor. Organized interests outside the bureaucracy also began to realize that being able to influence lawmaking and, especially, rulemaking offered enormous political opportunities. All you have to do is get your favored policy written into the rules and bureaucracy will enforce it well beyond the next election. These sorts of developments raise serious questions about the drawbacks of merit systems. As examples of how these concerns play out in state and local agencies, let us consider two issues: public labor unions and affirmative action.

Public Labor Unions

Public sector labor unions are a relatively new political force. Unions were almost exclusively a private sector phenomenon until the 1960s. This changed in 1962 when President John F. Kennedy issued an executive order that recognized the right of federal employees to join unions and required federal agencies to recognize them. The 1960s and 1970s saw a considerable expansion in the number of state and local employees joining unions. Today, roughly three to four times as many public sector as private sector workers belong to unions.[28]

The reasons for the expansion in public sector union membership are not hard to fathom. For much of their history, public employees received lower wages than their private sector counterparts. Public employees also had limited input in regard to personnel decisions. Despite the merit system, many still saw favoritism and good-old-boy networks having too much influence in pay and promotion decisions. Public sector labor unions pushed for **collective bargaining,** a process in which representatives of labor and management meet to negotiate pay and benefits, job responsibilities, and working conditions. The vast majority of states allow at least some public unions to bargain collectively.

What should not be missed here is that the outcomes of collective bargaining are important policy decisions. They are decisions that the voter—and sometimes the legislator—has little say in. Negotiations about pay and benefits for public employees are, in a very real sense, negotiations about taxes. A raise won by a public employee represents a claim on the taxpayer's pocketbook. And it is a claim that is worked out not in an open democratic process, but often in closed-door negotiations.

It is not just money. Collective bargaining agreements can result in fairly complex rules about what public employees are and are not expected to do. Such rules reduce the flexibility of agency managers—who are constrained from redirecting personnel from their assigned jobs—and reduce the responsiveness of bureaucracy to legislatures and elected executives.

COLLECTIVE BARGAINING

A process in which representatives of labor and management meet to negotiate pay and benefits, job responsibilities, and working conditions.

Labor unions have given public employees more than just collective bargaining muscle, they also have started to do some heavy lifting in electoral politics. Unions able to deliver their members' votes can have a powerful say in who holds office. Understandably, people seeking public office pay attention to the policy preferences of public sector unions. By raising money, mobilizing voters, even running independent campaigns, unions exercise considerable political clout. Consider the Wisconsin Education Association Council (WEAC). Long recognized as an important political actor in the state, WEAC has a well-thought-out set of legislative goals and supports candidates accordingly.[29] It also spends its money strategically. In the 2003–2004 state election cycle WEAC made $62,639 in political campaign contributions. That made this teachers' union Wisconsin's fifth largest campaign spender. Only the Republican Party of Wisconsin and three other political action committees spent more.[30]

Unions can have enough political clout to shape how the merit system actually works. A basic principle of the merit system is that competence is supposed to be rewarded. Expertise and job performance are supposed to be the basis of promotion and pay increases. In contrast, unions tend to advocate **seniority**—the length of time spent in a position. Public employees with more experience may—and often do—deserve such rewards. Yet it is not always the most senior employee who is the most productive or contributes the most to an agency's success. Even in the absence of unions, seniority plays a considerable role in the pay and benefits of public employees. This is much to the chagrin of critics who view civil service protections as failing the public interest. For example, some critics view tenure at colleges and universities as a system that rewards laziness and allows "dead wood"—unproductive faculty members—to collect healthy paychecks.[31]

Unions are far from all bad—they have fought successfully for reasonable compensation packages and safer work environments for people who perform some of society's toughest, dirtiest, and most thankless jobs. In most instances, they support the merit system as long as it also protects seniority. And unions are far from incompatible with effectiveness and productivity. Comparative studies of student performance and the strength of teachers' unions have found that states with the strongest teachers' unions also tend to have the highest student achievement scores.

The pros and cons of unions can be debated, but there is no doubt that they have helped politicize the bureaucracy. It is a different sort of politics than the favoritism and outright corruption that marked the spoils system, but it is politics nonetheless.

Affirmative Action

Public unions show how a political role for bureaucracy can be generated internally—public employees get organized and pursue their interests in the political arena. Yet bureaucracies can be politicized from the out-

SENIORITY

The length of time spent in a position.

side as well. Consider **affirmative action**, the set of policies used to get government to make a special effort to recruit and retain certain categories of workers who historically have been underrepresented in order to achieve better and more fair representation. It is illegal for government agencies to have employment, evaluation, or promotion practices that discriminate on the basis of race, age, color, creed, gender, physical disability, or other characteristics not related to the job or job performance. Yet even though such discrimination has been banned outright, public bureaucracies are not particularly diverse on a number of these factors, especially race and gender.

About 55 percent of state and local government employees are males and about 68 percent are white. Males hold roughly 63 percent of the top management jobs in public agencies, and more than 80 percent of the individuals—male or female—in these positions are white. In contrast, racial and ethnic minorities tend to be much more concentrated in lower ranking positions. They constitute about 19 percent of the top management jobs in state and local government, but more than 46 percent of the service and maintenance positions.[32] Consider the New York Police Department (NYPD), which in 2005 had approximately 680 officers at the rank of captain or above. Of these, approximately 10 percent were minorities. Yet at the time of the 2000 Census, minorities accounted for more than 50 percent of New York City's population.[33]

The lack of diversity in the NYPD's management is probably not due to the outright racism of individuals. A bigger problem is that the nondiscriminatory hiring practices foundational to the merit system are passive; they ensure access to hiring opportunities, but make no guarantees of jobs or promotions. In choosing who should be hired or promoted, the merit system looks at things like experience and qualifications. It does not account for gender, race, or ethnicity. The problem here is that minorities historically have had fewer educational opportunities. Less education means fewer qualifications. This translates into a tougher time gaining access to jobs. The end result is that even if race is not an explicit factor in hiring and promoting, whites tend to have more education and better connections in bureaucratic hierarchies.[34] This strikes many as unfair.

One of the remedies offered to this is affirmative action, which are policies that, in essence, are proactive attempts to increase diversity. Such policies are highly controversial—are they necessary to remove institutionalized racism from the merit system, or are they simply a way for certain groups to profit from a double standard that makes a mockery of the merit system? Defenders argue that such policies are necessary because of the political role of the bureaucracy.

There is more than the desire for multiracial balance behind this argument. There is a fairly long-standing theory in the field of public administration that suggests that more diverse bureaucracies actually may be more

AFFIRMATIVE ACTION

Policies designed to help recruit and promote disadvantaged groups.

This graduation ceremony at the police academy in New York reflects a highly diverse class of future law enforcement officers. There are proportionately fewer minorities, however, in the upper ranks of the New York Police Department.

effective bureaucracies. The theory of **representative bureaucracy** argues that public agencies that reflect the diversity of the communities they serve are more likely to account for the interests of all groups when managing programs and delivering services.[35] In order for bureaucracy to better serve a diverse and democratic society, affirmative action should be an important part of its hiring and promoting practices. Remember our street-level bureaucrat, the traffic cop deciding which speeders to stop? What if all the traffic cops were white and most of the speeders stopped were black—or vice versa? Regardless of who was going how fast, this sort of situation is likely to create friction. Some may view the agency as unfair, which can make the bureaucracy's job harder. If traffic cops are ethnically diverse, it is less likely that the bureaucracy is going to be seen as playing favorites, and it is better able to focus on its job.

Opponents of affirmative action reject such arguments. Males and whites often resent establishing preferential recruitment and promotion policies for women and/or racial and ethnic minorities. Some see the policies as little more than reverse discrimination. From this perspective, affirmative action represents the success of special interests in getting their favored agendas written into the law and the rules that run bureaucracies. In a merit system, technical qualifications and job performance—not race or gender—are supposed to drive personnel decisions in the ideal bureaucracy. Opponents of affirmative action argue that it produces quotas and favoritism for certain groups. In effect, it has bureaucracy wage politics on behalf of the favored groups. Speeders should be stopped, and the race or gender of the driver and of whoever issues the ticket should be irrelevant.

Which of these viewpoints is correct is a matter of fierce debate. Whatever the underlying pros and cons, the fight comes down to what is the best way to recruit and promote public employees, and who—if anyone—should be given preferential treatment. This is ultimately a political fight about who gets government jobs.

If Not Merit . . . Then What?

Traditional bureaucracy and the merit system have some clear advantages: equity, competence, and something approaching neutrality. They also have disadvantages: a measure of red tape and inefficiency, a lack of flexibility and accountability, and a political role that makes many uncomfortable. No clear answer exists on whether the pros outweigh the cons or vice versa, but this has not stopped the nearly constant search for a better way to do things. Bureaucratic reform is a perennial issue in American politics.

Many of the reform efforts are variations on a single theme that reflects a popular belief that government would be better if it were run more like a business. In practice this means introducing competition into the delivery of public programs and services, making the organizations that deliver these goods and services less hierarchical, and making greater use of the private sector to deliver public services.[36] The idea is to introduce the benefits of the market into the public sector, which in theory could lead to more efficiency through lower costs while increasing responsiveness, since competition means paying attention to your customers or going out of business. The great difficulty facing reformers is how to get these benefits without leaving behind the advantages of the traditional, tried and true merit-based bureaucracy?

Over the past two decades reformers have made a sustained effort to try to change the entire philosophy of delivering public programs and services from the use of a traditional bureaucracy to the use of a more business-based model. Although these reforms come in many different packages, collectively they often are described as New Public Management (NPM). NPM has six core characteristics that have been widely pursued and adopted by state and local governments:

1. A focus on productivity that emphasizes "doing more with less," that is, providing public services with fewer resources.

2. A market orientation that looks increasingly to the private sector to deliver public services. This typically is done through a process of competitive bidding, during which private companies vie to gain a government contract to run a public program.

3. A drive to improve customer satisfaction with public services.

4. A decentralization of decision-making power, an effort to push policy-making choices as close as possible to the people who are going to be affected by them.

5. A movement to improve the government's capacity to make, to implement, and to manage public policy and public programs.

6. An effort to maintain accountability, that is, to make the government deliver on its service promises.[37]

These characteristics all sound fairly positive when presented as a simple list. In practice, however, they have proven to be a mixed bag. It turns out that pursuing one of these goals often has negative implications for another. For example, in the effort to be more productive and to leverage the advantage of the market, many public policies and programs are now delivered through private sector contracts. So if a state government wants to implement a new mental-health care program, the NPM approach is to contract with private clinics and mental-health care professionals to deliver those services. This is considerably cheaper than building and staffing a mental-health care facility from scratch, since renting the expertise and facilities that already exist in the private sector costs a fraction of duplicating everything in the public sector.

Yet contracting public service delivery to the private sector can have considerable drawbacks. Consider the experience of Denver, Colorado. In the 1990s, the city shifted control of its public transportation services from a traditional bureaucracy to a system of competitive bidding from the private sector. Initially, eight companies submitted bids and three contracts were awarded, all to national transportation companies. The national companies submitted bids far below those submitted by local companies, and local operators essentially were cut out of the market. Two of the national companies that had been awarded bids soon merged, further reducing competition and leaving public transportation under the control of just two companies. Costs soon went up. In the late 1990s, another round of bidding yielded only three bids, all of which were awarded to a single company. Over a decade of contracting out, the costs of using private vendors turned out to be not that much different from using a public agency, the service quality was not noticeably different, and the public transportation services effectively ended up in the hands of a single for-profit company. The result, some critics argued, was a program that was more expensive, less effective, and less accountable than a traditional bureaucracy.[38]

> The basic problem with trying to run government more like a business is that government is not a business.

The basic problem with trying to run government more like a business is that government is not a business. For the most part, we do not like rules and red tape—until there is a problem or a scandal. Then we want to know what went wrong and who is to blame. We want government agencies to act more like a business until a bureaucracy takes a calculated risk—as businesses do routinely—and loses taxpayer money. We want bureaucrats to be given the freedom to be flexible and make choices—until those choices result in favoritism or program failure. We like the idea of competition and the profit motive. We like it until a private company contracted to provide public services puts profit above the public interest.

Although most efforts to make government bureaucracy more market-like have produced very mixed results, they have done little to reduce the widespread belief that government is best run as a business. This belief has spawned a veritable alphabet soup of business-oriented reform movements. Reinventing government (REGO) stresses making public agencies entrepreneurial. Total Quality Management (TQM) emphasizes having public programs and services designed and shaped by the clients who actually consume those services and focuses on preventing problems rather than reacting to them. Management by Objectives (MBO) and Performance Based Management (PBM) are approaches that focus on setting goals and achieving them. In 2001, the President's Management Agenda (PMA) set five government-wide goals, and quarterly scorecards report federal agencies' successes.

There are many other such movements. All originated in private sector management trends that do not fully account for the unique problems of the public sector. Support and enthusiasm for making government more like a business tend to fade when these systems are put into practice, and it becomes apparent that there are good reasons why government is not run like the typical 9-to-5 corporation.

As the problems with these proffered replacements for traditional bureaucracy become apparent, public agencies gravitate back to their tried and true bureaucratic ways of doing things. At least until they get swept up in the next big reform movement. Some of these movements are counterproductive from the beginning because they spread more confusion than efficiency and leave public managers with a vague or complicated set of guidelines that is difficult to implement and is based on concepts that are hard to understand. "I'm just not sure what it has to offer, but maybe that's just because I don't understand what it is," was a typical public manager's response to Balanced Scorecard (BSC), a management reform movement that gained popularity in 2002.[39] This constant cycle of reform by acronym breeds cynicism among public sector administrators. Some refer to all reform movements as BOHICA, as in "bend over, here it comes again." BOHICA implies that the best response to reform is to just go through the motions. This fad too shall pass.

Another big drawback to trying to replace the traditional merit-based bureaucracy is that its advantages get overlooked until they are no longer there. Many of the attempts to radically reform the bureaucracy by either making agencies more like businesses or eliminating the merit system end up doing little more than returning public programs and services to the spoils system. (See box on page 356.)

Policy in Practice: Florida Ends the Merit System

Frustrated with the drawbacks of traditional bureaucracy, the state of Florida has spent the past few years experimenting with an alternative to the merit system. On May 14, 2001, Florida governor Jeb Bush signed into law a civil service overhaul dubbed "Service First." Service First is technically a significant reform of public sector personnel policy. In practice, it eliminates the merit system.

Specifically, Service First does three things. First, it eliminates seniority for all state workers. Second, it classifies a large number of employees into a "serve at will" category, which means that their superiors can hire or fire them at will. Third, it prepares the way for a massive reorganization of job titles and pay, all in an effort to give public sector managers the power to decide the salary and benefits of their individual employees.

The law has been controversial, to put it mildly. To its supporters, Service First is a long overdue change in the policies that regulate how public employees are hired, fired, promoted, and managed. It gives public sector managers the flexibility they need to hire workers who do the best job and fire those who do not and to compensate these employees according to their talents and contributions. The ability of agency personnel heads to freely and quickly hire, promote, transfer, or offer raises to employees arguably gives them the ability to better manage public employees and makes government agencies more businesslike.

To its detractors, however, Service First is little more than a re-institution of the spoils system. For example, bureaucrats who work for regulatory and licensing agencies may put their jobs on the line when they pursue cases against politically well-connected businesses and individuals. The law also leaves higher-level bureaucrats exposed to the whims of budget cutters, who may be tempted to fire more experienced and higher salaried bureaucrats—not because of their job performance—but simply as an exercise in economizing.

There is evidence to suggest these concerns have merit. The shadow of a spoils system mentality is evident in who is *not* covered by the Service First law. Several groups of employees, including police, fire fighters, and dieticians, are exempt. Common among those groups: their unions supported Bush in his gubernatorial election campaigns. To Service First critics this smacks of the sort of political payoff that is the cornerstone of the spoils system—support the electoral winner and get a secure job. Oppose the winner and run the opposite risk. Even some groups that support Service First are opposed to these special exceptions.

Regardless of its pros and cons, there is no doubt Service First has created a firestorm of controversy and no small amount of resentment among public employees. Unions have fought the program in court, with mixed success. The American Federation of State, County and Municipal Employees (AFSCME) won a case when Florida's First District Court of Appeals ruled that more than sixteen thousand state employees transferred to exempt status under Service First deserved hearings to justify those transfers; fewer than three hundred workers took the opportunity. Another state appeals court ruled that Service First did not violate employees' right to collective bargaining. Many believe the law's main goal is to downsize government and shift more public services into the private sector. What's clear is that thousands of employees lost jobs under the Bush administration. Whether the result is a better or worse public bureaucracy remains to be seen.

Sources: Adapted from Jonathan Walters, "Civil Service Tsunami," *Governing* magazine, May 2003; Bill Cotterell, "Appeals Court Supports Service First; Ruling Finds Fault with Use of 2001 Legislative Budget," *Tallahassee Democrat*, October 24, 2003; and Cotterell, "Union Tired of Waiting," *Tallahassee Democrat*, November 10, 2003.

E-Government

The history of reform shows the difficulty in coming up with a viable alternative to traditional bureaucracy. This does not mean, however, that bureaucracy is not changing. Indeed, it is changing in fundamental ways. Perhaps the best example of this is how public agencies are increasing their use of information technology. The changes in technology are creating **e-government**, "the delivery of information and services online via the Internet or other digital means." [40] All fifty states and most local governments now have at least some e-government operations that allow citizens to do everything from applying for hunting licenses to submitting small business applications to filing their taxes. [41] Some states, responding to an increasingly wireless society, have taken electronic interaction with citizens a step further by disseminating urgent information, such as Amber Alerts, through e-mail or text messages. [42]

There are a number of key advantages to e-government. It is convenient for citizens—no more waiting in lines—and governments—shorter lines to deal with. It may even promote political participation by facilitating communication between the public and elected officials. A good example of this is the attempt by numerous states, especially in the Southwest, to make all of their Web sites available in Spanish as well as English to make it easier for nonnative speakers to get the information they need. In Texas, all state government Web sites can be accessed in Spanish simply by clicking "En Español." [43]

According to Brown University's 2006 E-Government study, 92 percent of state and federal government Web sites have e-mail addresses. Governments post everything from laws and proclamations to bus schedules. They also clearly hope that e-government will allow them to deliver information, public programs, and public services cheaper and faster. Although it is still too early to make a general statement about how well this goal is being achieved, governments have made significant progress in their efforts to interact virtually with their citizens. Nearly half now offer interactive communication features on their Web sites, such as message boards and chat rooms. [44] (See Table 9-5.)

States and localities, however, differ widely in their use of technology. A key indicator of the commitment to e-government is the extent to which the Web sites allow transactions. In 2006, 77 percent of government sites offered online services, up from 22 percent six years earlier; 24 percent of sites accepted credit cards to complete transactions. But just 3 percent were set up for digital

---

E-GOVERNMENT

The delivery of public services and programs via the Internet or other digital means.

TABLE 9-5

Best and Worst Performing E-Government States

State	Score (100-Point Scale)
Best	
Texas	51.7
New Jersey	51.5
Oregon	49.1
Michigan	48.5
Utah	48.1
Worst	
Alaska	28.3
Alabama	28.4
Wyoming	29.0
Mississippi	33.4
West Virginia	33.6

Source: Darrell M. West, "State and Federal E-Government in the United States, 2006," Taubman Center for Public Policy at Brown University, August 2006. www.insidepolitics.org/egovt06us.pdf (accessed February 4, 2007).

signatures.[45] Why are some state and local governments more techno-savvy than others? The most important factor to explain the differences in e-government reform seems to be professionalism of state government. Wealthier, more urban states also have been found to be more likely to be e-government innovators.[46]

Unlike many other reform movements, the rise of e-government does seem to be bringing about important and permanent changes in the administrative arm of government. It is changing how people interact with government, changing expectations of government, and changing how public agencies are run. For example, in the virtual world there are no boundaries between agencies—they are just a mouse click away. This is forcing those agencies to rethink how they work together. When you make it easier to do business with government online, one of the typical results is an increase in the workload of agency personnel. This can force a rethinking of who does what and why in a public agency. Management reform fads have had a very mixed impact on bureaucracy, but the shift toward e-government has brought broad changes that are here to stay.

Conclusion

Bureaucracy is in many ways the Rodney Dangerfield of government—it gets no respect. Although it often is despised and disparaged, it is also clear that government bureaucracy is underestimated and does not get the credit it actually deserves. A wide range of state and local agencies support and deliver the programs and services that make up our social and economic life as we know it. The comparative method shows us that bureaucracy is big, but only as big as we want it. If we want less bureaucracy, all we have to do is make fewer demands on government. The comparative method also shows that, for the most part, these bureaucracies do their jobs remarkably well. In contrast to the popular stereotype, most public agencies tackle difficult jobs that are unlikely to be done better by any other alternative. Perhaps the most astonishing thing about bureaucracy is how much we take it for granted. Public schools, safe drinking water, working utility grids, and roads are simply there. We rarely contemplate what an astounding administrative and logistical feat is required to make these aspects of everyday life appear so mundane.

Yet while bureaucracy almost certainly deserves more praise than criticism, there is cause for concern. Its growing role and responsibilities have raised worries about the power administrative agencies wield in a democratic society. Changes such as the rise of new information technology are forcing bureaucracy to change with the times. The high cost of public services and an ongoing debate about what government should do is shifting more of what was traditionally considered public administration toward the private sector.

Bureaucratic reform movements, at least in some ways, should be viewed with skepticism. Criticizing the bureaucracy is a traditional sport in American politics, and a lot of reforms turn out to be little more than fads that quickly fade when the pleasing rhetoric meets the real-life challenge of delivering the goods. Some reforms, like the rise of the merit system and of e-government, can radically reshape what bureaucracy is and what it does. One thing, however, will almost certainly remain constant. Whatever the government is, and whatever it does, it will rely on bureaucracy to get it done.

Key Concepts

affirmative action (p. 351)

bureaucracy (p. 329)

bureaucrats (p. 329)

collective bargaining (p. 349)

e-government (p. 357)

merit systems (p. 347)

neutral competence (p. 347)

patronage (p. 346)

policy implementation (p. 330)

professionalization (p. 329)

representative bureaucracy (p. 352)

rulemaking (p. 332)

seniority (p. 350)

spoils system (p. 346)

street-level bureaucrats (p. 331)

Suggested Readings

Goodsell, Charles. *The Case for Bureaucracy: A Public Administration Polemic.* 4th ed. Washington, D.C.: CQ Press, 2004. A classic argument for why bureaucracy works and why it does not deserve its negative reputation.

Kerwin, Cornelius M. *Rulemaking: How Government Agencies Write Law and Make Policy.* 3rd ed. Washington, D.C.: CQ Press, 2003. A comprehensive look at rulemaking and bureaucracy.

Lipsky, Michael. *Street-Level Bureaucracy.* New York: Russell Sage Foundation, 1980. This classic work examines the policymaking role of the street-level bureaucrat.

Suggested Web Sites

http://results.gpponline.org. Online results and additional information from the Government Performance Project.

www.aspanet.org. Official Web site of the American Society for Public Administration, the largest professional association for those who work for or study public agencies.

www.governing.com. Web version of *Governing* magazine, which is dedicated to covering state and local issues. Includes numerous stories and other resources on agency leaders and performance, e-government, and more.

www.insidepolitics.org. Web site detailing results of Brown University's annual e-government survey.

CHAPTER 10

Local Government

Function Follows Form

Ancient Greeks pledged allegiance to their city, not to any nation-state. There are plenty of people who still make a formal commitment to serve local government, including police officers and firefighters. Pictured here is the graduation ceremony of the 36th Alaska Law Enforcement Training class; these individuals will go on to work as municipal police officers and fire marshals and in other law enforcement posts in towns and cities across Alaska.

Why do local governments vary so much within and between states?

How and why have local governments changed over the years?

What are the positive and negative aspects of Dillon's Rule?

Ancient Greeks did not pledge allegiance to ancient Greece. At that time and place, the nation-state as we know it didn't really exist. Instead of the nation-state, the patriotic loyalty and civic duty of the Greeks was oriented toward city-states, such as Athens and Sparta. And, boy, did the Greeks take their civic duty seriously.

The Athenian Oath was recited by the citizens of Athens more than two thousand years ago and is still cited as a model code for civic responsibility. Citizens who took this oath pledged, "We will never bring disgrace on this our City by an act of dishonesty or cowardice. . . . We will revere and obey the City's laws, and will do our best to incite a like reverence and respect in those above us who are prone to annul them or set them at naught." [1]

Americans tend not to feel quite that level of civic commitment to their cities. But attitudes toward local government in the twenty-first century are not as far off from the Greek ideal as you might imagine. The United States has a long tradition of strong local government, which is unsurprising given the political system's founding principles of division and decentralization of power. Woven tightly into the country's political fabric is a mistrust of centralized power, and Americans generally prefer to keep government as close as possible to citizens, where they can keep an eye on it.

Government does not get any closer than local government: the cities, counties, and other political jurisdictions that exist at the substate level. It is this level of government that Americans tend to trust the most, and it is this level of government that citizens generally want to have more rather than less power. A 2006 survey, for example, found that roughly a third of those citizens who responded believe local government gives them the most for their money. In bang-for-buck assessments, local governments trump state governments (which received about 20 percent approval) and even the federal government (which received about 29 percent approval). This is important, the authors of the survey argued, because federalism is not just a way to organize a political system, but is founded on a set of beliefs about what government is and what it should do. [2] As a general rule, Americans prefer, value, and trust government down at the grassroots level, and the nation's strong traditions of local government reflect those beliefs.

Given those beliefs, it is thus somewhat paradoxical that local government is, technically speaking, the weakest level of government of all. The federal government and state governments are sovereign powers, equal partners in the federal system who draw their powers from their citizens. Pull a state out of the federal system and view it independently, however, and what you find is not a federal system, but a unitary system. (See Figure 10-1.) Hierarchically speaking, as discussed in some depth below, states are superior to local governments. Local governments are not sovereign; they can only exercise the powers granted to them from the central authority of the states.

An individual state, though, is a strange sort of unitary system. Whereas state government is clearly the seat of power, below the state is typically an astonishing number and variety of political jurisdictions, many of them piled on top of one another and related to one another in no clear organizational fashion. Indeed, many of them operate independently of each other even when they occupy the same geographic space and provide services to the same citizens. A city and a school district may overlap each other entirely, but they have different governance structures, different leaders, and different purposes. One of these governments is not the boss of the other; the city cannot tell the school what its tax rate should be any more than the school can tell the city to build another library.

> It is down here in the crazy quilt of local governments that much of the grunt work of the political system takes place.

It is down here in the crazy quilt of local governments that much of the grunt work of the political system takes place. Local governments provide law enforcement, roads, health services, parks, libraries, and schools; they are mostly responsible for regulating (or even providing) utilities, such as sewer and water; they run airports, public transportation systems, mosquito control programs, and community recreation centers. The list goes on. And on. Collectively they represent the public services we encounter most in our daily lives, generally take for granted, and almost certainly could not get along without. No wonder citizens tend

FIGURE 10-1 Sub-state "Unitary" System

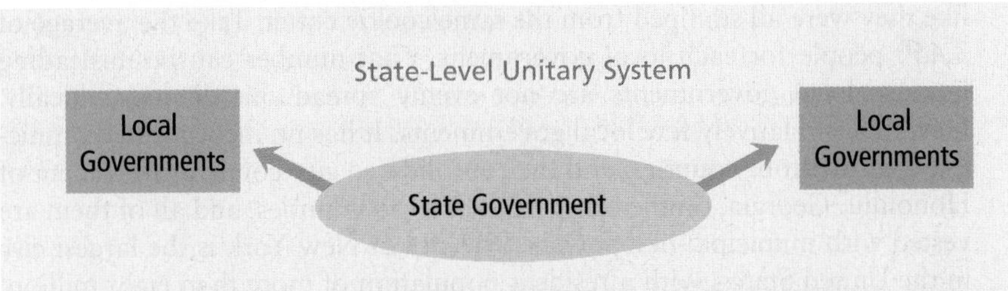

State-Level Unitary System

Local Governments ← State Government → Local Governments

At the state level, state government grants power to local governments

to think local governments give them good value for the money (well, at least compared to what they get from state and federal government).

Local governments, however, go well beyond just providing services. They must make political and philosophical decisions that affect their residents' quality of life and reinforce values. Many citizens believe local government has an obligation to provide a safety net for the poor, strike a balance between the need for sufficient revenues and public resistance to high taxation, and referee disputes over land-use planning that pit, say, developers against environmentalists or middle-income homeowners against low-income renters.

In short, local governments are worth getting to know. This chapter examines the powers, responsibilities, and specific forms of local government; how and why these forms evolved; how they differ by state and region; and how the political process works within the astonishing number and variety of substate governments.

The Many Faces of Local Government

The importance of local government to the American political system can be judged on one level by their sheer numbers. According to the U.S. Census Bureau, at last count there were more than eighty-seven thousand local governments operating in the United States (see Table 10-1). That works out to be roughly one local government for every 3,450 people.[3]

What form these local governments take, what responsibilities and powers they exercise, and how many of a particular kind exist in a given geographic or demographic area vary wildly from state to state. The number of local governments in a state's boundaries, for example, depends on a state's history, culture, and administrative approach to service delivery. New England states have a tradition of active civic participation and social spending that accommodates a large number of local governing units. By contrast, the South has much less of a tradition of civic engagement in local government, and even today a relatively small number of powerful county leaders dominate such services as school governance.

In terms of differences, local governments make state governments look like they were all stamped from the same cookie cutter. Take the average of 3,450 people for each local government. That number can be misleading because local governments are not evenly spread out demographically. Hawaii has relatively few local governments. It has no incorporated municipalities, just four counties, and the consolidated city-county government of Honolulu. Georgia, on the other hand has 159 counties, and all of them are vested with municipal-like powers. The city of New York is the largest city in the United States, with a resident population of more than eight million. The city of Hove Mobile Park, North Dakota, has a population of two. No that's not a typo. As of the last census, Hove Mobile was an incorporated

TABLE 10-1

Number of Governments Units, Ranked by State and Type

State	All Government Units	County	Municipal	Township	School Districts	All Special Districts
Illinois	6,903	102	1,291	1,431	934	3,145
Pennsylvania	5,031	66	1,018	1,546	516	1,885
Texas	4,784	254	1,196	-	1,089	2,245
California	4,409	57	475	-	1,047	2,830
Kansas	3,887	104	627	1,299	324	1,533
Ohio	3,636	88	942	1,308	667	631
Minnesota	3,482	87	854	1,793	345	403
Missouri	3,422	114	946	312	536	1,514
New York	3,420	57	616	929	683	1,135
Indiana	3,085	91	567	1,008	294	1,125
Wisconsin	3,048	72	585	1,265	442	684
Michigan	2,804	83	533	1,242	580	366
Nebraska	2,791	93	531	446	575	1,146
North Dakota	2,735	53	360	1,332	226	764
Iowa	1,975	99	948	-	386	542
Colorado	1,928	62	270	-	182	1,414
South Dakota	1,866	66	308	940	176	376
Oklahoma	1,798	77	590	-	571	560
Washington	1,787	39	279	-	296	1,173
Arkansas	1,588	75	499	-	310	704
Georgia	1,448	156	531	-	180	581
Kentucky	1,439	119	424	-	176	720
Oregon	1,439	36	240	-	236	927
New Jersey	1,412	21	324	242	549	276
Florida	1,191	66	404	-	95	626
Alabama	1,171	67	451	-	128	525
Idaho	1,158	44	200	-	116	798
Montana	1,127	54	129	-	352	592
Mississippi	1,000	82	296	-	164	458
North Carolina	960	100	541	-	-	319
Tennessee	930	92	349	-	14	475
New Mexico	858	33	101	-	96	628
Massachusetts	841	5	45	306	82	403

TABLE 10-1, continued

State	All Government Units	County	Municipal	Township	School Districts	All Special Districts
Maine	826	16	22	467	99	222
Vermont	733	14	47	237	283	152
Wyoming	722	23	98	-	55	546
South Carolina	701	46	269	-	85	301
West Virginia	686	55	234	-	55	342
Arizona	638	15	87	-	231	305
Utah	605	29	236	-	40	300
Connecticut	580	-	30	149	17	384
New Hampshire	559	10	13	221	167	148
Virginia	521	95	229	-	1	196
Louisiana	473	60	302	-	66	45
Delaware	339	3	57	-	19	260
Maryland	265	23	157	-	-	85
Nevada	210	16	19	-	17	158
Alaska	175	12	149	-	-	14
Rhode Island	118	-	8	31	4	75
Hawaii	19	3	1	-	-	15

Source: U.S. Census Bureau, *Census of Governments,* vol. 1, no. 1, Government Organization, Series GC02(1)-1), quinquennial. www.census.gov/govs/www/cog2002.html (accessed January 12, 2007).

municipality whose population consisted of an elderly married couple living in a trailer park.[4]

Local governments are not evenly spread out geographically, either. They range from villages covering less than a square mile to counties that cover nearly 125,000 square miles. Within or adjacent to their borders may be mountains, deserts, beaches, urban centers, or vast stretches of nothingness. These differences help explain why some local governments are interested in maintaining subways and others worry about maintaining clean beaches.

Political and cultural traditions also vary at the local level. For instance, the degree of loyalty that citizens display toward a local governing entity often depends on whether they personally identify with the area or whether they ignore their membership and regard the area as an artificial construct. Put another way, a Manhattanite probably feels more community pride than, say, a user of the Susquehanna and Delaware River Basin.

All of these differences provide multiple opportunities to put the comparative method into practice, but they also can be confusing. Local authority,

Strong attachments to localities are not unusual. New Yorkers love New York, of course, but the sentiment is familiar to any long (or even not-so-long) resident of virtually any city in the United States. These attachments are reflected in public attitudes toward government; local government tends to be more trusted than higher levels of government.

for example, overlaps—school districts sprawl across municipalities, which, in turn, are covered by counties. A couple may plan on getting married in the city of Chapel Hill, North Carolina, but their marriage certificate will carry the insignia of Orange County, North Carolina. That is because in most states the power to grant marriage licenses is vested in counties, not in cities. Adding to the confusion, the units of government at the substate level vary in their duties and obligations from state to state. Depending on where you live, you may rely on a different set of authorities to get a pothole filled on your street, arrange for a stop sign to be installed at a dangerous intersection, or register your opinion on a bond issue for a new high school.

Despite all these differences, however, there are only three general forms of local government: **counties, municipalities,** and **special districts**. Counties traditionally are viewed as geographic and administrative subdivisions of states. The exact definition of a municipality varies from state to state, although they generally are political units that are distinguished geographically from counties by being more compact and distinguished legally by being independent corporations rather than "branch offices" of state government. Special districts cover a huge range of local governments. Typically, special districts are single-purpose governments. Unlike counties and cities, which are general purpose governments, special districts usually are created to provide a specific public service rather than a range of services. School districts are a good example. These are geographically defined local units of government created to provide educational services. Other special districts include water management and sewage treatment districts.

COUNTIES

A geographic subdivision of state government.

MUNICIPALITIES

Political jurisdictions, such as cities, villages, or towns, incorporated under state law to provide governance to a defined geographic area. More compact and more densely populated than counties.

SPECIAL DISTRICTS

Local governmental units created for a single purpose, such as water distribution.

The Organization and Responsibilities of Local Governments

Even within each of the three basic categories of local government there is considerable variation in organizational structure, autonomy, and responsibilities. These categories are distinct enough, however, to wrangle those more than eighty-seven thousand local governments in the United States into an general understanding of what local governments are and why they take on the forms they do.

Between the County Lines

To find out what county government is all about it would be instructive to take a trip to your local county courthouse. There you are likely to find signs pointing you toward a variety of self-explanatory government offices: district attorney, coroner, sheriff, treasurer, and the like. You also may find signs for offices whose purposes are not quite so self evident. President Harry Truman once walked into the courthouse in Allegheny, Pennsylvania, and was taken aback by one of the signs he saw. "What the hell is a prothonotary?" he famously asked. Well, a prothonotary, Mr. President, is the chief record keeper of a civil court. Truman's bewilderment over this obscure county office encapsulates some of the confusion over what county government is and what it does. People might be asked to vote on a prothonotary come election time, but chances are it is a small minority who knows what the heck a prothonotary is or why the position is necessary.[5]

In your particular courthouse the prothonotary might travel under a less mysterious title, such as clerk of the civil court. Regardless, though, the office of prothonotary points out what county government is often about: the unglamorous, but undoubtedly necessary, administration of central (that is, state) government functions. Civil courts and criminal courts for the most part function under the framework of state rather than county authority. Yet at the county courthouse the court's record keeper, prosecutor, and judge are typically county-level elective offices. It is the county government that represents the local face of the central government.

The unglamorous, utilitarian governing unit known as the county grew out of a thousand-year-old tradition brought over from Mother England, where it was known as the shire. (English counties still carry this suffix; one of the authors of this book was born in the county of Oxfordshire.) In the United States, counties "are nothing more than certain portions of the territory into which the state is divided for the more convenient exercise of the powers of government," wrote U.S. Supreme Court chief justice Roger B. Taney, in *Maryland ex. rel. Washington County v. Baltimore & Ohio Railroad Co.* (1845).[6] Centralizing day-to-day governance for an entire state in the state capitol simply was, and largely still is, impractical. Thus, states divided themselves into smaller geographical units—counties—and created a governance structure within each to provide a local "branch office" of state government.

Called parishes in Louisiana and boroughs in Alaska, more than three thousand counties are drawn on the maps of the remaining forty-eight states. How many county governments reside within a state varies wildly. Rhode Island and Connecticut are the only states that have no county governments (as more geographically compact states there is less need for such administrative subunits of state governments). Some states have just a handful. Hawaii and Delaware, for example, have only three apiece. Supporting the claim that everything is bigger in Texas, the state has 254 counties, the most in the nation.

Geographically speaking, counties are typically the largest local governments, although, like their numbers, their size can vary enormously. Arlington County, Virginia, covers forty-two square miles, which is on the smallish side. North Slope Borough, Alaska, encompasses 142,224 mostly uninhabited square miles. Measured by population, counties cross the spectrum from 9.5 million in Los Angeles County, California, to 67 persons in Loving County, Texas.[7] (See Tables 10-2 and 10-3.)

Because they generally cover the largest geographical territory, counties bear much of the burden of providing services widely, if not lavishly. The majority of the million citizens in California's Sacramento County, for example, live in unincorporated territory. This means that their property is not part of any city, town, or township that can provide municipal services. Hence the burden falls on the county to provide these residents with such services as law enforcement, parks and recreation, and storm water management.

The autonomy and authority of county governments also varies considerably from state to state. There are some regional patterns to such differences. For example, in the Northeast, local government traditionally is centered on towns and villages. These are the units of government that attract the most participation, make the most high-profile decisions, and are the focus of most attention. County governments in this region are historically viewed as just the local offices of state government, representing a form of government and governance more remote than the village board.

In the South, counties are also technically creatures of state government, as they were formed and granted their authority by state legislatures. Yet,

TABLE 10-2

Twenty-five Largest U.S. Counties by Population, 2000

County, State	Population	Rank
Los Angeles, CA	9,519,338	1
Cook, IL	5,376,741	2
Harris, TX	3,400,578	3
Maricopa, AZ	3,072,149	4
Orange, CA	2,846,289	5
San Diego, CA	2,813,833	6
Kings, NY	2,465,326	7
Dade, FL	2,253,362	8
Queens, NY	2,229,379	9
Dallas, TX	2,218,899	10
Wayne, MI	2,061,162	11
King, WA	1,737,034	12
San Bernardino, CA	1,709,434	13
Santa Clara, CA	1,682,585	14
Broward, FL	1,623,018	15
Riverside, CA	1,545,387	16
New York, NY	1,537,195	17
Philadelphia, PA	1,517,550	18
Middlesex, MA	1,465,396	19
Tarrant, TX	1,446,219	20
Alameda, CA	1,443,741	21
Suffolk, NY	1,419,369	22
Cuyahoga, OH	1,393,978	23
Bexar, TX	1,392,931	24
Clark, NV	1,375,765	25

Source: U.S. Census Bureau. *County and City Data Book 2000,* Table B-1.

TABLE 10-3

Twenty-five Smallest U.S. Counties by Population, 2000

County, State	Population	Rank
Loving, TX	67	1
Kalawao, HI	147	2
King, TX	356	3
Kenedy, TX	414	4
Arthur, NE	444	5
Petroleum, MT	493	6
McPherson, NE	533	7
San Juan, CO	558	8
Blaine, NE	583	9
Loup, NE	712	10
Thomas, NE	729	11
Borden, TX	729	11
Grant, NE	747	13
Slope, ND	767	14
Logan, NE	774	15
Hooker, NE	783	16
Hinsdale, CO	790	17
Harding, NM	810	18
Banner, NE	819	19
Mineral, CO	831	20
McMullen, TX	851	21
Kent, TX	859	22
Treasure, MT	861	23
Wheeler, NE	886	24
Roberts, TX	887	25

Source: U.S. Census Bureau. *County and City Data Book 2000,* Table B-1.

Note: If two or more counties are tied, all counties are listed alphabetically by state.

in the South, county governments are much more likely to be a central focus of local government. County government here tends to be the form of local government that wields the most political power and policy influence and tends to be the focus of local political elites. The reason for these differences primarily has to do with the more urban nature of the Northeast compared to the historically more rural South. Rural areas by definition lack substantial urban centers; which means they lack large and powerful city or village governments. County governments thus occupy the center of local government, and the county seat—the place where county government is physically located—becomes the locus of local politics.

Counties are distinct from municipalities (which are discussed in-depth later), although these distinctions have blurred. County governments are historically rural governments that help conduct state government business. The quintessential county government is a keeper of public records, such as property deeds, birth and death certificates, and mortgages and an administrator of property taxes, local road maintenance, election results certification, criminal courts, and jails run by county sheriffs. The typical U.S. municipality, on the other hand, performs such day-to-day functions as police and fire protection; sewage disposal; sanitation; and the maintenance of public parks and other infrastructure facilities, including stadiums, airports, and convention centers.

In the messy real world, however, such clear distinctions often disappear. Many modern county governments—particularly urban ones—have their official fingers in these classic city functions as well. In many regions there is substantial overlap between county and city functions, and county and city governments operate cheek by jowl. For example, in Phoenix, Arizona, the city hall is directly across the street from the Maricopa County administration building.

As a general rule, though, counties tend to be kept on a tighter leash by state governments when compared to municipalities (especially large urban cities). In New Hampshire, for example, legislators still approve county budgets. In Texas, each county is required by the state to appoint a county judge-at-large and four commissioners, regardless of whether the county's population numbers in the hundreds or the millions. Counties, in other words, are still in theory and often in practice the administrative sub-units of state government.

Perhaps because they often are seen as extensions of state government, counties tend to be treated less generously when state and federal governments make appropriations to local governments. For many counties, this is a problem, especially given their responsibilities as "backstops" in providing such services as welfare, healthcare, housing, and mass transit. Counties, according to a 1992 U.S. Census Bureau study, spend almost three times as much as cities on social services and twice as much on administration, but less on public safety and less on the environment than cities. Counties often get stuck with responsibilities involving costs they cannot cap, or put a limit on. When the federal government appropriated funds to put more local cops on the beat in the 1990s, counties actually suffered. More city cops on the beat meant more offenders in county jails. There was money to hire more cops, but little thought and even fewer dollars were given to expanding and running county jails. The resulting rise in arrests meant more prisoners to support and guard in county jails.[8]

The primary funding source for county governments is the property tax, which nationally accounts for about 30 percent of county government income. Like everything else about local government, however, there is considerable variation in where county governments get their money and what they spend it on. Fairfax County, Virginia, gets about 40 percent of its revenues from property taxes, whereas Orange County, California, gets less than 10 percent of its revenues from property taxes. Other sources of revenue include sales taxes (although not all counties have the legal authority to levy a sales tax), state appropriations, and taxes on everything from cars to hotel rooms.[9]

Just as there are huge variations among counties in terms of revenue, there are similar variations in spending priorities. Where county governments focus their spending depends on geography, politics, and relations with neighboring jurisdictions. A significant chunk of county spending goes to basic social services; public welfare, hospitals, and other healthcare programs account for about 60 percent of county government expenditures. Other categories of expenditure range from roads to sewers to schools to general administration.[10]

The Structure of County Government. There are three basic forms of county government: commission, council-executive, and commission-administrator. What differentiates the three forms is the degree of separation between legislative and executive powers and who is responsible for the day-to-day administration of the executive side of government.

The most common form of county government is the **commission**, which concentrates legislative and executive functions into an elected board of commissioners. This elected body exercises legislative and executive powers. For example, it exercises legislative powers by passing county ordi-

North Carolina's local governments generated more than $27 billion in total revenue in 2002. Of that, nearly 39 percent came from state and federal governmental transfers, 26 percent from taxes, 26 percent from charges, and 5 percent from other miscellaneous sources, such as liquor store revenues.

COUNTY COMMISSION SYSTEM

A form of county governance in which executive, legislative, and administrative powers are vested in elected commissioners.

nances and approving the budget. It wields executive powers by being responsible for a broad range of hiring and firing decisions and by exercising considerable control over many administrative offices.

Depending on the state and the county, members of these county-level legislatures may be called county commissioners, supervisors, selectmen, county board members, or judges. In Louisiana these locally elected legislators are called parish jurors. In New Jersey they are boards of chosen freeholders. Whatever their official titles, commissioners are typically a small group elected to serve staggered two-year or four-year terms.

The most significant reform of county government since its inception has been to separate executive and legislative powers by creating an independent county-level executive office. **Council-executive** county governments typically have an independently elected officer who serves as the county-level equivalent of a governor. County executives frequently have powers to veto ordinances passed by the board of commissioners, and they have the authority to appoint key department heads. Thus the main difference between the commission and council-executive forms of government is their approach to separation of powers. (See Figure 10-2.)

Commission-administrator county governments stand somewhere between the commission and council-executive forms. In this form of government, an elected commission retains most legislative and executive powers but appoints a professional administrator to actually run the government. County administrators usually serve at the pleasure of the commissioners—they can be hired and fired as the county commission sees fit. In practice, commissioners typically delegate considerable powers to administrators, including the power to hire and fire department heads and to prepare a budget for the commission's approval.

Commission-administrator and, to an even greater extent, council-executive structures have been popular reforms to traditional commission forms of county government. Diffuse and ineffective decision making, and outright corruption, were the primary reasons for the shift away from commissions in the twentieth century. Reformers were concerned that under the commission approach power was so diffuse that county governments tended to drift in the absence of clear leadership, and that commissioners too often appointed friends to important positions. As a result, an increasing number of counties, as many as 15 percent, now are run by elected county executives who exert firm leadership on policy and hiring. This reduces the role of the commissioners to something closer to an advisory level. Another 12 percent of counties are led by appointed administrators. State policymakers have contributed to this trend—Arkansas, Kentucky, and Tennessee now mandate that their counties be headed by elected executives.

Although such reforms have reduced entrenched corruption, even today there are examples of county governments going very badly astray. When this happens, states are still known to step in and, in effect, put

Governing States and Localities

FIGURE 10-2 How It Works: The Structure of County Government

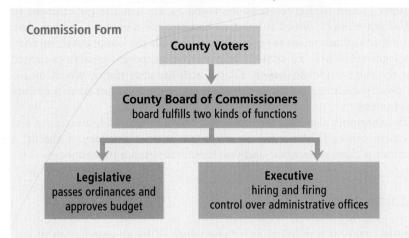

Commission Form

County Voters

↓

County Board of Commissioners
board fulfills two kinds of functions

Legislative
passes ordinances and
approves budget

Executive
hiring and firing
control over administrative offices

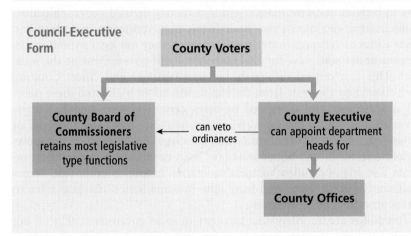

Council-Executive Form

County Voters

County Board of Commissioners
retains most legislative
type functions

← can veto ordinances ─

County Executive
can appoint department
heads for

↓

County Offices

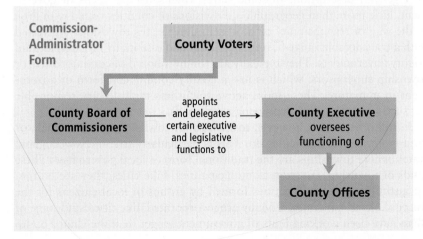

Commission-Administrator Form

County Voters

County Board of Commissioners

─ appoints and delegates certain executive and legislative functions to →

County Executive
oversees
functioning of

↓

County Offices

The three basic forms of county government differ on division of powers and in who is responsible for day-to-day administration of county government. In the commission form, voters elect county commissioners who exercise legislative and executive powers and exercise considerable authority over day-to-day administration. In the council-executive form, voters elect commissioners who exercise legislative powers and independently elect a county executive who wields executive powers and serves as the chief administrator. In the commission-administrator form, voters elect commissioners who retain most legislative and executive powers. However, they hire a professional manager to provide day-to-day administration of county government.

county government out of business. For example, in 1997, the Massachusetts House of Representatives voted to abolish the government of Middlesex County, which it believed had become a corrupt, debt-ridden, and expensive administrative burden. Although the county still survives as a legal venue and for other administrative purposes, legislators judged that the state could do better. That is still the case today, which means the most populous county in the Massachusetts does not have a county government.

Most counties also elect the heads of a broad range of administrative and executive offices. These typically include a district attorney, a sheriff, a treasurer, a clerk of records, and yes, sometimes even a prothonotary.

Municipalities

A municipality is a political jurisdiction formed by an association of citizens to provide self-governance within a clearly defined geographic area. Municipalities encompass two basic forms of government: townships and cities. **Cities** are corporations. In other words, they are legal entities incorporated under state law for the purpose of self-government at the local level. This is a central difference between counties and cities. Counties were created by the state from the top down; states mandated these political jurisdictions and delegated to them certain powers and functions. Cities are bottom up creations. A local community seeks the authority of self-governance by incorporating itself as a legal entity with certain powers and responsibilities under state law. Such corporate municipal governments also may be called villages, towns, or boroughs (although, somewhat confusingly, towns and boroughs in some states can also refer to nonincorporated governments).

Townships are an interesting category of local government that all but defy general description. In some states, townships are shells of government, little more than geographic subdivisions of counties vested with little in the way of responsibility or power. In other states townships are vested with a considerable range of responsibilities and essentially function as mini county governments. They typically are run by a board of commissioners or township supervisors, which is just a county commission form of government in miniature. These more active townships typically are responsible for such functions as snowplowing rural roads.

In still other states, however, townships (or towns) exercise as much, or even more, power than cities do. This is particularly true in New England states, where townships are the traditional form of local governance. These kinds of townships function as municipalities. Like cities, they are bottom up institutions, political entities formed by groups of local citizens for the purpose of self-governance. Many are incorporated, like cities, and some of them have been working units of government longer than the United States

CITIES

An incorporated political jurisdiction formed to provide self-governance to a locality.

TOWNSHIPS

A common type of local government whose powers, governance structure, and legal status vary considerably from state to state. In some states townships function as general purpose municipalities, in others they are geographic subdivisions of counties with few responsibilities and little power.

has been in existence. The Maine town of Dover-Foxcroft, for example, was incorporated in 1769, eight years before the Declaration of Independence was approved.[11] Townships, in other words, can be viewed as like counties, like cities, or like large geographic spaces with little in the way of a governance structure within them. Which of these descriptions is accurate depends on state law and traditions of local governance.

What distinguishes cities and the city-like townships from counties and county-like townships is that they are formed by associations of citizens rather than being brought to life as designated subunits of states. Municipalities are general purpose governments that provide a range of public services and address a variety of political issues at the local level. They are brought into existence because groups of citizens, usually those concentrated in compact urban areas, wanted to exercise a degree of political self-determination over their community. Accordingly, they incorporated, bringing to life a legal entity—a municipality—that grants them the right to a broad degree of self-governance.

Governance arrangements at the municipal level vary even more than at the county level. In municipalities there is variation in the powers of the executive, or **mayor**, and the legislature, typically a **city council**. A strong role often is played by an appointed administrator, or **city manager**, who is given day-to-day responsibility for running municipal operations. There are four municipal governance systems: the mayor-council system, the commission system, the city manager system, and the town meeting system.

Mayor-Council Systems

One of the most common forms of municipal governance is the **mayor-council system**. It is distinguished by a separation of executive and legislative powers. According to the International City/County Management Association (ICMA), approximately 43 percent of U.S. cities use this system. Executive power is vested in a separately elected mayor, although the powers a mayor actually is allowed to exercise vary considerably.

The mayor-council system can be broken down into **strong mayor** and **weak mayor** systems. In discussions of city governance, these terms have less to do with a politician's personality than with the powers that a given mayor enjoys when stacked up against the powers of the city council and the bureaucracy. Under the strong mayor system, the executive is roughly the municipal-level equivalent of a governor. Strong mayors exercise real power, and typically they have the authority to make appointments to key city offices, to veto council decisions, to prepare budgets, and to run the day-to-day operations of municipal government in general.

The strong mayor system is most common in the Northeast and the Midwest. One example of a strong mayor in action is Carleton S. Finkbeiner, who was elected mayor of Toledo, Ohio, in 1994. Early in his tenure, he overrode resistance from school authorities and placed uniform-

MAYOR
The elected chief executive of a municipality.

CITY COUNCIL
A municipality's legislature.

CITY MANAGER
An official appointed to be the chief administrator of a municipality.

MAYOR-COUNCIL SYSTEM
A form of municipal governance in which there is an elected executive and an elected legislature.

STRONG MAYOR
A mayor with the power to perform the executive functions of government.

WEAK MAYOR
A mayor who lacks true executive powers, such as the ability to veto council decisions or appoint department heads.

ed police officers in every junior high school and high school as a way to reduce violence. The policy has taken some cops off the street, but it also has created trust with students and has taken a preventive approach that has reduced drug and gang problems by providing mentors and role models for students. The U.S. Conference of Mayors cited the program as an example of best practice in 2000.[12] What Finkbeiner demonstrated was the ability of a strong mayor to independently make important policy decisions.

A weak mayor system retains the elected executive, but this is more of a ceremonial than a real policymaking office. In weak mayor systems real executive, as well as legislative, power is wielded by the council. Executives in weak mayor systems still can exercise considerable influence, but they have to do this using their powers of persuasion rather than the authority vested in their office. In many cities where mayors have limited powers, individuals with strong personalities have nevertheless been able to exert huge influence. They do this by fostering cooperative relationships with their powerful city managers. Examples are Pete Wilson, mayor of San Diego in the 1970s, and Henry Cisneros, mayor of San Antonio in the 1980s.

In both strong and weak mayor systems, the council serves as the municipal-level legislature and can wield extensive policymaking power. No major policy or program can get far in a city without massaging from the city council. Councils average six members, but there are twelve members to fourteen members elected in many large jurisdictions. Los Angeles, for example, has fifteen. Chicago has a whopping fifty council members, and New York City has fifty-one.

City councils exert major influence over a city's livability. They steer policies on such vital issues as zoning and urban renewal, as have the councils in Los Angeles and Philadelphia, for example. In recent years, they have been pivotal in the pursuit of public-private partnerships. In Indianapolis, for instance, the city council has worked with the city's mayor and administrators to save taxpayers $100 million by opening up service contracts to competitive bidding. The money saved by contracting out such services as wastewater treatment, asbestos abatement, recycling, street sweeping, and server billing goes toward public safety and airport improvements.[13]

In cities where councils lack discipline, however, quirky personalities can impede progress. In St. Louis, the board of aldermen has twenty-nine members. Back in the 1950s, these aldermen enjoyed a major say in decisions that affected zoning, development, and highway location. But by the start of the twenty-first century, critics complained that the board micromanaged and encouraged parochialism—a limitation of views or interests—and balkanization—the division of an area into small, often hostile, units.

Elected with as few as eight hundred votes, some of these personally ambitious individuals have embarrassed their communities by spending more time squabbling among themselves than teaming up to make princi-

FIGURE 10-3 Strong Mayor-Council Form of Government

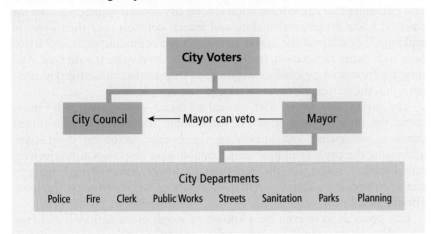

Source: John P. Pelissero, "The Political Environment & Cities in the 21st Century," in *Cities, Politics & Public Policy: A Comparative Analysis,* ed. John P. Pelissero (Washington, DC: CQ Press, 2003), 15.

FIGURE 10-4 Weak Mayor-Council Form of Government

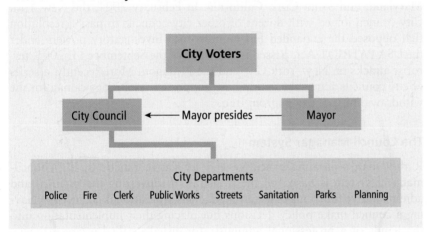

Source: John P. Pelissero, "The Political Environment & Cities in the 21st Century," in *Cities, Politics & Public Policy: A Comparative Analysis,* ed. John P. Pelissero (Washington, DC: CQ Press, 2003), 15.

pled decisions. For many aldermen, however, the personal stakes are higher than is commensurate with their actual power. Neighborhood **wards** have little influence, for example, on developers and corporations whose view of the city includes many wards. Ward aldermen can't implement a broad vision because the real power is in the mayor's office. In addition, they do not always know about deals being cut in other wards. Yet, sometimes, just one or two individuals can hold up a hand and make the entire city come to a halt.[14]

WARDS

Divisions of municipalities, usually representing electoral districts of the city council.

A survey taken in 2001 by the National League of Cities showed an array of issues that cause frustration among city council members across the country. Local leaders resent state and federal controls over their decision making. They chafe at the degree to which their communities are polarized over such issues as taxation, traffic abatement, development, and race. And they are frustrated by conflict within their own ranks, interest-group pressure, and the nature of media coverage.

The survey also found that council members—who work part-time—spend the bulk of their hours, in rank order, responding to constituent demands, reviewing and approving the budget, resolving complaints, addressing the city's "real problems," establishing objectives and priorities, establishing a vision for the community's future, establishing long-term goals, overseeing administrative performance, and overseeing program effectiveness.[15]

City councils have even been known to weigh in on national, and even international, issues with or without the approval of the mayor or city manager. In the 1980s, for example, when proposals for a joint U.S.-Soviet freeze on nuclear weapons was being discussed by U.S. arms control officials, "nuclear-free zones" were declared by city councils in Takoma Park, Maryland, and Santa Cruz, California. In February 2004, the New York City council joined with dozens of other city councils to pass a resolution that opposed the expanded FBI antiterrorism investigatory powers under the USA PATRIOT Act, passed in the wake of the September 11, 2001, terrorist attacks on New York City and the Pentagon. More recently, a series of city councils across the nation have supported resolutions calling for the withdrawal of U.S. troops from Iraq.

The Council-Manager System

COUNCIL-MANAGER SYSTEM

A form of municipal governance in which the day-to-day administration of government is carried out by a professional administrator.

Rather than separating executive and legislative functions, the **council-manager system** is based on the principle of separating the political and administrative functions of government. This separation is achieved by having a council make policy decisions but placing their implementation into the hands of a professional administrator, usually called a city manager, hired by the council. (See Figure 10-5.)

The origins of this system are in the Progressive reform movement that swept through government at all levels at the turn of the nineteenth century. As discussed elsewhere in the context of state-level party politics, a century ago, political machines ran the typical large city in the United States. Places like Boston, Chicago, and New York were governed by charismatic politicians who took advantage of ties to ethnic minorities, such as the Irish or the Italians. Patronage jobs were given out to personal friends whose chief qualification was that they were campaign supporters. Elections were fraught with partisanship, which produced high incumbent reelection rates. Many machine insiders got themselves elected as city commissioners, who

FIGURE 10-5 Council-Manager Form of Government

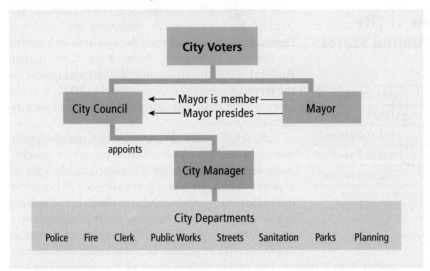

Source: John P. Pelissero, "The Political Environment & Cities in the 21st Century," in *Cities, Politics & Public Policy: A Comparative Analysis,* ed. John P. Pelissero (Washington, DC: CQ Press, 2003), 16.

were given authority to run individual departments, including police, fire, or sanitation services. This resulted in politically powerful, but often corrupt and incompetent, municipal governments.

During the first half of the twentieth century, reform groups began pressuring city governments to become more professionalized and less politicized. The National Municipal League (now the National League of Cities), which focuses on small to medium-sized cities, was one such group. The U.S. Conference of Mayors, whose members head larger cities, and the ICMA were two others. In the belief that the top vote-getters in a given city may not be the best managers, the National Municipal League drafted a model charter that laid out the powers of mayors, city councils, and administrators.

Dayton, Ohio, in 1913 became the first major U.S. city to create a position for a strong manager, largely in response to suburbanization—the establishment of residential communities on the outskirts of a city—and the rise of an educated middle class. The idea was that a government run by a professional city manager would be less prone to corruption and partisan favoritism than those led by the classic big-city mayor. Such managers are generally more interested in implementing organizational systems than they are in glad-handing voters and trolling for campaign cash.

This reform movement by no means eliminated urban political machines or the power wielded by strong executives. For example, Richard J. Daley, mayor of Chicago from 1955–1976, continued to run the city

TABLE 10-4

Most Common Forms of City Government in the United States, 2007*

Council-Manager	3,511 (49 percent)
Mayor-Council	3,116 (43.5 percent)
Commission	143 (2.0 percent)
Town Meeting	339 (4.7 percent)
Representative Town Meeting	62 (0.9 percent)

Source: International City/County Management Association. www.icma.org/upload/library/2007-04/{F55E2557-92E4-4791-9DFC-FB9D282E3DF1}.doc (accessed May 23, 2007).

*Represents only those cities with populations of 2,500 or greater.

with unequaled influence, even though Chicago had a supposedly independent city council. He swayed his city council members, the national Democratic Party, and the Chicago-area delegation to the U.S. Congress. New York City mayor Rudolph Giuliani, in leading the city's response to the terrorist attacks of September 11, 2001, was far more visible than any city council member or city administrator.

Still, while political machines did not disappear overnight and no administrative branch of government was ever completely de-politicized, the idea of a professional city manager took root. This is an individual who is appointed, not elected, and at least in theory can counter the powers of commissioners or city council members with nonpartisan technical administrative expertise. In some cities, this manager is paired with a mayor. The mayor acts as more of a ceremonial figurehead and seldom blocks anything wanted by the manager or the council members. Supported by a legislative body that is elected by popular vote and that meets about every two weeks to deal with policy issues, the manager is empowered to hire and fire all city employees, set pay scales, prepare an annual budget that is approved by elected officials and implemented by staff, and make policy recommendations.

Today, the council-manager system of city government is seen in more than 3,000 cities, or 48 percent of communities with populations of more than 2,500. (See Table 10-4.) It is most popular in medium-sized cities primarily in the South and the West. The reason council-manager cities concentrate in these population areas is because smaller cities cannot afford a full-time manager's salary, and big cities tend to want a more partisan mayor. However, there are exceptions to the rule. Large cities that use a manager-council system include Dallas, Texas, and San Diego and San Jose, California.[16]

And the trend toward professionalization continues. A survey conducted by the ICMA showed that the percentage of city managers with advanced degrees rose from 27 percent in 1971 to 73 percent in 1995. Managers are also less likely to use volunteer committees to farm out work and more likely to use a professional staff. They supervise the systems that provide detailed financial controls and reporting transparency. For example, in Phoenix, the city manager issues a monthly report that details the percentage of ambulance calls answered in less than ten minutes, the total number of nights individuals spent in homeless shelters, how many rounds of golf were played on public courses, and how many square miles of streets were swept.

Commission Systems

Similar to their county-level counterparts, municipal **commission systems** concentrate executive and legislative powers into a single elected body. These bodies are elected and make key policy decisions in the same way a legislature does. Yet each commissioner is also the head of an executive department. Commissioners run for office not to be representatives in a legislative body, but to run a particular city department: commissioner for public safety, commissioner for public works, and so on. Most commission systems also have a mayor, but this is not an independent executive office. The position usually is held by a commissioner chosen to preside over commission meetings; it is not an independent executive office, but more of ceremonial position.

As a form of municipal (as opposed to county) governance, the commission system originated in Galveston, Texas, in the early 1900s. Galveston had suffered a devastating hurricane that killed thousands and left the city in ruins. The existing city government proved ineffective in dealing with the aftermath of this disaster. In response, the Texas legislature approved a completely new form of municipal government—the commission system—to try to deal with the huge task of rebuilding the city. It proved successful. Galveston was rebuilt and put back on the civic track.

This success led other municipalities to follow Galveston's lead and adopt the commission form of governance. The commission system's success, however, has been limited, and only a relative handful of cities currently operate under it. Its main drawbacks are twofold. First, the merging of elected and administrative positions leads to commissioners becoming entrenched advocates of their departments. Second, winning an election and administering a large bureaucracy turn out to be very different skills. Good politicians, in other words, do not always make good department heads.

Only about 2 percent of municipalities with populations greater than 2,500 use the commission form of government.[17] The drawbacks of commission governments are much the same drawbacks of commission systems at the county level; executive authority is so diffuse it tends to produce a government with no real direction. As commissioners serve as the head of their own departments, with no real central authority above that position, commission systems at the municipal level function as a legislature consisting of elected executives. This can make coordinating departments difficult and providing a strong sense of direction for the government overall even harder.

Town Meetings

The **town meeting form of government** is largely unique to the United States and is mostly found in municipal-like towns in New England states.

The town meeting form of government is largely unique to the United States, and even in the United States is mostly confined to the Northeast. In this form of local governance, legislative powers are vested in citizens who exercise those powers during a town meeting of local residents. Here, residents in Strafford, Vermont, are meeting to discuss local issues and elect town clerks.

Although not a particularly widespread form of local governance, it is probably the oldest, and certainly the most democratic. Its origins are rooted in the religious communities that made up early colonial settlements in New England. A high premium was put on consensus in these communities, and the town meeting evolved as a means to reach such widespread agreement. Such meetings allowed citizens to have a direct role in deciding what laws they would pass and who would be responsible for implementing and enforcing these laws. In many cases the politics were worked out before the actual town meeting, with neighbor talking to neighbor across their fences and in taverns. The grassroots agreements hashed out in these informal discussions was expressed as community consensus in the town meeting.[18]

What all of this boils down to is that legislative functions are concentrated in the citizens themselves. A town meeting is convened through a warrant, or an announcement of the date, time, and place of the meeting, and the items to be discussed. It is open to all community citizens, and all have an equal vote in matters of town policy. Such legislative power often is exercised directly; for example, budgets are approved by town meetings. Some authority, however, may be delegated to a representative board, whose members are called selectmen. The board of selectmen exercises whatever authority is granted to it and is responsible for seeing that policies enacted in the town meeting are carried out.

Towns also have incorporated some elements of the council-manager system by voting to hire professional managers to handle the administrative side of government. The manager system seems to work well with this type of government; at a minimum it is widespread. For example, roughly 30 percent of the towns in Maine—most of them small communities with fewer than 2,500 residents—have managers but still hold town meetings as well.[19]

The town meeting is probably the most idealized form of government that has ever existed in the United States. Thomas Jefferson, for example, saw this grassroots democratic approach to self-governance as, "the wisest invention ever devised by man." [20] Alexis de Tocqueville, the nineteenth-century French aristocrat who wrote one of the most celebrated analyses of the American political system, referred to towns as the "fertile germ" of democracy.[21] For even modestly large communities, however, this approach simply isn't practical. A gathering of citizens that runs into the thousands will be too unwieldy, and the likelihood of getting broad agreement from such a large group on any number of policy issues is pretty low. This goes a long way toward explaining why this approach is thus largely confined to smaller communities in New England.

Special Districts

Special districts, for the most part, are fundamentally different from the other forms of local government already discussed. Counties and municipalities are general purpose governments that provide a broad range of public services within their given jurisdictions. Special districts, on the other hand, are mostly single-purpose governments. They are created to provide a specific service that, for whatever reason, is not being provided by a general purpose government.

With few exceptions special districts exist outside the consciousness of the average citizen. More than thirty thousand special districts have been created across the country—and often across borders of other units of government—to administer single programs or services. One of those exceptions, and the most common form of special district, are school districts. Next in line, and much lower in profile, are sewer and water systems, which account for about one-third of special districts nationwide. These are followed by districts for such purposes as fire protection, housing, education, and sanitation.

Still other districts administer transportation, soil conservation, mosquito control, water, and even libraries. Commuters may not know it, but hundreds of thousands of them use some pretty well known special districts every day. The Port Authority of New York and New Jersey, Boston's Massachusetts Bay Transportation Authority, and the Washington Metropolitan Area Transportation Authority of the District of Columbia collectively cover hundreds of square miles and cross dozens of government borders.

Oklahoma was one of five territories to gain statehood in the twentieth century. At one point, American Indians initiated efforts to create a state from land in the Indian and Oklahoma territories. Today, the state is home to the most members of recognized tribes in the country, and like other native groups in the United States, many of these have their own government and judicial systems.

Why use special districts to provide single programs or services? Why not just have a county or a municipality add that service to its governing portfolio? Well, in certain situations, single-purpose governments can seem attractive solutions to political and practical problems. For example, special districts sometimes are implemented as a way of heading off threats of political annexation of one local government by another. They also are used as a tool for community and business improvement. Freed of local tax authority, administrators of special districts often can get infrastructure items built and services provided without dipping into any one locality's funds. For example, farmers in special water districts, particularly in the West, are eligible for discounted federal loans to help them with irrigation. In addition, special districts can use private-sector business techniques in management, such as paying market rates instead of government rates to contractors.

Working within Limits: The Powers and Constraints of Local Government

Local governments, regardless of their particular form, differ from the state and federal government in a fundamentally important way: they are not sovereign. What this means is that local governments draw their power not from the citizens they serve, but from the government immediately above them. This means the state government, and it is why states considered in isolation were referred to as unitary governments in the introduction to this chapter.

This is not to say that local governments are powerless. Far from it. Local governments are charged with the primary responsibility for delivering a broad range of public services (education, law enforcement, roads, utilities, etc.), and they have broad authority to levy taxes and pass regulations and ordinances. (An ordinance is a law passed by a nonsovereign government.) Yet despite all their responsibilities and powers (not to mention their sheer numbers) all forms of local governments are, at least technically, not equal partners in government. They are subordinate to the state governments from which they are granted their power.

Why is this the case? The short answer is the Tenth Amendment to the U.S. Constitution. Local governments are not mentioned anywhere in the U.S. Constitution, which divides power between the federal and state governments. Despite the longstanding cultural practice of having strong local governments, legally they fall under the purview of the Tenth Amendment's guarantee of state sovereignty. This means the power to determine the scope of authority of local governments is among those "reserved to the States respectively, or to the people." In other words, states get to say what localities can and cannot do. They set the limits and define the terms.

Policy in Practice: Eminent Domain and Local Power

Although local governments are not sovereign, this does not mean they are powerless. Many local governments, for example, have the power of eminent domain, or the right to take private property without the owner's consent.

The Fifth Amendment to the U.S. Constitution compels any government exercising such powers to offer the owner just compensation for the property taken. That, however, often does little to mollify people who have their lives or communities uprooted to make way for a new road or a new development.

Eminent domain became a hot topic recently because of a U.S. Supreme Court decision. In *Kelo v. New London* (2002) the court ruled homeowners could be forced to sell not just to a city but to private developers who would add to the city's tax base. In effect, the court said that local governments have a central role in planning and that economic development cannot be halted simply because some property owner objects.

At first blush, this seems to be a significant boost to the power and reach of local governments. The political fallout from the *Kelo* ruling, however, also has provided an instructive lesson in Dillon's rule. In the wake of the court's decision a number of states immediately moved to curb local powers of eminent domain. There undoubtedly would have been more immediate action

by state legislatures except for the fact that many of them were not in session when the ruling was announced. A few states, including Nevada and Utah, anticipated the ruling and passed new restrictions on eminent domain before the Supreme Court made its decision.

Eminent domain, in other words, may be a real power exercised by local governments, but it is one of the most unpopular exercises of power taken by any level of government. Any time a local government uses eminent domain it often finds its power challenged, not by a court or another level of government, but by its own citizens. For example, when Cypress, California, decided to force a church to sell in order to make way for a Costco store the political fallout was so negative that local officials backed off and sought a less confrontational (and more expensive) settlement.

"Elected officials rightly know that they cannot go around taking property at will," says Indianapolis Mayor Bart Peterson, who has taken the lead on this issue for the National League of Cities. Eminent domain is an important and sweeping power given many local governments, and it remains an important tool to aid economic development. Like most powers exercised by local government, however, the power of eminent domain is far from absolute.

Source: Alan Greenblatt, "Land Law," *Governing,* magazine, August 2005.

Dillon's Rule

The legal doctrine that defines the division of power between state and local governments is known as **Dillon's Rule,** named after Iowa Supreme Court justice John F. Dillon. In addition to having a fine legal mind, Dillon was a highly respected and well-read scholar of local government. An argument he formulated in 1868 has served ever since as the basis for understanding and justifying the power—or, more accurately, the lack of power—of local government. The rule is built around the legal principle of *ultra vires*, which means "outside one's powers." In a nutshell, it states that local governments are limited to the powers expressly granted to them by their state and to

DILLON'S RULE

The legal principle that says local governments can exercise only the powers granted to them by state government.

those powers indispensable to the stated objectives and purposes of each local government.

What Dillon essentially did was build a legal argument that the Tenth Amendment secured power for the states, but not for local governments. As Dillon himself put it in his famous 1868 ruling in *City of Clinton v. the Cedar Rapids and Missouri Railroad*: local governments are "mere tenants at the will of their respective state legislatures." The rule has structured legal thinking on the power of local governments ever since, although it has always had its critics and opponents. It was challenged as early as the 1870s, when Missouri legislators rewrote the state constitution specifically to allow municipalities a degree of independence from the constraints of state government.[23]

For the most part, however, Dillon's Rule holds. In a nutshell, state power trumps local government power, which means state legislatures invariably win power struggles with local governments. In Virginia, for example, antitax lawmakers continually prevent localities from restructuring their tax systems to raise revenue. It should come as no surprise that ambitious state legislators hoard power over their county and city counterparts.

> In a nutshell, Dillon's Rule means state power trumps local government power, which means state legislatures invariably win power struggles with local governments.

Yet while Dillon's Rule says state governments can grant and retract powers to local government powers as they see fit, Dillon himself felt that it would be a bad idea for state governments to take full advantage of this legal authority. The bottom line is that the division of labor between local and state governments, broadly speaking, works. It makes sense, Dillon argued, for states to respect local government autonomy because of cultural tradition and sheer practicality. Accordingly, the independence and powers state governments grant to localities vary considerably. Some state governments are more willing than others to let local governments make their own decisions. Much of these differences can be explained by state culture and degree of citizen participation. Idaho and West Virginia reserve the most local powers to the state. Oregon and Maine give localities the most freedom.[24]

The powers granted to substate political jurisdictions, in other words, reflect the cultural traditions, politics, and practicalities of governance unique to each state. This variation is a difference that can make a difference. For example, it can make a difference in taxes. What local governments can or cannot tax, and by how much, is structured by state law. For example, Virginia allows cities with populations greater than five thousand to operate independently of the counties of which they are a part. It also gives these communities the right to impose sales taxes on meals, lodging, or cigarettes. On the other hand, counties in Virginia are heavily reliant on a single revenue source—property taxes—to pay their bills.[25] This can pose a serious dilemma for county leaders. When the housing market is booming, many homeowners watch their property assessments, and hence their annual taxes, rise relentlessly. In many cases, the property taxes rise faster than their incomes. These homeowners, subsequently, take it out on county leaders come election time.

It's not just taxes. State governments can, and sometimes do, place regulatory limits on local government in areas ranging from taxes to titles, from personnel to pensions. For example, the city of Buffalo, New York, is prevented from controlling the salaries and pensions of its uniformed workers because of New York State labor laws. The state limits the pool of candidates the city can consider when hiring managers. And state requirements for thorough hearings in cases of alleged disciplinary infractions by city employees make it tough for a city official to speedily fire an unsuitable staffer.

States also invoke Dillon's Rule to block localities from enacting what are called living wage laws. Living wage laws are part of a union-backed movement to require businesses that win contracts with a local government to pay prevailing area wages rather than just the federal minimum wage. This means that publicly financed workers can support a family without working multiple jobs. Such floors in wages can amount to twice the federal minimum wage. Proposals for such laws often clash with the desire of the business community to keep labor costs down.

Home Rule

Dillon's Rule establishes a clear legal hierarchy between state and local governments. Unlike federal and state governments, which are co-equal partners, local governments are unquestionably subordinate to state governments. Yet states, if they so choose, can grant considerable autonomy to local governments. Many states make such grants of autonomy formal through **home rule**, or the freedom to make local decisions without interference from state government. Home rule typically is enshrined in a **charter**, which spells out the powers and purposes of the local government. In effect, a charter is the municipal equivalent of a constitution.

The movement for such charters got started in the nineteenth century and peaked in the early 1970s. Charters can be adopted only after voters approve a council-approved or citizen-written petition. Thirty-six of the forty-eight states that use a county form of government allow charters or some form of home rule, according to the National Association of Counties (NACo). This can free these communities from both state and county obligations. Even under home rule, however, the state may place some strict limits on local government autonomy. Even those who might be thought of as natural advocates of home rule support keeping a measure of state control. For instance, city or county employees may prefer state protections to giving local mayor or city manager too much authority. Antitax groups often fear that independent cities free of state regulation will raise new taxes.

HOME RULE

The right of localities to self-government, usually granted through a charter.

CHARTER

A document that outlines the powers, organization, and responsibilities of a local government.

Local Focus: Sex and the City ... Charter

Unless the discussion turns to sex, an ancient document written by city founders laying out the powers of a community's government seldom makes for popular reading. And that applies in spades to the sprawling and formless municipality of Los Angeles. There, a charter originally drafted in 1925 was for decades ignored by most neighborhood citizens but exploited by business lobbyists and downtown insiders who wanted their development projects approved with only minimal public debate.

When the Los Angeles city charter was revised and put to the voters in July 1999, a *Los Angeles Times* poll conducted three months before the vote showed that nine out of ten respondents said they did not know enough about the proposed charter to judge the reforms.[a]

The idea of charter reform was the work of Mayor Richard Riordan who, although he would not remain in office to enjoy it, had wanted to strengthen the city's famously weak mayoral powers and clip the wings of city council members who, many felt, had built their own personal fiefdoms across L.A.'s disconnected geography.

With city council members skeptical, two competing commissions were set up to research and draft the reforms. One was run by a law professor and another by a neighborhood negotiator. The two might never have seen eye-to-eye were it not for a stepped-up threat in 1998 from activists in the San Fernando Valley. Many of the 1.5 million suburbanites in this area, packed onto reclaimed farmland north of downtown, have long wanted to secede from Los Angeles and form their own city.

The prospect of such a loss prompted the two commissions to agree on a set of reforms that would simplify an intricate document that had been amended four hundred times. Their changes would strengthen the office of the mayor, allow voters to consider expanding the fifteen-member city council in the future, restrict civil service protection for high-level officials, and set up a new network of neighborhood councils.

There was resistance among council members who were wary of concentrating too much power, such as the authority to fire department heads, with a mayor. Critics noted that the reforms would do nothing to exert more control over the vast Los Angeles Unified School System and that the new charter would leave intact the inconsistency between the Los Angeles planning commission boundaries and the political district boundaries used when electing the nonpartisan city council members. Finally, most neighborhood organizations were left as weakly organized as they had been before the reforms.

Still, the charter reforms passed with backing of 60 percent of L.A. voters. The new charter took effect in July 2002.[b]

Out of sight, out of mind. The next time many Los Angelinos would read about their new city charter was during a 2003 controversy over the regulation of strip clubs. Critics believe that the proliferation of "gentlemen's clubs" in certain L.A. neighborhoods has increased public drunkenness and harmed property values. Therefore, the city council unanimously passed an ordinance that banned the clubs from permitting male customers to go into private rooms and touch the female "lap dancers."

The adult entertainment industry stepped in, spending some $400,000 to make use of a provision in the city charter that allows any group of citizens to repeal a city ordinance if, within thirty days of its enactment, they gather signatures on a petition at a number equal to 10 percent of the people who voted for the mayor in the most recent election.

Under the threat of total repeal and leery of the costs of putting the measure to voters, the council retreated, working out a compromise with the clubs that included more narrow restrictions on sexual touching and stepped-up enforcement of rules in granting business permits.[c]

[a] Jim Newton, "Los Angeles: Voters Know Little of Candidates or Charter," *Los Angeles Times*, April 1, 1999. www.latimes.com (accessed January 14, 2004).

[b] William Fulton and Paul Shigley, "Putting Los Angeles Together," *Governing* magazine, June 2000.

[c] Robert Greene, "A Touch of Democracy: A Lap Dancer's Guide to Beating City Hall," *L.A. Weekly*, November 14–20, 2003. www.laweekly.com (accessed January 20, 2004).

Home rule can be granted in two basic forms. Legislatures may approve home rule in what are called **general act charters**, which apply to all cities, or **special act charters**, which affect only one community. Either type can be initiated by state legislators, local councils, or citizens groups. In cases of citizen initiatives, advocates gather the requisite number of signatures on petitions that are then converted to legislation or language for a ballot referendum that is put before voters.

For example, one fifth of all California cities are charter cities. In 2000, a ballot question for the city of Signal Hill asked voters whether the city should become a locally governed charter city, as opposed to a general law city that would be governed by all statewide laws. The question explained that the charter would serve as the city's constitution, giving it full control over its municipal affairs.

The ballot text specified that municipal affairs included "regulation of municipal utilities; procedures for bidding and contracting; regulation of parks, libraries, and other facilities; salaries of officers and employees; parking regulations; franchise and other fees; taxation; and zoning and election procedures." It also noted that the charter could exempt the city from some state sales taxes.

The city would remain subject to state law on "matters of statewide importance," however. This basically meant environmental regulations, General Plan requirements, open-meeting laws, public records, and redevelopment. Despite the complexity of the issue and the uncertainty about the fiscal impact of home rule, the charter city ballot question passed with 86 percent of the vote.[26] In principle, American voters are supportive of local government autonomy, even though with such autonomy comes new responsibilities.

While voters generally support the notion of local government autonomy, and generally oppose state or federal governments making decisions on behalf of local communities, there are benefits to state or federal oversight. What is lost in local control can be offset by the deeper pockets of the larger, sovereign governments. Much of what local leaders wish to accomplish requires infusions of funds from Washington and state capitols. So with oversight at least comes cold, hard cash. The superior capacities of state governments and the federal government to raise revenues is another limit on the powers of localities.

The important point here is that there are a set of trade-offs that go along with greater local government autonomy. County officials, for example, are responsible for the building and maintenance of extensive road systems, as well as for enforcing traffic and safety laws on those roads. That's an expensive proposition, and counties generally welcome state and federal money to support these critical public services. Yet the golden rule—he who gives the gold, gets to make the rules—means those funds inevitably come with strings. The obligations that come with the money in the form of state or federal mandates are not nearly as popular as the cash. This sets up a love-hate relationship between local authorities and the state and federal governments above them. On the one hand, state and federal governments are frustrating because they restrict the decision making freedom of local authorities. The restrictions and conditions, however, are often the price of intergovernmental grants that underwrite important local government functions.

Participation in Local Government

Local governments are not only distinguished from state and federal governments by their power (or lack thereof), but also by their politics. Comparatively speaking, state and federal politics are dominated by political parties, which contest elections, mobilize voters, and organize government. Things are different down at the local level: more than two-thirds of local governments are nonpartisan. Since the decline of the big-city political machines of the early twentieth century, candidates for county boards and city councils run on their personal competence for the most part rather than on ideology or past affiliation. Only 17 percent of city councils hold partisan elections, according to the ICMA. Yet in some cities, partisan labels that have been abolished officially continue to play a role unofficially. This occurred in Chicago. Officially abolished since the 1930s, partisan labels have remained in play as Democrats continue to dominate the heavily African American city.

Council members usually run in **ward, or district, elections.** The populations of such districts can reach as high as 246,000, as in Los Angeles, or 165,000, as in Phoenix. The advantage of such elections is that they assure each neighborhood of having a local on the city council who knows their streets and residents by name. This is especially important for minorities who may be grouped together by housing patterns.

Other jurisdictions permit candidates to run in **at-large elections.** This means that they can hail from any part of the jurisdiction. The advantage of having candidates run at-large, and the reason most cities opt for it, is that it makes room for a greater pool of highly qualified and talented people who, presumably, look at the interests of the city as a whole. Some city charters require a combination of ward representatives and at-large members. But it can get controversial. In 1991 in Dallas, court-ordered redistricting required a switch from an at-large system to fourteen members chosen by districts. The result was that more Hispanics and blacks won seats.

There is perhaps no better example of the unique nature of local politics than the town meetings that define local governance in New England. Usually held twice a year when the elected council or clerk issues a warrant, or agenda, these gatherings epitomize direct democracy in action. Citizens can do everything from pass a budget to resolve to oppose a developer's plan for a new golf course. There simply is no equivalent to this comprehensive citizen legislature at the state or federal level, nor, as a practical matter, could there be.

One of the paradoxes of local government is that although it is the level of government citizens support the most, it is the level of government they participate in the least. Turnout in local elections is often half of the national average of 55 percent voter turnout in a presidential election. This reflects a general indifference among many citizens toward the prosaic affairs of local government. Neighborhood volunteer and community development organizations, although often run by articulate and dedicated activists, often involve as little as 3 percent to 12 percent of the local population.[27]

Yet the absence of popular fervor in local issues does not mean that local offices are not important. Indeed, politics at this level can have implications for state and even national politics. For example, local government offices often serve as proving grounds for up-and-coming politicians who go on to higher office at the state or national level. New immigrants, particularly Asians and Latinos,

There are more females in the ranks of local officials these days, though women remain proportionally under-represented in key elective offices. For example, compared to males, there are relatively few female mayors, especially of major cities. Still, there are plenty of examples of successful female chief executives. Two are shown here: Laura Gasbarre, mayor of Leavenworth, Kansas, is pictured here speaking at a press conference in the state capitol. Allyson Adams is mayor of Virginia City, Montana. (The baby goat, by the way, is part of a plan to keep weeds down on city property without spraying potentially harmful chemicals.)

increasingly are working their way into public office. By the end of the twentieth century, a third of all cities with more than two hundred thousand residents had elected either a Hispanic or black mayor.[28] The number of Hispanic or Latino officials, according to the 2003 *Directory of Latino Elected Officials,* is 438 among county officials, 1,522 among municipal officials, 1,694 among school board members, and 168 among special district officials.

The increase in black local officials over the final third of the twentieth century was dramatic. According to the Washington-based Joint Center for Political and Economic Studies, from 1970 to 2001, the number of black mayors rose from 48 to 454, the number of black city council members rose from 552 to 3,538, and the number of black county commissioners rose from 64 to 820.

Women also have made great gains, although far from their proportion as half the total population. According to the Center for American Women and Politics in Washington, D.C., as of June 2003, there were fourteen female mayors among the largest one hundred U.S. cities. One is African American, Shirley Franklin of Atlanta, Georgia; and one is Latino, Heather Fargo of Sacramento, California.

Where partisan affiliations are allowed at the local level, there have been some historically important divisions among voters. For example, minority groups have tended to cast their ballots with Democratic candidates, who also drew Catholics and the liberal intelligentsia. Republicans tended to draw votes from WASPs, or white Anglo-Saxon Protestants; big business; and law-and-order enthusiasts. This is changing, however. In New York City in 2001, billionaire Michael Bloomberg, who had switched from the Democratic Party to the Republican Party, spent millions of dollars of his own money in an upset victory over Democratic public advocate Mark Green. Part of his success was that he was able to attract Hispanic voters.[29]

> The payoff for winning local office is more likely to come in the form of visibility and personal satisfaction than in cold, hard cash. Mayors, many of whom are part-time, earn an average of $8,400.

The payoff for winning local office is more likely to come in the form of visibility and personal satisfaction than in cold, hard cash. Mayors, many of whom are part-time, earn an average of $8,400. By contrast, mayors of large cities such as Chicago or New York can earn upwards of $200,000. Council members generally earn less than mayors. In most small and medium-sized cities, being a member of the city council is more of a public service than a part-time job. Even in large mayor-council cities—where being a member of the city council is a full-time job—the average compensation is less than $40,000 a year.[30] Professional city or county mangers, on the other hand, tend to be fairly well-compensated white-collar positions. According to the ICMA, city managers made about $92,000 a year in 2003, and county managers a little more.

The weekly average workload for council members in small, medium, and large cities is twenty, twenty-five, and forty-two hours, respectively. The typical number of hours they spend doing services for constituents rose to 35 percent of their time in 2001. In larger cities with mayor-council systems, more than 90 percent of elected officials have staffs at their disposal, compared with only half in smaller cities, says the National League of Cities.[31]

Not surprisingly, 66 percent of city council members in the National League of Cities survey said they wanted a raise. Many citizens oppose large salaries for their local officials, particularly at the school board level, because they feel the nominal fees they receive are not an hourly wage, but rather a stipend that honors public spiritedness.

The Road Ahead

The forms and functions of local governments have evolved through myriad permutations, nearly all of them designed to produce leaders and practices that maximize both efficiency and responsiveness to voters. Yet few local governments can go it alone. In the first five years of the twenty-first century local governments suffered considerably as recession squeezed budgets. By 2006 most local governments had significantly improved their fiscal outlooks, helped by a hot real estate market that improved property tax revenues. The real estate market, though, began to cool in 2006, signaling that market forces might begin to put downward pressure on the growth of property tax revenues.

Yet there is no question that local governments face a number of looming fiscal and policy challenges. Unfunded mandates and the escalating expenses associated with public employment are two prominent examples of such challenges. State officials often are heard to complain about unfunded mandates from the federal government, but local officials face a double whammy; they have to deal with unfunded mandates from state and federal governments. Nine in ten city officials say that unfunded mandates pose significant challenges to municipal government. Coupled with cuts or limits in state and federal aid, not to mention other laws limiting the revenue options at the local level, the actions at higher levels of government are boxing in the ability of local government to provide services.[32]

For example, local governments often are expected to help provide affordable housing for needy citizens. Yet block grants from the federal government to support affordable housing are being cut. At the same time, the federal government has passed laws limiting the use of franchise fees that cities can charge to cable companies, a significant source of revenue for municipalities. The demand for affordable housing has not dropped off—quite the opposite, in fact—and local governments are still

Policy in Practice: Phone Home for Revenue

Once upon a time, back before cell phones, cities charged phone companies franchise and right-of-way fees. The money was steady, and it helped underwrite city budgets. Cities still charge these fees, at least they try to. The money, though, is not as steady as it used to be.

The basic problem is that landlines seem to be going the way of the dinosaur. And if the tax laws are based on collecting revenues from century-old technology, they obviously do not capture the impact of new technologies that have freed the telephone from a cable or a wire. It's not just landlines that are disappearing, but the local tax revenue that goes along with them.

In 2005, roughly 8 percent of cell phone users dropped their landline phone services. As telecom companies switch from wires to wireless, they are less inclined to pay local governments for the privilege of stringing cable and planting telephone poles. For example, Portland, Oregon, has seen its revenues from Qwest, one of its two traditional telephone providers, drop by about 50 percent since 1999. That adds up to $3.1 million a year—a not insignificant chunk of change.

The Portland city council has tried unsuccessfully to update its tax code to pull all telephone providers into a tax net. "We viewed it as just taxing phone services no matter the technology," says Mary Beth Henry, Portland's deputy director of the Cable and Franchise Management Office. It's met with mixed success; taxes on the new communications technology have proven to be unpopular with telecom users who put pressure on state governments to take the issue out of the hands of local governments.

Some states are reacting to the changing telecom world by simplifying and centralizing their tax codes to reflect the new communications technologies. Typically this involves not only lowering tax rates, but also extending them to telephone technologies generally, not just landlines. Such changes also can involve states playing a more prominent role in collecting and distributing these fees and reducing the independent role of cities to manage this revenue stream.

Some cities are rebelling against such moves. St. Louis, Missouri, for example, has campaigned against a state proposal to implement a 5 percent telecom tax rate. This would be collected by the state and distributed to the cities, but the state wants to take a cut of the revenue in the form of a collection fee, and it also wants to require cities to drop all lawsuits filed against providers to recover back taxes. This is a big deal in Missouri, where many cities were suing telecom companies who have refused to pay telephone taxes.

The bottom line is that disappearing telephone lines are an important challenge for local governments. They somehow have to adapt to new technologies that effect—make that shrink—their revenue streams.

Source: Sarah Wheaton, "Ringing in Change," *Governing* magazine, June 2006.

expected to step up to the plate and respond to this demand. They have to do this, though, while facing reduced support from the federal government and federal laws that limit their ability to raise the cash to do it on their own.

A second major challenge looming for local governments, however, is less a function of federal or state decision making than of labor markets and poor planning. Some of the biggest pressure on local budgets comes from employee salaries and benefits. In a recent survey, nearly 90 percent of city officials cite these two factors as big budgetary challenges.[33] Like all big employers, municipal governments are struggling to cover healthcare benefits that are rising faster than inflation. They also are dealing with covering "legacy costs," or the obligations to cover pensions and benefits for public retirees. For years many local governments have approved benefit packages with little thought to how these benefits will pressure future budgets. In the past couple of years, it has become clear that the pressure will be considerable.

Despite such challenges, the current vibrancy and long-term durability of governments at the town, city, county, and special-district levels continue to be seen in the variety of ways each responds to circumstances of geography, economics, and political culture. And there is no shortage of candidates willing to pay the price in time, sweat, and sacrificed income that it takes to make a go of it in the modern world of local elected office. These small-scale leaders continue to debate and organize to provide valued services using a process consistent with a loftier vision of democracy. De Tocqueville noted nearly two hundred years ago that democracy in America was practiced unusually effectively at the local level where "inhabitants with the same interests" manage to provide "all the elements of a good administration." At least in this way, local government hasn't changed much at all.

Conclusion

De Tocqueville viewed local governments in the United States as sort of mini republics. He saw them as civic entities in which citizens were closest to government and government reflected accurately what citizens desired. In many ways, that perspective is still valid. Local governments wield real power, and they are responsible for important programs and services. They come in a bewildering variety of types, many of which reflect state or regional history, culture, and preferences. As a whole, all of these differences can seem confusing. Yet in any single place—your hometown, the local county—the government and what it does or does not do probably seems perfectly reasonable and natural.

Local government certainly remains the most common form of government in the United States, and it is still the form of government the average citizen is most likely to come into contact with on a day-to-day basis. Counties, municipalities, and special districts build and maintain roads, police those roads, run schools, manage libraries, and provide other programs and services too numerous to list. And they do all of this while employing very different approaches to government. Some are run by powerful executives, others by more egalitarian councils or commissions. Still others are mostly run by professional managers.

Yet local government is far from ideal. These mini republics are constrained by Dillon's Rule. They tend to have relatively low voter turnout for elections. The idiosyncrasies of local government structure can mean electing someone with no real administrative experience to run a complicated bureaucracy with a multimillion-dollar budget. Local governments face significant challenges that range from the urban dysfunction brought on by sprawl to finding the money to hold up their end of the war on terror. Just because the politics are local does not mean they are less difficult.

Key Concepts

at-large elections (p. 390)

charter (p. 387)

cities (p. 374)

city commission system (p. 381)

city council (p. 375)

city manager (p. 375)

commission-administrator system (p. 372)

council-executive (p. 372)

council-manager system (p. 378)

counties (p. 367)

county commission system (p. 371)

Dillon's Rule (p. 385)

general act charters (p. 389)

home rule (p. 387)

mayor (p. 375)

mayor-council system (p. 375)

municipalities (p. 367)

special act charters (p. 389)

special districts (p. 367)

strong mayor (p. 375)

town meeting form of government (p. 381)

townships (p. 374)

ward, or district, elections (p. 390)

wards (p. 377)

weak mayor (p. 375)

Suggested Readings

Garvin, Alexander. *The American City: What Works, What Doesn't,* 2nd ed. New York: McGraw-Hill, 2002. A comprehensive reference to urban planning and design in the United States that analyzes key projects initiated in 250 urban areas.

Kemp, Roger L., ed. *Model Government Charters: A City, County, Regional, State, and Federal Handbook.* Jefferson, N.C.: McFarland, 2003. Each chapter covers a different level of government and the sample charters provided describe the laws that form the basis of government.

Orfield, Myron. *Metropolitics: A Regional Agenda for Community and Stability.* Washington, D.C.: Brookings Institution, 1997. Using the example of the Twin Cities of Minneapolis and St. Paul, Minnesota, the author presents a system of regional government meant to improve schools, create affordable housing, and protect the environment and quality of life.

Pelissero, John P., ed. *Cities, Politics, and Policy: A Comparative Analysis.* Washington, D.C.: CQ Press, 2003. Through case studies and cross-sectional analyses of a variety of urban areas, this text shows how scholars find patterns and draw conclusions that offer insights beneficial to all communities.

Vogel, Ronald K., ed. *Handbook of Research on Urban Politics and Policy in the United States.* Westport, Conn.: Greenwood Press, 1997. This reference work provides access to research on urban politics and policy in the United States.

Suggested Web Sites

www.brookings.edu. Web site of the Brookings Institution, one of Washington, D.C.'s oldest think tanks, which pursues independent, nonpartisan research in such areas as metropolitan policy and governance.

www.census.gov. Web site of the U.S. Census Bureau, which is responsible for collecting and tabulating data on the population and demographics of the United States.

www2.icma.org/main/sc.asp. Web site of the International City/County Management Association, whose mission is to create excellence in local government by developing and fostering professional local government management worldwide.

www.naco.org. Created in 1935, the National Association of Counties is the only national organization that represents county governments in the United States.

www.natat.org. The National Association of Towns and Townships seeks to strengthen the effectiveness of town and township governments by exploring flexible and alternative approaches to federal policies to ensure that smaller communities can meet federal requirements.

www.nlc.org. Web site of the National League of Cities, the oldest and largest national organization representing municipal governments in the United States.

www.usmayors.org. The Web site of the U.S. Conference of Mayors, which is the official nonpartisan organization of the nation's 1,183 cities with populations of 30,000 or more.

CHAPTER 11

Metropolitics

The Hole Problem of Government

Critics of urban governance argue that there is a hole in local government. Not a hole quite as literal as this one, but rather the general absence of meaningful regional government. While many issues—such as transportation and highway maintenance—are essentially regional in nature, there is a notable lack of regional political jurisdictions.

11

What is the "hole" in government?

Why do the decisions of one local government affect the decisions of other local governments?

Why do patterns of growth create pressure for new forms of local government?

Allegheny County, Pennsylvania, has a lot of governments. There is the county government, of course. You've probably also heard of the county seat: Pittsburgh, a city famed for football (the Steelers are five-time Super Bowl champs), ketchup (headquarters of the H. J. Heinz Company), and steel (in the early twentieth century, Pittsburgh accounted for half of the nation's steel manufacturing). Pittsburgh is a major metropolitan city, with a general purpose government organized under a mayor-council system.

Chances are, though, that you can't name even a tiny fraction of all the governments in Allegheny County, even if you live there. If you can, you have a remarkably good memory. For example, there are more than one hundred municipalities in the county. Pittsburgh is the biggest, but there are eighty-five other cities or boroughs in the county limits. (In Pennsylvania a borough is a general purpose municipal government). Add to that forty-two townships and forty-four school districts. Then there is a mix of other special districts—everything from the West Mifflin Sanitary Sewer Municipal Authority to the Allegheny County Hospital Development Authority. If anyone bothered to count, and as it happens, someone has, that person would find a grand total of 273 local governments in Allegheny County.[1]

That works out to be 1 government for every 2.56 square miles, or 1 government for every 4,526 residents.[2] Like we said, Allegheny County has a lot of government. All those political jurisdictions add up to a lot of differences and, you guessed it, those differences make a difference. There are more than a hundred police departments and more than two hundred volunteer fire companies.[3] There are different public works departments, dispatch centers, library systems, purchasing operations . . . you get the point. There are a lot of differences. And how do they make a difference? Well, in taxes for one thing.

Consider that someone owning property valued at $100,000 in Pine Township on the county's northern edge will pay about $120 in municipal taxes annually. A similarly valued property in the city of Pittsburgh will cost its owner $1,080 in taxes.[4] In other words, the property tax burden can vary by a factor of ten depending on where the property is located within a county's borders. Of course, not everybody pays taxes for the same public services. What public services are available, and the quality of those services, also will vary from place to place.

Governing States and Localities

Keeping up with all this variation can cause a headache. So can trying to make rational sense of it. The problem with large urban areas like Pittsburgh and its immediate surrounding areas is that the fragmented political system is not really designed to deal with the realities of governing. In Allegheny County there are lot of governments engaged in providing the same services, and each has its own political leaders, governance structure, and bureaucracy. Some say this is a bad thing. Splitting the responsibilities of local government into literally hundreds of small slices adds up to a lot of redundant inefficiency.

It also makes it incredibly difficult to coordinate an effective response to a wide range of problems that have multi-jurisdictional causes and consequences. Consider traffic. Authorizing, say, the construction of a new industrial park means a lot of new commuters. Chances are that many of these commuters will live in other communities, which they will drive through on their way to work. Those communities face increased pressure on their transportation infrastructures and have to deal with the expensive consequences of a more heavily used transportation system. In other words, a decision by one local government can have important implications for other local governments. This not only makes coordination difficult, it can lead to a lot of hard feelings and conflict.

Other individuals, however, say "vive la difference." Pittsburgh and Allegheny County are like most other major metropolitan areas in that for a lot of people they are pretty terrific places to work, live, go to school, or raise a family. So what if there are a lot of local governments? The positive side to having a lot of different municipalities, townships, and counties with their different tax rates and levels of public services is choice, and lots of it. All those differences mean people can choose to live in a place that has the right mix of taxes and public services to suit their individual preferences. Of course, this assumes they actually have the resources and the knowledge to make such choices, an assumption that more than one political scientist has questioned.

This chapter explores the consequences of all these differences and what they mean for everything from effective environmental policies to dealing with racial segregation, poverty, crime, political inequality, and traffic congestion. Addressing such problems in places like Allegheny County is hard because it demands that not just one or two governments do something, but that dozens or even hundreds of governments do something. And whatever that something is, it needs to be effectively coordinated if it is going to provide a reasonable solution to the problem. And there's the rub. According to some, the organization and structure of government at the local level not only makes it hard to forge solutions to certain problems, it makes finding those solutions harder.

Chapter 10 discussed the number of different forms of local government and a number of different ways to organize local government. This chapter focuses more on the importance and difficulty of coordinating all those different localities. Most Americans live in urban areas like Allegheny County, areas where local governments are cheek to jowl and piled on top of one another. The central economic and social problems governments must address in these areas are regional rather than local in nature. Yet the United States has no tradition, and few examples, of regional government. It has a lot of local governments with limited abilities and limited incentives to act regionally. How to fashion coherent responses to regional problems is the central challenge of local governance in urban areas. It raises questions about how governments below the state level are organized, as well as fundamental questions of political power, questions that deal with who has the authority to make policy and who has to pay for it.

> How to fashion coherent responses to regional problems is the central challenge of local governance in urban areas. It raises questions about how governments below the state level are organized, as well as fundamental questions of political power, questions that deal with who has the authority to make policy and who has to pay for it.

As it turns out, rural areas are facing the same governance challenges, although for different reasons. Rural areas are being forced to grapple with regional-level coordination issues because shrinking populations cannot provide the tax base to support general purpose governments in small communities. Thus, local governments in rural areas, like local governments in urban areas, are feeling their way toward more cooperative arrangements, sharing the burden of providing public services, and even considering mergers. So, urban or rural, the biggest challenge of all is dealing with a world in which the problems are regional, but the governments are local.

The Missing Level of Government

You might not have noticed, but according to some scholars there is a hole in the organizational structure of the federal system. The basic organization of the federal government, and the powers and responsibilities of state and federal governments, is covered by the U.S. Constitution. The organization of state governments and the powers and responsibilities of state and local governments are covered by individual state constitutions. The "hole" is at the regional level. There is nothing in the Constitution, and virtually nothing in state constitutions, that addresses even the notion of regional government, let alone its organization or powers and responsibilities.

In some ways this is understandable. The federal arrangement set up by the Constitution is the bedrock of the U.S. political system and is deeply woven into the fabric of society. No one seriously proposes to fundamentally alter this arrangement. While standing on less legal authority—local governments, remember, are not sovereign—there is a strong tradition of local government. People tend to be oriented toward their local communities and tend to place more faith in city hall than in the state or national capitol. In contrast, there are no strong legal foundations for regional governments and no strong tradition of regional government either. It is the poor relation of the U.S. political system: little thought of, and outside the community of urban scholars and a handful of officials, not much loved.

Yet the majority of local governments in the United States are, like the 273 governments of Allegheny County, embedded in a larger metropolitan region. These regions have similar policy challenges and problems in that they have common sources and call for common solutions. This absence of some sort of regional umbrella government has been called a "fundamental flaw in America's governance structure." Why? Because "[m]etropolitan regions have become the most important functional units of economic and social life in almost all modern societies."[5] Labor and jobs, for example, rarely are concentrated in a single local political jurisdiction. At the local level, markets are interconnected across political boundaries, with people working in one place and living in another.

While key social and economic issues are regional in nature, in most cases there is no authority looking at these problems from a regional perspective. Local governments tend to view these problems, not unreasonably, from their own parochial perspectives. Pine Township in Allegheny County, for example, hardly can be blamed if it makes decisions in the best interests of the residents of Pine Township rather than for the residents of the city of Pittsburgh. As a local government, that is what it is supposed to do. The problem, of course, is that by making decisions independently the city of Pittsburgh and the municipalities that surround it may be working at cross purposes.

What about county government? Doesn't the county fill the hole between local and state governments? The short answer is no. Counties are divisions of state government meant to provide basic governance functions to less urbanized areas; although they have adapted to modern urban environments, this is not what they were designed for.

Allegheny County makes an instructive example. It is an urban county, but its borders do not define a metropolitan region. The metropolitan region sprawls over several counties, not one. According to the U.S. Census Bureau, a **metropolitan area** is a region with "a large population nucleus, together with adjacent communities having a high degree of social and economic integration with that core." It is important to note that this definition sees a metropolitan area as comprising "one or more entire counties."[6]

For data gathering and reporting purposes, the federal government formally defines metropolitan areas using the concept of a **metropolitan statistical area (MSA)**, an area with a city of fifty thousand or more people, together with adjacent urban communities that have strong ties to the central city. As of the 2000 census there were 362 metropolitan statistical areas in the United States. Roughly 80 percent of U.S. residents live

METROPOLITAIN AREA

A populous region typically comprised of a city and surrounding communities having a high degree of social and economic integration.

METROPOLITAN STATISTICAL AREA (MSA)

An area with a city of fifty thousand or more people, together with adjacent urban communities that have strong ties to the central city.

MAP 11-1 Pittsburgh Metropolitan Statistical Area and Surrounding MSAs

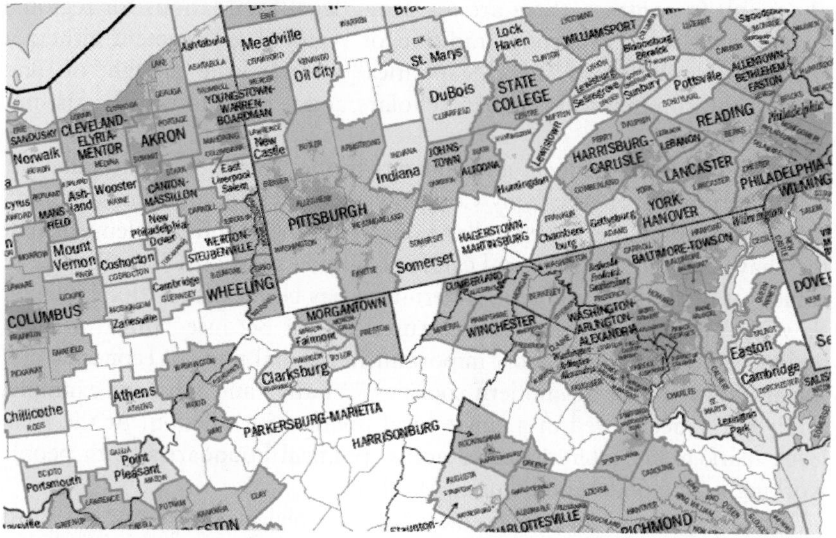

Source: U.S. Census Bureau, Population Division.

in such metropolitan areas, with 30 percent living in central cities.[7] Allegheny County, for example, is part of the Pittsburgh Metropolitan Statistical Area.

The core city of this metropolitan region, obviously, is Pittsburgh. The communities with strong social and economic ties to the core city of Pittsburgh, however, are not confined to Allegheny County. The Pittsburgh Metropolitan Statistical Area covers seven counties. Even this may be a somewhat conservative geographical description of the metropolitan region centered on Pittsburgh. For example, people outside of those seven counties—perhaps even in neighboring counties in Ohio and West Virginia—watch Pittsburgh television stations, read the Pittsburgh paper, and travel to the city for work purposes, to shop, or to watch a Steelers game. They have, in short, strong economic and social ties to the core city.

It is a basic fact of life for most local governments that, like it or not, they are tied socially and economically to a broad range of other local governments in an overarching metropolitan area. Cities, their suburbs, *their* neighboring cities and *their* suburbs, and the counties in which they are geographically located, all tend to blend together into a dense urban concentration. According to the U.S. Conference of Mayors, at the start of the twenty-first century nearly half of the fifty most populated cities in the United States were packed into just one hundred square miles. These population centers account for an astonishing 85 percent of U.S. employment.[8]

But there are even bigger units to consider. These dense metropolitan areas often bump into each other, forming an even larger urban geographi-

MAP 11-2 Metropolitan and Micropolitan Statistical Areas of the Continental United States

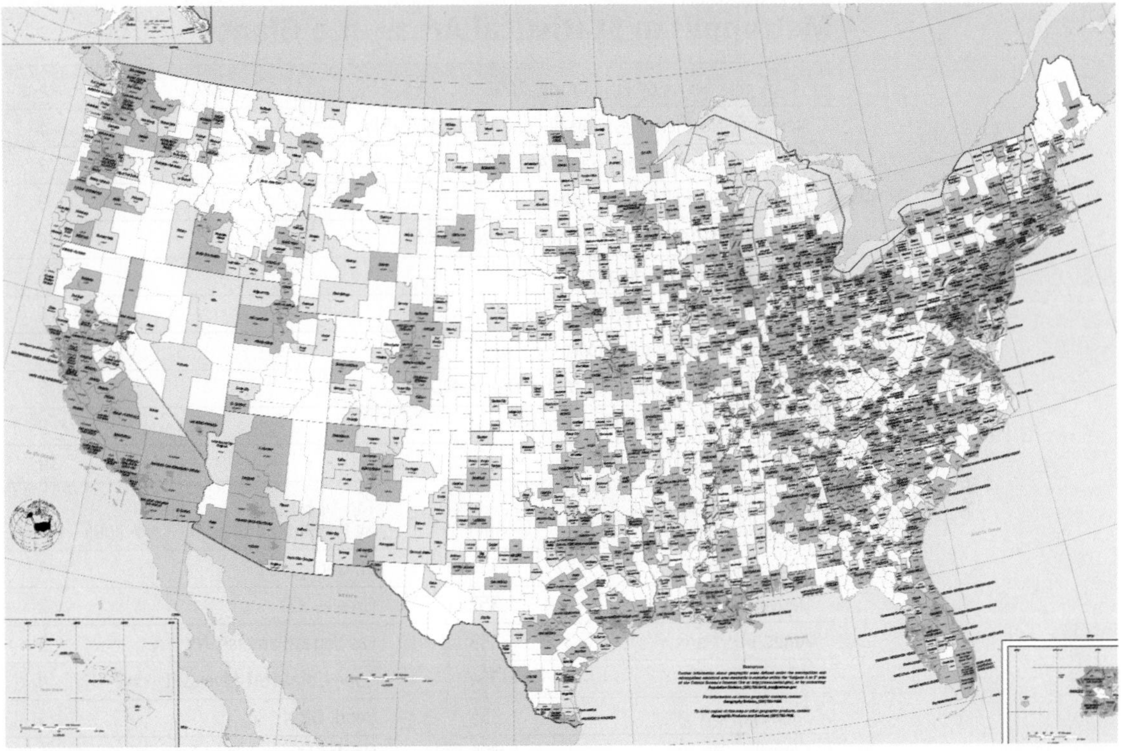

Source: U.S. Census Bureau, Population Division.

cal area referred to as a **megalopolis**. A megalopolis is an urban area made up of several large cities and their surrounding urban areas—in effect, a string of MSAs (see Map 11-2). Megalopolises are not confined by county borders, and they are not necessarily confined by state borders either. For example, one of the largest megalopolises in the country starts at Philadelphia, Pennsylvania, and runs through the state of New Jersey. They may not even be confined by national borders, as in the case of Detroit, Michigan, and Windsor, Ontario, in Canada. Another example of a cross-national megalopolis is El Paso, Texas, and Juarez, Mexico.

Because these metropolitan areas span not just county, but also state and even national borders, it is incredibly difficult to exercise any form of centralized planning over their growth and operation. Like Allegheny County, there are literally hundreds of governments making thousands of decisions, and these often are made with little coordination or thought to their regional effects. This fragmentation of political authority not only makes it hard to address regional problems, it is arguably the cause of some of them.

Take, for example, the rise of so-called **edgeless cities**. These are sprawling, unplanned office and retail complexes that are not pedestrian friendly

MEGALOPOLIS

An urban area made up of several large cities and their surrounding urban areas.

EDGELESS CITIES

Office and retail complexes without clear boundaries.

TABLE 11-1

Metropolitan Statistical Areas at a Glance

10 Largest MSAs by Population, 2005	Rank
New York-Northern New Jersey-Long Island, NY-NJ-PA	1
Los Angeles-Long Beach-Santa Ana, CA	2
Chicago-Naperville-Joliet, IL-IN-WI	3
Philadelphia-Camden-Wilmington, PA-NJ-DE-MD	4
Dallas-Fort Worth-Arlington, TX	5
Miami-Fort Lauderdale-Miami Beach, FL	6
Houston-Sugar Land-Baytown, TX	7
Washington-Arlington-Alexandria, DC-VA-MD-WV	8
Atlanta-Sandy Springs-Marietta, GA	9
Detroit-Warren-Livonia, MI	10

10 Smallest MSAs by Population, 2005	Rank	Top 10 MSAs by Percentage Change, 2000–2005	Rank
Cheyenne, WY	351	St. George, UT	1
Danville, IL	352	Greeley, CO	2
Ames, IA	353	Las Vegas-Paradise, NV	3
Great Falls, MT	354	Cape Coral-Fort Myers, FL	4
Sandusky, OH	355	Bend, OR	5
Corvallis, OR	356	Naples-Marco Island, FL	6
Columbus, IN	357	Provo-Orem, UT	7
Casper, WY	358	Riverside-San Bernardino-Ontario, CA	8
Hinesville-Fort Stewart, GA	359		
Lewiston, ID-WA	360	Port St. Lucie-Fort Pierce, FL	9
Carson City, NV	361	Raleigh-Cary, NC	10

Source: U.S. Census Bureau, Population Division.

and often become ghost towns at night. They do have obvious economic attractions: they mean jobs, sales taxes (people who work in them buy stuff, even if it is just gas and incidentals at a convenience store), and also property taxes (office complexes are valuable property).

Yet whatever local benefits they produce, they also export a set of costs to the larger region. Most of the people who work in edgeless cities commute home to greener residential areas. This means such developments segregate and put considerable geographical distance between where people live and where people work. The end result—traffic congestion, smog— affects all communities in the region, but individually there is not much any local government can do about such problems.

Sprawl: How Metropolitan Regions Grow

The fragmented nature of governance in metropolitan areas creates an interconnected set of problems that are difficult to address in a systematic and coordinated fashion. To understand the causes and consequences of these problems, as well as the challenges involved in effectively addressing them, it helps to have a little historical background on the roots of metropolitan growth.

Metropolitan areas are a relatively new concept. As recently as the 1920s, scholars recognized that the growth of suburbs, rapid and easily accessible transportation, and new forms of communication were transforming urban areas into a new social and economic phenomenon. They also recognized that existing forms of local government were ill equipped to deal with this new urban reality, and some even went so far as to call for a new form of metropolitan government to address the gap between state and local political jurisdictions.[9]

It was not until after World War II, however, that the country really saw the explosive growth of metropolitan areas and the broad-scale governance problems that accompanied this growth. In some ways this growth was inevitable. A population boom created enormous pressure for new development, and that development typically took place on the periphery of large cities or urban areas in the form of low-density suburban housing and commercial developments. This created an interrelated set of problems that can be traced to the catch-all phenomenon of **sprawl**. Often used as a generic term for the rapid growth of any metropolitan area, most urban scholars see sprawl as a particular type of growth. There is no universal definition, but this type of growth does have set of specific characteristics:

Single-use zoning. One of the central political powers of local government is control over land use. This power is typically exercised through **zoning laws**. These laws can allow land to be used for a mix of commercial, recreational, and residential developments, or for single uses, when land is used for single-purpose developments. Local governments in metropolitan areas have tended to favor the latter approach. The end result is geographic separation between the places where people work, live, and play.

Low-density development. The growth of metropolitan areas has not only been defined by single-use developments, but also by low-density developments. In effect, local governments have exercised their powers over land use to dictate that the growth in metropolitan areas will be out rather than up. Rather than multi-family developments like high-rise condominiums and apartments, suburbs and other urban municipalities have favored single-family developments. These developments make for lower population densities, but obviously they also require more land. For example, the population of the Milwaukee, Wisconsin, metropolitan area increased roughly 3 percent between 1970 and 1990. Geographically, it increased by

---

SPRAWL

The rapid growth of a metropolitan area, typically as a result of specific types of zoning and development.

ZONING LAWS

Regulations that control how land can be used.

LOW-DENSITY DEVELOPMENT

Development practices that spread (rather than concentrate) populations across the land.

---

38 percent. Los Angeles is a classic case of how low-density development can consume vast stretches of land. Population-wise, L.A. grew about 45 percent between 1970 and 1990. Land-wise, it grew by 300 percent.[10]

Leapfrog development. Leapfrog developments jump—or leapfrog—over established developments, leaving undeveloped or underdeveloped land between developments. This puts a particular strain on infrastructure, not just on roads, but also on water and sewer facilities. Developments that bypass undeveloped land mean that utilities have to be stretched out further to serve these developments.

Leapfrog development is partially driven by the economic incentives of developers. Most established municipalities like to create uniform requirements for developments within their own jurisdictions, for example, by enforcing specific building codes. They may even impose what are sometimes called **impact fees.** Municipalities charge builders of new housing or commercial developments impact fees to help offset the costs of extending services such as parks, schools, law enforcement, and fire protection services to these developments. A new housing development, for instance, may require the building of a new fire station, and impact fees can help offset that cost. It is not hard to see then why developers often favor building in unincorporated areas, typically on land with a geographic separation from municipal borders that is still close enough to make for an easy commute. The land in unincorporated areas tends to be cheaper, and there are fewer regulations to deal with.

Car-dependent living. Developing metropolitan areas through singe-use, low-density developments means citizens have to be highly mobile. To get from a suburban home to a job in a commercial office development, and from home to the kids' soccer game on the weekend, pretty much requires an automobile. In low-density housing developments it is often impossible—or at least impractical—to do something like "run to the corner store." Getting a six-pack to watch the game or a bag of sugar to bake cookies, or even arranging a play date for the kids, requires transportation. As public transportation systems are, for the most part, not set up for convenient and efficient transportation across large, multi-jurisdictional geographical areas, cars become all but a necessity for living in metropolitan areas.

Between 1950 and 1990 the population of the United States increased by about 40 percent, but the number of miles traveled in cars increased 140 percent. The imbalance between population growth and the growth in automobile use is a direct consequence of how land has been developed in metropolitan areas. The rise of car-dependent living exacts an environmental toll. Governments have done a reasonably good job of controlling "point" sources of pollution—concentrated sources of pollutants that tend to be limited in number, like factories or power plants—over the past three decades or so. However, so-called nonpoint sources of pollution are harder to identify and control because they consist of many sources, each putting

---

LEAPFROG DEVELOPMENT

Developments that jump—or leapfrog—over established developments, leaving undeveloped or underdeveloped land between developments.

IMPACT FEES

Fees that municipalities charge builders of new housing or commercial developments to help offset the costs of extending services.

CAR-DEPENDENT LIVING

An outcome of low-density development, when owning a car for transportation becomes a necessity.

out a relatively small amount of pollutants but collectively having a large-scale impact on the environment. Cars are a classic example of a non-point source of pollution and a major cause of air quality problems in metropolitan areas.[11]

Fragmentation of land use powers. A key characteristic of sprawl is the division of powers among local political jurisdictions, in particular the power over land use. Local governments frequently have strong incentives to use these powers in a way that provides local benefits for those within the particular local jurisdiction but creates costs for neighboring communities.

These basic characteristics have defined the growth and development of many major metropolitan areas in the United States during the past half century or so. The result is largely unplanned growth (no systematic coordination to balance local benefits with regional costs) that spreads out across ever-larger geographic regions, gobbling up previously rural areas and replacing them with low-density, single-use developments.

One of the consequences of development patterns in urban metropolitan regions is traffic congestion. Because people tend to live in one place and work in another, commuting by car is part of the daily routine for millions of Americans. Traffic back-up along Lake Shore Drive in Chicago is common for area drivers.

The Cons of Metropolitan Growth

By now it should be fairly obvious how metropolitan growth characterized by sprawl results in problems like traffic congestion and smog. Yet many academics who study urban politics and growth also believe these development patterns produce a wide range of other problems. These problems include the concentration of poverty and crime into certain neighborhoods, segregation by race and class, and inequality in public services, fiscal resources, and political power.

As new, low-density housing developments began popping up around core cities after World War II, the middle and upper classes began moving from the cities to the suburbs. There were "push" and "pull" reasons for the migration of the better-off classes to the suburbs. One was the lure of the lifestyle—the home with the white picket fence on a leafy suburban lane—that "pulled" people out of the city. Another was the racial desegregation of public schools in the 1960s and 1970s. Increasing numbers of less well-off nonwhites began to make up an ever greater proportion of urban schools, acting as an incentive to "push" whites out to the suburbs.

The racial—and perhaps racist—undertones of this demographic shift have been repeatedly noted by academics.[12] As the middle and upper classes were largely white, this demographic phenomenon became known as **white flight**. As whites left the dense, multi-use neighborhoods of cities for the lure of single-family homes on large lots in suburbia, minorities became concentrated in the core urban areas. As racial minorities also were much more likely to be less socioeconomically well-off than whites, this also meant that inner-city neighborhoods became poorer.

As neighborhoods became poorer, the remaining middle-class felt more pressure to decamp to the suburbs and a self-reinforcing trend set in: the poor and ethnic minorities became increasingly concentrated into core city neighborhoods. In the past couple of decades this trend has started to move out into the suburbs. Minorities who manage to get far enough up the socioeconomic ladder to move to an inner-ring suburb have triggered another round of white flight. As comparatively less white, less well-off people move into the inner-ring suburbs, the better-off move farther out. The end result is the increasingly racial and socioeconomic homogeneity of particular political jurisdictions.

Some local political jurisdictions are well-off and tend to have property values that support high-quality public services. Middle- and upper-class suburbs, for example, tend to have high-quality public schools. So do **exurbs**, or municipalities in more rural settings that serve as bedroom communities, with residents commuting in to jobs in the cities or suburbs during the day and returning to their homes after work. This tends to be in stark contrast with some inner-city neighborhoods and inner-ring suburbs in which poverty is concentrated. Property values are low in such neighborhoods, meaning that they cannot support high-quality public services.

It is important to note that the end result is economic *and* racial segregation based on housing patterns. This trend is made apparent by school districts. In some urban areas, for example, African Americans make up less than 3 percent of the total population, but constitute 70 percent of the enrollment in some school districts.[13] These are invariably schools that serve poor communities where crime and other social problems place enormous strains not just on public education, but also on social and economic opportunities in general. While people can, and do, experience challenge and struggle out in the suburbs, such communities are much more likely to have the fiscal capacity to support such public services as good school systems. And as good schools play an important role in determining where the middle-class wants to live, again it is easy to see a self-reinforcing trend.

In other words, here is a difference that makes a big difference to quality of life for millions of people. Place matters because wealth is segregated by community across metropolitan regions; communities that are themselves concentrated in different political jurisdictions. As one well-known study of metropolitan politics and policy concluded, where you live in a given metropolitan area affects both your quality of life and shapes your social and economic opportunities. Place affects access to jobs, public services, levels of personal security (crime tends to be higher in some socioeconomically stressed neighborhoods), availability of medical services, even the quality of the air you breathe (the people commuting in from the exurbs contribute to urban smog, but escape to the cleaner rural air after the work day is done).[14]

Take the issue of jobs. Two-thirds of all new jobs are created in suburbs (think of big-box stores like Wal-Mart and Home Depot that dot suburban landscapes—they represent a lot of jobs). The people who most desperately need some of those jobs, and the social and economic opportunities they represent, are concentrated in poorer inner-city neighborhoods. Three-quarters of all welfare recipients live either in central cities or in poorer rural areas.[15] These people cannot move to the suburbs where the jobs are because they cannot afford the expensive homes that typify low-density, single-use housing developments. Buying and operating a car also is an expensive proposition that can levy a harsh financial toll on those less well-off. That leaves public transportation, which because of the huge geographical spaces that have to be covered, is often an inefficient proposition.

> Place matters because wealth is segregated by community across metropolitan regions; communities that are themselves concentrated in different political jurisdictions. As one well-known study of metropolitan politics and policy concluded, where you live in a given metropolitan area affects both your quality of life and shapes your social and economic opportunities.

Critics of the consequences of sprawl argue that the end result are metropolitan areas that promote and reinforce economic and racial segregation and create disparities in tax base that lead to huge differences in the quality of public services among local political jurisdictions. On top of that, from a regional perspective, the patterns of metropolitan growth are economically inefficient (jobs and the labor market are disconnected) and environmentally dangerous (all those cars pump out a lot of toxic emissions).[16]

Government Reform in Metropolitan Areas

Racial and economic segregation, inequity in tax bases and public services, and, above all, political fragmentation that creates difficulty in coordinating rational and effective responses to regional challenges; the problems with governing in metropolitan areas are well known. But what can be done about them?

There are a number of strategies for rationalizing government in metropolitan areas, all of which either have been implemented or considered to various degrees in virtually all major urban areas. The **reform perspective**

REFORM PERSPECTIVE
An approach to filling gaps in service and reducing redundancies in local governments that calls for regional-level solutions.

Local Focus: Loudoun County, Virginia: Caught between Sprawl and Smart Growth

In a county with a long geographical reach, local leaders can find themselves refereeing a citizenry whose interests diverge among those who live in towns, expanding suburbs, or preserved rural landscapes. Such is the case of Loudoun County in northern Virginia. The county is a 517-square-mile area bordered by the Blue Ridge Mountains on the west and exploding high-tech development surrounding Dulles International Airport to the east. In fact, it was *the* fastest growing county in the entire country in terms of population by the early twenty-first century.

With quaint towns and "gentleman farmer" horse farms that date back to the eighteenth century, Loudoun has been torn by an ongoing cycle of zoning and land-use disputes since the early 1980s. Nearly every election for its board of supervisors hinges on the desirability of "smart growth" efforts to control encroaching suburban tracts and strip malls steadily pushed by developers eager to exploit Loudoun's commuting proximity to the nation's capital.

It was the arrival of such world-class employers as America Online and MCI that brought new demands to the county for housing, roads, and schools. So, in 1989, county officials drew up a 250-page 20-year growth vision with development guidelines that won the American Planning Association's "outstanding planning" award. It projected the likely impact of population growth, particularly the school-aged population, on demand for services, tax rates, and debt burden, as well as probable changes to infrastructure, water and air quality, and transportation needs. By the late 1990s, Loudoun was among the fastest-growing counties in the nation. Its population doubled in ten years, and its economy expanded at a meaty 32 percent a year.

In 1999, however, angry voters turned out a board of supervisors perceived as being too much in the pocket of developers who many felt were making a killing at the expense of Loudoun's historically serene ambience. The incoming board vowed to make Loudoun a "land-use planning showcase." It would do this by using its powers to zone areas between towns that are beyond the control of small towns within Loudoun, such as Purcellville, Middleburg, and Leesburg. This, the board stated, would help preserve the countywide vision voters wanted.

The smart-growth advocates had the backing of environmentalists and the "old money" landowners who wished to protect their idyllic heritage from the onslaught of traffic and cul-de-sacs lined with mini-

pushes for such rationalization and begins with the assumption that the key problems and challenges of governance in metropolitan areas are regional in nature, and as such, should be addressed regionally. Proponents also tend to argue that many of the problems are created by political fragmentation in the first place, as there are lots of smaller governments making decisions that may produce local benefits but export costs to other jurisdictions. If the root cause of these problems is political fragmentation, government consolidation is the obvious solution. In other words, new regional governing structures should be created to fill the hole in the federal system, governments that are better positioned to effectively respond to the interconnected problems of large metropolitan areas.[17]

There is no universal response to filling that hole, however. Instead there are a number of different strategies that range from creating new pan-regional governments to eliminating longstanding local jurisdictions.

mansions. Development would be restricted to compact, high-density areas. This encourages use of existing roads and sewer lines rather than the construction and digging of expensive new ones. Sprawl can bankrupt a county government, they argued. For every $1 in tax revenues a new home brings in, the county shells out $1.55 in roads, sewers, and other services. Included in these figures were the twenty-three new schools (at cost of $600 million) that Loudoun had had to plan for in recent years.[a]

But smart-growth restrictions on new subdivisions threaten to gore the oxen of developers, realtors, middle-class prospective homeowners, and longtime working farmers now ready to cash in on their land and retire. Their representatives warn against density packing, which they see as shifting all of the growth to eastern middle-class suburbs so that the gentry in the west can enjoy their horse country undisturbed.

"We're entitled to green space in the east as well," said one supervisor, adding that property owners have the right to sell their land for development.

In November 2003, the pro-growth Republican candidates from the eastern side of the county swept onto the board of supervisors. In January 2004, in a series of nineteen votes, six Republicans overrode the minority of two Democrats and one independent and voted to bring water and sewer services for planned home construction to a large chunk of central Loudoun. They set the stage for a new highway. They streamlined the business permit approval process and terminated public funding for a land preservation program that pays landowners who agree not to develop their property.

Finally, they promised to reduce government paperwork. The problem is "not the developers," said supervisor Stephen J. Snow. "It's the insidious growth of government."[b] Growth and development, however, has continued to be a flashpoint for political conflict. As of early 2007, Campaign for Loudon's Future, a local grassroots group dedicated to opposing urban development, continued to pressure local government with some success to slow down the approval process for large residential developments.

[a] Christopher Swope, "Sprawl: Rendezvous with Destiny," *Governing* magazine, March 2001, 32.
[b] Michael Laris and Maria Glod, "Loudoun GOP Eases Growth Restraints," *Washington Post,* January 6, 2004.

Regional Governments

Adherents to the reform perspective are strong advocates of creating regional authorities to address regional problems. This can be done in a couple of ways. First, new government structures can be created to sit above existing political jurisdictions and be given the authority to oversee regional land-use planning.

This sort of approach has been popular with a number of civic activists from the reform tradition, people such as former Albuquerque mayor David Rusk, Minnesota state representative Myron Orfield, and syndicated columnist Neal Pierce. All have been popular champions of pan-regional planning authorities. There are a couple of well-known examples of such regional planning authorities frequently cited by such advocates as examples of the benefits of taking a top-down approach to land-use regulation.

One of the best known of these is the Metropolitan Service District in Portland, Oregon, or "Metro." Metro is a true regional government that covers Clackamas, Multnomah, and Washington Counties, and the twenty-five municipalities in the Portland metropolitan area. It is governed by an elected legislature (a six-member council) and an elected executive (the council president).[18] Metro has real power, exercising regulatory authority in areas such as land-use planning, regional transportation, recycling and garbage disposal, and a host of other issue areas that are regional rather than local in nature.

A number of academic observers have concluded that the Portland top-down approach to regional planning has reaped considerable benefits compared to metropolitan areas that have no comparable regional governance. For example, white flight in Portland has been markedly less than in other cities. Compared to many other major cites, the middle class—especially young, highly educated individuals—tend to settle in the central city rather than in suburbs or nonmetropolitan areas.[19]

One of the notable characteristics about the Portland Metro is the presence of an **urban growth boundary (UGB)**. A UGB controls the density and type of development by establishing a boundary around a given urban area. Land inside the UGB is slated for high-density development, land outside the UGB is slated for lower-density, rural sorts of development. In effect, this is a planning regulation that forces cities to grow vertically rather than horizontally, and thus sets limits on sprawl and the problems it generates.

Critics of UGBs argue they have a significant downside. By limiting the land available for development, UGBs drive up prices for land in particular and real estate in general. The end results are high property values and limited supplies of affordable housing. This does not seem to have happened in Portland, however, at least to any extreme. In fact, property values there are considered reasonable compared with the rest of the West Coast. The success of the UGB in Portland has been used by reformers as an example to promote the adoption of similar policies in other urban areas. Three states—Oregon, Tennessee, and Washington—now mandate cities to establish UGBs.

Regional Councils

As discussed later in this chapter, creating new regional governments is difficult because it requires local jurisdictions to cede some of their authority. Accordingly, most metropolitan areas lack any form of regional government with the authority and standing of Portland's Metro. There are, however, a large number of regional planning authorities that provide at least some rudimentary form of coordination among the local governments packed into metropolitan areas.

Probably the most common attempt to rationalize local policymaking across multi-jurisdictional metropolitan areas is the formation of regional councils. A **regional council** is "a multi-service entity with state and locally-

URBAN GROWTH BOUNDARY (UGB)

The border established around urban areas that is intended to control the density and type of development.

REGIONAL COUNCIL

A planning and advisory organization whose members include multiple local governments. Region councils often are used to administer state and federal programs that are regionally targeted.

defined boundaries that delivers a variety of federal, state and local programs while continuing its function as a planning organization, technical assistance provider and 'visionary' to its member local governments." [20]

Regional councils are made up of member governments, such as municipalities and school districts, although other nonprofit, civic, private, or academic organizations also may be included. They originated in the 1960s and 1970s as a vehicle for delivering state and federal programs to regional areas. Since then they have grown to become an important means of making and coordinating regionwide policy and planning in such areas as land use, transportation, economic development, housing, and social services. In effect, regional councils are a way to recognize the fact that decisions made in one community can have knock-on effects in neighboring communities, and that it makes sense to address some problems regionally rather than locally. There are 516 such bodies in the United States, and of the roughly 39,000 general purpose local governments in the country (that includes counties, cities, municipalities, villages, boroughs, towns, and townships) about 35,000 are served by a regional council.[21]

A related form of regional authority is the **metropolitan planning organization (MPO)**. MPOs are regional organizations that decide how federal transportation funds are allocated within a regional area. MPOs are interesting because they represent a specific recognition by federal law that regions—as opposed to localities—are central, functional policy units. The Intermodal Surface Transportation Efficiency Act of 1991 (ISTEA) mandated that every metropolitan region had to identify an institution (an MPO) to serve as the central coordinating authority for federal transportation funds in that area. MPOs have the responsibility of developing transportation plans and programs for their metropolitan regions. All transportation projects involving federal money—which is to say virtually all major transportation projects—have to be approved by an MPO. Some MPOs administer billions of dollars in federal transportation grants, and control over such amounts of money, coupled with its authority over critical transportation programs, translates into real political clout.[22]

Regional councils and MPOs, however, should not be confused or equated with Portland's Metro. They are different in the sense that they are more a vehicle for intergovernmental cooperation than an actual form of government with executive and legislative authority independent of local government interests. Formal organizations of local governments in metropolitan areas have existed in some form or another for decades, and regional councils and MPOs are just the more common and better-known examples. Hashing out roles and responsibilities, not to mention making decisions, is often a complicated—and often contentious—give-and-take among the local governments that constitute the membership of these regional bodies.

For example, most formal organizations of local governments—in metropolitan areas at least—began by allowing every member to have an equal

METROPOLITAN PLANNING ORGANIZATION (MPO)

A regional organization that decides how federal transportation funds are allocated within a regional area.

MAP 11-3 California's Metropolitan Planning Organizations' Boundaries

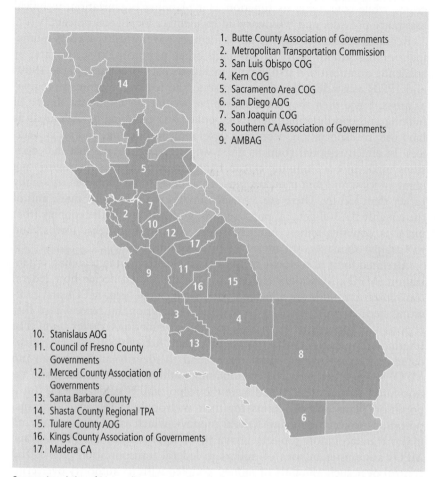

1. Butte County Association of Governments
2. Metropolitan Transportation Commission
3. San Luis Obispo COG
4. Kern COG
5. Sacramento Area COG
6. San Diego AOG
7. San Joaquin COG
8. Southern CA Association of Governments
9. AMBAG

10. Stanislaus AOG
11. Council of Fresno County Governments
12. Merced County Association of Governments
13. Santa Barbara County
14. Shasta County Regional TPA
15. Tulare County AOG
16. Kings County Association of Governments
17. Madera CA

Source: Association of Metropolitan Planning Organizations. http://terrains.com/gallery/ampo/ampo_map.php (accessed April 11, 2007).

voice in the organization. What this meant was that a small, rural township had exactly the same influence on regional issues as a core city, even though it had a fraction of the population. Figuring out more representative, equitable, and democratic decision making in these regional bodies has been, to put it mildly, a challenge. Smaller jurisdictions are, understandably, loathe to give up their influence to bigger neighbors for fear of having their interests take a back seat. The bigger neighbors resent having their interests yoked to the interests of much smaller communities.

The end results are some complicated, and often still not fair, decision-making processes. For example, the Southwestern Pennsylvania Commission (SPC) serves as the regional coordinating body for Allegheny County and ten other counties in and around the Pittsburgh Metropolitan Statistical Area.

The smallest county in this regional body has 3 percent of the region's population, but 12 percent of the voting power in the commission. In the mid-1990s Allegheny County had 24 percent of the vote in the commission, even though it had 58 percent of the population and 64 percent of the market value of the entire region.[23]

Intergovernmental institutions such as regional councils are, at best, confederal sorts of regional governments that are creatures of the often conflicting interests of their members. This complicates decision making and makes it harder for these bodies to exert firm regulatory authority over critical areas such as land use. Still, in most parts of the country they come the closest to filling the "hole" in the organizational structure of the federal system. At a minimum there has been growing support for regional planning efforts that emphasize **smart growth**, a term that describes development practices that emphasize more efficient infrastructure and less dependence on automobiles. Smart growth is reflected in regional, or even single-jurisdiction, policies that promote mixed-use developments that are pedestrian and bicycle friendly, emphasize building community rather than just bricks and mortar, and consciously account for development's impact on the environment.

SMART GROWTH

Environmentally friendly development practices, particularly those that emphasize more efficient infrastructure and less dependence on automobiles.

Outside of cooperating on land-use plans, many local governments engage in looser, informal cooperative arrangements rather than create formal institutions. Such arrangements frequently take the form of contracting services. For example, a town may contract with the county for law enforcement services or at least for dispatch services.

Government Consolidation

One way to regularize or rationalize governance in a metropolitan region is to create a pan-regional institution. As already discussed, this can be done either through the creation of a new form of government (such as Portland's Metro) or through a formal institution of intergovernmental cooperation, such as a regional council. Rather than creating new government institutions, a second approach is to reduce the number of governments through merger or consolidation. This is typically done by merging a city with a county.

On the face of it, this makes a good deal of sense. Cities and urban counties share the same geographic space and provide similar services. A classic example is law enforcement services. Think of an urban county sitting on top of a large city. The county will have a sheriff's office, the city a police department. Each can have its own jails, dispatch centers, training facilities, and purchasing departments. It strikes many that there is a lot redundancy and inefficiency in duplicating these services in such close quarters. Why not consolidate at least some of these functions?

That is exactly what Des Moines, Iowa, and Polk County did with their city and county jails. The county and city jails sat on opposite sides of the

Des Moines River—directly across from each other—and consolidating facilities and operations just seemed to make sense.

If consolidating operations can reduce redundancy and improve efficiency, why not go the whole hog and merge municipal and county governments into a single government? Cities and counties often duplicate bureaucracies and paperwork, so there seems to be an obvious logic to **city-county consolidation**. With as many as 75 percent of all major urban areas in the United States contained within single counties, it would seem to make sense that such mergers would be common and easy. They aren't, and it isn't.

According to the National Association of Counties, of the nation's more than three thousand counties only thirty-three—roughly 1 percent—have consolidated with cities. Since 1990 there only have been about six successful mergers, although many more have been considered.[24] Unsuccessful efforts during the past decade or so include Gainesville, Flordia, with Alachua County and Spokane, Washington, with Spokane County.

Despite the glacial pace of city-county consolidation, it is an idea that has been around for a long time. The earliest consolidation dates back to 1805, when the city of New Orleans was consolidated with New Orleans Parish (remember, in Louisiana, counties are called parishes). The practice even enjoyed an era of popularity in the 1960s and 1970s.

Proposals for consolidation often come in response to a state initiative or a regional challenge. For example, the citizens of Jacksonville, Florida, in Duval County, were experiencing industrial waste in their river, underachieving high schools, and clashes between city and county officials during the 1960s. Local business leaders lobbied the state legislature for help. The legislature created a commission that proposed a consolidation plan. The plan was approved in 1967 by the legislature and, subsequently, was approved by the voters in a referendum.

For the most part, this merger has worked for the two governments involved. But even after it, there were municipalities in Duval County (Atlantic Beach, Baldwin, Jacksonville Beach, and Neptune Beach) but outside Jacksonville city limits that continued as independent local governments. These communities periodically have considered splitting off from Jacksonville/Duval and forming a new county (Ocean County) as a means to recover a county government less tied to the city of Jacksonville. Thus far, however, these efforts have not progressed beyond the discussion stage, and all of the municipalities remain a part of Duval County.

Still, only thirty-three mergers in two hundred years and a lot of cities and counties sitting right on top of each other duplicating services? Why haven't city-county consolidations happened more often? A lot of it has to do with who supports and who opposes mergers when they are proposed.

Consolidation typically is favored by business groups and others who favor efficiency in government spending and regulation over local control of government. These individuals seek a reorganization of government to reduce bureaucratic redundancy and to allow communities to speak "with

CITY-COUNTY CONSOLIDATION

The merger of separate local governments in an effort to reduce bureaucratic redundancy and service inefficiencies.

TABLE 11-2

Consolidated City-County Governments

City-counties operating primarily as cities		Metropolitan governments operating primarily as cities		Areas with county-like offices in other governments (city, township, special district, state)	
Alaska	City and borough of Anchorage	Tennessee	Hartsville and Trousdale County	Florida	County of Duval (City of Jacksonville)
	City and borough of Juneau		Lynchburg and Moore County	Georgia	County of Clarke (City of Athens)
	City and borough of Sitka		Nashville and Davidson County		County of Muscogee (City of Columbus)
	City and borough of Yakutat				County of Richmond (City of Augusta)
California	City and county of San Francisco			Hawaii	County of Kalawao (State of Hawaii)
Colorado	City and county of Broomfield			Indiana	County of Marion (City of Indianapolis)
	City and county of Denver			Kentucky	Lexington-Fayette Urban County
Hawaii	City and county of Honolulu			Louisiana	Parish of East Baton Rouge (City of Baton Rouge)
Kansas	Unified Government of Wyandotte County and City of Kansas City				Parish of Lafayette (City of Lafayette)
Montana	Anaconda-Deer Lodge County				Parish of Orleans (City of New Orleans)
	Butte-Silver Bow County				Terrebonne Parish Consolidated Government
				Massachusetts	County of Nantucket (Town of Nantucket)
					County of Suffolk (City of Boston)
				New York	Counties of Bronx, Kings, New York, Queens, and Richmond (all part of the City of New York)
				Pennsylvania	County of Philadelphia (City of Philadelphia)

Source: *2002 Census of Governments,* vol. 1, no. 1, Government Organization, GC02(1)-1 (Washington, D.C.: United States Department of Commerce, Bureau of Census), Appendix B.

one voice." The politics of consolidations, however, are tricky. Middle-class suburbanites may be concerned that mergers mostly will benefit downtown residents while raising taxes in the suburbs; inner-city minorities may fear their voting power will be diluted. Elected officials reflect these concerns, and perhaps add some of their own. Consolidated governments mean fewer

A Difference that Makes a Difference: Marrying a City with a County

January 2003 saw the birth of the Louisville-Jefferson Metro Government. The new government was the result of a long-disputed merging of Kentucky's most developed and populous entities—the city of Louisville and Jefferson County. Advocates of what would become the largest such consolidation in the United States since 1970 had finally driven home their case after three failed attempts to persuade voters going back to the 1950s.

The hope is that consolidation will allow struggling downtown Louisville to share the benefits of the job growth previously concentrated in the suburbs. Rivalry between competing bureaucracies should ease, paperwork for businesses in such areas as building codes should shrink, and regional planning to relieve traffic congestion should be streamlined.

No longer will the county, run by a judge-executive with authority over more than eighty municipalities, have veto power over tax and annexation proposals. Under the new rules, if both the county and the city have a law on the books for a certain issue, the county law prevails. If the city has a given law and the county doesn't, then the existing city law now covers both areas.

The idea seemed so promising that representatives from cities such as Fresno, California; Buffalo, New York; Milwaukee, Wisconsin; and Cedar Rapids, Iowa, came to study its implementation.[a]

For cities with expansion potential that is "inelastic," in the phrase of author and former Albuquerque mayor David Rusk, consolidation becomes a tempting alternative to annexation or boundary change. Rusk said in his 1995 book *Cities without Suburbs* that consolidation is a way to amplify economic power and project it over a greater area.

Resistance most commonly comes from suburbanites who do not feel attracted to forming a common identity with a city that in many cases is impoverished and suffering from crime and bad public schools. Perhaps suburban taxpayers are reluctant to pay for infrastructure improvements in other jurisdictions—urban sewer and water lines, for example—when many residents of rural areas and newly suburbanized neighborhoods paid for their own septic tanks and wells.

Politically, many urban minorities feel that their autonomy and influence would be diluted in a greater metropolitan entity. Those in surrounding unincorporated areas may feel left out of the political mix altogether.[b] Indeed, with the Louisville merger, the percentage of African Americans in the total population shrank from 34 percent to 19 percent.

But there are grounds for optimism. With the area in square miles rising from 60 to 386, and the population tripling from 256,231 to 693,784, the average education levels, the median income, home price, homeownership rates, and employment rates all rose. The number of high school graduates rose from 76 percent to 82 percent, median household income rose from $28,843 to $39,457, and home ownership rates rose from 52.5 percent to 64.9 percent.

[a] Alan Greenblatt, "Louisville: Anatomy of a Merger," *Governing* magazine, December 2002.
[b] *Handbook of Research on Urban Politics and Policy in the United States,* Ronald K. Vogel, ed. (Westport, Conn.: Greenwood Press, 1997), 139.

elected politicians and, most likely, fewer public employees. This creates internal pressure to resist merger movements.

There is also plain, old-fashioned community loyalty. The point has been made before about the strong tradition of local government in the United States. People identify with their local governments and tend to trust them (at least when compared to state and federal governments). There is no tradition of regional government, and citizens and public officials treat these new and unknown entities with a degree of mistrust.

All of this combines to make city-county consolidations a tough political undertaking, even when most objective observers agree they make a good deal of sense. Allegheny County and the city of Pittsburgh, for example, have been flirting with the issue of consolidation for more than a decade. A series of blue ribbon panels, committees, and commissions have studied the pros and cons of an Allegheny-Pittsburgh consolidation, and they have mostly come to the same conclusion. "There's no question you could save money and provide much better service," David O'Laughlin, who served on one such panel.[25]

There has been some progress. The city and county have managed to consolidate some operations, for example, 9-1-1 call centers, finger printing duties, and some court functions. A full-scale merger, despite its apparent advantages, still seems a long way off. In 2006, yet another panel was formed to study city-county consolidation, but veterans of previous efforts are skeptical. Paul Renne, a former chief financial officer at H. J. Heinz Co., and chair of a panel formed to do more or less the same thing in 2002, did not express much optimism. The problem, he suggests, is not the technical difficulties but rather the political ones. "It seems like such an obvious thing. There are duplications of services, and it's just a question of will on the part of the leaders."

That said, there are some difficult technical issues to deal with as well. Pittsburgh, for example, carries a bigger debt burden than Allegheny County. If they merge, do the non-Pittsburgh residents have to help pick up that tab? The bottom line is that people do not want to give up their local government and replace it with some regional entity; the consolidated government may benefit the region, but no one is sure what the local benefits or costs will be.[26]

Like a good marriage, the consolidation of a city and a county may depend on partners who trust each other and can make equal contributions to the merger. For example, Phoenix, Arizona, has won awards for its state-of-the-art management innovations. Surrounding Maricopa County, on the other hand, has a reputation for management inefficiency. Good luck getting those two governments down the aisle.[27]

Annexation

Rather than forming new governments like Metro or merging old ones, another option for dealing with the problems of sprawl, traffic congestion, and uneven economic development is to make the existing political jurisdictions bigger. **Annexation** is the legal incorporation of one jurisdiction or territory into another. Usually, the jurisdiction that does the annexing is the more politically powerful, whereas the "annexee" is weaker and may not be enthusiastic about becoming the latest addition to a larger municipal neighbor. This approach is relatively common in the South and West, regions where there are large tracts of unincorporated land adjacent to

ANNEXATION

The legal incorporation of one jurisdiction or territory into another.

major cities. Cities such as El Paso, Houston, and Phoenix have annexed hundreds of square miles and in doing so have turned themselves into regional governments by sheer geographic size. Oklahoma City, for example, has more than six hundred square miles within its city limits, with much of that added over the years through annexations.[28]

Annexation is principally a tool for municipalities that want to control development along their peripheries and engage in planned expansions of their tax bases. Remember that cities like to create uniform requirements on area developers, whereas developers tend to favor unincorporated areas where land is cheaper and there are fewer regulations. One option for cities to put a stop to this and impose a more coherent and orderly plan to metropolitan growth is to simply annex that unincorporated land.

A city government that wishes to annex a tract of land must organize the citizens of an unincorporated area to sign a petition. Some communities seek to expand by annexing prospectively, working to incorporate a still-undeveloped parcel of land farther out from a suburban parcel already being transformed from woods or farmland into subdivisions. This, in turn, may alienate rural landowners, including farmers, who value their traditional identity separate from that of the city.[29] Annexing, in short, can create a lot of conflict, with some residents of unincorporated areas seeing it as a land grab that threatens to develop their rural communities out of existence.

Given this sort of conflict, it should not be too surprising to find that states make it tough for cities to annex new land. For example, in 1963 the California legislature created fifty-eight local agency formation commissions (LAFCOs) as boundary watchdogs to discourage annexation. Among other things LAFCOs are supposed to discourage urban sprawl. However, as urban sprawl pretty much describes metropolitan growth in the past four decades in large parts of the state, many Californians believe that these commissions are too weak to deal with rapid suburbanization.

Annexation can make sense from a big picture perspective in that it can help impose the orderly expansion of urban municipalities, but there is no getting around the fact that it creates losers as well as winners. And the losers often are not interested in losing at all. For example, in Ohio, townships and counties are pushing for more say over annexations, deliberately trying to limit the ability of municipalities to gobble up unincorporated land in the name of development.[30]

Annexation also has natural limits: there has to be land available to annex. While municipalities tend to have the upper hand over sparsely populated, unincorporated territories, if they bump up against another city, it's a different story. Unlike cities in the South and West, cities in the North and East are more likely to be ringed by incorporated suburbs; in effect, core cities are fenced in by other cities, with no real option to expand. Pittsburgh, for example, covers about fifty-eight square miles—a fraction of Oklahoma City's six-hundred-plus square miles. Outside of a merger with Allegheny County, it is unlikely that Pittsburgh is going to grow to anywhere near the geographic size of Oklahoma City.

Even in the South and West there are limits to how much land can be annexed or developed. The Las Vegas metropolitan area, for instance, seems to have land in abundance; the urban area sits, more or less, in a vast open area and the availability of cheap land has fueled construction of many classic, low-density developments. However, even though Las Vegas is the fastest growing metro area in the nation, some analysts say this growth is going to hit its limit in the next decade or so. The metro area is spreading out toward areas where development will be difficult or impossible; mountains, military bases, Native American communities, and land that is home to protected species (notably the desert tortoise). It is hard to think of go-go Las Vegas being halted in its tracks by a desert tortoise but that, at least partially, is the case. Growth is consuming about six thousand to seven thousand acres a year, and at that rate of consumption the supply of cheap land in the metro area is just about exhausted.[31]

The Case against Reform: Public Choice and the Tiebout Model

While metropolitan areas undoubtedly have problems, not everyone agrees that these problems require stronger regional governments. Indeed, some argue that some of the underlying problems are exaggerated, or at least not balanced adequately against the benefits of metropolitan growth.

Backing this argument is the fact that cities are, for the most part, pretty decent places to live. Core cities have not been swirling down into a uniform death spiral of relentless flight to the suburbs, leaving poverty, racial segregation, and crime. In many MSAs, the core cities remain the economic and social hubs of the region. Scholars and musicians, business leaders and actors—people in a wide range of fields are still more likely to be attracted to the city to pursue their opportunities and dreams than to an exurb or single-use housing tract. Core cities remain exciting places, centers of innovation and culture, shopping and business activity.

In fact, most people living in cities have a fairly decent standard of living. Mention core city or urban area and most people think of large cities in the North and East. But there are plenty of large and growing cities in the South and West, including Phoenix and Oklahoma City. Truth be told, cities in the South and West have had to worry less about urban decay than urban growth. And while cities in the North and East, such as Pittsburgh, have endured some rough economic times over the past twenty or thirty years, many have bounced back. Heinz Field—home of the Pittsburgh Steelers—was a $281 million development that opened in the Pennsylvania city in 2001. A similarly ultramodern stadium was built for the city's baseball team (the Pittsburgh Pirates) at the same time. Developments such as

In June 2006, Anaheim, California, became the first major U.S. city to go wireless. Residents can subscribe to the service on a monthly basis, and visitors can purchase temporary usage capabilities.

these generate enormous economic activity and provide a city with prestige and civic identity and civic pride that is hard to find in the exurbs.

So, despite the undeniable downsides to growth patterns in metropolitan areas, there are also some positives, at least for some people. First and foremost are quality of life benefits. That house in the suburbs can be a pretty darn nice house, in a pretty darn nice neighborhood. Good-quality schools are not hard to find in the suburbs, and neither are relatively crime-free developments with nice parks and maybe even a golf course nearby. This looks pretty attractive to those who have the means to take advantage of such opportunities. The same developments that often are castigated by academic critics of urban planning (or the lack thereof) can be job generating machines. And not all new housing projects are single-family McMansions that make a large ecological footprint for the benefit of a few while passing on the costs to many.

For example, many consider Levittown in Nassau County, New York, to be the original "cookie cutter" modern suburban housing development. Eventually totaling more than seventeen thousand homes, Levittown was built in an unincorporated area in the late 1940s and early 1950s. It was, literally, a community built from the ground up. First came the housing development, then public services (schools, parks) followed. Levittown served as a model for suburban growth across the United States, and what is notable about it for present purposes is that it was designed as an affordable housing development. The houses were nothing fancy—brand-new they cost under $8,000, which even by the standards of the early 1950s was a good price for a single-family home. What they offered was not economic segregation for the moneyed class, but instead the American dream of home ownership to a generation of World War II veterans.[32] Although they get less attention, there are modern counterparts to Levittown still being built, and they continue to hold out the possibility of home ownership to lower-income people.[33]

And the middle- and upper-classes have not abandoned every neighborhood in every city. Indeed, some decaying urban areas have undergone a renaissance, with old warehouses being turned into upscale condos and downtown neighborhoods becoming the focus of thriving cultural scenes. This process of physical rehabilitation of urban areas, which attracts investment from developers and drives up property values, is known as **gentrification**. Gentrified neighborhoods do present something of a double-edged sword, though. While gentrification clearly can resuscitate decaying areas, the rise in property values means that poorer people can no longer afford to live there. In essence, gentrification creates pockets of middle-class wealth within cities.

In short, there is a glass half-full perspective that sees innovation and vitality, high standards of living, and social and economic opportunities that is in contrast to the glass half-empty perspective that focuses on segregation, smog, and economic inequality. There are also strong theoretical

GENTRIFICATION

The physical rehabilitation of urban areas, which attracts investment from developers and drives up property values.

reasons that argue against any large-scale movement to replace multiple local jurisdictions with larger, regional governance structures.

Public choice is a model of politics that views governments and public services in market terms. In public choice models, governments are seen as producers of public services and citizens are seen as consumers. As in most markets, competition among producers is seen as a good thing. With lots of local jurisdictions citizens can choose their favored "producer" by moving to the city or town that has the mix of taxes and public services that suits them best. If that local government fails to satisfy the individual citizen consumer—in other words, its taxes go too high or its public services drop too low—they can vote with their feet and move to another jurisdiction with a more attractive tax-public service package.

Multiple jurisdictions mean multiple producers, a set of competing "products" in the form of different mixes of taxes and public services. That competition keeps governments responsive to their constituents and puts pressure on these governments to be efficient and to keep the quality of public services as high as possible and taxes as low as possible. If local governments are inefficient, that is, their taxes are high and their public services are poor, they risk having their constituents move to another jurisdiction that offers a better deal.

From a public choice perspective, concentrating local governments into regional governments, either through formal or informal mechanisms, risks a considerable downside. Government consolidation basically represents the creation of monopoly service providers and brings with it all the problems of monopolies that are well understood from private markets: lack of response to consumers, high costs, and indifferent quality.

This perspective on local government was most famously articulated by Charles Tiebout in the 1950s. The **Tiebout model** of local government calls for a metro area made up of a series of micropolitical jurisdictions. If each jurisdiction can control its tax-service packages, fully mobile citizens will respond to that mix of packages by gravitating to the one that suits them best. Or, as Tiebout put it, the mobility of citizens will provide "the local public goods counterpart to the private market's shopping trip." [34]

In addition to highly mobile citizens, the Tiebout model also requires informed citizens. If people do not know what different governments are offering in the way of alternative tax-service packages they are not going to be very good local government "shoppers," and local governments may be able to take advantage of that ignorance by becoming lazy and inefficient producers of public goods and services.

> **PUBLIC CHOICE MODEL**
> A model of politics that views governments and public services in market terms; governments are seen as producers of public services and citizens are seen as consumers.

> In short, there is a glass half-full perspective that sees innovation and vitality, high standards of living, and social and economic opportunities that is in contrast to the glass half-empty perspective that focuses on segregation, smog, and economic inequality.

> **TIEBOUT MODEL**
> A model of local government based on market principles wherein a metro area is made up of a series of micropolitical jurisdictions that, on the basis of their services and costs, attract or repel certain citizens.

If the mobility and information requirements are met, the Tiebout model makes a strong theoretical case for political fragmentation in metropolitan areas, obviously arguing against the reform perspective of pushing for different forms of government consolidation. From the Tiebout model perspective a regional government or a merged city and county represents a big monopoly, which is something that is likely to produce a large, inefficient bureaucracy that is unresponsive to citizens and that has little pressure to keep quality high and costs low.

The "if" on the mobility and information requirements, however, is a big one. A number of scholars have argued that citizens are not fully mobile, nor are they fully informed. The constraints on mobility are fairly obvious: where you can live is determined by how much you can make. This means the well-off, if they so choose, can be fairly mobile. The less well-off, on the other hand, are more likely to find their mobility limited by their pocketbooks. They simply cannot afford to move to better neighborhoods, even if they want to, because property prices are too high. There are some important implications here. The Tiebout model, remember, makes a good case that local governments will be responsive to people who have a real exit option, in other words, people who can pack up and move if they do not like what the local government is doing. If those people are defined by wealth, it means governments in metropolitan areas are likely to be more responsive to the concerns of the well-off than to those of the poor.

The requirement that citizens be informed also turns out to be a fairly restrictive burden on using the Tiebout model as a practical template for metropolitan governance. As it turns out, most people have only a vague notion of the details of the tax-service packages offered by their own local government, let alone what the tax-service packages of neighboring local governments offer. Three political scientists, William Lyons, David Lowery, and Ruth Hoogland DeHoog, undertook one of the more comprehensive field tests of the Tiebout model in the early 1990s. They surveyed citizens who lived in what they termed "monocentric" metropolitan areas (areas where there was a consolidated city-county government) and "polycentric" metropolitan areas (places defined by a range of smaller political jurisdictions). They found there was no difference in citizens' reported satisfaction with public services in the two types of metropolitan settings, that mobility was extremely low in both settings (the probability of moving was 2.66 percent in polycentric areas and 1.32 percent in monocentric settings), and that citizens were better informed in monocentric than polycentric settings.[35] These findings raise considerable questions about whether the Tiebout model can serve as a practical guide to governance in metropolitan areas.

In the 1990s the Tiebout model was reworked by a group of political scientists who argued that the central idea did not require *all* citizens to be mobile and highly informed. It just required *enough* citizens to have these characteristics to force government to be responsive to their interests. The question, of course, was what sort of citizens would be motivated enough to inform themselves about local government and be willing to use that knowledge to form the basis of buying property.

The logical test case for this argument seemed to be school districts. Schools are an important consideration in buying real estate, and, if anyone was going to have the motivation to bone up on local government it would be parents moving into a new school district. A survey of people who recently had bought homes in Suffolk County, New York, revealed that these recent movers were more informed than long-time residents. If wealthy movers tend to be highly informed it suggests there might be a subgroup of citizens who resemble those in the Tiebout model.[36] Whether this small subgroup is enough to create market-like pressures for efficiency on local governments, however, remains a point of contention.[37]

Regardless, what the Tiebout demonstrates is that there is a theoretical case to be made for political fragmentation in metropolitan areas. Coupled with high suburban standards of living and gentrification in the core cites, there is a reasonable counterargument to the calls for more centralized government in metropolitan areas.

Rural Metropolitics

Rural governments frequently face a different set of challenges than the urban areas discussed thus far. For example, some rural counties are dealing with shrinking and aging populations, as younger people shift from rural agricultural areas to more metropolitan areas in search of educational, social, and economic opportunities.

Consider that in Kansas roughly three-quarters of the state's 105 counties lost population between 2000 and 2004.[38] This reflects a population exodus that tracks a massive consolidation in agriculture as family farms give way to massive corporate operations. Fewer farms means fewer agricultural jobs, which means that younger people move to the cities where the jobs are, leaving smaller rural communities with fewer shoppers, fewer schools, and fewer businesses. That is a recipe for decline that can be hard to reverse.

Rather than white flight, rural states such as Iowa, Kansas, and Nebraska face **rural flight**, the movement of the young and the middle class to more urban areas. While the underlying cause is different, the end result can be pressure for solutions that would sound familiar to any veteran of the political battles over urban growth: regional government. Iowa, for example, is a mostly rural state. It has a population of roughly three million and roughly a thousand general purpose governments. That works out to be thirty-six general units of government for every one hundred thousand residents.[39] Most counties in Iowa do not have a lot of people; what

RURAL FLIGHT

The movement of rural youth and middle classes to more urban areas.

MAP 11-4 Population Changes by County, Iowa, 1990–2000

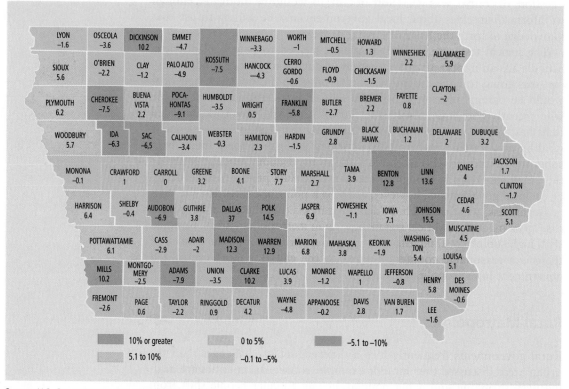

Source: U.S. Census Bureau, Population Division.

they have is a lot of government. (See Map 11-4 for county-by-county population changes in Iowa.)

That makes government tremendously inefficient; in rural areas there are redundant layers of government sitting on stagnant tax bases. That puts upward pressure on property taxes, and it also creates incentives to make government more efficient. Consolidating governments is one way to do this, and this is an option that increasingly is being considered in rural states. Schools are typically among the first sets of merger candidates. As student populations decrease in a rural community, it is harder to fund a comprehensive school K–12 school system. If there is another community within busing distance, it can make a good deal of financial sense to split educational services; for example, have elementary schools in both communities, the junior high in one town, and the high school in the other.

These sorts of pressures have made for a steady stream of school district consolidations in rural states. As recently as the mid-1980s, for example, Nebraska had more than a one thousand school districts. As of 2006, it

Governing States and Localities

had roughly a quarter of that number.[40] School consolidations make financial sense from the standpoint of the statewide taxpayer; larger districts can take advantage of economies of scales, rationalize class sizes, and lower per-pupil spending. From a community perspective, however, school consolidations are less about dollars and cents than identity, or even survival. A rural community that loses its school loses a central social and cultural institution, and the loss of teachers also means losing a significant chunk of a town's middle class. Many see the loss of a school, especially a high school, as a devastating blow to a rural community.

When economics run into strong loyalties to local governments, the local loyalties often win, but those victories mean higher property taxes and fewer public services. In 2005, Iowa governor Tom Vilsack argued that his state simply had too much public infrastructure. Iowa has 99 counties, 948 cities, and 2,000 towns; a lot of government for a state with a population of less than 3 million. Vilsack proposed a truly radical solution to the problem of too many governments relative to the size of the population: his plan proposed replacing the grab bag of local governments with about fifteen regional governments. These regional governments, Vilsack reasoned, would not only be cheaper, they would be better positioned to drive economic development in rural areas. His plan landed with a thud; local governments—and their constituents—didn't exactly flock to support it. Vilsack's innovative plan to sweep away the traditional local government infrastructure and replace it with regional governments got a chilly reception in the legislature.[41]

While the plan for a new system of regional government did not pass in Iowa, many officials in rural communities recognize that size does matter. Simply put, smaller rural communities, especially those facing population drains, simply have not got the tax base to support layer upon layer of government. People remain fiercely loyal to their local schools and local towns, but while they may not express much enthusiasm for out-and-out consolidation, there are increasing trends toward cooperative agreements, and an increasing recognition that in some circumstances consolidation makes too much sense to ignore.

For example, Adams County, Iowa, has three communities within its borders, none with a population of more than 200, and the population of the entire county is about 4,400. A survey of Adams County residents found that most people recognized the difficulties created by the mismatch between too few people and too much government. "You could just have one government for 4,400 people and call it good," says county supervisor Mark Olive.[42]

Rural flight is a demographic phenomenon whose causes and consequences tend to attract less scholarly and media attention than white flight and the problems it causes for core cities and urban areas. The governance and political issues it raises, however, clearly have distinct parallels with the broader story of metropolitics told in larger urban areas.

Conclusion

The central issue of metropolitics—and its rural equivalent—boils down to the gap that exists between local and state governments. Local governments were founded and organized in a horse and buggy era, and those organizational structures do not always make for a rational fit with twenty-first century realities.

Political fragmentation in urban areas, and dispersed and shrinking populations in urban areas, raise a tough set of questions: How many governments are too many? What exactly should they have the power to do? Should new institutions be created to fill the hole between local government and state government? The questions resist easy answers in rural areas just as they resist easy answers in metropolitan ones.

The questions, however, cannot be ignored. A broad array of social and economic challenges are essentially regional in nature, and the hole in government organization means that in most places there is no strong, central government taking a regional perspective on these problems. The politics of metropolitan areas—and in many cases, in rural areas—boils down to difference on what, if anything, should fill that hole. A true regional government, with the authority to develop and effectively enforce policy solutions to problems of transportation, land use, and the like, means established local governments must cede their power to this new government. In the case of consolidation, they have to, in effect, put themselves out of business. The politics involved can be contentious.

Despite the difficulties, however, the realities on the ground are pushing local governments toward regional perspectives through cooperative agreements and joint action. The social and economic challenges that are regional in nature demand the hole in government be filled. The unanswered question is how.

Key Concepts

annexation (p. 421)

car-dependent living (p. 408)

city-county consolidation (p. 418)

edgeless cities (p. 405)

exurbs (p. 410)

gentrification (p. 424)

impact fees (p. 408)

leapfrog development (p. 408)

low-density development (p. 407)

megalopolis (p. 405)

metropolitan area (p. 403)

metropolitan planning organization (MPO) (p. 415)

metropolitan statistical area (MSA) (p. 403)

public choice model (p. 425)

reform perspective (p. 411)

regional council (p. 414)

rural flight (p. 427)

smart growth (p. 417)

sprawl (p. 407)

Tiebout model (p. 425)

urban growth boundary (UGB) (p. 414)

white flight (p. 410)

zoning laws (p. 407)

Suggested Readings

Dreier, Peter, John Mollenkopf, and Todd Swanstrom. *Place Matters: Metropolitics for the Twenty-First Century.* Lawrence: University of Kansas Press, 2001. Three distinguished urban scholars argue that geography plays a central role in determining social and economic opportunities. Their central theme is that inequality is at least partially a product of the policy choices rooted in a structure of governance that includes little in the way of real regional political jurisdictions.

Miller, David. *The Regional Governing of Metropolitan America.* Boulder, Colo.: Westview Press, 2002. An excellent primer on the political, legal, and historical foundations of local government. Also includes an original study on the comparative power of regional governments across the United States.

Orfield, Myron. *American Metropolitics: The New Suburban Reality.* Washington, D.C.: Brookings Institution, 2002. One of the best-known studies on the regional nature of the problems facing urban areas, and also one of the most widely cited arguments for regional government.

Suggested Web Sites

www.ampo.org. AMPO is the national organization for metropolitan planning organizations. It is mainly oriented toward transportation issues, but the Web site includes downloadable studies and publications on a range of issues facing metropolitan areas.

www.census.gov/population/www/estimates/metrodef. html. The U.S. Bureau of the Census Web site that contains definitions and descriptions of all metropolitan statistical areas in the United States.

www.metro-region.org. Web site of Portland's Metro, a rare example of a true regional government in the United States. Includes history behind the formation of Metro and information on a range of Metro's activities.

www.narc.org. The National Association of Regional Councils is an organization of metropolitan planning organizations that seeks to promote cooperation between governments. It covers urban, suburban, and rural governments.

CHAPTER 12

Finance

Filling the Till and Paying the Bills

Will that be cash or charge? Either way, these shoppers at the Mall of America in Bloomington, Minnesota, got a break from sales tax on their clothing purchases. Minnesota is one of numerous states that consider clothing an essential item and, therefore, waive any sales taxes. Other states, such as New Hampshire, have no sales tax at all, which makes their malls and shopping outlets very popular with shoppers from neighboring states.

12

What are the differences between progressive and regressive tax systems?

Why are many state and local politicians against Internet sales?

Why are property taxes so important to communities?

Tennessee is a state that prides itself on its low taxes. According to the Washington, D.C.-based Tax Foundation, residents of the Volunteer State pay 8.6 percent of their incomes in state and local taxes—the fourth lowest tax rate in the country.[1]

Only Alaska, which derives nearly 40 percent of its general **revenues** from taxes on the huge Prudhoe Bay oil field, New Hampshire, and Delaware have lower **tax burdens**. Tennessee is also one of only nine states with no income tax. Instead, Tennessee has long relied on a sales tax to generate most of the state's revenues. Back when the state sales tax rate hovered at 6 percent that seemed like a good bargain to most Tennesseans. That was before Tennessee decided in 2002 to increase its sales tax from 6 percent to 7 percent—and that's before local governments tack on their own levies. In many parts of the state, residents pay almost 10 percent sales tax on most purchases.

During the long economic boom of the 1990s, a decade in which Americans shopped like never before, Tennessee's sales tax more or less sufficed. But when the economy slid into recession in the spring of 2001, sales tax revenues dried up. By the summer of 2001, Tennessee found itself with an $880 million **budget shortfall**.

For the federal government, a budget shortfall is an embarrassment, not a crisis. Congress and the president usually agree to cover the shortfall by borrowing money, that is, by selling U.S. Treasury bonds. The situation at the state level is very different. Like virtually every state, Tennessee is required by law to balance its operating budget every year. As a result, its shortfall presented Tennessee legislators and Gov. Don Sundquist with some very difficult choices. Policymakers could either slash programs or raise taxes, or do some combination of both.

Governor Sundquist, a Republican, had been elected governor in 1994 and then again in 1998 due in large part to his opposition to a state income tax. After winning reelection, however, Sundquist changed his position and proposed replacing the state's 6 percent sales tax with a 3.75 percent sales tax and a 3.75 percent income tax.

Sundquist's proposal would have made Tennessee's tax system more **progressive**. Low-income Tennesseans would have gained more from the sales tax reduction than they would have lost from the new income tax. High-income residents would have had their taxes increased. Of course, the new income tax also would have raised considerably more money for the state overall, increasing the state's tax burden.

At first, the legislature resisted this proposal. By the afternoon of July 12, 2001, however, a majority of the state legislature was on the verge of accepting the governor's position. That is when Marsha Blackburn, a Republican state senator from Nashville, got on the phone. Blackburn, a vehement opponent of a state income tax, called two of Nashville's most popular—and most conservative—radio talk show hosts to sound the tax alarm.

Within forty minutes, more than two hundred protesters had entered the capitol building. Chants of "No new taxes!"—and other, more explicit, phrases—filled the building and disrupted the debate. Soon an estimated two thousand protesters had converged on the building. State police locked them out, which made the crowd even angrier. As protestors pounded on the doors, someone hurled a rock through the window of the governor's office. Not surprisingly, the legislature decided to hold off on Governor Sundquist's income tax proposal.[2]

Tennessee's **tax revolt** was unusual, but strong feelings about taxes are not. Few things arouse stronger feelings among voters than taxes. Personal income taxes and property taxes are among the most visible and the most controversial. Yet many people have only a vague understanding of how state and local governments raise money.

That is because the taxes that state and local governments impose are less visible than, say, the federal income tax, which claims a large portion of most people's paychecks every two weeks. The largest source of money for state and local governments comes from the sales tax, which is much less visible.[3] State and local governments also raise substantial sums from charges for tuition, sewage and water treatment, utilities, highway tolls, and various **user fees**. A $19 resident fishing license may not sound like much, but fees of that sort do add up.

In 2006, residents of the United States paid approximately $12,122 in local, state, and federal taxes per person.[4] State and local taxes and user fees raised about $1.45 trillion.[5] State and local governments use these funds and a substantial influx of funds from the federal government to finance local schools and state universities, provide health insurance to very low-income families and people with disabilities, and build highways and mass transit. The money also helps maintain correctional facilities that house more than two million people a year[6] and provides police and fire protection to the remaining approximately three hundred million of the population. In short, state and local taxes pay for the programs that Americans care most about and most directly affect their daily lives.

There is a tendency to think of taxes and budgets as dry, technical, and, yes, boring. That is a pretty good description of much of the literature on this subject, but a very mistaken view of the subject itself. Actually, budgets are the subject of some of the most intense political struggles in state and local politics. It is not simply that people care about money, although they certainly do. Budgets are fundamentally about policy. In many ways, they are the central policy documents of government. They determine and reflect much of the policy orientations of elected leaders. If you want to know what your state or local government's priorities are, its budget will tell you.

This chapter discusses how state and local governments raise money, how they decide to spend it via the budget process, and what they spend it on. It examines why state and local governments make such different taxing and spending choices and explores the consequences of these very different choices. The chapter concludes with a discussion of how budgetary constraints and challenges are forcing many state and local governments to rethink how they pay for public services.

Show Me the Money: Where State Revenues Come From

Roughly half of the money that state and local governments took in in 2002, that is, about $905 billion, came from six primary taxes.[7] These were sales taxes, including **excise taxes,** often referred to as **sin taxes,** on tobacco and alcohol; property taxes; income taxes, motor vehicle taxes, **estate taxes,** also called death taxes; and **gift taxes.**

Sales Taxes

In 2002, state and local governments took in $324 billion from **sales taxes**—about 36 percent of total state and local government tax revenues. About 81 percent of the money raised by sales taxes goes to state governments. But like Tennessee, most states allow at least some counties and cities to levy additional sales taxes. Currently, about 7,500 localities do. Some states, such as California, return a small percentage of sales taxes to the areas in which the purchases were made. Overall, sales tax revenues account for nearly 17 percent of local government tax revenues nationwide.[8]

State governments, and, to a much lesser extent, local governments, also take in significant sums from gasoline taxes and sin taxes on tobacco and alcohol. Different states interpret this type of tax very differently. Other factors often influence what gets taxed and for how much. North Carolina has a large tobacco-growing industry and a tax of only thirty cents on each pack of cigarettes. New Jersey has no large-scale tobacco industry and levies a tax of $2.40 per pack of cigarettes sold.[9]

Politicians like sales taxes because they tend to be less visible than an income tax. As such, they are less likely to cause voters to retaliate against them at the polls. Economists like sales taxes because they are **focused consumption taxes** that do not distort consumer behavior. That is, sales taxes, even relatively high ones, often do not cause consumers to buy less.

This does not mean that they do not receive their share of criticism. Many liberals and advocates for low-income people complain that sales taxes are **regressive**. If Bill Gates buys a grande latte on his way to work, he pays about twenty-eight cents in sales taxes. Freshmen at the University of Washington pay exactly the same.

The tax is the same but the students are paying a much higher percentage of their incomes to the government than Mr. Gates is. Put another way, if Bill Gates's income were even a mere $5 million a year, and a typical student's income is $2,500 a year, guess how much Bill Gates would have to pay in sales taxes to face the same tax burden as a typical student? Give up? His grande latte would have to cost him a whopping—but tax-proportionate—$566.20. Of course, as already noted, it doesn't really work that way. If and when Bill Gates goes to a coffee shop, he pays the same price—and the same sales tax—as anyone else.

States often do attempt to make their sales tax less of a burden on low-income residents by exempting necessities such as food, clothing, and electric and gas utilities from taxation. In general, however, states that rely heavily on a sales tax tend to have more regressive tax systems than other states.

Take Tennessee again. Rich and poor alike paid a 7 percent sales tax at the cash register in 2003. However, Memphis residents earning $25,000 a year or less paid an average of 7 percent of their incomes in state and local taxes. That is about $1,757. In contrast, those residents earning $150,000 or more a year paid only 5.6 percent, or $8,369, of their incomes in taxes.[10] So, whereas it *looks* like the $150,000 wage earners paid more, the low-income residents paid a higher percentage of their incomes in taxes than they might have if they lived in a state that relied more on income taxes. That makes Tennessee's tax system highly regressive.

Sales taxes have another problem—they simply are not bringing in as much revenue as they used to. In the words of James Hine, a finance expert at Clemson University, relying on the sales tax "is like riding a horse that is rapidly dying."

What that basically means is that the sales tax base is slowly eroding. Two factors seem to account for this. First, services have become a much more important part of the economy. In 1960, 41 percent of U.S. consumer dollars were spent on services. By 2000, that percentage had risen to 58 percent. Yet most sales taxes are skewed toward the purchase of products rather than the purchase of services. Buy a robotic massage chair at the Mall of America in Bloomington, Minnesota, and you'll pay $97.49 in sales tax on that $800 item. Hire an acupuncturist for an hour from a holistic medical center in Bloomington, and you'll pay no sales tax.

> Budgets are fundamentally about policy. In many ways, they are the central policy documents of government. They determine and reflect much of the policy orientations of elected leaders. If you want to know what your state or local government's priorities are, its budget will tell you.

Hawaii, New Mexico, and South Dakota have changed their tax codes so that sales taxes now cover most professional and personal services. However, most states have been reluctant to follow suit. Taxing services could put them at a competitive disadvantage. For instance, if Illinois starts to tax accounting services, there probably would be a sudden boom in business for CPAs in nearby Indiana.[11]

The second factor behind faltering sales tax revenues is the rise of the Internet and online shopping. In 1992, the U.S. Supreme Court ruled that states could not force companies to collect sales taxes for them in places where the companies had no physical presence. As a result, most online purchases are tax-free. A study by William F. Fox and Donald Bruce of the University of Tennessee, Knoxville put the overall losses of sales tax revenue from Internet sales between $15.5 billion and $16.1 billion in 2003 and predicted losses as great as $33.7 billion a year by 2008.[12]

For states such as Texas and Tennessee that don't have income taxes and rely heavily on sales tax revenue, this trend is a big problem. To make up for the kind of revenue loss that Fox and Bruce predict, Texas would have to raise its current statewide sales tax rate from 6.25 percent to 7.86 percent.[13]

The U.S. Congress has rejected states' pleas to stop exempting online retailers from collecting the taxes, citing the difficulty the companies would have complying with very different state sales tax codes. In 2004, Congress extended the moratorium on online taxation until 2007. Absent federal intervention, states have banded together to collect online taxes. Dozens of states joined the Streamlined Sales Tax Project, agreeing to simplify their tax codes in exchange for the chance to convince retailers to voluntarily collect the taxes. The project went live in October 2005, with 150 retailers signing on in 18 states.[14] By January 1, 2007, the effort had picked up steam, with more than one thousand companies participating in twenty-one states.[15]

Property Taxes

The second largest source of tax revenue for state and local governments comes from property taxes. In 2002, property taxes raised approximately 31 percent, or $279 billion, of total state and local government tax revenues. Most sales tax revenues go to state governments, but almost all property taxes go to local governments. As a result, property taxes are by far the most important source of revenue for local government. Approximately 73 percent of local government revenues, but only a tiny fraction—2 percent— of state tax revenues, come from property taxes.[16]

Just about every local government relies on property tax revenues, but property tax rates vary widely from community to community. Most Americans who own homes or condominiums face an effective tax rate of about 1.5 percent.[17] The word "effective" simply acknowledges that some places have exemptions and adjustments that make the effective tax rate lower than the nominal tax rate. You can figure out the nominal tax rate by dividing the amount of tax paid by the amount of taxable income. The effective tax rate is found by dividing the amount of tax paid by the amount of total economic income.

In other words, if you own a condo worth $100,000, you probably pay about $1,500 a year in property taxes. In Manchester, New Hampshire, however, you'd pay $2,570 in property taxes on that same condo. That's because New Hampshire has an effective tax rate of 2.57, which is one of the highest in the country. Why are New Hampshire's property tax rates so high? Largely because the state has no income tax and no sales tax. That limits the state government's ability to raise funds. It also means that the state does not offer its towns the levels of financial support that most state governments do. As a result, whereas most local governments receive 25 percent of their total revenues from property taxes, local governments in New Hampshire are forced to rely on property taxes for 47 percent of their total revenues.[18]

The Education Connection. Property taxes are important for another reason. They pretty much finance elementary and high school education. On average, school districts receive about 43 percent of their funding from local governments.[19] In most states, where you live determines how many education dollars your children receive.

Wealthy communities with high housing values raise the most money from property taxes. School districts in these areas tend to have the most educational resources. Conversely, school districts in the poorest areas have the fewest resources. For instance, in New York during the 2002–2003 school year, the most prosperous school districts spent about $2,280 more per student than the least prosperous school districts.[20]

In recent years, this funding gap has begun to narrow. State governments have taken larger roles in financing public education in response to a string of lawsuits that challenged the constitutionality of financing arrangements that provide the poorest children with the fewest resources. Nationwide, school districts with the highest levels of poverty spent $907 less per student during the 2002–2003 school year than school districts in areas with the lowest levels of poverty.[21]

Hawaii's state government has taken over financing local schools completely. Many view such a system as more equitable than a traditional, property tax–supported system. However, efforts to equalize school finances also can have unintended consequences, as the state of California discovered. (See box on page 440.)

The Pros and Cons of Property Taxes. Property taxes generally are paid twice a year as a large lump fee. As such, they tend to be highly visible and extremely unpopular with the public. However, local officials like them because property tax receipts are less volatile and more predictable than other types of taxes. Local revenue departments assess the value of houses and businesses and then send their owners a bill, so they know exactly how much revenue a property tax will yield.

Policy in Practice: California's Misguided Effort to Equalize School Funding

Policymakers often look at different types of taxes and see interchangeable ways to raise revenue. Sometimes, however, the way policymakers decide to fund a program can have a dramatic impact on how the program itself works—or whether it works at all.

One example of a well-intentioned reform gone awry is California's effort to provide equal educational funding for all students in kindergarten through twelfth grade. In 1970, the California Supreme Court ruled in *Serrano v. Priest* that the state's existing education financing scheme was unconstitutional.

The system relied on local property taxes to support local schools. There was only one problem. Relying on property taxes meant that children in "property rich" communities often attended lavishly financed schools while children in "property poor" communities had to make do with facilities and instruction that were often completely inadequate.

In 1977, after years of such litigation, the California legislature responded. It voted to funnel money from the state's large budget surplus to local schools. However, the legislation didn't stop there. The state also required communities that wanted to boost school spending by raising local property taxes to share the additional funds they brought in with other school districts.

In hindsight, this "district power equalization" was ill conceived. Californians no longer had any incentive to raise local property taxes to pay for education. In fact, any incentive was to do just the opposite. Under the new system, each district received a base level of support regardless of its local tax revenue and tax rate. As a result, every district had an incentive to set its local property tax rate as low as possible. In other words, instead of raising education spending to a new, higher level for most students, equalization actually may have lowered the average amount spent on education.

By breaking the link between local property taxes and local school spending, some economists believe that the 1970 *Serrano* decision laid the groundwork for Proposition 13, which capped property taxes and banned reassessment of a house's value so long as the owner stayed in it. The result was less money for everyone.

New Mexico, South Dakota, and Utah—other states that have tried to equalize school funding by confiscating "extra" revenues raised by local school districts—also have ended up driving school funding *down* rather than up.

According to Harvard economist Caroline Hoxby, "It appears that some students from poor households would actually have better funded schools if their states had not attempted such complete equalization." *

* See Caroline Hoxby's paper, "All School Finance Equalizations Are Not Created Equal," *Quarterly Journal of Economics* 116, no. 4 (November 2001), and William Fischel's "How Judges Are Making Public Schools Worse," *City Journal,* Summer 1998.

In most instances, taxes seem worse when the economy is bad. Property taxes are the exception. They tend to rise most sharply when a town or city is experiencing an economic boom and housing prices are soaring. In these circumstances, an upsurge in property values can lead to a backlash.

The most famous of such backlashes occurred in California in 1978. In response to years of rising property values and related taxes, Californians passed Proposition 13. This piece of legislation capped the property tax rate at 1 percent of a property's purchase price and froze property assessments at their 1978 levels until the property is resold. Newcomers have to pay property taxes based on the actual value of the house.

To this day, Proposition 13 is hotly debated. Conservatives have long praised the movement that gave rise to it. They say that it was the harbinger of the conservative politics that former California governor Ronald Reagan would bring to Washington three years later. Most experts, however, believe that its effects have been devastating. These individuals point to Proposition 13 as the sole reason California transformed from one of the most generous contributors to public education to one of the least generous.

Even the most liberal electorates can be goaded into atypical action by rising property tax rates. In 1980, Massachusetts voters passed Proposition 2¹/₂. Property tax increases were capped at, you guessed it, 2¹/₂ percent. As a result, towns that want to increase spending by more than that, for such needs as increased funding for education, have to hold special override sessions. Towns also have come to rely on user fees, a phenomenon examined later in this chapter.

Many state and local governments have attempted to ease the burden of property taxes on senior citizens and, in some cases, on other low-income individuals. In about fifty Massachusetts towns, senior citizens can reduce their property taxes by performing volunteer work. Cook County, Illinois, limits property tax rate increases by tying them to the national rate of inflation.[22]

Despite these efforts, tensions between retirees living on fixed incomes and parents eager to spend more on local schools are commonplace. These pressures can be particularly acute in areas with large numbers of retirees living on fixed incomes. Indeed, some "active-adult retirement communities" ban children altogether.

It's worth noting another hidden cost of property taxes. You might think that commercial and residential property owners are the only ones who pay, right? You're off the hook if you rent, right? Wrong! Most economists believe that landlords pass the cost of property tax increases to renters in the form of rent increases.

Eunice McTyre, one of the original activist proponents of Proposition 13, poses in front of her Los Angeles–area home with her property tax bill in February 2003. For individuals on fixed incomes, many of them elderly, Proposition 13 has been a tremendous financial boon. For parents, the legislation has been a disaster. Most communities use property taxes to pay for their public schools. Property taxes capped at rates well below the value of the property mean millions of dollars less for education.

> Most economists believe that landlords pass the cost of property tax increases to renters in the form of rent increases.

Income Taxes

Personal **income taxes** account for 22 percent of all state and local tax revenues.[23] That makes income tax revenue the third most significant source of state and local government income. In some ways, however, this figure con-

INCOME TAXES
Taxes on income.

ceals more than it reveals. Almost all income tax revenues go to state governments.[24]

Of course, this is not true for every state. As previously mentioned, nine states make do without income taxes. Alaska, Florida, Nevada, South Dakota, Texas, Washington, and Wyoming impose no income taxes at all. New Hampshire and Tennessee impose taxes only on certain types of income.

As discussed earlier, states that do not have an income tax usually rely heavily on the sales tax. But Alaska, Delaware, Montana, New Hampshire, and Oregon have no sales tax. Oregon has managed this by—drum roll, please—relying heavily on a state income tax. In fact, in 2002, Oregon's income tax provided approximately three-fourths of its total tax revenues—the most of any state.[25]

So, Alaska and New Hampshire have neither income taxes nor sales taxes. How can that be? For Alaska, the answer is the Prudhoe Bay oilfields.[26] New Hampshire makes do. According to Donald Boyd of the Rockefeller Institute, New Hampshire's state government simply does less than most state governments. The state relies almost exclusively on local governments to finance elementary and secondary education rather than raising state revenue for this purpose. Unlike many other states, it also has managed to avoid court orders to spend dramatically more on secondary school education. It is able to do all of this, in part, because the income of the average New Hampshire resident is one of the highest in the country. People are able to pay for a lot of goods and services for themselves.

These states are the exceptions. On average, Americans pay about $747 a year in state income taxes.[27] However, residents of states with high taxes, such as Maryland, Massachusetts, New York, and Oregon, face much higher state income tax burdens. (See Table 12-1.)

Other Tax Revenue Sources: Cars, Oil, and Death

Car registrations, death, and oil and other natural resources also are major sources of state revenues. In 2002, car registration fees brought in more than $18 billion to state and local governments. Estate taxes, sometimes called death taxes, and gift taxes brought in another $7.5 billion.[28]

Thirty-nine states levy **severance taxes** on natural resources that are removed, or severed, from the state. Some states are quite creative about devising severance taxes. Washington, for example, taxes oysters and salmon and other game fish caught in state. But despite some creative taxing, the only states that raise real money from severance taxes are states with significant coal, oil, and natural gas reserves, such as Wyoming and Alaska.

Other Sources of Income: Fees, Charges, and Uncle Sam

The total tax revenues discussed so far add up to about $905 billion. That is a lot of money, but it accounts for less than half of the $2 trillion that

SEVERANCE TAXES

Taxes on natural resources.

TABLE 12-1

State Individual Income Tax Rates, 2007

State	Tax Rate (percentage)		Number of Brackets	Income Brackets		Personal Exemption[b]			Federal Tax Deductions
	Low	High		Low	High	Single	Married	Children	
Alabama	2.0 –	5.0	3	500 [b] –	3,000 [b]	1,500	3,000	300	*
Alaska	No State Income Tax								
Arizona	2.59 –	4.57	5	10,000 [b] –	150,000 [b]	2,100	4,200	2,300	
Arkansas [a]	1.0 –	7.0 [e]	6	3,599	–	30,100	22 [c]	44 [c]	22 [c]
California [a]	1.0 –	9.3 [w]	6	6,622 [b] –	43,468 [b]	91 [c]	182 [c]	285 [c]	
Colorado	4.63		1	—Flat rate—		—None—			
Connecticut	3.0 –	5.0	2	10,000 [b] –	10,000 [b]	12,750 [f]	24,500 [f]	0	
Delaware	2.2 –	5.95	6	5,000 –	60,000	110 [c]	220 [c]	110 [c]	
Florida	No State Income Tax								
Georgia	1.0 –	6.0	6	750 [g] –	7,000 [g]	2,700	5,400	3,000	
Hawaii	1.4 –	8.25	9	2,400 [b] –	48,000 [b]	1,040	2,080	1,040	
Idaho [a]	1.6 –	7.8	8	1,198 [h] –	23,964 [h]	3,400 [d]	6,800 [d]	3,400 [d]	
Illinois	3.0		1	—Flat rate—		2,000	4,000	2,000	
Indiana	3.4		1	—Flat rate—		1,000	2,000	1,000	
Iowa [a]	0.36 –	8.98	9	1,343 –	60,436	40 [c]	80 [c]	40 [c]	*
Kansas	3.5 –	6.45	3	15,000 [b] –	30,000 [b]	2,250	4,500	2,250	
Kentucky	2.0 –	6.0	6	3,000 –	75,000	20 [c]	40 [c]	20 [c]	
Louisiana	2.0 –	6.0	3	12,500 [b] –	25,000 [b]	4,500 [i]	9,000 [i]	1,000 [i]	*
Maine [a]	2.0 –	8.5	4	4,550 [b] –	18,250 [b]	2,850	5,700	2,85	
Maryland	2.0 –	4.75	4	1,000 –	3,000	2,400	4,800	2,400	
Massachusetts [a]	5.3		1	—Flat rate—		4,125	8,250	1,000	
Michigan [a]	3.9		1	—Flat rate—		3,300	6,600	3,300	
Minnesota [a]	5.35 –	7.85	3	21,310 [j] –	69,991 [j]	3,400 [d]	6,800 [d]	3,400 [d]	
Mississippi	3.0 –	5.0	3	5,000 –	10,000	6,000	12,000	1,500	
Missouri	1.5 –	6.0	10	1,000 –	9,000	2,100	4,200	1,200	* r
Montana [a]	1.0 –	6.9	7	2,300 –	14,500	1,980	3,960	1,980	* r
Nebraska [a]	2.56 –	6.84	4	2,400 [k] –	27,001 [k]	106 [c]	212 [c]	106 [c]	
Nevada	No State Income Tax								
New Hampshire	State Income Tax Is Limited to Dividends and Interest Income Only.								
New Jersey	1.4 –	8.97	6	20,000 [l] –	500,000 [l]	1,000	2,000	1,500	
New Mexico	1.7 –	5.3	4	5,500 [m] –	16,000 [m]	3,400 [d]	6,800 [d]	3,400 [d]	
New York	4.0 –	6.85	5	8,000 [b] –	20,000 [b]	0	0	1,000	
North Carolina [n]	6.0 –	8.0	4	12,750 [n] –	120,000 [n]	3,400 [d]	6,800 [d]	3,400 [d]	
North Dakota [a]	2.1 –	5.54 [o]	5	30,650 [o] –	336,550 [o]	3,400 [d]	6,800 [d]	3,400 [d]	
Ohio [a]	0.649 –	6.555	9	5,000 –	200,000	1,400 [p]	2,800 [p]	1,400 [p]	
Oklahoma	0.5 –	5.65 [q]	7	1,000 [b] –	10,000 [b]	1,000	2,000	1,000	* q
Oregon [a]	5.0 –	9.0	3	2,750 [b] –	6,851 [b]	159 [c]	318 [c]	159 [c]	* r

TABLE 12-1, continued

State	Tax Rate (percentage)		Number of Brackets	Income Brackets		Personal Exemption[b]			Federal Tax Deductions
	Low	High		Low	High	Single	Married	Children	
Pennsylvania	3.07		1	—Flat rate—		—None—			
Rhode Island	25.0% Federal Tax Liability [s]			–		–	–	–	–
South Carolina [a]	2.5 – 7.0		6	2,570 – 12,850		3,400 [d]	6,800 [d]	3,400 [d]	
South Dakota	No State Income Tax								
Tennessee	State Income Tax Is Limited to Dividends and Interest Income Only.								
Texas	No State Income Tax								
Utah	2.30 – 6.98 [t]		6	1,000 [b] – 5,501 [b]		2,550 [d]	5,100 [d]	2,550 [d]	★ [t]
Vermont [a]	3.6 – 9.5		5	30,650 [u] – 336,551 [u]		3,400 [d]	6,800 [d]	3,400 [d]	
Virginia	2.0 – 5.75		4	3,000 – 17,000		900	1,800	900	
Washington	No State Income Tax								
West Virginia	3.0 – 6.5		5	10,000 – 60,000		2,000	4,000	2,000	
Wisconsin [a]	4.6 – 6.75		4	9,160 [v] – 137,411 [v]		700	1,400	700	
Wyoming	No State Income Tax								
Dist. of Columbia	4.5 – 8.7		3	10,000 – 40,000		2,400	4,800	2,400	

Source: The Federation of Tax Administrators, from various sources. www.taxadmin.org/fta/rate/ind_inc.html (accessed May 30, 2007).

[a] 17 states have statutory provision for automatic adjustment of tax brackets, personal exemption or standard deductions to the rate of inflation. Massachusetts, Michigan, Nebraska and Ohio indexes the personal exemption amounts only.

[b] For joint returns, the taxes are twice the tax imposed on half the income.

[c] tax credits.

[d] These states allow personal exemption or standard deductions as provided in the IRC. Utah allows a personal exemption equal to three-fourths the federal exemptions.

[e] A special tax table is available for low income taxpayers reducing their tax payments.

[f] Combined personal exemptions and standard deduction. An additional tax credit is allowed ranging from 75% to 0% based on state adjusted gross income. Exemption amounts are phased out for higher income taxpayers until they are eliminated for households earning over $56,500.

[g] The tax brackets reported are for single individuals. For married households filing separately, the same rates apply to income brackets ranging from $500 to $5,000; and the income brackets range from $1,000 to $10,000 for joint filers.

[h] For joint returns, the tax is twice the tax imposed on half the income. A $10 filing tax is charged for each return and a $15 credit is allowed for each exemption.

[i] Combined personal exemption and standard deduction.

[j] The tax brackets reported are for single individual. For married couples filing jointly, the same rates apply for income under $31,150 to over $123,751. A 6.4% AMT rate is also applicable.

[k] The tax brackets reported are for single individual. For married couples filing jointly, the same rates apply for income under $4,000 to over $50,001.

[l] The tax brackets reported are for single individuals. For married couples filing jointly, the tax rates range from 1.4% to 8.97% (with 7 income brackets) applying to income brackets from $20,000 to over $500,000.

[m] The tax brackets reported are for single individuals. For married couples filing jointly, the same rates apply for income under $8,000 to over $24,000. Married households filing separately pay the tax imposed on half the income.

[n] The tax brackets reported are for single individuals. For married taxpayers, the same rates apply to income brackets ranging from $21,250 to $200,000. Lower exemption amounts allowed for high income taxpayers. Tax rate scheduled to decrease after tax year 2007.

[o] The tax brackets reported are for single individuals. For married taxpayers, the same rates apply to income brackets ranging from $51,200 to $336,551. An additional $300 personal exemption is allowed for joint returns or unmarried head of households.

[p] Plus an additional $20 per exemption tax credit.

[q] The rate range reported is for single persons not deducting federal income tax. For married persons filing jointly, the same rates apply to income brackets ranging from $2,000 to $15,000. Separate schedules, with rates ranging from 0.5% to 10%, apply to taxpayers deducting federal income taxes.

[r] Deduction is limited to $10,000 for joint returns and $5,000 for individuals in Missouri and to $5,000 in Oregon.

[s] Federal Tax Liability prior to the enactment of Economic Growth and Tax Relief Act of 2001.

[t] One half of the federal income taxes are deductible. Taxpayer has an option of using the standard brackets and rates with all deductions, or paying a flat 5.35% of income with limited deductions.

[u] The tax brackets reported are for single individuals. For married couples filing jointly, the same rates apply for income under $51,200 to over $336,551.

[v] The tax brackets reported are for single individuals. For married taxpayers, the same rates apply to income brackets ranging from $12,210 to $183,211. An additional $250 exemption is provided for each taxpayer or spouse age 65 or over.

[w] An additional 1% tax is imposed on taxable income over $1 million.

state and local governments spent in 2002. The rest of the money came from user fees and other charges, insurance trust money, and intergovernmental transfers.

In 2002, state and local governments raised $419 billion from "charges and miscellaneous fees." That is $95 million more than they raised from sales taxes.[29] Little charges like university tuitions, public hospital charges, airport use fees, school lunch sales, and park permits make a big difference. Recently, states have increased fees to help close budget deficits and avoid more prominent tax increases. The pattern kept up even after tax revenue rebounded: enacted 2007 budgets included $279 million in fee increases.[30] State and local governments earned another $107 million from utility fees and, yes, from liquor sales and licenses.[31] (See Table 12-2.)

TABLE 12-2

The Five States Most Reliant on Revenue from Fees, Charges, and Interest

State	Percentage of Total Revenue
Alaska	33.8
Delaware	30.5
Alabama	25.5
West Virginia	24.9
South Carolina	24.0
U.S. Average	18.6

Source: *Governing* magazine, *State and Local Sourcebook, 2006,* supplement to *Governing* magazine, 36.

Insurance Trust Funds

Looking at a pay stub before any deductions are taken out can be pretty impressive. Looking at the actual amount of the paycheck can be a bit disappointing. What people may not realize is that they are not the only ones paying these taxes and fees. Their employers often have to match these payroll taxes and deductions. These **insurance trust funds** go to their state governments and to the federal government. Ultimately, the contributions are invested to support Social Security and retirement programs, workers' compensation and disability programs, and other related insurance programs that benefit employees.

Intergovernmental Transfers

The final portion of state and local government revenues comes from **intergovernmental transfers** of money. In the case of state governments, that means transfers from the federal government. In the case of local governments, that means transfers from state governments. Localities do receive some funds directly from the federal government, but not much. In 2004, the federal government provided some $426 billion to state and local governments. All told, federal funding made up approximately 32 percent of total state and local expenditures.[32] (See Map 12-1.)

Approximately 90 percent of federal funds go to specific state programs. Medicaid, the joint state-federal health insurance program for low-income people and people with disabilities, is by far the largest recipient. It receives about 44.6 percent of all federal funds that go to state governments.[33] Education (both K–12 and post-secondary), transportation projects, and public

INSURANCE TRUST FUNDS

Money collected from contributions, assessments, insurance premiums, or payroll taxes.

INTERGOVERNMENTAL TRANSFERS

Funds provided by the federal government to state governments and by state governments to local governments.

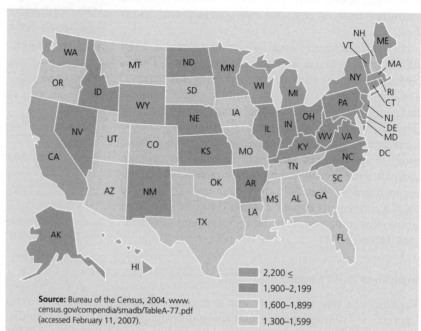

MAP 12-1 Federal Aid to State and Local Governments, Per-Capita Ranges by State, Fiscal Year 2004

Legend:
- 2,200 ≤
- 1,900–2,199
- 1,600–1,899
- 1,300–1,599

Source: Bureau of the Census, 2004. www.census.gov/compendia/smadb/TableA-77.pdf (accessed February 11, 2007).

welfare also receive significant federal funding. Most of these funds cannot be used on just anything. States must spend them on certain programs and often in a certain fashion.

During the 1960s, local governments and some neighborhood organizations also received substantial federal funding. Many of these programs have since ended or have been scaled back drastically. Today, local governments get only about 4 percent of their total revenues from the federal government. However, as the federal government has reduced support, state governments have stepped up their levels of assistance. In 2002, intergovernmental revenue transfers from state governments accounted for 33 percent of total local government revenues.[34]

Localities generally have welcomed the money, but the relationship between state governments and county and city governments has not always been an easy one. Over the course of the past decade, many city and county governments have found themselves stuck with unfunded mandates. These requirements have been imposed upon them by federal or state legislation that forces them to perform certain tasks but fails to provide them with the money to carry out those tasks.

Even worse—from the perspective of local governments—some state governments have dealt with their own revenue shortfalls by cutting assistance to local budgets, shifting responsibilities from the state to the local level, or raiding local budgets outright. When Wisconsin's economy slid into recession in 2001, Gov. Scott McCallum proposed to close the state's budget shortfall by eliminating the state's ninety-year-old system of revenue sharing. This move would have cost localities $1.1 billion. The legislature ultimately turned back McCallum's proposal. Less sweeping transfers of money and responsibilities, however, continue to be commonplace during economic downturns.[35] (For more on this trend, see box on page 448.)

Taxing Variations among State and Local Governments

Generalizations about state and local finances should not obscure the fact that different states and localities tax themselves in very different ways and at very different rates. The first striking difference concerns the very different tax burdens that states choose to impose on themselves. In 2006, Connecticut residents paid the most per capita in state and local taxes of any state in the country—$6,018. However, Maine residents faced the largest tax burden. They returned 13.5 percent of their incomes to state and local governments. This was the highest percentage of any state in the country. In contrast, residents of Alaska, New Hampshire, Tennessee, and Texas face some of the lowest state and local tax burdens in the country. On average, residents pay 10.6 percent or less of their incomes a year in state and local taxes.[36]

State and local governments do not just choose to tax themselves at different rates. They also choose to tax themselves in different ways. Residents of many Tennessee counties pay sales taxes of almost 10 percent. New Hampshire relies on property taxes to generate 27 percent of its total state tax revenue. In contrast, property taxes do not contribute anything to state coffers in thirteen states, although localities rely heavily on them.[37]

In thinking about a state's tax burden, it is helpful to distinguish between its **tax capacity** and its **tax effort**. In Newport Beach, California, for example, the median house price is a staggering $1.4 million. The typical family earns $124,979 a year and spends almost $9,000 on vacations. Even low sales and property taxes are going to bring in serious money.[38] Conversely, Odessa, Texas, with a median home price of $66,700, is not going to generate a lot of property tax revenue, no matter how high its rates are. Newport Beach's tax capacity is high. Odessa's tax capacity is low.

Many political scientists prefer to look at a different measurement—tax effort, or tax burden. Basically, measurements of tax effort seek to determine the proportion of its income that a given community chooses to pay out in taxes. A community's tax effort is also a good proxy for its appetite for public services. Some communities are willing to pay for street cleaning, and some communities are not. Some communities, such as Cambridge, Massachusetts, even are willing to pay a government employee to drive around and announce that street cleaning is about to commence.

Tax capacities and tax efforts often diverge markedly. Consider Massachusetts and New Hampshire. Both are comparatively affluent states. Per-

TAX CAPACITY

Measurement of the ability to pay taxes.

TAX EFFORT

A measure of taxes paid relative to the ability to pay taxes.

Policy in Practice: Campaign Daydreams vs. Fiscal Reality

Bill Owens earned, and wore proudly, his antitax credentials. As a Colorado legislator, he sponsored the state's Taxpayer Bill of Rights, better known as TABOR. The constitutional amendment prevented the state from raising taxes without an affirmative vote of the electorate and mandated that state spending increase in any year not more than the level of inflation plus population growth, and never more than 6 percent. According to TABOR, any surplus must be returned to the taxpayers. As governor, Owens took his TABOR success on the road, encouraging other states to adopt similar measures.

His road show took on a different tone in 2004, when TABOR's full effect became clearer. The amendment kept the state's government from growing large during flush times, true, but it also amplified the budget crisis that began in 2001. When revenues fell, Colorado, like many states, cut program budgets accordingly. But TABOR's strict 6 percent cap on annual spending increases meant that as conditions improved, the state could grow budgets 6 percent only from the bottom, not from where they started in better times.

The state's budget constraints were further complicated by Amendment 23, another budget initiative approved by voters that committed Colorado to increasing primary and secondary education spending by 1 percent more than the inflation rate every year for ten years and then by at least the rate of inflation every year after. In 2003, for example, the state's deficit reached $500 million, but the state school budget grew by 11 percent. Colorado simply couldn't make the numbers work, and business leaders began voicing concerns that the state's higher education and highway systems were faltering.

Owens's answer was to suspend some of TABOR's provisions. He forged a deal with state Democrats that was approved by voters in November 2005, which allowed the state to retain some $3.1 billion through 2010 to help fund education, healthcare, and transportation. "I'm a conservative Republican," Owens said, "but I do what I have to do to run a state." That Owens continued to tout his tax-cutting bona fides mattered little to the antitax crusaders who quickly criticized his plan as tantamount to a tax increase.

Faced with the realities of finding a way through the worst state budget crisis since World War II, half a dozen other governors and hundreds of state legislators reneged on pledges not to raise taxes. Several Republican governors broke ranks to support tax increases they considered necessary to balance their books, including Alabama's Bob Riley, Nevada's Kenny Guinn, Kentucky's Ernie Fletcher, and Indiana's Mitch Daniels—an architect of President George W. Bush's federal tax cuts.

Their actions didn't go unnoticed by antitax groups, which spent time, money, and energy to discredit the lawmakers—despite their previous status as allies. Americans for Tax Reform (ATR), the most vocal antitax organization in state politics, says that more than 1,300 state legislators have signed its pledge not to increase taxes; pledge breakers are named in its "Hall of Shame" and "Heroes and Enemies" list.

But while the backing of groups such as ATR has helped lift antitax candidates and ballot initiatives to election day success, breaking their pledges doesn't usually hurt politicians, says David Brunori, a tax analyst for State Tax Notes. The recently broken pledges signal a shift away from the influence of antitax activists, although not necessarily away from low-tax policy, he says. "There are times when the government simply needs more money, and even the most ardent low-tax conservative recognizes that. They recognize that the government's got to raise taxes, and they're not punished."

Sources: Adapted from Alan Ehrenhalt, "Optional Illusions," *Governing* magazine, June 2004; Zach Patton, "Taxophobe Targets," *Governing* magazine, May 2005; and Alan Ehrenhalt, "Rewriting the Formula," *Governing* magazine, February 2006.

sonal income per capita in 2005 was $44,289 in Massachusetts and $38,408 in New Hampshire.[39] In other words, the two states have very similar tax capacities.

However, they make very different tax efforts. New Hampshire has the second lightest tax burden in the country. Its residents pay about $3,133 a year in state and local taxes. In contrast, residents of neighboring Massachusetts pay about $4,217.[40]

Explaining Tax Variations

What accounts for such differences? Primarily, the two states have very different political cultures. New Hampshire prides itself on its rugged individualism. Its motto is "Live Free or Die." Residents tend to want the government to stay out of their way.

In contrast, Massachusetts was founded as a commonwealth. The founding document of the Massachusetts Bay Colony described a single "Body Politic" dedicated to the "general good" of the colony.[41] In this tradition, state and local governments are seen as effective ways of advancing that general good. Higher taxes and larger governments are more acceptable.

Political culture is not the only important variable that explains the very different tax efforts among states. Factors such as geography, geology, demographics, and history also influence the choices that state and local governments make.

Geography. One obvious, but easy to overlook, factor that influences state tax policies is geography. Some states use sales tax policy as a competitive edge—Delaware proudly recruits shoppers from nearby Mid-Atlantic states to its outlet malls with its "no sales tax" advertisements—Hawaii charges a 4.5 percent tax on nearly everything sold, including many services. How does it get away with the practice? Well, unless residents are willing to fly to the mainland for their sundries, they don't have much choice but to pay up.

Geology. Geology plays an important role in some state economies too. This is most notably true in oil-rich and natural-gas-rich states like Alaska and Wyoming. Thanks in large part to Prudhoe Bay, state and local governments in Alaska were able to spend $13,172 per person in 2002 while maintaining the lightest tax burden in the country.[42] Indeed, Alaska's Permanent Fund sends each eligible citizen a yearly **dividend** check—typically, for around $1,500—as a way of distributing the oil wealth.

DIVIDEND

A payment made to stockholders, or in Alaska's case, residents, from the interest generated off an investment.

Demographics. Demographics play an important role in determining the attitudes of state and local governments toward taxes. This is particularly true at the local level. Consider a city with a strong local economy and rising house prices. Such a city attracts large numbers of young workers with children. These are people who might very well want to spend more money on local schools and are willing to deal with rising property tax revenues. However, as mentioned previously, for seniors living on fixed incomes, rising house prices and rising property taxes might spell disaster. During economic booms, conflicts between parents and retirees are a common feature of local politics.

The Economic Cycle. Even when states make similar tax efforts and have similar cultures, state and local finances are distributed very differently from state to state. That is because different states and cities have very different economies.

Different states are situated at different points on the economic cycle. Industrial states, such as Michigan and Indiana, experience economic downturns first. Texas historically has had a counter-cyclical economy. When rising oil prices threaten to push industrial states into recession, Texas tends to do well. The same is true of Wyoming and Alaska.

> When higher energy prices threaten to push industrial states into recession, states rich in natural resources, such as Alaska, Nevada, and Texas, tend to do well.

Yet as important as demographics, geography, history, and political culture are, these variables do not always explain the actual financial choices that state and local governments make.

Take Mississippi. One of the most religious and politically conservative states in the country, Mississippi is the buckle of the Bible Belt. In 1990, however, Mississippi passed riverboat gambling legislation. This legislation allowed casino operators to build full-sized casinos on barges moored permanently to the shoreline. The goal was to turn the northwestern town of Tunica, which had gained a measure of renown after the television show *60 Minutes* profiled it as the poorest city in America, into Las Vegas East.

Nevada and Mississippi have completely different political cultures. Political scientist Daniel Elazar described Mississippi as a traditionalistic state and Nevada as an individualistic state. In short, Nevada has the kind of political culture that one might expect to produce, well, Las Vegas. Mississippi does not. Today, however, the hamlet of Tunica has more casino square footage than the East Coast gambling hotspot, Atlantic City, in the individualistic state of New Jersey. Clearly, political culture isn't everything.

BONDS

Certificates that are evidence of a debt on which the issuer promises to pay the holder a specified amount of interest for a specified length of time and to repay the loans on their maturity.

Bonds

The final source of money for state and local governments comes from bonds. These are financial instruments with which state and local governments promise to pay back borrowed money at a fixed rate of interest on a specified date. The interest rates paid by the governments depend largely on the government's bond ratings. The ratings are issued by three private companies—Moody's, Standard and Poor's, and Fitch—and are based on the

450

governments' fiscal health; many states' bond ratings fell during the recent budget crisis. A rating of AAA is the best, whereas anything lower than BBB is considered "junk bond status" and would send a government's interest rates skyrocketing. No state has ever fallen below BBB.[43]

State and local governments, as well as quasi-governmental entities like utility and water authorities, use bonds to finance **capital investments**, typically infrastructure upgrades such as new roads, new schools, or new airports. There are two types of bonds—**general obligation bonds**, which are secured by the taxing power of the jurisdiction that issues them, and **revenue bonds**, which are secured by the revenue from a given project, such as a new toll road. For state governments, that means projects like highways, power plant construction and pollution control, or even land conservation. Because general obligation bonds must be approved by voters, state and local governments turn to revenue bonds much more often. In 2002, they issued nearly twice as many revenue bonds as they issued general obligation bonds.[44]

Local governments use bonds to finance programs like school construction, sewage and water lines, airports, and affordable housing. Investors like them too. The earnings from most state bonds are exempt from state income taxes.

In 2002, state and local governments issued $356 billion in bonds.[45] **Municipal bonds**, or "munis" to bond traders, are generally safe and attractive investments, particularly for the rich. Municipal bond holders usually are exempted from paying federal or state taxes on income they receive from bonds. Sometimes, however, municipal finances go disastrously awry. In 1994, Orange County, California, one of the nation's largest and richest counties, announced huge investment losses and defaulted on its bond payments after risky pension fund investments went bad.

The Budget Process

Once state and local governments have raised money from taxes, user fees, and bonds and have received money from intergovernmental transfers, they must decide how to spend it. These decisions are made during the **budget process.**

Most state and local governments budget for one **fiscal year.** Unfortunately for fans of simplicity in government, the fiscal year is not the same as the calendar year. The federal government's fiscal year runs from October 1 to September 30. Most state and local governments generally begin the fiscal year on July 1. Alabama, Michigan, New York, and Texas are the exceptions. As a result, when legislatures debate the budget, they are almost always debating the budget for the coming fiscal year.[46] Twenty-one states pass two-year budgets.[47]

Budget timelines do vary from state to state, but the budget process itself is quite similar. It begins with instructions from the governor's budget office

CAPITAL INVESTMENTS
Investments in infrastructure, such as roads.

GENERAL OBLIGATION BONDS
Investments secured by the taxing power of the jurisdiction that issues them.

REVENUE BONDS
Investments secured by the revenue generated by a state or municipal project.

MUNICIPAL BONDS
Bonds issued by states, counties, cities, and towns to fund large projects as well as operating budgets. They are exempt from federal taxes and from state and local taxes for the investors who live in the state where they are issued.

BUDGET PROCESS
The procedure by which state and local governments assess revenues and set budgets.

FISCAL YEAR
The accounting period used by a government.

Boston's Central Artery/Tunnel Project, dubbed the "Big Dig" by locals, is the most expensive project of its kind in the United States. As of 2007, it had cost roughly $15 billion. Construction began in 1991, and as of early 2007 was still ongoing. The ten-lane, one-of-a-kind Leonard P. Zakim Bunker Hill Bridge, opened in 2003, has helped reduce traffic congestion and made for an imposing addition to the city skyline.

or the mayor's budget office. The executive branch agencies are told to draw up funding requests for the upcoming year. During the fall, the budget office reviews the spending requests and helps the chief executive develop a unified budget for the executive branch.

Most chief executives unveil their budgets in state-of-the-state addresses in January. In forty-five states, governors and mayors are required by law to submit a **balanced budget** to the legislature or city council. The legislative body reviews the budget, authorizes spending on certain programs, appropriates the necessary money, and presents its budget to the chief executive to sign into law.

As a guard against fiscal excess and abuse, forty-nine states have statutory or constitutional requirements that state legislatures must enact a balanced budget. Only Vermont is free to run up debts as it pleases.[48] All but five states also have laws that require lawmakers to save a certain portion of state revenues in so-called rainy day, or budget stabilization, funds. States can draw on these funds during times of recession, when revenues fall. Although rainy day funds rarely offset the revenue drops that occur during a recession, they do provide some cushion for the lawmakers who have to balance state budgets. Between 2001 and 2003, for example, rainy day funds helped close about a quarter of states' budget gaps—billions that would have otherwise had to come from program cuts or tax increases.[49] (See box on page 461 for more.) Many local governments face similar requirements due to state requirements or their own municipal codes.

BALANCED BUDGET

A budget in which current expenditures are equal to or less than income.

Governing States and Localities

There are, of course, exceptions. In states such as Arkansas, Mississippi, and South Carolina, legislatures take the lead role in formulating the initial budget plan. Legislative bodies also take the lead in county and city governments with weak chief executives, such as Los Angeles, California. In many western states, citizens and special interests have become players in the budgeting process via ballot initiatives.

Expenditures, or Where the Money Goes

In fiscal year 2004, state and local governments spent approximately $7,712 for every man, woman, and child in the country.[50] (See Table 12-3.) So, where did the money go?

Wages. Salaries are the single largest source of **expenditures** for state and local governments—roughly $611 billion in 2002. State and local governments are the biggest employers in the United States. In 2006, state governments employed 5.2 million people nationwide. Local governments employed another 14.4 million people.[51]

What do all of these employees do? There is a good chance that someone from one large category of state government employees—a professor or lecturer—is teaching you this course.

Education. Education has long been the single largest functional spending category for state and local governments. In 2004, state and local governments spent $645 billion on education. Approximately 73 percent of that went to elementary and secondary schools. The remaining 27 percent went to community colleges and state universities.[52]

Primary and secondary education traditionally has been the preserve of local governments. In most states, elected local school boards hire superintendents and principals, select curriculums that align with state standards, and develop school budgets. Local governments typically spend about 38 percent of their funds on schools.[53]

State governments now provide half of all funding for K–12 education. State dollars increasingly are used to train teachers, reduce the number of students in classrooms, promote the use of computers and high-speed Internet access, and fund "accountability" and testing regimes. In 2005, 21.8 percent of state expenditures went to K–12 education.[54]

State governments also devote a portion of their expenditures to higher education—10.6 percent of total expenditures in 2005.[55] Spending on higher education is the third largest item on state budgets. Tuition covers about 32 percent of the costs of higher education.[56]

Unlike highways, which have their own dedicated stream of funding from gasoline taxes, legislatures typically appropriate funding for higher education from general revenue funds. This is known as **discretionary spending**. When economic times are good, institutions of higher learning

EXPENDITURES

Money spent by government.

Arkansas's spending grew 25.2 percent between 2005 and 2006. North Carolina's spending dropped 5 percent during the same period.

DISCRETIONARY SPENDING

Spending controlled in annual appropriations acts.

TABLE 12-3

State and Local Revenues, Expenditures, and Debt, 2004 (in millions of dollars)

State	Total Revenues	Total Expenditures	Total Debt Outstanding at End of Fiscal Year
Alabama	32,065	31,268	21,629
Alaska	11,038	10,019	8,626
Arizona	38,388	36,072	29,844
Arkansas	18,027	16,323	10,409
California	358,673	328,029	269,935
Colorado	38,744	34,395	33,841
Connecticut	29,295	28,837	30,516
Delaware	7,102	6,922	6,053
Florida	129,687	115,547	108,764
Georgia	57,902	58,435	34,848
Hawaii	9,983	9,870	9,027
Idaho	9,754	8,426	4,021
Illinois	100,247	95,421	102,304
Indiana	40,977	39,333	29,583
Iowa	22,545	20,634	11,335
Kansas	18,550	18,361	16,122
Kentucky	26,834	26,871	29,143
Louisiana	34,107	31,089	22,165
Maine	11,131	10,031	6,919
Maryland	44,288	38,540	27,795
Massachusetts	60,795	58,208	72,898
Michigan	80,185	77,621	57,609
Minnesota	42,956	42,144	33,670
Mississippi	20,670	19,450	10,189
Missouri	40,033	35,571	30,408
Montana	7,088	6,198	4,297
Nebraska	15,479	14,075	8,829
Nevada	16,888	16,182	17,851
New Hampshire	8,703	8,346	8,135
New Jersey	75,083	72,660	64,272

TABLE 12-3, continued

State	Total Revenues	Total Expenditures	Total Debt Outstanding at End of Fiscal Year
New Mexico	14,918	14,068	9,724
New York	224,429	219,325	219,358
North Carolina	63,458	56,543	37,973
North Dakota	6,524	4,486	3,143
Ohio	105,382	89,598	57,898
Oklahoma	23,954	20,879	13,265
Oregon	33,734	28,215	24,753
Pennsylvania	102,238	94,598	96,374
Rhode Island	9,665	8,937	8,237
South Carolina	30,547	30,451	25,940
South Dakota	5,593	4,612	3,849
Tennessee	42,125	41,760	24,320
Texas	153,761	144,880	146,009
Utah	18,917	16,707	14,265
Vermont	5,266	4,812	3,327
Virginia	54,162	47,801	40,006
Washington	54,738	54,317	50,370
West Virginia	14,117	12,201	8,214
Wisconsin	48,698	42,410	35,272
Wyoming	6,816	5,080	1,835

Source: *Governing* magazine, *State and Local Sourcebook, 2006,* supplement to *Governing* magazine, 30, 38, 40.

and the voters and future voters who enroll in them often benefit from considerable largesse. Between 1996 and 2001, states such as California and Virginia increased higher education budgets by more than 10 percent a year.

When the economy slides into recession, however, the fact that institutions of higher education do not have a dedicated source of funding makes them particularly vulnerable to cutbacks. The economy stopped growing in the spring of 2001. State revenues plunged, and legislators responded in a familiar way. They cut higher education spending. The result in many states was higher tuitions at a time when family incomes and job prospects often were uncertain. According to the State Higher Education Executive Officers, tuition costs rose 13 percent between 2001 and 2005.

Healthcare. Since the late 1990s, healthcare spending has surged dramatically. In 2003, state and local governments spent $358 billion.[57] For state governments, spending on healthcare is now greater than for any other single item.

Medicaid is the largest and most expensive state-run health program. When established in 1965, it was viewed as a limited safety net for the very poor and disabled. However, the number of low-income, uninsured Americans has grown, and medical care has become more expensive. The program has grown at an enormous rate as a result. In 1970, state governments spent $2 billion on the program, and the federal government kicked in another $3 billion. By 2005, states and the federal government spent $283 billion on the program, up from $261 billion just a year earlier.[58] State Medicaid programs now provide health insurance to approximately fifty-nine million people and account for 22.9 percent of total state spending.[59] And healthcare costs are growing faster than any other category of government expenditures.

The Medicaid program is an excellent example of **fiscal federalism**. The federal government picks up most of the program's costs, while states take responsibility for administering the program itself.

Medicaid is also an **entitlement** program. Most programs receive a specific appropriation during the budget process and can spend no more. Entitlements like Medicaid are different. States and the federal government are obligated by law to provide health insurance to low-income individuals who qualify for the program, regardless of the cost. If states have an unexpected surge of applicants and they have not set aside enough money for Medicaid, tough.

States do have some leeway in determining how generous they want their state Medicaid programs to be. They enjoy similar discretion with another joint state-federal program, the State Children's Health Insurance Program (SCHIP). In most states, this program provides health insurance for children living in families whose primary wage earner makes up to twice the federal poverty level. In 2007, this amount was $41,300 for a family of four.[60] (See Table 12-4.)

During the boom of the late 1990s, some states made a major effort to extend health insurance via Medicaid and SCHIP. Mississippi raised its Medicaid eligibility to 135 percent of the federal poverty level—the highest in the country.

Many healthcare advocates saw Medicaid and SCHIP expansions as the most promising approach to extending health insurance to some of the roughly forty-five million Americans who do without it. By 2003, 10.1 percent of low-income children were uninsured, down from 12.6 percent two years earlier. When the economy slid into recession in early 2001, however, states scaled back these efforts, sometimes dramatically. Three states froze SCHIP enrollment; one-third changed enrollment policies, making it more difficult for families to apply; and half began charging or raised cost-sharing amounts.[61]

FISCAL FEDERALISM

The system by which federal grants are used to fund programs and services provided by state and local governments.

ENTITLEMENT

A service that government must provide, regardless of the cost.

Medicaid increasingly serves another function as well. It is the only governmental program that pays for long-term care, such as nursing homes and assisted living facilities. Private nursing homes and assisted living facilities can cost as much as $3,500 a month. Few seniors or disabled individuals can afford these costs for very long. As the number of Americans age 85 and older increases from about 5.1 million in 2005 to a projected 8 million in 2025,[62] a growing number of elderly citizens will find themselves in need of such services.

Local governments spend much less on healthcare than state governments, or only about 7 percent of total expenditures. This is not to say that local governments do not make an important contribution. In 2002, state and local governments spent $50 billion supporting local public hospitals, which is almost as much as they spent on police protection.[63] All of these funds came directly from the local governments. Many of these hospitals serve as healthcare providers of last resort to people without health insurance. In the event of a terrorist attack involving biological weapons, many of these hospitals would serve as society's defense of first resort.

TABLE 12-4

Department of Health and Human Services Poverty Guidelines, 2007

Size of Family Unit	48 Contiguous States and Washington, D.C.	Alaska	Hawaii
1	$10,210	$12,770	$11,750
2	$13,690	$17,120	$15,750
3	$17,170	$21,470	$19,750
4	$20,650	$25,820	$23,750
5	$24,130	$30,170	$27,750
6	$27,610	$34,520	$31,750
7	$31,090	$38,870	$35,750
8	$34,570	$43,220	$39,750
For each additional person, add	$ 3,480	$ 4,350	$ 4,000

Source: *Federal Register*, vol. 72, no. 15, January 24, 2007, 3147–3148.
Note: Amounts listed are maximum yearly income.

Welfare. The topic of welfare has been one of the most contentious issues in U.S. politics for a long time. Welfare is an entitlement program. While states have some leeway to determine eligibility, they cannot deny or restrict benefits to qualified individuals. From 1965 to 1996, women with young children were eligible to receive monetary assistance through a welfare program known as Aid to Families with Dependent Children (AFDC).

In 1996, Republicans in Congress and President Bill Clinton joined forces to pass the Personal Responsibility and Work Reconciliation Act, which abolished AFDC and replaced it with the Temporary Assistance for Needy Families (TANF) program. TANF disbursed federal money to states in block grants and gave them considerable freedom in determining how they wanted to spend those funds. Many liberals predicted that such welfare "reform" would result in disaster. Instead, the number of people on welfare rolls declined dramatically. Between 1994 and 1999, the welfare caseload declined by nearly 50 percent, from approximately four million people to two million people.[64]

Welfare continues to be a politically contentious issue. Yet from a financial viewpoint, it is actually a pretty minor program. In 2005, state governments spent a total of $24.7 billion on TANF, that is, about 2 percent of total state expenditures.[65]

FIGURE 12-1 How It Works: A Year in the Life of a State Budget: Idaho's Budgetary Process

Most folks first hear about state budget priorities through their governor's state of the state address, the forum in which most state budgetary news is presented. In reality, budget planning begins well in advance of this address and involves all three branches of government to some degree. In Idaho, each year in May (after the last of the potatoes have been planted), that state's Division of Financial Management (DFM) starts sowing its own seeds: overseeing the development of that state's budget for the coming fiscal year. This is the beginning of what is really an eighteen-month process: the planning for fiscal year 2010, for instance, will actually get underway about mid-year in 2008.

This chart shows how the process works in Idaho:

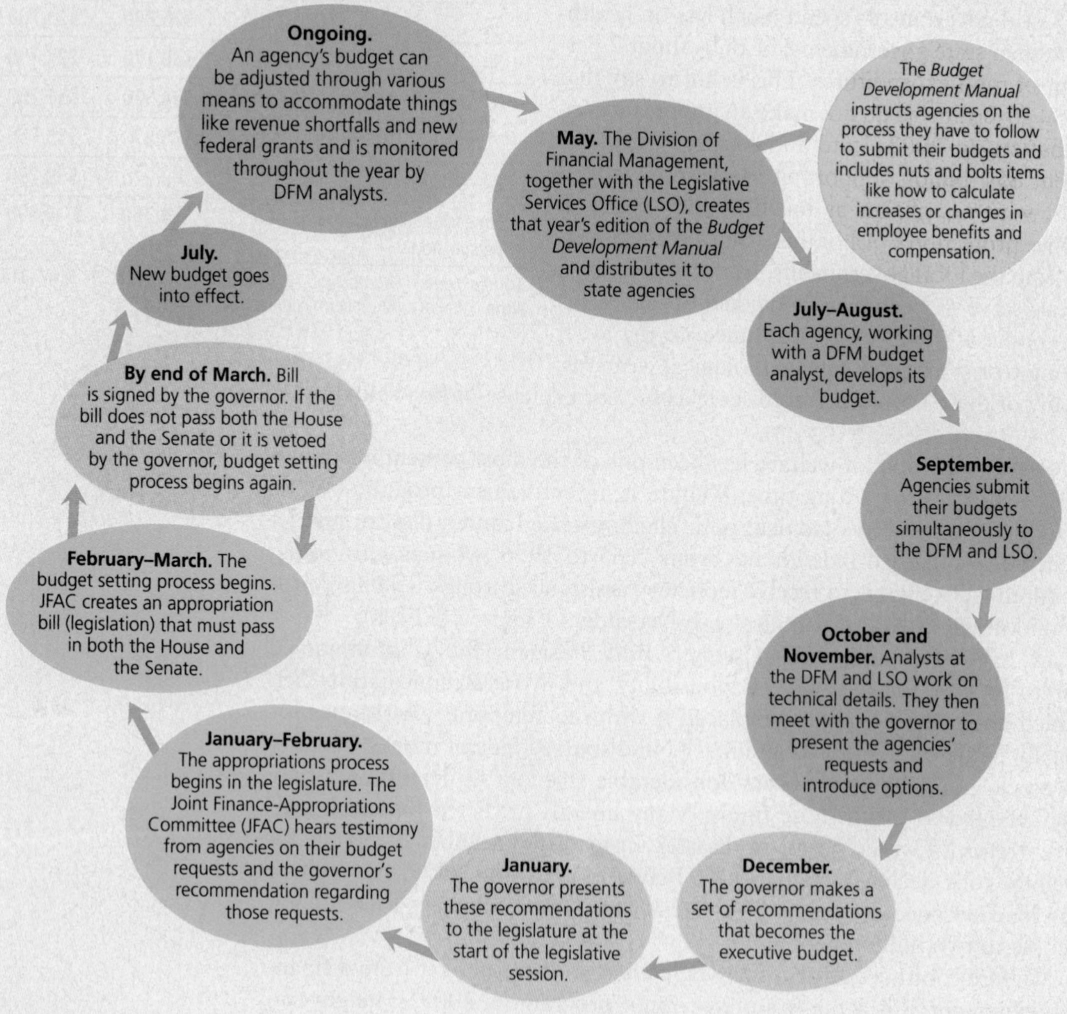

Ongoing. An agency's budget can be adjusted through various means to accommodate things like revenue shortfalls and new federal grants and is monitored throughout the year by DFM analysts.

May. The Division of Financial Management, together with the Legislative Services Office (LSO), creates that year's edition of the *Budget Development Manual* and distributes it to state agencies

The *Budget Development Manual* instructs agencies on the process they have to follow to submit their budgets and includes nuts and bolts items like how to calculate increases or changes in employee benefits and compensation.

July. New budget goes into effect.

July–August. Each agency, working with a DFM budget analyst, develops its budget.

By end of March. Bill is signed by the governor. If the bill does not pass both the House and the Senate or it is vetoed by the governor, budget setting process begins again.

September. Agencies submit their budgets simultaneously to the DFM and LSO.

February–March. The budget setting process begins. JFAC creates an appropriation bill (legislation) that must pass in both the House and the Senate.

October and November. Analysts at the DFM and LSO work on technical details. They then meet with the governor to present the agencies' requests and introduce options.

January–February. The appropriations process begins in the legislature. The Joint Finance-Appropriations Committee (JFAC) hears testimony from agencies on their budget requests and the governor's recommendation regarding those requests.

January. The governor presents these recommendations to the legislature at the start of the legislative session.

December. The governor makes a set of recommendations that becomes the executive budget.

Source: State of Idaho's Division of Financial Management, "Budget Process." http://dfm.idaho.gov/citizensguide/ budgetprocess.html (accessed May 16, 2007).

Fire, Police, and Prisons. In 2002, state and local governments spent $90 billion on fire and police protection. They spent an additional $55 billion on prisons and correctional facilities.[66] State and local government spending on police protection and prisons varies widely. New York City, a city of eight million people, employs a police force of thirty-nine thousand. That works out to one police officer for every 205 people. In contrast, Los Angeles, a city of 3.8 million, employees only 9,200 police officers. That equals only one police officer for every 413 people.

States also have very different levels of enthusiasm for funding prisons. In fiscal year 2005, the Texas state government devoted 5.5 percent of state spending to prisons. That is a level of spending 2 percent higher than the national average and reflects Texas's incarceration rate, which is the second highest in the country. In contrast, West Virginia's state government spent only 1 percent of its state budget on corrections.[67]

Highways. In 2005, state and local governments spent $106 billion on highways and roads.[68] Most of this money came from dedicated revenue sources, such as the gasoline tax. In addition, the federal government kicked in another $32 billion from the federal highway trust fund and other sources.

Not surprisingly, states with wide open spaces spend more money on highway construction and transportation. In 2005, Alaska devoted 18.1 percent of total state expenditures to transportation. This was the highest percentage of any state in the country, followed by Louisiana at 15.6 percent and Wyoming at 15.3 percent. Nationwide, state governments spent 8.6 percent of total revenues on transportation in 2005.[69]

Restraints on State and Local Budgeteers

Politicians and journalists usually talk about "the budget" in the singular tense, as if elected officials meet every year or two to divvy up a single pot of money. That's misleading. State and local officials cannot actually lay their hands on all the revenues flowing into state and local coffers. Most federal funds are devoted to specific programs, such as Medicaid. Revenue streams from many state sources, such as the car registration tax, are likewise dedicated to specific purposes, such as highway construction. State and local officials develop their budgets under several additional restraints as well.

GASB. States conduct their accounting and financial reporting according to standards set by the GASB, or the Governmental Accounting Standards Board. In 2004, the organization issued GASB 45, a rule that mandated that by December 2006 states tally and disclose the cost of healthcare benefits pledged to current and retired state employees. As if that were not daunting enough, the states also have to find a way to begin saving enough to cover their liabilities, or the risks damaging their credit ratings. One analyst estimates the cumulative shortfall could hit $500 billion—more than twice what states are paying now for Medicaid.[70]

Unfunded Mandates. For years, state officials complained bitterly about the federal government's habit of mandating that states achieve a goal, such as an environmental clean-up, but then failing to provide any money to pay for it. State officials viewed such unfunded mandates as an affront to the notion of federalism itself. In 1995, Congress did something surprising. It passed legislation that curtailed dramatically the practice of imposing unfunded mandates on state governments. This measure alleviated some of the pressures on states, but it did not end the problem. Ironically, in the late 1990s, state governments increasingly imposed unfunded mandates on county and city governments. Evidently, many state governments were no more able to resist the temptation to set goals and make someone else pay for them than the federal government had long been.

The United States is a federation. Under this federal system, state governments and the federal government are co-equals, at least in theory. If the federal government encroaches too much on state prerogatives, the U.S. Supreme Court can step in and strike federal actions down.

But states are not federations. Local governments are not equal partners with state governments. In most cases, state governments are free to intervene in local arrangements as they please. Beginning in the late nineteenth century, many states did extend the sovereign powers of government to local governments by passing legislation that provided for home rule. Communities could enact charters and ordinances, change their names, and annex their neighbors without the permission of the legislature. They also controlled their own budgets and property taxes.

At the time, California was one of the strongest home-rule states. In recent years, however, that has changed. California cities now control less than half of their discretionary spending. The state tells them what they must do with the rest. The situation is even worse for California's counties. They now have the final say over less than one-third of the money they spend.[71]

Ballot Initiatives and the Budget Process. California's experience illustrates one of the most significant trends in state finances—the growing use of ballot initiatives to shape and restrain state tax systems. According to Bill Piper of the Initiative and Referendum Institute, voters put 130 tax initiatives on ballots nationwide between 1978 and 1999. Roughly two-thirds of them were antitax initiatives that cut, limited, or eliminated taxes in some way. Of these, forty-one passed. In fact, a whopping 67 percent of all antitax initiatives that came up for a vote between 1996 and 1999 passed.

When citizens put their hands directly on the tax levers, it often gets much harder for state and local governments to pay the bills. California is just one name on a list of states that are choking on tax policies put in place by voters. Colorado, Oregon, and Washington are only a few of the other

Policy in Practice: Saving for a Rainy Day . . . or Any Day

Forty-seven states have some sort of budget stabilization fund that is designed as a savings account of last resort. States put the so-called rainy day funds to good use between 2001 and 2003, when revenues fell dramatically. Thanks to the tens of billions they'd socked away during the flush days of the late 1990s, they were able to draw on at least $30 billion to help close budget gaps and prevent more drastic program cuts and tax and fee increases.

The states had nurtured their rainy day funds to an average of 10.4 percent of expenditures before they began draining them down to 3.2 percent in 2003. With revenues back on the increase in the years since then, they once again are putting money in their piggy banks—almost $60 billion between year-end balances and rainy day funds already. Pressure from other parts of their operating budgets is making it tough to build a much larger pile of reserves, however. In many cases, the rainy day funds have turned into temporary holding areas for monies destined to pay for ongoing expenses, including education and healthcare.

"I don't see a significant increase in the number of states making new deposits into these funds," says Corina Eckl, head of the fiscal affairs program at the National Conference of State Legislatures. The Center on Budget and Policy Priorities and the Government Finance Officers Association have recommended that states dedicate as much as 15 percent of general fund revenues to the accounts, but attaining that goal seems unlikely. "Politically, 5 percent is probably about as high as you can go before people complain that you're sitting on all this cash," says Scott Pattison, executive director of the National Association of State Budget Officers.

Some states, though, are getting aggressive about restoring their depleted reserve accounts. At the end of fiscal year 2006, thirty states had year-end balances of 10 percent or more of total expenditures; another 11 had between 5 percent and 9.99 percent. In 2003, Virginia wrote its priorities into a statute aimed at adding extra deposits in addition to the normal formula-driven deposits the state makes. In the Midwest, Minnesota had saved about $1 billion by the end of 2006. It had made the decision to direct surpluses into rainy day funds and other cash-flow accounts after battling a $5 billion deficit in 2003—well before positive tax revenues began flowing back into its coffers.

Sources: Alan Greenblatt, "Rebalancing Act," *Governing* magazine, November 2005, and *The Fiscal Survey of the States,* National Governors Association and National Association of State Budget Officers, December 2006.

states that have dealt with financial problems caused by ballot initiatives—problems that grew more severe during the budget crises of 2001–2004 (see box on this page).

These maneuvers have influenced individual tax changes. They also have been known to paralyze state legislatures and local governments. Fifteen states have passed initiatives or referendums that require more than 50 percent of the vote, or supermajorities, on tax decisions made by the state legislatures. In Montana, for example, a supermajority is three-quarters of the legislature. Roy Brown, House majority leader for the state, sees changing tax policy as pretty much impossible. "We can't even get a three-fourths majority vote to go to the bathroom," he told the *Billings Gazette* in November 2002.[72]

Conclusion

State and local governments rely on six major types of taxes to fund the operations of government—property taxes; income taxes; sales taxes; sin, or excise, taxes; user fees; and gift taxes. Each of these taxes has distinct pros and cons. Local governments like property taxes because they set the rates and thus control exactly how much revenue is raised. However, when property taxes rise, seniors and people on fixed incomes often suffer. Income taxes tend to be more progressive; sales taxes are more regressive. The exact configuration of taxes in any given state reflects that state's history and political culture. Tax revenues, in turn, support the budget process by which state and local governments set their spending priorities.

State and local government finances can be difficult to unravel. However, it is an area that citizens are well advised to watch. Not only do the budget decisions of state and local governments determine the services individuals enjoy and how much they pay in taxes, this also is often the arena in which the priorities of public life are sorted out. Is it fair or unfair to ask wealthy citizens to pay a higher percentage of their income in taxes? States such as Texas and Florida that have no income taxes have in a sense decided that it is unfair. States like California, which has an income tax, have reached a different conclusion. Should everyone pay more in taxes to extend healthcare to low-income citizens? Massachusetts's tax policies suggest that its answer is yes. Many states in the Deep South have reached different conclusions. In short, the consequences of budget decisions are very real.

There is another reason to pay close attention to state and local finances. Barring a repeat of the economic boom of the 1990s, they almost certainly will need to change. States like Tennessee that rely heavily on sales tax revenues face particularly serious challenges. As Internet sales and dollars spent on untaxed services continue to grow, sales tax revenues in particular will most likely continue to falter. This will create a need for new revenue-raising measures. Yet states with ballot initiatives may well find new approaches blocked by antitax sentiments at the voting booth.

Many states have turned to the federal government for help. In particular, states have asked Congress to relieve them of some of the fiscal burdens of Medicaid. Yet for now, large-scale federal assistance seems unlikely. As a result, in the coming years states will have to focus as never before on the programs and priorities that drive their taxing and spending decisions. The following three chapters examine some of the most important state and local government programs in more detail. In many states, they almost certainly will need to change soon.

Key Concepts

balanced budget (p. 452)

bonds (p. 450)

budget process (p. 451)

budget shortfall (p. 434)

capital investments (p. 451)

discretionary spending (p. 453)

dividend (p. 449)

entitlement (p. 456)

estate taxes (p. 436)

excise, or sin, taxes (p. 436)

expenditures (p. 453)

fiscal federalism (p. 456)

fiscal year (p. 451)

focused consumption taxes (p. 436)

general obligation bonds (p. 451)

gift taxes (p. 436)

income taxes (p. 441)

insurance trust funds (p. 445)

intergovernmental transfers (p. 445)

municipal bonds (p. 451)

progressive tax system (p. 434)

regressive taxes (p. 437)

revenue bonds (p. 451)

revenues (p. 434)

sales taxes (p. 436)

severance taxes (p. 442)

tax burden (p. 434)

tax capacity (p. 447)

tax effort (p. 447)

tax revolt (p. 435)

user fees (p. 435)

Suggested Readings

State and Local Government Sourcebook. Washington, D.C.: *Governing* magazine. Annual publication that provides easy access to a wide range of information on state and local government finances.

State Expenditure Report. Washington, D.C.: National Association of State Budget Officers. Report printed annually since 1987 details state expenditure data.

Suggested Web Sites

www.cbpp.org/state/index.html. Web site of the Center on Budget and Policy Priorities. Founded in 1981, the center studies fiscal policy and public programs at the federal and state levels that affect low-income and moderate-income families and individuals. An excellent source of information on state budget controversies and debates.

www.census.gov/prod/www/statistical-abstract.html. The U.S .Census Bureau provides an on-line version of the *Statistical Abstract of the United States.* Section 8, "State and Local Government Finances and Employment," provides a wealth of information on state and local government revenue and spending.

www.nasbo.org. Web site of the National Association of State Budget Officers.

CHAPTER 13

Education
Reading, Writing, and Regulation

States are finding that new federal standardized testing requirements can make it difficult to balance their education budgets. Connecticut, for example, estimates it could cost the state $40 million or more to comply with federal testing mandates. The conflict over who sets educations standards and who has to pay for them will shape the educational futures of Connecticut grade school students like Madeline Kumm (right) and Joseph Oriz (left) for a long time.

13

Why are some school systems so much stronger than others?

Why do curriculums vary so much from state to state?

Why are there so many different brands of school reform?

Why has the federal government increased its involvement in education, traditionally a function of local and state government?

Connecticut officials don't oppose standardized testing. In fact, the state has long tested all of its students in grades four, six, and eight. But under the **No Child Left Behind Act (NCLB)**, signed into law in January 2002, all states receiving federal education funding must test students once a year in grades three through eight and once in high school—a requirement that doubles the frequency of Connecticut's tests.

NO CHILD LEFT BEHIND ACT (NCLB)

Federal law enacted in January 2002 that introduced new accountability measures for elementary and secondary schools in all states that wish to receive federal aid.

Those tests come with a price tag. The federal government increased education spending 50 percent between 2001 and 2006, a jump of $4.6 billion. That funding fell some $7 billion short of the amount authorized by Congress, however. This led to an outcry from many states, which were battling their worst budget shortfalls since World War II just as NCLB's bills began coming due.[1] One report in Connecticut estimated that the state would fall $41.6 million short in paying for NCLB's requirements through 2008.[2] When the federal Department of Education denied the state's request for flexibility to continue its previous testing schedule, state attorney general Richard Blumenthal took Connecticut's complaints to the next level: the courts. In August 2005, the state of Connecticut sued the U.S. Department of Education, charging that the federal government inadequately funded NCLB. A federal judge ruled that the court could not reverse the Education Department's denial of Connecticut's request but allowed part of the case challenging the department's administrative procedures to move forward.

Connecticut is not the only state pushing back against NCLB. Months before Connecticut filed its lawsuit, the National Education Association, along with school districts in Michigan, Texas, and Vermont, filed a similar suit that was dismissed in U.S. District Court in Michigan. Utah enacted a bill giving priority to its own state education law over NCLB in the case of conflict.[3] A study by the Civil Society Institute, a nonpartisan advocacy group, found twenty-one states considering legislation critical of NCLB.[4]

More than five years after the enactment of NCLB, implementation remains a work in progress, and the law is due for reauthorization in 2007. The main tenets of the law have not changed: all students must be proficient according to each state's standards by 2014, and schools must make "adequate yearly progress" in bringing students of all races and ethnic backgrounds to proficiency or risk penalties. Some states have had better luck working with the feds than Connecticut, though. As part of a pilot program in 2006, the U.S. Education Department approved changes to how North

Carolina and Tennessee track students' progress—a change that would have resulted in forty more North Carolina schools meeting the standard for adequate progress in 2005.[5]

NCLB is a classic example of the push and pull of federalism. Since the days of Horace Mann, nineteenth-century Massachusetts education chief and the father of the American **common school**, education has been a function of state and local governments. As president, Ronald Reagan even proposed eliminating the federal Department of Education. The advent of NCLB, however, dramatically boosted the federal role in education, intensified accountability pressures, and did much to place all state and local school entities on a similar path toward change.

At a time when schooling was reserved mostly for families able to afford tutors or boarding schools, Mann's endeavor was school reform for radicals. The one-room schoolhouses he inspected as the first secretary of Massachusetts's **state board of education** were crude and ill-equipped. Many of the teachers were poorly paid and trained, and regular attendance by students was not even required by law. Through personal advocacy and his widely circulated writings, Mann did much to build up the state as the primary actor in the fledgling experiment of public education in the United States.

A century and a half of impassioned debate has passed since Mann's time. The years have yielded few certainties in American education. What is undisputed, however, is the way the quest for good schools is intertwined with democratic civic ideals. The everyday rough-and-tumble over curriculum and budgets pays constant heed to this country's founding ideals of individual dignity, the promise of social mobility, and government by consent of the governed.

It was not just for public relations that President Lyndon B. Johnson viewed education as "the answer to all our national problems."[6] A former teacher himself, Johnson launched what he called the Great Society initiative. This was a series of new federal programs designed to curb poverty and expand opportunities to the nation's disadvantaged. It rested, as he said in one speech, on "abundance and liberty for all" and led the federal government to make its first major forays into education policy.

Given the variety of policy approaches permitted under the U.S. system of federalism, education has always been governed, to the extent possible, by states and localities. In 2005, elementary and secondary education accounted for the largest share of state government spending—35.8 percent of general funds—according to the National Association of State Budget Officers.[7] Members of all parties and followers of various philosophical leanings agree that education has the most impact on economic growth and civic engagement.

The nation's universal compulsory education laws mean that all taxpayers, not just families with school-age children, are required to support society's bid for an educated citizenry. Education is a field that brings out panic

COMMON SCHOOL

In a democratic society, a school in which children of all income levels attend at taxpayer expense.

STATE BOARD OF EDUCATION

Top policymaking body in each of the fifty states, usually consisting of appointees selected by governors.

BACK TO BASICS

A movement against
modern education "fads"
and a return to an
emphasis on traditional
core subjects such as
reading, writing, and
arithmetic.

STANDARDS

Fixed criteria for learning
that students are
expected to reach in
specific subjects by
specific grade years.

HIGH-STAKES
STANDARDIZED TESTING

Testing of elementary
and secondary students
in which poor results can
mean either that the
student fails to get pro-
moted or that the school
loses its accreditation.

SCHOOL BOARDS

Elected or appointed
bodies that determine
major policies and
budgets for each of the
nation's school districts.

DEPARTMENTS OF
EDUCATION

State-level agencies
responsible for over-
seeing public education.

in some parents who feel their child's whole future is at stake with every report card. It is a field that allows ambitious politicians to make names for themselves by vowing to make schools more accountable. Candidates promise to get better results in the classroom from taxpayer dollars. They do this despite occasional resistance by professional educators who value autonomy and resent burdensome regulation.

The stakes have always been high. But it was in the final decades of the twentieth century that political leaders and many in the general public shifted to a mindset that public education was in dire and ongoing need of fixing. The 1983 report *A Nation at Risk* was commissioned by the Reagan administration. It declared that the United States was just that because a rising tide of mediocrity in schools invited defeat by a foreign power.

That report set in motion a continual movement with such themes as **back to basics**, new curriculum **standards**, and **high-stakes standardized testing**. The movement involved not just teachers and parents, but also federal and state legislators, local **school boards**, courts, advocacy groups, even the national political parties. And this wave of reform that continues well into the twenty-first century.

Organization and Leadership: Schools Have Many Bosses

The United States is one of the few industrialized countries with no national ministry of education. The U.S. Department of Education was created in 1978, but the primary authority for running schools rests with the fifty states. This is in accordance with the Tenth Amendment edict that the powers not delegated by the Constitution to the federal government are reserved to the states. An exception is the District of Columbia. Its board of education derives its funds from the city's appropriation from Congress.

As far back as the 1780s, state legislatures were tasked with schooling the citizenry. For example, in 1857, Minnesota's constitution proclaimed that the "stability of a Republican form of government depend[ed] upon the intelligence of the people, it is the duty of the legislature to establish a general and uniform system of public schools." [8] In other words, the consensus was that creating a well-educated population not only helped individual citizens prosper, it also helped entrench the democratic process.

Fifty varying traditions make for a lot of bosses in a democratic approach to education. A system that permits local innovations and variations is a far cry from systems in Europe. Legend has it that a national education chief there can look at a clock on any given weekday and know precisely what lesson is being taught in classrooms across a country.

Modern state legislatures, working with state **departments of education,** are the players who deal with major state policy questions and large-scale resource issues. A state legislature can raise teacher salaries statewide, equalize funding among districts, and set up health benefits and retirement plans for the state's pool of teachers. It can borrow money by "floating" state bonds to provide schools with construction funds, which commits taxpayers to long-term debts.

The states are also the main players in determining **teacher licensure procedures**. For example, they determine whether or not teacher candidates take a standardized test and how schools are awarded **accreditation**.

The more complex state decisions are proposed and implemented by an experienced educator who is the chief state school officer. The governor can appoint these officials, as in Iowa, Maine, and New Jersey. They can be appointed by a state board of education, as in Louisiana, Utah, and Vermont. Sometimes, they are elected on a partisan ballot, as in North Carolina and Oklahoma or on a nonpartisan ballot, as in North Dakota and Oregon. They work closely with state boards of education. These boards also can be appointed or elected, depending on the state, and their members usually represent each region of a state.

Further down the chain are the **local education agencies (LEAs)**, which have been formed in nearly fifteen thousand **school districts** scattered over cities, counties, and townships. School districts are staffed with full-time professionals, but they carry out policies set by school boards or other locally elected officials.

The extent of policymaking authority enjoyed by each LEA or district is determined by a state's legislature. In Horace Mann's region of New England, local control is strong. The population of states in the Deep South traditionally has been poor and rural. Many citizens are suspicious and untutored in the workings of government. As a result, the legislatures of these states have retained a more centralized role.

Even within states, there are huge differences in economies, traditions, and demographics. Think of rural, mountainous northern California versus densely populated, arid southern California, which some want to turn into separate states. Northern Virginia, an affluent suburban area of Washington, D.C., that favors active government, is very different from Virginia's rural areas, in which folks favor limited government.

The degree of flexibility states can give to localities in education depends greatly on scale. It also depends on the degree to which local citizens feel passionate about participating in school governance. The nation's school districts are a patchwork quilt that evolved as individually as the states themselves. Texas, for example, contains more than one thousand school districts. These vary widely, from the liberal college town of Austin to the conservative business center of Dallas. By contrast, rural, and still largely undeveloped, Hawaii is administered as one district.

In large cities such as Los Angeles, schools are administered under a centralized authority. This is why the district is called Los Angeles Unified. New York City, the nation's largest school district with more than one million students, has tried both centralized and decentralized approaches. In 2002, Mayor Michael Bloomberg won approval from the state legislature to eliminate the city's thirty-two separate school boards and centralize control. The intent was to reduce what some viewed as administrative bloat so that the new chancellor, Joel Klein, could experiment with such reforms as charter schools and be held accountable for results.

> Legend has it that a national education chief in Europe can look at a clock on any given weekday and know precisely what lesson is being taught in classrooms across a country.

While it is still too early to declare New York's experiment a complete success, it is working well enough for the mayor of Los Angeles to cite it as a model as he pushed for a mayoral takeover of Los Angeles Unified. In the end, the bill signed by California governor Arnold Schwarzenegger gave Mayor Antonio Villaraigosa less authority than Bloomberg has in New York, but he and the twenty-six other mayors of cities within the school district were to have had increased control over the school budget and the hiring (and firing) of the superintendent. Villaraigosa was to have had direct control of three high schools and the elementary and middle schools that feed into them.[9] That was until an April 2007 court ruling nullified the law granting this long-sought authority. Villaraigosa now says he will work with other officials and special interest groups toward the ultimate goal of better schools for all LA students. Also in April 2007, the mayor of Washington, D.C., Adrien Fenty, won the approval of the city council to take over the city's troubled school system from the city school board.

School boards are quintessentially U.S. democratic institutions that got their start in the Progressive Era at the end of the nineteenth century. These citizen boards were envisioned as a way to end the spoils system. Individu-

Large urban school districts in New York and Los Angeles have been experimenting with centralizing control over public schools. In 2006 Los Angeles mayor Antonio Villaraigosa, pictured here, successfully sought more authority over the Los Angeles Unified School District until a 2007 court decision struck down his efforts.

als would no longer be able to show partisan and political favor by awarding jobs to their followers. This would make way for the shared pursuit of effective public education.

Looking back now, that promise seems quaint, given that political interest groups continue to target school board elections. In Virginia, for example, school board elections were abolished in the early 1950s because southern white traditionalists feared that too many candidates were sympathetic to the then-growing school desegregation movement. It was not until 1992 that elected members once again would replace appointed members. In addition, during the 1990s, conservative Christian political activists zeroed in on school board elections as battlegrounds for the agenda of promoting school prayer and eliminating sex education.

Some critics say school boards actually produce fewer school improvements than they do campaign bumper stickers. (See box on page 472.) That is one reason they were curbed by city governments during the 1990s in Boston, Chicago, Cleveland, Detroit, and, to a lesser extent, the District of Columbia.[10] Faced with stagnating test scores and an exodus of families to private or parochial schools, urban leaders argued that emergency action to arrest the decline of the schools was more important than the democracy of a thousand voices.

The idea is that a centralized authority figure, such as a mayor or school chief, is accountable in the mystifying field of school reform. Appointees from an elected mayor are more likely to take decisive action and worry less about glad-handing, returning campaign favors, and seeking reelection. The jury is still out on such propositions, and proposals to abolish elected school boards tend to appear only in districts that are in dire straits.

The challenges facing school boards are formidable. Keep in mind that by law a public school must accept all students who live within its jurisdiction. This makes planning tricky. School boards do not have taxing authority, but most prepare budgets for approval by the county board or city council, which must balance education spending against spending on police and fire protection and transportation. It is the board that hires the superintendent . . . who hires the principals . . . who hire the teachers who taught you to read.

Money Matters

The lion's share of school funding comes from the states. On average, states paid for 47.1 percent of a school's costs in 2004, according to the U.S. Census Bureau's Annual Survey of Local Government Finances. This is in comparison to 43.9 percent from local jurisdictions and just 8.9 percent from the federal government.

Many states and localities raise school funds from income tax and sales taxes. Twenty-four states dedicate funds raised through the morally con-

Policy in Practice: Do School Board Races Improve Education or Simply Create More Bumper Stickers?

At the bottom of the ballot, far below the household names seeking the presidency or a seat in Congress, appear the names of candidates for your local school board. Most, rest assured, are fine people. But with voter turnout often as low as 20 percent in off-year elections, school board races are sometimes derided as wasteful exercises dominated, in the worst cases, by personally ambitious, underqualified, single-issue ideologues.

According the National School Boards Association (NSBA), 93 percent of the members of the nation's 14,890 school boards are elected, 2.8 percent are appointed. The remainder serve on boards with both elected and appointed members.

Today, only 10 percent of the country's ninety-five thousand school board members declare a party affiliation. Most run and pay for their bumper stickers using their own funding, without the typical baggage of campaign donations from business groups or trade unions (other than teachers' associations). In large cities, such as San Diego, Milwaukee, and Los Angeles, candidates can spend tens of thousands of dollars. In the poorer communities of the Deep South, fundamentalist candidates may rely instead on tactical support from the Costa Mesa, California-based National Association of Christian Educators.

Although some complain that school board incumbents are firmly entrenched, school board races actually seem competitive. Compared with congressional races, that is. An NSBA survey shows that from 1998 to 2001, 47.4 percent of the races produced no defeats for incumbents. In the U.S. Congress, the incumbency retention rate is well over 90 percent. Turnout for school board elections is highly influenced by the presence of state and national races, with turnout improving substantially when school board races take place at the same time as those other more visible races. (See Table 13-1.) The average school board term of office is four years; the average member serves six or seven years. Many win a second term, serve, and then go on to run for higher office. Those whose children have graduated, however, can find themselves losing energy and credibility.

Among the most vocal critics of elected school boards are superintendents, whose function as chief executive officers of school districts sometimes can be thwarted by boards, which have power to hire and fire them. They argue that school board members, who are paid little or nothing, often take office with little understanding of nuts-and-bolts management issues and that many need training. Writes William J. Price, a former superintendent in Michigan:

troversial practice of running a state lottery. Those gambling dollars add up: In California, the lottery generates 2 percent of the state's education funding, and in 2005, the Florida lottery transferred more than $1 billion to the schools.[11] The bulk of school funds, however, come from the local property tax. This tax is based on the assessed value of a taxpayer's home, usually a percentage of each $100 in assessed value.

There is logic to this. All taxpayers in a given community are believed to benefit from a quality school system—it helps maintain attractive real estate values and helps create an educated workforce. And the tax system is progressive, meaning that homeowners whose property is worth more pay more in nominal amounts, although all pay the same percentage. Most mortgage companies inconspicuously collect most of these tax funds for

With some exceptions for members who serve purely as a civic duty, many board members' interests are either ideological, political, or both. The more highly politicized and single issue-oriented the school board election is, the more difficult it is to create a governance culture in which the school board operates within a carefully defined and crafted set of role expectations, while maximizing the role of the CEO.[a]

Princeton University molecular biology professor Lee Silver, after a frustrating term as an elected school board member in his college town, proposed that boards be abolished and replaced by a committee of professional educators. "There isn't a single thing school boards do well," he wrote. "On the contrary, what they do more often than not is to get in the way of school district administrators who are perfectly able to run the schools by themselves."[b]

But abolition of elected school boards is unlikely in today's political climate. So-called education experts don't carry much weight among average citizens—and many of today's pushy baby-boomer parents simply will call in another expert with opposing views. Parents want a role in picking the superintendent and assigning budget priorities, which is why they value board members who seek their votes. And the low turnout for school board elections could easily be a sign that constituents are satisfied with the way boards run things.

TABLE 13-1

Voter Turnout and the Timing of School Board Elections

	Percentage Turnout when School Board Elections Are		Percentage Increase when Board Elections Are Held on the Same Day as
	Always Held on the Same Day as	Never Held on the Same Day as	
National or State Elections	43.8	25.8	+18.0
Mayoral or City Council Elections	41.8	29.1	+12.7

Source: Frederick M. Hess, "School Boards at the Dawn of the 21st Century: Conditions and Challenges of District Governance," National School Boards Association, 2002.

Note: Turnout percentage is respondents' estimate of the percentage of registered voters who voted in the most recent local school board election.

[a] William J. Price, "Policy Governance Revisited," *School Administrator* Web edition, February 2001.
[b] Lee M. Silver, "Why I'm Giving Up on School Boards," *School Administrator,* Web edition, February 1998.

homeowners. The money is then kept in a homeowner's personal escrow account until the tax is due.

The downside of property taxes is that as property values gain in value, the assessment and corresponding property taxes also rise—irrespective of whether a homeowner's income is rising along with it. As mentioned in Chapter 12, this vicious circle is what fueled passage of California's famous Proposition 13 in 1978. This statewide ballot measure capped property taxes and ignited a tax revolt.

An even deeper problem with funding schools via the property tax is the fact that wealthier districts are able to keep theirs attractively low as a percentage rate and still produce enough revenue dollars to support good schools. For example, in affluent Beverly Hills, California, property was—

and still is—very expensive. Yet the tax rate cited in *Serrano v. Priest* (1971), a famous school funding equity case, was only $2.38 per $100 in assessed value.

Place this up against the $5.48 per $100 in the low-income Baldwin Park area. Schools were demonstrably inferior, and the community was able to spend only half of what was spent in Beverly Hills. The California Supreme Court agreed that families in Baldwin Park were being denied a "fundamental right" to quality schools.[12] The court ordered the legislature to find a way to make school funding more equitable.

A slightly different principle was spelled out by the U.S. Supreme Court in the 1973 ruling in *San Antonio Independent School District v. Rodriguez.* In this case, attorneys for a largely Mexican American population found that their clients were paying a tax rate 25 percent higher than nearby affluent school districts. These less affluent districts, however, were only able or willing to fund schools at only 60 percent of that enjoyed by wealthy San Antonio neighborhoods.

The Supreme Court acknowledged the disparities but ruled that equal school funding is not a federal constitutional right: "The Equal Protection Clause does not require absolute equality or precisely equal advantages," the justices wrote. Despite this ruling, the precedent was set. State courts began to see themselves as protectors of poor and rural students, and the school funding equity movement at the state level gathered more steam.

These two cases launched a decades-long movement of constitutional litigation on school funding that has spread to nearly every state. It pits the principle of local control against pressures to close the gap between wealthy and poor districts. Jurists, educators, parents, and tax activists continue to fight over the key to school equity.

In the 1970s, most courts, like California's, ruled in favor of greater equalization among districts. After some judicial setbacks, the momentum slowed in the 1980s before gaining ground again in the courts of the 1990s. Nowhere was this drama played out more visibly than in Vermont, where a 1997 state supreme court ruling prompted the legislature to enact the controversial Act 60. The act forces wealthier districts that want to upgrade their schools to share their added funds with schools in poor districts.

Understandably, citizens in affluent districts like to see their tax dollars spent in their own communities, and they will lobby and push to keep their schools the best. Many middle-class and upper-class taxpayers say they paid extra for their homes so that their children could attend schools that do not lack for essentials. Citizens in poor districts, by contrast, argue that dilapidated school buildings, meager resources, and teachers at the low end of the profession's already low pay scale are the chief reasons for the achievement gap between their children and those in wealthier districts. (See Map 13-1.) They assert that resources should be distributed among all districts so that all students receive an essentially equitable level of education. Should individuals from less affluent areas be denied access to a good education? Must

MAP 13-1 **Spending per Student by State, 2002–2003**

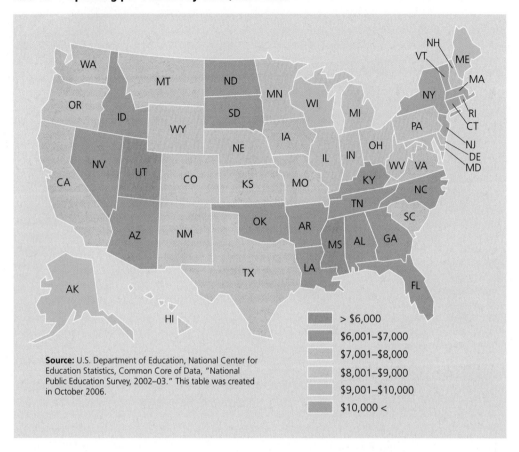

Source: U.S. Department of Education, National Center for Education Statistics, Common Core of Data, "National Public Education Survey, 2002–03." This table was created in October 2006.

Legend:
- > $6,000
- $6,001–$7,000
- $7,001–$8,000
- $8,001–$9,000
- $9,001–$10,000
- $10,000 <

funneling more resources into disadvantaged communities require "penalizing" affluent communities?

Responses among state legislatures to court orders on school funding have varied. The issue has not always broken down easily along conservative-liberal lines. Indeed, the percentage of per-pupil expenditures has risen most steeply during periods of conservative ascendancy, such as the 1920s and 1950s.[13] This all demonstrates the degree to which creating quality schools is a near-universal value.

Researchers examining the role that money plays in learning have created models that attempt to factor in such variables as a school's percentage of student dropouts, graduation rates, teacher salaries, and enrollment. (See Map 13-2.) These models also look at the percentage of children living in poverty and those in female-headed households, how many students have disabilities and how many of these have severe disabilities, and how many students possess limited English proficiency.[14] Few believe that pouring

MAP 13-2 **Student Enrollment in Public Schools by State, Fall 2002**

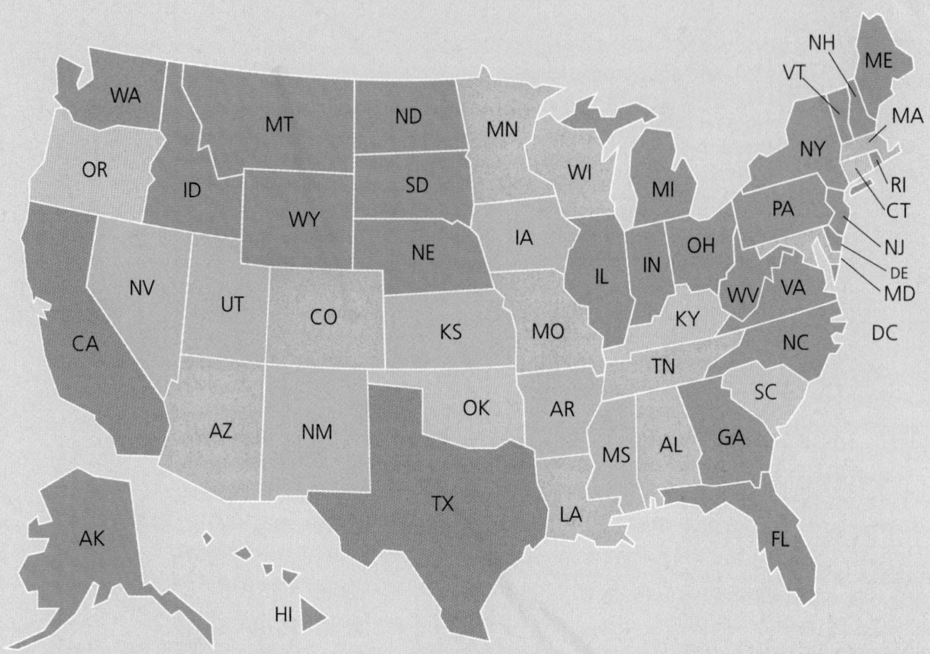

Source: U.S. Department of Education, National Center for Education Statistics, Common Core of Data, "National Public Education Survey, 2002–03." This table was created in October 2006.

Legend:
- ≤ 300,000
- 300,001–500,000
- 500,001–700,000
- 700,001–1,000,000
- 1,000,001–3,000,000
- 3,000,000 ≤

money into a school district automatically produces improvements. As a result, they also attempt to consider such human factors as the degree of cooperation among teachers, rates of absenteeism, and the extent of disruptive behavior in classrooms.

Most important, researchers try to isolate precisely how monies are best spent inside schools to derive the most benefit. Areas in which increased funding translates into student learning gains, according to one study, included spending on instruction, central office administration, and teacher-student ratios. Areas that demonstrated less of a payoff included funds for school-level administration, overall **capital outlays** and salaries for teachers with advanced degrees.[15]

Since the movement for new standards and accountability gained ground in the 1990s, school funding battles have shifted from an emphasis on equalization toward an effort to achieve adequacy, or what is required to get students to meet high standards.[16] To determine how much per-pupil

CAPITAL OUTLAYS

A category of school funding that focuses on long-term improvements to physical assets.

Governing States and Localities

spending is adequate for a school district, some states convene a panel of experts who use their professional judgment to pick the resources needed by schools, determine the costs of acquiring these resources, and then adjust their recommendations in favor of the needier districts. Examples of such states are Maine, Oregon, and Wyoming. Other states use the **successful schools model**, wherein groups of schools whose students have done well according to state standards are examined for their average per-pupil costs, which are then applied across the state. Examples of these states are Illinois, Mississippi, and Ohio.[17]

The funding appropriated by state legislatures depends on the input expected of localities. New York State, for example, reports the nation's largest disparity in per-pupil spending between affluent and less affluent districts, with the richer areas spending $2,280 more.[18] The amounts also vary by regional costs of living and a state's philosophy on the proper reach of government.

Furthermore, affluent suburban communities often differ from their urban counterparts in funding priorities. Parents in downtown Detroit or Cleveland, for example, may want extra monies for crime prevention and building upgrades, whereas suburbanites in places such as Bloomfield Hills, Michigan, and Shaker Heights, Ohio, want more money spent on computer technology and extracurricular programs.

Rural districts in states such as South Dakota or Wyoming have their own problems. They may have trouble raising teacher salaries, for example, if it means pushing those salaries out of line with comparable local salaries in other professions.

Wyoming has the fewest enrolled students (88,116 in 2002–2003). California has the most (6,353,667).

Looking strictly at per-pupil spending, the state offering the least was Utah at $5,008. The state spending the most was the New Jersey at $12,981.[19] The District of Columbia ranked third, spending $12,801 per student, but unfortunately for the nation's capital, its high per-pupil spending for years has been accompanied by some of urban America's lowest student test scores. This has made it a favorite whipping boy for conservatives who argue the futility of "throwing money at problems." (See box on page 478.)

Understandably, school funding is affected by economic downturns. Nearly all states are required to balance their budgets. As a result, they must choose among raising taxes, drawing from budget stabilization (rainy day) funds, or cutting spending in areas such as corrections and welfare. In the fall of 2002, states suffered their weakest two-year growth rates since the recession of the early 1980s.

In 2003, California stopped paying $10,000 merit awards to mid-career teachers who earned national certification.[20] Washington State suspended teacher cost-of-living salary hikes for two years. Oregon, faced with a protracted funding crisis and a legislature determined not to raise income taxes, watched as its largest communities around Portland approved a new, temporary sales tax to narrowly avoid having to end the school year early.

Local Focus: Got an Alternative to Throwing Money at Schools? Tell It to Kansas City

In August 2003, a judge in Kansas City, Missouri, issued a ruling that ended a labyrinthine, high-profile lawsuit over school desegregation and unequal funding between the city's urban and suburban schools. The postmortems offered by attorneys and educators were eye-popping: In twenty-six years, $2 billion had been spent; multiple court rulings had gone back and forth that had required tax increases and redrawing of boundaries; and fifty-five dilapidated schools were renovated while seventeen new ones were built, including a new $32 million magnet high school designed to attract suburban students by featuring, among other assets, an Olympic-sized pool and indoor track. Magnet schools place a strong emphasis in a particular subject area, for example, music, science, drama, or math. Students are selected through an application process instead of being assigned based on residence as in traditional public schools.

The main goals of the litigation, however—the recruitment of more white students to the mostly black inner-city schools and improved academic achievement by minorities—went largely unfulfilled. One of the series of judges who handled the epic case was reported to have confessed, "Maybe I created too expensive a school system." [a]

The degree to which money should factor as an ingredient in any recipe for school improvement is among the least settled disputes in education research.

Conservatives have long argued against the futility of "throwing money at problem schools." Indeed, school districts plagued by "bureaucratic bloat," embezzlement scandals, and rigid regulation and paperwork do not inspire school reformers to push additional funds as a panacea. If a funding shortage is the cause of underperformance, critics ask, how do you explain the fact that students often perform better at private and Catholic schools, some with tuitions of less than $3,000? How to explain the fact that students in the other countries of the Organization for Economic Cooperation and Development outperform American children on reading and math tests, even though the per-pupil spending rates in these mostly European countries are nearly half the U.S. average? [b]

Such critics argue that competently run schools provide "added value." This, they say, has as much to do with academic rigor as with simple dollars. They offer case studies in which infusions of cash failed to prompt a noticeable rise in test scores. [c]

Backers of increased school spending argue that in most cases, higher test scores are linked to affluent districts. They dramatize the "savage inequalities" in resources between districts, using a phrase coined from Jonathan Kozol's 1991 book of the same name. Who wants to teach or learn inside a run-down and filthy building? Liberals emphasize that greater spending is needed in districts with a preponderance of children from low-income homes and uneducated parents. They note that some children also are more expensive to educate—the National Center on Education Statistics calculates that special education students need 2.3 times the student average, poor students need 1.2 times the average.

The lack of consensus on this question is one reason the fifty states and the District of Columbia vary so widely in what they spend. (See Map 13-1.) The jury is still out on measuring the role of funding. As the Kansas City drama confirmed, money may not be a guaranteed solution to troubled schools. But most communities feel obliged to spend goodly amounts in the course of finding one.

[a] Donna McGuire," Judge Ends Desegregation Case after 26 Years and $2 Billion," *Kansas City Star,* August 14, 2003.

[b] Center for Education Reform, "Spending More but Educating Less" www.edreform.com (accessed October 24, 2003). See also Thomas B. Fordham Foundation, "Spending More while Learning Less: U.S. School Productivity in International Perspective," report by Herbert J. Walberg, 1998. www.edexcellence.net (accessed October 24, 2003).

[c] Eric A. Hanushek, "Assessing the Effects of School Resources on Student Performance: An Update. *Educational Evaluation and Policy Analysis* 19 (1997):141–164.

To school reformers, these state funding cuts were embarrassing. They came at a most inopportune time, too—just as the states needed to invest more resources to show progress under the No Child Left Behind Act.

New Pressure to Perform

Except in the minds of some nostalgists, it is doubtful there ever was a halcyon era of consensus among education's disparate stakeholders. There are far too many views about the nation's public schools to have all parties agree that they at some point achieved a satisfactory level of quality. Today's charge that schools are going to the proverbial hell in a hand basket also was heard throughout the 1940s and 1950s.

This charge intensified in 1957 after the Soviet Union launched its *Sputnik* satellite. Americans feared that U.S. students had fallen behind the country's cold war rivals in science and math. Traditionalists who hearken back to the classic education taught in the early twentieth century sometimes forget that in 1900, only 6 percent of children in the United States finished high school. Back then, the best that most could count on was a solid job in, say, manufacturing. For many college wasn't an option.[21]

> Traditionalists who hearken back to the classic education taught in the early twentieth century sometimes forget that in 1900, only 6 percent of children in the United States finished high school.

The current crisis over performance was set in motion during the early 1980s by the Reagan administration. Education secretary Dr. Terrell Bell lit a fire under sometimes resentful educators in 1983 by publishing *A Nation at Risk*. This report ranked states by school achievement data. Today, there are continuing laments that test scores are plummeting, kids don't know U.S. history, and that graduates arrive in college or in the workplace unable to write a declarative sentence.

It is true that school test scores have been stagnant for many years. It is hard to argue that a yawning achievement gap has not persisted between the preponderance of black and Hispanic students at the lower end of the achievement scale and the frequently more affluent whites and Asians near the top. Yet, test scores are not locked into a downward spiral. Those who choose to see the school performance glass as half full point to the nation's ever-replenishing supply of successful entrepreneurs. Look at the country's proliferation of Nobel Prize winners, they say. Step back and admire how its corporations continue to dominate the world economy. If public education plays a foundational role in supporting the economy and promoting new knowledge, clearly America's schools are doing something right.

Yes, a disturbing 68 percent of respondents to the annual Gallup Poll for *Phi Delta Kappan* magazine gave the nation's overall school system a grade of less than A or B. But defenders point out that far more assigned good grades to the performance of their own local schools.[22] Is it fair to blame a school for its students' performance, defenders ask, without considering each child's opportunity to learn? What about the income disparities that subject poorer kids to inferior schools? Schools that, however well-intentioned their staff, present a less rigorous curriculum, underqualified teachers, low expectations, resource disparities, and a disruptive climate? These students also tend to suffer from performance anxiety, negative peer influences, racial discrimination, sketchy preschool attendance, and homes in which the value of learning is not emphasized. Back and forth—the debate roars on.

Teaching to the Test

Meanwhile, on the front lines of education, the main performance indicator for schools remains not grades, not satisfaction surveys, not oral exams, but rather the standardized test—an indicator that has taken on new significance in the era of No Child Left Behind. Critics bemoan the trend of "teaching to the test," which skews classroom time toward the subjects covered on the tests, often at the expense of classes such as art and music. In early 2006, nearly three-fourths of school districts reported reducing elementary school instructional time in at least one subject to make more time for reading and math, the subjects tracked by NCLB.[23]

A thriving commercial testing industry has grown up to supply schools with inexpensive, mass-produced tests for quick, computerized scoring of large numbers of students from kindergarten to twelfth grade. Familiar giants in the multibillion-dollar industry include the Comprehensive Test of Basic Skills; the Iowa Test of Basic Skills; and the Stanford Achievement Test, or SAT (but not the SAT many of you took when applying to colleges).

Each publisher has developed procedures to continually rotate questions, keep the tests statistically valid and as free as possible from cultural bias, and minimize scorekeeping errors. And all for good reason. When things go awry, the result can be lawsuits. Some of these tests are **criterion referenced** and are intended to measure mastery of a given subject as defined by state standards. Most, however, are **norm referenced**, meaning that students are graded on how well they approach the mean student score on that same test administered across the country.[24]

A large number of states have their own tests. Resistance among advocates of local control to proposals made in the 1990s for a national student test caused such tests to continue to be permitted under the No Child Left Behind Act. Florida has its Florida Comprehensive Assessment Test (FCAT), Virginia has its Standards of Learning, and New York has its Regents Exam. Critics still question whether these tests are properly aligned with a given district's or state's curriculum and if such tests are comparable to those used in other states.

CRITERION REFERENCED TESTS

Standardized tests designed to gauge a student's level of mastery of a given set of materials.

NORM REFERENCED TESTS

Standardized tests designed to determine how a student's mastery of a set of materials compares with that of a specially designed sampling of students determined to be the national "norm" for their age group.

After eight decades of standardized testing, sometimes it seems that the more experts learn, the more they learn there is to learn. In New York State, for example, a special panel of math and testing experts concluded in October 2003 that the state's new high school end-of-course tests were of unacceptably bad quality. They came to this conclusion after a poor showing on state tests by high school seniors. The tests were the first under No Child Left Behind. Unfortunately, the experienced professionals who had prepared them ignored their own guidelines for the number of students needed for a valid sample in testing the questions.

In an effort to provide some uniformity and continuity in testing, the federal government has administered its own test since 1969—the **National Assessment of Educational Progress (NAEP)**. Nicknamed "the nation's report card," it is administered in volunteer sample districts to students in grades four, eight, and twelve. Over the years, NAEP scores have remained essentially flat, with subgroups' scores rising and falling. Since the early 1990s, fourth- and eighth-graders have shown improvement in math but little change in reading ability. The federal government has not released twelfth graders scores in recent years, as fewer high schools have agreed to participate in the testing.[25]

Another key performance indicator coordinated by the U.S. Department of Education is the **Trends in International Mathematics and Sciences Study (TIMSS)**. Designed to compare the academic achievement of students in forty-six countries, the 2003 TIMSS study found, for example, that the scores for U.S. eighth graders exceeded the averages for those of industrialized countries. Students in the United States beat out those in Italy and Lebanon in math, but trailed Japan and Singapore in science.[26] And although U.S. school reform advocates frequently point out the superior academic performance of students in many other countries as a sign of an urgent need to introduce more resources and more accountability measures, the 2003 TIMSS results showed that American students made significant progress in both math and science between 1995 and 2003.

Many of the countries that participate in TIMSS run schools that are rigidly tracked between a college-bound elite of students and the remainder who normally attend vocational schools. In the United States, all students have an equal opportunity to advance, at least in theory. (See box on page 482.)

Most students applying to college endure the stomach-churning tests known as the SAT and the less widely used ACT, which is used primarily in the Midwest. Designed by the private nonprofit Educational Testing Service and run by the private nonprofit College Board, the SAT is designed to be a predictor of college achievement. The test has been renamed and recalibrated on several occasions. What began as the Scholastic Aptitude Test became the Scholastic Assessment Test. Thirty years of annual scores from this test have prompted much anguish.

In the early 1980s, a study found that average scores had fallen by 81 points from 1963–1977—from 478 down to 429 on the verbal test and

NATIONAL ASSESSMENT OF EDUCATIONAL PROGRESS (NAEP)

Known as the "nation's report card," this is the only regularly conducted independent survey of what a nationally representative sample of students in grades four, eight, and twelve know and can do in various subjects.

TRENDS IN INTERNATIONAL MATHEMATICS AND SCIENCE STUDY (TIMSS)

Launched by the United States in 1995, it is a regularly updated study that compares performance in science and mathematics of students from forty-six countries.

Policy in Practice: How College Tuition Gets Raised

College students who get irked when tuition goes up should nail down one key detail before rounding up their dorm mates to stage a protest. Who has the power to make education more expensive?

The answer depends on the state and its policies on the question of who pays for whom to gain access to public higher education.

In the decade ending in 2005–2006, average tuition and fees at public and private four-year colleges and universities climbed a steep 54 percent and 37 percent, respectively, according to an initiative of the American Council on Education.

Tuition hikes grew thicker and faster with the economic downturn and state budget crunches during the first few years of the twenty-first century. Twenty-two state higher education appropriations were cut in 2002–2003, at just the time the children of the baby boomers were creating record-size freshman classes. All but one state raised tuition at public colleges and universities to bridge the gap.[a] In 2003, the average increase was 14 percent, but several public institutions imposed larger hikes. UCLA led the pack with a 43.1 percent increase, while the University of Arizona system raised tuition at all three major campuses by 39 percent.

Some students don't take it lying down. In Arizona, four students in 2003 filed suit against the Arizona Board of Regents to challenge the legality of the $1,010 tuition hike.[b] The Arizona students said the hike violated the state constitution's provision that tuition be "as nearly free as possible."

A whopping 77 percent of college students in the United States attend taxpayer-funded public institutions. This means that most family pocketbooks are squeezed by tuition decisions made by legislators, governors, and public higher education boards.

Tuition at private colleges is set by the board of trustees in consultation with administrators. In the public system, tuition is set using governance structures worked out over the decades by state statute. Nine states vest their legislatures with full authority on tuition. Twenty-eight states give that authority to a statewide higher education system coordinating body, and thirteen allow tuition to be set by institutional governing boards, which are composed of distinguished volunteers either appointed by the governor or elected.[c]

In some cases the decision-making authority on tuition is total, in others it is shared. In South Carolina and Washington State, for example, the legislature has complete decision-making authority for state colleges and universities. In North Carolina, the legislature considers recommendations from the governor and university board of governors and sets tuition rates as part of its annual appropriations bill. In Connecticut and Wisconsin, the authority resides with system boards, but the legislature can appropriate funding to freeze tuition rates and, in times of economic hardship, require increases.

Victims of tuition hikes point to an increasing chunk of the American family's income that is required to finance college—more than $11,000 on average for

from 502 to 470 on the math test. During the 1990s and early part of the twenty-first century, however, the College Board had reason to be upbeat: in an August 2003 report, the board reported the highest level of math scores in thirty-five years. Then the College Board revised the test once again, adding a writing section and including higher-level math. The class of 2006 posted the greatest year-over-year decline in scores since 1975, with combined reading and math scores down seven points.[27]

Beyond standardized testing—and both before and after passage of the No Child Left Behind Act—one performance indicator that is gaining

public institutions and $27,000 for private institutions. That is just tuition, fees, and room and board. That's like buying a new car every year. They complain that colleges have become profligate spenders. The burden on students and parents clearly has grown. Tuition in 1990 covered 20 percent of public institutions' costs; by 2005 that share had risen to 36.7 percent, and state and local support per student had fallen to a 25-year low.[d] That pattern seems unlikely to change. A 2006 study by the Kansas Board of Regents forecasted that by 2010, tuition would comprise 25 percent of its six public universities' operating budgets; state support is expected to fall to 24 percent.[e]

It is true that colleges feel pressure to remain competitive in attracting students by outfitting campuses with health facilities, entertainment centers, and state-of-the-art electronic and computer equipment. There also is constant pressure to raise professors' salaries. Tuition, however, does not begin to cover the actual cost per student. This means that all students are to some extent subsidized. For example, public medical schools derive a mere 3 percent of their revenues from student tuition payments, according to the American Medical Student Association (AMSA). Because their state appropriations have been dropping for two decades, public colleges and universities have been striving for efficiencies and creating alternative sources of revenue such as university-affiliated foundations.

Those who raise tuition are aware of the pain they inflict. In Arizona, the 39-percent hike was combined with a 140-percent increase in need-based student aid, and the tuition increase was done after the regents conducted a comprehensive study of the missions, strengths, and finances of the state schools, along with the needs of the state economy.

Having rebounded from their fiscal crises, in 2005 forty-three states increased state and local funding for higher education. But for all their good intentions, their share of college funding still dropped, due to enrollment growth and inflation that outpaced the increases in their investments. Nationwide surveys show there is consensus that all of society benefits from widespread access to college—but the United States lacks consensus on how to pay that ever-growing bill.

[a] Putting College Costs into Context," American Council on Education, 2004. www.acenet.edu/bookstore/pdf/2004_college_costs.pdf (accessed September 25, 2006).

[b] *Arizona Republic,* August 27, 2003.

[c] *Survey of State Tuition, Fees, and Financial Assistance Policies, 2003,* State Higher Education Executive Officers. www.sheeo.org (accessed October 22, 2003).

[d] Paul E. Lingenfelter, David L. Wright, and Takeshi Yanagiura, *State Higher Education Finance FY 2005* (Boulder, Colo.: State Higher Education Executive Officers, 2005).

[e] Mara Rose Williams and James Hart, "Kansas' Share of College Funding Drops," *Kansas City Star,* September 20, 2006.

ground is the measurement of high school graduation rates. The states are a patchwork of methods for figuring these rates, which has led to a policy conundrum. Experts point out that it is tempting for districts to arrive at a school's rate simply by subtracting the number of dropouts from the number collecting a diploma. The problem with that is that some dropouts transfer to other schools in a **General Equivalency Degree (GED) program,** get their GEDs on their own, or are incarcerated.

These missing students are hard to track down. Only ten states have spent the money required to perform a longitudinal study of the fate of such

GENERAL EQUIVALENCY DEGREE (GED) PROGRAM

A series of tests that can be taken to qualify for a high school equivalency certificate or diploma.

students. Some schools are embarrassed by such "failures" and choose to sweep them under the rug. Indeed, in 2003, the school district for Houston, Texas, previously run by former education secretary Roderick Paige, suffered under the glare of the national spotlight when it was revealed that the city's high schools had been underreporting dropout rates in order to perform better under the state's accountability plan.

The underreporting—a citywide dropout rate of 1.5 percent, when the actual figures were between 25 percent and 50 percent—was uncovered by a principal. His school reportedly had had no dropouts. Unfortunately, he personally knew of some. Fallout from the scandal caused several high officials to be fired.[28]

For these reasons and others, graduation rates are not fully reliable. Methods for creating uniform measures are still works in progress. For instance, if raising standards merely creates pressure that produces more dropouts, it should not count as true education reform.[29]

Many Brands on the School Reform Shelf

It is one thing to theorize on how to improve schools and quite another to implement real-world programs that get results. Decades of promising techniques—and sometimes utopian promises—have rotated through solutions that span everything from site-based management to early-reading programs to smaller class sizes, to name just a few. No consensus has materialized, only more debate. Still, the main schools of thought on school reform can be boiled down to the following:

Standards and Accountability

The standards movement first drew attention at a 1989 education summit in Charlottesville, Virginia. Attended by the elder George Bush and state governors, including future president Bill Clinton, the summit created a national panel to set and monitor education targets that would become Goals 2000, or the Educate America Act. That same year, the Kentucky Supreme Court struck down the entire state education system, which prompted the enactment of the Kentucky Education Reform Act the following year. This paved the way for the standards movement nationwide.

The premise was simple. Standards mean laying out in advance what students should be able to do at each grade in each subject, aligning tests to that content, and then evaluating who reaches the standard. Without question, determining what students should know in each subject area was a task for professional associations. The National Council of Teachers of Mathematics produced the earliest standards. As momentum built in the early 1990s, the Clinton administration worked to give the movement a national framework in its reauthorization of the **Elementary and Secondary Education Act,** originally passed in 1965.

Prodding from governors and the business community produced much progress on the integration of a standards-based approach. Fully forty-nine states laid out standards. Iowa—the lone holdout—proudly leaves standards to local school districts. By summer 2002, forty-seven states were issuing "report cards" on student achievement. Not quite half were breaking the data down by racial subgroups, level of income, or limited English proficiency. Among teachers, according to an *Education Week* survey, eight in ten reported that their curricula were now more demanding. Six out of ten said their students were writing more.

Not that this was not all to the good, but the problem with standards, teachers say, is that there are too many to cover in one school year.[30] There is no consensus that standardized tests truly measure learning, given that some children who perform well in written and oral and problem-solving situations do not test well, perhaps due to pressure. Plus, many who test well forget what they memorized soon after.[31] Recent data have shown a disconnect between state standards and states' ability to make adequate yearly progress, as defined by NCLB. For example, almost 75 percent of Florida's schools failed to make adequate yearly progress in 2003–2004, but less than 10 percent earned grades of "D" or "F" according to the state system.[32] (See Table 13-2.)

There is also the issue of textbooks and curriculum development. Twenty-nine states are open territory states that allow individual districts to purchase their own textbooks and develop their own curriculums. This means that children are using different learning materials in different grades at different schools, even if the state has subject standards. Actual learning levels may not be represented accurately on standardized tests, state-authored or otherwise.

The other twenty-one states are adoption states. This means that not only are there state standards, there is also a standard statewide curriculum. Often, the state legislature or a specially appointed panel determines what books will be used at every grade in every public school in the state. Even among adoption states, however, curriculums and standards vary widely. This also can cause students' education levels to be misrepresented. For example, a student moving from Texas to California (both adoption states) will not have learned the same material in the same grade. Forced to take a standardized test, especially a state-sponsored one, the child may fail.

Open territory state or adoption state, at the high school level, standardized tests are truly high stakes. By 2006, twenty-five states had policies in place to deny diplomas to students who fail end-of-course exams.[33] That means students can fail to graduate even if they had passing grades. This not only breaks the hearts of families, it can cost a student a college acceptance. It also opens schools up to embarrassment from lowered

ELEMENTARY AND SECONDARY EDUCATION ACT

Federal law passed in 1965 as part of President Johnson's Great Society initiative; steered federal funds to improve local schools, particularly those attended primarily by low-income and minority students.

TABLE 13-2

No Child Left Behind Results, School Years 2004–2005 and 2005–2006

State	School Year 2004–2005[a]		School Year 2005–2006	
	Percentage of Schools that Did Not Make AYP[b]	Percentage of Schools in Need of Improvement	Percentage of Schools that Did Not Make AYP	Percentage of Schools in Need of Improvement
Alabama	47	34	12	34
Alaska	41	38	39	39
Arizona	13	9	34	3
Arkansas	22	22	29	29
California	39	19	35	23
Colorado	25	6	—	—
Connecticut[c]	20	16	36	15
Delaware	26	21	24	19
District of Columbia	55	51	82	60
Florida[d]	64	32	71	31
Georgia	18	17	21	15
Hawaii	66	48	65	61
Idaho	43	15	34	27
Illinois	26	17	—	—
Indiana	41	5	51	9
Iowa	9	6	—	—
Kansas	9	1	—	—
Kentucky	25	11	34	13
Louisiana	16	11	—	—
Maine	23	8	—	—
Maryland[e]	23	17	22	15
Massachusetts	43	24	—	—
Michigan	12	12	15	9
Minnesota	13	4	—	—
Mississippi	11	9	17	7
Missouri	35	6	37	6
Montana	7	9	—	—
Nebraska	10	5	—	—
Nevada	53	29	36	36
New Hampshire	47	42	40	20
New Jersey	38	25	29	26
New Mexico	53	30	54	44

TABLE 13-2, continued

State	School Year 2004–2005[a]		School Year 2005–2006	
	Percentage of Schools that Did Not Make AYP[b]	Percentage of Schools in Need of Improvement	Percentage of Schools that Did Not Make AYP	Percentage of Schools in Need of Improvement
New York	18	16	—	—
North Carolina[f]	42	9	40	9
North Dakota	9	4	8	4
Ohio	24	13	39	28
Oklahoma	3	7	—	—
Oregon	35	28	31	4
Pennsylvania	19	10	18	10
Rhode Island	56	18	—	—
South Carolina	50	15	—	—
South Dakota	16	15	22	13
Tennessee	7	10	19	6
Texas	12	3	9	4
Utah	13	1	—	—
Vermont[g]	14	21	21	7
Virginia	17	6	23	4
Washington	20	9	—	—
West Virginia	17	5	14	4
Wisconsin	2	2	4	2
Wyoming	21	4	13	6

Source: As first appeared in *Quality Counts, 2006, Education Week*. www.edweek.org/media/04ayp.pdf (accessed September 20, 2006). Reprinted with permission from Editorial Projects in Education.

Notes:

AYP = Adequate Yearly Progress

—Not available. These states had not yet publicly released their AYP data under the No Child Left Behind Act for the 2005–2006 school year at press time.

[a] New Hampshire, Rhode Island, and Vermont suspended much of their testing programs during the 2004–2005 school year as they made the transition to a fall testing cycle. For 2004–2005, the percentage of elementary and middle schools making AYP was primarily based on attendance. High school results for 2004–2005 are based on assessment data and graduation rates. For these states, the table only reflects the percentages of high schools making adequate yearly progress, not making AYP, and identified as in need of improvement.

[b] All states must include Title I schools in their designation of schools "in need of improvement." Federal law allows states to choose whether non-Title I schools are assigned a school improvement status and whether federal consequences apply to those schools. As a result, some schools rated for AYP may not receive a school improvement designation.

[c] 2005–2006 figures represent data for elementary and middle schools only. High school data will be released at a later date.

[d] This table counts schools labeled "provisional AYP" by Florida (828 in 2004–2005 and 1,240 in 2005–2006) as not making AYP. These schools earned an A or B under Florida's A+ Plan but did not make AYP under the federal system.

[e] 2005–2006 figures represent data for elementary and middle schools only. High school data will be released at a later date.

[f] 2005–2006 elementary and middle school AYP designations do not include information on mathematics because of the administration of new math assessments in spring 2006.

[g] 2005–2006 figures represent data for elementary and middle schools only. High school data will be released at a later date.

graduation rates. Such fears are the reason that Alaska, Arizona, and Maryland delayed implementation of high-stakes tests.[34]

The achievement aims expressed in the standards movement were undeniably noble. Goals 2000 included such aspirations as all children beginning school ready to learn and then graduating with demonstrated competencies. It vowed that there should be more professional development for teachers and greater parental involvement. Graduation rates were to be increased to 90 percent. All schools would be drug-free and violence-free, and U.S. students would rocket to first place in the world in math and science.

The question the standards movement never fully answered, however, dealt with accountability. What happens if students fail? Should students, teachers, principals, schools, or all of the above be penalized? As the turn of the millennium came and went, no one could argue that whoever was accountable had done their jobs. Nor could anyone claim that the lofty goals had been achieved. All of this became a somewhat moot point, however, when the George W. Bush administration abolished the Goals 2000 infrastructure to make way for the No Child Left Behind program.

Recruiting Good Teachers

Recent research has demonstrated that the single most important factor in student learning, more important than curriculum, family income, student health, or parental involvement, is good teaching.[35] (See Table 13-3.) Economists have even quantified the effect, estimating that the best teachers give their students an extra year's worth of learning and perhaps fifty points on standardized tests.[36] This is particularly true for minorities, so many of whom enter school socially or economically disadvantaged.

Problem is, demographic projections point to a shortage of teachers that could exceed two million during the first decade of the twenty-first century. The absence of qualified teachers also is worse in high-poverty schools. These schools suffer from heavy turnover, and the number of teachers with less than three years experience is 20 percent versus 15 percent for other school districts.

The shortage is acute in certain subject areas: special education, mathematics, science, bilingual education, and technology. This is in part due to the fact that teacher salaries often are too low to attract candidates who can earn more at high-tech firms and corporations. School districts must make do, then, with who they have. The use of teachers by school districts, however reluctantly, to instruct in areas in which they do not hold degrees affects between 4 and 16 percent of high school students in the liberal arts, says the Department of Education.[37]

One piece of the No Child Left Behind Act aims at improving this record. It originally called for all teachers of core subjects to be "fully qualified"— defined broadly as holding a teaching license and showing command of the subjects they teach—by the 2005–2006 school year. When the U.S. Depart-

TABLE 13-3

Quality Counts, Grades at a Glance, 2006

State	Standards and Accountability	Efforts to Improve Teacher Quality	School Climate	Resource Equity
Alabama	B	B	C–	C+
Alaska	C–	D	D+	D+
Arizona	B	D	C+	D+
Arkansas	C+	A–	C+	B–
California	B+	B–	C	B–
Colorado	B	C	B	C–
Connecticut	B–	A–	B–	C
Delaware	B+	C+	B	B–
District of Columbia	C+	D	C–	N/A*
Florida	A	C	C	B–
Georgia	A–	C+	C+	C
Hawaii	B+	C–	C	N/A*
Idaho	B	D	C+	F
Illinois	B+	C	C+	D+
Indiana	A	B–	C	B–
Iowa	F	C+	B–	B+
Kansas	C	B+	B–	C+
Kentucky	B+	B	C	C
Louisiana	A	A	C–	B
Maine	C	D	B	C–
Maryland	A–	C+	D+	C–
Massachusetts	A	C	B–	C–
Michigan	B	D	C–	C–
Minnesota	C+	C	B	B
Mississippi	C+	C	D+	C–
Missouri	D+	B–	B	C
Montana	D	D+	C–	D–
Nebraska	D	C	C+	C+
Nevada	B–	C	C–	A–
New Hampshire	C	C–	B–	D
New Jersey	B+	B	B–	C–
New Mexico	A	B	C	B+

TABLE 13-3, continued

State	Standards and Accountability	Efforts to Improve Teacher Quality	School Climate	Resource Equity
New York	A	B–	C	C
North Carolina	B	B	C+	C–
North Dakota	C–	D+	C	D–
Ohio	A–	B	C+	C
Oklahoma	B+	B	C+	B–
Oregon	C+	D	C+	C–
Pennsylvania	B–	B	C	C–
Rhode Island	C	C–	B	D
South Carolina	A	A	C+	C
South Dakota	B–	D+	C+	C+
Tennessee	B	C+	C+	C
Texas	B–	C–	C	C–
Utah	C+	C–	C	B+
Vermont	B–	C–	B–	F
Virginia	B	B+	C	D+
Washington	B	C	C+	C
West Virginia	A	B	C+	B
Wisconsin	B–	C+	B	B–
Wyoming	D	D+	B	C+

Source: As first appeared in *Quality Counts, 2006, Education Week* www.edweek.org/media/ew/qc/2006/17sos.h25.sg.pdf (accessed August 26, 2006). Reprinted with permission from Editorial Projects in Education.

*Because Hawaii and the District of Columbia are single districts, it is not appropriate to measure district-level equity.

ment of Education realized most states were unlikely to meet the deadline, it declared them compliant if they could demonstrate "good faith and effort" toward meeting the goal. All but seven passed the test.[38] A survey of states and school districts revealed, however, that few believe the NCLB requirement has significantly improved teacher quality.[39]

Colleges and universities that have schools of education are working to improve the quality of their graduates and to provide aspiring educators with more substantive knowledge and less jargon and abstract pedagogy. Many current researchers believe that teachers with the most content knowledge in their field are most effective in raising student achievement. This suggests that the techniques of working with young people and diagnosing student impediments are best acquired on the job.[40]

Alternative licensure programs that provide appropriate training, mentoring, and testing to interested individuals now are permitted in twenty-four states and the District of Columbia. Examples of such programs include Troops to Teachers, which opens up classroom jobs to former military personnel, and Teach for America, which involves recent college graduates who want to fight poverty. Tens of thousands of teachers enter the profession through these programs each year.

Many Schools, Few Resources

Teach for America places its newly minted teachers in urban and rural schools, a boon to districts that have difficulty recruiting and retaining quality instructors. On average, teachers in rural school districts earn 88 percent of the salaries of their nonrural counterparts. While rural schools do have lower crime and dropout rates than urban schools, teachers in rural districts must also contend with the perpetual challenges of few opportunities for professional development, limited curricula, and threats of school and district consolidation.[41]

The problem of shrinking teacher numbers has many in education feeling like they are banging their heads against the wall. Or, in this case, the table. DeSoto, Texas, Independent School District Athletic Director Fred Hedgecoke pretty much sums up the frustration and helplessness felt by recruiters at this poorly attended teacher career day at the University of Texas in April 1998. The years that have passed since then haven't changed the seriousness of the teacher shortage situation.

Consolidation of small, rural schools has been controversial since it began back in the days of Horace Mann and his one-room schoolhouse. The practice, often pursued by states and districts in search of cost savings, picked up steam throughout the twentieth century. According to the National Center for Education Statistics, the nation's 117,108 school districts in the 1937–1938 school year were cut back to 14,928 by 1999–2000. During that same time period, enrollment grew from 25.5 million students to 46.9 million.[42] States continue to propose consolidation plans, despite lacking hard evidence that the strategy is successful. In 2006, Vermont education commissioner Richard Cate recommended reducing the state's school districts by 75 percent, although the legislature failed to approve the plan.

Such plans have moved forward in other states, including West Virginia, where more than three hundred schools closed between 1990 and 2005, and Iowa, which consolidated 14 percent of its districts during the same period.[43] Backlash against further consolidation has some districts and states rethinking their strategies, however, and turning, yet again, to technology. Distance learning is more than correspondence courses; it encompasses video conferencing and online learning modules and can vastly expand learning opportunities for both students and teachers.[44] This is not to say that computers are a panacea for all of the ills plaguing rural school districts—after all, they still have to come up with the money to invest in the technology—but proponents argue that it is a strong alternative to closing schoolhouse doors.

Choosing Wisely: Alternatives to Public Schools

School choice, always guaranteed to stir up emotions, has been brought to the forefront of the education debate by the No Child Left Behind Act. Schools that fail to make adequate yearly progress for two consecutive years are deemed "in need of improvement," giving parents the right to transfer their children to another public school. Few parents, however, have taken advantage of that option. In 2005, just 38,000 students—less than 1 percent of those eligible—transferred out of struggling schools.[45] Polls show the public would rather reform the public school system from within. Alternatives such as charter schools and voucher programs excite varying levels of support.[46] Nevertheless, reformers continue to promote school choice.

Charter Schools

CHARTER SCHOOLS

Public schools, often with unique themes, managed by teachers, principals, social workers, or nonprofit groups. The movement was launched in the early 1990s.

Entrepreneurs who want to launch their own schools with public money have been applying to run **charter schools** since the early 1990s. These schools are less an educational philosophy than a variation on school governance. Charter schools range in theme from Montessori to the fact-based niche curriculum called Core Knowledge to ranching to online (distance) learning. Sponsors have included former public and private school principals, parent groups, universities, social service agencies, and nonprofits such as the YMCA. By 2005, more than three thousand charter schools had sprung up in thirty-nine of the forty states that have enacted charter laws, with more than seven hundred thousand students enrolled.[47]

In principle, students who attend charter schools are given the same per-pupil expenditure as students in mainstream schools, although the founders often must scrounge to find facilities. The willingness of a state to encourage the establishment of charter schools depends on the condition of its public schools and the energies of would-be charter school founders. Some states set up special chartering boards. Others allow local school boards to approve applications.

Overall, state charter laws vary. Arizona's loose regulations provide start-up funds, a fifteen-year authorization, and the freedom for existing private schools to convert to charter status. States with strict charter laws, such as Kansas, provide no start-up funds, allow only a three-year term before a charter school must seek a renewal, and cap the number of schools permitted.

Backers see charter schools as laboratories of innovation that bypass staid bureaucracies and satisfy the parental desire for choice. Evidence of the academic achievement of charter schools is modestly favorable, but not spectacular. Some have been forced to close due to corruption, such as embezzlement by administrators, or a failure to attract enough families or maintain a physical facility. California's largest charter school operator announced in August 2004 that it would be closing at least sixty campuses. This left ten thousand children stranded just weeks before the start of the school year.

In addition, critics worry that charter schools will balkanize public education and that they may be exploited as a way to avoid dealing with unionized teachers. They also fear that these schools may present an administrative headache to those school superintendents charged with monitoring against abuses of funds. The growth of charter schools in Washington, D.C., led the district superintendent to call for a moratorium on new charters. More than seventeen thousand D.C. public school students—nearly one in four—attend the city's fifty-one charter schools, using $140 million a year that would otherwise flow to traditional schools, several of which have closed in recent years to help balance the city's budget.[48]

To determine whether charter schools should be scaled up and duplicated throughout the country, researchers do not just want to know whether a charter's own students' test scores improve. They also want to know if the schools these children's families chose to leave are using the departures as an incentive to do better.[49] To that end, studies have been carried out. Advocates of charter schools, including the George W. Bush administration, suffered a blow in August 2006, when a long-awaited study of test scores by the U.S. Department of Education revealed that fourth graders in charter schools scored significantly lower than their peers in traditional public schools. (See Table 13-4.)

Some studies suggest that tracking students over time might present more favorable findings. Tom Loveless, director of the Brown Center on Education Policy at the Brookings Institution, conducted a 2-year study of 569 charter schools in 10 states. He found that although charter school students do score lower on state tests, over time they progress faster than students in traditional public schools. Other proponents believe that students in charter schools also score lower in part because they were farther behind to begin with in their previous, traditional schools.[50]

There are plenty of individual charter school success stories. They have been embraced by the chancellor of the nation's largest school system, that of New York City. For all of this, the jury is still out on whether the concept of charter schools will emerge as a strong force behind future school reform.

Vouchers

Considered a more radical reform than charter schools, **school vouchers** have been proposed in some form since the 1950s. The idea is to mimic government grants used in higher education by giving interested families a set amount of public money that can be used at any accredited school—public, private, or parochial (religious). Voucher enthusiasts want to provide parents with more choice, to break up the "monopoly" of the public education bureaucracy to boost competition, and, more recently, to advance the rescue of low-income black families from failing schools in low-income neighborhoods as a civil right.

SCHOOL VOUCHERS

Movement dating to the 1950s to allow taxpayer dollars to be given to families to use at whatever public, private, or parochial schools they choose.

TABLE 13-4

Charter School Scores

| | Percentage of Fourth Graders at or above Basic Level in... | | | |
| | Math | | Reading | |
	Charter Schools	Other Public Schools	Charter Schools	Other Public Schools
Gender				
Male	69	77	55	58
Female	68	75	60	65
Race				
White	84	87	73	74
Black	51	54	37	39
Hispanic	58	62	45	43
Income				
Eligible for Public Lunch	53	62	39	45
Not Eligible	81	88	72	76
Location				
Central city	58	67	50	51
Non-central City	79	80	66	66

Source: U.S. Department of Education, Institute of Education Sciences, National Center for Education Statistics, National Assessment of Educational Progress (NAEP), 2003 Reading Charter School Pilot Study, December 2004.

Opponents worry that vouchers spell the beginning of the end of society-wide efforts to maintain and improve universal public education. They note that private schools can be selective about which students they accept. In addition, the proposed amounts for vouchers are often less than half of actual tuition. In some communities, the number of available slots at area private schools sometimes is insufficient for the number of interested applicants. Voucher proponents aren't without counter-arguments, though. They assert that the programs create competition that forces public schools to improve, and that they give lower-income students opportunities they might not otherwise have.[51]

Critics also object to the potential for religious indoctrination at parochial schools. Despite these concerns, in June 2002, the U.S. Supreme Court ruled that vouchers can go to a religious school as long as the school's chief purpose is education. In other words, a school that offers a comprehensive secular curriculum, albeit with religious rituals and instructors, as opposed to a Sunday school or bible study.

For each of these reasons, vouchers generally have failed when put to voters on state ballot initiatives, including votes in Michigan and California in 2000. Since the early 1990s, however, voucher experiments have been underway at long-troubled and racially isolated schools in Cleveland, Ohio, and Milwaukee, Wisconsin. Measures of success have varied, but both programs were recently expanded. Cleveland's voucher program, which served 5,800 students during the 2005–2006 school year, was folded into Ohio EdChoice. This statewide voucher program offers fourteen thousand renewable scholarships to students attending schools considered in "academic emergency" or on "academic watch," the state's two lowest rankings for school performance.[52]

Milwaukee's program offers vouchers worth up to $6,500 to low-income families who may send their children to 1 of 125 participating private schools. The program included only secular schools to start, but in 1995 expanded to include parochial schools, a measure protected by the 2002 Supreme Court ruling. By 2006, religiously affiliated schools comprised about 70 percent of the participating schools. In 2006, Wisconsin governor Jim Doyle signed a bill to raise the number of vouchers issued annually from 15,000 to 22,500 in exchange for increased accountability, including standardized testing and accreditation.[53]

Many studies have been released that document achievement gains among students using vouchers.[54] Certainly any program that is selected by parents eager for change has an improved chance for students to gain ground. But studies by the U.S. Department of Education and by University of Illinois researchers found public and private school students perform similarly when test scores are adjusted for race and other factors, and a congressionally requested study by the Government Accountability Office of the Milwaukee and Cleveland experiments "found little or no difference in voucher and public school students' performance" in the schools of those two cities.[55]

Home Schooling

A major school reform movement gaining popularity is **home schooling**. According to a 1999 survey by the U.S. Department of Education, an estimated 850,000 students were taught at home. By 2004, that number had jumped by 29 percent to 1.1 million. This is according to the National Center for Education Statistics (NCES), a part of the U.S. Department of Education.

Home schooling champions have organized a legal defense network and a lobbying effort. They put out national publications, including *Homeschooling Today* and *Homeschooling Helper*. As the movement has grown, it has organized sports leagues, field trips, proms, and graduation ceremonies. And there are plenty of home-school success stories, including Harvard acceptances and solid scores on standardized tests.

HOME SCHOOLING

The education of children in the home; a movement to grant waivers from state truancy laws to permit parents to teach their own children.

Home schooling advocates are a diverse group, but the two main strands are fundamentalist Christians and "free-school" advocates who favor more student choice of subject matter. Parents who can make the time to home-school like the security and personal imprint they can leave on their youngsters. The NCES study found that 30 percent of those surveyed wanted the flexibility to teach moral or religious lessons. Another 31 percent cited concerns about the environment of traditional schools.

Of course, throughout the history of this country, there always have been those who have chosen to teach their children at home. The modern movement, however, really started taking off in the 1980s. State governments have accommodated home schoolers to varying degrees. Some require parents to have a bachelor's degree to home-school. Others require a curriculum to be submitted for approval, and still others give parents a choice whether to give their children a standardized test selected by the school district or to hire their own qualified evaluator.

Michael Farris, leader of the Purcellville, Virginia-based Home School Legal Defense Association, has been at the forefront of the national movement. His organization ranks states based on how tightly or loosely they regulate home schooling. States with no requirements for notifying state authorities include Idaho, Michigan, and Texas. States with low regulation include Alabama, Kentucky, and Mississippi. Most other states in the Southeast moderately regulate home schooling, whereas most states in New England regulate more intensively.[56]

Critics fear that home-schooled students miss important opportunities for social development and that many parents are not qualified to teach. They also worry that some parents isolate their children and instill them with religious prejudice. Some state and local officials consider home schooling an inconvenience. It forces them to come up with policies on home visits, gauge assessments that may be out of sync with conventional report-card grades, and wrestle with dilemmas such as whether a home-schooled student can play in the public high school band. Finally, there have been some reported cases of severe child abuse among home schoolers. These are cases that short-staffed state education departments can't always track.

For those who choose to home school their children, the rewards can be great. Christine and Paul Pressau (far left and second from left, respectively) have home schooled each of their four daughters since pre-kindergarten. Oldest daughter Tatiana (far right) graduated from Geneva College in 2004 and now works as a human resources analyst. Jacquelyn (second from right) attends college and will enter a nursing program in spring 2008. Eighteen-year-old Arielle (third from left) graduated in June 2007 and will enter college in fall 2007. Sixteen-year-old Desirée (third from right) continues to be educated at home and also through the Cedar Brook Academy in Clarksburg, Maryland, from which Tatiana, Jacquelyn, and Arielle's diplomas were issued. The academy was started in 1983 as a resource for families who home school. More than 550 students from 250 families take part in classes, sports, and other activities offered by the academy.

Can't Tell the Players without a Program: Groups that Influence Public Education

When the Texas Supreme Court struck down school funding disparities in *Edgewood Independent School District v. Kirby* (1989), it declined to specify a precise solution to the problem. Instead, it opted to launch a dialogue with legislators and education officials. In Kentucky, the state supreme court was even more activist. As previously discussed, that same year it declared the state's school system unconstitutional and not adequate to meeting "an efficient system of public schools." The court went on to lay out a set of goals and ability standards to be pursued.[57]

In both cases, judges knew that no legal ruling on the subject of education would hold sway without public support and buy-in from key stakeholders. That meant going far beyond a small elite of education officials. In Texas, for example, the Mexican-American Legal Defense and Education Fund (MALDEF) played an influential role in developing and supporting the state's new education reforms.

In Kentucky, the legislation and landmark school reform program that resulted from the state court's ruling gained ground largely because of support from such players as newspaper editorialists and a group of education and business leaders called the Prichard Committee for Academic Excellence. Such groups as these are common participants in the educational debate and are part of the following roster of the familiar players in the education dramas that unfold across the country.

Teachers' Unions

For decades, the major **teachers' unions** have been the National Education Association (NEA), which boasts 2.8 million members, and the American Federation of Teachers (AFT), reporting more than 1.3 million members as of 2006. These groups organize employees from the pre-school level to the K–12 level to the university level to form state and local affiliates. They engage in collective bargaining, lobby for resources, and seek to upgrade teacher professionalism through training and publications.

For years, the two Washington, D.C.-headquartered unions have flirted with a merger, but style differences always intervene. The AFT was quicker than the NEA to join the school reform parade, for example, by participating in creation of standards and charter schools. By the late 1990s, however, both had turned sour on the school choice movement, which they consider a threat to public education and their members' livelihoods. They're critical, too, of No Child Left Behind, with the NEA leading the charge in lawsuits challenging the federal government's administration of the law. Both unions align themselves with the Democratic Party, one reason most Republicans blame them for obstructing school reform.

TEACHERS' UNIONS

Primarily the National Education Association and the American Federation of Teachers, both headquartered in Washington, D.C.

Parents' Groups

The **National PTA**, with six million members, bills itself as the "largest volunteer child advocacy organization in the United States." For decades, this umbrella group for local parent-teacher associations and organizations was stereotyped as a klatch of moms putting on bake sales. Today, however, the PTA has school-based state and national organizations that combine to form a sophisticated lobbying and policy force. For the most part, the organization works to boost parent involvement and to encourage parent-teacher cooperation.

The PTA is under strict rules to remain nonpartisan. Despite this, occasional endorsement of state legislative candidates based on school funding commitments has gotten some locals in hot water. Other parent groups have emerged over the years to focus on narrower issues, such as the school desegregation efforts of the Mississippi-based Parents for Public Schools.

National Political Parties

For much of the latter part of the twentieth century, education was Democratic Party turf, mostly because of the Great Society legislation pushed through in the mid-1960s. The Democrats traditionally wanted to expand government spending to close the gap between affluent and low-income schools. Republicans, on the other hand, emphasized local control and social issues, such as efforts to overturn the ban on school prayer. During the Reagan administration, Republicans vowed to abolish the federal Department of Education set up by President Jimmy Carter. Many of them opposed proposals made during the mid-1990s to introduce a national standardized test. They based their protests on the need to preserve local control of schools.

By 2000, however, Texas governor George W. Bush moved the Republicans dramatically to the center of the education debate while campaigning for the Oval Office. His eventual victory in enacting the No Child Left Behind Act, which is modeled in part on the system used since the early 1990s in Texas and borrows its name from the liberal Children's Defense Fund, was attributable to support from key Democratic lawmakers.

Sen. Edward M. Kennedy, D-Mass., and Rep. George Miller, D-Calif., carry a lot of weight in their respective congressional houses, and they were able to sway others in their party to cross partisan lines. Polls soon after showed that Republicans had caught up with Democrats on the question of which party was the "education party." Republican efforts to woo Democrats on the more controversial proposals for school vouchers have been less successful. This is due in great part to the strong support Democrats depend on from anti-voucher teachers' unions and their general skepticism about market-based alternatives to government programs.

Business Groups

Corporations and small businesses have been among the most vocal in pushing for school reform. They cite what they perceive as a decline in the writing and math skills of young job applicants as industry has become more complex technologically. Business leaders, such as former IBM chief executive Louis V. Gerstener Jr., have joined with business groups, such as the Business Roundtable and the National Alliance of Business, to meet with governors, educators, and school reform activists to press for higher standards for students and teachers. In 2007, the Business Coalition for Student Achievement, led by the Business Roundtable and the U.S. Chamber of Commerce, issued recommendations to improve No Child Left Behind, including a call to focus on college and workplace readiness, and to strengthen science, math, and technology curriculums.[58]

Professional and Advocacy Groups

Within the education "establishment," each of the managerial groups—administrators, principals at the elementary and secondary levels, and school boards—have their own associations. These official decision makers usually win their jobs through a prerequisite set of academic credentials, years of experience in the classroom, and dues paid on the front lines of management.

In addition, there are research groups, such as the Washington, D.C.-based Education Trust. This organization performs research to encourage higher education to help with elementary and secondary school reforms. There are also professional development providers for teachers and school design consultants, such as Arlington, Virginia-based New American Schools, that advocate for design changes to school buildings that compliment education reform. Then there are the advocacy groups, such as the Center for Education Reform, which promotes school choice, and the Public Education Network, which organizes local funds to improve public engagement in school reform.

Finally, there are the single-issue activists, most prominent of whom are Texas textbook critics Mel and Norma Gabler. For forty years, this fundamentalist Christian couple has been the bane of the multimillion-dollar school textbook industry, taking advantage of the fact that Texas is a "bellwether" state in the intricate nationwide school textbook adoption process. Focused and persistent, the Gablers challenge books for factual errors, forcing the publishers, in some cases, to tone down discussions of such tricky topics as evolution or to emphasize abstinence in sex education lessons.[59]

Issues to Watch

As if the battles over instruction, school choice, and testing weren't enough, debates on social policy and changes in the nation's demographics are playing out in the American classroom.

Evolution and Instruction

American students' achievement in science—or lack thereof—has long been central to the United States' competition with other countries, as seen in the TIMSS results. But the average American science classroom is also central to a domestic dispute: the debate over the teaching of **intelligent design**, the idea that the universe is so complex that it must be explained by more than evolution.

Almost nowhere has the debate raged more fiercely than in Kansas, where the state board of education rewrote science standards around evolution and intelligent design three times in six years. After the board approved standards in 2005 that opened the door once again to intelligent design, the 2006 elections moved the majority of the board toward pro-evolution members, setting the state up for yet another possible revision of standards.[60]

Farther east, a federal judge in Pennsylvania struck down the teaching of intelligent design in the Dover, Pennsylvania, school system, saying that the curriculum violated the separation of church and state. That ruling led Ohio's Board of Education in early 2006 to remove its direction that high school biology classes include a critical analysis of evolution. The board's decision was not the last word on intelligent design in the Buckeye State, though. Just a few months later, it was considering a curriculum proposal that would encourage students to have "open discussion" in the classroom, which is language that critics said was meant to cast doubt on such widely accepted theories as evolution.[61]

A Growing Minority

White students consistently score better than minority students on the nation's standardized tests. In 2005, 90 percent of white fourth graders scored at or above the basic level in math on the NAEP, compared to just 68 percent of Hispanic fourth graders. Those numbers represented gains for both groups—twelve years earlier, 73 percent of white students and 33 percent of Hispanic students scored at or above average—but the improvements still are not enough to meet the demands of No Child Left Behind, which requires that schools close this cultural and ethnic performance gap.[62]

That challenge looms large, given both NCLB's tight timeframe and the direction of the nation's demographics. Four in ten public school students are members of a minority group, including 19 percent Hispanic. The U.S.

INTELLIGENT DESIGN
The theory that certain features of the universe and of living things are best explained by an intelligent cause, not an undirected process such as evolution.

In Michigan's Detroit school district, children of color constitute 97 percent of the enrollments.

Census Bureau estimates that by 2020, almost half of all school-age children will be children of color—no longer minorities. Nearly one in four students will be Hispanic.

The performance gap at the elementary and middle school levels trickles upward. A 2001 report by researchers at Arizona State University revealed that in 2000, Hispanics earned just 12 percent of the bachelor's degrees earned statewide, despite comprising a quarter of the state's population. In 2004, some of the same researchers took a closer look at Arizona's schools, 37 percent of which had enrollments of Hispanic students of 50 percent or higher. They found that schools with high percentages of minority or poor student populations were not doomed to failure. A handful, in fact, far outperformed other schools across the state. The most successful schools used data extensively—not just annual data, as NCLB directs, but monthly, weekly, and even daily data to track achievement per classroom, teacher, and student.[63]

Conclusion

Although each state has its own internal timeline for success, No Child Left Behind requires that all schools bring every single student to proficiency by the 2013–2014 school year. Until that day comes, it is a safe bet that the debates over performance, accountability, funding, and teacher quality will continue to passionately invoke lofty themes of democracy and civic ideals. Efforts at strengthening the federal role in public education will continue to run up against a centuries-old tradition of local control. Advocates of increased funding targeted at the poor will still lock horns with those who stress reforms in pedagogy and new incentives.

If Horace Mann is watching from school-reformers' heaven, he probably isn't surprised that ancient debates over school reforms remain unsettled. The governance system of the U.S. public education system is rooted in local control and wide variations in state and community traditions. This guarantees that it always will be characterized by diverse approaches and active political maneuvering. The quest for the ideal school continues to be more art than science. The results? They are as glorious—and as messy—as democracy itself.

Key Concepts

accreditation (p. 469)

back to basics (p. 468)

capital outlays (p. 476)

charter schools (p. 492)

common school (p. 467)

criterion referenced tests (p. 480)

departments of education (p. 468)

Elementary and Secondary Education
   Act (p. 485)

general equivalency degree (GED) program
   (p. 483)

Goals 2000 (p. 484)

high-stakes standardized testing (p. 468)

home schooling (p. 495)

intelligent design (p. 500)

Kentucky Education Reform Act (p. 484)

local education agencies (LEAs) (p. 469)

National Assessment of Educational Progress
   (NAEP) (p. 481)

National PTA (p. 498)

No Child Left Behind Act (NCLB) (p. 466)

norm referenced tests (p. 480)

school boards (p. 468)

school districts (p. 469)

school vouchers (p. 493)

site-based management (p. 484)

standards (p. 468)

standards movement (p. 484)

state board of education (p. 467)

successful schools model (p. 477)

teacher licensure procedures (p. 469)

teachers' unions (p. 497)

Trends in International Mathematics and
   Sciences Study (TIMSS) (p. 481)

Suggested Readings

Boswell, Matthew H. *Courts as Catalysts: State Supreme Courts and Public School Finance Equity.* Albany, N.Y.: State University of New York Press, 2001. Examines the effectiveness of state supreme courts in Kentucky, North Dakota, and Texas in achieving funding equity between rich and poor public school districts.

Rothman, Robert. *Measuring Up: Standards, Assessment, and School Reform.* San Francisco: Jossey-Bass, 1995. Examines the shift in thinking about testing, including a look at assessment programs in California, Colorado, Kentucky, and Vermont. Also explores the problems reformers encounter.

Rothstein, Richard. *The Way We Were?: The Myths and Realities of America's Student Achievement.* New York: Century Foundation, 1998. Provides a counter-argument to the claim that education in the United States is bad and getting worse.

Smith, Kevin. *The Ideology of Education: The Commonwealth, the Market, and America's Schools.* Albany, N.Y.: State University of New York Press, 2003. The author examines the ideological underpinnings of school choice and other market-based reforms in education.

Tyack, David, and Larry Cuban. *Tinkering toward Utopia: A Century of Public School Reform.* Cambridge: Harvard University Press, 1995. Explores some of the basic questions of education reform.

Suggested Web Sites

www.aasa.org. Web site of the American Association of School Administrators. Founded in 1865, AASA has more than thirteen thousand members worldwide. Its mission is to support and develop individuals dedicated to the highest quality public education for all children.

www.aft.org. Web site of the American Federation of Teachers, which represents the economic, social, and professional interests of classroom teachers. The AFT has more than 3,000 local affiliates nationwide, 43 state affiliates, and more than 1.3 million members.

www.cep-dc.org. Web site of the Center on Education Policy, a national, independent advocate for more effective public schools.

www.charterfriends.org. Website of the Charter Friends National Network, which has helped start charter support organizations in states that are passing and strengthening charter school laws.

www.ed.gov. Web site of the U.S. Department of Education, which oversees the federal government's contributions to public education.

www.edexcellence.net. The Web site of the Thomas B. Fordham Foundation, the mission of which is to advance understanding and acceptance of effective reform strategies in primary and secondary education.

www.edreform.com. Web site of the Center for Education Reform, a national organization dedicated to the promotion of more choices in education and more rigorous education programs.

www.edweek.org. The Web site of *Education Week,* a weekly publication devoted to primary and secondary education and funded by Editorial Projects in Education. Education Week publishes *Quality Counts,* an annual evaluation of K–12 education in all fifty states.

www.nea.org. Web site of the National Education Association, which is dedicated to advancing public education. The organization has 2.8 million members at every level of education, from preschool to university graduate programs, and affiliates in every state, as well as in more than thirteen thousand local communities across the United States.

www.nsba.org. Web site of the National School Boards Association, a not-for-profit federation of state associations of school boards across the United States.

CHAPTER 14

Crime and Punishment

Just because these women got their cake and were allowed to eat it too doesn't mean that crime pays. In fact, these female chain gang members were headed back to their work details in downtown Phoenix, Arizona, in August 1998. All are residents of Maricopa County, Arizona, sheriff Joe Arpaio's "Tent City." Arpaio opened the outdoor tent compound in 1994 as an inexpensive way to battle prison overcrowding. About 185,000 individuals have been incarcerated in the facility since then. In 2004, the facility housed nearly two thousand men and women and there are plans to expand. Supporters laud Arpaio as a criminal justice hero for his creative strategy. Critics say his tactics are too harsh.

14

Why did different types of policing develop in
the United States?

Why has creative problem solving become so important
to law enforcement?

How does political culture affect law enforcement in
the different states and localities?

Think back for a moment and consider this question: Over the past decade or two, did state or local governments do anything really notable? Something to improve the lives of everyone in the country in an unquestionably good way?

Anything come to mind? No? If not, then criminologist George Kelling thinks you're missing something pretty big. "The most impressive achievement of city governance during the urban renewal of the 1990s," writes Kelling, "was the enormous decline in crime."[1] The numbers speak for themselves. In 1990 alone, 23,438 people were murdered in the United States. By 2000, that number had fallen to 15,586—and this at a time when the population of the country as a whole grew by 40 million people.[2]

Overall, violent crime rates declined to less than half that of 1973. Property crimes, robbery, burglary, and auto theft, which make up 75 percent of total crimes committed, fell by a similar amount. The lives, trauma, and money saved by this crime reduction are immense. New York City alone experienced approximately sixty thousand fewer crimes than it would have if crime rates had not declined.[3]

This crime drop of the mid-1990s to late 1990s was one of the most welcome developments of the past decade, and state and local officials and law enforcement were quick to take the credit. But is it really their accomplishment to boast about? To many, including Kelling, the answer is clearly yes. They credit the crime reduction to a revolution in policing. Further reductions are possible, advocates believe, as more police departments adopt the new methods. Given that the vast majority of law enforcement officers in the United States work for local police departments, county sheriffs' offices, and state law enforcement agencies, it might seem reasonable to credit local and state governments with this improvement.

However, not all criminologists are applauding. Many doubt that improved law enforcement had much at all to do with the crime decline. University of Cincinnati criminologist John Eck summed up the resurgent conventional wisdom, "The bottom line is that one can't really give a lot of credence to the strong statement about the police having a huge *independent* role in reducing crime, particularly homicide."[4] In the view of Eck and other criminologists, crime rates are primarily the function of larger societal trends like the changing nature of the drug market, changing demographics, improved economic conditions, and increased incarceration rates. Still other researchers attribute the crime drop to such factors as improved trauma procedures in hospital emergency rooms and even legalized abortion.[5] And many criminologists believe that the crime drop is over and that rising crime rates, such as those seen between 2004 and 2005, will be the norm for the future.

For anyone new to the field, the wide divergence in opinions about what happened, what works, and what is likely to occur in law enforcement may be startling. Welcome to the fractious world of the criminal justice system. This chapter is about the U.S. criminal justice system, which for most Americans translates to their local police departments and their state prison systems. It explores not just how the system works but also whether it works. Can police reduce crime? Do tougher penalties and longer jail terms deter criminals? Do Americans as a society have or want to have a penal system that emphasizes punishment? Or one that stresses correction instead?

The chapter also explores how states and localities approach solutions to crime differently. Should we be concerned that 13 percent of African American males currently cannot vote because of state laws that penalize criminal activity? Is capital punishment fair or racially biased? Are antidrug laws too tough? Why is crime so much higher in some cities and states than in others? How can successful crime reduction strategies be replicated in other areas? These questions are not only the basis for a tour of the criminal justice system, they also help explore the causes of crime in a world where the connections between crime and punishment are often uncertain and unclear.

Gangs, guns, murder, drugs, and hard time are just some of what this chapter examines. Exploration of the criminal justice system also offers an opportunity to investigate our society's most basic values. After all, crime is about the transgression of a society's ethical norms, and punishment is about the enforced adherence to them. Understanding how a society disciplines itself and punishes people also provides insights into the nature and limits of state power, into the society's conception of justice, and ultimately, into the nature of democracy itself.

Private Wrongs, Public Justice

Americans are fascinated with crime. Books about private eyes, detectives, and the courts regularly top the best-seller lists. Television shows about cops top the Nielsen charts. In fact, anyone who watches TV has a pretty good idea of how the criminal justice system in the United States works: the police enforce the law and make arrests.

However, they do not have the power to punish. That authority rests with the state. District attorneys initiate prosecutions. Elected at the county level—except in Alaska, Connecticut, and New Jersey, where they are appointed by the governor—these individuals represent the state's interests in a case. Most of the time, the defendant is represented by either a defense

These days the local news is filled with stories of unexpected crimes happening in unexpected places and involving unexpected individuals. Pure sensationalism? Not quite. While alarming, those reports actually do reflect the fact that while crime rates have declined in cities, they are on the rise in suburban areas. Alda Larios lives in the quiet neighborhood of South Miami, Florida. In January 2004, one of her children's eleven-year-old playmates and her mother were arrested for the dealing and possession of heroin.

attorney or a public defender and agrees to a plea bargain without ever going to trial.

If a case does go to trial, a jury decides the guilt or innocence of the accused. If the accused is found guilty—and most are—then a circuit judge metes out a penalty in accordance with relevant law. Judges may be appointed or elected, depending on the state, but their responsibilities are the same in this situation. Defendants who believe they received an unfair trial may file an appeal request with an appeals court or even with the state supreme court.

That is the U.S. criminal justice system—as seen on *CSI* or *Law and Order*. It's a pretty accurate picture, as far as it goes. The problem is, it doesn't go very far. In fact, Americans' very familiarity with the system obscures some basic facts about it. Take, for instance, the fact that punishment is a public function at all.

One of the most (pardon the pun) arresting features of the U.S. criminal justice system is that the state initiates and dispenses punishment for such crimes as homicide, assault, robbery, and burglary. To Americans, this seems entirely natural. People in the United States instinctively note the differences between civil and criminal affairs. Civil disputes are private. Your neighbors knock down your fence and then refuse to put it back up or pay to repair it. You've never much liked them, so you decide to sue. The state offers a forum for the dispute—the court—and carries out the penalty, but the dispute is between two private individuals and their lawyers, and the penalty is a fine. No one expects the county district attorney to initiate criminal proceedings against your neighbors. No matter how precious your fence or how guilty your neighbors, you cannot lock them away. In short, a civil offense is a crime against an individual.

Criminal offenses are thought of in an entirely different way. These are offenses not just against an individual, but also against society itself. As a result, the state initiates the punishment—and the punishment can be severe. It can take the form of imprisonment or **probation**. Cruel and unusual punishment, such as torture, may not be allowed, but for the most serious offenses, death is still an option.

When you stop to think about it, however, the distinction between civil and criminal cases is not really an obvious one at all. It's all well and good to say that the guy who pulls a gun on you, takes your wallet, and whacks you upside the head has committed a crime against "the public order." Yet you might be forgiven for thinking that what he really has done is commit

PROBATION

Supervised punishment in the community.

Governing States and Localities

a crime against *you*. If you happen to actually know the guy who mugged you, it might seem natural, just, and appropriate for you to try to punish him. If he hurts you, you might want to hurt him. As it says in the Book of Deuteronomy, "An eye for an eye, a tooth for a tooth, a hand for a hand, a foot for a foot."

A look at the historical record reveals something interesting—the beliefs that Americans see as natural are, in fact, not natural at all. For most of human history, from ancient Greece to monarchical Europe, private prosecution was the norm.[6] In medieval Britain, the attorney general initiated cases only for the king. Justices of the peace began prosecutions only when there was no private individual to initiate punishment.

Until comparatively recently, governments of most nations simply set the rules for how offended parties should pursue justice. Their role was essentially that of umpire. Governments had to fight long and hard to establish that they had the *exclusive* right to punish wrongdoers.[7] A key figure in this transference of the right of retaliation from the wronged party to the state was the public prosecutor. For reasons that historians still do not fully understand, public prosecutors first appeared in North America—in Great Britain's Atlantic colonies.

On the whole, the state's successful monopoly on punishment has brought enormous benefits to the United States. Conflicts like those between the Hatfields and McCoys notwithstanding, the nation is essentially free of ongoing feuds or vendettas. However, there are also drawbacks to such efforts to monopolize authority. Today, for instance, state and local governments in forty-eight states actively conceal what may be the greatest power U.S. citizens enjoy.

The feud between the Hatfields of West Virginia and the McCoys of Kentucky would come to involve the U.S. Supreme Court and the National Guard before the families agreed to end the conflict in 1891.

Common Law, Sovereign Power

The criminal justice system in the United States is rooted in the tradition of English **common law**. Forty-nine states operate within this common law tradition. (The exception is Louisiana. As a former French colony, the state instead operates under the Napoleonic code. Emperor Napoleon I put forth this body of law in the early nineteenth century.) The common law tradition makes the U.S. system quite unlike the legal systems of most other countries. In most of the world, law is enacted by a single sovereign power, be that a legislature, a monarch, or some other combination.

This is partially true in the United States as well, of course. The nation is a federation in which the federal government and the state governments are both sovereign. Congress and state legislatures both make laws—as do county and city governments—at the discretion of the state. Citizens must obey these laws or risk punishment. However, lawmakers are not the only source of laws. Americans are governed by a mixture of formal—or statute—law

COMMON LAW

Law composed of judges' legal opinions that reflects community practices and evolves over time.

and case—or common—law. The common law is made up of legal opinions written by judges that recognize commonly accepted community practices and evolves gradually over time as a community's ideas change.

One of American society's most important inheritances from the common law tradition is the institution of the jury. Serving on a jury is *the* defining act of citizenship. It is just about the only thing every citizen must do. (Men between the ages of eighteen and twenty-five must also register with the Selective Service in the event that the government needs to reinstitute the draft.) In most states, ignoring a jury summons is a crime. Failing to appear for jury duty without being properly exempted constitutes contempt of court and may present a somewhat less appealing opportunity to experience the criminal justice system, such as fines or even imprisonment. Unless you commit a crime or have the misfortune of being one of the roughly five million people who fall victim to a crime every year, serving on a jury probably will be your primary mode of interaction with the criminal justice system.[8]

> Americans are governed by a mixture of formal—or statute—law and case—or common—law. The common law is made up of legal opinions written by judges that recognize commonly accepted community practices and evolves gradually over time as a community's ideas change.

As discussed in Chapter 8, there are two types of juries. In most states east of the Mississippi River, a grand jury determines whether there is sufficient evidence for the state to prosecute someone for a crime. In states west of the Mississippi, district attorneys usually have the authority to take someone to trial on their own. Presented with a less clear instance of wrongdoing, a prosecutor also may impanel an investigative grand jury to study the evidence and determine exactly who should be targeted for prosecution. Once a grand jury or the district attorney has indicted an individual, another trial begins and another jury is formed to hear the case.

So what is the role of a juror? Most are given clear instructions by the presiding judge. The word **verdict** comes from the Latin phrase *vera dicere,* "to speak the truth." Jurors usually are told that their role is to determine exactly what the truth of a case is. They are to apply the law, regardless of whether they personally agree with it or not. As a result, the role of the juror often is that of a cog—albeit a very important one—in the criminal justice machine.

VERDICT
A jury's finding in a trial.

This official story conceals the fact that the role of jurors historically has not been limited to deciding whether the prosecutor's charges are true or not and delivering a verdict. Since the seventeenth century, jurors, like judges, also have enjoyed the legal right to set aside laws. (See on page 510.) The effort to limit juries to mere fact-finding bodies is part of an ongoing and largely hidden struggle between the state and the citizenry over who should wield the power to punish.

The jury system is not the only inheritance left to the United States by the British legal system. Many of the other institutions that characterize the

U.S. criminal justice system have their roots in the English justice system as well. County sheriffs are the most notable example. More than one thousand years old, the office of sheriff is the oldest law enforcement office within the common law system. The King of England appointed a representative called a "reeve" to act on behalf of the King in each shire or county. The "shire reeve," or King's representative, became the "sheriff" as the English language changed. These days, sheriffs remain the primary law enforcement official in most communities.

The Texas Rangers are the nation's oldest law enforcement agency, unofficially organized in 1823 and formally created in 1835.

Together with state law enforcement agencies like the highway patrol, county sheriffs make up the vast bulk of law enforcement capacity in the United States. In most states, each law enforcement agency focuses on maintaining order in a specific geographic area, although agencies frequently do cooperate.

The Purpose of Punishment

The criminal justice system of nearly every state comes out of the same English common law tradition. As a result, most states share an idea of what is permitted and what is a crime. The ancient Greeks may have tolerated slavery while harshly cracking down on the crime of hubris—not knowing your place in society—but even Minnesota and Mississippi more or less agree on what constitutes a crime these days.

This is much less true of punishment, however. Here the differences among the states become more evident. The Deep South, for instance, imprisons people at a much higher rate than other parts of the country. (See Map 14-1.) In one sense, this is not surprising. Different states and localities do have very different political cultures. It should come as no shock that they define some crimes differently and punish them differently.

Still, efforts to better understand this dynamic have produced some interesting findings. Studies have shown that the percentage of African American residents in a state's population correlates closely with the severity of penalties. The more black residents a state has, the tougher its laws tend to be.[9] Social scientists question the degree to which what is supposed to be an objective, color-blind criminal justice system—one that is administered largely by whites—systematically disadvantages blacks.[10]

The severity of punishment also is tied closely to the political parties. States with more Democratic legislators tend to have less severe penalties than states with more Republican legislators. Not surprisingly, election years tend to produce calls for tough new penalties as well.[11] The fairness and effectiveness of these penalties is a hotly debated issue that is taken up later in this chapter.

Cultural differences cannot be dismissed when studying criminal justice at the state and local levels. They play an important role in explaining why states approach crime differently. New England, with its Puritan heritage,

A Difference that Makes a Difference:
Jury Power: What the Courts Don't Want You to Know

The origins of the modern jury go back to the early 1200s, when the English crown enlisted the most notable men in local communities across England into administrative divisions called "hundreds." Twice a year, the king's circuit court judges would meet with these hundreds of notable individuals and ask them to identify all of the miscreants in each village who had violated the king's peace. Fines and other forms of punishment were allotted accordingly.

By the fourteenth century, it had become clear that this approach was subject to abuse. As a result, it was decided that jury verdicts had to be unanimous. The presiding judge could punish juries that could not come to an agreement. Despite the strong arming, the right to issue a verdict remained firmly in the hands of the local juries.[a]

In the mid-sixteenth century, the criminal justice system took a big step toward law and order as it is known today when Queen Mary decreed that henceforth justices of the peace had the power to investigate accusations, take statements from the accused and the accuser, and indict potential criminals. Justices of the peace were then to present their findings to the jury. They even could instruct the jury on how to proceed. In short, the state was asserting ever more control over the way the criminal justice system worked.

But sometimes, juries refused to play along. This was particularly true when it came to enforcing laws about religion. In 1670 William Penn, a Quaker, was brought to trial for illegally preaching to the public. Under English law, only state-sanctioned Anglican priests could preach in public. Penn admitted that he had broken the law, but he argued that the law itself was illegal. He asked the jury to acquit him. It did, despite instructions from the presiding judge to enforce the law.

The Crown was profoundly displeased, for in a sense the jury's challenge raised a very fundamental issue: Who really held sovereign power? When a jury could set aside laws made by the Queen in Parliament, the clear implication was that the jury, not the government, was the ultimate power in society. To demonstrate where power really lay, all twelve jury members were fined.

Juryman Bushel, however, refused to pay. His appeal went to the court of Chief Justice Robert Vaughan, who ruled in favor of the stubborn juror. He rejected the practice of penalizing jurors for ruling in defiance of the law, and his opinion established something remarkable. Juries truly became the final authority in English society. It had been rather vague until that moment, which marked a turning point in judicial

has always been a region that took a strong interest in saving people's souls, whether they wanted saving or not. During the nineteenth century, it was the center of the national abolitionist movement. The region exported missionaries, built universities, and fostered the temperance movement. It also sent hundreds of thousands of emigrants west, where they settled much of the Upper Midwest and Pacific Northwest. As a result, these regions share many cultural similarities. To use the typology of the political scientist Daniel Elazar, they all have a strong moralistic streak.[12]

Given this cultural background, it should be evident why New Englanders and their descendants and other moralistic groups, such as Quakers, view punishment in a certain light. By the early nineteenth century, a growing number of people in the Northeast were turning against the viewpoint

history. Today, the practice whereby juries set aside laws or penalties they disagree with is known as jury nullification. The right to a trial by jury is one of the basic constitutional rights, enshrined in the Sixth Amendment of the U.S. Constitution.

William Penn went on to establish the colony of Pennsylvania in North America. Like Penn, jury nullification also quickly jumped across the Atlantic. In the tumultuous years leading up to the Revolutionary War, American juries repeatedly refused to convict John Hancock and other agitators who were brought to trial on charges of smuggling. Their activities were viewed as principled acts of defiance rather than as crimes. During the 1850s, juries in the North regularly refused to enforce the Fugitive Slave Act, which had been passed at the insistence of the South in 1850 and made it illegal for anyone to assist a runaway slave.[b] Southern anger at Northern "lawlessness" and Northern anger at Southern "overreach" became major issues of contention in the years leading up to the Civil War.

The practice of jury nullification and the spirit of civil disobedience that inspired it also inspired other, less savory actions. For instance, in the 1950s and 1960s, many white juries in the South would not convict citizens who assaulted and sometimes killed civil rights workers. The federal government responded by enacting new guidelines for jury selection that made juries more representative of the community as a whole. Women, minorities, and poor whites began to sit on juries after centuries of nonrepresentation.

Despite the important role that jury nullification has played, no government in the United States is keen on letting folks know about it. Forty-eight states bar defense lawyers and judges from even mentioning that jurors may set aside a law. Indiana and Maryland are the exceptions. As in the days of Juryman Bushel, the state remains uneasy about the discretion that juries enjoy.

Does the fact that jurors can find whatever they want mean that they should? Not necessarily. Chief Justice Vaughan upheld the right of an English jury to reject laws promulgated by a thoroughly undemocratic monarchical government. In contrast, the United States today is a democracy in which nearly every adult citizen has the right to vote. Today, jury nullification can be seen as a profoundly undemocratic act. After all, laws are passed by democratically elected bodies. However, it is also a right that jurors can continue to enjoy it. It may be a secret, but under the U.S. system of law, the jury is still sovereign.

[a] Danielle S. Allen, *The World of Prometheus: The Politics of Punishing in Democratic Athens* (Princeton: Princeton University Press, 1999), 7.
[b] Ibid., 5–6.

that painful punishments deterred crime and were fitting "just desserts" for criminal activity. Instead, they embraced a new idea—protecting society while rehabilitating criminals.

A new kind of institution soon spread across the landscape—the penitentiary. Unlike prisons, penitentiaries were designed for correction, not for punishment. The most famous penitentiary in early America was located in Philadelphia. Eastern State Penitentiary was designed to force criminals to face their consciences. It operated under a system of maximum solitary confinement. The facility went to extremes to achieve its goal. For example, until 1903, inmates were required to wear face masks when they left their cells. An unfortunate side effect of this "reform" was that many inmates, faced with such extreme isolation, suffered mental breakdowns.[13] It would

MAP 14-1 Incarceration Rates per 100,000 Population, 2004

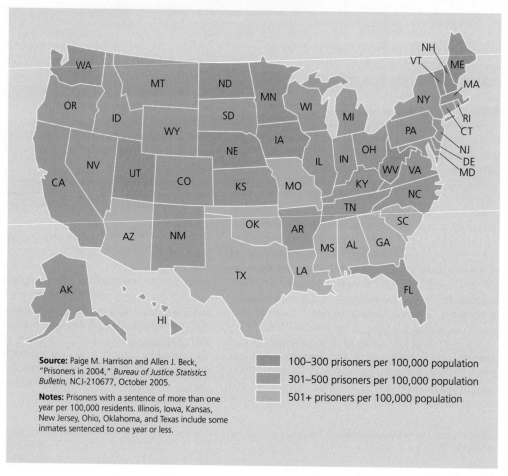

Source: Paige M. Harrison and Allen J. Beck, "Prisoners in 2004," *Bureau of Justice Statistics Bulletin*, NCJ-210677, October 2005.

Notes: Prisoners with a sentence of more than one year per 100,000 residents. Illinois, Iowa, Kansas, New Jersey, Ohio, Oklahoma, and Texas include some inmates sentenced to one year or less.

100–300 prisoners per 100,000 population

301–500 prisoners per 100,000 population

501+ prisoners per 100,000 population

not be the last well-intentioned, but ultimately unsuccessful criminological reform.

Of course, correction and penance are not the only purposes a criminal justice system serves. There is also deterrence, incapacitation, and even vengeance. The debate over the proper purpose of punishment is very old. Different societies have addressed it in different ways at different times. Three centuries before the birth of Christ, in ancient Athens, public punishment was administered to salve the wounds and ease the anger of the injured party. The philosopher Socrates was the first Athenian to argue that public punishment should aim at correcting the deficiencies of the criminal and not just at revenge. For his efforts, Socrates eventually was tried and sentenced to die by drinking poison hemlock for "corrupting youths" and for heresy.

Here in the United States, punishments also have changed to reflect evolving political cultures. To Pennsylvania Quakers, accustomed to silent contemplation, forcing inmates to confront their misdeeds in silent isolation was a natural idea. In the traditionalistic Deep South, governments chose another model of correction. Facilities like Parchman Farms in Mississippi and Angola Prison in Louisiana were organized as working plantations until well into the twentieth century. For their overwhelmingly African American inmate populations, the similarities to antebellum slavery were unmistakable.[14] Different histories and cultures produced very different institutions. Nonetheless, reformers believed that correction, not punishment, was the future. Then came the 1960s.

New Freedoms, New Fears

The 1960s was a decade of extremes. Its early years saw the birth of arguably the two most significant social movements of recent times—the civil rights movement and the modern feminist movement. Congress started to dismantle the Jim Crow laws that states had erected during the 1890s. Federal monitors were placed at polling stations throughout the South. Housing and real estate discrimination were outlawed. Women, who identified themselves as feminists, persuaded both Congress and most state legislatures to outlaw the practice of paying women less than men who performed the same job.[15]

Yet despite these accomplishments, the decade ended in a social inferno. A wave of riots nearly snuffed the life out of several inner city neighborhoods, jump-started the move to the suburbs, and ushered in a new era focused largely on public safety issues. The first such urban disturbance occurred in the summer of 1964 in the historically African American neighborhood of Harlem in New York City. The event that triggered it all was the police shooting of a fifteen-year-old African American boy.

The shooting tapped into a widespread belief that law enforcement in minority neighborhoods was arbitrary, ineffective, and sometimes brutal. One year later, a police stop in the Los Angeles neighborhood of Watts set off riots that lasted six days, cost thirty-nine people their lives, and caused hundreds of millions of dollars in damages. In the summer of 1967, large swaths of Newark, New Jersey, and Detroit, Michigan, went up in flames.

Then, on April 4, 1968, Martin Luther King Jr. was assassinated in Memphis, Tennessee. Within days of King's death, Washington, D.C., Chicago, Illinois, and many other cities were torn apart by riots. By one estimate, 329 "important" racial disturbances took place in 257 cities between 1965 and 1968. The result was nearly three hundred deaths, eight thousand injuries, sixty thousand arrests, and hundreds of millions of dollars in property losses.[16] The decade-long increase in crime showed no sign of stopping.

The riots that swept the Watts neighborhood of Los Angeles in August 1965 confirmed the beliefs of many nationwide that the law enforcement system needed an overhaul. In a spiral of violence, a police action started a retaliatory backlash from blacks that caused further violence on the part of law enforcement. Nearly four thousand people, like the young man in this picture, were arrested for looting and destruction of property.

Confronted by the specter of race riots, most social scientists concluded that racism and inequality were the real fuel behind violence in urban America. These experts argued that, far from solving the problem, the police actually inflamed it on occasion with discriminatory and sometimes violent misconduct. The idea that better policing might be an appropriate response to the riots and rising crime rates was largely dismissed.

To support the belief that the police had little to do with the crime rate, researchers pointed to a decade of studies that documented what police actually did on the job. These seemed to show that the answer was, well, not much. Police officers spent most of their time walking around, talking to people, and occasionally mediating disputes. They did little actual crime fighting. Social scientists suggested that cities should look for other solutions that did not involve law enforcement. Programs to address inner-city poverty and a society-wide effort to reduce income inequality were the solutions.

Federal money began to flow to neighborhood community groups, with few apparent results. One possible reason for this is that all of this funding was going to sometimes erratic community groups that were primarily interested in advocacy. This "me first" attitude did not accomplish much. Another reason for the lack of success was that many mayors resented the fact that federal money was flowing to someone other than them. The result was dissension and not much else.

No massive redistribution of income from wealthy Americans to poor Americans was ever tried. It is impossible to know if such a large-scale move would have worked. Empowering neighborhood groups did not. Crime continued to rise throughout the 1970s. (See Figure 14-1.) In many U.S. cities, there was a belief that authority was collapsing and anarchy was at hand. Nowhere was this sense of imminent disaster more apparent than in New York.

On the evening of July 13, 1977, lightning strikes, coupled with a Con Edison repair mistake, plunged the city into darkness. In many neighborhoods, riots and looting broke out. Thousands of fires were set. Although the police ultimately arrested more than three thousand people, much of the city experienced what *Time* magazine described as "a night of terror." [17] The country was entering a world of fear that would last for several decades.

FIGURE 14-1 The Rise and Fall of Crime Rates: Aggravated Assault, Robbery, and Homicide Rates per 100,000 Residents, 1960–2004

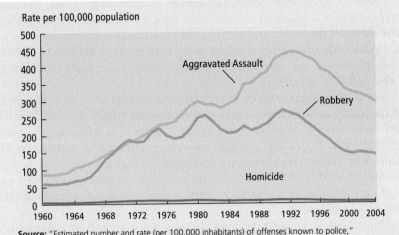

Source: "Estimated number and rate (per 100,000 inhabitants) of offenses known to police," *Sourcebook of Criminal Justice Statistics Online*. www.albany.edu/sourcebook/pef/t31062004.pdf (accessed October 10, 2006).

The War on Drugs

As policymakers cast about for a way to make sense of the growing crime problem in the United States, one problem in particular stood out—illegal drugs. By 1978, one-third of all kids ages twelve to seventeen admitted to having tried an illegal drug.[18] In the country's inner cities, heroin usage was a particular problem. Many government officials first viewed the upsurge in drug use as a public health issue. However, as a strong link between illegal drug use and crime became clear, most turned to the criminal justice system for solutions.

Faced with a seemingly unstoppable rise in violence, more and more cities responded by increasing the penalties for dealing and possessing drugs. Nelson Rockefeller, the liberal Republican governor of New York State, led the way. In 1973, Rockefeller and the New York state legislature agreed to impose new drug laws that were among the toughest in the nation. Suddenly, anyone found in possession of four or more ounces of a narcotic like heroin or cocaine faced the likelihood of a *mandatory* fifteen-year prison sentence. Selling as little as two ounces of the same narcotic could result in similar penalties. The hope was that such harsh penalties would drive up prices and deter potential users. New York's strategy was an application of **deterrence theory,** the belief that if the punishment is severe enough, it will keep people from committing the crime.

Other states and many cities quickly followed suit. State legislatures upped the penalties for the possession of illegal narcotics. Local and

DETERRENCE THEORY

A theory advanced by criminologists that harsh penalties will deter people from committing crimes.

county law enforcement officers focused their resources on catching dealers.[19]

However, sometimes efforts did seem to be at cross-purposes. The same year Governor Rockefeller and the New York state legislature created tough new penalties for heroin and cocaine, they essentially decriminalized the use and possession of small portions of marijuana. In New York today, possession of less than eight ounces of marijuana typically leads to a small fine for a first-time offender.[20]

By contrast, in the state of Arkansas, possession of more than one ounce of marijuana can open you up to prosecution on felony charges. Penalties can range from four years to ten years in prison. In Montana, first-time offenders can face a life sentence for selling a pound of marijuana. The maximum penalty for selling ten thousand pounds of marijuana is three years in New Mexico.[21] Why such wide variations in penalties? At least part of the answer can be traced back to the differing political cultures of these states.

Unfortunately, toughening laws did not work as well as policymakers hoped. Efforts to deter drug use and dealing by setting draconian penalties probably did drive up prices somewhat. Higher prices probably stopped at least some casual users from experimenting with illegal drugs. However, for the hard-core user, the "high" of heroin or the rush of cocaine was worth the fairly long-shot chance of a stint in prison.[22]

All in all, the tough new penalties directed against drug users had a minor effect at best on drug use. What they did succeed in doing is putting a lot more people in jail. In 1973, New York State incarcerated approximately ten thousand people. By 1980, that number had reached twenty thousand. To many, it seemed that things could hardly get worse. By the mid-1980s, they were.

Crack Cocaine

In the early 1980s, intrepid drug dealers discovered that they could add baking soda and water to high-quality powder cocaine and bake up small rocks. These rocks could be smoked in homemade pipes. Nicknamed "crack," for the crackling sound the rocks made when broken, it could be bagged and sold for as little as $5. Cocaine had been a "yuppie" drug available only to those with the right connections and the right amount of cash. Now it could be bought for a week's allowance.

Crack delivered a potent high at a bargain price. As a result, it quickly found users—with devastating results. Many heroin addicts managed to maintain functioning lives while also indulging their habit. That drug provides a comparatively gentle high. Crack was different. Highly concentrated, the craving it created in most users was so intense that they would do almost anything to get more. Children were abandoned. Prostitution was

Policy in Practice:
Is It Time to Admit Defeat in the War on Drugs?

Listen to the nightly news or read the daily paper and it's easy to conclude that the "war on drugs" has been something of a disaster. Billions of dollars spent and tens of thousands of Americans in prison, and yet drug usage remains constant. The price of drugs actually has gone down. So is it time to raise the white flag and do something different?

Most criminologists would say, yes, it is time to do something different. However, few see the most commonly proposed solution—legalization—as a good answer. The problem with legalizing drugs is who uses them. Basically, it is a disproportionate number of young people who do. The number of eighth-grade students who report using marijuana within the last year nearly doubled between 1991 and 2005. Use among high school seniors rose 40 percent.

Even if drugs are legalized, these are not the people society wants using drugs, just as it currently does not want teenagers to smoke cigarettes. So most likely, even if most narcotics were legalized, say, for people twenty-one years old and up, there would still be a serious illegal drug problem. Which leads University of Cal-

ifornia, Los Angeles, criminologist Mark Kleiman to this opinion about legalizing marijuana:

My view is that the risks [related to cannabis use] are substantially greater than most of my well-educated boomer friends believe. Taking the entire population of people who have used cannabis at least five times, the risk in that group of becoming a heavy daily cannabis user for a period of at least months is something like one in nine. . .

That seems a strong enough reason to oppose the legalization of marijuana on any commercial basis. Think about how aggressively tobacco and alcohol already are marketed. Imagine what big business could do with legalized marijuana.

The federal government hasn't moved toward legalization, instead using the Office of National Drug Control Policy (ONDCP) to aggressively market an anti-drug message through print advertising and television and radio spots. At the end of 2006, the campaigns could claim some success: in 2005, fewer eighth-grade, tenth-grade and twelfth-grade students had used marijuana in the last year.

Sources: Mark Kleiman, "Revenge of the Killer Weed," www.markarkleiman.com, October 9, 2002 (accessed December 11, 2003); Lloyd D. Johnston, Patrick M. O'Malley, Jerald G. Bachman, and John E. Schulenberg, "Monitoring the Future National Results on Adolescent Drug Use, Overview of Key Findings, 2005," U.S. Department of Health and Human Services, National Institute on Drug Abuse, www.monitoringthefuture.org/pubs/monographs/overview2005.pdf (accessed April 10, 2007); and "Teen Drug Use Continues Down in 2006, Particularly among Older Teens; but Use of Prescription-type Drugs Remains High," University of Michigan News Service, December 21, 2006, www.monitoringthefuture.org/pressreleases/06drugpr.pdf (accessed April 10, 2007).

embraced. Condemned buildings were broken into and stripped of their contents, even their pipes, just so users could make some extra money.

A new urban type was born—the "crackhead" or "fiend." On their best days, crack addicts resembled urban zombies. In particularly hard hit neighborhoods, police recount seeing dozens of addicts wandering the streets in search of their next "fix." At their worst, they could be very violent. Hardcore crack users would rob the grandmother next door or do much worse.

To serve this new market, open-air drug markets sprang up on street corners across urban America. In drug-infested neighborhoods, teenagers often occupied the perfect dealing niche. Many were juveniles and thus were hard to arrest. But dealing drugs on a street corner could be a violent business. These open-air drug markets were profitable. Street-level dealers became popular robbery targets. So they started carrying handguns. Neighborhood fistfights and gang brawls turned into running gun battles. Homicides, which had been rising slowly for years, skyrocketed.

Harsher Punishments and Penalties: Prison Nation

State and local government officials responded to this frightening surge in violence and crime in much the same way that legislators had responded to drug use concerns a decade earlier. They imposed tough new penalties for the use and possession of crack. Many states also made fundamental changes to their sentencing practices. For most of the post–Second World War era, U.S. courts had enjoyed considerable leeway in determining the severity of punishment they delivered. In academic-speak, this was known as indeterminate sentencing.

By the 1980s, however, the public's rising fears led to more strident demands to get tough on crime. Most judges obliged, if only to placate voters. Federal judges are nominated by the president and approved by the Senate for life service. However, most states rely at least in part on elections to select judges—even state supreme court justices.[23]

Stories of judges releasing hardened criminals with little more than a slap on the wrist resulted in a growing number of states moving toward determinate sentencing. "Truth in sentencing" laws were passed. These restricted a judge's ability to set penalties and curtailed a parole board's freedom to release prisoners early. Some states went even further. Fourteen states abolished discretionary parole and parole boards altogether. In 1994, California voters approved a "three strikes" law. Individuals arrested and convicted of three felony crimes must be imprisoned for a minimum of twenty-five years, if not for the rest of their lives. In 2004, the U.S. Supreme Court further constrained judges' sentencing flexibility but also set the stage for potentially shorter sentences when it ruled that only juries, not judges, can increase sentences beyond the maximums suggested by sentencing laws.

Nevertheless, the increased reliance on incarceration had a big effect on state budgets. In 1978, state governments spent about $5 billion on maintaining prisons and jails. By 2000, prison spending had risen to $40 billion. Two million people were under lock and key. (See Figure 14-2.) States now spend an average of 7 percent of total general revenue funds—$1 out of every $14—on prisons.[24]

Not everyone felt the weight of determinate sentencing equally. By 1995, 7 percent of all black males in the United States were serving time either in a state prison or in a city or county jail on any given day. This was double the percentage of a decade earlier. It also was in sharp contrast to the 1 per-

FIGURE 14-2 U.S. Incarceration Rate, 1920–2004

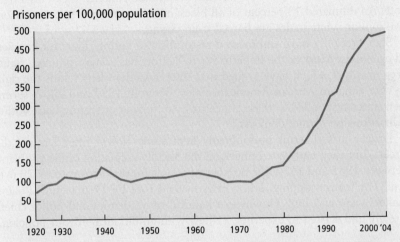

Prisoners per 100,000 population

Sources: M. W. Cahalan, *Historical Corrections Statistics in the United States, 1850–1984* (Washington, D.C.: U.S. Department of Justice, 1986) and Bureau of Justice Bulletins, *Prisoners in 2000, 2001, 2002, 2003, and 2004.*

cent of white males jailed during the same period. Every day, nearly one-third of all black males ages twenty to twenty-nine were either in prison or under some form of supervision, such as probation or **parole**. A black male currently has a 32 percent chance of going to prison at some point in his life. In contrast, Hispanic males born that same year have a 17 percent chance of being imprisoned, and white males have a 5.9 percent chance.[25]

Many of those men have a good chance of repeating their time, too. For too many, prison now functions as a kind of criminal finishing school. It is an educational facility whose graduates usually return to a life of crime. Roughly two-thirds of the people who leave prison after serving time for a felony return within three years. That percentage is growing. Unless state and local governments figure out an effective strategy to reverse this recidivism, millions of those locked away during the "tough on crime" 1980s and 1990s will almost certainly commit crimes again.

The high incarceration rate for black males has meant that many no longer can vote. Forty-eight states—Maine and Vermont being the exceptions—have laws that prohibit prisoners from voting. Felons on probation or out on parole are barred from voting in thirty-seven states. The exceptions are Hawaii, Illinois, Indiana, Massachusetts, Michigan, Montana, New Hampshire, North Dakota, Ohio, Oregon, Pennsylvania, and of

PAROLE

Supervised early release from prison.

> A black male currently has a 32 percent chance of going to prison at some point in his life. In contrast, Hispanic males born that same year have a 17 percent chance of being imprisoned, and white males have a 5.9 percent chance.

course, Maine and Vermont. Kentucky and Virginia deny convicted felons the right to vote *ever* again. As a result, 5.3 million Americans can no longer vote. An estimated 13 percent of all black men cannot vote. In comparison, two million white males are barred from voting.

States recently have embraced a restoration of voting rights for convicted criminals. Most of the impetus for this effort has come from civil rights organizations, which have argued that state laws that deny felons the right to vote penalize African American males. Between 1997 and 2007, seventeen states responded to these concerns by removing or scaling back voting restrictions on former convicts.[26]

Longer prison terms undoubtedly kept some violent offenders off the streets, but they had little impact on the rapidly escalating crime problem. Between 1985 and 1992, the number of people incarcerated rose by 79 percent. Far from dropping, crime rates instead rose by 17 percent.[27] Policymakers were at a loss. However, a handful of academics and police chiefs already had started to experiment anew with an old idea—better policing.

The Return of Policing

In the 1820s, Sir Robert Peel founded London's Metropolitan Police, the first recognizably modern police department. "The basic mission for which the police exist," wrote Peel, "is to prevent crime and disorder."[28] Peel's vision defined policing until the 1960s. Race riots and rising drug abuse convinced criminologists and many police departments that there was little they could do to reduce crime in the face of shifting demographic trends.[29] By the 1970s, however, a handful of people began to rethink the role that law enforcement agencies should play. In time, these ideas would revolutionize the practice of policing.

The first big idea came in the late 1970s. Put forward by Herman Goldstein, a professor at the University of Wisconsin Law School in Madison, it argued that the proper role of the police was not to enforce the law. It was to solve problems. Goldstein's work encouraged police chiefs in cities such as Madison, Wisconsin, and Newport News, Virginia, to think in more creative ways about how to deal with such issues as street-level drug problems. He urged local officials to search for ways to solve underlying societal problems. This philosophy came to be known as problem-oriented policing. Although it would be more than a decade before Goldstein's theory began to take root in police departments, the idea that police ought to function as creative problem solvers eventually would transform the way in which many departments thought about policing.

The second breakthrough came in the early 1980s. Political scientist James Q. Wilson and criminologist George Kelling hatched an idea that changed the future of policing in the United States. Arguably, it changed the future of urban America. Their basic premise was simple: minor disorders, such as shoplifting and vandalism, often give rise to much more serious types of disorder and crime, such as robbery and arson.

To support this claim, Wilson and Kelling pointed to a famous experiment conducted by Stanford psychologist Philip Zimbardo in the 1960s. Zimbardo took two identical cars, popped their hoods, and then abandoned them on two very different streets. One car was left on a high crime street in the Bronx neighborhood of New York City. The other car was parked in Stanford's hometown of Palo Alto, California. The two cars met with very different fates. Within ten minutes of its being abandoned, vandals—most of whom were respectably dressed, clean-cut whites—began to strip the car left in the Bronx. One day later, virtually everything of value had been removed. In contrast, the car in Palo Alto sat untouched, hood up, for an entire week.

Then Zimbardo changed the equation. He smashed out the windshield of the car in Palo Alto. Within hours, the car had been turned upside down and essentially destroyed. Once again, most of the perpetrators were whites. He concluded that untended property—particularly property that looks as if it actually has been neglected—sends the signal that disorder is tolerated. This quickly gives rise to more serious forms of disorder.

Wilson and Kelling extended this idea to neighborhoods as a whole. They theorized that seemingly minor signs of neglect, such as graffiti, trash, or broken windows, signal that authority is absent and give rise to much more serious problems such as violent crime. The two criminologists went on to make a larger point about policing. Those police officers whom researchers in the 1950s observed walking around and resolving disputes actually might have been doing something important. By their very presence, they had been maintaining order. It was time, Wilson and Kelling wrote, to go back to the future.[30]

Community Policing vs. the Professional Model

Wilson and Kelling argued for a dramatic break from the **professional model** of policing. This approach to crime emphasizes squad cars and quick response times. Police departments across the country embraced it during the 1970s. The reason was an important new innovation—the 9-1-1 emergency number. Cops who had once walked the beat and played the role of friendly neighborhood supervisor now were put into squad cars. Response time—how quickly the police responded to a call for assistance—became the criterion by which departments were judged as successes or failures. It was an all-or-nothing situation, since there simply were not enough police officers available to both monitor neighborhoods and answer emergency calls.

The professional model originated on the fast-growing West Coast. Long before the advent of 9-1-1, many West Coast police departments

PROFESSIONAL MODEL POLICING

An approach to policing that emphasizes professional relations with citizens, police independence, police in cars, and rapid responses to calls for service.

The first police car went on patrol in Akron, Ohio, in 1899. It was electric powered and could reach speeds of sixteen miles per hour.

emphasized technology. They prided themselves on their small, highly mobile forces. The influence of the Los Angeles Police Department (LAPD) in particular on police technique nationwide cannot be understated. For many years, it was seen as the prototype for effective police departments. Its cool professionalism ("Just the facts, ma'am.") was captured in the TV show *Dragnet*. The department was the first to buy helicopters. It pioneered the use of the now ubiquitous Special Weapons and Tactics, or S.W.A.T., teams.

When widespread use of 9-1-1 pushed things even further toward the professional model, East Coast departments changed the most because they had been most unlike the professional model in the first place. West Coast officials long had thought of East Coast police departments as dinosaurs with troubling opportunities for corruption. With many more police officers per capita than West Coast police departments, East Coast departments were portrayed as sources of patronage jobs, not as effective law enforcement agencies. A beat cop walking past the same gambling den or house of ill repute every day could be tempted all too easily to accept payoffs and look the other way.

West Coast police departments were convinced that they could do the same job better—or at least as well. Good tactics and high-tech equipment would prevail. And, for a while, departments such as the LAPD did maintain order, but at a cost. Their smaller forces used aggressive tactics—sometimes in a very arbitrary fashion. Senseless stops by the police became an all too familiar experience for residents of many predominantly minority areas. Consequently, a considerable number of African Americans and Hispanic Los Angelinos came to mistrust the police department.

This state of affairs was underscored by violence that broke out following the 1992 acquittal of police officers involved in the beating of Rodney King.[31] Earlier that year, a bystander had videotaped LAPD officers violently subduing King, a black motorist who had led them on a high-speed chase and then resisted arrest.[32] When an all-white jury found the officers not guilty, riots erupted throughout the city. For six days, the police force, caught unprepared in part because of political maneuvering in its top levels, struggled to regain control.

A Return to Community Policing

COMMUNITY POLICING

An approach that emphasizes relationships with neighborhoods and collaborative problem solving.

By the early 1990s, it was obvious that a different model was needed. That model was **community policing**. In a sense, it represented a return to one of Sir Robert Peel's earliest ideas—the belief that police officers should walk a beat and get to know their neighborhoods. Community policing emphasizes the importance of good relations with local neighborhoods and the need for residents and police officers to solve problems jointly. Isolated experiments with community policing began to appear in a handful of police departments, including that of San Francisco, California, as early as the late 1960s.

Momentum did not begin to build, however, until the late 1980s and early 1990s. Departments like those in Madison, Wisconsin, and Houston, Texas, embraced and developed the model during this period.[33] The Rodney King riots spotlighted the problems of the professional model. They also pushed other departments toward the community policing model. The most significant variation on community policing appeared in New York. During the early 1990s, Mayor David Dinkins introduced its precepts to the nation's largest police department, the New York Police Department (NYPD).

At the same time the NYPD was experimenting with community policing, the city's transit police were attempting to test James Q. Wilson and George Kelling's belief that disorder left unattended bred crime. **Broken windows policing**, which emphasizes the maintenance of public order, was instituted. The result was immediate and dramatic. The transit police discovered that many of the vandals and turnstile jumpers they arrested were ex-felons who also were carrying guns or skipping out on warrants. By getting to these people early, the police were, in effect, disarming them. After two years in which crime underground had increased by 48 percent, the transit police under the leadership of Chief Bill Bratton managed to bring it down by 40 percent.[34]

Bratton's successes caught the attention of an equally ambitious U.S. attorney, Rudolph Giuliani. Two years later, Giuliani won a close race to become mayor of New York. Reducing crime was one of his major priorities. The young chief who had done so much with the transit police immediately went to the top of Giuliani's list to head the NYPD. What secured the job offer for Bratton was his promise to Giuliani. If he offered Bratton the job, Bratton would deliver a 40 percent crime reduction for the whole of New York City within three years.

It was an unprecedented and—in the eyes of most criminologists—outlandish commitment. Most experts believed that other factors, such as demographics, were far more important than any type of policing. And the demographics were bad. The problem was young people. People between the ages of eighteen and twenty-five commit crimes at disproportionate rates—more than five times the rate of people age thirty-five and older. (See Figures 14-3a and 14-3b.) During the 1990s, the proportion of

The community policing model is based on the idea of building good relationships with neighborhoods. Bensalem, Pennsylvania, police officer Theresa Nelson is doing exactly that by stopping to chat with 8-year-old Victoria McDaniel.

FIGURE 14-3a Violent Crime, Arrests by Age, 1993–2005

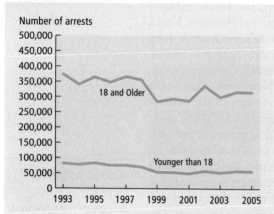

Number of arrests

Source: *Crime in the United States 1993–2005,* Federal Bureau of Investigation.

Note: Gun violence is a frequent topic of discussion in the United States, with good reason: arrests for gun-related murders rose 40 percent among people aged eighteen to twenty-four between 1976 and 2004. More encouraging, though, is that all violent crime, including gun-related murders, committed by people younger than eighteen years of age has dropped significantly.

FIGURE 14-3b Homicide, Arrests by Age and Weapon, 1976–2004

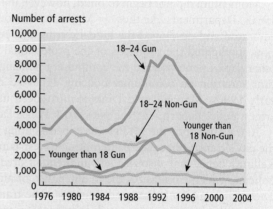

Number of arrests

Sources: Jeffrey A. Butts and Jeremy Travis, *The Rise and Fall of American Youth Violence: 1980 to 2000* (Washington, D.C.: Urban Institute, 2000) and James Alan Fox and Marianne W. Zawitz, "Homicide trends in the U.S.," U.S. Department of Justice, Bureau of Justice Statistics, www.ojp.usdoj.gov/bjs/homicide/homtrnd.htm (accessed October 10, 2006).

SUPERPREDATORS

Ultra-violent youths whom experts predicted would further drive up the nation's crime rate.

young people in the population as a whole was growing fast. Demographers described it as "the echo of the baby boom." Criminologists saw it in different terms—they predicted the coming of juvenile **superpredators**.

Fortunately for New York City, Mayor Giuliani was not much interested in criminology's conventional wisdom. Bratton's bold offer and the promise that broken windows policing had shown underground appealed to the new mayor. Bratton got the nod. When he resigned two years later, homicides in New York had fallen by 39 percent.

So what happened? Officials in the NYPD say the answer is simple—better policing. The key innovation was a new computerized crime-mapping system known as Compstat. This system allowed the police to map crime in virtual real time, identify patterns or problems, and then shift resources and devise solutions accordingly. Before the creation of Compstat, the NYPD compiled crime statistics every quarter. Compstat provided fresh numbers every week and allowed police commanders to look for crime patterns and "hot spots." It also encouraged officers to try new tactics and introduced an element of accountability to policing.[35] Today, nearly 70 percent of large police departments in the United States use some version of this system. More police officers and a focus on broken windows, or quality of life offenses, rounded off the prescription for success.

In the mid-1990s and late 1990s, these concepts were exported to other cities nationwide. Former NYPD officials were hired as consultants in such

chattanoogaRESULTS

Departmental Performance Indicators:
Citywide Crime

During Q3 2007, CPD recorded a total of 2,994 crimes committed—a 14.29% decrease under crimes committed in Q3 2006. Calendar year to date, crimes committed in CPD are up by 5.28% compared to 2006.

Of the 2,994 crimes committed in Q3, 2,632 or 87.9% were non-violent crimes and 362 or 12.09% were violent crimes. Non-violent crimes include burglary, larceny, and auto theft. Violent crimes are murder, rape, robbery, and aggravated assault. During Q3, larceny accounted for 73.14% of non-violent crimes committed—a 11.70% decrease under the Q3 2006 crimes committed. Calendar year to date, larceny crimes committed are up by 5.74% compared to 2006. In violent crimes, aggravated assault accounted for 69.3% of violent crimes committed—a 3.83% decrease under the Q3 2006 crimes committed. Calendar year to date, aggravated assault is up 3.17% compared to 2006.

Crime Type	Q3 '2007	Q3' 2006	% change	CYTD '07	CYTD '06	% change
Burglary	474	647	−26.74%	484	414	+16.91%
Larceny	1,925	2,180	−11.70%	1972	1865	+5.74%
Auto Theft	233	261	−10.73%	244	265	−7.92%
Non-violent	2,632	3,088	−14.77%	2,700	2,544	+6.13%
Murder	3	5	−40.00%	3	2	+50.00%
Rape	20	11	+81.82%	20	17	+17.65%
Robbery	88	128	−31.25%	88	102	−13.73%
Aggravated Assault	251	261	−3.83%	260	252	+3.17%
Violent	362	405	−10.62%	371	373	−0.54%
Crime Committed	2,994	3,493	−14.29%	3,071	2,917	+5.28%

**The CYTD totals include April figures

Like Compstat, chattanoogaRESULTS is a computer-based crime mapping system that provides up-to-date information on what crimes are being committed and where they are being committed. This allows police departments to quickly identify trends and target law enforcement efforts to "hot spots" of criminal activity.

cities as New Orleans, Louisiana; Newark, New Jersey; Philadelphia, Pennsylvania; and Baltimore, Maryland. These consultants put NYPD-style techniques into place. Many of these transplants generated dramatic results, especially at first. However, another dynamic soon became evident that caught public officials off guard. Many cities that had done nothing to improve their police departments also were enjoying dramatically falling crime rates.

Los Angeles was a case in point. Once one of the most admired police forces in the country, by the early 1990s, the LAPD had fallen on hard times. In the years that followed the Rodney King riots, the department went through two chiefs and struggled with sagging officer morale. Yet

FIGURE 14-4 Homicides in Large U.S. Cities, 1995, 2000, 2005

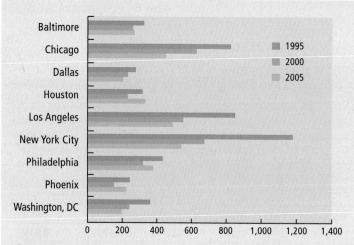

Legend:
- 1995
- 2000
- 2005

Cities (top to bottom): Baltimore, Chicago, Dallas, Houston, Los Angeles, New York City, Philadelphia, Phoenix, Washington, DC

X-axis: 0, 200, 400, 600, 800, 1,000, 1,200, 1,400

Sources: Jeremy Travis and Michelle Waul, "Reflections on the Crime Decline: Lessons for the Future?" Urban Institute, 2002, www.urban.org/uploadedpdf/410546_crimedecline. pdf (accessed May 13, 2003); and "Crime in the United States," Federal Bureau of Investigation, 2005.

despite all of this, homicides in LA fell from 983 in 1990 to 425 in 1999. (See Figure 14-4.)

As crime fell almost everywhere, regardless of policing techniques, questions about Bratton's accomplishment in New York and his philosophy of crime reduction reappeared. Criminologists began to look for factors other than improvements in policing. They explored such areas as changes in the structure of urban drug markets, demographics, the economic boom of the 1990s, and the high rates of incarceration during the 1980s and 1990s.[36]

The dispute between those who give the police most of the credit for the crime reduction of the 1990s and those who do not continues. There is, however, a more subtle and widely accepted explanation for what happened in New York and across the country that both sides more or less agree with. It's called the "tipping point." This concept comes from epidemiology, the study of diseases. Early in the history of the discipline, epidemiologists noted that diseases do not tend to spread in a linear fashion. Rather, a handful of people come down with a disease, then a few more, and then BOOM!, doctors are dealing with a full-fledged epidemic.

Moreover, the scientists noted that epidemics often end suddenly too. Some diseases spread too fast and then "burn out" or, if checked by quarantine, die out as infected people are isolated from the rest of the population. As a result, epidemiologists developed the concept of the tipping point, literally, the number at which a disease either "tips" into a full-fledged epidemic or burns out.

Many observers now see the crack-fueled violent crime wave of the 1980s as a kind of epidemic. An epidemic that eventually burned out as a new generation saw how addictive the narcotic really was and stayed clear and as the police developed new techniques that reduced related violent crimes. Under this model, no single factor caused the crime reduction. Rather, a series of interventions were tried, each of which had some effect. First, the at-risk population came to appreciate the dangers of the "disease," and then—at some point—violent crime "tipped." The epidemic crashed, and crime rates plummeted.

Governing States and Localities

Crime, Punishment, and the Essence of Modern America

At the beginning of this chapter, we stated that the way a society chooses to define crime and mete out punishment offers fundamental insights into the nature of that society. When the young French nobleman Alexis de Tocqueville decided in the early 1830s to visit and investigate the fledgling democracy of the United States, his first stop was the prisons. When British author Charles Dickens visited in 1842, he too sought out prisons and asylums.

Today, many Europeans view punishments like the death penalty as evidence of American cruelty and racism. They use the death penalty to argue against American "justice" in much the same way that critics of U.S. actions in the Middle East seized on the abuses at Abu Ghraib to criticize the U.S. occupation of Iraq. Most U.S. citizens these days are shielded from the reality of the nation's criminal justice system. It operates largely out of sight. Only a small percentage of Americans see what modern punishment looks like in this country. A tour of its state prisons and county and city jails may prove enlightening.

First, the system is rife with violence. A report by Human Rights Watch estimated that approximately 20 percent of all inmates are sexually assault-

Prisons can be dangerous places. A surprise sweep of the Big Muddy Correctional Center in Ina, Illinois, in March 1998 resulted in more than thirty positive drug tests and the discovery of one weapon. Prisoners often find creative ways to manipulate the system to gain access to forbidden items.

ed in some way and at least 7 percent are raped. That equals approximately one million assaulted individuals over the past twenty years. For many of these prisoners, rape may be just the beginning. Prisoners who are passive or effeminate may end up as slaves, forced to do menial jobs and sometimes "rented out" to other inmates to satisfy their sexual needs.[37]

Second, the prison population is a sick population. In the 1960s, most states disbanded the psychiatric hospitals that held many of society's mentally ill. At the time, the goal was to replace the old, often cruel, networks of state mental hospitals with more humane, community-based clinics. Unfortunately, the states did away with the hospitals without building the clinics. An estimated 56 percent of state prisoners and 64 percent of local jail inmates suffer from a mental health disorder, including serious illnesses like schizophrenia, bipolar disorder, and depression. That's more than one million mentally ill prisoners and inmates—far more than there are patients in mental hospitals. What's more, about three-quarters of those inmates with mental illnesses also are addicted to drugs or alcohol.[38]

Once in prison, do people with mental illnesses receive adequate treatment? Although more than a quarter of state prisoners report having taken medications prescribed to treat mental illnesses since entering prison, for the most part, the answer is no. In the words of another report by Human Rights Watch,

> across the nation, many prison mental health services are woefully deficient, crippled by understaffing, insufficient facilities, and limited programs. All too often, seriously ill prisoners receive little or no meaningful treatment. They are neglected, accused of malingering, treated as disciplinary problems.[39]

A century-and-a-half ago, many visitors to the United States praised the prisons and asylums. Today, they do not. A recent study by the international human rights group Amnesty International stated,

> The death penalty continued to be used extensively. There were reports of police brutality and unjustified police shootings and of ill treatment in prisons and jails. Human rights groups and others voiced concern at the lack of public information given about the circumstances under which more than 1,200 people, mainly foreign nationals, were detained during investigations into the . . . attacks [of September 11] on the Pentagon and World Trade Center. . . .[40]

The organization found that more than twenty thousand prisoners continued to be held in conditions of extreme isolation in **supermax security prisons**. Between 1976 and 2006, 1,047 people have been executed in the United States. Roughly 34 percent of those executed have been black.[41]

What most shocks the rest of the developed world, however, is this country's treatment of children. According to Amnesty International, the United States has "continued to use life imprisonment without the possi-

SUPERMAX SECURITY PRISONS

High-security prisons designed for violent criminals.

bility of parole against defendants who were under eighteen at the time of the crime, in violation of international law." Amnesty International estimates that over the course of the past decade, the United States executed roughly two-thirds of the total children age seventeen and under who were put to death worldwide. Until the U.S. Supreme Court ruled the practice unconstitutional in 2005, the United States was the only developed country that made child execution a regular part of its criminal justice system.[42] The nation also leads the world in the execution of people with mental impairments.

Issues to Watch

After the long crime decline of the 1990s, most experts are uncertain about what to expect in the future. Crime rates in the United States still are well above the post–Second World War rate. Granted, the world has changed a lot since the 1950s. It may seem unrealistic and idealist to think that such an old benchmark is relevant anymore. Crime rates remain remarkably lower than the dark days of the early 1990s, but it seems that the decline is over and that crime is increasing. The FBI reported a 2.3 percent increase in violent crime, including a 3.4 percent increase in homicides, during 2005. In 2006, murder rates rose even further in cities across the country, including Boston, which just a few short years earlier was a model for declining crime rates. The police chief of Washington, D.C., declared a crime emergency after thirteen people were killed in an eleven-day span.

But if the 1990s showed anything, it was that making predictions about the direction of crime rates is an uncertain thing. Radical improvement is still the goal in cities such as Los Angeles. Today, the city has one of the country's highest homicide rates. The LAPD estimates that approximately sixty thousand of LA County's residents are gang members, one of the largest populations in the nation. Yet despite these daunting numbers, Los Angeles's elected leadership insists that it is committed to making the city the nation's safest. With enough law enforcement personnel and creative problem solving, it just might happen. Even with the inherent uncertainty of predicting the future, some important trends already are evident in LA and nationwide.

Policing

Experts predict that the retreat from the professional model of policing will continue. The belief that the professional model was a misguided reform is now conventional wisdom. Even the West Coast, the one-time citadel of the professional model, now is trying to revamp its departments. Given its commitment to improved safety, it should be no surprise that the biggest change is taking place in Los Angeles. In the fall of 2002, Mayor James Hahn hired

Bill Bratton of New York City fame to head LA's police force. After taking over, Bratton introduced his Compstat to the city and pushed hard to put an additional three thousand officers on the payroll.

Yet despite Bratton's efforts, the legacies of the professional model linger. Even now, residents of East Coast cities continue to enjoy a far higher level of protection than residents of West Coast cities. To police a city of nearly 4 million people, the LAPD relies on approximately 9,300 officers. New York City has a population of eight million and thirty-seven thousand police officers. That is more than twice the number of police officers per capita for New York than for Los Angeles. Granted, Los Angeles and New York are extreme examples of (comparatively) small and large police forces, but such differences are visible between other cities as well. Cities in the Upper Midwest, including Chicago, Illinois; Milwaukee, Wisconsin; and Detroit, Michigan, tend to have larger police departments, in line with the size of East Coast forces. Cities in the Southwest and the Southeast, such as Dallas and El Paso, Texas; Phoenix, Arizona; Charlotte, North Carolina; and Memphis, Tennessee, often have smaller departments comparable to West Coast cities like Los Angeles and Las Vegas.[43]

The End of Federal Support

This chapter has discussed crime and punishment as almost an entirely local matter. Basically, this is true. According to the Bureau of Justice Statistics, there are roughly 708,000 state and local law enforcement officers nationwide and only 106,000 federal law enforcement officers. This does not mean that the federal contribution to law enforcement is insignificant. Federal agencies take the lead in responding to crimes that cross state boundaries. They also are in charge of certain categories of crime, including counterfeiting, and, to a lesser extent, gun trafficking. Sometimes the division of responsibility between federal law enforcement, such as the Drug Enforcement Agency or the FBI, and state and local agencies can be quite unclear.

The most significant federal contribution to state and local law enforcement, however, has been financial. During the late 1960s, the federal government created the Law Enforcement Assistance Administration. This agency funneled hundreds of millions of dollars to local law enforcement agencies. In the mid-1990s, President Bill Clinton and Republicans in Congress passed legislation that provided nearly $20 billion to states and localities to build more prisons and helped localities add about seventy thousand police officers to their forces.

Today, the picture is very different. At a time when many departments are facing a manpower crisis as police officers hired in the 1970s begin to retire, direct federal funding of local departments has virtually ended. This is in part because of longstanding Republican antipathy toward such funding and plain old belt-tightening.[44]

The New Criminal Frontier

There also is a sense that the locus of crime is shifting. During the 1960s, 1970s, and 1980s, the notion of the city as a dangerous place established a powerful hold on the American mind. *Law and Order* is not set in Oklahoma City, Oklahoma, or suburban Indianapolis, Indiana. It is set in New York City. These days, more and more of these images of danger are just that—creations of the imagination. Today, New York is one of the safest cities, not just in the country, but also in the world. Although gun crimes are still much, much more rare in European cities, London residents are more than twice as likely to be victims of crime than New Yorkers.

In fact, a new dynamic is now at play in cities that reduced their rates of violent crime dramatically during the 1990s. These communities have exported much of their crime to their surrounding suburbs. Guns, gangs, and drug problems are no longer limited to large cities; cities with populations of 100,000 to 249,999 experienced a 12.5 percent increase in the number of murders between 2004 and 2005.[45]

The countryside is not as quiet as the stereotype portrays it, either. Urban crime rates continue to be higher than rural, but violent crime in rural communities grew more than 50 percent between 1983 and 1997.[46] Police departments in small towns increasingly fight the same battles against drugs and gangs as their urban neighbors. Those departments lack many of the resources of their city counterparts, though. A survey conducted for the National Institute of Justice found that fewer than a quarter of small and rural police departments had the capability to use computers to aid criminal investigations, and that they underutilized other technologies, such as digital fingerprint imaging and global positioning systems.

Many rural areas connect a rise in crime to the rise of methamphetamine, a drug often made at home using the same ingredients found in cold medicine. Meth's popularity exploded in such states as Montana, Nebraska, and Oklahoma in the late 1990s. A recent survey by the National Association of Counties ranked it as the top drug problem for 48 percent of its responding counties. By 2005, states across the country had attempted to curtail the drug's availability by moving medicines containing pseudoephedrine, meth's main ingredient, behind the counter. In October 2005, Oregon passed a law to begin requiring a prescription for these previously over-the-counter drugs. The states were ahead of the federal government, which passed a law limiting the distribution and sales of pseudoephedrine in March 2006.

There is some evidence that these laws are helping reduce the number

MY SISTER ALWAYS LOOKED UP TO ME. EVEN AFTER I MADE HER AN ADDICT.

METH
NOT EVEN ONCE.

Methamphetamine, or meth, is the top drug problem facing many rural law enforcement agencies. The Montana Meth Project is a public education campaign that uses real people to try to dissuade teens from trying the drug.

of small-scale meth labs, but hard-core meth addicts may be looking elsewhere for their fix. One Oklahoma sheriff reported an increase in imports of "ice," a meth product from Mexico and labs in southern California. Ice is vastly more expensive than homemade meth, leading to an increase in crimes by addicts who need money to pay for the drug similar to those once committed by those addicted to crack.[47]

Moreover, suburban communities are dealing with these problems without the resources or the experience of big city police departments. The next decade may need to witness an explosion of suburban public safety creativity to match the urban innovations of the 1990s.

The Uncertain Future of the Death Penalty

In 1972, the U.S. Supreme Court found that the application of the death penalty in many states had been cruel, arbitrary, and unconstitutional. A moratorium, or indefinite delay, was placed on all executions. Four years later, the Court lifted the moratorium. By then, the states had passed sentencing guidelines that addressed the Court's concern that the death penalty was being applied in an arbitrary fashion. Today, the statutes of thirty-eight states allow prosecutors to request the death penalty. More than 1,000 prisoners have been executed since capital punishment was reinstated, and another 3,366 people were on death row in 2006.[48]

The fact that most states sanction capital punishment does not mean that they use it in a similar way. Some counties and states are much more enthusiastic than others. A 1999 *USA Today* investigation found that suburban counties tend to apply the death penalty with more zeal than urban counties. For example, San Mateo County, a suburb of San Francisco, had seventeen people on California's death row at the time. San Francisco itself, a larger city with twice as many murders, had sentenced only four people to death. The newspaper found that "fifteen counties account for nearly a third of all prisoners sentenced to death but only one-ninth of the population of the states with capital punishment."[49] One reason for this may be the rising crime rates in suburban areas and a "fight back" reflex felt by residents who have seen their safe communities become danger zones.

During the 1990s, a scientific breakthrough—DNA testing—shook up the capital punishment systems of most states. In state after state, lawyers and public interest groups convinced courts and prosecutors to reexamine forensic evidence. What they found was that innocent people had been convicted for crimes they had not committed. By October 2006, post-conviction DNA testing had cleared 183 Americans. Fourteen of these people had been sentenced to death; 106 of them were African Americans.[50] The impact of this new research has been felt. In January 2000, Illinois governor George Ryan, a Republican and an avowed supporter of capital punishment, became the first governor in the nation to halt executions.

Other states began examining the most widely used method of execution—lethal injection—after the U.S. Supreme Court ruled in June 2006 that lower courts must consider the possibility that the process can be cruel and painful—a standard that would make the procedure unconstitutional. Several states proposed adding an anesthesiologist to monitor executions and confirm that the three-drug process, intended to sedate, paralyze, and finally kill the prisoner, was working properly. There was just one problem: Anesthesiologists balked at the idea of presiding over executions that went against their Hippocratic Oath "to do no harm." When California could not find a workable solution, the death penalty went on trial. In December 2006, a federal judge found California's method of lethal injection unconstitutional, but said the system could be fixed.[51]

Although another national moratorium seems unlikely, support for the death penalty process as it is currently constructed is waning. Jeb Bush, Florida's governor at the time of the California ruling, suspended executions in Florida the same day as the ruling. A legislative commission in New Jersey recommended in January 2007 that the state abolish the death penalty, a move favored by Gov. Jon Corzine. A May 2006 Gallup poll found that 65 percent of Americans support capital punishment, down from 80 percent in 1994.

A New Interest in Alternative Punishment

A serious curtailment of executions seems unlikely, but other changes to state criminal justice systems already are becoming evident. It is yet to be seen if these will do more harm than good. For instance, during the 2001–2002 economic recession, many states concluded that they could no longer afford to warehouse ever-growing numbers of prisoners. Some states, notably Oregon and Alabama, responded with a simple but perhaps shortsighted solution—they released inmates early. Given current recidivism rates, law enforcement officials may be placing many of these individuals back behind bars for other crimes. By letting criminals out of jail early, states may save some money in the short term, but at a potentially high cost in the long run.

Early release programs are not the only option states are exploring. During the late 1980s and early 1990s, states such as Arizona and Georgia pioneered the use of military-style boot camps for offenders. The camps reflected the belief that many young individuals lack direction, discipline, and self-control. Exposure to military-style discipline might correct that. However, while studies found some evidence of improved attitudes, boot camp seemed to have no impact on future criminal activities. Recidivism rates for juveniles who had gone through boot camps were no lower than recidivism among juveniles who did not. Since the mid-1990s, the number of juvenile boot camps has declined by a third.[52]

In recent years, state and local governments have experimented with a number of other promising options. One initiative that got underway dur-

Policy in Practice: Does Gun Control Work?

The late 1980s and early 1990s witnessed a huge surge in homicide rates. The rising numbers can be attributed to just one thing—the rise in the use of handguns by people twenty-five years of age and younger. Between 1985 and 1993, firearm homicides increased by 53 percent. Other homicides actually declined slightly.[a] Handgun homicides committed by juveniles eighteen years of age and younger *quadrupled*.[b]

The huge surge in juvenile gun violence in the mid-1980s raises an obvious question: Would tougher gun control laws have saved lives? For some people, the answer is obvious. In 1992, the United States suffered 13,200 gun-related homicides. Countries with strict gun control laws, such as Great Britain and Japan, suffered thirty-three and sixty gun-related deaths, respectively.

For others, the very suggestion of outlawing handguns is outrageous. Many gun owners view firearms ownership as a basic constitutional right. The Second Amendment proclaims, "A well-regulated militia being necessary for the security of a free state, the right to keep and bear arms shall not be infringed." Some have even attempted to argue that allowing citizens to carry concealed weapons would improve overall public safety. They claim that the country would be safer if more Americans carried guns, although the research supporting these claims has largely been undermined.

In general, the courts have not agreed with this more expansive interpretation of the Constitution. States and individual cities enjoy considerable discretion to restrict gun laws as they see fit—or not at all. As a result, the right to bear arms depends very much on where you live. Twenty-nine states essentially require law enforcement agencies to provide a concealed weapon license to any law-abiding citizen who applies. Fourteen states—Alabama, California, Delaware, Georgia, Hawaii, Iowa, Maryland, Massachusetts, Michigan, Minnesota, New Jersey, New York, Rhode Island, and South Carolina—give law enforcement agencies the discretion to issue or deny weapons based on a variety of factors. In most of these states, relatively few permits are issued. Only Illinois, Kansas, Missouri, Nebraska, New Mexico, Ohio, and Wisconsin ban concealed weapons altogether.[c] In Vermont, no permit is needed to carry a concealed weapon. Many cities also have passed laws banning concealed firearms, although in gun-friendly states, state preemption laws typically mean that people with concealed weapon licenses do not have to disarm before entering otherwise "firearm-free" cities.

Both sides believe that their position will increase public safety. Advocates of gun ownership point out that localities with strict gun control laws often have very high crime rates and that all bans on handgun do

---

DRUG COURTS

An alternative forum for sentencing nonviolent drug offenders.

COMMUNITY, OR RESTORATIVE, JUSTICE MOVEMENT

A movement that emphasizes nontraditional punishment.

ing the Clinton administration involves **drug courts**. Drug courts are special tribunals that offer nonviolent drug offenders a chance to reduce or dismiss charges in exchange for undergoing treatment or other rehabilitation. As of December 2005, more than 1,500 drug courts were operating in all fifty states, and 391 new drug courts were planned. Enrolling a participant in a drug court program costs about $6,000, but the U.S. Justice Department recently reported that the programs save, on average, more than $3,600 per participant in avoided criminal justice and victimization costs over a thirty-month period.[53]

Drug courts are closely connected with the **community**, or **restorative, justice movement**. The movement's basic goal is to give neighborhoods a voice in determining what kinds of criminals that prosecutors should choose to pursue. In practice, community justice initiatives range from the modest—placing prosecutors in local police stations where they can see

is ensure that only criminals have guns. Gun control advocates acknowledge the problems but say the real problem is that borders are porous and other surrounding jurisdictions often have very weak gun control laws. Handguns may be banned in Washington, D.C., but cross the Potomac into Virginia and anyone can buy an assault rifle as long as no criminal record shows up in a background check.

In fact, according to criminologist Garen Wintemute at the University of California–Davis, a dispassionate look at the evidence seems to support key claims of both sides. Studies have shown that certain types of gun restrictions—waiting periods, background checks, and some level of screening for gun buyers—work. In Wintemute's words, "they reduce rates of criminal activity involving guns and violence among people who are screened out and denied purchase of a gun—about 25 percent to 30 percent of those who are screened." Others, such as gun "buybacks," do not. They often encourage people to turn in old, sometimes inoperable guns.

Some measures, such as requiring gun manufacturers to install trigger-locks on new handguns, are still too new to fully evaluate. However, the argument for treating gun violence as a public health problem is a strong one. Gun-related deaths, mainly accidental, are the second leading cause of death in the United States, second only to automobile accidents.[d] At the same time, there is no evidence to suggest that gun control laws reduce violent crime. Which raises an intriguing question: How can gun control laws work and yet not work at the same time?[e]

Source: John Buntin, *Assertive Policing, Plummeting Crime: The NYPD Takes On Crime* (1530.0), case study written for use by the John F. Kennedy School of Government, Harvard University (0799). Copyright © 1999 by the Presidency and Fellowes of Harvard College.

[a] Jeremy Travis and Michelle Waul, "Reflections on the Crime Decline: Lessons for the Future?" *Proceedings from the Urban Institute Crime Decline Forum,* August 2002, p. 2.
[b] Alfred Blumstein, "Why Is Crime Falling—Or Is It?" February 14, 2001, presentation.
[c] Figures come from www.bradycampaign.org/facts/faqs/?page=ccwfaq and www.packing.org.
[d] See David Hemenway, *Private Guns, Public Health* (Ann Arbor: University of Michigan Press, 2004), for a discussion of the public health approach to gun violence.
[e] Wintemute's answer is this: "The resolution of the apparent paradox is that under current criteria so few people are denied the purchase of a firearm under Brady and its state level analogs relative to the number of people who purchase guns every year that an impact on that select group is too small at the population level to be noticed." Travis and Waul, "Reflections on the Crime Decline," 16.

neighborhood needs firsthand—to the ambitious—alternative courts that may require juvenile offenders to apologize to the people they harmed and perform community service in an attempt to rectify the harm done by the crime committed.

More Young People, More Crime?

For the past twenty years, the proportion of eighteen- to twenty-four-year-olds in the overall population has declined. However, that trend is now beginning to reverse. During the first decade of the twenty-first century, the proportion for that same age group will increase. The proportion of young African American males, a group who commits and suffers from crimes at a much higher rate than the population as a whole, will continue to increase through 2020.

From the standpoint of a criminologist, this is bad news. As mentioned earlier, young people, particularly young men, commit crimes at a much higher rate than older people.[54] Young people are also much more likely to be victims of crime than older people. According to the Centers for Disease Control, homicide is the second leading cause of death among young people ages fifteen to twenty-four.[55] As a result, more young people usually means more crime.

Of course, demography is not destiny. During the mid-1990s, society dodged the dreaded juvenile superpredator and managed to actually reduce crime during "the echo of the baby boom." In Boston, an interagency team of police, probation officers, corrections officers, social workers, and others agencies targeted a rapidly growing juvenile violence epidemic fed by gangs with guns. Probation officers inspected the homes of gang members with police officers at the ready. Corrections officials and cops kept track of who was being released when. Social workers talked with gang members and warned them that gun play would result in constant police attention. The result was a dramatic reduction in juvenile gun violence. In 1990, seventy-three people under the age of twenty-four were murdered in Boston. By 1997, that number had fallen to fifteen.[56]

But soon after the turn of the century, complacency set in, the number of teens living in the city grew, and Boston's collaboration crumbled. Once again, crime rates involving juveniles headed north. To reverse them, in Boston and elsewhere, may require another outburst of creative policing and community problem-solving. Otherwise, look for crime to return once more to the top of the public agenda.

Conclusion

Crime is one of the most complex—and contentious—issues in public policy. Its causes are not well understood, and the fairness of the criminal justice system and the best strategies for responding to crime are hotly debated. Nevertheless, the past decade has been a period of remarkable progress. Such innovations as community and broken windows policing and Compstat have given law enforcement agencies new tools and a new sense of purpose. Contrary to some alarmist predictions, crime rates have fallen sharply and youth violence also has declined. However, serious issues, notably the high incarceration and victimization rates of African American males, remain. Moreover, the future remains uncertain. Will new innovations push crime back down, or is the crime decline of the 1990s finally over? Only time will tell.

Key Concepts

broken windows policing (p. 525)

common law (p. 509)

community, or restorative,
   justice movement (p. 536)

community policing (p. 524)

deterrence theory (p. 517)

drug courts (p. 536)

parole (p. 521)

probation (p. 508)

professional model policing (p. 523)

supermax security prisons (p. 530)

superpredators (p. 526)

verdict (p. 510)

Suggested Readings

Blumstein, Alfred, and Joel Wallman. *The Crime Drop in America.* New York: Cambridge University Press, 2000. Presents a comprehensive overview of current thinking on a wide range of issues.

Gladwell, Malcolm. *The Tipping Point: How Little Things Can Make a Big Difference.* Little, Brown and Co., 2000. Gladwell details examples of tipping points in society.

Goldstein, Herman. *Problem-Oriented Policing.* New York: McGraw-Hill, 1990. One of the classics of modern policing.

Sherman, Lawrence W., et al. "Preventing Crime: What Works, What Doesn't, What's Promising," National Institute of Justice, July 1998.

Simon, David, and Edward Burn. *The Corner: A Year in the Life of an Inner-City Neighborhood.* New York: Broadway, 1998. Offers a gripping and sympathetic account of life in a troubled Baltimore neighborhood.

Wilson, James Q., and George Kelling. "Broken Windows," *Atlantic Monthly,* March 1982. The authors set forth what became an extremely influential vision of policing. Available online at www.theatlantic.com/politics/crime/windows.htm.

Suggested Web Sites

http://virlib.ncjrs.org/Statistics.asp. The Web site of the National Criminal Justice Reference Service provides statistics on a variety of topics involving crime.

www.amnesty.org. Amnesty International's Web site gives readers a sense of how the rest of the world views the criminal justice system of the United States through recent and archived material.

www.fbi.gov. Web site of the Federal Bureau of Investigation, which offers information on national and international criminal activities as well as crime prevention tips.

www.manhattan-institute.org. The Manhattan Institute's Web site includes archived articles from the institute's *City Journal,* which addresses such issues as the affects of racism.

www.ojp.usdoj.gov/nij/welcome.html. The National Institutes of Justice is the research, development, and evaluation agency of the U.S. Department of Justice. The agency researches crime control and justice issues, particularly at the state and local levels.

www.sentencingproject.org. The Sentencing Project's Web site offers data and information about racial disparities in the U.S. criminal justice system.

CHAPTER 15

Health and Welfare

State, Heal Thyself!

Open up and say, "Ahhh . . . ." Undeniably, the patients aren't the only ones who are sick in the U.S. healthcare system. The system itself will need more than an aspirin and an apple a day to heal itself. While the debate continues to rage over a national healthcare plan, states and localities are forced to pick up the slack. And the flu doesn't care if someone has insurance or not. Here, Beverly Cowart, a nurse at NAN Healthcare in Hattiesburg, Mississippi, checks for signs of influenza in 6-year-old Devon Kraeger in January 2003.

15

Why is long-term healthcare becoming more important?

Why does access to care vary so widely across
the country?

What roles do state and local governments play in
maintaining public health?

Perris, California, is located eighteen miles south of the city of Riverside. Headquarters of the Riverside County fire department and not much else, the town has a rural, easygoing feel to it.

On December 14, 1998, however, the slow tempo of Perris was disrupted dramatically.

At approximately 4:30 P.M., the director of special education at an elementary school in the small town opened a letter. Inside, he found a moist paper towelette and a note that read, "You have been exposed to anthrax."

Anthrax is an infectious disease caused by the spore-forming bacterium *Bacillus anthracis*. In the wild, it primarily infects sheep. People who come in close contact with infected animals or infected animal products—such as wool—also may contract it. In its early stages, anthrax can be treated with antibiotics, but it can be fatal if left untreated. Consequently, many people employed in occupations that require them to work closely with animals receive anthrax vaccinations.

There's more. The spore form of the bacterium is extremely durable and can be delivered as an aerosol. It is largely invisible—at best, a fine dust—and hence difficult to detect. Symptoms typically do not appear for one to five days. The evidence is extremely limited, but mortality rates from anthrax inhalation may exceed 85 percent.[1] This all means that anthrax is well suited for use as a biological weapon.

Even before September 11, 2001, government officials had become increasingly concerned about the dangers of chemical and biological weapons. So when the Riverside County fire department got a call about a possible anthrax attack, it treated the situation seriously. Firefighters arrived in Level B protective gear—essentially, full-protection suits with self-contained breathing gear. Then they quarantined everyone who might have been exposed to the purported anthrax.

In keeping with the standard protocol for dealing with people exposed to hazardous materials, the fire department proceeded to decontaminate everyone on the scene. With the temperature hovering below thirty degrees Fahrenheit, people were forced to take off of all their clothes. Their garments were sealed in plastic bags. Quarantined individuals then had to stand in small inflatable plastic containers like child-sized swimming pools while they were hosed down with a bleach solution. At the end of the process, they were issued temporary clothing.[2]

Once FBI agents arrived on the scene, however, they quickly ascertained that the letter was almost certainly a hoax. Even if it had been a real incident of terrorism involving anthrax, local officials were not really doing the right thing. Anthrax is not a dangerous chemical that needs to be washed off with a strong solution. Proper treatment involves antibiotics. Local first responders were responding to a novel and frightening public health threat in a traditional—and ineffectual—way.

The reaction of the Riverside County fire department underscores one of the most important functions of government—protecting **public health.** Public health is the area of medicine that deals with the protection and improvement of citizen health and hygiene by government agencies. Since the earliest days of the United States, state and local governments have met this need. This is especially true in regard to the poorest and to the disabled members of society.

State and local governments also have taken the lead in responding to public health crises. In practice, this includes responses as simple as making sure an ambulance or fire truck responds to a 9-1-1 call and responses as complex as managing an epidemic. A century ago that might have involved yellow fever, cholera, or influenza. A flu outbreak in 1918 killed an estimated six hundred thousand Americans and one hundred million people worldwide.[3]

Today, such a crisis may stem from a twenty-first century danger such as a chemical or biological weapon. Only three years after Riverside County's anthrax scare, the residents of New York, New York; Washington, D.C.; and Boca Raton, Florida, were victims of real anthrax attacks. More likely, though, is that diseases will pose continued threats. Avian flu, first found in Hong Kong in 1997, has spread to humans in at least 10 countries and killed more than 160 people, according to the World Health Organization. The federal government estimates that a **pandemic** flu could kill as many as two million Americans. As a result, state and local governments spend an increasing amount of time planning for such crises, and carrying out drills intended to simulate public health emergencies.

Just how active state and local governments should be on these issues is often a source of heated debate. Terrorism experts warn that the United States has far too few hospital beds in the event of a real emergency.[4] Many communities cannot even keep an adequate blood supply available to healthcare facilities when things are quiet and uneventful. Despite the dangers posed by illnesses like avian flu, most counties maintain only skeletal public health departments.

Pandemic flu, anthrax, and the specter of bioterrorism are frightening new developments in the field of public health. But they are not the only threats to the public. Sometimes the public is its own worst enemy. The impact of recent "outside" health threats pales beside more long-standing public health concerns. According to the Surgeon General, smoking causes more than four hundred thousand deaths a year in the United States. And a growing percentage of Americans are overweight or suffer from **obesity.**

PUBLIC HEALTH

Government agencies' protection and improvement of citizen health and hygiene.

Twelve states ban smoking in all bars and restaurants. Washington, D.C.'s ban went into effect at the stroke of midnight on January 2, 2007.

PANDEMIC

An outbreak of a disease that spreads across a large geographic area.

OBESITY

A medical term used to describe people who are excessively overweight.

Some governors, including former governor Mike Huckabee of Arkansas —who has himself lost more than a hundred pounds—have made combating obesity a major priority. They have pushed for educational programs for parents and have restored physical education classes in schools while removing soft drink machines. Others pooh-pooh the problem. Some states are generous providers of assistance to their low-income citizens to cover the expenses associated with illness and hospitalization. Other states are much more restrictive. Explanations for these differences are explored in this chapter.

For all the variation among state and local governments, it is clear that over the course of the past decade they have become much more assertive. During the economic boom of the mid-and late 1990s, the states worked with the federal government to find new ways to extend health insurance to low-income parents and children. When the economy slipped into recession, states led the effort to find ways to reduce the costs of medical care, particularly prescription drugs, and to improve the quality of care.

The newfound activism on the part of the states regarding prescription drug costs reflects what may prove to be a momentous realignment of the United States' system of federalism. Forty years ago, most states were minor players in the nation's healthcare system. Proponents of expanded health coverage and healthcare reform looked to the federal government for solutions. Today, the situation is very nearly reversed. A decade of inaction and partisan division in Washington has shifted the most important—and most difficult—healthcare issues to state and local governments. The lawmakers tackling tough issues like rising rates of obesity, health insurance for the uninsured, rising prescription drug costs, long-term care, HIV and other sexually transmitted diseases, and drug use are more likely to be sitting in state capitols than under the Capitol dome in Washington, D.C.

In addition, states have taken the lead in rethinking such safety net programs as welfare. In 1996, Congress abolished the existing **Aid to Families with Dependent Children (AFDC)**, or welfare, program and replaced it with a system of block grants to the states, called **Temporary Assistance to Needy Families (TANF)**. These grants gave state governments the leeway to design their own personalized, work-oriented, time-limited welfare programs. The result has been a profusion of sometimes very different welfare-to-work programs.

For instance, Oklahoma, a traditionalistic state, used TANF funds to train government workers and religious volunteers to administer a program developed by the U.S. military and designed to strengthen the marriages of people moving from welfare to work. In contrast, states like New York have downplayed so-called family formation policies. Part of this difference in emphasis reflects states' different political cultures. However, the structure of state government also plays an important role. New York's welfare system is decentralized. It relies on county governments to administer programs. So does Colorado. Despite having a political culture that would seem to be supportive of "family formation," Colorado has made few

AID TO FAMILIES WITH DEPENDENT CHILDREN (AFDC)

The original federal assistance program for women and their children, started under Roosevelt's New Deal.

TEMPORARY ASSISTANCE TO NEEDY FAMILIES (TANF)

The next-generation welfare program that provides federal assistance in the form of block grants to states, which have great flexibility in designing the program.

efforts in that direction, largely because its decentralized structure makes the system unresponsive to directives of any sort.[5]

The Influence of Culture

How state governments define public health has a lot to do with a given region's distinctive political culture. All public health officials would agree that certain issues, such as terrorism and AIDS, are important public health issues. No one would argue that a flu epidemic or the contamination of a major watershed also qualifies.

Other topics are not so easily categorized. Is gun violence a public health issue? Researchers at the Centers for Disease Control and Prevention (CDC) think so. They point out that gun-related deaths, most of which are accidental, are the country's second leading cause of death. The American Medical Association (AMA) now advises doctors to talk with patients about the proper handling and storage of any guns they may own. Many gun owners, however, vehemently reject the idea that guns are a public health issue.

On other health fronts, some cities have attempted to reduce the transmission of dangerous blood-born illnesses like HIV and Hepatitis C by providing addicts with clean needles. Others

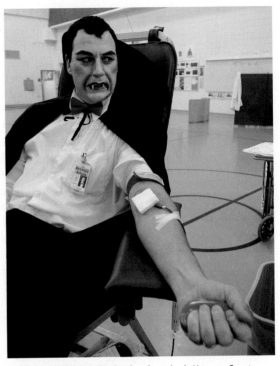

Vampires usually take blood rather than give it. Yet even Count Dracula (actually Marshfield, Wisconsin, American government teacher Troy Schmitt) is willing to donate a pint for a worthy cause. Local community blood drives are a central source of blood supplies and an important element of the nation's healthcare system. Marshfield High School does two such drives a year, each collecting between eighty and ninety pints of blood.

have rejected these needle exchange programs. They charge that such programs give rise to disorder and crime and send the message that intravenous drug use is okay.

Then there is the always controversial question of sexual health and education. Should parents, educators, and other adult role models emphasize **abstinence** or teach teenagers to use condoms? Or is instruction in a variety of options that includes both abstinence and birth control the answer? What role should government play in providing access to contraception?

As these examples demonstrate, state and local governments are being asked to respond to a variety of public health challenges. And they are doing so in very different ways. Often these different positions reflect very different political cultures. Oregon has granted terminally ill patients the right to physician-assisted suicide. Most other states continue to classify such an action as a felony, even if it is rarely prosecuted. Nebraska passed legislation to ban late-term abortions, and even though the U.S. Supreme

ABSTINENCE

Refraining from sexual activity, usually intercourse.

New Hampshire announced plans to offer a free vaccine to prevent the virus that causes most cervical cancer to all girls between the ages of eleven and eighteen. Other states mandate use of the vaccine.

MEDICAID

A joint state and federal health insurance program that serves low-income mothers and children, the elderly, and people with disabilities.

Court later struck down the law, the voters had made their preferences known.

Different states have very different notions about the roles state governments should fill. Wisconsin's innovative early attempts at welfare reform in the late 1980s and early 1990s, laid the groundwork for the federal decision to junk welfare altogether in 1996 and return most welfare responsibilities to the states. States such as Massachusetts and Maine have sought to expand healthcare coverage to nearly every resident, whereas other states have shown no great enthusiasm for providing healthcare to low-income citizens.

Yet even states that have shown little interest in taking on new responsibilities have found that healthcare is *the* unavoidable issue. This is due largely to **Medicaid**, the joint state-federal health insurance program for low-income mothers and children, the elderly, and people with disabilities. When Congress created the program in 1965, it was supposed to be a modest program that served only a small number of extremely poor people. It hasn't worked out that way.

As soon as it was created, Medicaid expenditures started growing quickly—and never stopped. Today, it provides health insurance and services to approximately fifty-seven million Americans. This includes 27 million children, 15.5 million elderly and people with disabilities, and 14 million adults in low-income families.[6] States now devote an average of about 17 percent of their general revenue funds to Medicaid.[7]

The continuing growth of Medicaid has huge implications for the future of state governments. There are good reasons to believe the program will continue to grow at near double-digit rates, meaning that healthcare eventually will become the major function of state governments. That means either higher taxes or less money for other state priorities like education, transportation, and criminal justice.

County and city governments spend significant amounts on healthcare as well. In many parts of the country, hospitals and clinics funded by counties and cities continue to function as a critical social safety net for people without health insurance. These are people who earn too much to qualify for Medicaid but too little to pay for private health insurance. If the United States ever experiences a large-scale biological attack or influenza pandemic, the capacities of these facilities will determine how well this society survives such a crisis.

How Government Got into the Healthcare Biz

Any serious discussion of healthcare soon arrives at a basic question: "Who should pay for what?" Over the past decade, the answer has varied widely. During the early 1990s, the solution offered by many Democrats was, "The federal government should provide health insurance to everyone who does not have it."

By the early twenty-first century, a lot of those same Democrats were arguing that state governments, not the federal government, should lead the way. Universal—or nearly universal—coverage, they stated, should be created by gradually extending existing health insurance programs, notably Medicaid. Such programs should be expanded to encompass various populations not currently eligible for it. In contrast, some Republicans argued that health insurance should be extended via federal tax credits. How much health insurance should be provided has been another hotly contested topic.

It wasn't always so complicated. For most of the nation's history, elected officials believed that the government should serve as the health and welfare provider of last resort for society's poorest and sickest members. The level of government that officials had in mind, however, was not the federal government. Not even state governments. It was local government.

The role of local governments in health and welfare goes back to the very beginning of U.S. history. In colonial America, local communities maintained almshouses to feed and clothe people who could not care for themselves and who had no families to care for them. Back then few distinctions were made between the sick, the mentally ill, and people without a means of support. As sociologist Paul Starr has noted, almshouses "received dependent persons of all kinds, mixing together promiscuously the aged, the orphaned, the insane, the ill, the debilitated." [8] Those with infectious diseases, such as typhoid fever and cholera, were sent to pesthouses to survive as best they could.

That began to change in the nineteenth century. By the middle of the century, elected officials, social reformers, and physicians—who were just beginning to establish themselves as a respectable profession—came to believe that mixing juveniles, beggars, the mentally ill, widows, and others in almshouses was no longer the best course of action. In effect, physicians and public officials began to distinguish between the sick and the destitute. A new institution was needed—the hospital.

From the early to mid-1800s, cities like Philadelphia and New York transformed some of their almshouses into hospitals.[9] Privately organized charitable hospitals, many run by religious groups, appeared in many cities too. Even state governments made a modest foray into healthcare. By 1860, most states had established mental hospitals and homes for the blind and the deaf.

Like almshouses, the first hospitals were institutions for unfortunates without money or family. For people with families or money, a house call

> Even states that have shown little interest in taking on new responsibilities have found that healthcare is *the* unavoidable issue. This is due largely to Medicaid ... When Congress created the program in 1965, it was supposed to be a modest program that served only a small number of extremely poor people. It hasn't worked out that way.

from the doctor was the preferred form of medical care. According to Starr, "[a]lmost no one who had a choice sought hospital care."

Hospitals were regarded with dread, and rightly so. They were dangerous places, in part because of the medical and hygienic practices of the time. Sick people were safer at home. The few who became patients went into hospitals because of special circumstances. They might be seamen in a strange port, travelers, the homeless, or the solitary aged. Individuals who, whether traveling or destitute, were unlucky enough to fall sick without family, friends, or servants to care for them.[10]

Hospitals and physicians made a spirited effort to improve their image. Hospitals moved their sickest residents—as well as patients who were dissolute or morally objectionable—to other institutions. In 1847, for instance, Bellevue Hospital in New York decided to move the penitentiary and almshouse off its grounds and concentrate on medical care.[11] The hospital was beginning to emerge as a distinct institution.

As hospitals sought more respectable clientele, almshouses took on a harder edge. During the seventeenth and eighteenth centuries, many almshouses were patterned on conventional homes and sought to serve as a kind of surrogate family for their residents. During the nineteenth century, however, local governments refashioned almshouse to serve a different purpose. Such facilities now were used to illustrate the consequences of idleness, sinfulness, and poverty and to shame their residents. Shabby facilities and neglect became commonplace.[12]

The Idea of a Social Safety Net

This arrangement continued in the United States until well into the twentieth century. The duty of providing healthcare and welfare remained firmly in the hands of local governments. States assisted with those with mental illnesses and people with disabilities. The federal government ran a compulsory health insurance system for the merchant marine, so that sick sailors could get care in any port, and provided pensions and healthcare to military veterans.

By the end of the nineteenth century, a new idea was percolating in progressive circles. Many social reformers came to believe that the federal government should take a much larger role in securing healthcare and pensions for the working class.

Such an idea first arose in Germany. In 1883, the conservative government of German chancellor Otto von Bismarck created the world's first compulsory sickness and unemployment insurance fund, which required employees and employers to set aside money to cover the costs of medical treatment for workers. Bismarck later created a compulsory retirement program, whose cost was divided among employees, employers, and the national government, in much the same way that it is done in the United States today.

These innovations were momentous in the development of the state. Before Bismarck, talk of healthcare, unemployment insurance, and pensions had been largely the arena of socialists and communists. He showed that conservative, capitalist countries could enact such programs too. Indeed, they could take the lead in developing a generous social safety net. Over the course of the next thirty years, other European countries followed Germany's lead.

The United States, however, did not. During the heyday of the Progressive movement in the early twentieth century, discussions about national health insurance were widespread. Eventually, opposition from physicians and from the country's largest labor union, the American Federation of Labor (forebearer of today's AFL-CIO), fearful of government control of the healthcare system, effectively derailed the idea. During the 1920s, many states took the small, first steps toward creating a social safety net by setting up workers' compensation funds for injured workers. However, amidst the affluence of the times, there was little support for a more ambitious social safety net.[13] That changed with the start of the Great Depression.

The Birth of the American Safety Net

On Thursday, October 24, 1929, the stock market in New York City collapsed in what the *New York Times* called "the most disastrous trading day in the stock market's history."[14] By the spring of 1933, it was clear that the United States had entered an unprecedented economic slump—the Great Depression.

In response to this economic disaster, the federal government for the first time took on some of the social safety net functions that European governments had pioneered decades earlier.[15] In 1935, President Franklin Delano Roosevelt and Congress teamed up to pass the Social Security Act. This act established two social safety net programs. The first was a joint federal-state program of unemployment compensation. The second was a federally run program of retirement benefits for senior citizens, which soon would be known simply as Social Security.

The federal government also created the Aid to Families with Dependent Children program. AFDC's purpose was to provide monetary assistance to widowed women with children, women who had been abandoned by their husbands, or women who were in some way incapacitated. Funded by the federal government, the program was administered by the states.

The Roosevelt administration briefly considered adding a compulsory health insurance program to the Social Security Act as well. However, given the medical industry's continued vehement opposition to the idea for fear of too much government control, the proposal was eventually dropped as too controversial. Instead, the Social Security Act provided federal grants to help states pay for programs for the disabled and the aged and to provide child welfare services, public health services, and vocational rehabilitation.[16] As a result, responsibility for providing a healthcare safety net remained in the hands of state and local governments.

A Multibillion-Dollar Afterthought

State governments became major participants in the U.S. safety net system almost by accident. After the assassination of President John F. Kennedy in 1963, Lyndon B. Johnson ascended to the Oval Office. Johnson and congressional Democrats were determined to pass legislation that would cover hospital costs for senior citizens. Congressional Republicans, however, had a different proposal in mind. They supported a voluntary health insurance program that would cover the cost of physician visits for seniors. So in 1965, the two parties decided to compromise in classic Washington fashion—by doing both. The result was **Medicare**, the federal health insurance program for the elderly.

But Congress didn't stop there. While it was on a roll, it also created Medicaid. Despite their very similar names, Medicare and Medicaid are very different programs. Medicare is run and paid for entirely by the federal government. As with Social Security, every senior who worked for ten years and paid taxes—or whose spouse worked for ten years and paid taxes—is eligible to participate, as are people with certain types of disabilities. The program is financed in part by a small payroll tax. Most retirees, however, take far more out of Medicare than they contribute.[17] Understandably, Medicare almost immediately became a popular program.

Medicaid, on the other hand, is a joint state-federal program that is paid for in part by the general revenue funds of state and local governments. The federal government does pick up most of the cost, however. On average, it covers 57 percent of Medicaid expenditures. For poorer areas, the percentage is higher. Arkansas, Mississippi, Montana, New Mexico, Utah, and West Virginia all receive more than 70 percent of their Medicaid expenditures from the federal govern-

MEDICARE

The federal health insurance program for elderly citizens.

IMPLEMENTING MEDICARE

1. Getting the People 65 or Over Ready
2. Getting Hospitals and Other Institutions Ready
3. Arranging for Participation of Physicians
4. Tooling Up for Internal Operations

With the strong backing of President Lyndon Johnson, Congress created Medicare in 1965. The federal health insurance program for the elderly has proven to be wildly popular, but also has proven to be incredibly expensive for state governments. Pictured here is John Gardner, Johnson's Secretary of Health, Education, and Welfare. His outline for implementing Medicare notably says nothing about who is covering the costs.

ment.[18] Wealthier states split the cost 50–50. States do not have to participate. However, since 1982—when Arizona finally signed on—all states have.

Therefore, Medicaid is not an unfunded mandate. The federal government does not force states to participate in it. It is, however, an entitlement
program. That is, it does create legally enforceable rights. In fact, it is a double entitlement program. For one, states have a right to a certain amount of
federal money every year. And then, individuals who meet its eligibility
thresholds are entitled to its services, regardless of the cost. States are
required to provide coverage to certain populations, including children in
families with income below the **poverty line,** or **poverty threshold,** and parents who qualify for TANF.[19]

Beyond these basics, the states enjoy considerable leeway to setting those
eligibility standards. (See Table 15-1.) They have created healthcare safety
nets with very different levels of generosity. As of July 2005, Alabama and
Arkansas were the least generous states in the country. They allowed only
those earning less than 19 percent of the federal poverty level—the threshold set by the U.S. Bureau of the Census to measure poverty—to receive
Medicaid. That means that a working parent with two children who earned
more than $255 a month—slightly more than $3,000 a year—earned too
much to qualify. Few states want to be stingy when it comes to health coverage. But they need to balance their budgets, and paring back eligibility
levels is one way to make the numbers work, especially when Medicaid
expenditures increase by double-digit percentages every year.

The most generous state was Minnesota. It allowed families earning up
to 275 percent of the federal poverty level to receive Medicaid benefits. In
other words, a working parent with two children could earn up to $3,687
a month—more than $44,000 a year—and still qualify for Medicaid. Even
controlling for the fact that most parts of Alabama and Arkansas have considerably lower costs of living than Minnesota, that is a dramatic difference.
The United States may have one safety net for seniors, but for everyone else,
it is a country with fifty-one safety nets.

**POVERTY LINE, OR
POVERTY THRESHOLD**

An annual income level,
set by the federal
government, below
which families cannot
afford basic necessities.

Oops!: The Unexpected Cost of Health Insurance

Medicare and Medicaid were structured very differently, but the two programs soon revealed a common trait. They both quickly proved to be fan-
tastically expensive. From 1965 to 1970, the annual rate of increase in state
and federal health expenditures was 20.8 percent. By fiscal year 2005, the
federal government and state governments spent more than $300 billion on
Medicaid alone.[20]

Even as state officials were watching with alarm as Medicaid spending
soared, another disturbing trend was becoming evident. The number of
women with children receiving financial assistance under the AFDC program was soaring too. After two decades of slow growth, the number of

TABLE 15-1

Amount a Working Parent with Two Children Applying for Publicly Funded Coverage May Earn and Still Be Eligible for Medicaid (as of July 1, 2005)

State	Monthly Income-Eligibility Threshold	Annual Income-Eligibility Threshold	Percentage of 2005 Federal Poverty Line
Alabama	$255	$3,057	19%
Alaska	$1,357	$16,289	81%
Arizona	$2,682	$32,180	200%
Arkansas	$255	$3,057	19%
California	$1,435	$17,216	107%
Colorado	$510	$6,114	38%
Connecticut	$2,105	$25,261	157%
Delaware	$1,435	$17,216	107%
District of Columbia	$2,682	$32,180	200%
Florida	$805	$9,654	60%
Georgia	$751	$9,010	56%
Hawaii	$1,543	$18,510	100%
Idaho	$402	$4,827	30%
Illinois	$2,574	$30,893	192%
Indiana	$375	$4,505	28%
Iowa	$1,059	$12,711	79%
Kansas	$496	$5,953	37%
Kentucky	$912	$10,941	68%
Louisiana	$268	$3,218	20%
Maine	$2,105	$25,261	157%
Maryland	$523	$6,275	39%
Massachusetts	$1,783	$21,400	133%
Michigan	$778	$9,332	58%
Minnesota	$3,687	$44,248	275%
Mississippi	$456	$5,471	34%
Missouri	$563	$6,758	42%
Montana	$858	$10,298	64%
Nebraska	$805	$9,654	60%
Nevada	$1,126	$13,516	84%
New Hampshire	$778	$9,332	58%

TABLE 15-1, continued

State	Monthly Income-Eligibility Threshold	Annual Income-Eligibility Threshold	Percentage of 2005 Federal Poverty Line
New Jersey	$1,341	$16,090	100%
New Mexico	$898	$10,780	67%
New York	$2,011	$24,135	150%
North Carolina	$751	$9,010	56%
North Dakota	$898	$10,780	67%
Ohio	$1,207	$14,481	90%
Oklahoma	$590	$7,080	44%
Oregon	$1,341	$16,090	100%
Pennsylvania	$845	$10,137	63%
Rhode Island	$2,574	$30,893	192%
South Carolina	$1,301	$15,607	97%
South Dakota	$791	$9,493	59%
Tennessee	$1,086	$13,033	81%
Texas	$402	$4,827	30%
Utah	$670	$8,045	50%
Vermont	$2,574	$30,893	192%
Virginia	$416	$4,988	31%
Washington	$1,086	$13,033	81%
West Virginia	$496	$5,953	37%
Wisconsin	$2,574	$30,893	192%
Wyoming	$791	$9,493	59%
U.S. Median	**$898**	**$10,780**	**67%**

Source: Adapted from "Income Eligibility for Parents Applying for Medicaid by Annual Income as a Percent of Federal Poverty Level, 2005," Kaiser statehealthfacts.org (accessed November 28, 2006).

Note: Federal poverty level for a family of three was $16,090 for the forty-eight contiguous states, $18,510 for Hawaii, and $20,110 for Alaska. Monthly and annual income thresholds rounded to the nearest dollar.

AFDC beneficiaries took off in the late 1960s, rising from slightly more than two million recipients in 1960 to more than ten million recipients by 1972.

The composition of AFDC recipients also was changing. The widows of the 1940s were being replaced by divorced and separated women with children as well as single mothers who had never been married. By 1979, single mothers made up nearly 80 percent of all AFDC recipients.[21]

As those benefiting from welfare changed, the program became increasingly unpopular with the public. During the late 1970s and early 1980s,

Ronald Reagan and other conservative politicians railed against what they saw as the excesses of the welfare state. They evoked images of "welfare queens" who drove Cadillacs and paid for steak dinners with fat rolls of food stamps.[22] Reagan's welfare queen proved to be more of a myth than reality, but it was arguably true that the United States had created a set of permanent dependents of the sort that Franklin Delano Roosevelt had warned against when he called government relief "a narcotic, a subtle destroyer of the human spirit."[23]

The 1970s were a difficult decade for proponents of expanding the nation's social safety net. As the boom of the 1960s gave way to the stagflation of the 1970s, cities such as New York ran into serious problems. These were urban centers that had long prided themselves on generous housing subsidies and social programs. However, as manufacturing jobs vanished and businesses and middle-class residents abandoned many urban downtowns, cities were forced to radically scale back their efforts. In 1976, after years of lavish overspending and declining federal subsidies, New York City was forced to declare bankruptcy. Even state and local governments that had not attempted to forge comprehensive social safety nets were forced to dramatically reduce their social welfare programs.

The Devolution Revolution

Supporters of Ronald Reagan weren't the only people fed up. State and local officials were too. Many were frustrated by the high-handed way that the federal government administered welfare and Medicaid. Medicaid was theoretically a joint state-federal program, but the federal government always held the whip over state governments. The Centers for Medicare and Medicaid Services (CMS) is the federal agency responsible for administering both Medicare and Medicaid. Formerly the Health Care Financing Administration, this agency monitors state governments in much the same way that a reform school principal might monitor juvenile offenders.

Of course, the federal government sometimes had reason to be suspicious. Many states, most notably Louisiana, have long sought to shift as many Medicaid expenses to the federal side of the ledger as possible. Indeed, in 2004, the federal government chided both Louisiana and Missouri for improper reimbursements totaling $116 million and $87 million, respectively.[24]

Despite sometimes questionable actions on the part of the states, such as Louisiana, even federal officials began to come around during the 1980s. Maybe the states should be given greater freedom to experiment with their welfare and Medicaid programs. In the late 1980s, the U.S. Department of Health and Human Services, the parent organization of the CMS, began to grant states "demonstration waivers." This allowed states to experiment with how they provided welfare and healthcare. By 2006, every state had received at least one waiver for a portion of its Medicaid program. States were able to extend or augment health insurance to more than seven million individuals who otherwise would not have been able to receive it.[25] The 2005 Deficit Reduction Act increased both states' responsibility for and flexibility over Medicaid (see box on page 556).

Welfare Reform

One of the first states to take advantage of federal flexibility was Wisconsin. In 1987, Tommy Thompson entered the governor's office. One of Thompson's first acts was to bring together about a dozen people for lunch at the executive mansion to discuss one of the most contentious topics in American politics—welfare reform. Thompson's first lunch underscored that he was eager to think outside the box and achieve real reform. Unlike most governors, Thompson didn't invite policy wonks or advocates, either pro or con. Instead, he invited welfare mothers so that he could hear first-hand about obstacles that made it difficult for them to get and keep jobs.[26]

Thompson took the answers he got that day and during his subsequent yearly lunches and set out to radically reorient welfare in Wisconsin. In doing so, he managed to avoid the dead ends that previous reformers had encountered. In the past, most states had attempted to move welfare recipients into the job market by providing training and education opportunities. All of these programs were expensive. Only some were successful. Thompson decided to focus on getting welfare recipients a job. Any job. Virtually all recipients were required to work. If they were unable to find a job, then a subsidized one or one in community service was made available.

If welfare recipients needed childcare or transportation to get to work, the state provided it. Essentially, Thompson subverted one of the major arguments for ending welfare—namely, that welfare recipients were free riding on the taxpaying public. Instead, he actually increased funding for childcare, healthcare, and transportation. Once recipients were working, they were provided with one-on-one job counseling, education, training, and other support services.[27]

Not all of Thompson's actions to reform welfare were as touchy-feely as his yearly lunches or as supportive as providing childcare and transportation. Some of them were downright coercive. Funds were cut off to parents of truant children. Marriage incentives were created for teenage parents.

By forcing welfare recipients to get jobs *and* offering them the support they realistically needed to enter the job market, Thompson disarmed both conservative and liberal critics and pointed the way to workable reforms to the system. Other states soon followed suit. Work requirements were strengthened and time limits on benefits were imposed. New assistance with

A Difference that Makes a Difference: Waiving Goodbye to Traditional Medicaid

Tennessee made headlines in 1994 when the Clinton administration approved a first-of-its kind waiver that allowed the state to reshape its Medicaid program to include everyone close to or below the federal poverty line. TennCare, as the new program was known, went on to cover as much as 25 percent of Tennessee's population and reduced the number of uninsured residents dramatically.

Today, TennCare has been dismantled, done in by rapidly rising costs. But the federal government continues to make deals with states interested in redesigning their Medicaid programs, although the Bush administration approached waivers differently than the Clinton White House did. These days, the Centers for Medicaid and Medicare Services (CMS) tends to favor proposals that cap program costs rather than add thousands of near-poor people to the rolls—and this approach shifts the risk of cost overruns to the states.

States, interested in finding ways to reduce their own Medicaid-related costs, have brought a wide variety of proposals to CMS, ranging from narrowly constructed reforms of prescription drug programs to full-blown reforms to statewide systems of care.

In 2005, Vermont struck a ground-breaking deal with the feds. In exchange for more flexibility in managing and distributing Medicaid funds, the state agreed to limit the amount of federal Medicaid funds it will receive through 2009. Total Medicaid spending will be capped at $4.7 billion, with the federal government contributing about 60 percent of the funds. The state will have to eat any costs above that threshold, but optimistic officials estimate that overruns won't happen. In fact, they believe the deal will end up saving them about $165 million, thanks in part to patients' lengthened terms of eligibility, which the state expects will enable doctors to treat chronic conditions more proactively—and cheaply.

West Virginia is in search of savings with its revised Medicaid program, too. During the summer of 2006, CMS approved the state's plan to reward healthy and responsible Medicaid beneficiaries with additional benefits, as allowed by the federal Deficit Reduction Act of 2006, which gives states unprecedented flexibility with their Medicaid programs. Patients who miss appointments or don't join weight-loss or anti-smoking programs will be denied some services, a feature of the

childcare and transportation was offered. By the summer of 1996, more than forty states had received statewide waivers that allowed them to vary work requirements for AFDC recipients.[28]

Thompson's reforms, coercive or otherwise, were remarkably effective. Providing services such as childcare and transportation increased per capita welfare costs in the short run, but in the long run it paid off. State welfare costs fell by about 65 percent over the course of the decade. The state saved more than $1 billion. Such successes later earned Thompson the position of secretary of health and human services under President George W. Bush.

It was in 1996 that Congress and President Bill Clinton formally embraced the reforms that states had initiated. The AFDC program was replaced with TANF. As part of this new program, the Personal Responsibility and Work Opportunity Reconciliation Act put a five-year cap on fed-

plan denounced by critics. As this book goes to press, the plan is being rolled out in three counties, and it is too early yet to tell what the ultimate results will be.

Critics have been vocal, too, about Florida's new Medicaid program. With the state's Medicaid costs escalating 20 percent or more a year, changes undeniably needed to be made to prevent the program from eating the entire state budget. The plan devised by the state—introduced in a pilot phase to two counties in 2006—is possibly the most radical reform proposed in Medicaid's forty-year history. Beneficiaries will be given what amount to vouchers to buy health plans offered by private insurance companies. The amount of each voucher will be set depending on the patient's health status; elderly and seriously ill patients will receive more than healthy adults. The insurers will provide preventive services and meet the federally required minimum service level, but then they—not the state—will have newfound flexibility to determine the scope of benefits.

Taking yet another step toward the private insurance model, Florida's revised Medicaid program will come with a maximum benefit level for each recipient. Once that level is reached, beneficiaries will have to pay out of pocket or go without. Critics worry this feature will overburden those unable to pay and lead to a sicker population that simply turns to the hospital system, driving up costs across the medical system, but the state says a catastrophic care fund will be established to help such recipients pay for necessary care.

States are experimenting with new and different ideas to pay for residents' healthcare to see if they make sense. More than a decade ago, TennCare made sense. The more recent Medicaid reforms may fare better than TennCare, both fiscally and politically—or they may not. What's certain is that the other states will be watching.

Sources: Adapted from Penelope Lemov, "Drowning in Choices," *Governing* magazine, November 2005; Zach Patton, "Vermont Accepts a Medicaid Cap," *Governing* magazine, December 2005; Kevin Kelley, "State to Roll the Dice in Medicaid Deal," *Vermont Business Magazine,* December 1, 2005; Penelope Lemov, "Capping Medicaid Costs," *Governing* magazine, March 2006; and Eric Eckholm, "Medicaid Plan Prods Patients toward Health," *New York Times,* December 1, 2006.

eral payments to welfare recipients. It also required states to put a large portion of welfare recipients to work.

What the new legislation was most notable for, however, was for what it did not require. Gone were most of the requirements that the federal government sign off on state plans. TANF gave states the freedom to set benefit levels, eligibility requirements, and financial incentives and penalties as they saw fit.

TANF also converted welfare from an **entitlement program** to a block grant program. In the past, people who met eligibility guidelines had been legally entitled to welfare, no matter the cost. Now, the federal government would provide only a finite amount of money to the states. At first, the federal payout was quite generous. The intent was to give states plenty of funds to devise and implement the support programs of their choice. Over time, however, the federal contribution grew smaller and smaller.

ENTITLEMENT PROGRAM

A government-run program that guarantees unlimited assistance to those who meet its eligibility requirements, no matter the cost.

Opponents of the reforms were deeply upset by the loss of the entitlement aspect of welfare. This seemed to announce a retreat from the progressive goal of expanding the social safety net. Democratic senator Daniel Patrick Moynihan warned of children in the streets and "something approaching the Apocalypse." [29]

So far, such predictions have proven to be off base. The number of welfare recipients declined sharply, from approximately six million in 1996 to about four million in 2006. Poverty rates for single-parent households also fell during this period. By and large, the alarming predictions have failed to materialize.

The fact that this happened during the longest economic expansion since the Second World War undoubtedly played an important part in the success of welfare reform. However, even when the economy slid into recession in the spring of 2001, the number of people on welfare rolls stayed low. So too did the expansion of the Earned Income Tax Credit and the expansion of Medicaid in many states.

However, as with the AFDC program, states have created TANF programs with very different levels of benefits. (See Map 15-1.) A dollar in Mississippi goes a lot farther than a dollar in California. Even a cursory look at the map reveals that states' TANF spending tends to track their political orientation. Simply put, Democratic states continue to spend more on welfare than Republican states.

The Feds Falter

When Bill Clinton took office in 1993, he and his administration were prepared to let states take the lead on welfare reform. After all, the president's previous job had been governor of Arkansas. However, the president and his wife, Hillary, did see the problem of the uninsured as primarily a federal one. In early 1994, Clinton introduced the Health Security Act. This was legislation that would have provided universal health insurance to all Americans.

Senate Republicans initially countered with a proposal that would have extended health insurance coverage dramatically but would still have fallen short of universal health insurance. Clinton rejected this counterproposal, vowing to veto any measure that failed to provide 100 percent coverage.[30] Politics being politics, the two major parties were unable to find common ground. Nine months later, the Clinton health insurance proposal went down in defeat.[31]

Fast forward a decade. In 2005, there were an estimated forty-six million Americans sixty-five years of age and younger without health insurance—seven million more than had been uninsured just five years earlier. (See Map 15-2.) The Kaiser Commission on Medicaid and the Uninsured estimates that some 20 percent of uninsured residents are noncitizens, who often work in low-wage jobs that do not include health coverage.[32] Since the defeat of the Health Security Act, the federal government has largely given up the effort to find a federal solution to the problem of the uninsured or such new problems as the soaring cost of prescription drugs. In the absence of federal initiative, the states have stepped up to the plate once again.

> The federal government has largely given up the search for a solution to the problems of the uninsured or soaring prices of prescription drugs. In its absence, the states have stepped up to the plate once again.

The Rise of the Healthcare State

The collapse of healthcare reform efforts at the federal level left states in a tricky position. They were being squeezed between the pincers of the rising costs of state Medicaid programs and the rising demands for assistance from citizens struggling with drug costs and a lack of health insurance.

MAP 15-1 TANF Income Eligibility Thresholds, 2005

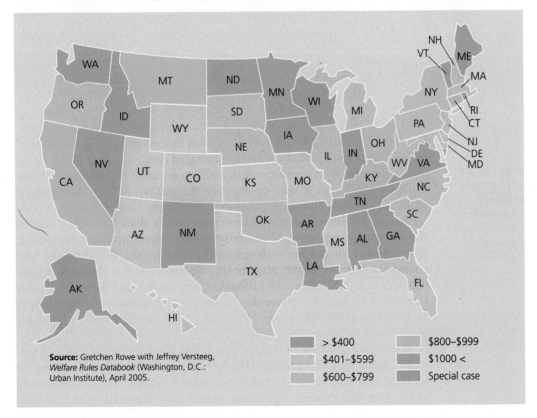

Source: Gretchen Rowe with Jeffrey Versteeg, *Welfare Rules Databook* (Washington, D.C.: Urban Institute), April 2005.

Legend:
- > $400
- $401–$599
- $600–$799
- $800–$999
- $1000 <
- Special case

MAP 15-2 Rates of Uninsurance among Non-Elderly, 2006

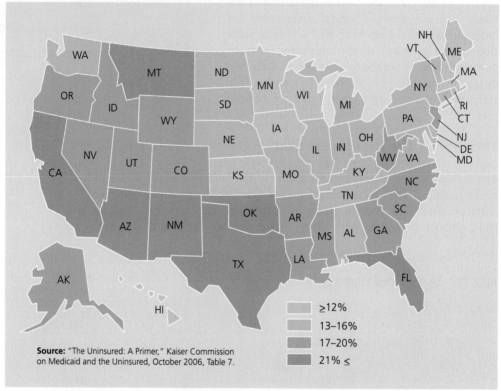

Legend:
- ≥12%
- 13–16%
- 17–20%
- 21% ≤

Source: "The Uninsured: A Primer," Kaiser Commission on Medicaid and the Uninsured, October 2006, Table 7.

MANAGED CARE

An arrangement for the provision of healthcare whereby an agency acts as an intermediary between consumers and healthcare providers.

Finally, in the mid-1990s, states found what looked like a good way to both contain costs and expand coverage—**managed care.**

Proponents of managed care originally saw health maintenance organizations (HMOs) as a way to improve the quality of care that patients received. Most medical care patients receive in the United States is poorly coordinated. Different doctors often cannot easily share a patient's medical records. Physicians have little incentive to offer preventive services because they get paid for dealing with sickness. Paul Ellwood, the physician who coined the phrase "health maintenance organization" in the early 1970s, believed that HMOs would rationalize and coordinate the care patients received. This would improve the quality of the healthcare the members of an HMO received. Moreover, HMOs would reduce costs by emphasizing preventive healthcare.

Under managed care, instead of paying doctors a fee for each service provided, states typically paid an HMO a flat fee for each Medicaid patient enrolled in a plan. The fee that states offered HMOs was designed to be lower than the expenses the states would have incurred if patients had remained in a traditional "fee for service" Medicaid program. HMOs agreed to these lower rates because they believed that even with lower reimbursement rates, they would still be able to squeeze inefficiencies out of the system and turn a profit.

Medicaid beneficiaries benefited too. They were able to join health plans that gave them access to physicians and services that often had been unavailable under the old program. Traditional Medicaid reimbursement rates are so low that many physicians simply refuse to see Medicaid beneficiaries. Ultimately, the states saved money, at least theoretically.[33]

Some states pocketed the savings. Others viewed the windfall as an opportunity to achieve more ambitious goals. In 1994, Tennessee governor Ned McWherter, a Democrat, converted Tennessee's entire Medicaid program into a managed care program—TennCare. The new program was opened up to an estimated four hundred thousand people who lacked health insurance but earned too much to qualify for Medicaid. That same year Oregon governor John Kitzhaber received permission from the U.S. Department of Health and Human Services to try an even more radical approach: Oregon was allowed to explicitly ration its healthcare dollars to cover as many people as possible in the most cost-effective fashion possible.

A Promising Beginning

For a while, the HMO approach seemed to work. By 1998, approximately half of all Medicaid recipients nationwide were in managed care programs.[34] As enrollment increased, health costs slowed. Between 1995 and 1999, Medicaid expenditures grew at the relatively modest rate of 4.3 percent annually. This was dramatically lower than the unprecedented 27 percent growth of the early 1990s.[35] In addition, as the economic expansion that began in the early 1990s gained momentum and swelled state coffers, a growing number of state officials and healthcare advocates began to think about addressing other problems of the uninsured.

Who should do what? In 1993, Democrats and other advocates of universal health insurance had said that nothing less than universal coverage would do. After the defeat of the Health Security Act, however, many advocates set their sights on a different model. Instead of a new federal program, they sought a new state-federal partnership. The first goal—to extend health insurance to uninsured children in families that earned too much to qualify for Medicaid but too little to pay for healthcare on their own.

In August 1997, Congress created the **State Children's Health Insurance Program** at the behest of President Clinton. SCHIP (as it came to be known) was designed to provide health insurance to roughly 6.5 million children in low-income families without health insurance.[36] As with Medicaid, SCHIP would be designed and administered by the states and paid for primarily by the federal government. The federal government would spring for about 80 percent of total costs.

STATE CHILDREN'S HEALTH INSURANCE PROGRAM (SCHIP)

A joint federal-state program designed to expand coverage to children whose parents earned income above the poverty line but still were too poor to afford insurance.

The states were given considerable flexibility in designing their child health programs. They were free to fold SCHIP into their Medicaid programs or create stand-alone SCHIP programs. As with Medicaid, they determined eligibility levels. They also could cap SCHIP enrollments and force recipients to pay some of the costs for the health insurance they received.[37]

Not surprisingly, states have taken full advantage of this flexibility. Twenty-three states currently allow children living in families earning up to 200 percent of the federal poverty level to qualify for SCHIP. Nine states cover children in families with even higher incomes—sometimes significantly higher. Connecticut, Maryland, New Hampshire, New Jersey, and Vermont all set their eligibility levels from 300 percent to 350 percent of the federal level. Other states, including Montana and North Dakota, set much lower eligibility thresholds.[38]

What effect do these different policies have on the residents of these states? It's hard to say. Not having health insurance does not necessarily translate into no healthcare. Government-supported community health clinics provide healthcare to more than six million uninsured Americans in thousands of communities across the country every year. These clinics treat people regardless of their ability or inability to pay. In addition, hospitals are required to provide treatment to people who come into their emergency rooms, whether these people can pay or not.

Along with community health clinics, public hospitals have long assumed a particularly important role in providing services to the uninsured. For many low-income individuals, the emergency room of a public hospital is their first and only way to access medical care. Many public hospitals border high-crime neighborhoods and provide essential advanced emergency and trauma services, as well as outpatient clinics for these same communities.

These are critically important functions. They are not, however, very profitable ones. The Urban Institute estimates it costs hospitals about $40 billion a year to treat uninsured patients. The 1990s were a tough decade for public hospitals. HMOs squeezed hospitals' fees and private competitors scooped up desirable patients with private health insurance. Between 1996 and 2002, the number of public hospitals in the 100 largest cities fell from 730 to 645.[39] (See box on page 564.)

Access to care is not an issue limited to cities and suburbs. Rural areas long have been plagued by fragmented healthcare systems and shortages of doctors and nurses. Even worse, rural residents tend to be older and poorer than their urban and suburban counterparts, factors that often translate into a greater need for healthcare services.[40] It's not a formula for a healthy population.

The problem has not gone unnoticed. In partnership with the federal government, all fifty states have established offices of rural health. For instance, the Appalachian Regional Commission is a federal-state partnership that addresses economic and social issues in West Virginia and parts of twelve other states. This partnership advocates telemedicine as a strategy for residents to gain access to specialists and for doctors in rural areas to gain needed continuing education. In one instance, eleven sites in northeastern New York State have been equipped with computers and other technology to create a "virtual pediatric center" serving three counties where poverty is high, transportation is difficult, and healthcare is insufficient.[41]

Researchers have found a strong link between health insurance and access to and use of healthcare.[42] Giving more people access to public healthcare probably is the most direct way to increase their healthcare use. Connecticut and Vermont are two states that have made major efforts to expand eligibility for public health insurance. Subsequently, they have lower numbers of uninsured children than states like Idaho or Montana. However, that is not universally the case. During the 2004–2005 fiscal year, "generous" New Jersey had an 11 percent uninsured rate among children; 10 percent of kids were uninsured in "stingy" North Dakota.[43] Such a paradox as this can be caused by a combination of factors: the availability of jobs offering health insurance, parents' awareness of programs for which their children qualify, and the cost of insurance for those just beyond the eligibility thresholds.

Does It Work?

By the late 1990s, many health policy experts and advocates had come to see the gradual expansion of Medicaid and SCHIP and of the state-federal partnership as the best way to address the widespread lack of health insurance in the United States. The Robert Wood Johnson Foundation reported in 2006 that the number of uninsured children had dropped by 20 percent since SCHIP's introduction.[44]

That is clearly a significant accomplishment. Unfortunately, the SCHIP approach has not reached everyone it is supposed to reach. The Urban Institute estimates that more than a quarter of all poor children—those in families with incomes below 100 percent of the federal poverty level—continue to go without insurance. Indeed, data from 2005 showed that 12 percent of children in the United States are not covered by insurance. Among poor children—who make up about one-fifth of all children—that figure is significantly higher. This is despite the fact that almost all of this population qualifies for SCHIP.[45]

Why? The problem seems to be that families in certain states simply have not signed up. Knowledge of Medicaid and SCHIP varies substantially across states, and as states endured budget crises in the early years of this decade, many cut costs by curtailing outreach and program simplification efforts.[46] In Texas, only 41 percent of low-income families had heard of these programs. In Massachusetts, 71 percent had. As a result, in Massachusetts, the vast majority of people eligible for Medicaid and SCHIP participate. Subsequently, only 6 percent of children in Massachusetts lack

Local Focus: Rising from a Hospital's Ruins: Milwaukee

It was the "hospital of last resort." For 135 years, County General—later Doyne Hospital—served the poor of Milwaukee. The suburban county hospital was as solid in its commitment to providing care as its massive brick-and-stone architecture. It mattered not if the patient was from the inner city or from across the street.

By the 1980s, however, that commitment got expensive. Hospital managers had to make regular visits to the county board of supervisors to report yet another budget shortfall. The county bailed the hospital out, but the board was growing increasingly tired of the ritual.

By 1995, the supervisors had had enough. They closed Doyne, an act that cut a psychological hole in the fabric of the community. Generations of families had been born or treated there. The fear was that the poor would have nowhere to go when they got sick or just needed to get a prescription filled.

Fears of closures similar to that of Doyne have been running through neighborhoods in Austin, Texas; Boston, Massachusetts; Detroit, Michigan; Tampa, Florida, and dozens of other places in which public hospitals have closed recently or been turned over to private management. With the dramatic upheaval and rising costs in the healthcare industry, more and more local governments are getting out of the hospital business. An Urban Institute survey conducted after these conversions found that most hospital patients were equally or more satisfied with the new arrangements. However, respondents also expressed fear over diminished access in the future.

For local officials, closing a public hospital is politically risky. The hospital—its history, its difficulties, and its successes—is often a symbol of the community itself. Just ask Anthony Williams, mayor of Washington, D.C., from 1999 to 2007. Facing budget woes, Williams sought to close D.C. General, the city's lone public hospital for nearly two hundred years. Many African American residents relied on the hospital for care, and they were proud of the generations of black physicians who

had been trained there. Williams eventually won the battle and the hospital closed in June 2004. The residents of the District's east side, the most frequent users of D.C. General, were left with few nearby medical centers.

In early 2007, it appeared likely that the public hospital network in Prince George's County, Maryland, just over the border from D.C., would close as well. This would add to the scarcity of available medical options for several hundred thousand individuals, many of whom are low-income, unemployed, or homeless. Given a reprieve by the county council until mid-2008, the hospital's owner and its administration face an uphill battle to secure sufficient funding to convince the county council to keep it and several other smaller hospitals open after that time.

Since Doyne's closing, Milwaukee is looking pretty good. The county was able to convince the area's private hospitals and clinics that all health providers, not just the county, were responsible for the healthcare safety net. All of the area's private hospitals and neighborhood clinics signed contracts with the county to treat the medically indigent.

The county's medically indigent have, by most accounts, roughly the same access to medical care that they had before. For some residents, particularly in the inner city, access actually has improved. What's more, the nature of that care is changing for the better. Fewer people use emergency rooms and more people visit clinics for preventive care.

And all of this is being accomplished for less money and with a more stable budgeting process. This does *not* mean that the burden comes cheap. The hospitals especially have had to suck up big financial losses to make it work. "When Doyne was there, it was easy for other hospitals to say that the uninsured and underinsured were Doyne's problem," says former county health director Paula Lucey, who also worked as a nurse at Doyne for twenty years. "Now, taking care of the poor is everybody's problem."

Sources: Adapted from Christopher Swope, "Rising from a Hospital's Ruins," *Governing* magazine, September 2001; Susan Levine, "A D.C. Neighborhood Finds Itself in Unhealthy Condition," *Washington Post,* November 24, 2006.

health insurance. In contrast, roughly 20 percent of children in Texas lacked health insurance in 2005.

As Medicaid spending accelerated and state revenues shriveled, states retreated from plans to expand their SCHIP programs and shifted their emphasis to containing costs as best they could. Caught in the budgetary crossfire: waivers allowing states to cover adults who didn't qualify for Medicaid through SCHIP. Federal officials expected the program to cover 2.7 million uninsured adults, but states simply couldn't afford to expand coverage. By 2004, programs under the waivers added just about 200,000.[47]

The Decline of Managed Care

After the initial surge of success mentioned earlier in this section, many HMOs failed to meet the high hopes of their boosters. Consumers were dismayed by the ways in which HMOs limited their choices of doctors to a small group of physicians who had agreed to lower reimbursement rates. In some cases, the programs demanded that doctors receive pre-approval before performing certain procedures. By the late 1990s, many consumers had turned against HMOs.

Eager to separate themselves from the HMOs they had initially supported, state legislators acted on their residents' desires. Many states passed "patients' bill of rights" legislation. These laws made it easier for patients to sue HMOs and generally made it more difficult for managed care plans to restrict healthcare. Such acts may have curbed some of the HMOs' more egregious practices, but they also came with a cost of their own. By making it harder for HMOs to limit care and access to physicians, lawmakers also deprived HMOs of negotiating leverage and reduced their ability to hold down costs. Costs were again on the rise by the late 1990s.

TennCare, Tennessee's innovative program that used managed care to expand insurance coverage to 25 percent of the state's population, crumbled due to reliance on unstable HMOs and rapidly escalating costs. One study projected that TennCare would require 91 percent of Tennessee's tax appropriations by 2008. In 2005, eligibility was scaled back dramatically, and more than three hundred thousand adults fell off the rolls. TennCare as the state had known it was dead.[48]

Issues to Watch

The cost of healthcare dominated the discussion in the late 1990s and first years of the twenty-first century. Rapidly increasing healthcare bills, coupled with falling revenues, led every state to implement cost-containment measures. States are back on more solid fiscal footing, but they continue to watch healthcare's bottom line. Meanwhile, they are taking steps to increase the quality of care and meet new public health demands.

The Return of Rising Costs

In late 1999, health inflation began to revive. In fiscal year 2000, Medicaid expenditure grew by 9 percent. By 2002, it was running at 12.8 percent.

What was behind this surge in healthcare spending? Two factors stand out: prescription drugs, and the growing numbers of people in need of "long-term care," such as nursing homes, assisted living, or at-home care. By early 2003, states were experiencing the most dramatic revenue decreases in history. Some states saw income tax revenues fall by as much as 25 percent in a matter of months. State cost-saving measures included politically unpopular moves, such as rolling back SCHIP and Medicaid eligibility levels. They've since begun to restore those cuts, and some states are rethinking the idea that they should play the leading role in expanding the health insurance safety net. In other words, the answer to the question, "Who should do what?" may be about to change yet again.

There was a glimmer of good news in 2006: Medicaid spending increased just 2.8 percent that year, the first time since 1998 that state revenue growth outpaced Medicaid, according to the Kaiser Family Foundation. It was a welcome reprieve for governments that are reasonably sure the program will return to higher growth rates as the population ages.

Prescription Drugs

One of the primary forces behind rocketing drug spending is the appearance of a new generation of prescription drugs. In 2003, forty states named prescription drugs as the primary factor contributing to the escalating rate of healthcare expenditures.[49] Consumers naturally want the newest and best products, particularly when they don't directly bear the costs. Subsequently, seniors with arthritis ask for Celebrex at $2.20 a pop rather than Advil, which costs five cents a pill. Drug manufacturers have brought more and more innovative but expensive prescription drugs to market, and state Medicaid programs and private health insurance plans alike have devoted ever more of their limited resources to buying these products.

It is somewhat difficult to gauge the true costs of rising prescription drug usage. While new drugs are often very expensive, drug companies and some health economists have argued that many seemingly "expensive" drugs actually pay for themselves by mitigating the effects of a condition, preempting surgical care, and reducing hospital admissions and lengths of hospital stays.[50]

Few states have much time for this claim. Some officials, so enraged by the fact that prescription drugs in the United States cost so much more here than in Canada or Mexico, began importing drugs for government

A reenactment of the Boston Tea Party—although this time the patriots are throwing prescription medications rather than caffeinated beverages overboard. The Massachusetts Senior Action Players staged this skit as part of campaign to pressure the federal government to allow U.S. citizens to buy Canadian prescription drugs. Drugs in Canada are often drastically cheaper than their U.S. equivalents.

employees from Canada—in blatant violation of the rules of the U.S. Food and Drug Administration, which contends that it cannot guarantee the drugs' safety. In Illinois, where prescription drug costs jumped by an average of 15 percent a year between 2001 and 2006, Gov. Rod Blagojevich unveiled I-SaveRx, a plan to import Canadian drugs for state seniors and uninsured residents. A 2006 state audit criticized the program not for its lawlessness, but for its wastefulness—the state auditor reported that the state had spent more than $1 million on a program that had served just 3,700 residents.[51]

State Medicaid programs are legally entitled to receive the "best available price." In practice, many don't. Private sector customers actually get bigger discounts than state Medicaid programs. A study by the Lewin Group estimated that the biggest HMOs buy drugs for 30 to 39 percent below retail. That is at least twice as much as the discounts state Medicaid programs receive.[52]

Not surprisingly, a growing number of states are attempting to do something about this. Nearly all stepped up efforts to encourage doctors to prescribe less-expensive generic drugs. In Delaware, state purchases for Medicaid and state employees constitute one-third of the state's prescription drug market. By consolidating purchasing for the two groups, the state was able to negotiate better rates that saved $3.5 million in 2004 alone. Many states, including Delaware, joined multi-state purchasing pools to further capitalize on bulk purchasing. Louisiana estimated its participation in one such program saved it $27 million in Medicaid costs in 2006; Maryland and West Virginia together attributed an additional $35 million in savings to the same pool.[53]

Long-Term Care

Unlike private sector health insurance plans, state Medicaid programs have an additional responsibility. Medicaid provides long-term care to the elderly and other services to people with disabilities. These services can range from providing nursing home care for low-income Medicaid recipients to developing rehabilitation plans for people with disabilities. All of these services are extremely expensive. Although the elderly and disabled make up only about 25 percent of the people enrolled in Medicaid programs, they account for 70 percent of total Medicaid spending.

Moreover, the cost of long-term care is growing fast. According to the Congressional Budget Office, caring for elderly and disabled Medicaid beneficiaries accounted for more than 72 percent of the program's cost increases between 1975 and 2002.

Some states, such as Oregon, have kept costs down by shifting the elderly away from expensive care in nursing homes and toward less expensive at-home care and assisted-living centers. Seniors overwhelmingly support such alternatives to nursing homes. However, the strong nursing home lobby and the legislation that created Medicaid have hobbled the efforts. The nursing home lobby obviously does not want to lose its bread and butter, and the legislation provides explicit coverage only for nursing homes.

Even if these problems can be resolved, states will continue to face a daunting challenge—demographics. According to the Census Bureau, the number of people eighty-five years of age and older will grow by 20 percent by 2010. By 2050, that population is expected to grow by more than 300 percent. As it does, the number of people with serious disabilities will almost certainly increase also. Many of these people will be unable—or unwilling—to pay for long-term care on their own. (See box on page 569.)

Groups such as the National Governors Association have petitioned lawmakers in Congress to relieve states of the burden of providing long-term care in particular. As former Kentucky governor Paul Patton told the Senate Special Committee on Aging in March 2002,

> At a time when state Medicaid budgets are rising annually at double digit inflation rates and most states face budget deficits, we must find long range solutions or we will be ill-prepared to meet the long-term care needs of seventy-seven million **baby boomers** when they retire.... This is not an issue that can be put on the back burner until Social Security and Medicare are reformed. It is an issue that will not wait.[54]

However, with deficits at the federal level rising, a grand bargain of this sort seems unlikely.

BABY BOOMERS

Generation of nearly eighty million individuals born after World War II, between 1946 and 1964.

Lofty Goals

Despite the financial challenges states' healthcare programs face, many have not abandoned their mid-1990s goal to expand insurance coverage to more

Policy in Practice: Felonious Seniors

In 2002, about seven million older Americans needed long-term care in the form of home health aides, nursing homes, or assisted-living facilities. By 2020, experts estimate that number will jump to nearly twelve million.

How much will it cost? According to a survey by the AARP (formerly the American Association of Retired Persons), most Americans don't have a clue. Only about 20 percent of responders came close to guessing the actual monthly cost of a nursing home (nearly $6,000 a month) or of an assisted living facility (about $2,500). Needless to say, most Americans underestimate these costs.

Moreover, a considerable portion of Americans believe that their private health insurance covers long-term care services. It doesn't. Long-term care requires a separate policy, and less than 10 percent of the population has purchased such a policy.

The general lack of knowledge about long-term care means that families often are unprepared for when a family member requires such care. Many people are shocked to discover that Medicare provides for only very limited long-term care services. Medicaid pays for long-term care, but only for individuals who qualify.

Many senior citizens are forced to spend all of their money on medical care and then, when sufficiently impoverished—typically, seniors must have less than $2,000 in assets—receive care through Medicaid. However, a small but not insignificant group of seniors choose another course of action. They break the law by transferring their assets to their children on the sly in order to qualify for Medicaid faster.

Sources: Linda L. Barrett, "The Costs of Long-Term Care: Public Perceptions versus Reality," AARP Research Center, December 2001; "Tax Incentives for Long-Term Care Insurance Haven't Worked, University of Hawaii at Manoa Study Shows," *U.S. Fed News*, November 28, 2006.

---

residents. In recent years, Maine and Massachusetts unveiled universal (or near-universal) healthcare plans.

When Dirigo, Maine's plan, began in 2004, 14 percent of the state's residents lacked health insurance, and 80 percent of the uninsured worked for small businesses that could not afford to provide coverage. Private insurers agreed to provide coverage, which the state would administer and, for the first year, subsidize. In the first phase of enrollment, geared toward small businesses and self-employed workers, 250 businesses and 1,000 individuals signed up. By September 2006, Dirigo covered more than eleven thousand Mainers, and Gov. John Baldacci estimated that the plan had saved the state $78 million.[55]

The Massachusetts plan is even more ambitious. It requires every resident of the state to have health insurance by July 2007, or face tax penalties. Under the law, every resident below the federal poverty line can receive insurance fully subsidized by the state; subsidies are extended on a sliding scale to those earning between 100 percent and 300 percent over the established federal poverty line. Businesses that do not provide health insurance are required to pay the state $295 per employee per year, which will be used to fund the coverage subsidies. It's true, though, that "universal healthcare" isn't exactly accurate. State officials estimate the law will extend health

Dirigo, the name of Maine's universal healthcare plan, means "I lead" in Latin, Maine's state motto.

insurance coverage to as much as 95 percent of the state's population. They expect that the remaining residents will accept the tax penalties rather than pay for insurance that may still be too expensive, despite the government subsidies.[56]

The Return of Public Health

As Medicaid costs have risen and SCHIP has emerged as the major means for expanding health insurance coverage, states have become major players in the field of healthcare. However, local governments at both the county and city levels continue to play important roles as well. In many parts of the country local governments, unlike state governments, are direct healthcare providers.

In the wake of September 11, 2001, many government officials have come to view the public health system in a new light. Individuals in this field now are seen as first responders to possible biological terrorism, pandemics, and natural disasters such as Hurricane Katrina. "Any community that fails to prepare and expects the federal government will come to the rescue is tragically wrong. It's not because we don't care, don't want to, or don't have the money, but because it's logistically impossible," Mike Leavitt, the U.S. Secretary of Health and Human Services, told state and local officials in 2006.[57] Some experts now believe that instead of downsizing public hospitals, governments should look for ways to keep them available in case a crisis generates high numbers of casualties.[58]

State and local governments have started drawing up emergency response plans, giving special attention to preparing for a bird flu pandemic. The National Association of City and County Health Officials, anticipating as much as one-third of the population falling ill in such an epidemic, issued a guide to planning for local governments, but there is much still to be done. One study by the Centers for Disease Control and Prevention found that a lack of direction from the federal government had hindered states' planning efforts, which vary widely. Government officials continue to plug away at their preparations, writing new plans and conducting emergency response drills, hoping they will be ready if and when a public health crisis hits.

Another controversial issue in many communities involves sexual health and education. One in nine girls between the ages of sixteen and nineteen currently becomes pregnant outside of marriage, yet a considerable number of parents remain opposed to their children learning about sexuality in the classroom. These parents have resurrected abstinence-only sex education programs, which have received $1 billion in federal funding since 1998, when only 2 percent of schools offered such programs. By 2002, the number of schools teaching abstinence as the only way to avoid sexually transmitted diseases and pregnancy had risen to 23 percent, despite the dearth of evidence that abstinence-only sex education works.[59]

Some advocates of abstinence say this effort is working. A report by the Centers for Disease Control and Prevention found that 53 percent of high school students graduating in 2005 claimed to be virgins. Forty-seven percent did not. A decade earlier, those percentages were reversed. Of course, lower pregnancy rates could reflect the fact that sex education has taught teenagers something about contraception as well.

States are the battlegrounds in the debate over access to contraception. At least twenty-five states have passed laws that require insurers that cover prescription drugs to include coverage of contraceptives. Fourteen of the states, however, allow an exemption for employers who oppose such coverage for religious reasons.[60] The Food and Drug Administration approved sales of emergency contraception to women ages eighteen and older without a prescription in September 2006, but nine states had allowed pharmacists to sell the drugs on their own in advance of the FDA's ruling. Access to these drugs is not universal, though: At least four states, Arkansas, Georgia, Mississippi, and South Dakota, have passed conscience clauses that protect pharmacists who refuse to dispense the medication.[61]

What Is Good Health Anyway?

As if these issues were not enough, local health officials are increasingly wrestling with another question that was touched upon earlier in the chapter. What exactly constitutes a health issue anyway?

Consider obesity. Media attention has turned to this issue more and more as an ever-growing list of health studies appears to proclaim just how out of shape Americans are. The documentary film *Super Size Me!* addresses people's obsession with fast food. The latest figures show that two-thirds of all adults in the United States are overweight or obese. Kids are getting heavier too. In the past two decades, the number of overweight and obese children has nearly tripled. Today, according to the Centers for Disease Control and Prevention, roughly 19 percent of children between the ages of six years and eleven years are overweight—up from just 4 percent thirty years ago. That number falls just slightly to 17 percent for adolescents between the ages of twelve and nineteen, but that too is a significant change from three decades ago, when just 6 percent of teens weighed too much. (See Map 15-3)

Obesity contributes to a variety of ailments, among them heart disease, certain types of cancer, diabetes, stroke, arthritis, breathing problems, and psychological disorders such as depression. Overweight individuals suffer from these and other related conditions at a much higher rate than people who are not overweight. Indeed, researchers attribute about three hundred thousand deaths to obesity each year in the United States alone. Obesity in the United States cost about $92.6 billion in 2003.[62] Former Arkansas governor Mike Huckabee estimated that his state could save more than $24

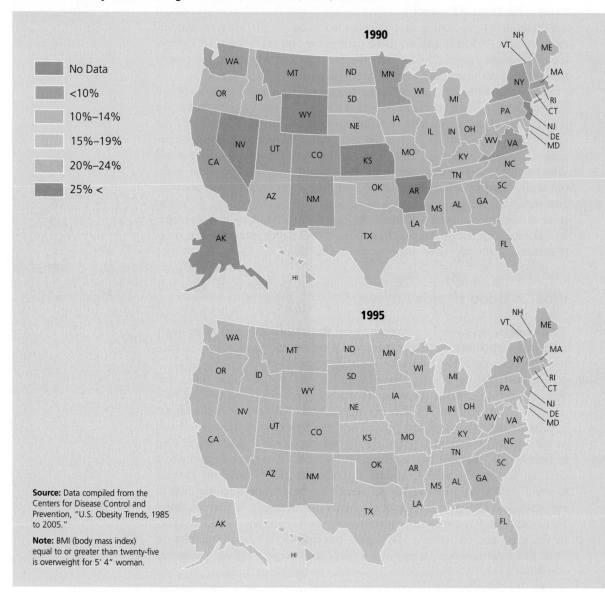

1990

No Data
<10%
10%–14%
15%–19%
20%–24%
25% <

1995

Source: Data compiled from the Centers for Disease Control and Prevention, "U.S. Obesity Trends, 1985 to 2005."

Note: BMI (body mass index) equal to or greater than twenty-five is overweight for 5' 4" woman.

million a year simply by convincing state employees to stop smoking, lose weight, and exercise.[63]

In 2006, New York City reignited the debate over government's role in promoting healthy eating habits when it banned the use of transfats, some of the most dangerous fats, in city restaurants. Soon after, other cities and states began to consider similar legislation. Parent groups and health organizations

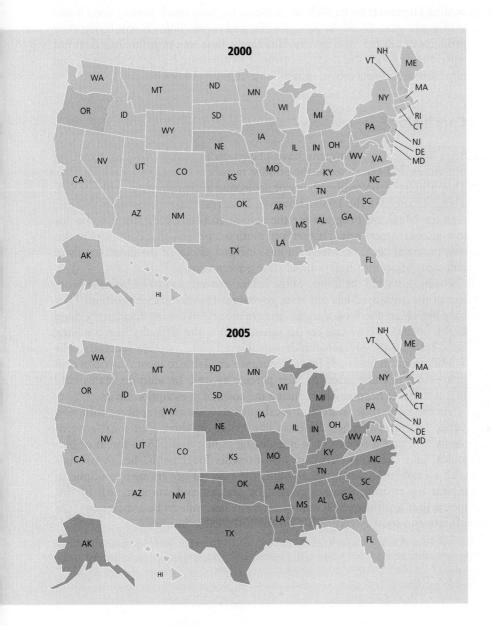

demanded better, healthier fast-food options. Fast-food restaurants quickly took notice. McDonald's, the world's largest fast-food chain, received such a negative rap for its unhealthy products that it had strong pressure to take immediate action. It began expanding its "healthy" meal options with great fanfare, began shooting Ronald McDonald commercials showing Ronald with children rollerblading and exercising instead of inside eating, and began posting fact sheets on its Web site announcing how much healthy food it had sold worldwide. Wendy's, KFC, Chili's, and other chains began frying their products in oils free of transfats. Ultimately, however, transfats-free does not equal health food, and doctors continue to advocate less drive-through, and more fruits and vegetables, in the battle against obesity.

Conclusion

State and local governments have played an important role in providing healthcare and assistance to the poorest members of society for a long time. They also have the responsibility of protecting and promoting public health. Things changed in the 1960s, however. Congress passed legislation that created the Medicare program for the elderly and the Medicaid program for low-income Americans. This set into motion a process that continues to this day. In recent decades, Medicaid has emerged as one of the most expensive and most important functions of state government.

Rising costs and the failure of the federal government to address the problem of the uninsured has put state governments in a difficult position. They have been forced to look for ways to save money on the one hand and extend health insurance coverage on the other. Despite the difficulty in reconciling these tasks, state governments have achieved some notable successes. The SCHIP program has made health insurance available to most American children—and, in some cases, to their parents as well. In addition, states have begun to make headway in reducing the costs of prescription drugs.

At the same time, state and local governments are grappling with new public health challenges. Illnesses like avian flu show that local governments still have a role to play in guarding public health. The threat of biological and chemical terrorism also presents local public health officials with a grave new threat. Meanwhile, the bills for government continue to mount for treating diseases caused by obesity and smoking. All of this means that healthcare will almost certainly continue to be a major concern of state and local governments for the foreseeable future.

Key Concepts

abstinence (p. 545)

Aid to Families with Dependent
Children (AFDC) (p. 544)

baby boomers (p. 568)

entitlement program (p. 557)

managed care (p. 560)

Medicaid (p. 546)

Medicare (p. 550)

obesity (p. 543)

pandemic (p. 543)

poverty line, or poverty threshold
(p. 551)

public health (p. 543)

State Children's Health Insurance
Program (SCHIP) (p. 561)

Temporary Assistance to Needy Families
(TANF) (p. 544)

Suggested Readings

Cutler, David. *Your Money or Your Life.* New York: Oxford University Press, 2003. For a sophisticated and sometimes eye-opening introduction to healthcare policy.

Gingrich, Newt. *Saving Lives, Saving Money.* Washington, D.C.: Alexis de Tocqueville Institution, 2003. Former House Speaker Gingrich provides a spirited, conservative review of healthcare and possible future innovations.

Starr, Paul. *The Social Transformation of American Medicine.* New York: Basic Books, 1992. Provides a wonderful account of the evolution of American healthcare.

Weil, Alan. "Ten Things Everyone Should Know about Welfare Reform," Urban Institute, May 9, 2002. Provides a concise yet thorough overview of welfare reform. Available online at www.urban.org/url.cfm?ID=31048.

Suggested Web Sites

www.familiesusa.org. Web site of FamiliesUSA, a liberal advocacy group that promotes a more activist government policy.

www.healthyamericans.org. Web site of Trust for America's Health, a nonprofit organization dedicated to protecting public health.

www.kff.org. Web site of the Henry J. Kaiser Family Foundation that offers a wealth of detail on state healthcare initiatives in general and Medicaid in particular.

www.statehealthfacts.kff.org. This Kaiser Family Foundation site provides detailed information on state healthcare policies.

Notes

Chapter 1

1. Wendy Koch, " 'Go-getter,' 18, Ousts Mayor in Michigan," *USA Today,* March 15, 2006. www.usatoday.com/news/nation/2005-11-09-kid-mayor_x.htm (accessed March 15, 2006).

2. Karl T Kurtz, Alan Rosenthal, and Cliff Zukin, "Citizenship: A Challenge for All Generations" (Denver: National Conference of State Legislatures, 2003).

3. "The American Freshman: National Norms for Fall 2004" (Los Angeles: Higher Education Research Institute at the University of California, 2005).

4. Bureau of the Census. www.census.gov/population/www/socdemo/voting (accessed March 10, 2006).

5. Statistical profile taken from National Center for Education Statistics, *Digest of Education Statistics* (Washington, D.C.: Department of Education, 2001); Institute of Politics, "Attitudes toward Politics and Public Service: A National Survey of College Undergraduates," Harvard University, 2000; Higher Education Research Institute, "CIRP Freshman Survey," 2001, www.gseis.uscla.edu/ heri/01_press_release.htm (accessed March 21, 2002); and Bureau of the Census, *Statistical Abstract of the United States, 2001* (Washington, D.C.: U.S. Government Printing Office, 2001).

6. "Total Fall Enrollment in Degree-Granting Institutions, by Attendance Status, Sex of Student, and Control of Institution: Selected Years, 1947 to 2002," *Digest of Education Statistics.* http://nces.ed.gov/programs/digest/d04/tables/dt04_171.asp (accessed March 21, 2006).

7. "Current-fund Revenue of Public Degree-granting Institutions, by Source of Funds: Selected Years, 1980–81 to 2000–01," *Digest of Education Statistics.* http://nces.ed.gov/programs/digest/d04/tables/dt04_332.asp (accessed March 21, 2006).

8. "Undergraduates Enrolled Full-time and Part-time, by Aid Status, Source of Aid, and Control and Type of Institution: 1999–2000." *Digest of Education Statistics.* http://nces.ed.gov/programs/digest/d04/tables/dt04_320.asp (accessed March 21, 2006).

9. National Center for Education Statistics, "Average Amounts of Federal, Institutional, or State Aid Received by Undergraduates: 1999–2000," 2000. www.nces.ed.gov/surveys/npsas/table_library/tables/npsas.04.asp (accessed March 25, 2002).

10. "Enrollment in Grades 9 to 12 in Public and Private Schools Compared with Population 14 to 17 Years of Age: Selected Years, 1889–90 to Fall 2005," *Digest of Education Statistics.* http://nces.ed.gov/programs/digest/d04/tables/dt04_056.asp (accessed March 21, 2006).

11. National Center for Education Statistics, "Enrollment in Educational Institutions, by Level and by Control of Institution: 1869–70 to Fall 2010," 2002. http://nces.ed.gov/pubs2001/digest/dt003.html (accessed March 27, 2002).

12. Kenneth J. Meier, *Politics and the Bureaucracy* (Pacific Grove, Calif.: Brooks/Cole, 1993), 2.

13. Christopher Z. Mooney, "Why Do They Tax Dogs in West Virginia? Teaching Political Science through Comparative State Politics," *PS: Political Science & Politics* 31 (June 1998): 199–203.

14. Federation of Tax Administrators, "State Tax Guide." www.taxadmin.org/fta/rate/sl_sales. html (accessed March 13, 2002).

15. Based on a standard OLS regression analysis in which average tuition bills at public, four-year universities are the dependent variable and state appropriations as thousands of dollars per enrolled student is the dependent variable. Data taken from the National Center for Education Statistics's *Digest of Education Statistics.* http://nces.ed.gov/programs/digest/d04_tf.asp (accessed March 20, 2006).

16. Bureau of the Census, "State and County Quick Facts." http://quickfacts.census.gov/qfd/ (accessed March 22, 2006).

17. Bureau of the Census, "100 Fastest Growing Counties." www.census.gov/popest/housing/ HU-EST2005-top100.html (accessed March 22, 2006).

18. Bureau of the Census, "Population Estimates by County." www.census.gov/popest/counties/ tables/CO-EST2005-01-31.xls (accessed March 22, 2006).

19. Daniel Elazar, *American Federalism: A View from the States* (New York: Crowell, 1966). This book has gone through three editions, the most recent of which was published in 1984.

20. Ibid, 88.

21. Maureen Moakley, "New Jersey," in *The Political Life of the American States,* ed. Alan Rosenthal and Maureen Moakley (New York: Praeger, 1984), 222.

22. Associated Press, "Many in N.J. Don't Know Enough about Politics to Complain," *Daily Journal* (Vineland, N.J.), June 3, 2003, 4A.

23. Quoted in Robert D. Putnam, *Bowling Alone* (New York: Simon & Schuster, 2000), 293.

24. Russell Hanson, "Political Culture Variations in State Economic Development Policy," *Publius* 21, no. 2 (Spring 1991): 63–81, and Kevin B. Smith, *The Ideology of Education* (Albany: SUNY Press, 2003).

25. Figures calculated by author using state rankings 2004 and 2005 data from the Bureau of the Census. www.census.gov/statab/www/ranks.html (accessed March 28, 2006).

26. Phillip W. Roeder, *Public Opinion and Policy Leadership in the American States* (Tuscaloosa: University of Alabama Press, 1994).

27. Bruce Wallin, "State and Local Governments Are American Too," *Political Science Teacher* 1 (1988): 1–3.

28. Bureau of the Census, *Statistical Abstract of the United States,* 2006, Table 455. www.census. gov/prod/2005pubs/06statab/stlocgov.pdf (accessed March 25, 2006).

29. Ibid.

30. Evan J. Ringquist and James C. Garand, "Policy Change in the American States," in *State and Local Politics,* ed. Ronald E. Weber and Paul Brace (New York: Chatham House, 1999).

31. David Osborne and Ted Gaebler, *Reinventing Government: How the Entrepreneurial Spirit Is Transforming the Public Sector* (New York: Plume, 1993).

Chapter 2

1. "Mayor to Feds: 'Get off Your Asses'," CNN.com, September 2, 2006. www.cnn.com/ 2005/US/09/02/nagin.transcript (accessed June 1, 2006).

2. Jonathan Walters and Donald Kettl, "The Katrina Breakdown," *Governing* magazine, December 2005.

3. Jonathan Walters, "Contention over Catastrophes," *Government Executive* magazine, December 2005.

4. Cass Sunstein, "The Return of States' Rights," *American Prospect.* www.prospect.org/print/ V11/24/sunstein-c.html (accessed November 27, 2002).

5. The Constitution was adopted by a convention of the states in 1787 and met the requirements for ratification in 1788. The First Congress under the Constitution assembled in 1789.

6. James Collier and Christopher Collier, *Decision in Philadelphia* (New York: Random House, 1986), 3.

7. Ellen Perlman, "The Preemption Beast: The Gorilla that Swallows State Laws," *Governing* magazine, August 1994, 46–51.

8. Harry Scheiber, "The Condition of American Federalism: An Historian's View," in *American Intergovernmental Relations,* ed. Laurence J. O'Toole Jr. (Washington, D.C.: CQ Press, 2000), 71.

9. Ibid.

10. Kala Ladenheim, "History of U.S. Federalism." www.cas.sc.edu/poli/courses/scgov/History_of_Federalism.htm (accessed May 18, 2006).

11. Scheiber, "The Condition of American Federalism."

12. Ellis Katz, "American Federalism, Past, Present and Future," *Issues of Democracy* 2, no. 2 (1997). usinfo.state.gov/journals/itdhr/0497/ijde/katz.htm (accessed May 21, 2006).

13. Paul L. Posner, *The Politics of Unfunded Mandates: Whither Federalism?* (Washington, D.C.: Georgetown University Press, 1998), 13.

14. David S. Broder, "President's Unfunded Mandates Criticized," *Washington Post,* March 11, 2004, A25.

15. Timothy Conlon, "Federalism and Competing Values in the Reagan Administration," *Publius: The Journal of Federalism* 16, no. 4 (1986): 29–47.

16. Thomas J. Anton, "New Federalism and Intergovernmental Fiscal Relationships: The Implications for Health Policy," *Journal of Health Politics, Policy and Law* 22, no. 3 (1997).

17. Richard L. Cole and John Kincaid, "Public Opinion and American Federalism: Perspectives on Taxes, Spending and Trust," *Spectrum: The Journal of State Government* 74, no. 3 (2000): 14–18.

18. "Same-Sex Marriage: Federal and State Authority," *Congressional Digest* 75 (November 1996): 263.

19. Rueben Morales, "Federalism in the Bush Administration," *Spectrum: The Journal of State Government* 75, no. 2 (2001): 5–6.

20. John Dinan and Dale Krane, "The State of American Federalism, 2005: Federalism Resurfaces in the Political Debate." *Publius: The Journal of Federalism* 36, no. 3 (2006). publius.oxfordjournals.org/cgi/reprint/36/3/327 (accessed June 5, 2006).

21. Ibid.

22. Bardon Aronson, "The Rising Tide of Federalism," CNN.com. www.cnn.com/2001/LAW/02/columns/fl.aronson.federalism.02.01/ (accessed November 25, 2002).

23. Michael S. Greve, *Real Federalism: Why It Matters, How It Could Happen* (Washington, D.C.: AEI Press, 1999), 17.

24. Jeffrey G. Homrig "*Alden v. Maine:* A New Genre of Federalism Shifts the Balance of Power," *California Law Review* 89, no. 1 (2001): 183–205.

25. David G. Savage, "Justices Rule U.S. Can Ban Medical Pot," *Los Angeles Times,* June 7, 2005.

26. Brady Baybeck and William Lowry, "Federalism Outcomes and Ideological Preferences: The U.S. Supreme Court and Preemption Cases," *Publius: The Journal of Federalism* 30, no. 1 (2000): 73–96.

27. Greg Shaw and Stephanie Reinhart, "Devolution and Confidence in Government," *Public Opinion Quarterly* 65, no. 2 (2001): 369–388.

Chapter 3

1. Bill Rufty, "High-Speed Rail Authority Still Exists," *The Ledger,* May 13, 2005.

2 Tom Blackburn, "Hogging the Constitution," *Palm Beach Post,* November 10, 2002.

3. See Chapter 1 for a discussion of Elazar's typology.

4. Donald Kettl, "Governor Rehnquist," *Governing* magazine, July 1999.

5. Christopher Hammons, "Was James Madison Wrong? Rethinking the American Preference for Short, Framework-Oriented Constitutions," *American Political Science Review* 93, no. 4 (December 1999): 837.

6. Ibid., 840.

7. Ibid. See also John G. Kester, "Amendment Time," *Washingtonian,* March 1995.

8. Janice C. May, "Trends in State Constitutional Amendment and Revision," in *The Book of the States 2003* (Lexington, Ky.: Council of State Governments, 2003), 8.

9. Robert J. Taylor, ed., *Massachusetts, Colony to Commonwealth* (New York: Norton, 1961).

10. Willi Paul Adams, *The First American Constitutions: Republican Ideology and the Making of the State Constitutions in the Revolutionary Era* (Chapel Hill: University of North Carolina Press, 1980).

11. Ibid.

12. Ibid., 207

13. Alan Tarr, *Understanding State Constitutions* (Princeton, N.J.: Princeton University Press, 1998), 121.

14. W. B. Stouffer, Cynthia Opheim, and Susan Bland Day, eds., *State and Local Politics: The Individual and the Governments* (New York: HarperCollins College Publishers, 1996).

15. Bruce Sundlun, "R.I.'s Martyr for Democracy," *Providence Journal-Bulletin,* August 11, 2002.

16. Delaware is the only state that does not refer constitutional amendments to the electorate as a whole. The legislature may enact constitutional amendments on its own if a measure receives support in two consecutive legislative sessions.

17. *The Book of the States 2001* (Lexington, Ky.: Council of State Governments, 2001), 5. In South Carolina, a majority of both houses of the legislature must vote to approve a constitutional amendment a second time, after it has passed a popular referendum, before it can go into effect.

18. Initiative and Referendum Institute. www. iandrinstitute.org (accessed March 12, 2006). The institute's Web site includes detailed timelines of initiative and referendum activity in each state.

19. Juan B. Elizondo Jr., "Ratliff: Time to Rewrite Constitution; Lawmaker Joined by Watchdog," *Austin American-Statesman,* October 28, 1999.

20. *The Book of the States 2003,* 3–4.

21. Warren Richey, "Unique Law Lets Florida Voters Make Changes to Constitution," *Christian Science Monitor,* May 8, 1998.

22. Alan Ehrenhalt, "Vermont's Judicial Distillery," *Governing* magazine, February 2000.

23. Hammons, "American Preference," 839.

24. Joni James, "Voters Hold Key to Big Shake-Up in State Cabinet: The Revision Would Eliminate Three Posts, Give the Governor More Power, and Shift Control of Education Policy," *Orlando Sentinel,* October 20, 1998, D1.

25. Stuart MacCorkle and Dick Smith, *Texas Government* (New York: McGraw-Hill, 1960).

26. Daniel Elazar, *American Federalism: A View from the States,* 3rd ed. (New York: Harper & Row, 1984).

27. Hammons, 846.

28. See Hammons for a more complete argument along these lines.

29. Melinda Gann Hall, "State Judicial Politics: Rules, Structures, and the Political Game," in *American State and Local Politics,* eds. Ronald Weber and Paul Brace (New York: Chatham House, 1999).

30. Ibid., 136.

31. Andrew Taylor, "Line Item Budget Barely Trims Spending at State Level," *Denver Rocky Mountain News,* January 15, 1995.

32. Scott Milfred, "Some Want to Clip Gubernatorial Wings: A Resolution in the Legislature Would Curtail Wisconsin Governor's Exceptionally Broad Veto Power," *Wisconsin State Journal,* September 23, 2001, A1.

33. Virginia Gray, Herbert Jacob, and Kenneth N. Vines, eds. *Politics in the American States: A Comparative Analysis* (Boston: Little, Brown, 1983).

34. In 2003 the U.S. Supreme Court invalidated laws prohibiting sodomy. Until that time, Alabama, Florida, Idaho, Louisiana, Massachusetts, Mississippi, North Carolina, South Carolina, Utah, and Virginia had laws that explicitly prohibited sodomy. Kansas, Oklahoma, and Texas prohibited only same-sex sodomy. Lambda Legal Defense and Education Fund Web site: www.lambda.org.

35. Alexander Hamilton, James Madison, and John Jay, *The Federalist Papers,* eds. Charles Kesler and Clinton Rossiter (New York: Penguin Putnam, 1961).

36. Hamilton, Madison, and Jay envisioned other safeguards as well. One is the well-known principle of the separation of powers among the three branches of government. The other was the large size of the republic itself. Previous theorists of democracy had worried about republics that became too large to govern. In *The Federalist,* No. 10, Madison makes the novel claim that a more extensive republic would be less likely to succumb to factionalism than the smaller republics of old.

37. David Broder, *Democracy Derailed: Initiative Campaigns and the Power of Money* (New York: Harcourt, 2000), 27.

38. Ibid.

39. *The History of Initiative and Referendum in the United States,* Initiative and Referendum Institute. www.iandrinstitute.org (accessed February 8, 2007).

40. Richard Ellis, *Democratic Delusions: The Initiative Process in America* (Lawrence: University Press of Kansas, 2002).

41. Broder, *Democracy Derailed.*

42. Keon S. Chi, "Emerging Trends Shaping State Governments: 2005 and Beyond," in *The Book of the States 2005* (Lexington, Ky.: Council of State Governments, 2005).

43. Broder, *Democracy Derailed.*

44. Daniel A. Smith, "Was Rove Right? The Partisan Wedge and Turnout Effects of Issue 1, Ohio's 2004 Ballot Initiative to Ban Gay Marriage," prepared for presentation at the University of California Center for the Study of Democracy/USC-Caltech Center for the Study of Law and Politics/Initiative and Referendum Institute, Newport Beach, California, January 14–15, 2005. law.usc.edu/academics/centers/cslp/conferences/direct_democracy_05/documents/smith.pdf (accessed June 21, 2006).

45. Lawrence F. Keller, "Municipal Charters," *National Civic Review* 91, no. 1 (Spring 2002): 155–161.

Chapter 4

1. "CNN Larry King Live," December 8, 2004; transcript available at: http://transcripts.cnn.com/TRANSCRIPTS/0412/08/lkl.01.html.

2. Tom Zeller, "One State, Two State, Red State, Blue State," *New York Times,* February 8, 2004, 4:16.

3. David Brooks, "The New Red-Diaper Babies," *New York Times,* December 7, 2004, A7.

4. Sabin Russell, "A Junction of Red and Blue Blood Vessels," *San Francisco Chronicle,* December 15, 2006, A5.

5. Laura Litvan, "Santorum, Republicans Find Philadelphia Suburbs 'Ground Zero,'" *Bloomberg,* October 17, 2006, www.bloomberg.com/apps/news?pid=20601103&sid=aL0XNMxd38nE&refer=us.

6. Steven Hill, *Fixing Elections* (New York: Routledge, 2002), 119.

7. "Q&A with Bob Levey," *Washington Post,* September 16, 2003. http://discuss.washingtonpost.com/wp-srv/zforum/03/r_metro_levey091603.htm (accessed December 8, 2004).

8. Caroline J. Tolbert, John A. Grummel, and Daniel A. Smith, "The Effects of Ballot Initiatives on Voter Turnout in the American States," *American Politics Research,* 29, no.6 (2001): 625–648.

9. Interview with author, December 11, 2006.

10. Kevin J. Coleman, Thomas H. Neale, and Joseph E. Cantor, "The Election Process in the United States," Congressional Research Service, Washington, D.C., July 6, 1995, 69.

11. National Conference of State Legislatures, "Straight-Ticket Voting." www.ncsl.org/programs/legismgt/elect/straight_ticket.htm (accessed December 26, 2006).

12. Election Data Services, *The Election Data Book: A Statistical Portrait of Voting in America* (Lanham, Md.: Bernan Press, 1992), Appendix.

13. Kay Lawson, "How State Laws Undermine Parties," in *Elections American Style,* ed. A. James Reichley (Washington, D.C.: Brookings Institution, 1987), 241.

14. Cited in William C. Binning, Larry E. Esterly, and Paul A. Sracic, *Encyclopedia of American Parties, Campaigns, and Elections* (Westport, Conn.: Greenwood Press, 1999), 95.

15. Phone interview, September 11, 2003.

16. "Jimmy Carter Supports Ballot Access Reform," *Ballot Access News,* August 1, 2003, 3. www.ballot-access.org/2003/0801.html (accessed December 10, 2004).

17. Lawson, "State Laws," 246.

18. Binning, Esterly, and Sracic, *American Parties,* 95.

19. Phone interview, September 4, 2003.

20. Phone interview, September 11, 2003.

21. Interview with author, April 2006.

22. Alan Greenblatt, "Slow March to the Polls," *Governing* magazine, June 2006, 17.

23. Barbara G. Salmore and Stephen A. Salmore, *New Jersey Politics and Government*, 2nd ed. (Lincoln: University of Nebraska Press, 1998), 128.

24. See Liberal Arts Instructional Technology Services, University of Texas at Austin, "Texas Politics." http://texaspolitics.lamc.utexas.edu/html/exec/index.html (accessed December 10, 2004).

25. Associated Press, "The Decatur Daily on Windom Candidacy," October 4, 2001.

26. Rob Gurwitt, "The Lone Comptroller," *Governing* magazine, October 2003, 68.

27. Quoted in Alan Greenblatt, "Where Campaign Money Flows," *Governing*, magazine, November 2002, 44.

28. Alan Greenblatt, "The Avengers General," *Governing* magazine, May 2003, 54.

29. Zach Patton, "Robe Warriors," *Governing* magazine, March 2006, 34.

30. Initiative and Referendum Institute. www.iandrinstitute.org (accessed December 8, 2004).

31. John F. Camobreco, "Preferences, Fiscal Policy, and the Initiative Process," *Journal of Politics* 60, no. 3: (August 1998): 822.

32. James Dao, "Same-Sex Marriage Key to Some G.O.P. Races," *New York Times,* November 4, 2004, P4.

33. Simon Jackman, "Same-Sex Marriage Ballot Initiatives and Conservative Mobilization in the 2004 Election," presentation available at http://jackman.stanford.edu/papers/RISSPresentation.pdf.

34. Alan Greenblatt, "Some Presidential Politics Is Local," *New York Times,* October 10, 2004, 4:5.

35. Alan Greenblatt, "Total Recall," *Governing* magazine, September 2003, 27.

36. Erin Neff, "I've Seen Enough—Gibbons Must Go," *Las Vegas Review-Journal,* March 13, 2007, 9B.

37. Phone interview, August 7, 2003.

38. V. O. Key, *Public Opinion and American Democracy* (New York: Knopf, 1964), 7.

39. Interview with author, November 15, 2006.

40. See especially Robert S. Erikson, Gerald C. Wright, and John D. McIver, *Statehouse Democracy: Public Opinion and Policy in the American States* (New York: Cambridge University Press, 1993).

41. Paul Brace et al., "Public Opinion in the American States: New Perspectives Using National Survey Data," *American Journal of Political Science* 46, no. 1 (January 2002): 173–189.

42. Susan Herbst, "How State-Level Policy Managers 'Read' Public Opinion," in *Navigating Public Opinion: Polls, Policy, and the Future of American Democracy,* eds. Jeff Manza, Fay Lomax Cook, and Benjamin I. Page (New York: Oxford University Press, 2002), 176.

43. Phone interview, September 3, 2003.

44. Phone interview, September 10, 2003.

Chapter 5

1. Gabriel Garcia Marquez, *One Hundred Years of Solitude,* trans. Gregory Rabassa (New York: Everyman's Library, 1995), 171.

2. Karen Tumulty, "The End of a Revolution," *Time,* October 16, 2006, 30.

3. Alan Greenblatt, "The Disengaging Voter," *CQ Weekly,* October 24, 1998, 2880.

4. Ed Kilgore, "Diagnosing Dems," *Blueprint* magazine, May 17, 2006. www.ndol.org/ndol_ci.cfm?kaid=127&subid=171&contentid=253867 (accessed March 27, 2007).

5. Jonathan Raban, "Cracks in the House of Rove," *New York Review of Books,* April 12, 2007, 4.

6. Alan Greenblatt, "Wired to Win," *Governing* magazine, October 2006, 26.

7. Quoted in Alan Greenblatt, "Politics and Marketing Merge in Parties' Bid for Relevance," *Congressional Quarterly Weekly Report,* August 16, 1997, 1967.

8. Jeff Greenfield, "Hayes's Ride," *Washington Monthly,* March 2003.

9. Alvin Kess, *Politics in New York State* (Syracuse, N.Y.: Syracuse University Press, 1965), 29.

10. David R. Mayhew, *Placing Parties in American Politics: Organization, Electoral Settings and Government Activity in the 20th Century*

(Princeton, N.J.: Princeton University Press, 1986), 24ff.

11. Quoted in Bertil L. Hanson, "County Commissioners of Oklahoma," *Midwest Journal of Political Science* 9 (1965): 396.

12. Joel H. Sibley, "The Rise and Fall of American Political Parties, 1790–1990," in *The Parties Respond: Changes in the American Party System*, ed. L. Sandy Maisel (Boulder, Colo.: Westview Press, 1990), 9.

13. Mayhew, *Placing Parties,* 105.

14. Ibid., 185.

15. John F. Bibby and Thomas M. Holbrook, "Parties and Elections," in *Politics in the American States: A Comparative Analysis,* 7th ed., eds. Virginia Gray, Russell L. Hanson, and Herbert Jacobs (Washington, D.C.: CQ Press, 1999), 71.

16. John F. Bibby, "State and Local Parties in a Candidate-Centered Age," in *American State and Local Politics: Directions for the 21st Century,* eds. Ronald E. Weber and Paul Brace (New York: Chatham House, 1999), 198.

17. Rhodes Cook, "Republican Brawls through the Century Helped Define Party for Years to Come," *Congressional Quarterly Weekly Report,* April 6, 1996, 942.

18. Alan Greenblatt, "History: Winds of War Blew through Chicago." *Congressional Quarterly Weekly Report,* August 17, 1996, 23.

19. Bibby "State and Local Parties," 1999, 199.

20. Peter W. Wielhower and Brad Lockerbie, "Party Contacting and Political Participation, 1952–90," *American Journal of Political Science* 38 (February 1994): 213.

21. See John H. Kessel, "Ray Bliss and the Development of the Ohio Republican Party during the 1950s," in *Politics, Professionalism and Power: Modern Party Organization and the Legacy of Ray C. Bliss,* ed. John C. Green (Lanham, Md.: University Press of America, 1994), 49–50.

22. Interview with Lee Herrington, September 2002.

23. Leon D. Epstein, *Political Parties in the American Mold* (Madison: University of Wisconsin Press, 1986), 155.

24. Malcolm E. Jewell and Sarah M. Morehouse, *Political Parties and Elections in American States,* 4th ed. (Washington, D.C.: CQ Press, 2001), 76.

25. Bibby, "State and Local Parties," 1999, 198.

26. Bibby and Holbrook, "Parties and Elections," 1999, 70.

27. Ibid., 71.

28. Quoted in Ruth Marcus, "Party Spending Unleashed; Justices Say Independence from Candidate Is Key," *Washington Post,* June 27, 1996, A1.

29. Alan Greenblatt, "Soft Money: The Root of All Evil or a Party-Building Necessity?" *Congressional Quarterly Weekly Report,* September 26, 1997, 2064.

30. Don Van Natta Jr. and Richard A. Oppel Jr., "Parties Set Up Groups to Elude Soft Money Ban," *New York Times,* November 2, 2002, A1.

31. Agustín Armendariz and Aron Pilhofer, "McCain-Feingold Changes State Party Spending," Center for Public Integrity, May 26, 2005. www.publicintegrity.org/partylines/report.aspx?aid=690 (accessed March 7, 2007).

32. Interview with Larry J. Sabato, May 2002.

33. Tim Storey and Gene Rose, "GOP #1 First Time in 50 Years," *State Legislatures* 12 (December 2002).

34. Jewell and Morehouse, *Political Parties and Elections,* 22–23.

35. "Changing Hands," *Governing* magazine, January 2003, 24.

36 Mayhew, *Placing Parties,* 291.

37. Ibid., 292–293.

38. David S. Broder, "Edwards Criticizes Bush's Policies on Family," *Washington Post,* March 13, 2003, A8.

39. Jason Szep, "Youth Turnout in Election Biggest in 20 Years," Reuters, November 8, 2006.

40. Alan Greenblatt, "California House Race Shapes Up as a Duel of Interest Groups," *Congressional Quarterly Weekly Report,* January 17, 1998, 1172.

41. Alan Ehrenhalt, "Political Pawns," *Governing* magazine, July 2000, 20.

42. Alan Greenblatt, " 'Big Tent' Advocates Look Likely to Defeat Abortion Measure," *Congressional Quarterly Weekly Report,* January 10, 1998, 89.

43. Martin P. Wattenberg, *The Decline of American Political Parties, 1952–1992* (Cambridge, Mass.: Harvard University Press, 1994), x.

44. Quoted in Joel Siegel, "Party's over for Liberals," *Daily News,* February 24, 2003, 20.

45. Greenblatt, "Politics and Marketing," 1967.

46. Larry M. Bartels, "Partisanship and Voting Behavior, 1952–1996," *American Journal of Political Science* 44 (January 2000): 35.

47. Ibid., 36–37

48. Quoted in Greenblatt, "Politics and Marketing."

49. Phone interview with author, July 2006.

50. Paul S. Herrnson, Ronald G. Shaiko, and Clyde Wilcox, *The Interest Group Connection: Electioneering, Lobbying and Policymaking in Washington,* 2nd ed. (Washington: CQ Press, 2004), xiii.

51. Frank J. Sorauf, *Political Parties in the American System* (Boston: Little, Brown, 1964), 13.

52. Clive S. Thomas and Ronald J. Hrebenar, "Interest Groups in the States," in *Politics in the American States: A Comparative Analysis,* 8th ed., eds. Virginia Gray and Russell L. Hanson (Washington, D.C.: CQ Press, 2004), 114–115.

53. Alan Rosenthal, *The Third House,* 2nd ed. (Washington: CQ Press, 2001).

54. Sarah Laskow, "State Lobbying Becomes Billion-Dollar Business," The Center for Public Integrity, December 20, 2006. www.publicintegrity.org/hiredguns/report.aspx?aid=835 (accessed February 27, 2007).

55. Virginia Gray and David Lowery, "Interest Representation in the States," in *American State and Local Politics: Directions for the 21st Century,* eds. Ronald E. Weber and Paul Brace (New York: Chatham House, 1999), 267.

56. Quoted in Rosenthal, *The Third House,* 17

57. Alan Greenblatt, "Squeezing the Federal Turnip," *Governing* magazine, March 2003, 28.

58. Christopher Swope, "Winning without Steaks and Cigars," *Governing* magazine, November 2000.

59. Rosenthal, *The Third House,* 78.

60. Ibid., 45.

61. Quoted in Alan Greenblatt, "Secondhand Spokesmen," *Governing* magazine, April 2002.

62. Quoted in Rosenthal, *The Third House,* 61.

63. Clive S. Thomas and Ronald J. Hrebenar, "Lobby Clout," *State Legislatures,* April 1999.

64. Thomas and Hrebenar, "Interest Groups in the States," 121–122.

65. Alan Greenblatt, "Real Power," *Governing* magazine, June 2006, 46.

66. Phone interview with author, February 6, 2007.

Chapter 6

1. Alan Greenblatt, "Segway Rolls," *Governing* magazine, September 2002, 18.

2. National Conference of State Legislatures, "Overview: Public Health Preparedness," July 22, 2002.

3. Rob Gurwitt, "The Riskiest Business," *Governing* magazine, March 2001, 21.

4. Interview with bill status clerk, New York legislature, March 15, 2007.

5. Interview with Montana Legislative Services Division, March 13, 2007.

6. Associated Press, "Wisconsin Governor Signs Bill to Increase Efforts to Kill Deer to Fight Fatal Disease," May 20, 2002.

7. Alan Greenblatt, "Fit to Be Tied," *Governing* magazine, August 2001, 20.

8. Judith C. Meredith, *Lobbying on a Shoestring,* 2nd ed. (Dover, Mass.: Auburn House Publishing Company, 1989), 4.

9. Alan Greenblatt, "Health Crusader," *Governing* magazine, November 2001, 33.

10. Greenblatt, "Fit to Be Tied," 20.

11. Richard Perez-Pena, "Legislating the New York Way in a Chronic Case of Gridlock," *New York Times,* October 19, 2002, 1.

12. Virginia Gray and David Lowery, "Where Do Policy Ideas Come From? A Study of Minnesota

Legislators and Staffers," *Journal of Public Administration Research and Theory* 10 (January, 2000): 573–597.

13. See Gary F. Moncrief, Joel A. Thompson, and Karl T. Kurtz, "Old Statehouse Ain't What It Used to Be," *Legislative Studies Quarterly* 21, no. 1 (February 1996): 57–72.

14. Interview with Rosalind Kurita, October 7, 2002.

15. Alan Rosenthal, *Governors and Legislatures: Contending Powers* (Washington, D.C.: CQ Press, 1990), 187.

16. Diane D. Blair, *Arkansas Politics and Government* (Lincoln: University of Nebraska Press, 1988), 182, cited in Rosenthal, *Governors and Legislatures.*

17. Alan Rosenthal et al., *Republic on Trial: The Case for Representative Democracy,* (Washington, D.C.: CQ Press, 2003), 26.

18. Wes Clarke, "The Divided Government and Budget Conflict in the U.S. States," *Legislative Studies Quarterly* 23, no. 1 (February 1998): 5.

19. Greenblatt, "Fit to Be Tied."

20. Meredith, *Lobbying on a Shoestring,* 34.

21. Edmund Burke, "The English Constitutional System," in *Representation,* ed. Hannah Pitkin, (New York: Atherton Press, 1969).

22. Christopher Swope, "Winning without Steak and Cigars," *Governing* magazine, November 2000, 40.

23. Quoted in Alan Ehrenhalt, "Putting Practice into Theory," *Governing* magazine, November 2000, 6.

24. Alan Ehrenhalt, *The United States of Ambition: Politicians, Power and the Pursuit of Office* (New York: Times Books/Random House, 1991), 158.

25. Foster Church, "Just Like a Woman," *Governing* magazine, September 1990, 26.

26. Richard A. Clucas, "Principal-Agent Theory and the Power of State House Speakers," *Legislative Studies Quarterly* 26, no. 2 (May 2001): 319–338.

27. Alan Greenblatt, "The Mapmaking Mess," *Governing* magazine, January 2001, 23.

28. Ibid., 22.

29. David Rosenbaum, "Campaign Season," *New York Times,* October 3, 2002, 24.

30. Rosenthal et al., *Republic on Trial,* 69.

31. Howard Troxler, "Choice for Attorney General Not So Easy," *St. Petersburg Times,* October 18, 2002.

32. Alan Greenblatt, "The Regency Shuffle," *Governing* magazine, March 2001, 31.

33. Otis White, "Making Laws Is No Job for Lawyers These Days," *Governing* magazine, June 1994, 27.

34. Kathleen Dolan and Lynne E. Ford, "Change and Continuity among Women Legislators: Evidence from Three Decades," *Political Research Quarterly* 50 (March 1997): 137–152.

35. "Women in State Legislatures 2007," Center for American Women and Politics. www.cawp. rutgers.edu/Facts/Officeholders/stleg.pdf (accessed March 19, 2007).

36. Interview with Barbara Lee, October 8, 2002.

37. Thomas H. Little, Dana Dunn, and Rebecca E. Dean, "A View from the Top: Gender Differences in Legislative Priorities among State Legislative Leaders," *Women and Politics* 22, no. 4 (2001): 29–50.

38. Whistler and Ellickson, "Women," 84.

39. Ibid.

40. Michael B. Berkman and Robert E. O'Connor, "Do Women Legislators Matter: Female Legislators and State Abortion Policy," *American Politics Quarterly* 21, no. 1 (January 1993): 105.

41. Kerry L. Haynie, *African American Legislators in the American States* (New York: Columbia University Press, 2001), 19.

42. Ibid., 2.

43. Ibid., 25.

44. Bernard Grofman and Lisa Handley, "Impact of the Voting Rights Act on Black Representation in Southern State Legislatures," *Legislative Studies Quarterly* 16 (1991): 111–128.

45. Malcolm E. Jewell and Samuel C. Patterson, *The Legislative Process in the States* (New York: Random House, 1966), 138.

46. William Pound, "State Legislative Careers: Twenty-Five Years of Reform," in *Changing Patterns in State Legislative Careers,* eds. Gary

F. Moncrief and Joel A. Thompson (Ann Arbor: University of Michigan Press, 1992).

47. James D. King, "Changes in Professionalism in U.S. State Legislatures," *Legislative Studies Quarterly* 25, no. 3 (May 2000): 327–343.

48. Wade Rawlins, "Lawmakers Adjourn," *News and Observer* (Raleigh), October 4, 2002.

49. Ellen Perlman, "The 'Gold-Plated' Legislature," *Governing* magazine, February 1998, 37.

50. Bob Mahlburg, "Special Session to Cost Taxpayers $25,000 a Day," *Orlando Sentinel*, April 30, 2002, A1.

51. Alan Ehrenhalt, "An Embattled Institution," *Governing* magazine, January 1992, 30.

52. "Legislative Webcasts of Floor Proceedings, Committee Hearings, and Archiving of Webcasts," National Conference of State Legislatures. www.ncsl.org/programs/lis/webcasts.htm; (accessed March 16, 2007).

53. Interview with John Hibbing, October 15, 2002.

54. William Powers, "The Saturation Fallacy," *National Journal*, September 7, 2002, 2565.

55. Jonathan Walters, "How to Tame the Press," *Governing* magazine, January 1994, 30.

56. Charles Layton and Jennifer Dorroh, "The State of the American Newspaper," *American Journalism Review* (June 2002): 18.

57. Peverill Squire, "Professionalization and Public Opinion of State Legislatures," *Journal of Politics* 55, no. 2 (1993): 479–491.

58. Interview with Gary Moncrief, October 2, 2002.

59. Christopher Swope, "Instant Influence," *Governing* magazine, July 2005, 23.

60. Christopher Swope, "Queen of the State Blogs," 13th Floor. http://governing.typepad.com/13thfloor/2007/04/queen_of_the_st.html#more (accessed April 24, 2007).

60. Anita Chadha and Robert A. Bernstein, "Why Incumbents Are Treated So Harshly: Term Limits for State Legislators," *American Politics Quarterly* 24 (1996): 363–376.

61. Rosenthal et al., *Republic on Trial*, 52.

62. Patricia Lopez, "Coleman's Journey Crosses Typical Divide," *Minneapolis Star Tribune*, October 16, 2002. www.startribune.com/stories/462/ 3367928.html (accessed April 4, 2003).

63. Rob Gurwitt, "Southern Discomfort," *Governing* magazine, October 2002, 32.

64. Ibid.

Chapter 7

1. Lynda Gledhill, "Taxes—or Fees—in New Health Plan Raise Critics' Ire," *San Francisco Chronicle*, January 22, 2007, B1.

2. Quoted in Larry J. Sabato, *Goodbye to Good-Time Charlie*, 2nd ed. (Washington, D.C.: CQ Press, 1983), 4.

3. Lynn R. Muchmore, "The Governor as Manager," in *Being Governor: The View from the Office*, eds. Thad Beyle and Lynn R. Muchmore (Durham, N.C.: Duke University Press, 1983), 83.

4. Terry Sanford, *Storm over the States* (New York: McGraw-Hill, 1967), 185–188, as quoted in Eric B. Herzik and Brent W. Brown, "Symposium on Governors and Public Policy," *Policy Studies Journal* 17 (1989): 761.

5. David Nitkin, "Maryland's Governor Ranks Second to None in Chief Budget Power," *Baltimore Sun*, January 21, 2004, 4B.

6. E. Lee Bernick, "Gubernatorial Tools: Formal vs. Informal," *Journal of Politics* 42 (1979): 661.

7. Quoted in Alan Rosenthal, *Governors & Legislatures: Contending Powers* (Washington, D.C.: CQ Press, 1990), 14.

8. Muchmore, "Governor as Manager," 13.

9. Quoted in H. Edward Flentje, "The Political Nature of the Governor as Manager," in *Being Governor: The View from the Office*, eds. Thad Beyle and Lynn R. Muchmore (Durham, N.C.: Duke University Press, 1983), 89.

10. Alan Greenblatt, "Steady in a Storm," *Governing* magazine, November 2006, 28.

11. Bill Ritter, veto message to Colorado House, February 9, 2007. www.colorado.gov/governor/press/february07/HB1072-veto-message.html (accessed April 25, 2007).

12. "Gov. Ehrlich, Pitchman," *Washington Post*, May 21, 2006, B6.

13. Alan Ehrenhalt, "Myths and Realities of Statehouse Power," *Governing* magazine, December 2002, 6.

14. Sabato, *Goodbye*, 4.

15. See Muchmore, "Governor as Manager."

16. Alan Greenblatt, "Tug of War," *Governing* magazine, August 2004, 32.

17. Alan Greenblatt, "Posse Politics," *Governing* magazine, December 2006, 18.

18. Rob Gurwitt, "The Governor's People," *Governing* magazine, March 1991, 28.

19. Daniel C. Vock, "Govs Enjoy Quirky Veto Power," Stateline.org, April 24, 2007. www.stateline.org/live/details/story? contentId=201710.

20. Alan Greenblatt, "Why Are We Meeting Like This?" *Governing* magazine, August 2002, 40.

21. Rosenthal, *Governors & Legislatures*, 28.

22. Garry Young and Vicky M. Wilkins, "The Influence of Governors on Veto Override Attempts: A Test of Pivotal Politics," *Legislative Studies Quarterly* 27, no. 4 (November 2002): 557.

23. Laura A. Van Assendelft, *Governors, Agenda Setting and Divided Government* (Lanham, Md.: University Press of America, 1997), 1.

24. Wes Clarke, "Divided Government and Budget Conflict in the U.S. States," *Legislative Studies Quarterly* 23, no. 1 (February 1998): 5.

25. Quoted in Van Assendelft, *Governors*, 71.

26. Raphael J. Sonenshein, "Can Black Candidates Win Statewide Elections?" *Political Science Quarterly* 105 (1990): 219.

27. We are indebted for these figures to Professor Thad Beyle of the University of North Carolina, who compiled them for a forthcoming edition of *The Book of the States.*

28. Quoted in Thomas Clouse, "Kempthorne at the Helm," *Idaho Statesman,* January 5, 1999, 1A.

29. Interview with author, January 5, 2004.

30. Quoted in Alan Greenblatt, "Where Campaign Money Flows," *Governing* magazine, November 2002, 44.

Chapter 8

1. Sandra Day O'Connor, "The Threat to Judicial Independence," *Wall Street Journal,* September 27, 2006.

2. The full text of Senator Kennedy's speech is available at: http://tedkennedy.com/journal/ 72/senator-kennedys-floor-speech-on-the-nuclear-option.

3. George F. Will, "In Florida, 'Uniform' Foolishness," *Washington Post,* March 23, 2006, A23.

4. Sandra Day O'Connor, "The Threat to Judicial Independence," *Wall Street Journal,* September 27, 2006.

5. National Center for State Courts Online *Examining the Work of State Courts, 2003.* www.ncsconline.org/D_Research/CSP/2005_files/3-EWOverview_final_1.pdf (accessed November 28, 2006).

6. David Rottman et al., *State Court Organization, 2004* (Washington, D.C.: Bureau of Justice Statistics, 2004), www.ojp.usdoj.gov/bjs/pub/pdf/sco04.pdf (accessed November 28, 2006).

7. William Glaberson, "Broken Bench," *New York Times,* September 25, 2006.

8. William Glaberson, "Big Plan for Small Courts: Seeking Money to Fix Them," *New York Times,* January 30, 2007.

9. Diana Penner, "Judge: Jurors Antics Harmless," *Indianapolis Star,* November 30, 2006, 1

10. Rottman, Table 2: Courts and Judges.

11. Victor Flango and Carol Flango, "A Taxonomy of Appellate Court Organization," *Caseload Highlights: Examining the Work of the State Courts,* vol. 3, no. 1 (July 1997), citing R. Leflar, *Internal Operating Procedures of Appellate Courts* (Chicago: American Bar Foundation, 1976).

12. Sari S. Escovitz, *Judicial Selection and Tenure* 4 (Chicago: American Judicature Society, 1975).

13. Caleb Nelson, "A Re-Evaluation of Scholarly Explanations for the Rise of the Elected Judiciary in Antebellum America," *American Journal of Legal History* 37 (April 1993).

14. Larry C. Berkson, "Judicial Selection in the United States: A Special Report," *Judicature* 64, no. 4, (October 1980, updated in 1999 by Seth Andersen): 176–193. www.ajs.org/selection/berkson.pdf (accessed June 2, 2004).

15. G. Alan Tarr, "Rethinking the Selection of State Supreme Court Justices," *Willamette Law Review* 39, no. 4 (Fall 2003): 1445.

16. Ibid.

17. February 2007 Pennsylvania Keystone Poll, produced by Franklin & Marshall College in Lancaster, Pennsylvania. Polls and other analysis available at http://politics.fanm.edu.

18. Mark S. Hurwitz and Drew Noble Lanier, "Women and Minorities on State and Federal Appellate Benches: A Cross-Time Comparison 1985 to 1999," *Judicature,* 85 (September–October 2001): 84.

19. National Center for State Courts, "African American Justices Serving the State Supreme Courts," and "Women Justices Serving on State Courts of Last Resort and Intermediate Appellate Courts," 2002 (last comprehensive revision May 2003).

20. Molly McDonough and Debra Cassens Weiss, "Huge Defeat for 'Jail 4 Judges;' Female judicial candidates win big," *ABAJournal.Com,* November 9, 2006. www.abanet.org/journal/redesign/n8elect.html (accessed November 14, 2006)

21. American Judicature Society, "Judicial Selection in the States: Appellate and General Jurisdiction Courts" (1986, revised October 2002). www.ajs.org/js/judicialselectioncharts.pdf (accessed June 2, 2004).

22. Ibid.

23. David B. Rottman, Anthony Champagne, and Roy A. Schotland, *Call to Action: Statement of the National Summit on Improving Judicial Selection* (Williamsburg, Va.: National Center for State Courts, 2002).

24. Frontline, "Justice for Sale: Interview with Justices Stephen Breyer and Anthony Kennedy." www.pbs.org/wgbh/pages/frontline/shows/justice/interviews/supremo.html (accessed, June 10, 2004).

25. Ibid.

26. Paul Brace and Melinda Gann Hall, "Studying Courts Comparatively: The View from the American States," *Political Research Quarterly* 48 (1995): 5–29.

27. Ibid.

28. Gerald F. Uelmen, "Crocodiles in the Bathtub: Maintaining the Independence of State Supreme Courts in an Era of Judicial Politicization," *Notre Dame Law Review* 72 (1997): 1133, 1135–1142.

29. Ibid., 1133, 1137.

30. Stephen J. Ware, "Money, Politics and Judicial Decisions: A Case Study of Arbitration Law in Alabama," *Journal of Law and Politics* 15 (1999): 645.

31. Adam Liptak and Janet Roberts, "Campaign Cash Mirrors a High Court's Rulings," *New York Times,* October 1, 2006.

32. Ibid.

33. Molly McDonough and Debra Cassens Weiss, "Huge Defeat for 'Jail 4 Judges; Female judicial candidates win big," *ABAJournal.com,* November 9, 2006. www.abanet.org/journal/redesign/n8elect.html (accessed November 14, 2006).

34. Kaplan, "Justice for Sale," *Common Cause Magazine,* May–June 1987, 29–30.

35. Rottman, Champagne, and Schotland, *Call to Action.*

36. Uelman, "Crocodiles in the Bathtub."

37. Behrens and Silverman, "Case for Adopting."

38. Zach Patton, "Robe Warriors," *Governing* magazine, March 2006.

39. Charles H. Sheldon and Linda S. Maule, "*Choosing Justice: The Recruitment of State "and Federal Judges* (Pullman: Washington State University Press, 1997).

40. Rottman, Champagne, and Schotland, *Call to Action.*

41. Behrens and Silverman, "Case for Adopting."

42. "Judicial Selection in the States: Appellate and General Jurisdiction Courts," *American Judicature Society,* 1986 (updated January 2004). www.ajs.org/js/ judicialselectioncharts.pdf (accessed June 10, 2004).

43. Behrens and Silverman, "Case for Adopting."

44. Berkson, "Judicial Selection.

45. Ibid.

46. Behrens and Silverman, "Case for Adopting."

47. Ibid., 303.

48. Ibid.

49. Rottman, Champagne, and Schotland, *Call to Action.*

50. Behrens and Silverman, "Case for Adopting."

51. Luke Bierman, "Beyond Merit Selection," *Fordham Urban Law Journal* 29 (2002): 851, 864–865.

52. Ibid., citing, American Bar Association, "An Independent Judiciary, Report of the Commission on Separation of Powers and Judicial Independence" (1997), 48–49, and Henry J. Abraham, *The Judicial Process: An Introductory Analysis of the Courts of the United States, England, and France*, 6th ed. (New York: Oxford University Press, 1993), 42.

53. Brace and Hall, "Studying Courts Comparatively."

54. Drew Noble Lanier and Roger Handberg, "In the Eye of the Hurricane: Florida Courts, Judicial Independence, and Politics," *Fordham Urban Law Journal* 29 (2002): 1033.

55. Robert L. Misner, "Recasting Prosecutorial Discretion," *Journal of Criminal Law and Criminology* 86 (1996): 717, 741.

56. Steve Weinberg, "Inside an Office: An Elected Prosecutor Explains," *The Center for Public Integrity*. www.publicintegrity.org/pm/default.aspx?act=sidebarsa&aid=28 (accessed August 3, 2006).

57. Steven W. Perry, "Prosecutors in State Courts 2005," *Bureau of Justice Statistics Bulletin*, NCJ-213799, July 2006.

58. Ibid.

59. Misner, "Recasting."

60. Carol J. DeFrances, "State Court Prosecutors in Large Districts 2001," *Bureau of Justice Statistics Special Report*, NCJ-191206, December 2001.

61. Ibid. "About two-thirds of Part I Uniform Crime Report (UCR) offenses reported to the police in 1998 occurred in the prosecutorial district served by these offices."

62. Misner, "Recasting."

63. Shelby A. Dickerson Moore, "Questioning the Autonomy of Prosecutorial Charging Decisions: Recognizing the Need to Exercise Discretion—Knowing There Will Be Consequences for Crossing the Line," *Louisiana Law Review* 60 (Winter 2000): 371, 374.

64. Wayne R. LaFave, "The Prosecutor's Discretion in the United States," *American Journal of Comparative Law* 18 (1970): 532, 533.

65. Misner, "Recasting."

66. William T. Pizzi, "Understanding Prosecutorial Discretion in the United States: The Limits of Comparative Criminal Procedure as an Instrument of Reform," *Ohio State Law Journal* 54 (1993): 1325, n.88 citing a telephone interview with Kenneth Noto, the deputy chief of the narcotics section at the U.S. Attorney's Office for the Southern District of Florida.

67. John M. Dawson, "Prosecutors in State Courts," 1990, *Bureau of Justice Statistics Bulletin*, NCJ-134500, March 1992.

68. Moore, "Questioning."

69. Floyd D. Weatherspoon, "The Devastating Impact of the Justice System on the Status of African-American Males: An Overview Perspective," *Capital University Law Review* 23 (1994): 23, 43.

70. Steven K. Smith and Carol J. DeFrances, "Indigent Defense," *Bureau of Justice Statistics Selected Findings*, NCJ-158909, February 1996.

71. Carol J. DeFrances and Marika F. X. Litras, "Indigent Defense Services in Large Counties 1999," *Bureau of Justice Statistics Bulletin*, NCJ-184932, November 2000.

72. Ibid.

73. Carol S. DeFrances, "State Funded Indigent Defense Services 1999," *Bureau of Justice Statistics Special Report*, NCJ-188464, September 2001.

74. DeFrances and Litras, "Indigent Defense Services in Large Counties."

75. Ibid. Public defenders offices in the largest 100 counties employed more than 12,700 individuals during 1999, including more than 6,300 assistant public defenders; 1,200 investigators; 300 social workers; 21,700 support staff; and nearly 400 paralegals.

76. Criminal Justice Standards Committee, *Standards for Criminal Justice: Providing Defense Services*, 3d ed. (Chicago: American Bar Association, 1992).

77. Smith and DeFrances, "Indigent Defense."

78. Ibid.

79. Adele Bernhard, "Take Courage: What the Courts Can Do to Improve the Delivery of Criminal Defense Services," *University of Pittsburgh Law Review* 63 (2002): 293, 305.

80. DeFrances and Litras, "Indigent Defense Services in Large Counties."

81. Brian Ostrom, Robert LaFountain, and Neal Kauder, "Profiling Felony Cases in the NACM

Network," *Caseload Highlights: Examining the Work of State Courts*, 7, no. 1 (August 2001). In seventeen courts surveyed, nearly three-quarters of all felony cases resulted in pleas of guilty by the defendant.

82. *Improving Criminal Justice Systems through Expanded Strategies and Innovative Collaborations: Report of the National Symposium on Indigent Defense*, NCJ-181344, (Washington, D.C.: U.S. Department of Justice, Office of Justice Programs, 2000); Richard Klein and Robert Spangenberg, *The Indigent Defense Crisis* (Washington, D.C.: ABA Section of Crime Justice 1993), 25.

83. David Cole, *No Equal Justice: Race and Class in the American Justice System* (New York: New Press, 1999), 92.

84. Andrew Rachlin, "Rights of Defense," *Governing* magazine, January 2007.

85. ACLU press release, "ACLU Files Class-Action Lawsuit against Montana's Indigent Defense Program," February 14, 2002.

86. Kevin Clermont and Theodore Eisenberg, "Trial by Jury or Judge: Transcending Empiricism," *Cornell Law Review* 77 (1992): 1124.

87. See *Williams v. Florida*, 399 U.S. 78 (1970), approving six-member juries; *Apodaca v. Oregon*, 406 U.S. 404 (1972), allowing nonunanimous verdicts.

88. David Rottman et al., *State Court Organization, 2004*.

89. *New Directions from the Field: Victims' Rights and Services for the 21st Century*, Executive Summary (Washington, D.C.: U.S. Department of Justice, Office of Justice Programs, Office for Victims of Crime, 1998).

90. Wayne A. Logan, "Through the Past Darkly: A Survey of the Uses and Abuses of Victim Impact Evidence in Capital Trials," *Arizona Law Review* 41 (1999): 143, 177–178.

91. See *Payne v. Tennessee*, 501 U.S. 808 (1991), which reversed *Booth v. Maryland*, 482 U.S. 496 (1987).

92. Robert Mosteller, "New Dimensions in Sentencing Reform in the Twenty-First Century," *Oregon Law Review* 92 (2003): 1, 13.

93. Ibid., 14–15.

94. In *Ring v. Arizona*, 536 U.S. 584 (2002), the Supreme Court invalidated Arizona's capital sentencing procedures, holding that the jury, not the judge, must find the aggravating factors necessary to impose the death penalty. Similar procedures in Colorado, Idaho, Montana, and Nebraska also were ruled unconstitutional.

95. Rottman et al., *State Court Organization 1998*.

96. Michael M. O'Hear, "National Uniformity/Local Uniformity: Reconsidering the Use of Departures to Reduce Federal-State Sentencing Disparities," *Iowa Law Review* 87 (2002): 721, 756.

97. Ibid., 749.

98. Robert Mosteller, "New Dimensions in Sentencing Reform in the Twenty-First Century," *Oregon Law Review* 92 (2003): 1, 16–17.

99. Arizona, California, Delaware, Florida, Illinois, Maine, Minnesota, Mississippi, New Mexico, North Carolina, Ohio, Virginia, and Washington have adopted determinate sentencing laws. *1996 National Survey of State Sentencing Structures* NCJ-169270 (Washington, D.C.: Bureau of Justice Assistance, 1998), 4–5.

100. Marguerite A. Driessen and W. Cole Durham Jr., "Sentencing Dissonances in the United States: The Shrinking Distance between Punishment Proposed and Sanction Served," *American Journal of Comparative Law* 50 (2002): 623, 635.

101. Bureau of Justice Statistics, National Corrections Reporting Program 1999. www.ojp.usdoj.gov/bjs/abstract/ncrp92.htm (accessed March 22, 2007).

102. *1996 National Survey of State Sentencing Structures*, exhibit 1-1.

103. Rottman et al., *State Court Organization, 2004*.

104. Driessen and Durham, "Sentencing Dissonances."

105. Rottman et al., *State Court Organization, 2004*.

106. *1996 National Survey of State Sentencing Structures*.

107. Rottman et al., *State Court Organization, 2004*.

108. Ibid., Table 47.

109. Michael M. O'Hear, "National Uniformity/Local Uniformity."

110. Ibid., n.70, citing Ralph Ranalli, "Crack Sentence Debate Reopened: Proof Whites, Blacks Treated Equally Asked," *Boston Globe*, September 26, 1999, B1.

111. B. Ostrom, N. Kauder, and R. LaFountain, *Examining the Work of the State Courts, 1999–2000: A National Perspective from the Court Statistics Project* (Williamsburg, Va.: National Center for State Courts, 2000).

112. Judith S. Kaye, "The State of the Judiciary, 2003: Confronting Today's Challenge" (annual address, Albany, N.Y., January 13, 2003), 4.

113. Alan Greenblatt, "Docket Science," *Governing* magazine, June 2001, 40

114. Ibid.

115. Ibid.

116. Ibid.

117. Rottman, Champagne, and Schotland, *Call to Action*.

Chapter 9

1. Larry Hannan, "Police Shut Down Girl's Lemonade Stand: City Later Offers Free Permit," *Naples Daily News*. www.bonitanews.com/03/ 06/naples/ d945350a.htm (accessed June 20, 2003).

2. H. H. Gerth and C. Wright Mills, *Max Weber: Essays in Sociology* (New York: Oxford University Press, 1943).

3. Ronald C. Moe and Robert S. Gilmour, "Rediscovering Principles of Public Administration: The Neglected Foundation of Public Law," *Public Administration Review* 55, no. 2 (March/April 1995): 135–146.

4. John J. Gargan, "Introduction and Overview of State Government Administration," in *Handbook of State Government Administration,* ed. John J. Gargan (New York: Marcel-Dekker, 2000).

5. Jerrell D. Coggburn and Saundra K. Schneider, "The Quality of Management and Government Performance: An Empirical Analysis of the American States," *Public Administration Review* 63, no. 2 (March/April 2003): 206–213.

6. Jason Hill and Frank Johnson, "Revenues and Expenditures for Public Elementary and Secondary Education: School Year 2002–03," National Center for Education Statistics, October 2005. http://nces.ed.gov/pubs2005/ 2005353.pdf (accessed April 15, 2006).

7. Charles Barrilleaux, "Statehouse Bureaucracy: Institutional Consistency in a Changing Environment," in *American State and Local Politics,* eds. Ronald E. Weber and Paul Brace (New York: Chatham House, 1999).

8. Michael Lipsky, *Street-Level Bureaucracy* (New York: Russell Sage Foundation, 1980).

9. Cornelius Kerwin, *Rulemaking: How Government Agencies Write Law and Make Policy,* 3rd ed. (Washington, D.C.: CQ Press, 2003).

10. Deil S. Wright, Chung-Lae Cho, and Yoo-Sun Choi, "Top-Level State Administrators: Changing Characteristics and Qualities," *The Book of the States 2002* (Lexington, Ky.: Council of State Governments, 2002).

11. Charles T. Goodsell, *The Case for Bureaucracy: A Public Administration Polemic,* 4th ed. (Washington, D.C.: CQ Press, 2003).

12. Ibid.

13. George W. Downs and Patrick D. Larkey, *The Search for Government Efficiency* (Philadelphia: Temple University Press, 1986).

14. Elliott Sclar, *You Don't Always Get What You Pay For* (Ithaca, N.Y.: Cornell University Press, 2000).

15. J. Norman Baldwin, "Public versus Private Employees: Debunking Stereotypes," *Review of Public Personnel Administration* 12 (Winter 1991): 1–27.

16. Barrilleaux, "Statehouse Bureaucracy," 106–107.

17. John J. DiIulio Jr., Gerald Garvey, and Donald F. Kettl, *Improving Government: An Owner's Manual* (Washington, D.C.: Brookings Institution, 1993).

18. The Government Performance Project. results.gpponline.org/ProjectTeam.aspx (accessed April 20, 2006).

19. Coggburn and Schneider, "Quality of Management," 206–213.

20. Dennis Cauchon, "Bad Moves, Not Economy behind Busted State Budgets," *USA Today,* June 23, 2003, P1A.

21. Kenneth J. Meier, "Bureaucracy and Democracy: The Case for More Bureaucracy and Less Democracy," *Public Administration Review* 57, no. 3 (May/June 1997): 193–199.

22. Katherine Barrett and Richard Greene, "Time for a Check Up," *Governing* magazine, November 2005.

23. Elizabeth G. Hill, "California Legislative Analyst's Office: An Isle of Independence," *Spectrum: The Journal of State Government* 6, no. 4 (2003): 26–29.

24. Barrett and Greene, "Time for a Check Up."

25. Barbara Romzek and Melvin Dubnick, "Accountability in the Public Sector: Lessons from the Challenger Tragedy," *Public Administration Review* 47, no. 3 (May/June 1987): 227–238.

26. Alfred Steinberg, *The Bosses* (New York: MacMillan, 1972).

27. Dwight Waldo, *The Administrative State* (New York: Holmes and Meier, 1948).

28. "Union Membership Edges Up, but Share Continues to Fall," *Monthly Labor Review*, January 1999, 1–2.

29. Wisconsin Democracy Campaign, "2003–2004 Committee Contributions to Candidates and LCCs," 2005. www.wisdc.org/WEB_PAC_Amt 2004.php (accessed April 17, 2006).

30. WEAC's legislative goals are available on its Web site: www.weac.org/capitol/2005-06/legagenda/main.htm.

31. Charles J. Sykes, *Profscam: Professors and the Demise of Higher Education* (New York: St. Martin's Press, 1989).

32. Bureau of the Census, *Statistical Abstract of the United States 2003,* (Washington, D.C.: U.S. Government Printing Office, 2003), Table 454.

33. Jennifer 8. Lee, "In Police Class, Blue Comes in Many Colors," *New York Times,* July 8, 2005.

34. C. J. Chivers, "For Black Officers, Diversity Has Its Limits," *New York Times,* April 2, 2001.

35. Sally Selden, *The Promise of Representative Bureaucracy: Diversity and Responsiveness in a Government Agency* (Armonk, N.Y.: M. E. Sharpe, 1997).

36. Donald F. Kettl, *The Global Public Management Revolution: A Report on the Transformation of Governance* (Washington, D.C.: Brookings Institution, 2000).

37. H. George Frederickson and Kevin B. Smith, *The Public Administration Theory Primer* (Boulder, Colo.: Westview Press, 2003), 215.

38. Sclar, *You Don't Always Get,* 84–88.

39. Jonathan Walters, "The Buzz over Balance," in *Governing: Issues and Applications from the Front Lines of Government,* ed. Alan Ehrenhalt (Washington, D.C.: CQ Press, 2002).

40. D. M. West, "Assessing E-Government: The Internet, Democracy and Service Delivery by State and Federal Governments," World Bank, 2000. www1.worldbank.org/publicsector/egov/Egov ReportUs00.htm (accessed May 15, 2003).

41. Ramona McNeal et al., "Innovating in Digital Government in the American States," *Social Science Quarterly* 84, no. 1 (March 2003): 52–70.

42. Darrell M. West, "State and Federal E-Government in the United States, 2006," Taubman Center for Public Policy at Brown University, August 2006. www.insidepolitics.org/egovt06us.pdf (accessed February 4, 2007).

43. Ellen Perlman, "eGovernment Special Report," *Governing* magazine, 2002. www.governing.com/archive/2002/sep/eg2c.txt (accessed June 3, 2003).

44. West, "State and Federal E-Government in the United States, 2006."

45. Ibid.

46. Karen Mossberger, Caroline Tolbert, and Ramona McNeal, "Developing E-Government in the Fifty States 2000–2004," presented at the 2005 State Politics and Policy Conference, East Lansing, Mich., May 14, 2005. http://polisci.msu.edu/sppc2005/papers/satam/MossbergerTolbertMcNealSPPC.doc (accessed April 22, 2006).

Chapter 10

1. National League of Cities. www.nlc.org/about_cities/cities_101/146.cfm (accessed September 16, 2006).

2. Richard Cole and John Kincaid, "Public Opinion on U.S. Federal and Intergovernmental Issues in 2006," *Publius: The Journal of Federalism* 36, no. 3 (May 2006): 443–459.

3. This figure is based on an estimated total population of three hundred million.

4. City-Data.com. www.city-data.com/city/Hove-Mobile-Park-North-Dakota.html (accessed September 5, 2006).

5. David Miller, *The Regional Government of Metropolitan America* (Boulder, Colo.: Westview Press, 2002).

6. Jonathan Walters, "Cry, the Beleaguered County," *Governing* magazine, August 1996.

7. See the National Association of Counties Web site, www.naco.org/Template.cfm?Section=About_Counties (accessed Feb. 5, 2004). See also Roger L. Kemp, ed. *Model Government Charters: A City, County, Regional, State, and Federal Handbook* (Jefferson, N.C.: McFarland, 2003), 55.

8. Walters, "Cry."

9. "A Brief Overview of County Government," National Association of Counties, August 2003. www.naco.org/Content/NavigationMenu/About_Counties/County_Government/Default271.htm (accessed August 4, 2004).

10. Ibid.

11. Miller, "Regional Government," 26.

12. U.S. Conference of Mayors Web site. www.usmayors.org (accessed January 12, 2004).

13. Penelope Lemov, "Infrastructure Conference Report: Building It Smarter, Managing It Better," *Governing* magazine, October 1996.

14. Rob Gurwitt, "Are City Councils a Relic of the Past?" *Governing* magazine, April 2003.

15. National League of Cities, "Serving on City Councils," *Research Brief on America's Cities,* Issue 2003–5, September 2003.

16. Kemp, *Model Government,* 10.

17. William Hansell, "Evolution and Change Characterize Council-Manager Governmment," *Public Management,* vol. 82 (August 2000): 17–21.

18. Michael Zuckerman, *Peaceable Kingdoms: The New England Towns of the 18th Century* (New York: Knopf, 1970).

19. Miller, "Regional Government," 41.

20. Anwar Syed, *The Political Theory of the American Local Government* (New York: Random House, 1966), 40.

21. Alexis De Tocqueville, *Democracy in America: A New Translation,* translated by George Lawrence, edited by J. P. Mayer (New York: HarperCollins, 2000).

22. Lemov, "Infrastructure."

23. Ibid., 40.

24. *Handbook of Research on Urban Politics and Policy in the United States,* ed. Ronald K. Vogel (Westport, Conn.: Greenwood Press, 1997), 133.

25. Kemp, *Model Government,* 59.

26. League of Women Voters of California. http://smartvoter.org (accessed January 20, 2004).

27. *Cities, Politics, and Policy: A Comparative Analysis,* ed. John P. Pelissero (Washington, D.C.: CQ Press, 2003), 81.

28. Ibid., 162.

29. Ibid., 71.

30. National League of Cities, "Compensation and Workload for Local Elected Officials," www.nlc.org/About_Cities/cities_101/147.cfm (accessed September 16, 2006).

31. Ibid.

32. National League of Cities, "City Officials Disapprove of Federal and State Tax Policies," *Research Brief on America's Cities,* Issue 2005–2, July 2005.

33. National League of Cities, "City Fiscal Conditions in 2005," *Research Brief on America's Cities,* Issue 2006–1, January 2006.

Chapter 11

1. Christopher Briem, "A Primer on Local Government Fragmentation and Regionalism in the Pittsburgh Region." www.pitt.edu/~cbriem/pittsburghindex.htm (accessed October 1, 2006).

2. Figures calculated by author from U.S. Census Bureau data. http://quickfacts.census.gov/qfd/states/42/42003.html (accessed October 1, 2006).

3. Advisory Commission on Intergovernmental Relations, "Metropolitan Organization: The Allegheny County Case," 1992.

4. www.county.allegheny.pa.us/munimap/ (accessed November 1, 2006).

5. Anthony Downs, "The Devolution Revolution: Why Congress Is Shifting a Lot of Power to the Wrong Levels," Policy Brief #3, Brookings Institution, 1996. www.brookings.edu/index/scholarwork.htm?scholar=Downs*Anthony** (accessed September 30, 2006).

6. U.S. Census Bureau, "Metropolitan Statistical Area." http://quickfacts.census.gov/qfd/meta/long_metro.htm (accessed October 1, 2006).

7. U.S. Bureau of the Census, *Statistical Abstract of the United States 2000* (Washington, D.C.: U.S. Government Printing Office, 2000).

8. Ronald K. Vogel, *Handbook of Research on Urban Politics and Policy in the United States* (Westport, Conn.: Greenwood Press, 1997), 133.

9. David Miller, *The Regional Governing of Metropolitan America* (Boulder, Colo.: Westview Press, 2002), 1.

10. David Cieslewits, "The Environmental Impacts of Sprawl," in *Urban Sprawl: Causes, Consequences, and Policy Responses,* ed. Gregory D. Squires, (Washington, D.C.: Urban Institute Press, 2002).

11. Ibid.

12. See, for example, Myron Orfield, *American Metropolitics: The New Suburban Reality* (Washington, D.C.: Brookings Institution, 2002).

13. Ibid, 41.

14. Peter Dreier, John Mollenkopf, and Todd Swanstrom, *Place Matters: Metropolitics for the Twenty-First Century* (Lawrence: University of Kansas Press, 2001).

15. Ibid., 67.

16. Orfield, *American Metropolitics,* 10.

17. G. Ross Stephens and Nelson Wikstrom, *Metropolitan Government and Governance: Theoretical Perspectives, Empirical Analysis, and the Future* (New York: Oxford University Press, 1999).

18. About Metro. www.metro-region.org/pssp.cfm?ProgServID=62 (accessed November 1, 2006).

19. Heike Mayor and John Provo, "The Portland Edge in Context," *The Portland Edge: Challenges and Successes in Growing Communities,* ed. Connie P. Ozawa (Washington, D.C.: Island Press, 2004).

20. National Association of Regional Councils, "What Is a Regional Council?" http://narc.org/regional-councils-mpos/what-is-a-regional-council.html (accessed October 20, 2006).

21. Ibid.

22. Miller, *Regional Governing,* 103.

23. Ibid., 104.

24. National Association of Counties. www.naco.org/Content/ContentGroups/Publications1/County_News1/20035/6-2-03/Successful_City-County_Consolidations.htm (accessed November 1, 2006).

25. Jeffrey Cohan, "Reports Outline Options in Merging Pittsburgh-Allegheny County Services," *Pittsburgh Post-Gazette,* April 2, 2004.

26. Lara Brenckle, "City, County Study Merger . . . Again," *Pittsburgh Tribune-Review,* October 20, 2006. www.pittsburghlive.com/x/pittsburghtrib/news/cityregion/s_475861.htm (accessed October 23, 2006).

27. National League of Cities, "Serving on City Councils," *Research Brief on America's Cities,* Issue 2003–5, September 2003.

28. David Rusk, *Cities without Suburbs,* 2nd ed. (Washington, D.C.: Woodrow Wilson Center Press, 1995).

29. Vogel, *Handbook,* 139.

30. Rob Gurwitt, "Annexation: Not So Smart Growth," *Governing* magazine, October 2000.

31. John Ritter, "Las Vegas Closing in on Full House," *USA TODAY,* November 13, 2006, 3A.

32. Barbara Kelly, *Expanding the American Dream: Building and Rebuilding Levittown* (Albany: SUNY University Press, 1993).

33. An interesting counterpoint to academic criticisms of the problems caused by metropolitan growth can be found in Andrew Kirby's review of Myron Orfield's *American Metropolitics,* a well-known study cited throughout this chapter. See Andrew Kirby, "Metropolitics or Retropolitics?" *Antipode* 36, no. 4, (September 2004): 753–759.

34. Charles Tiebout, "A Pure Theory of Local Expenditures," *Journal of Political Economy* 64, no. 5 (October 1956): 416–424.

35. William Lyons, David Lowery, and Ruth Hoogland DeHoog, *The Politics of Dissatisfaction: Citizens, Services, and Urban Institutions* (Armonk, N.Y.: M. E. Sharpe, 1992).

36. Paul Teske et al., "Establishing the Micro Foundations of a Macro Theory: Information, Movers and the Competitive Local Market for

Public Goods," *American Political Science Review* 87, no. 3 (September 1993): 702–713.

37. Paul Teske et al., "The Empirical Evidence for Citizen Information and a Local Market for Public Goods," *American Political Science Review* 89, no. 3 (September 1995): 707–709.

38. Dave Ranney, "State's Rural Population Continues to Shrink," *Lawrence Journal-World*. www2.ljworld.com/news/2005/dec/13/states_rural_population_continues_shrink/ (accessed August 15, 2006).

39. Alan Greenblatt, "Little Mergers on the Prairie," *Governing* magazine, July 2006, 48–54.

40. "Class I School District Consolidation Ballot Refendum," *Cornhusker Economics,* University of Nebraska–Lincoln Extension, November 9, 2005. http://agecon.unl.edu/pub/cornhusker/11-09-05.pdf (accessed November 21, 2006).

41. Greenblatt, "Little Mergers," 49–50.

42. Ibid, 54.

Chapter 12

1. "State and Local Tax Burdens Compared to Other U.S. States 2006," Tax Foundation. www.taxfoundation.org/taxdata/show/336.html (accessed July 11, 2006).

2. Jason Zengerle, "Radio City Dispatch," *New Republic,* August 9, 2001.

3. Alaska, Delaware, Florida, Nevada, South Dakota, Texas, Washington, and Wyoming have no personal income taxes. New Hampshire imposes a 5 percent tax on interest and dividend income only. Tennessee also only imposes an income tax on certain types of interest, dividend, and partnership income.

   See Tracy C. Von Ins's, "Some Cities Turning to Local Income Taxes for Revenue," July 9, 2001, published by the National League of Cities, for information on local income taxes.

4. "Local, State and Federal Taxes Per Capita, 2006," Tax Foundation, April 18, 2006. www.taxfoundation.org/taxdata/show/1441.html (accessed August 19, 2006).

5. These figures and many that follow come from the U.S. Census Bureau's *Statistical Abstract of the United States, 2006* and refer to the fiscal year that concluded in 2002, one of the last years for which such data are available.

6. Bureau of Justice Statistics, 2004. www.ojp.usdoj.gov/bjs/correct.htm#findings (accessed August 14, 2006).

7. *Statistical Abstract, 2006,* 281.

8. Ibid.

9. "State Excise Tax Rates on Cigarettes," Federation of Tax Administrators. www.taxadmin.org/FTA/rate/cigarett.html (accessed July 3, 2006).

10. *Statistical Abstract, 2006,* 301.

11. Katherine Barrett et al., "The Way We Tax: A 50-State Report," *Governing* magazine, February 2003.

12. Donald Bruce and William F. Fox, "State and Local Sales Tax Revenue Losses from E-Commerce: Estimates as of July 2004." Center for Business and Economic Research, University of Tennessee, Knoxville, July 2004. cber.bus.utk.edu/ecomm/Ecom0704.pdf (accessed July 13, 2006).

13. Cited in Penelope Lemov, "The Untaxables," *Governing* magazine, July 2002.

14. Alan Greenblatt, "The Sales Tax Goes Online," *Governing* magazine, December 2005.

15. Gail Perry, "Streamlined Sales Tax Plan Slowly Gaining Momentum," *Accounting Today* 24 no. 3 (2006): 3.

16. *Statistical Abstract, 2006,* 281, 293, and 297.

17. The effective tax rate information for the nation and New Hampshire can be found in the *Statistical Abstract, 2006,* 301.

18. *Statistical Abstract, 2006,* 297.

19. *2004 State Expenditure Report,* National Association of State Budget Officers, 14.

20. *The Funding Gap: Low-Income and Minority Students Shortchanged by Most States* (Washington, D.C.: Education Trust, 2005). Based on 2002–2003 U.S. Department of Education and U.S. Census Bureau data.

21. Ibid.

22. Alan Greenblatt, "The Loathsome Local Levy," *Governing* magazine, October 2001.

23. *Statistical Abstract, 2006*, 281. Corporate income taxes account for an additional 4 percent of state and local tax revenues.

24. Fifteen states allow certain localities to impose income taxes as well, but for the most part, income tax receipts are a minor source of funds for cities and counties.

25. *Statistical Abstract, 2006*, 294.

26. Recently, however, Alaska's oil-dependent tax structure has been shaken. Alaska entered 2003 with the most serious revenue shortfall of any state.

27. "State Individual Income Tax Collections, 2005," Tax Foundation, June 1, 2006. www.taxfoundation.org/taxdata/show/282.html (accessed August 19, 2006).

28. *Statistical Abstract, 2006*, 281.

29. Ibid.

30. *The Fiscal Survey of States*, National Governors Association and National Association of State Budget Officers, 14.

31. *Statistical Abstract, 2006*, 280–281.

32. *Statistical Abstract, 2006*, 275.

33. *2005 State Expenditure Report*, National Association of State Budget Officers, 9.

34. *Statistical Abstract, 2006*, 297.

35. Alan Greenblatt, "Enemies of the State," *Governing* magazine, June 2002.

36. "Local, State and Federal Taxes Per Capita, by State, 2006," and "State and Local Tax Burdens Compared to Other States, 2006," Tax Foundation, April 2006. www.taxfoundation.org/taxdata/topic/86.html (accessed August 19, 2006).

37. *Statistical Abstract, 2006*, 293.

38. CNNMoney, "The Best Places to Live 2006." http://money.cnn.com/magazines/moneymag/bplive/2006/index.html (accessed July 23, 2006).

39. *State and Local Sourcebook, 2006*, supplement to *Governing* magazine, 5.

40. "State and Local Tax Collections per Capita, 2004," Tax Foundation, June 1, 2006. www.taxfoundation.org/taxdata/show/279.html (accessed July 3, 2006).

41. See the Mayflower Compact for further insights into the mindset of the founders of the Massachusetts Bay Colony.

42. *Statistical Abstract, 2006*, 285, and "State and Local Tax Burdens Compared to Other States, 2002," Tax Foundation, April 2006. www.taxfoundation.org/files/burdens_compared-20060412.pdf (accessed August 19, 2006).

43. John E. Petersen, "Guide to Municipal Finance: Credit Raters Make Their Mark," *Governing* magazine, June 2005.

44. *Statistical Abstract, 2006*, 288.

45. Ibid.

46. See *Budget Processes in the States*, National Association of State Budget Officers, Washington, D.C., January 2002, for a detailed discussion of the state budget process.

47. These states are Arizona, Arkansas, Connecticut, Hawaii, Indiana, Kentucky, Maine, Minnesota, Montana, Nebraska, Nevada, New Hampshire, North Carolina, North Dakota, Ohio, Oregon, Texas, Virginia, Washington, Wisconsin, and Wyoming. www.stateline.org (accessed July 3, 2006).

48. See "Legislative Budget Procedures: A Guide to Appropriations and Budget Processes in the States, Commonwealths and Territories," National Conference of State Legislatures, for a detailed discussion of state balanced budget requirements. www.ncsl.org/programs/fiscal/balbud2.htm (accessed December 15, 2003).

49. Robert Zahradnik, "Rainy Day Funds: Opportunities for Reform," Center on Budget and Policy Priorities, March 9, 2005. www.cbpp.org/3-9-05sfp.htm (accessed July 19, 2006).

50. "State and Local Spending Per Capita, 2004," Tax Foundation, June 1, 2006. www.taxfoundation.org/taxdata/show/276.html (accessed August 19, 2006).

51. *Governing Sourcebook, 2006*, 47–48.

52. *Governing Sourcebook, 2006*, 14–15.

53. *Statistical Abstract, 2006*, 299.

54. *2005 State Expenditure Report*, 4.

55. Ibid.

56. Paul E. Lingenfelter, David L. Wright, and Takeshi Yanagiura, *State Higher Education*

Finance FY 2005 (Boulder, Colo.: State Higher Education Executive Officers).

57. "2002–2003 State Health Care Expenditure Report," National Association of State Budget Officers, June 2005. www.milbank.org/reports/05NASBO/index.html#total (accessed August 19, 2006).

58. *2005 State Expenditure Report,* 49.

59. *2005 State Expenditure Report,* 44.

60. *Federal Register* 72 no. 15, January 24, 2007, 3147–3148.

61. Ian Hill, Holly Stockdale, and Brigette Courtot, "Squeezing SCHIP: States Use Flexibility to Respond to the Ongoing Budget Crisis," Urban Institute, June 2004. www.urban.org/publications/311015.html (accessed July 20, 2006).

62. *Statistical Abstract, 2006,* 14.

63. *Statistical Abstract, 2006,* 281.

64. Cynthia Miller, "Leavers, Stayers, and Cyclers: An Analysis of the Welfare Caseload," Manpower Demonstration Research Corporation, November 2002. Submitted to the Office of the Assistant Secretary for Planning and Evaluation, U.S. Department of Health and Human Services. See also Alan Weil's "Ten Things Everyone Should Know about Welfare Reform," Urban Institute, May 9, 2002, for a full discussion of the effects of welfare reform.

65. *2005 State Expenditure Report,* 30.

66. *Statistical Abstract, 2006,* 285.

67. *2005 State Expenditure Report,* 59.

68. *Governing Sourcebook, 2006,* 74.

69. *2005 State Expenditure Report,* 69.

70. Pamela M. Prah, "Accounting Rule Could Bust State Budgets," Stateline.org, June 28, 2006.www.stateline.org/live/ViewPage.action?siteNodeId=137&languageId=1&contentId=123266 (accessed August 3, 2006).

71. Alan Greenblatt, "Enemies of the State," *Governing* magazine, June 2002.

72. This section is adapted from the February 2003 *Governing* special issue on state tax systems. See Katherine Barrett et al., "The Way We Tax."

Chapter 13

1. Margaret E. Goertz, "State Education Policy in the New Millennium," *The State of the States* (Washington, D.C.: CQ Press, 2006), 153.

2. Associated Press, "Connecticut Challenges No Child Left Behind," August 23, 2005. www.msnbc.msn.com/id/9042496/ (accessed August 29, 2006).

3. John Dinan and Dale Krane, "The State of American Federalism, 2005: Federalism Resurfaces in the Political Debate," *Publius: The Journal of Federalism* 36, no. 3 (2006). http://publius.oxfordjournals.org/cgi/reprint/36/3/327 (accessed June 5, 2006).

4. Alexandra Marks, "Local Discontent with 'No Child Left Behind' Grows," *Christian Science Monitor,* August 19, 2005.

5. Diana Jean Schemo, "Flexibility Granted Two States in No Child Left Behind," *New York Times,* May 18, 2006.

6. David Tyack and Larry Cuban, *Tinkering toward Utopia: A Century of Public School Reform* (Cambridge: Harvard University Press, 1995), 2.

7. *2005 State Expenditure Report* (Washington, D.C.: National Association of State Budget Officers), 5.

8. Michael A. Rebell, "Fiscal Equity Litigation and the Democratic Imperative," *Journal of Education Finance* 24, no. 1 (Summer 1998): 23–50.

9. Duke Helfand and Howard Blume, "Gov. Signs Mayor's Dream into Law," *Los Angeles Times,* September 19, 2006.

10. Charles Mahtesian, "Too Much Democracy," Governing.com, January 24, 2000. www.governing.com/view/vu012400.htm (accessed November 14, 2003).

11. Education Commission of the States, February 2006. www.ecs.org/clearinghouse/57/32/5732 .htm (accessed September 5, 2006).

12. Rebell, "Fiscal Equity."

13. Tyack and Cuban, *Tinkering toward Utopia,* 47.

14. William Duncombe, John Ruggiero, and John Yinger, "Alternative Approaches to Measuring the Cost of Education," in *Holding Schools Accountable: Performance-Based Reform in*

Education, ed. Helen F. Ladd (Washington, D.C.: Brookings Institution, 1996), 338. See also Christopher B. Swanson, "Ten Questions (and Answers) about Graduates, Dropouts, and NCLB Accountability," Urban Institute, 2003.

15. Harold Wenglinsky, "School District Expenditures, School Resources and Student Achievement: Modeling the Production Function," in *Developments in School Finance, 1997— Does Money Matter?* ed. William J. Fowler Jr. (Washington, D.C.: National Center for Education Statistics, 1998).

16. Allan Odden, "Equity and Adequacy in School Finance Today," *Phi Delta Kappan* (October 2003): 120–125.

17. "Money Matters: A Reporter's Guide to School Finance," Education Writers Association, 2003, 5.

18. *The Funding Gap: Low-Income and Minority Students Shortchanged by Most States* (Washington, D.C.: Education Trust, 2005). Based on 2002–2003 U.S. Department of Education and U.S. Census Bureau data.

19. "Per Pupil Amounts for Current Spending of Public Elementary-Secondary School Systems by State: 2003–04," *Annual Survey of Local Government Finances* (Washington, D.C.: U.S. Census Bureau), 8.

20. "Quality Counts 2003," *Education Week,* January 9, 2003, 22.

21. Richard Rothstein, *The Way We Were: The Myths and Realities of America's Student Achievement* (New York: Century Foundation, 1998), 19.

22. Lowell C. Rose and Alec M. Gallup, "The 38th Annual Phi Delta Kappa/Gallup Poll of the Public's Attitudes toward the Public Schools," *Phi Delta Kappan* (September 2006).

23. Diane Stark Rentner et al., "From the Capital to the Classroom: Year 4 of the No Child Left Behind Act," Center on Education Policy, March 2006. www.cep-dc.org/nclb/Year4/CEP-NCLB-Report-4.pdf (accessed September 3, 2006).

24. Robert Rothman, *Measuring Up: Standards, Assessment, and School Reform* (San Francisco: Jossey-Bass, 1995), 53.

25. Nancy Kober, "A Public Education Primer," Center on Education Policy, July 2006.

www.cep-dc.org/pubs/publiceducationprimer/PublicEducationPrimer.pdf (accessed September 1, 2006).

26. National Center for Education Statistics. www.NCES.ed.gov/timss/results03.asp (accessed September 14, 2006).

27. Associated Press, "SAT Records Biggest Score Drop in 31 Years," August 29, 2006. www.msnbc.msn.com/id/14569572/ (accessed August 29, 2006).

28. "The Texas Miracle," CBSNEWS.com. www.cbsnews.com/stories/2004/01/06/60II/main591676.shtml (accessed August 13, 2004).

29. Swanson, "Ten Questions (and Answers)."

30. "Quality Counts 2001," *Education Week,* January 2001.

31. Kevin Smith, *The Ideology of Education: The Commonwealth, the Market, and America's Schools* (Albany: SUNY Press, 2003), 59.

32. Margaret E. Goertz, "State Education Policy in the New Millennium," 152.

33. Nancy Kober et al., "States High School Exit Exams: A Challenging Year," Center on Education Policy, August 16, 2006. www.cep-dc.org/pubs/hseeAugust2006/HSEE2006FINAL.pdf (accessed September 4, 2006).

34. Gayler et al., "State High School Exit Exams," 8.

35. Kati Haycock, "Good Teaching Matters: How Well-Qualified Teachers Can Close the Gap," *Thinking K–16* 3, no. 2 (Summer 1998).

36. Economists Steven G. Givkin and Eric A. Hanushek cited, along with researcher William Sanders, in "Quality Counts 2003," *Education Week,* 10.

37. John Wirt et al., "The Condition of Education 2004: Out-of-field Teacher in Middle and High School Grades," U.S. Department of Education, 2004.

38. Bess Keller, "Most States Pass Federal Review on Highly Qualified Teachers," *Education Week,* August 17, 2006.

39. Stark Rentner et al., "From the Capital to the Classroom."

40. Michael Allen, "Eight Questions on Teacher Preparation: What Does the Research Say?" Education Commission of the States, July 2003.

41. Vicki Hobbs, "The Promise and the Power of Distance Learning in Rural Education" (Arlington, Va.: The Rural School and Community Trust, 2004).

42. "Anything but Research-Based–State Initiatives to Consolidate School Districts," *Rural Policy Matters,* March 2006.

43. Joe Bard et al., "Rural School Consolidation Report," prepared for the National Rural Education Association Executive Board, April 1–2, 2005.

44. Hobbs, "The Promise and the Power of Distance Learning in Rural Education."

45. Susan Saulny, "Few Students Seek Free Tutoring," *New York Times,* April 6, 2006.

46. Lowell C. Rose and Alec M. Gallup, "38th Annual Phi Delta Kappa/Gallup Poll." www.pdkintl.org/kappan/kpollpdf.htm (accessed December 12, 2006).

47. See USCharterSchool.org, run by a consortium of educational associations with an interest in providing information and promising practices about charter schools, for more statistics about charter schools.

48. Lori Montgomery and Jay Mathews, "The Future of D.C. Public Schools: Traditional or Charter Education?" *Washington Post,* August 22, 2006.

49. Brian P. Gill et al., *Rhetoric versus Reality: What We Know and What We Need to Know about Vouchers and Charter Schools* (Santa Monica, Calif.: RAND Corporation, 2001), xviii; Charles S. Clark, "Charter Schools," *CQ Researcher,* December 20, 2002.

50. Diana Jean Schemo, "Nation's Charter Schools Lagging Behind, U.S. Test Scores Reveal," *New York Times,* August 17, 2003. www.nytimes.com/2004/08/17/education/17charter.html?hp (accessed August 17, 2004).

51. Kenneth Jost, "School Vouchers Showdown," *CQ Researcher,* 12, no. 6, February 15, 2002.

52. Angela Townsend, "More than 2,500 in Ohio Apply for School Vouchers," *Cleveland Plain Dealer,* July 4, 2006.

53. Amanda Paulson, "Milwaukee's Lessons on School Vouchers," *Christian Science Monitor,* May 23, 2006.

54. See the work of Paul Peterson at Harvard University School of Education. Paul E. Peterson and David E. Campbell, eds., *Charters, Vouchers, and Public Education* (Washington, D.C.: Brookings Institution Press, 2001).

55. "School Vouchers: Publicly Funded Programs in Cleveland and Milwaukee," GAO-01-914, Government Accountability Office, 2001, 4; Zachary M. Seward, "Long-Delayed Education Study Casts Doubt on Value of Vouchers," *Wall Street Journal,* July 15–16, 2006

56. Home School Legal Defense Association. www.hslda.org/laws/default.asp (accessed September 13, 2006).

57. Matthew H. Boswell, *Courts as Catalysts: State Supreme Courts and Public School Finance Equity* (Albany: SUNY Press, 2001), 125.

58. "Position Statement," Business Coalition for Student Achievement, February 15, 2007. www.biz4achievement.org/about_the_coalition/position_statement.html (accessed April 8, 2007).

59. Charles S. Clark, "School Censorship," *CQ Researcher,* February 19, 1993, 159; Gabler Web site, www.textbookreviews.org (accessed September 13, 2006).

60. "Kansas School Board Redefines Science," CNN.com, November 8, 2005. www.cnn.com/2005/EDUCATION/11/08/evolution.debate.ap/ (accessed August 1, 2006).

61. "One More Victory for Evolutionary Science," *Star Tribune,* February 16, 2006; Jodi Rudoren, "Ohio Board Undoes Stand on Evolution," *New York Times,* February 15, 2006; Patrick Cain, "Science Theories May Face Scrutiny," *Beacon Journal,* September 7, 2006.

62. See *A Public Education Primer,* by the Center on Education Policy, for more statistics about white and minority students across the country: www.cep-dc.org.

63. For these two reports, "Five Shoes Waiting to Drop on Arizona's Future" and "Beat the Odds," please see the Morrison Institute for Public Policy at Arizona State University. www.asu.edu/copp/morrison/APC01New.pdf and www.asu.edu/copp/morrison/LatinEd.pdf (accessed September 15, 2006).

Chapter 14

1. George Kelling and Ronald Corbett, "This Works: Preventing and Reducing Crime," *Civic Bulletin* 32 (March 2003): 1.

2. "Crime in the United States by Volume and Rate per 100,000 Inhabitants, 1986–2005," *Uniform Crime Report 2005* (Washington, D.C.: Federal Bureau of Investigation), Table 1.

3. Kelling and Corbett, "This Works," 3.

4. Jeremy Travis and Michelle Waul, "Reflections on the Crime Decline: Lessons for the Future?" *Proceedings from the Urban Institute Crime Decline Forum,* August 2002.

5. See John Donohue and Steven Levitt's National Bureau of Economic Research working paper, "The Impact of Legalized Abortion on Crime," November, 2000. www.nber.org/papers (accessed July 13, 2004).

6. Danielle S. Allen, *The World of Prometheus: The Politics of Punishing in Democratic Athens* (Princeton: Princeton University Press, 1999), 3.

7. See Sir Frederick Pollock and F. W. Maitland's *History of English Law before the Time of Edward I* (Cambridge: Cambridge University Press, 1969) for a brilliant discussion of how this transformation came to pass.

8. Marc Mauer, "The Crisis of the Young African American Male and the Criminal Justice System." Presentation to the U.S. Commission on Civil Rights in Washington, D.C., April 15–16, 1999, 6.

9. Kevin Smith, "The Politics of Punishment: Evaluating Political Explanations of Incarceration Rates," *Journal of Politics* 66, no. 3 (August 2004): 925.

10. Katherine Beckett, *Making Crime Pay: Law and Order in Contemporary Politics* (New York: Oxford University Press, 1997).

11. Smith, "Politics."

12. Daniel J. Elazar, *American Federalism: A View from the States* (New York: Crowell, 1972), 106–107.

13. See Norman Johnston's *The Crucible of Good Intentions* (Philadelphia: Philadelphia Museum of Art, 1994), for more details on nineteenth-century views of incarceration and on the Quakers' longstanding opposition to corporal punishment.

14. See David Oshinsky's *Worse than Slavery: Parchman Farm and the Ordeal of Jim Crow Justice* (New York: Free Press, 1996). As Oshinsky's title makes clear, the author is no fan of Parchman Farm. It is therefore interesting that he concludes in the book's final chapter that the modern penal institution that replaced the farm in the 1970s is in many ways worse.

15. Discrimination, however, persists. Women continue to earn only three quarters of what men with similar backgrounds and experience earn. Francine Blau and Lawrence Kah, "The Gender Pay Gap," in the *National Bureau of Economic Research Report* (Summer 2001).

16. Stephan Thernstrom, remarks, Heritage Foundation symposium on the Kerner Commission, March 13, 1998. www.heritage.org/Research/PoliticalPhilosophy/ hl619.cfm (accessed July 13, 2004).

17. "Night of Terror," *Time Magazine,* July 25, 1977.

18. This figure—from the Office of National Drug Control Policy—does not include alcohol, which is considered the most popular drug of all.

19. See Robert MacCoun and Peter Reuter's *Drug War Heresies: Learning from Other Vices, Times, and Places* (New York: Cambridge University Press, 2001), 26, 29.

20. See the National Organization for the Reform of Marijuana Laws for state-by-state drug laws. www.norml.org (accessed July 12, 2004).

21. Eric Schlosser, *Reefer Madness: Sex, Drugs, and Cheap Labor in the American Black Market* (Boston: Houghton Mifflin, 2003), 26.

22. See David Simon and Edward Burns's *The Corner: A Year in the Life of an Inner-City Neighborhood* (New York: Broadway Books, 1998), for an exploration the drug culture in one inner city Baltimore neighborhood. Later made into an HBO mini-series.

23. Kathleen Hunger, "Money Mattering More in Judicial Elections," Stateline.org, Wednesday, May 12, 2004. www.stateline.org/live/ViewPage.action?siteNodeId=136&languageId=1&contentId=15646 (accessed April 6, 2007).

24. *The Fiscal Survey of States,* 2006 (Washington, D.C.: National Governors Association and National Association of State Budget Officers), 1.

25. "Lifetime Likelihood of Going to State or Federal Prison," Bureau of Justice Statistics, Criminal Offenders Statistics. www.ojp.usdoj.gov/bjs/crimoff.htm (accessed October 13, 2006).

26. Information comes from the Sentencing Project, including "A Decade of Reform: Felony Disenfranchisement Laws in the United States." www.sentencingproject.org (accessed October 12, 2006).

27. Mauer, "The Crisis."

28. Kelling and Corbett, "This Works."

29. See Fred Siegel's *The Future Once Happened Here: New York, D.C., LA, and the Future of America's Big Cities* (New York: Free Press, 1997), for an account of how well-intentioned policies went horribly wrong.

30. James Q. Wilson and George L. Kelling, "Broken Windows: The Police and Neighborhood Safety," *Atlantic Monthly,* March 1982.

31. For an account of the Rodney King beating and the LAPD, see Lou Cannon's, *Official Negligence: How Rodney King and the Riots Changed Los Angeles and the LAPD* (New York: Westview Press, 1999).

32. Ibid.

33. See George L. Kelling and Mary A. Wycoff's "Evolving Strategy of Policing: Case Studies of Strategic Change," National Criminal Justice Reference Center Document No. 198029, for a detailed account of early experiments with community policing and problem-oriented policing.

34. William Bratton, *Turnaround: How America's Top Cop Reversed the Crime Epidemic* (New York: Random House, 1998), 143, 180.

35. See John Buntin's "Assertive Policing, Plummeting Crime: The NYPD Takes on Crime in New York City," Kennedy School of Government Case Study, Harvard University, August 1999, for an account of how Compstat was created and how it is used.

36. This section draws from an August 2002 seminar at the Urban Institute, "Reflections on the Crime Decline: Lessons for the Future," 12–19.

37. Robert Weisberg and David Mills, "Violence Silence: Why No One Really Cares about Prison Rape." *Slate,* October 1, 2003. See also "No Escape: Male Rape in U.S. Prisons," Human Rights Watch, 2001. www.hrw.org/reports/2001/prison/report.html (accessed July 13, 2004).

38. Doris J. James and Lauren E. Glaze, "Mental Health Problems of Prison and Jail Inmates," U.S. Department of Justice, Bureau of Justice Statistics, September 2006.

39. "Ill-Equipped: U.S. Prisons and Offenders with Mental Illnesses," Human Rights Watch, 2003. www.hrw.org/reports/2003/usa1003 (accessed July 12, 2004).

40. "Amnesty International's Concerns Regarding Post-September 11 Detentions in the U.S.," Amnesty International, March 14, 2002.

41. Death Penalty Information Project. www.deathpenaltyinfo.org (accessed October 5, 2006).

42. "Rights of Children Must Be Respected," Amnesty International, April 25, 2003. Currently, eighty child offenders await execution in the United States for crimes committed when they were sixteen or seventeen years old. Nineteen children were executed in the United States between 1995 and 2003.

43. Brian A. Reaves and Matthew J. Hickman, "Police Departments in Large Cities, 1990–2000," *Bureau of Justice Statistics Special Report,* NCJ-175703, May 2002.

44. Benjamin Wallace-Wells, "Bush's War on Cops" *Washington Monthly,* September 1, 2003, 30.

45. "Crime Trends by Population Group 2004–2005," *Uniform Crime Report 2005,* (Washington, D.C.: Federal Bureau of Investigation), Table 12.

46. "The Context of Rural Crime," National Center on Rural Justice and Crime Prevention. http://virtual.clemson.edu/groups/ncrj/about.htm (accessed April 10, 2007).

47. Jim Barnett, "Bush Signs Legislation to Fight the Spread of Meth across U.S.," *The Oregonian,* March 10, 2006; Chris Casteel, "Meth Imports Rising, Sheriff Says," *The Oklahoman,* July 19, 2006.

48. Figures are current up to November 5, 2003. They are compiled from "Death Row USA," a quarterly report by the Criminal Justice Project, the NAACP Legal Defense, and the Educational Fund, Summer 2003, and from the Death Penalty Information Project, www.deathpenaltyinfo.org (accessed May 2004).

49. Richard Willing and Gary Fields, "Geography of the Death Penalty," *USA Today,* December 20, 1999, A1.

50. "Facts on Post-Conviction DNA Exoneration," The Innocence Project. www.innocenceproject.org/docs/DNAExonerationFacts_WEB.pdf (accessed October 19, 2006).

51. Denny Walsh, "Judge: Rethink Lethal Injection," *Sacramento Bee,* December 16, 2006.

52. "Correctional Boot Camps: Lessons from a Decade of Research," National Institute of Justice, U.S. Department of Justice, June 2003.

53. "Drug Courts: The Second Decade," U.S. Department of Justice, Office of Justice Programs, National Institute of Justice, June 2006. www.ojp.usdoj.gov/nij (accessed October 6, 2006).

54. In 2000, 44 percent of the 625,243 people arrested nationwide were ages twenty-four or younger. Jeremy Travis and Jeffrey Butts, "The Rise and Fall of Youth Violence," Urban Institute, March 2002, 9.

55. Fact sheet, National Center for Injury Prevention and Control, Center for Disease Control. www.cdc.gov/nchs/data/nvsr/nvsr54/nvsr54_19.pdf (accessed October 6, 2006).

56. John Buntin, "A Community Responds: Boston Confronts an Upsurge of Youth Violence," Kennedy School of Government Case Study, Harvard University, June 1998.

Chapter 15

1. Internal memorandum from G. Marshall Lyon, M.D., National Center for Infectious Diseases, Centers for Disease Control and Prevention, January 21, 1999. The medical evidence strongly suggests that people who have inhaled anthrax can be successfully treated with antibiotics within twenty-four hours of the incident and perhaps later.

2. John Buntin, "Anthrax Threats in Southern California," Case No. 1577, a part of the Case Program: Case Studies in Public Policy and Management, Harvard University, John F. Kennedy School of Government, May 2000.

3. John Barry, *The Great Influenza: The Epic Story of the Deadliest Plague in History* (New York: Viking Penguin, 2004).

4. "Third Annual Report to the President and Congress of the Advisory Panel to Assess Domestic Response Capabilities for Terrorism Involving Weapons of Mass Destruction," RAND Corporation, December 15, 2001, 44.

5. Gary Bryner, "Welfare Reform in Utah," Nelson A. Rockefeller Institute of Government, Report No. 14, August 2002. See also Deborah A. Orth and Malcolm L. Goggin, "How States and Counties Have Responded to the Family Policy Goals of Welfare Reform," Report to the U.S. Department of Health and Human Services, Administration for Children and Families (Grant No. 90XP0028/01), Nelson A. Rockefeller Institute of Government, State University of New York, 2003.

6. The Kaiser Family Foundation Web site has a host of Medicaid-related facts and statistics at www.kff.org.

7. *2005 State Expenditure Report* (Washington, D.C.: National Association of State Budget Officers), November 2006.

8. Paul Starr, *The Social Transformation of American Medicine* (New York: Basic Books, 1992), 149.

9. Ibid., 72.

10. Ibid.

11. NYU Medical Center. www.med.nyu.edu/Bellevue (accessed July 20, 1994).

12. Starr, *Social Transformation,* 150.

13. Samuel Gompers, the head of the AF of L, viewed compulsory health insurance as "paternalistic" and worried that it might weaken the labor movement by causing workers to look to employers instead of to unions for benefits. Starr, *Social Transformation,* 254–255.

14. "Stocks Collapse in 16,410,30-Share Day, but Rally at Close Cheers Brokers," *New York Times,* October 30, 1929.

15. Scholars such as Theda Skocpol have argued that the federal government's first major foray into safety net programs actually came much earlier in the form of lavish pensions for Union veterans of the Civil War. Theda Skocpol, "America's First Social Security System: The Expansion of Benefits for Civil War Veterans," *Political Science Quarterly* 108 (Spring 1993): 85–86.

16. *Columbia Encyclopedia,* 6th ed. (New York: Columbia University Press, 2001). Entry for "social security."

17. Jay Bhattacharya and Darius Lakdawalla, "Does Medicare Benefit the Poor? New Answers to an Old Question," working paper w9280, National Bureau of Economic Research, October 2002.

18. Daniel C. Vock, "Medicaid: Biggest Insurer is a Budget Buster," Stateline.org, August 3, 2006. www.stateline.org/live/ViewPage.action ?siteNodeId=136&languageId=1&contentId= 131622 (accessed November 14, 2006).

19. "An Introduction to Medicaid," Center for Budget and Policy Priorities," October 2, 2006. www.cbpp.org/10-2-06health.htm (accessed November 28, 2006).

20. John Klemm, "Medicaid Spending: A Brief History," *Health Care Financing Review* 22, no. 1 (Fall 2000). For more recent data, see Statehealthfacts.org by the Kaiser Family Foundation.

21. By 1983, the number of single mothers had fallen back to about 50 percent of AFDC recipients. By 1992, that number had crept back up to 55 percent of AFDC recipients. *Evaluating Welfare Reform in an Era of Transition,* (Washington, D.C.: National Academy of Sciences, 2001), 17.

22. Steven Roberts, "Food Stamps Program: How It Grew and How Reagan Wants to Cut It Back," *New York Times,* April 4, 1981.

23. Lou Cannon *Governor Reagan: His Rise to Power* (New York: Public Affairs, 2003), 349. Of course, FDR made this statement to argue for government-funded work programs—a measure that Reagan never supported as president.

24. General Accountability Office, "Medicaid: Improved Federal Oversight of State Financing Schemes Is Needed," GAO-04-228, February 2004.

25. Andy Schneider, *Medicaid Resource Book* (Washington, D.C.: Kaiser Commission on Medicaid and the Uninsured, July 2002), 97–98.

26. "Public Officials of the Year: Leading in Good Times and in Bad," *Governing* magazine, December 1997.

27. Charles Mahtesian, "Captains of Conservatism," *Governing* magazine, February 1995.

28. *Evaluating Welfare Reform,* 19.

29. Mickey Kaus, "Has Welfare Reform Worked? Yes, Smashingly." *Blueprint Magazine,* January/February 2002.

30. See Haynes Johnson and David Broder's *The System: The Way of American Politics at the Breaking Point* (New York: Little, Brown 1996), for a comprehensive account of the healthcare debate.

31. Ibid.

32. "The Uninsured: A Primer," Kaiser Commission on Medicaid and the Uninsured, October 2006. www.kff.org/uninsured/upload/7451-021.pdf (accessed November 2, 2006).

33. In practice, states might not save money if HMOs managed to enroll the healthiest Medicaid recipients who would not have used many medical services anyway—a practice known as "risk selection."

34. Christopher Swope, "The Medicaid Windfall: Enjoy It While It Lasts," *Governing* magazine, September 1998.

35. Medicaid expenditures grew at an annual rate of 27.1 percent between 1990 and 1992. "Medicaid 101 Briefing Charts," Kaiser Commission on Medicaid and the Uninsured/Alliance for Health Care Reform, February 28, 2003.

36. "Enrolling Uninsured Low Income Children In Medicaid and SCHIP," Kaiser Commission on Medicaid and the Uninsured, May 2002

37. National Conference of State Legislatures, "NCSL Resources—SCHIP General Information." www.ncsl.org/programs/health/ sncs/web.htm (accessed November 15, 2006).

38. "50 State Comparisons: Income Eligibility Levels for Children's Separate SCHIP Programs." www.statehealthfacts.org/cgibin/healthfacts.cgi? action=compare&category=Medicaid+% 26+SCHIP&subcategory=Children%27s+

Medicaid+and+SCHIP+Eligibility&topic=
Income+Eligibility+%2d%2dSeparate+
SCHIP+Program (accessed November 16, 2006).

39. Katherine Vogt, "Public Hospitals Seen Slipping Away, Changing into Other Entities," Amednews.com, September 12, 2005. www.amaassn.org/amednews/2005/09/12/bise0912.htm (accessed November 14, 2006).

40. "Rural Health Care," Agency for Healthcare Research and Quality, U.S. Department of Health and Human Services. www.ahrq.gov/news/focus/focrural.htm (accessed April 16, 2007).

41. "How Technology is Being Used to Enhance the Delivery of Healthcare Services," Appalachian Regional Commission. www.arc.gov/index.do?nodeID=2043 (accessed April 17, 2007).

42. John Holahan and Brend Spillman, "A Strong Safety Net Is Not the Same as Insurance," Urban Institute, January 15, 2002. www.urban.org/url.cfm?ID=31041.

43. "Health Insurance Coverage of Children 0–18," www.statehealthfacts.org/cgi-bin/healthfacts.cgi?action=compare&category=Health+Coverage+%26+Uninsured&subcategory=Health+Insurance+Status&topic=Children+%280%2d18%29 (accessed November 18, 2006).

44. "The State of Kids' Coverage," prepared for the Robert Wood Johnson Foundation by the State Health Access Data Assistance Center, University of Minnesota, August 9, 2006.

45. Dubay, Hill and Kenney, "Five Things Everyone Should Know about SCHIP."

46. Vernon K. Smith and David M. Rousseau, "SCHIP Enrollment in 50 States," Kaiser Commission on Medicaid and the Uninsured, September 2005.

47. Katherine Barrett, Richard Greene, and Michele Mariani, "Insurance Coverage: Access Denied," Governing magazine, February 2004.

48. Ibid; Penelope Lemov, "Setting Limits on Medicaid," Governing magazine, March 2005.

49. Katherine Barrett, Richard Greene, and Michele Mariani, "Prescription Drugs: Bitter Pills," Governing magazine, February 2004.

50. J. R. Kleinke, "The Price of Progress: Prescription Drugs in the Health Care Market," Health Affairs, September/October 2001.

51. Crystal Yednak and Rick Pearson, "Audit Slams State Drug Plan," Chicago Tribune, September 19, 2006.

52. John Buntin, "Rx RELIEF: With Prescription Drug Costs Soaring, States Are Taking Bold Steps to Bring Them Down," Governing magazine, September 2000, provides more details.

53. "Pharmaceutical Bulk Purchasing: Multi-state and Inter-agency Plans, 2006," National Conference of State Legislatures, November 13, 2006. www.ncsl.org/programs/health/bulkrx.htm (accessed November 29, 2006).

54. March 21, 2002, testimony by Kentucky governor Paul E. Patton before the Senate Special Committee on Aging. National Governors Association. www.nga.org/nga/legislativeUpdate/1,1169, C_TESTIMONY%5ED_3671,00.html (accessed on June 7, 2004).

55. Katherine Barrett, Richard Greene, and Michele Mariani, "Insurance Coverage: Access Denied;" Penelope Lemov, "Maine's Medical Gamble," Governing magazine, November 2004; "Dirigo Agency Reaches Deal with Anthem to Extend Dirigo Choice," Associated Press, September 22, 2006.

56. Anna C. Spencer, "Massachusetts Going for Full Coverage," State Health Notes, April 17, 2006. www.ncsl.org/programs/health/shn/2006/sn465.htm (accessed December 2, 2006).

57. Aimee Curl, "Bracing for Bird Flu," Federal Times, April 10, 2006.

58. Statement by Janet Heinrich, GAO, "Public Health and Medical Preparedness." Testimony before the Subcommittee on Public Health, Committee on Health, Education, Labor, and Pensions, U.S. Senate, Tuesday, October 9, 2001.

59. Nicholas Kristof, "Shaming Young Mothers," New York Times, August 23, 2002, and Jane Brody, "Abstinence-Only: Does It Work?" New York Times, June 1, 2004.

60. "50 State Summary of Contraceptive Laws," National Conference of State Legislatures, August 2006. www.ncsl.org/programs/health/contraceplaws.htm (accessed November 28, 2006).

61. Daniel C. Vock, "FDA Ruling Puts Pharmacists in Crossfire," Stateline.org, September 6, 2006. www.stateline.org/live/details/story?contentId= 139338 (accessed September 6, 2006).

62. Eric A. Finkelstein, Ian C. Fiebelkorn, and Guijing Wang, "National Medical Spending Attributable to Overweight and Obesity: How Much, and Who's Paying?" *Health Affairs*, May 14, 2003.

63. Alan Greenblatt, "HHS Chief: Fixing Health Care Costs 'Imperative,'" Governing.com, February 27, 2006.

State Capitals and Date of Admission to the Union

State	Capital	Date	State	Capital	Date
Alabama	Montgomery	December 14, 1819	Montana	Helena	November 8, 1889
Alaska	Juneau	January 3, 1959	Nebraska	Lincoln	March 1, 1867
Arizona	Phoenix	February 14, 1912	Nevada	Carson City	October 31, 1864
Arkansas	Little Rock	June 15, 1836	New Hampshire	Concord	June 21, 1788
California	Sacramento	September 9, 1850	New Jersey	Trenton	December 18, 1787
Colorado	Denver	August 1, 1876	New Mexico	Santa Fe	January 6, 1912
Connecticut	Hartford	January 9, 1788	New York	Albany	July 26, 1788
Delaware	Dover	December 7, 1787	North Carolina	Raleigh	November 21, 1789
Florida	Tallahassee	March 3, 1845	North Dakota	Bismarck	November 2, 1889
Georgia	Atlanta	January 2, 1788	Ohio	Columbus	March 1, 1803
Hawaii	Honolulu	August 21, 1959	Oklahoma	Oklahoma City	November 16, 1907
Idaho	Boise	July 3, 1890	Oregon	Salem	February 14, 1859
Illinois	Springfield	December 3, 1818	Pennsylvania	Harrisburg	December 12, 1787
Indiana	Indianapolis	December 11, 1816	Rhode Island	Providence	May 29, 1790
Iowa	Des Moines	December 28, 1846	South Carolina	Columbia	May 23, 1788
Kansas	Topeka	January 29, 1861	South Dakota	Pierre	November 2, 1889
Kentucky	Frankfort	June 1, 1792	Tennessee	Nashville	June 1, 1796
Louisiana	Baton Rouge	April 30, 1812	Texas	Austin	December 29, 1845
Maine	Augusta	March 15, 1820	Utah	Salt Lake City	January 4, 1896
Maryland	Annapolis	April 28, 1788	Vermont	Montpelier	March 4, 1791
Massachusetts	Boston	February 6, 1788	Virginia	Richmond	June 25, 1788
Michigan	Lansing	January 26, 1837	Washington	Olympia	November 11, 1889
Minnesota	St. Paul	May 11, 1858	West Virginia	Charleston	June 20, 1863
Mississippi	Jackson	December 10, 1817	Wisconsin	Madison	May 29, 1848
Missouri	Jefferson City	August 10, 1821	Wyoming	Cheyenne	July 10, 1890

Glossary

abstinence. Refraining from sexual activity, usually intercourse. (Chapter 15)

accreditation. Certification process in which outside experts visit and evaluate a school or college to vouch for minimum quality standards. (Chapter 13)

activist judge. A judge who is said to act as an independent policymaker by creatively interpreting constitutions and statutes. (Chapter 8)

ad hoc federalism. The process of choosing a state-centered or nation-centered view of federalism on the basis of political or partisan convenience. (Chapter 2)

affirmative action. Policies designed to help recruit and promote disadvantaged groups. (Chapter 9)

Aid to Families with Dependent Children (AFDC). The original federal assistance program for women and their children, started under Roosevelt's New Deal. (Chapter 15)

alternative dispute resolution. A way to end a disagreement by means other than litigation. It usually involves the appointment of a mediator to preside over a meeting between the parties. (Chapter 8)

annexation. The legal incorporation of one jurisdiction or territory into another. (Chapter 11)

appeal. A request to have a lower court's decision in a case reviewed by a higher court. (Chapter 8)

appointment powers. A governor's ability to pick individuals to run state government, such as appointing cabinet secretaries. (Chapter 7)

apportionment. The allotting of districts according to population shifts. The number of congressional

districts a state has may be reapportioned every ten years. (Chapter 6)

appropriations bills. Laws passed by legislatures authorizing the transfer of money to the executive branch. (Chapter 3)

assigned counsel. Private lawyers selected by the courts to handle particular cases and paid from public funds. (Chapter 8)

at-large elections. Elections in which city or county voters vote for council or commission members. (Chapter 10)

baby boomers. Generation of nearly eighty million individuals born after World War II, between 1946 and 1964. (Chapter 15)

back to basics. A movement against modern education "fads" and a return to an emphasis on traditional core subjects such as reading, writing, and arithmetic. (Chapter 13)

balanced budget. A budget in which current expenditures are equal to or less than income. (Chapter 12)

ballot initiatives. Process through which voters directly convey instructions to the legislature, approve a law, or amend the constitution. (Chapter 3)

bench trials. Trials in which no jury is present and a judge decides the facts. (Chapter 8)

bicameral legislatures. Legislatures that possess two chambers, typically a house of representatives, or assembly, and a senate. (Chapter 3)

Bill of Rights. The first ten amendments to the Constitution. These amendments set limits on the power of the federal government and set out the rights of individuals and, to a lesser extent, the states. (Chapter 2)

blanket primaries. Elections in which all voters may cast ballots for any candidate for any office regardless of party. (Chapter 5)

block grants. Federal grants-in-aid given for general policy areas that leave states and localities with wide discretion on how to spend the money within the designated policy area. (Chapter 2)

bonds. Certificates that are evidence of a debt on which the issuer promises to pay the holder a specified amount of interest for a specified length of time and to repay the loans on their maturity. (Chapter 12)

broken windows policing. Policing that emphasizes maintaining public order. (Chapter 14)

budget process. The procedure by which state and local governments assess revenues and set budgets. (Chapter 12)

budget shortfall. When the money coming into the government falls below the money being spent. (Chapter 12)

bureaucracy. Public agencies and the programs and services they implement and manage. (Chapter 9)

bureaucrats. Employees of public agencies. (Chapter 9)

candidate-centered politics. Politics in which candidates promote themselves and their own campaigns rather than relying on party organizations. (Chapter 5)

capital investments. Investments in infrastructure, such as roads. (Chapter 12)

capital outlays. A category of school funding that focuses on long-term improvements to physical assets. (Chapter 13)

car-dependent living. An outcome of low-density development, when owning a car for transportation becomes a necessity. (Chapter 11)

casework. The work undertaken by legislators and their staffs in response to requests for help from constituents. (Chapter 6)

categorical grants. Federal grants-in-aid given for specific programs that leave states and localities with little discretion on how to spend the money. (Chapter 2)

caucus. A closed meeting of members of a political party. (Chapter 6)

cause lobbyist. A person who works for an organization that tracks and promotes an issue, for example, environmental issues for the Sierra Club or gun regulation for the National Rifle Association. (Chapter 5)

centralized federalism. The notion that the federal government should take the leading role in setting national policy, with state and local governments to help implement the policies. (Chapter 2)

charter. A document that outlines the powers, organization, and responsibilities of a local government. (Chapter 10)

charter schools. Public schools, often with unique themes, managed by teachers, principals, social workers, or nonprofit groups. The movement was launched in the early 1990s. (Chapter 13)

cities. An incorporated political jurisdiction formed to provide self-governance to a locality. (Chapter 10)

city commission system. A form of municipal governance in which executive, legislative, and administrative powers are vested in elected city commissioners. (Chapter 10)

city council. A municipality's legislature. (Chapter 10)

city-county consolidation. The merger of separate local governments in an effort to reduce bureaucratic redundancy and service inefficiencies. (Chapter 11)

city manager. An official appointed to be the chief administrator of a municipality.

civil cases. Cases that involve disputes between private parties. (Chapter 8)

closed primaries. Nominating elections in which only voters belonging to that party may participate. Only registered Democrats can vote in a closed Democratic primary, for example. (Chapter 5)

coalition building. The assembling of an alliance of groups to pursue a common goal or interest. (Chapter 6)

collective bargaining. A process in which representatives of labor and management meet to negotiate pay and benefits, job responsibilities, and working conditions. (Chapter 9)

colonial charters. Legal documents drawn up by the British crown that spelled out how the colonies were to be governed. (Chapter 3)

commission-administrator system. A form of county governance where executive and legislative powers reside with an elected commission, which hires a professional executive to manage the day-to-day operations of government. (Chapter 10)

common law. Law composed of judges' legal opinions that reflects community practices and evolves over time. (Chapter 14)

common school. In a democratic society, a school in which children of all income levels attend at taxpayer expense. (Chapter 13)

community, or restorative, justice movement. A movement that emphasizes nontraditional punishment. (Chapter 14)

community policing. An approach that emphasizes relationships with neighborhoods and collaborative problem solving. (Chapter 14)

compact theory. The idea that the Constitution represents an agreement among sovereign states to form a common government. (Chapter 2)

comparative method. A learning approach based on studying the differences and similarities among similar units of analysis (such as states). (Chapter 1)

concurrent powers. Powers that both federal and state government can exercise. These include the right to tax, borrow, and spend. (Chapter 2)

confederacy. A political system in which power is concentrated in regional governments. (Chapter 2)

constituents. Residents of a district. (Chapter 6)

constituent service. The work done by legislators to help those in their voting districts. (Chapter 6)

constitutional amendments. Proposals to change the constitution, typically enacted by a supermajority of the legislature or through a statewide referendum. (Chapter 3)

constitutional convention. An assembly convened for the express purpose of amending or replacing a constitution. (Chapter 3)

constitutional revision commissions. Expert committees formed to assess a constitution and suggest changes. (Chapter 3)

contract attorneys. Private attorneys who enter into agreements with a state, a county, or a judicial district to work on a fixed-fee basis per case or for a specific length of time. (Chapter 8)

contract lobbyist. A person who works for different causes for different clients in the same way that a lawyer will represent more than one client. (Chapter 5)

cooperative federalism. The notion that it is impossible for state and national governments to have separate and distinct jurisdictions and that both levels of government must work together. (Chapter 2)

council-executive. A form of county governance where legislative powers are vested in a county commission and executive powers are vested in an independently elected executive. (Chapter 10)

council-manager system. A form of municipal governance in which the day-to-day administration of government is carried out by a professional administrator. (Chapter 10)

counties. Geographic subdivisions of state government. (Chapter 10)

county commission system. A form of county governance in which executive, legislative, and administrative powers are vested in elected commissioners. (Chapter 10)

court of first instance. The court in which a case is introduced and nothing has been determined yet. (Chapter 8)

criminal cases. Cases that involve violations of the law. (Chapter 8)

criterion referenced tests. Standardized tests designed to gauge a student's level of mastery of a given set of materials. (Chapter 13)

crosscutting requirements. Constraints that apply to all federal grants. (Chapter 2)

crossover sanctions. Federal requirements mandating that grant recipients pass and enforce certain laws or regulations as a condition of receiving funds. (Chapter 2)

crossover voting. When members of one party vote in another party's primary. This practice is not allowed in all states. (Chapter 2)

dealignment. When no one party can be said to dominate politics in this country. (Chapter 5)

delegates. Legislators who primarily see their role as voting according to their constituents' beliefs as they understand them. (Chapter 6)

departments of education. State-level agencies responsible for overseeing public education. (Chapter 13)

determinate sentencing. The judge sentences an offender to serve a specific amount of time in prison depending on the crime. (Chapter 8)

deterrence theory. A theory advanced by criminologists that harsh penalties will deter people from committing crimes. (Chapter 14)

devolution. The process of taking power and responsibility away from the federal government and giving it to state and local governments. (Chapter 1)

Dillon's Rule. The legal principle that says local governments can exercise only the powers granted to them by state government. (Chapter 10)

direct democracy. The means for citizens to make laws themselves, rather than relying on elected representatives. (Chapters 3 and 4)

direct lobbying. A form of lobbying in which lobbyists deal directly with legislators to gain their support. (Chapter 5)

discretionary jurisdiction. The power to decide whether or not to grant review of a case. (Chapter 8)

discretionary spending. Spending controlled in annual appropriations acts. (Chapter 12)

districts. Geographical areas represented by members of a legislature. (Chapter 6)

dividend. A payment made to stockholders, or in Alaska's case, residents, from the interest generated off an investment. (Chapter 12)

drug courts. An alternative forum for sentencing nonviolent drug offenders. (Chapter 14)

dual constitutionalism. A system of government in which people live under two sovereign powers. In the United States this is the government of their state of residence and the federal government. (Chapter 3)

dual federalism. The idea that state and federal governments have separate and distinct jurisdictions and responsibilities. (Chapter 2)

edgeless cities. Office and retail complexes without clear boundaries. (Chapter 11)

e-government. The delivery of public services and programs via the Internet or other digital means. (Chapter 9)

electorate. Individuals who can vote. (Chapter 3)

Elementary and Secondary Education Act. Federal law passed in 1965 as part of President Johnson's Great Society initiative; steered federal funds to improve local schools, particularly those attended primarily by low-income and minority students. (Chapter 13)

en banc. Refers to appeals court sessions in which all of the judges hear a case together. (Chapter 8)

entitlement. A service that government must provide, regardless of the cost. (Chapter 12)

entitlement program. A government-run program that guarantees unlimited assistance to those who meet its eligibility requirements, no matter the cost. (Chapter 15)

enumerated powers. Grants of authority explicitly given by the Constitution. (Chapter 2)

estate taxes. Taxes levied on a person's estate or total holdings after that person's death. (Chapter 12)

excise, or sin, taxes. Taxes on alcohol, tobacco, and other similar products that are designed to raise revenues and reduce usage. (Chapter 12)

exclusive powers. Powers given by the Constitution solely to the federal government. (Chapter 2)

executive orders. Rules or regulations with the force of law that governors can create directly under the statutory authority given them. (Chapter 7)

expenditures. Money spent by government. (Chapter 12)

exurbs. Municipalities in rural areas that ring suburbs. They typically serve as bedroom communities for the prosperous, providing rural homes with easy access to urban areas. (Chapter 11)

factional splits, or factions. Groups that struggle to control the message within a party; for example, a party may be split into competing regional factions. (Chapter 5)

federalism. Political system in which national and regional governments share powers and are considered independent equals. (Chapter 2)

felony. A serious crime, such as murder or arson. (Chapter 8)

filibusters. Debates that under Senate rules can drag on, blocking final action on the bill under consideration and preventing other bills from being debated. (Chapter 6)

fiscal federalism. The system by which federal grants are used to fund programs and services provided by state and local governments. (Chapter 12)

fiscal year. The accounting period used by a government. (Chapter 12)

focused consumption taxes. Taxes that do not alter spending habits or behavior patterns and therefore do not distort the distribution of resources. (Chapter 12)

for cause challenge. Occurs when a lawyer asks the judge to excuse a potential juror because the individual appears to be biased or unable to be fair. (Chapter 8)

formal powers. The powers explicitly granted to a governor according to state law, such as vetoing legislation or appointing heads of state agencies. (Chapter 7)

Fourteenth Amendment. Amendment that prohibits any state from depriving individuals of the rights and privileges of citizenship and requires states to provide due process and equal protection guarantees to all citizens. (Chapter 2)

the franchise. The right to vote. (Chapter 3)

full faith and credit clause. The constitutional clause requiring states to recognize each other's public records and acts as valid. (Chapter 2)

general act charters. Charters that grant powers, such as home rule, to all municipal governments within a state. (Chapter 10)

general elections. The decisive elections in which all registered voters cast ballots for their preferred candidates for a political office. (Chapter 5)

general equivalency degree (GED) program. A series of tests that can be taken to qualify for a high school equivalency certificate or diploma. (Chapter 13)

general jurisdiction trial courts. Courts that hear any civil or criminal cases that have not been assigned to a special court. (Chapter 8)

general obligation bonds. Investments secured by the taxing power of the jurisdiction that issues them. (Chapter 12)

general revenue sharing grants. Federal grants-in-aid given with few constraints, leaving states and localities almost complete discretion over how to spend the money. (Chapter 2)

general welfare clause. An implied power giving Congress the authority to provide for the "general welfare." (Chapter 2)

gentrification. The physical rehabilitation of urban areas, which attracts investment from developers and drives up property values. (Chapter 11)

gerrymanders. Districts clearly drawn with the intent of pressing partisan advantage at the expense of other considerations. (Chapter 6)

gift taxes. Taxes imposed on money transfers made during an individual's lifetime. (Chapter 12)

Goals 2000. The Educate America Act, signed into law in March 1994, that provided resources to states and communities to ensure that all students reached their full potential. (Chapter 13)

grand jury. A group of between sixteen and twenty-three citizens that decides if a case should go to trial; if yes, an indictment is issued. (Chapter 8)

grants-in-aid. Cash appropriations given by the federal government to the states. (Chapter 2)

habitual offender laws. These statutes impose harsher sentences for offenders who previously have been sentenced for crimes. (Chapter 8)

high-stakes standardized testing. Testing of elementary and secondary students in which poor results can mean either that the student fails to get promoted or that the school loses its accreditation. (Chapter 13)

home rule. A form of self-governance granted to towns and cities by the state. (Chapter 3); the right of localities to self-government, usually granted through a charter. (Chapter 10)

home schooling. The education of children in the home; a movement to grant waivers from state truancy laws to permit parents to teach their own children. (Chapter 13)

impact fees. Fees that municipalities charge builders of new housing or commercial developments to help offset the costs of extending services. (Chapter 11)

impeachment. A process by which the legislature can remove executive branch officials, such as the governor, or judges from offices for corruption or other reasons. (Chapter 7)

implied powers. Broad, but undefined, powers given to the federal government by the Constitution. (Chapter 2)

income taxes. Taxes on income. (Chapter 12)

incumbent. A person holding office. (Chapter 6)

independent expenditures. Ad campaigns or other political activities that are run by a party or an outside group without the direct knowledge or approval of a particular candidate for office. (Chapter 5)

indeterminate sentencing. The judge sentences an offender to a minimum and a maximum time in prison. A parole board decides how long the offender actually will remain in prison. (Chapter 8)

indictment. A formal criminal charge. (Chapter 8)

indirect lobbying. A form of lobbying in which lobbyists build support for their cause through the media, rallies, and other ways of influencing public opinion with the ultimate goal of swaying legislators to support their cause. (Chapter 5)

individualistic. A political culture that views politics and government as just another way to achieve individual goals. (Chapter 1)

informal powers. The things a governor is able to do, such as command media attention or persuade party members, based on position, not on formal authority. (Chapter 7)

insurance trust funds. Money collected from contributions, assessments, insurance premiums, or payroll taxes. (Chapter 12)

intelligent design. The theory that certain features of the universe and of living things are best explained by an intelligent cause, not an undirected process such as evolution. (Chapter 13)

interest groups. Individuals, corporations, or associations who seek to influence the actions of elected and appointed public officials on behalf of specific companies or causes. (Chapter 5)

intergovernmental transfers. Funds provided by the federal government to state governments and by state governments to local governments. (Chapter 12)

intermediate appellate court. A court that reviews court cases to find possible errors in their proceedings. (Chapter 8)

interstate commerce clause. The constitutional clause that gives Congress the right to regulate interstate commerce. This clause has been broadly interpreted to give Congress a number of implied powers. (Chapter 2)

Jim Crow laws. Measures passed in the last decade of the nineteenth century that sought to legally and systematically separate blacks and whites. (Chapter 3)

judicial federalism. The idea that the courts determine the boundaries of state-federal relations. (Chapter 3)

judicial review. The power of courts to assess whether a law is in compliance with the constitution. (Chapter 3)

jury nullification. Occurs when a jury returns a verdict of "Not Guilty" even though jurists believe the defendant is guilty. The jury cancels out a law that it believes is immoral or was wrongly applied to the defendant. (Chapter 8)

Kentucky Education Reform Act. The 1990 law passed in response to court findings of unacceptable disparities among schools and considered the most comprehensive state school reform act to date. (Chapter 13)

laboratories of democracy. A term used for the states that emphasizes their ability to engage in different policy experiments without interference from the federal government. (Chapter 1)

leapfrog development. Developments that jump— or leapfrog—over established developments, leaving undeveloped or underdeveloped land between developments. (Chapter 11)

legislative over-criminalization. The tendency of government to make a crime out of anything the public does not like. (Chapter 8)

liability. A legal obligation or responsibility. (Chapter 8)

limited, or special jurisdiction, trial courts. Courts that hear cases that are statutorily limited by either the degree of seriousness or the types of parties involved. (Chapter 8)

line-item veto. The power to reject a portion of a bill while the rest remains intact. (Chapter 3)

local education agencies (LEAs). School districts, some of which may be cities, or counties, or subsets thereof. (Chapter 13)

low-density development. Development practices that spread (rather than concentrate) populations across the land. (Chapter 11)

magistrates. Local officials or attorneys granted limited judicial powers. (Chapter 8)

majority-minority districts. Districts in which a minority group, such as African Americans or Hispanics, make up a majority of the population or electorate. (Chapter 6)

majority rule. The process in which the decision of a numerical majority is made binding on a group. (Chapter 6)

malapportionment. A situation in which the principle of equal representation is violated. (Chapter 6)

managed care. An arrangement for the provision of healthcare whereby an agency acts as an intermediary between consumers and healthcare providers. (Chapter 15)

mandatory jurisdiction. Occurs when a court is required to hear every case presented before it. (Chapter 8)

mandatory minimum sentences. The shortest sentences that offenders may receive upon conviction for certain offenses. The court has no authority to impose a shorter sentence. (Chapter 8)

mayor. The elected chief executive of a municipality. (Chapter 10)

mayor-council system. A form of municipal governance in which there is an elected executive and an elected legislature. (Chapter 10)

Medicaid. A joint state and federal health insurance program that serves low-income mothers and children, the elderly, and people with disabilities. (Chapter 15)

Medicare. The federal health insurance program for elderly citizens. (Chapter 15)

megalopolis. An urban area made up of several large cities and their surrounding urban areas. (Chapter 11)

merit systems. Systems in which employment and promotion in public agencies are based on qualifications and demonstrated ability, which blends very well with the organizational characteristics of bureaucracy. (Chapter 9)

metropolitan area. A populous region typically comprised of a city and surrounding communities having a high degree of social and economic integration. (Chapter 11)

metropolitan planning organization (MPO). A regional organization that decides how federal transportation funds are allocated within a regional area. (Chapter 11)

metropolitan statistical area (MSA). An area with a city of fifty thousand or more people, together with adjacent urban communities that have strong ties to the central city. (Chapter 11)

misdemeanor. A less serious crime, such as shoplifting. (Chapter 8)

model constitution. An expert-approved generic or "ideal" constitution that is sometimes used by states as a yardstick against which they can measure their existing constitutions. (Chapter 3)

moralistic. A political culture that views politics and government as the means to achieve the collective good. (Chapter 1)

municipal bonds. Bonds issued by states, counties, cities, and towns to fund large projects as well as operating budgets. They are exempt from federal taxes and from state and local taxes for the investors who live in the state where they are issued. (Chapter 12)

municipal charter. A document that establishes operating procedures for local governments. (Chapter 3)

municipalities. Political jurisdictions, such as cities, villages, or towns, incorporated under state law to provide governance to a defined geographic area. More compact and more densely populated than counties. (Chapter 10)

National Assessment of Educational Progress (NAEP). Known as the "nation's report card," this is the only regularly conducted independent survey of what a nationally representative sample of students in grades four, eight, and twelve know and can do in various subjects. (Chapter 13)

National PTA. Founded in 1897, this umbrella organization of state-based and school-based parent-teacher associations consists of volunteers who work to improve and support schools. (Chapter 13)

national supremacy clause. The constitutional clause stating that federal law takes precedence over all other laws. (Chapter 2)

nation-centered federalism. The belief that the nation is the basis of the federal system and that the federal government should take precedence over the states. (Chapter 2)

natural, or higher, law. A set of moral and political rules based on divine law and binding on all people. (Chapter 3)

necessary and proper clause. An implied power giving Congress the right to pass all laws considered "necessary and proper" to carry out the federal government's responsibilities as defined by the Constitution. (Chapter 2)

neutral competence. The idea that public agencies should be impartial implementers of democratic decisions. (Chapter 9)

New Federalism. The belief that states should receive more power and authority and less money from the federal government. (Chapter 2)

No Child Left Behind Act (NCLB). Federal law enacted in January 2002 that introduced new accountability measures for elementary and secondary schools in all states that wish to receive federal aid. (Chapter 13)

nonpartisan ballots. Ballots that do not list candidates by political party; still often used in local elections. (Chapter 5)

nonpartisan elections. Elections in which candidates do not have to declare party affiliation or receive a party's nomination; local offices and elections are often nonpartisan. (Chapter 4)

norm referenced tests. Standardized tests designed to determine how a student's mastery of a set of materials compares with that of a specially designed sampling of students determined to be the national "norm" for their age group. (Chapter 13)

nullification. The process of a state rejecting a federal law and making it invalid within state borders. (Chapter 2)

obesity. A medical term used to describe people who are excessively overweight. (Chapter 15)

office group (Massachusetts) ballot. Ballots in which candidates are listed by name under the title of the office they are seeking. (Chapter 4)

open primaries. Election races that are open to all registered voters regardless of their party affiliation. (Chapter 5)

oversight. The role the legislature takes in making sure that the implementation of its laws by the executive branch is being done properly. (Chapter 6)

pandemic. An outbreak of a disease that spreads across a large geographic area. (Chapter 15)

panels. Groups of (usually) three judges who sit to hear cases in U.S. courts of appeal. (Chapter 8)

parole. Supervised early release from prison. (Chapter 14)

party column (Indiana) ballot. Ballots in which the names of candidates are divided into columns arranged according to political party. (Chapter 4)

party conventions. Meetings of party delegates called to nominate candidates for office and establish party agendas. (Chapter 5)

patronage. The ability of elected officials or party leaders to hand out jobs to their friends and supporters, rather than hiring based on merit. (Chapter 5); the process of giving government jobs to partisan loyalists. (Chapter 9)

peremptory challenges. Used by lawyers to dismiss potential jurors for any reason except race or gender. (Chapter 8)

plea bargain. An agreement in which the accused admits guilt, usually in exchange for a promise that a particular sentence will be imposed. (Chapter 8)

plural executive system. A state government system in which the governor is not the dominant figure in the executive branch, but instead is more of a first among equals, serving alongside numerous other officials who were elected to their offices rather than appointed by the governor. (Chapter 4)

plurality. The highest number of votes garnered by a candidate for a particular office but short of an outright majority. (Chapter 4)

policy implementation. The process of taking the expressed wishes of government and translating them into action. (Chapter 9)

political action committees. Groups formed for the purpose of raising money to elect or defeat political candidates. They usually represent business, union, or ideological interests. (Chapter 5)

political culture. The attitudes and beliefs broadly shared in a polity about the role and responsibility of government. (Chapter 1)

political machines. Political organizations controlled by a small number of people and run for partisan ends; controlled party nominations for public office and rewarded supporters with government jobs and contracts. (Chapter 5)

political parties. Organizations that nominate and support candidates for elected offices. (Chapter 5)

poverty line, or poverty threshold. An annual income level, set by the federal government, below which families cannot afford basic necessities. (Chapter 15)

precedent. In law, the use of the past to determine current interpretation and decision making. (Chapter 8)

preemption. The process of the federal government overriding areas regulated by state law. (Chapter 2)

prejudicial error. An error that affects the outcome of a case. (Chapter 8)

primary elections. Elections that determine a party's nominees for offices in general elections against other parties' nominees. Participation in primary elections is sometimes limited to voters registered as members of that particular party. (Chapter 5)

privileges and immunities clause. The constitutional clause prohibiting states from discriminating against citizens of other states. (Chapter 2)

probation. Supervised punishment in the community. (Chapter 14)

professionalization. The process of making legislators' positions full-time jobs. (Chapter 6); bureaucratic employees earn their jobs based on qualifications and merit. (Chapter 9)

professional model policing. An approach to policing that emphasizes professional relations with citizens, police independence, police in cars, and rapid responses to calls for service. (Chapter 14)

progressive tax system. System in which the tax rate paid reflects the ability to pay. (Chapter 12)

prosecutor. A government official who conducts criminal cases on behalf of the people. (Chapter 8)

public choice model. A model of politics that views governments and public services in market terms; governments are seen as producers of public services and citizens are seen as consumers. (Chapter 11)

public defender. A government lawyer who provides free legal services to those accused of a crime who cannot afford to hire a lawyer. (Chapter 8)

public health. Government agencies' protection and improvement of citizen health and hygiene. (Chapter 15)

pure appointive systems. Judicial selection systems in which the governor appoints judges alone without a nominating commission. (Chapter 8)

rank-and-file members. Legislators who do not hold leadership positions or senior committee posts. (Chapter 6)

ratification. A vote of the entire electorate to approve a constitutional change, referendum, or ballot initiative. (Chapter 3)

realignment. When popular support switches from one party to another. (Chapter 5)

recall. An occasion for citizens to collect signatures and then vote on the ouster of an incumbent politician prior to the next regularly scheduled election. (Chapter 4)

recall election. A special election allowing voters to remove an elected official from office before the end of his or her term. (Chapter 7)

recidivism. A return to, or relapse into, criminal behavior. (Chapter 8)

Reconstruction. The period following the Civil War when the southern states were governed under the direction of the Union Army. (Chapter 3)

redistricting. The drawing of new boundaries for congressional and state legislative districts, usually following a decennial census. (Chapters 4 and 6)

referendums. Procedures that allow the electorate to either accept or reject laws passed by the legislature. (Chapter 3)

reform perspective. An approach to filling gaps in service and reducing redundancies in local governments that calls for regional-level solutions. (Chapter 11)

regional council. A planning and advisory organization whose members include multiple local governments. Region councils often are used to administer state and federal programs that are regionally targeted. (Chapter 11)

regressive taxes. Taxes levied on all taxpayers, regardless of income or ability to pay; they tend to place proportionately more of a burden on those with lower incomes. (Chapter 12)

representation. When individual legislators act as the voices of their constituencies within the House or Senate. (Chapter 6)

representative bureaucracy. The idea that public agencies reflecting the diversity of the communities they serve will be more effective. (Chapter 9)

representative government. A form of government in which citizens exercise power indirectly by choosing representatives to legislate on their behalf. (Chapter 2)

responsible party model. The theory that political parties offer clear policy choices to voters, try to deliver on those policies when they take office, and are held accountable by voters for the success or failure of those policies. (Chapter 5)

retention elections. Judges run uncontested, and voters are asked to vote "yes" if they wish to retain a judge in office for another term or "no" if they do not. (Chapter 8)

revenue bonds. Investments secured by the revenue generated by a state or municipal project. (Chapter 12)

revenues. The money governments bring in, mainly from taxes. (Chapter 12)

riders. Amendments to a bill that are not central to its intent. (Chapter 6)

rocket docket. Fast-track cases that often have limited, specific deadlines for specific court procedures. (Chapter 8)

rulemaking. The process of translating laws into written instructions on what public agencies will or will not do. (Chapter 9)

runoff primary. An election held if no candidate receives a majority of the vote during the regular primary. The two top finishers face off again in a runoff to determine the nominee for the general election. Such elections are held in some states, primarily in the South. (Chapter 5)

rural flight. The movement of rural youth and middle classes to more urban areas. (Chapter 11)

sales taxes. Taxes levied by state and local governments on purchases. (Chapter 12)

school boards. Elected or appointed bodies that determine major policies and budgets for each of the nation's school districts. (Chapter 13)

school districts. Local administrative jurisdictions that hire staff and report to school boards on management of area public schools. (Chapter 13)

school vouchers. Movement dating to the 1950s to allow taxpayer dollars to be given to families to use at whatever public, private, or parochial schools they choose. (Chapter 13)

secession. The process of a government or political jurisdiction withdrawing from a political system or alliance. (Chapter 2)

secret (Australian) ballot. Ballots printed by the states that allow voters to pick and choose among different candidates and party preferences in private. (Chapter 4)

seniority. The length of time spent in a position. (Chapter 9)

separation of powers. The principle that government should be divided into separate legislative, executive, and judicial branches, each with its own powers and responsibilities. (Chapter 3)

settlement. A mutual agreement between parties to end a case before going to trial. (Chapter 8)

severance taxes. Taxes on natural resources. (Chapter 12)

site-based management. Movement to increase freedom for building administrators such as school principals to determine how district funds are spent at a given school. (Chapter 13)

smart growth. Environmentally friendly development practices, particularly those that emphasize more efficient infrastructure and less dependence on automobiles. (Chapter 11)

sociodemographics. The characteristics of a population, including size, age, and ethnicity. (Chapter 1)

soft money. Money that is not subject to federal regulation that can be raised and spent by state parties. A 2002 law banned the use of soft money in federal elections. (Chapter 5)

sovereign immunity. The right of a government to not be sued without its consent. (Chapter 2)

special act charters. Charters that grant powers, such as home rule, to a single municipal government. (Chapter 10)

special districts. Entities created by state legislatures that enjoy some attributes of government. (Chapter

3); local governmental units created for a single purpose, such as water distribution. (Chapter 10)

spoils system. The right of an electoral winner to decide who works for public agencies. (Chapter 9)

sprawl. The rapid growth of a metropolitan area, typically as a result of specific types of zoning and development. (Chapter 11)

standards. Fixed criteria for learning that students are expected to reach in specific subjects by specific grade years. (Chapter 13)

standards movement. Effort to create benchmarks of adequate learning in each subject for each grade level so that students and teachers can be evaluated on mastery of this predetermined material. (Chapter 13)

state board of education. Top policymaking body in each of the fifty states, usually consisting of appointees selected by governors. (Chapter 13)

state-centered federalism. The belief that states are the basis of the federal system and that state governments should take precedence over the federal government. (Chapter 2)

State Children's Health Insurance Program (SCHIP). A joint federal-state program designed to expand coverage to children whose parents earned income above the poverty line but still were too poor to afford insurance. (Chapter 15)

states' rights. The belief that states should be free to make their own decisions with little interference from the federal government. (Chapter 2)

state supreme court. The highest level of appeals court in a state. (Chapter 8)

straight ticket. Originally, ballots that allowed voters to pick all of a party's candidates at once; today, straight ticket voting is the practice of voting for all of one party's candidates for various offices—for instance, voting for all Democrats or all Republicans. (Chapter 4)

street-level bureaucrats. Lower-level public agency employees who actually take the actions that represent law or policy. (Chapter 9)

strong mayor. A mayor with the power to perform the executive functions of government. (Chapter 10)

successful schools model. Education model that uses observed spending levels in the highest-performing schools as models from which to calculate necessary spending in other, lower-performing schools. (Chapter 13)

supermajority vote. A legislative vote of much more than a simple majority, for instance, two-thirds of a legislative chamber voting to override a governor's veto. (Chapter 7)

supermax security prisons. High-security prisons designed for violent criminals. (Chapter 14)

superpredators. Ultra-violent youths whom experts predicted would further drive up the nation's crime rate. (Chapter 14)

swing voters. Individuals who are not consistently loyal to candidates of any one party. They are true independents whose allegiance is fought for in every election. (Chapter 5)

tax burden. A measurement of taxes paid. (Chapter 12)

tax capacity. Measurement of the ability to pay taxes. (Chapter 12)

tax effort. A measure of taxes paid relative to the ability to pay taxes. (Chapter 12)

tax revolt. A reaction to high taxes that often results in ballot initiatives to cap tax growth. (Chapter 12)

teacher licensure procedures. The academic degrees, work experience, and performance on adult standardized tests a state requires before a teacher candidate can be certified to work in a school district. (Chapter 13)

teachers' unions. Primarily the National Education Association and the American Federation of Teachers, both headquartered in Washington, D.C. (Chapter 13)

Temporary Assistance to Needy Families (TANF). The next-generation welfare program that provides federal assistance in the form of block grants to states, which have great flexibility in designing the program. (Chapter 15)

Tenth Amendment. Amendment that guarantees a broad, but undefined, set of powers be reserved for the states and the people, as opposed to the federal government. (Chapter 2)

ticket splitting. When voters or districts vote for different parties' nominees for different offices—for instance, supporting a Republican for president, while supporting a Democrat for Congress. (Chapter 5)

Tiebout model. A model of local government based on market principles wherein a metro area is made up of a series of micropolitical jurisdictions that, on the basis of their services and costs, attract or repel certain citizens. (Chapter 11)

town meeting form of government. A form of governance where legislative powers are held by local citizens. (Chapter 10)

townships. A common type of local government whose powers, governance structure, and legal status vary considerably from state to state. In some states townships function as general purpose municipalities, in others they are geographic subdivisions of counties with few responsibilities and little power. (Chapter 10)

traditionalistic. A political culture that views politics and government as dominated by elites. (Chapter 1)

Trends in International Mathematics and Science Study (TIMSS). Launched by the United States in 1995, it is a regularly updated study that compares performance in science and mathematics of students from forty-six countries. (Chapter 13)

trial court. The first level of the court system. (Chapter 8)

trustees. Legislators who believe they were elected to exercise their own judgment and to approach issues accordingly. (Chapter 6)

truth-in-sentencing laws. These laws give parole boards less authority to shorten sentences for good behavior by specifying the proportion of a sentence an offender must serve before becoming eligible for parole. (Chapter 8)

unfunded mandates. Federal laws that direct state action but provide no financial support for that action. (Chapter 2)

unicameral legislatures. Legislatures that possess only one chamber. Nebraska is currently the only state with a unicameral legislature. (Chapter 3)

unitary systems. Political systems in which power is concentrated in a central government. (Chapter 2)

urban growth boundary (UGB). The border established around urban areas that is intended to control the density and type of development. (Chapter 11)

user fees. Charges levied by governments in exchange for services; a type of hidden tax. (Chapter 12)

variance. The difference between units of analysis on a particular measure. (Chapter 1)

verdict. A jury's finding in a trial. (Chapter 14)

veto. The power to reject a proposed law. (Chapter 7)

voir dire. The interviewing and examination of potential jurors. (Chapter 8)

voter identification. When a voter consistently identifies strongly with one of the parties and can be considered, for example, a Democrat or Republican. (Chapter 5)

voter turnout. The percentage of eligible citizens who register to vote and do vote. (Chapter 4)

ward, or district, elections. Elections in which voters in a municipal ward vote for a candidate to represent them on a council or commission. (Chapter 10)

wards. Divisions of municipalities, usually representing electoral districts of the city council. (Chapter 10)

weak mayor. A mayor who lacks true executive powers, such as the ability to veto council decisions or appoint department heads. (Chapter 10)

white flight. A demographic trend in which the middle and upper classes leave central cities for predominately white suburbs. (Chapter 11)

zoning laws. Regulations that control how land can be used. (Chapter 11)

Index

NOTE: Page numbers with *f* indicate figures; with *m*, maps or cartograms; with *t*, tables.

Centers for Disease Control and
Prevention (CDC), 187, 188,
538, 545, 570, 571
Centers for Medicare and Medicaid
Services (CMS), 554, 556
Centralized federalism, 47, 49f,
50–51
Chard, Nancy, 71
Charles II, king of England, 74, 76
Charter of Privileges, in
Pennsylvania, 76
Charters
constitutions vs., 95
home rule and, 388, 390–391
Charter schools, 492–493, 494t
Cheadle, Don, 169
ChattanoogaRESULTS, 527
Checks and balances. See Separation
of powers
Chemical terrorism, 542
Chesapeake Climate Action
Network, 171
Chicago, Ill.
city council, 377
crime decline in, 528f
partisan elections in, 391
political machine in, 147
riots of 1968 in, 515
school boards in, 471
Chicago Tribune, 146
Child abuse, home schooling and,
496
Children. See also State Children's
Health Insurance Program
criminal, punishments for,
530–531
obese, 571
Children's Defense Fund, 498
Chili's restaurants, 574
Christian Coalition, 163, 292
Christian political activists, school
boards and, 471
Cisneros, Henry, 377
Cities. See also Local governments;
Municipalities
benefits of living in, 423–425
edgeless, 405–406
gun control laws in, 536–537
legal definition of, 375
Cities without Suburbs (Rusk), 420

Citizens Property Insurance, Florida,
246–247
City councils, 376, 377, 394
City-county consolidation, 418–421,
419t
City manager systems, 118, 376
City of Clinton v. the Cedar Rapids
and Missouri Railroad (1868),
387
Civil cases, 278, 508
Civil disobedience, 513
Civil rights movement, race riots
and, 515–516
Civil Society Institute, 466
Civil unions, 83, 275. See also Gay
marriage
Civil War, 31, 133, 513
Civil War Amendments, 39
Civil War veterans, 45
Clean needle programs, 545
Clements, Bill, 121
Cleveland, Ohio
school boards in, 471
school vouchers in, 495
Clinton, Bill
criminal justice system funding
and, 532
gubernatorial elections in 1994
and, 257
gubernatorial experience of, 53
Health Security Act and, 558
SCHIP and, 561
welfare reform and, 457
Clinton, Hillary Rodham, 265, 558
Closed primaries, 149–150
Coalition building, 184
Cole, David, 311
Coleman, Garnet, 191
Collective bargaining, 349
College Board, 481, 482
College students. See also Young
people
demographic profiles of, 4, 6
political engagement by, 4
state government subsidies for,
5–7
tuition rates for, 482–483
voter turnout among, 106
Colonial charters, 73–74
Colorado
ballot initiatives in, 80, 460–461

city-county consolidations in,
419t
geography of, 18
judicial selection in, 295
legislative sessions in, 216
magistrates in, 321
TANF programs in, 544–545
Taxpayer's Bill of Rights in,
448
term limits in, 221, 222
women as legislators in, 211
Commerce Clause, 40–41t, 58
Commission-administrator systems,
372, 373, 374f
Commission systems
county, 372–373, 374f
municipal, 382
Committees, legislative, 185, 202,
204
Common law, 509–510
Common schools, 467
Communication, governors' abilities
for, 252–253
Community health clinics, 562
Community justice movement,
536–537
Community policing, 524–528
Compact theory of federalism, 44
Comparative method for study
of culture and history, 11–12,
14–15, 15m, 16t
of economy, 15–18, 17m
of geography and topography,
18–19
on politics and women's status,
13
of sociodemographics, 9–11
as systemic approach, 7–9
Comprehensive Test of Basic Skills,
480
Compromises, 186, 229
Compstat, 526–527
Concurrent powers, 38, 42f
Confederacies (confederal systems),
30f, 31
Congress, U.S.
handling of domestic issues by,
218
on taxes for Internet shopping,
438
Congressional Budget Office, 568

Governing States and Localities

Good, common or public, public opinion on, 221, 224
Gore, Al, 58–59, 140, 166, 221, 276
Governing (magazine), 338
Government Accountability Office, 495
Governmental Accounting Standards Board (GASB), 459–460
Government Finance Officers Association, 461
Government lobbyists, 169–170
Government Performance Project (GPP), 338–340
Governors. *See also* Appointments; Executive branch; Veto power
as chief legislator, 232–234
as chief spokesperson, 235–236
communication ability of, 252–253
election of, 118, 158–159, 257, 260–261
formal and informal powers of, 246–247, 253, 256
formal powers of, 238, 239–241, 242–243t
as head of state agencies, 234–235
informal powers of, 238, 248, 251–253
institutional powers of, by state, 2007, 249–250t
job of, 230–238
keeping and leaving office, 261–263
legislative process and, 190
lessons learned about, 269–270
minor party, 166
as National Guard commander-in-chief, 237–238
pardons by, 244–245
party support in legislature for, 248, 251–252
personal powers of, by state, 2007, 254–255t
as political actors, 228–230
popular support for, 248
as presidents, 264–265
public opinion and, 132–133
qualifications and election of, 256–257
selection rules for, 88

special sessions and, 245, 247, 248
as state party chief, 236–237
on term limits, 222
who's who among, 258–259t
Grand juries, 306, 510
Grand Old Party (GOP), 140. *See also* Republican Party
Grannis, Alexander, 189
Grants-in-aid. *See also* Block grants
centralized federalism and, 47, 50–51
New Federalism and, 51
Great Britain. *See* United Kingdom
Great Depression, 46–47, 49f, 140, 549
Great Society initiative, 47, 467, 498
Greece, ancient, 361, 363, 511, 514
Green, Mark, 393
Green, Paul, 207
Green Party, 166
Gregoire, Christine, 190
Greve, Michael, 37
Griffin, Margaret, 197
Griswold v. the State of Connecticut (1965), 91
Groscost, Jeff, 153
Guinn, Kenny, 339, 448
Gun control laws, violent crime and, 536–537
Gun violence, public health and, 545

H

Habitual offender laws, 317
Hahn, James, 531–532
Halfway houses, 318
Hall, Melinda Gann, 290, 296
Hamilton, Alexander, 33, 42–43, 139, 185. *See also Federalist, The*
Hammonds, Christopher, 71, 96
Hancock, John, 513
Harris, Katherine, 108
Haskell, Dean, 71
Hatch, Orrin, 274
Hatfields and McCoys, 509
Hawaii
appellate courts in, 284
city-county consolidations in, 419t
culture and history of, 11

education funding in, 439
geography of, 18
gubernatorial elections in, 260
gun control laws in, 536
judicial selection in, 296
legislation on public health response to disasters in, 188
local governments in, 365, 370
party competition for governor in, 158
per-capita expenditures of bureaucracy in, 336, 337t
political party allegiances in, 101
professional and personal services taxes in, 438
same-sex unions in, 54
school districts in, 469
voting by felons in, 521
Haynie, Kerry L., 212
Healthcare. *See also* Public health
goals for, 568–569
issues to watch, 565–571
long-term care, 568, 569
managed care decline and, 565
Medicaid and SCHIP performance, 563, 565
prescription drug costs, 544, 566–567
public hospital closings and, 564
rising costs, 566
spending, 456–457
state, rise of, 559–563
Health Care Financing Administration, 554
Health maintenance organizations (HMOs), 560–561. *See also* Insurance companies; Managed care
Health Security Act, 558, 559, 561
Healthy Air Coalition, 171
Heart of Atlanta Motel v. United States (1964), 57
Heineman, Dave, 132, 264–265
Help America Vote Act (HAVA, 2002), 108
Henry, Mary Beth, 395
Hepatitis C, as public health issue, 545
Herbst, Susan, 131
Hibbing, John, 218
Hickel, Walter, 166

Hierarchies, in bureaucracy, 330, 343
Higher Education Research Institute, 4
Higher law, 69
High school graduation rates, 483–484, 485, 488
High-stakes standardized testing movement, 468, 480–484
Highway patrol, 511
Highways, funding for, 459
Hiler, Bob, 164
Hill, Steven, 105, 113, 116
Hine, James, 437
Hispanic(s). *See also* Persons of color; Minorities
  elected city officials, 392–393
  governors, 256
  incarcerated, 521
  mistrust of police departments by, 524
  in public schools, 500–501
  redistricting and, 209
  state legislators, 214–215*t*
  voter participation among, 117
History of states and localities
  culture and, 11–12, 14–15
  state constitutions and, 86–87
HIV transmission, needle-exchange programs and, 545
Hockey rinks, public, 327
Homeland security, states and localities and, 61
Home rule, 95, 388, 390–391, 460
Home schooling, 495–496
Homeschooling Helper, 495
Homeschooling Today, 495
Home School Legal Defense Organization, 496
Homicides
  gun-related, 536–537
  in Los Angeles, 531
  violent, arrests by age and weapon, 526*f*
Hospitals, public, 564
House arrest, 318
House of Representatives (states), 199, 201
House of Representatives, U.S., 218
Houston, Tex.
  annexations by, 422
  community policing in, 525

crime decline in, 528*f*
  school dropouts in, 484
Hoxby, Caroline, 440
Hrebenar, Ronald H., 178
Huckabee, Mike, 264, 544, 571–572
Human Rights Watch, 529–530
Humphrey, Hubert H., 150–151
Hunkers, 140
Hunt, Guy, 261
Hunter, Tye, 311
Huntsman, Jon, Jr., 55
Hurricane Katrina, 20–21, 35, 235, 238
Hurst, Julia, 265

I

Ice (methamphetamine product), 534
Idaho
  appellate courts in, 284
  budgetary process in, 458*f*
  home schooling in, 496
  judicial elections in, 89, 289
  local powers in, 387
  No Child Left Behind Act and, 55
  political parties in, 101, 133, 141
  public health services in, 563
  term limits in, 222
Ideology, Supreme Court federalism rulings and, 60–61
Illinois. *See also* Chicago, Ill.
  African Americans legislators in, 212
  ballot initiatives in, 92
  constitution on environmental goals of, 280
  Cook Co., property taxes, 441
  court system in, 281, 282
  education funding in, 477
  gun control laws in, 536
  judicial elections in, 89, 289
  party competition in, 158
  prescription drug plan in, 567
  prison sentences in, 318
  state capital reporters in, 220
  voting by felons in, 521
Immigrants
  as elected city officials, 392–393
  illegal, ballot initiatives on services for, 94
Impact fees, 408

Impeachment, 261, 291
Implied powers, 38. *See also* Reserved powers
Incarceration rates, 514*m*. *See also* Prisons
Income, voting and, 113
Income taxes
  proposed, in Tennessee, 434–435
  as revenue source, 436, 441–442
  school funds from, 471
  Sixteenth Amendment and, 46
  state rates for individuals, 2006, 443–444*t*
  Texas and, 215
Incumbents, 175, 196, 472
Independence Party, Minnesota's, 166
Independent candidates
  ballot access regulations and, 111–112
  difficulties of building support for, 166–167
  factors in disadvantages for, 165–166, 180
  major party support for, 167–168
Independent expenditures, 155
Indeterminate sentencing, 316–317, 520
Indiana
  attorney general's election, 2000, 122
  city council in Indianapolis, 377
  city-county consolidations in, 419*t*
  constitutional amendment process in, 79
  constitutional convention provisions, 80
  gubernatorial elections in, 77, 257
  judicial elections in, 289
  legislators in, 209
  voting by felons in, 521
Indiana ballot, 107, 110
Indictments, 306
Indirect lobbying, 173–174
Individualistic cultures
  characteristics, 12, 16*t*
  scrutiny of politician's record in, 133
  states with, 15*m*
  voter participation in, 114
Individual lobbyists, 170

Influenza. *See* Bird flu; Flu outbreak of 1918
Informal powers, of governors, 238
Informed citizens, in Tiebout model, 425–427
Institute for Women's Policy Research (IWPR), 13
Insurance commissioners, elections of, 120
Insurance companies, 188–189. *See also* Health maintenance organizations
Insurance trust funds, 445
Intelligent design theory, 500
Intensive probation, 318
Interagency Working Group on Federalism, 54–55
Interest groups. *See also* Business groups; Lobbies
  characteristics, 168–180
  definition of, 139
  judicial elections and, 292, 322
  political parties vs., 144
  political party competition and, 160, 162–163
  on preemption, 37
  public education and, 497–499
  public opinion shaping by, 132
  state and local decision-making authority and, 21–22
  ten most influential in states, 2002, 175*t*
  voter preferences and, 102
Intergovernmental transfers, 445–447
Intermediate appellate courts
  associate justices' salaries, by rank, 2006, 303*t*
  initial judicial selection for, 288*m*
  role in state court system, 278, 281–285
  terms of office and reappointment methods by state in 2007, 299–300*t*
Intermodal Surface Transportation Efficiency Act (ISTEA, 1991), 415
International City/County Management Association (ICMA), 376, 380, 381, 391, 393

Internet
  e-government, 358–359, 358*t*
  shopping, sales tax revenues and, 438
Interstate commerce clause, 57
Investigative grand juries, 510
Iowa
  chief state school officer in, 469
  constitutional amendment process in, 79
  government consolidation in, 417–418, 429
  gun control laws in, 536
  political party allegiances in, 101
  redistricting in, 208
  rural flight in, 427–428, 428*m*
  schools consolidation in, 491
Iowa Test of Basic Skills, 480
Iraq war, city councils on, 379
I-SaveRx program, 567

J

Jackman, Simon, 126
Jackson, Andrew, 140, 286, 347
Jacksonville, Fla., city-county consolidation and, 418
JAIL 4 Judges, 276
James I, king of England, 73
Jamestown (Va. colony), 73
Japan, gun-related homicides in, 536
Jarvis, Howard, 93
Jasper, Cindy, 179
Javits, Jacob, 167
Jefferson, Thomas, 43, 139, 140, 384
Jefferson, Wallace, 294
Jenness v. Fortson (1971), 111
Jessica's Law, 190
Jim Crow laws, 77, 515
Johanns, Mike, 264–265
Johnson, Gary, 244
Johnson, Lyndon B., 47, 53, 150, 467, 550. *See also* Great Society initiative
Johnson, Tim, 100–101
Johnson, Virgil, 194*f*
Johnson & Johnson, 177–178
Johnston, Henry, 261
Joint Center for Political and Economic Studies, 393

Jubelirer, Robert, 204
Judges. *See also* State court systems
  activist, 274–275, 276
  appointment systems, 285, 286
  compensation, 302–303, 303*t*
  elections for, 123
  managerial, 320–321
  merit selection, 286–287, 295
  retention elections for, 89, 287, 293, 296
  selection of, 89, 118, 285–287, 288*m*, 289–293, 295–296
  selection reforms, 321–322
  terms of office, 296, 297–302*t*
Judicial branch. *See* State court systems
Judicial federalism, 67
Judicial review, 83
Juries, 312–313, 510, 512–513
Jury nullification, 306, 513
Justice at Stake, 292
Justices. *See also* Judges; State court systems
  associate state, salaries by rank, 2006, 303*t*
Justices of the peace, 509, 512

K

Kaiser Commission on Medicaid and the Uninsured, 558–559
Kaiser Family Foundation, 566
Kansas
  city-county consolidations in, 419*t*
  college tuition–setting in, 483
  Democratic Party in, 101
  educational equity and constitution of, 70
  education policies in, 500
  gubernatorial elections in, 158, 260
  gun control laws in, 536
  judicial selection in, 287, 289
  recall elections in, 128
  rural flight in, 427
  school funding laws in, 193
Katz, Vera, 206
Katzenback v. McClung (1964), 57
Kaye, Judith S., 282
Kelling, George, 506, 522–523, 525

federalism and, 33–34, 363–365

fragmentation of land use powers among, 409

healthcare spending by, 457

as laboratories of democracy, 21–24

municipalities, 375–384, 378*f*, 380*f*, 381*t*, 383*f*

New Federalism and, 53

operating procedures for, 95

participation in, 391–394

powers and constraints of, 385–388, 390

powers of, 364–365

public health role for, 547, 570–571

public opinion on effectiveness of, 363

regional political jurisdictions and, 398

special districts, 384–385

statistics and demographics, 365, 366–367*t*, 367–368

taxing variations among, 447, 449–450

Tiebout model for, 425–427

unfunded mandates and, 460

Local political parties, 141, 152

Local politics

comparative method of studying, 7–10

daily impact of, 5–7

policymaking constraints on, 22–23

Locke, Gary, 190, 256

Loeb, William, 161

Logrolling, 184

London, Metropolitan Police of, 522

Long, Huey, 148

Long-term health care, 457, 566, 568, 569

Lorillard Tobacco Co. v. Reilly (2001), 59, 59*t*

Los Angeles (city). *See also* Los Angeles Police Department

budget process in, 453

city charter, 389

city council, 377

crime decline in, 527, 528*f*

low-density development in, 408–409

police force of, 459

public schools' administration in, 469, 470

school board elections in, 472

voting districts in, 391

Watts riots of 1965, 515, 516

Los Angeles County, district attorney's office staff, 305

Los Angeles Police Department, 524, 527, 531–532

Lotteries, state, 471–472

Loudoun Co., Va., sprawl, smart growth and, 412–413

Louisiana. *See also* New Orleans, La.

blogging about state legislative process in, 220–221

chief state school officer in, 469

city-county consolidations in, 419*t*

constitutional convention provisions, 81

constitution of, 71

gubernatorial elections in, 257

Hurricane Katrina response, 28

judicial elections in, 89, 289

jury verdict regulations in, 312–313

Medicaid programs in, 554

Napoleonic code in, 509

parishes in, 370

parish jurors in, 373

political culture in, 160–161

prescription drug costs under Medicaid in, 567

primary elections in, 150

prison sentences in, 318

transportation spending by, 459

Louisville-Jefferson Metro Government, Ky., 420

Loveless, Tom, 493

Low-density development, 407–408

Lowery, David, 426

Lucey, Paula, 564

Lunsford, Jessica Maria, 190

Lynch, John, 256

Lyons, William, 426

M

Madison, James, 31, 39, 91–92, 95. *See also Federalist, The*

Magistrates, 321

Magna Carta, 74

Maine

chief state school officer in, 469

constitutional convention provisions, 81

education funding in, 477

gubernatorial elections in, 111–112, 158

healthcare coverage in, 546

judicial appointments in, 293

legislative power in, 206

legislators in, 210–211

lieutenant governor of, 266

local powers in, 387

public campaign financing in, 156

public defenders in, 310

term limits in, 222

third party governor in, 166

town governments in, 384

townships in, 376

universal healthcare in, 569

voting by felons in, 522

Majority leaders, 201–202

Majority-minority districts, 209

Majority rule, 184

Malapportionment, 208

Managed care, 560–561, 565. *See also* Health maintenance organizations

Management by Objectives (MBO), 356

Managerial judges, 320–321

Mandatory jurisdiction, 284

Mandatory minimum sentences, 317

Mann, Horace, 467, 469, 491, 501

Marble cake federalism, 48*f*

Marijuana, 59–60, 124, 518, 519

Markham, William, 76

Marriage. *See also* Gay marriage

licenses for, local governments and, 368

Marshall, John, 43, 56

Maryland

Cedar Brook Academy, Clarksburg, 496

constitution of, 71

crime decline in Baltimore, 528*f*

EPA's enforcement of clean air rule and, 170

governors' influence on state budget for, 233

election of 2006 in, 144–145
fiscal year in, 451
geography of, 18
gun control laws in, 536
habitual offender sentencing in, 317
home schooling in, 496
judicial elections in, 89, 289, 292, 293
on No Child Left Behind Act, 466
party competition for governor in, 158
political parties in, 148
prison sentences in, 318
school vouchers in, 495
voting by felons in, 521
Microtargeting, 101–102
Mid-America Regional Council (MARC), 34, 35
Midwest (region). *See also* Plains states; Upper Midwest
criminal justice systems in, 512
moralistic cultures in, 12
strong mayors in, 376
unions in, 193
Migration patterns
metropolitan growth and, 409
political culture and, 12, 159
Tiebout model on, 425–427
Millenson, Daniel, 168–169
Miller, George, 498
Miller, Mike, 202
Milwaukee, Wis.
Doyne Hospital closing in, 564
low-density development in, 408–409
school board elections in, 472
school vouchers in, 495
Minimum wage, ballot initiatives on, 126
Minnesota
alternative dispute resolution in, 321
campaign financing in, 156
competitive elections in, 118
constitution and political culture of, 87
constitution on public education in, 468
daily newspapers in Twin Cities of, 196, 219

gun control laws in, 536
healthcare safety net in, 551
how bill becomes state law in, 194–195f
independent candidates as governor in, 111–112
judicial elections in, 289
legislative ideas in, 193
legislators' responses to public opinion in, 133
lobbying regulations in, 173
minor parties in, 167
political culture in, 160–161
political party regulation in, 155
professional legislators in, 215–216
sales tax waivers in, 432
third party governor in, 166
voter registration in, 115
voter turnout in, 113
women as legislators in, 211
Minorities. *See also specific groups*
as jurors, 513
students in public schools, 500–501
Minority leaders, 201
Minor (minority) parties. *See also* Third party candidates
ballot access regulations and, 111–112
state government role for, 153
Misdemeanors, 307
Mississippi
African Americans legislators in, 212
ballot initiatives in, 80, 92
budget process in, 453
constitutional convention provisions, 80
education funding in, 477
emergency contraceptives law in, 571
gambling operations and economy of, 450
gubernatorial elections in, 77, 257
home schooling in, 496
judicial elections in, 89, 289
jury selection regulations in, 313
lieutenant governor's power in, 266
Medicaid program in, 550–551

Parents for Public Schools, 498
per-capita gross state product, 15–16
politics and women's status in, 13
Reconstruction and executive powers in, 83
tort laws in, 193
unions in, 193
Missouri. *See also* St. Louis, Mo.
criminal sentencing in, 315
gubernatorial elections in, 257
gun control laws in, 536
judicial elections in, 89, 289
jury selection regulations in, 313
legislators in, 201
Medicaid programs in, 554
school desegregation and education funding in Kansas City, 478
Missouri Compromise (1820), 44–45
Missouri Plan, for judicial selections, 89, 287
Moakley, Maureen, 12
Moberly, Harold, 210
Mobility of citizens. *See* Migration patterns
Model constitutions, 87–88
Molnau, Carol, 265
Moncrief, Gary, 220
Montana
appellate courts in, 283
city-county consolidations in, 419t
constitutional convention provisions, 81
court decision on 2004 election in, 166
geography of, 18
gubernatorial elections in, 257
judicial elections in, 289
legislature of, bills in 2006 before, 190
Medicaid program in, 550–551
methamphetamines in, 533
political parties in, 141
privacy rights in, 91
public health services in, 563
SCHIP program in, 562
state superintendent of education in, 269
tax system in, 442

governor's veto power in, 244
gubernatorial elections in, 257
gubernatorial terms in, 229, 262
judicial selection in, 293, 295
judicial terms of office in, 296
lieutenant governor of, 266
political culture in, 161
political party allegiances in, 101
population characteristics of, 10
professional legislators in, 216
SCHIP program in, 562
tax capacity and tax effort in, 447, 449
taxes per capita in, 447
tax system in, 432, 439, 442
voting by felons in, 521
women as legislators in, 211

New Jersey
African Americans legislators in, 212
appellate courts in, 284
boards of chosen freeholders in, 373
chief state school officer in, 469
constitutional convention provisions, 80
constitution on schools in, 70, 280
district attorneys in, 507
education funding in, 477
executive branch elections in, 119
gubernatorial elections in, 257
gun control laws in, 536
individualistic culture of, 12, 14
Jersey City, party machine in, 147–148
judicial appointments in, 293
legislative sessions in, 213
lieutenant governor of, 263, 266
lobbyists in, 178
Newark, 1967 riots in, 515
political parties in, 147–148, 154
public health services in, 563
redistricting in, 208
same-sex unions in, 61
SCHIP program in, 562
Senate leadership powers in, 202
statewide officials, 263
supreme court on gay marriage in, 276
taxation in, 7
tobacco sales taxes in, 436

New Judicial Federalism, 280
New Mexico
constitution on bilingual education in, 280
education funding in, 440
gun control laws in, 536
judicial selection in, 295
mandatory minimum sentencing in, 317
Medicaid program in, 550–551
political party allegiances in, 101
professional and personal services taxes in, 438
state superintendent of education in, 269

New Orleans, La.
city-county consolidation and, 418
Hurricane Katrina and, 20–21, 28–29
political machine in, 148

New Public Management (NPM), 354–355
Newsom, Gavin, 131
Newspapers
on governors' pronouncements, 252
on legislative budget deadlines, 216
metropolitan daily, 196
partisan, 146
state capitol reporters for, 219

New York (city)
anthrax attacks in, 543
bankruptcy of, 554
Bellevue Hospital, 548
blackout of 1977, 516
charter schools in, 493
city council, 377
community policing in, 525
court system in, 281
crime decline in, 506, 528f
culture of, 11
government for, 365
Harlem riots of 1964, 515
police force of, 459
public health programs in, 547, 572–573
public schools' administration in, 469–470
safety of, 533
voter identification in, 393

New York (city) Police Department, 352, 353, 525, 526–527, 532
New York (state)
ballot access rules in, 111, 165, 167
city-county consolidations in, 419t
constitutional amendment process in, 79
constitutional revision commission in, 82
constitution of, 67
court system in, 282–283
divided legislature in, 193, 207
drug laws in, 517–518
education funding in, 439
fiscal year in, 451
governors' influence on state budget for, 233
gun control laws in, 536
Integrated Domestic Violence Court, 320
judicial elections in, 289
judicial selection in, 296
judicial terms of office in, 296
legislative sessions in, 213
legislature of, bills in 2006 before, 190
Levittown, benefits of living in, 424
local powers in, 388
merit system in, 348
redistricting in, 207
Regents Exam, 480
rural health services in, 563
standardized education testing in, 481
state capital reporters in, 219–220
TANF programs in, 544
tax system in, 442
New York Times, 281, 291
Nineteenth Amendment, 77, 112
Nixon, Richard M., 49f, 50, 53, 219
No Child Left Behind Act (NCLB)
achievement testing in states and, 464–465, 480
Bush's New Federalism and, 55, 498
business groups on, 499
Connecticut's suit on, 466–467
Goals 2000 and, 488

Q

Quakers, 76, 512, 515
Quam, David, 238

R

Raban, Jonathan, 144
Race, voter turnout and, 113, 115, 116
Race riots of 1960s, 515–516
Racial discrimination
  incarceration and, 520–521
  indeterminate sentencing and, 316
  metropolitan growth and, 409–410
  in prosecution of local crimes, 307
Railroads, federal regulation of, 45, 49f
Rainy day funds, 452, 461
Rank-and-file members, 204–206
Rants, Christopher, 247
Ratification, 79, 82
Raytheon, 205
Reagan, Ronald
  Democratic Party supporters and, 141–142
  on Dept. of Education, 467
  election of 1980 and, 100
  gubernatorial experience of, 53, 264
  New Federalism and, 49f, 51, 52–53
  Proposition 13 and, 441
  Supreme Court appointments by, 57
  taxpayer revolt of 1978 and, 93
  on welfare state, 554
REAL ID Act (2005), 55
Realignment, 153
Realtor lobbying, 179–180
Recall elections, 126, 128, 228, 261, 262t
Recht, Don, 317
Recidivism, 320, 521, 535
Reconstruction, 83, 86, 105
Records and files maintenance, bureaucracies and, 330, 343
Redistricting. See also Districts
  computer-assisted, 132–133

process of, 207
safe vs. swing districts and, 164
Red states, 100–101
Red tape, 329–330, 336, 346
Referendums. See also Ballot initiatives
  for amending constitutions, 80
  in California, 67
  direct democracy and, 93–94, 123–126
  for policy decisions by voters, 118
  popular initiatives vs. popular, 123
  states provisions for, 127–128t
Reform Party, 165–166
Reform perspective, for metropolitics, 411–412
Regional councils, 414–417
Regional governments, 413–414
Regressive taxes, 436–437
Rehnquist, William, 49f, 57, 67
Reinventing government (REGO), 356
Reno v. Condon (2000), 59t
Representation, 191–193, 196
Representative bureaucracy, 353
Representative governments, 33, 91–92, 95
Reproductive rights, 125
Republican Attorneys General Association (RAGA), 121, 267–268
Republican government, constitutional enforcement of, 40–41t
Republican National Committee, 141, 164
Republican Party
  attorneys general and, 121–122, 267
  congressional, welfare reform and, 457
  criminal justice system funding and, 532
  Democratic Party compared to, 138
  elections of 2002 and, 157–158
  factions in, 142, 144
  formation of, 140
  gubernatorial elections and, 260
  judicial elections and, 123

national character, evolution of, 105
  in Ohio, 153
  organization in Ohio and Cuyahoga Co., 143f
  periods of dominance of, 153
  political cultures and, 160
  red states and, 100
  state legislative leadership and, 202
  state organizations, 152
  on teachers' unions and school reform, 497
  voter identification with, 167–168
Republican Party of Minnesota v. White (2002), 292, 322
Reserved powers, 39–41, 40–41t, 199. See also Tenth Amendment
Residency requirements, voting and, 114
Responsible party model, 146
Restorative justice movement, 536–537
Retention elections, for judges, 89, 287, 293, 296
Revenue bonds, 451
Revenues. See also Finance
  bonds, 450–451
  definition of, 434
  fees and charges, 442, 445
  income taxes, 441–442, 443–444t
  insurance trust funds, 445
  intergovernmental transfers, 445–447, 446m
  other taxes, 442
  property taxes, 438–441
  sales taxes, 436–438
  state and local, 2004, 454–455t
  taxing variations among states, 447, 449–450
Revenue sharing, 50
Revolutionary War, 31–32, 33, 49f
Rhode Island
  appellate courts in, 283
  constitutional convention in, 81
  governor's appointment powers in, 240
  governor's veto power in, 244
  gun control laws in, 536
  illegal constitutional convention of 1841, 77–78